The Christian Bed & Breakfast Directory

1999-2000 Edition

Dan Harmon, Editor

BARBOUR
PUBLISHING, INC.
Uhrichsville, Ohio

The Christian Bed & Breakfast Directory

1999-2000 Edition

ISBN 1-57748-442-8

Published by Barbour Publishing, Inc., P.O. Box 719, Uhrichsville, Ohio 44683
http://www.barbourbooks.com

Printed in the United States of America.

Table of Contents

How to Use This Book

Have you ever dreamed of spending a few days in a rustic cabin in Alaska? Would you like to stay in an urban town house while taking care of some business in the city? Would your family like to spend a weekend on a midwestern farm feeding pigs and gathering eggs? Maybe a romantic Victorian mansion in San Francisco or an antebellum plantation in Mississippi is what you've been looking for. No matter what your needs may be, whether you are traveling for business or pleasure, you will find a variety of choices in the 1999-2000 edition of *The Christian Bed & Breakfast Directory*.

In the pages of this guide you will find over 1,400 bed and breakfasts, small inns, and homestays. All of the information has been updated from last year's edition, and many entries are listed for the first time. Although not every establishment is owned or operated by Christians, each host has expressed a desire to welcome Christian travelers.

The directory is designed for easy reference. At a glance, you can determine the number of rooms available at each establishment and how many rooms have private (PB) and shared (SB) baths. You will find the name of the host or hosts, the price range for two people sharing one room, the kind of breakfast that is served, and what credit cards are accepted. There is a "Notes" section to let you know important information that may not be included in the description. These notes correspond to the list at the bottom of each page. The descriptions have been written by the hosts. The publisher has not visited these bed and breakfasts and is not responsible for inaccuracies.

General maps are provided to help you with your travel plans. Included are the towns where our bed and breakfasts are located, some reference cities, major highways, and major recreational lakes. Please use your road map for additional assistance and details when planning your trip.

It is recommended that you make reservations in advance. Many bed and breakfasts have small staffs or are run single-handedly and cannot easily accommodate surprises. Also ask about taxes, as city and state taxes vary. Remember to ask for directions, and if your special dietary needs can be met, and confirm check-in and check-out times.

Whether you're planning a honeymoon, family vacation, or business trip, *The Christian Bed & Breakfast Directory* will make any outing out of the ordinary.

DAN HARMON, EDITOR

ALABAMA

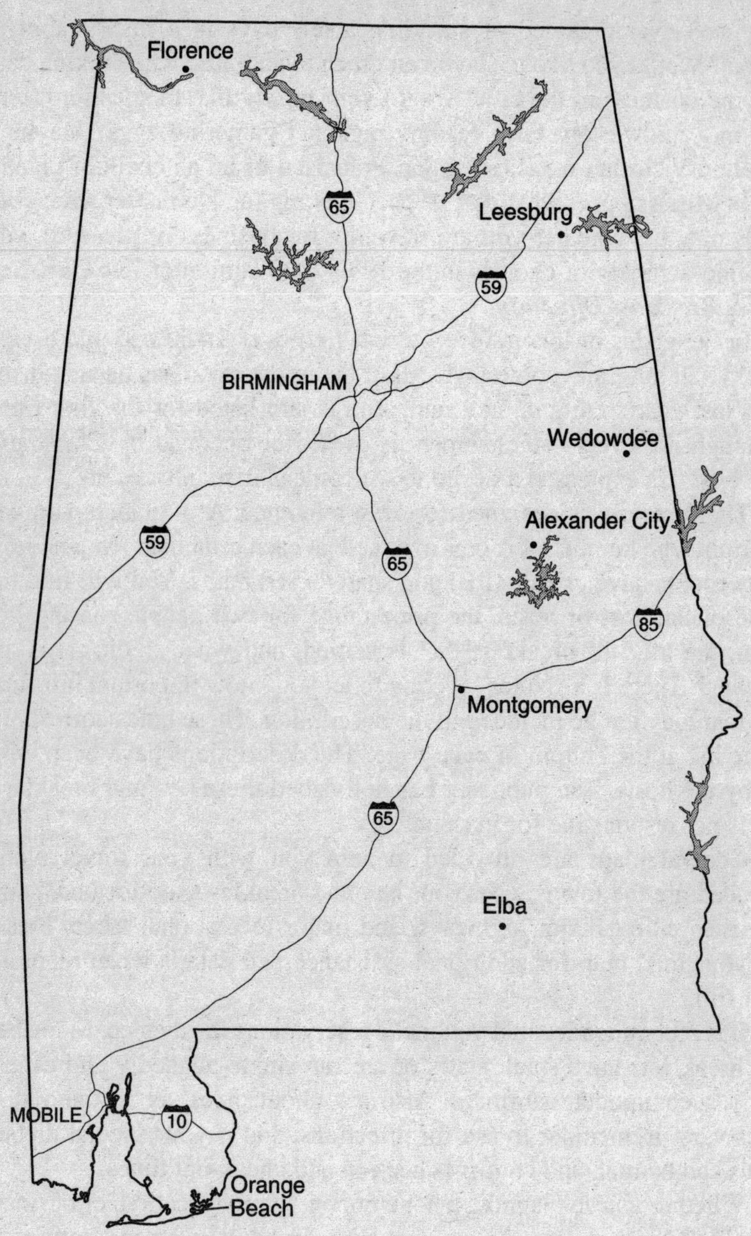
Florence
65
Leesburg
59
BIRMINGHAM
Wedowdee
Alexander City
59
65
85
Montgomery
65
Elba
MOBILE
10
Orange
Beach

Alabama

Natchez Trace Bed and Breakfast Reservation Service

PO Box 193, **Hampshire, TN** 38461
(615) 285-2777; (800) 377-2770

This reservation service is unusual in that all the homes listed are close to the Natchez Trace, the delightful National Parkway running from Nashville, Tennessee, to Natchez, Mississippi. Kay Jones can help you plan your trip along the Trace, with homestays in interesting and historic homes along the way. Locations of homes include Ashland City, Columbia, FairView, Franklin, Hohenwald, and Nashville, **Tennessee;** Florence and Cherokee, **Alabama;** and Church Hill, Corinth, French Camp, Kosciusko, Lorman, Natchez, New Albany, Tupelo, and Vicksburg, **Mississippi.** Rates $60-125.

Mistletoe Bough Bed and Breakfast

ALEXANDER CITY

Mistletoe Bough B&B

497 Hillabee Street, 35010
(256) 329-3717; FAX (256) 234-0094
Web site: http://www.bbonline.com/al/mistletoe

Mistletoe Bough is an elegant Queen Anne house built in 1890 for the family of Reuben Herzfeld. The bed and breakfast offers guests a retreat into years gone by with all the comforts and conveniences of modern days. Listed on the National Register of Historic Places, this lovely Victorian home offers elegance and charm you sense the moment you enter.

Hosts: Carlice E. and Jean H. Payne
Rooms: 5 (PB) $85-110
Full Breakfast
Credit Cards: none
Notes: 2, 5, 7 (over 10), 9, 10, 12

NOTES: Credit cards accepted: A Master Card; B Visa; C American Express; D Discover; E Diners Club; F Other; 2 Personal checks accepted; 3 Lunch available; 4 Dinner available; 5 Open all year; 6 Pets welcome; 7 Children welcome; 8 Tennis nearby; 9 Swimming nearby; 10 Golf nearby; 11 Skiing nearby; 12 May be booked through travel agent.

ELBA

Aunt B's Bed and Breakfast

717 W. Davis Street, 36323
(334) 897-6918 (voice and FAX)

This historic country Victorian built in 1910 has survived two floods, in 1920 and 1990. It was restored in 1993. Aunt B's has three guest rooms: the Angel Room (king-size bed decorated with Battenburg lace), the Cowboy Room (two full-size beds decorated with handmade quilts), and the Mayberry Room (twin or king-size beds decorated with ruffles). All guest quarters have private baths. The shaded backyard invites you to enjoy the hammock near the goldfish pond. We serve a country breakfast. Before you leave, you may shop at "Aunt B's Closet" for gifts, baskets, and collectibles.

Hosts: Barbara and Bobby Hudson
Rooms: 3 (PB) $50
Full Breakfast
Credit Cards: A, B
Notes: 2, 5, 7, 8, 9, 10, 12

FLORENCE

Wood Avenue Inn

658 N. Wood Avenue, 35630
(205) 766-8441

This grand Victorian mansion, built in 1889, is 13 miles off the Natchez Trace Parkway in the heart of historic Florence. Guests can walk to restaurants, art galleries, and shopping areas, or relax in our lovely gardens and enjoy songbirds. Golf, tennis, swimming, and the Tennessee River are nearby. Romantic, quiet, elegant, and comfortable. Business guests welcome!

Hosts: Gene and Alvern Greeley
Rooms: 5 (4PB; 1SB) $63-98
Full Breakfast
Credit Cards: A, B
Notes: 2, 5, 8, 9, 10, 12

The Secret Bed and Breakfast Lodge

LEESBURG

The Secret Bed and Breakfast Lodge

2356 Highway 68 W., 35983-4000
(205) 523-3825
E-mail: secret@peop.tds.net
Web site: http://www.bbonline.com/al/thesecret

At The Secret Bed and Breakfast Lodge, guests have a 180-degree panoramic view of seven cities and two states, overlooking Weiss Lake from the Lookout Mountain Parkway. Rooftop swimming pool. Vaulted ceiling in lodge area and bedrooms. King/queen-size beds, TVs, VCRs, private baths, balconies. AAA star rating. A special place—a secret—with a view as spectacular in the day as it is enchanting at night. Come. Discover. Enjoy!

Hosts: Carl and Diann Cruickshank
Rooms: 5 (PB) $95-150
Full Country Breakfast
Credit Cards: A, B
Notes: 2, 5, 8, 9, 10

NOTES: Credit cards accepted: A Master Card; B Visa; C American Express; D Discover; E Diners Club; F Other; 2 Personal checks accepted; 3 Lunch available; 4 Dinner available; 5 Open all year; 6 Pets

MONTGOMERY

Red Bluff Cottage

551 Clay Street; PO Box 1026, 36101
(334) 264-0056; (888) 551-2529;
FAX (334) 263-3054
E-mail: RedBlufBnB@aol.com
Web site: http://www.bbonline.com/al/redbluff

Share the comforts and pleasures of Red Bluff Cottage, high above the Alabama River in Montgomery's historic Cottage Hill District. Red Bluff is a raised cottage, built in 1987 as a B&B inn. The guest rooms are on the ground floor, with easy access from the parking area, gazebo, and fenced play yard. The kitchen, dining room, living room, sitting room with TV, and music room with piano and harpsichord are on the second floor for guests to enjoy. A deep upstairs porch offers a panoramic view of the river plain and downtown Montgomery, including a unique view of the state capitol. Each guest room is furnished with family antiques.

Hosts: Anne and Mark Waldo
Rooms: 4 (PB) $75
Full Breakfast
Credit Cards: A, B, D, E
Notes: 2, 7

ORANGE BEACH

The Original Romar House

23500 Perdido Beach Boulevard (Highway 182), 36561
(334) 974-1625; (800) 487-6627;
FAX (334) 974-1163
E-mail: original@gulftel.com
Web site: http://www.bbonline.com/al/romarhouse

Wake up to rediscover romance in a charmingly historic atmosphere, as the sun streams through the stained glass windows of your art deco-furnished room. After breakfast, take a morning swim or stroll along the beach collecting seashells, curl up in a cypress swing or hammock and read a book, or relax in the hot-tub whirlpool spa. You are only minutes by car to gift shops, golf courses, seafood restaurants, and entertainment. Break away from your everyday world. Come, be a part of the history at The Original Romar House bed and breakfast inn.

Host: Darrell Finley
Rooms: 6 + cottage (PB) $79-129
Full Breakfast
Credit Cards: A, B, C
Notes: 2, 5, 8, 9, 10

WEDOWEE

Friendship House Bed and Breakfast

PO Box 608, 36278
(256) 357-4092

A country bed and breakfast with the feel of going to your grandparents' house. The home is near beautiful, 10,000-acre Lake Wedowee, where the fishing is great. It is only a short drive to Cheaha State Park, highest point in Alabama, and the Talladega National Forest. Birmingham and Atlanta are only about 90 minutes away. There are several antique shops in Randolph and adjoining counties.

Hostess: Joyce Cantrell
Rooms: 2 (PB) $45-65
Continental Breakfast
Credit Cards: none
Notes: 2, 5, 6 (small), 7, 9, 11 (water skiing)

ALASKA

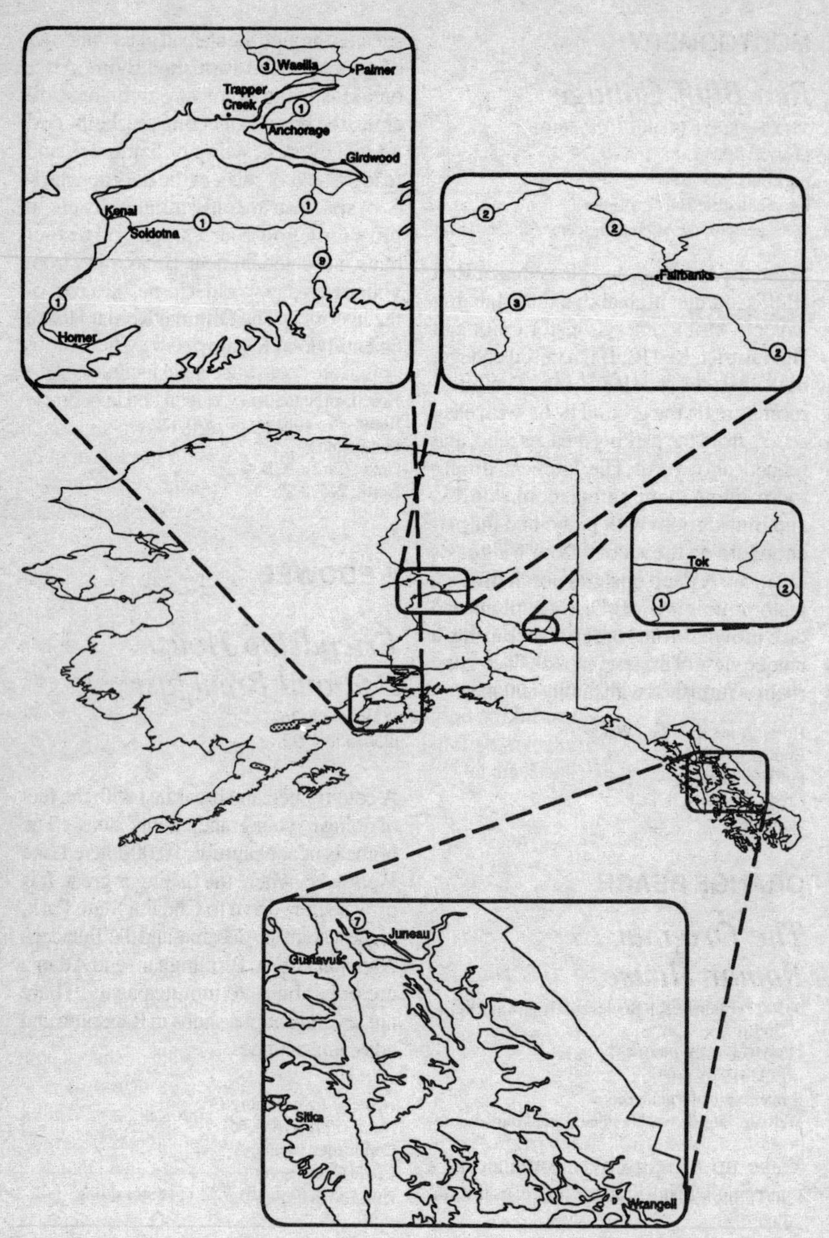
3
Wasilla
Palmer
Trapper Creek
1
Anchorage
Girdwood
1
Kenai
Soldotna
1
9
1
Homer
2
2
Fairbanks
3
2
Tok
1
2
7
Juneau
Gustavus
Sitka
Wrangell

Alaska

ANCHORAGE

Arctic Loon B&B

PO Box 110333, 99511
(907) 345-4935; FAX (907) 345-9495
E-mail: arcticln@alaska.net
Web site: www.alaska.net/~arcticln

Refined elegance set amid Chugach Mountains awaits pampered guests. Breathtaking views of Mt. McKinley, the Alaska Range, and the Anchorage skyline greet guests in the rosewood dining room and each spacious private room. A healthy breakfast on English bone china. Hot tub, sauna, world-class hiking trails, and golf complete a memorable stay. Fully licensed, private, quiet, and secure.

Hosts: Janie and Lee Johnson
Rooms: 3 (PB) $85-110
Full Breakfast
Credit Cards: A, B
Notes: 2, 5, 7, 8, 9, 10, 11, 12

Camai Bed and Breakfast

3838 Westminster Way, 99508-4834
(907) 333-2219
E-mail: camai@alaska.net
Web site: www.alaska.net/~camai

Enjoy old-fashioned hospitality in luxurious, contemporary suites in our home. Quiet Anchorage neighborhood nestled on Chester Creek's green belt, where moose often are seen. Each suite includes private bath, private entry, queen bed in bedroom, and day bed (converts to two singles) in sitting room. One suite has kitchenette. Craig and Caroline are active in their church, where Caroline is organist and directs the handbell choir.

Hosts: Craig and Caroline Valentine
Rooms: 2 (PB)
Full Breakfast (summer)
Credit Cards: none
Notes: 2, 5, 7, 8, 9, 10, 11 (cross-country), 12

Chickadee Bed and Breakfast

961 Coral Lane, 99515
(907) 345-4164 (voice and FAX); (888) 350-4164
E-mail: nest@alaska.net
Web site: www.alaskan.com/chickadee

Find reasonable rates, a warm welcome, and a hearty home-cooked breakfast at our Alaskan homestay bed and breakfast. Queen or twin beds, down comforters, robes, telephones, private or shared bath. Semiprivate entrance. Sitting room, VCR/TV, Alaska tape and book library. Minikitchen with sink, microwave, refrigerator,

---

NOTES: Credit cards accepted: A Master Card; B Visa; C American Express; D Discover; E Diners Club; F Other; 2 Personal checks accepted; 3 Lunch available; 4 Dinner available; 5 Open all year; 6 Pets welcome; 7 Children welcome; 8 Tennis nearby; 9 Swimming nearby; 10 Golf nearby; 11 Skiing nearby; 12 May be booked through travel agent.

and dining area. Freezer space available. Suite available for family or small group. Retired story-telling fisherman in residence. Easy highway access, trails, shopping, churches, dining nearby.

Hostess: Nancy Grant
Rooms: 3 (2PB; 1SB) $70-85
Full Breakfast
Credit Cards: A, B
Notes: Discounts available

Elderberry B&B

8340 Elderberry, 99502
(907) 243-6968 (voice and FAX)
E-mail: 103260.3221@compuserve.com

Elderberry B&B is located by the airport and has three guest rooms with private baths. We cater to each guest on an individual basis. Situated on the green belt in Anchorage, where moose often can be spotted. We serve full, home-cooked breakfasts. The hosts love to talk about Alaska and are very active in their church.

Hosts: Norm and Linda Seitz
Rooms: 3 (2PB; 1SB) $60-80
Full Breakfast
Credit Cards: A, B
Notes: 2, 5, 7, 11, 12

Hospitality Plus

7711 Anne Circle, 99504-4601
(907) 333-8504 (voice and FAX; call first)
E-mail: jbudai@alaska.net
Web site: http://www.alaska.net/~jbudai

Envision a comfortable home, delightful and thematically decorated rooms, caring and knowledgeable hosts, a sumptuous breakfast elegantly served every morning, a mountain range within reach, a profusion of wildflowers, and moose in the yard. Add to that years of various and intriguing Alaskan adventures, a Hungarian refugee's escape story, exceptional tour and guiding experience, an avid fisherman, story-telling experts, and artistic achievements, and then sum it all up in one word: *hospitality*.

Hostess: Joan Budai
Rooms: 3 (1PB; 2SB) $60-85
Full Breakfast
Credit Cards: D
Notes: 2, 5, 7, 8, 9, 11, 12

The Tree House Bed and Breakfast

13000 Admiralty Place, 99515
(907) 345-5421 (voice and FAX)
E-mail: treehouse@servcom.com
Web site: www.AlaskaOne.com/treehouse

The Tree House is a good place to start your vacation. Come in and relax in a lovely private home in south Anchorage where the robes are fluffy, the beds are covered in down comforters, and the cats are friendly. Each room has a phone and an amenity basket. Begin the day with a full, gourmet breakfast and end it in the Jacuzzi hot tub! Close to airport, hiking, golfing, parks, bus. Reasonable rates.

Hostess: Andrea Woods
Rooms: 3 (1PB; 2SB) $70-80
Full Breakfast
Credit Cards: A, B, D

FAIRBANKS

7 Gables Inn

PO Box 80488, 99708
(907) 479-0751; FAX (907) 479-2229
E-mail: gables7@alaska.net
Web site: http://www.alaska.net/~gables7

Centrally located between major attractions, 7 Gables Inn is a Tudor home with a

NOTES: Credit cards accepted: A Master Card; B Visa; C American Express; D Discover; E Diners Club; F Other; 2 Personal checks accepted; 3 Lunch available; 4 Dinner available; 5 Open all year; 6 Pets

floral solarium, antique stained glass, indoor waterfall, and meeting room. Soak in a soothing Jacuzzi bath or browse through our balcony library—or view an Alaskan video. Amenities include gourmet breakfasts, cable TV/VCRs, private phone/FAX/modem lines, bikes, canoes, and laundry facilities.

Hosts: Paul and Leicha Welton
Rooms: 9 (PB) $50-150 (seasonal)
Full Breakfast
Credit Cards: A, B, C, D, E
Notes: 2, 5, 7, 11, 12

Cook's Cove B&B

424 Glacier Avenue, 99701
(907) 452-3442
E-mail: bcook@mosquitonet.com

The Cook family crest bears the inscription "He showeth a safe road"—an appropriate direction for the weary traveler seeking a safe night's lodging. Located in the "Golden Heart of Alaska," Cook's Cove is decorated in the style of a Victorian country cottage. The atmosphere is peaceful and cozy, and the hospitality of your hosts is warm and friendly. Dick loves to share Alaska stories, and Betty serves up a hearty breakfast, with fresh-baked scones a specialty.

Hosts: Dick and Betty Cook
Rooms: 2½ (SB) $50-65
Full Breakfast
Credit Cards: none
Notes: 2, 5, 7, 9 (indoor), 10, 11 (winter)

Lennie's Lair B&B

2034 Eagan Avenue, 99701
(907) 456-5931

You'll find our bed and breakfast in the heart of the city, with a partial forest setting. Close to Alaskaland, public bus routes, and restaurant.

Hostess: Lennie Johnson
Rooms: 2 (PB) $50-65
Continental Breakfast
Credit Cards: A, B
Notes: 2, 5

"A Cross Country Meadows" Bed and Breakfast

GIRDWOOD

"A Cross Country Meadows" Bed and Breakfast

Timberline and Alta Drive; PO Box 123, 99587-0123
(907) 783-3333; FAX (907) 783-3335
E-mail: XCountryBB@aol.com
Web site: www.AlaskaOne.com/crosscountry

The "A Cross Country Meadows" Bed and Breakfast was designed and built specifically as a B&B and furnished for the convenience of our guests. We cater to those who seek quiet, peaceful accommodations with a luxurious and private atmosphere. Our home is a place for guests to rest from their travels or regroup for another nearby adventure. Our B&B is a great place for staging day trips, for a romantic retreat, or for just mixing business with pleasure. Sylvia and Brent's warm hospitality and their love of crafts graciously accent this cozy, charming B&B. Their home is decorated beautifully. All the top-floor guest rooms have a panoramic view of surrounding meadows, Alyeska ski slopes, and awesome, snowcapped glaciers. Each deluxe bedroom has cathedral ceilings and shares a private loft and sitting area.

Hosts: Brent and Sylvia Stonebraker
Rooms: 2 (PB with king beds) $85-125 (seasonal)
"Country Style" Continental Breakfast
Credit Cards: A, B, C
Notes: 5, 11, 12

GUSTAVUS

Good River Bed and Breakfast

Box 37, 99826
(907) 697-2241 (voice and FAX)
E-mail: river@thor.he.net
Web site: http://thor.he.net/~river

Spectacular Glacier Bay. Sixteen tidewater glaciers, whales, fishing, kayaking, wilderness—great B&B. Elegant log house, comfy beds, handmade quilts—reasonable rates. Delicious food—fresh-baked bread and goodies every day. Free bikes. Perfect accommodations for independent travelers. We provide free planning and reservation service so you'll get the most out of your visit. There are no "package tours"; we just make the arrangements for the things you choose to do; no extra cost.

Hostess: Sandy Burd
Rooms: 4 (SB) $80; guest cabin $60
Full Breakfast
Credit Cards: none
Notes: 2, 7, 10, 12

HOMER

Victorian Heights Bed and Breakfast

PO Box 2363, 99603
(907) 235-6357 (voice and FAX)
E-mail: Clays@xyz.net
Web site: http://akms.com/victorian

This beautiful two-story hillside home was built specifically for having guests. We offer five lovely guest rooms, each one spacious and comfortable. We also offer a studio apartment complete with kitchenette and laundry facilities. The spectacular views from our home include mountains, glaciers, and Kachemak Bay. Our guests enjoy a delicious breakfast with a view. We recently received a three-diamond rating by AAA. Come experience life on the last frontier in the land of the midnight sun!

Hosts: Phil and Tammy Clay
Rooms: 6 (4PB; 2SB) $100-120
Full Breakfast
Credit Cards: A, B
Notes: 2, 5, 7, 8, 9, 10, 11, 12

JUNEAU

Adlersheim Wilderness Lodge

PO Box 35541, 99803-5541
(907) 723-4447; FAX (907) 789-5888
E-mail: akmagic@alaska.net
Web site: www.alaska.net/~akmagic

Located in the heart of the Tongass National Rainforest just 34 miles north of Juneau, the lodge is set on a secluded, oceanfront property with 9 acres. Activities available through Adlersheim are salt-

NOTES: Credit cards accepted: A Master Card; B Visa; C American Express; D Discover; E Diners Club; F Other; 2 Personal checks accepted; 3 Lunch available; 4 Dinner available; 5 Open all year; 6 Pets

water and freshwater fishing, kayaking, boating, hiking, whale-watch tours, white-water rafting, helicopter "flight-seeing," city tours, and glacier cruises. Because of our large number of returning guests each season, we recommend you make your reservations well in advance.

Hosts: Tom and Heide Island
Rooms: 4 + 3 cabins (SB) $85-105
Continental Breakfast
Credit Cards: A, B
Notes: 2, 3, 4, 5, 6, 7, 11, 12

Alaska Wolf House

PO Box 21321, 99802
(907) 586-2422
E-mail: akwlfhs@ptialaska.net
Web site: http://www.wetpage.com/akwlfhse

Alaska Wolf House is a 4,000-square-foot western red cedar log home located 1 mile from downtown Juneau. Built on the side of Mt. Juneau, it features a southern exposure enabling the viewing of sunrises and sunsets over busy Gastineau Channel and the moon rising over the statuesque mountains of Douglas Island. Hosts Philip and Clovis Dennis serve an excellent breakfast in the Glassroom overlooking the channel and mountains. Within a short walk is the glacier hiking-jogging-biking trail and public transportation. Smoke-free rooms are available with private or shared bathrooms. Suites have kitchens. Plan to enjoy all the amenities of home while experiencing "Our Great Land of Foreverness."

Hosts: Philip and Clovis Dennis
Rooms: 6 (4PB; 2SB) $75-135
Full Breakfast
Credit Cards: A, B
Notes: 2, 5, 7, 8, 9, 10, 11, 12

Pearson's Pond Luxury Inn/Garden Spa/Travel Service

4541 Sawa Circle-CD, 99801-8723
(907) 789-3772; FAX (907) 789-6722
E-mail: pearsons.pond@juneau.com
Web site: http://www.juneau.com/pearsons.pond

Private studio/suites on scenic pond. Hot tub under the stars, rowboat, bicycles, BBQ, guest kitchenette. Complimentary cappuccino, fresh breads, gourmet coffee, and popcorn. Near glacier, fishing, rafting, skiing, ferry, airport, and Glacier Bay departures. Smoke-free. Quiet, scenic, with lots of privacy in fully equipped studio with private entrance and deck. In-room dining and TV, VCR, and stereo tapes provided. Hosts will make travel, tour, and excursion arrangements. Guests say it's a definite "10," where great expectations are met quietly. Winner of AAA and ABBA excellence awards.

Hosts: Steve and Diane Pearson
Rooms: 3 (PB) $89-239
Full Breakfast
Credit Cards: A, B, C, D, E, F
Notes: 2, 5, 8, 9, 10, 11, 12

KENAI

Eldridge Haven Bed and Breakfast

2679 Bowpicker Lane, 99611
(907) 283-7152 (voice and FAX)

Eldridge Haven Bed and Breakfast is hospitality at its best! Peaceful, clean, friendly. Excellent food: giant Alaskan pancake, steaming gingered bananas, stuffed scones, etc. It's in a wooded area surrounded by prime habitat for moose, caribou, bald eagles, and waterfowl. You can walk to the beach. Cross-country skiing is convenient. The lodging is close to all Peninsula points, including Seward and Homer. So eliminate packing and unpacking; stay with the best and visit the rest. Children are treasured; guests are pampered. Eldridge Haven Bed and Breakfast is open year-round. We've been serving satisfied guests since 1987.

Hosts: Marta and Barry Eldridge
Rooms: 2 (1PB; 1SB) $65-80
Full Breakfast
Credit Cards: A, B
Notes: 2, 5, 7, 8, 9, 10, 11 (cross-country), 12

PALMER

Hatcher Pass Bed and Breakfast

HC 05, Box 6797-D, 99645
(907) 745-6788; FAX (907) 745-6787
E-mail: Hejl@micronet.net

Relax and enjoy your own log cabin nestled at the base of beautiful Hatcher Pass. The area is home to winter activities such as skiing and snowmachining and a multitude of summer activities that include hiking, berry picking, gold panning, biking, rock climbing, and visiting the historic Independence Mine. Each guest cabin is private and completely self-contained, offering all the modern conveniences of a bathroom and kitchen. Your choice of a full or continental breakfast will be served in the privacy of your cabin. Summer guests can relax in the hot tub after a day of hiking or traveling nearby. Your stay at Hatcher Pass will truly be a highlight of your visit to Alaska.

Hosts: Dan and Liz Hejl
Rooms: 3 (PB) $65-75
Full or Continental Breakfast
Credit Cards: A, B
Notes: 2, 5, 6, 7, 11, 12

SITKA

Alaska Ocean View B&B

1101 Edgecumbe Drive, 99835
(907) 747-8310 (voice and FAX)
Web site: http://www.wetpage.com/oceanview

An outstanding lodging rated one of "Alaska's best!" Drift off to sleep in an exceptionally comfortable king/queen bed under a fluffy down comforter after a relaxing, massaging soak in the patio Jacuzzi. Wake to the wonderful aroma of a generous, delicious breakfast. Cable TV (51 channels), VCR, stereo, and phone in your room. Some rooms have sofa, refrigerator, and microwave. Enjoy the extensive library, lush rock gardens, magnificent view, and warm hospitality.

Hosts: Carole and Bill Denkinger
Rooms: 3 (PB) $89-139
Full Breakfast
Credit Cards: A, B, C
Notes: 2, 5, 7, 8, 9, 12

SOLDOTNA

Denise Lake Lodge

PO Box 1050, 99669
(907) 262-1789; (800) 478-1789;
FAX (907) 262-7184
E-mail: Jehanson@ptialaska.net
Web site: http://www.bbonline.com/ak/deniselake

We are located in a quiet setting of white birches on Denise Lake, 3 miles from

NOTES: Credit cards accepted: A Master Card; B Visa; C American Express; D Discover; E Diners Club; F Other; 2 Personal checks accepted; 3 Lunch available; 4 Dinner available; 5 Open all year; 6 Pets

Soldotna and the Kenai River. Our immaculate rooms and cabins all have private bathrooms. A full, cooked breakfast is included. We have a coin-operated laundry and an exercise room, and there is a handicap entrance to the lodge. Both the spacious dining and living room areas have picture windows with a view of the lake. God bless you.

Hostess: Elaine Hanson
Rooms: 12 (PB) $98-149
Full Breakfast
Credit Cards: A, B, C, D
Notes: 2, 7, 10, 12

TRAPPER CREEK

McKinley Foothills Bed and Breakfast Cabins

PO Box 13089, 99683
(907) 733-1454 (voice and FAX);
(888) 770-7052
E-mail: mckinley@matnet.com
Web site: www.matnet.com/~mckinley

Rustic, fully furnished wilderness cabins south of Mt. McKinley. Guests enjoy dog mushing, cross-country skiing, and snowmobiling in the winter; fishing in the summer; hiking, gold panning. Great birding experience. We speak Spanish. Wonderful view of Mt. McKinley and the northern lights. Our best assets: hospitality and food.

Hosts: Robert and Vilma Anderson
Rooms: 3 cabins (1PB) $75-85
Full Breakfast
Credit Cards: A, B, C
Notes: 4, 5, 6, 7, 12

WASILLA

Abbey on the Lake

PO Box 876332, 99687-6332
(907) 357-6332 (voice and FAX)
E-mail: abbeyonthelake@compuserve.com

Welcome to the most serene setting in the most beautiful country at an inn run by delightfully interesting people. The owners have been in the B&B business for 7 years and can't think of anything they love doing more! Jackie came to Alaska in 1975 and is full of wonderful suggestions—and her hobby is cooking! You are definitely in for a treat. You'll be fed from the organic garden of this 5-acre bed and breakfast on Finger Lake.

Hostess: Jackie Williams
Rooms: 2 (PB) $95-125
Full Breakfast
Credit Cards: A, B
Notes: 2, 5, 7, 9, 10, 11

Yukon Don's B&B Inn

1830 E. Parks Highway, Suite 386, 99654
(907) 376-7472; (800) 478-7472;
FAX (907) 376-7470
E-mail: yukondon@alaska.net
Web site: http://www.alaskaone.com/yukondon

When you're traveling in Alaska, or to and from Denali National Park, you don't want to miss staying at Yukon Don's Bed and Breakfast, "Alaska's most acclaimed B&B inn." Each spacious, comfortable guest room is decorated with authentic Alaskana. Stay in the Iditarod, Fishing, Denali, or Hunting rooms, or select the Matanuska or Yukon executive suites. Our guests relax in the Alaska Room, complete with an Alaskan historic library, video library, pool table, cable TV, and gift bar.

The all-glass-view room on the second floor offers a grand view in the Matanuska Valley, complete with fireplace, chairs, and observation deck. We provide phones in each room, Yukon Don's own expanded continental breakfast bar, sauna, exercise room, and, according to Commissioner Glenn Olds (world traveler) "the grandest view he has ever seen from a home." Judge William Hungate of St. Louis, Missouri, said, "It's like seeing Alaska without leaving the house." Wasilla is home of the international Iditarod sled dog race.

Hosts: Don and Beverly Tanner
Rooms: 8 (3PB; 5SB) + cabin $79-125
Continental Breakfast
Credit Cards: A, B, C, D
Notes: 2, 5, 7, 8, 10, 11, 12

WRANGELL

Grand View B&B

PO Box 927, 99929
(907) 874-3225 (voice and FAX)
Web site: http://www.GrandviewBnB.com

Nestled in the woods, quiet and secluded. Courtesy transportation. Three guest rooms with private baths and entrances. Common dining, living, kitchen area with kitchen privileges. Rooms include cable TV, VCR, touchtone phone, XL twin or queen beds. Smoke-free environment, view with lots of maritime activity to watch, and beautiful sunsets. We will work with you to customize a package for the activities that best suit your needs, such as charter fishing, kayaking, jet boat tours, guided walking tours, golf, tennis, or swimming. We enjoy hosting our guests and look forward to sharing our community and lifestyle with them.

Hosts: Judy and John Baker
Rooms: 3 (PB) $65-90
Full or Continental Breakfast
Credit Cards: none
Notes: 2, 3, 5, 8, 9, 10, 12

Grand View Bed and Breakfast

Arizona

Advance Reservations Inn Arizona/Mi Casa Su Casa/Old Pueblo Homestays B&B RSO

PO Box 950, **Tempe,** 85280-0950
(602) 990-0682; (800) 456-0682 (reservations);
FAX (602) 990-3390
E-mail: micasa@primenet.com
Web site: http://www.micasa.com

Since 1981, we have listed inspected, clean, comfortable homestays, inns, cottages, and ranches in the southwestern U.S. We list about 200 modest-to-luxurious, historic-to-contemporary B&Bs. **Arizona** listings include Ajo, Benson, Bisbee, Cave Creek, Cottonwood, Flagstaff, Globe, Mesa, Page, Patagonia, Paradise, Payson, Phoenix, Prescott, Rimrock, Scottsdale, Sedona, Sierra Vista, Sonoita, Tempe, Tombstone, Tucson, Willcox, Williams, and other cities. (See also our entries in Nevada, New Mexico, and Utah.) We also represent two luxury villas, one in Puerto Vallarto, **Mexico,** and the second in the Costa Brava area of **Spain.** Most rooms have private baths and range from $50 to $275, based on double occupancy. Continental to gourmet breakfasts. A book with individual descriptions and pictures is available for $9.50. Ruth Young, coordinator.

Arizona Trails B&B Reservation Service

PO Box 18998, **Fountain Hills,** 85269-8998
(602) 837-4284; (888) 799-4284;
FAX (602) 816-4224
E-mail: aztrails@arizonatrails.com
Web site: http://www.arizonatrails.com

A respected resource for B&B accommodations. More than eighty properties, all inspected and approved. Statewide coverage includes traditional homestays, B&Bs, country inns, and historic properties. Romantic getaways, luxury B&B experiences. Travel packages, corporate travelers, and small groups are accommodated. Prices range from modest to luxury. Free service. All major credit cards accepted. Roxanne Boryczki, owner.

FLAGSTAFF

Birch Tree Inn Bed and Breakfast

824 W. Birch Avenue, 86001-4420
(520) 774-1042; (888) 774-1042;
FAX (520) 774-8462
E-mail: birch@flagstaff.az.us
Web site: http://www.birchtreeinn.com

"A traditional bed and breakfast" located a fraction of a mile from downtown, this

ARIZONA

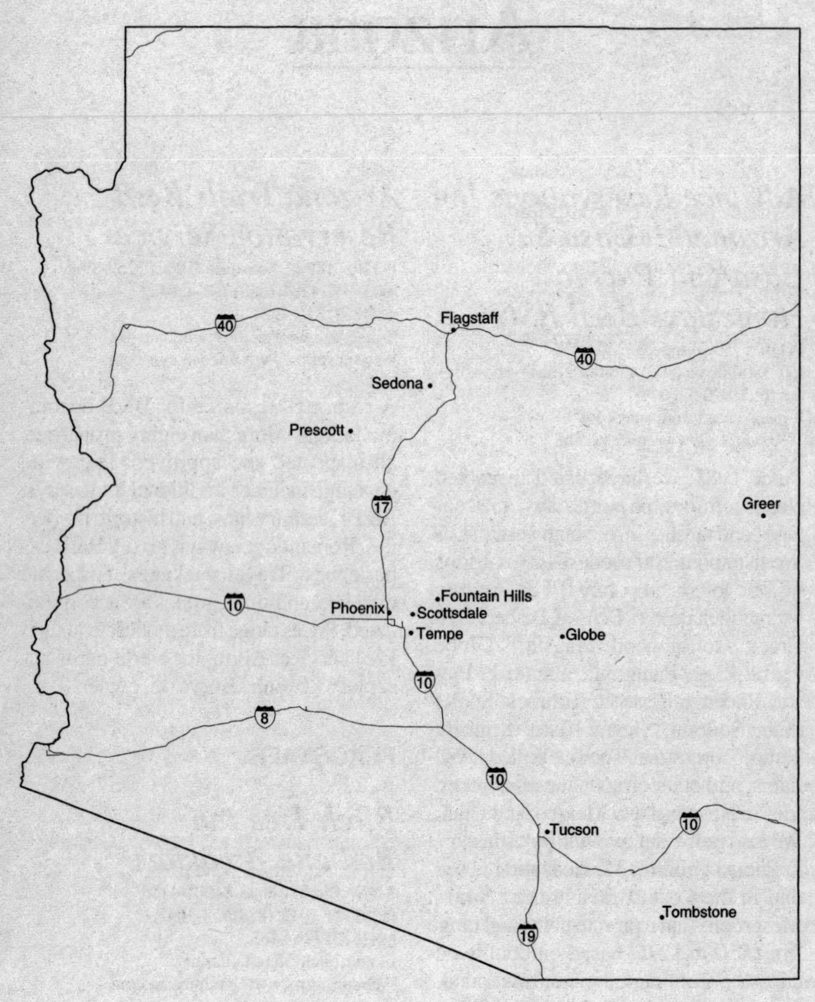
40
Flagstaff
40
Sedona
Prescott
17
Greer
Fountain Hills
10
Phoenix
Scottsdale
Tempe
Globe
10
8
10
Tucson
10
Tombstone
19

Birch Tree Inn Bed and Breakfast

1917 home has five rooms upstairs. Fireplace downstairs; pool table for guests' use. Hot tub outdoors. Rates include full breakfast, afternoon refreshments.

Hosts: Rodger and Donna Pettinger, Sandy and Ed Znetko
Rooms: 5 (3PB; 2SB) $69-109
Full Breakfast
Credit Cards: A, B, C, D
Notes: 2, 5, 8, 10, 11

Comfi Cottages

1612 N. Aztec Street, 86001
(520) 774-0731; (888) 774-0731;
FAX (520) 779-1008
E-mail: Comfie@infomagic.com
Web site: http://www.virtualflagstaff.com/comfi

Near the Grand Canyon, great for families. Six individual cottages with antiques and English country motif. Three cottages are two-bedroom, one bath; one is a one-bedroom honeymoon cottage; and two are three-bedroom, two baths. All have gas fireplaces. Fully equipped with linens, towels, blankets. Kitchens have dishes, pots, pans, coffeepot, etc. Ready-to-prepare breakfast foods in fridge. Color cable television and telephone. Bicycles on premises, washer/dryer, picnic tables, and barbecue grills at each cottage. Recommended by *Fodor's*, 1998. *Arizona Republic's* choice as "Best Weekend Getaway" for November 1995.

Hosts: Pat and Ed Wiebe
Rooms: 6 cottages (PB) $95-195 (entire cottage)
Self-Catered Full Breakfast
Credit Cards: A, B, D
Notes: 2, 5, 7, 8, 9, 10, 11, 12

Comfi Cottages

Fall Inn to Nature

8080 N. Colt Drive, 86004
(520) 714-0237

A touch of nature inside and out is what Flagstaff and this bed and breakfast have to offer. Built in 1996 on a spacious 2½ acres surrounded by Ponderosa Pines and wildflowers with a panoramic view of Mt. Elden and the peaks right out your window. Conveniently located on the way to the Grand Canyon, Sunset Crater, Lake Powell, and the Painted Desert, and just a few minutes from town. Horseback riding and hiking trails are close by.

Hosts: Annette and Ron Fallaha
Rooms: 2 (PB) $80-89
Continental Breakfast
Credit Cards: A, B, F
Notes: 2

NOTES: Credit cards accepted: A Master Card; B Visa; C American Express; D Discover; E Diners Club; F Other; 2 Personal checks accepted; 3 Lunch available; 4 Dinner available; 5 Open all year; 6 Pets welcome; 7 Children welcome; 8 Tennis nearby; 9 Swimming nearby; 10 Golf nearby; 11 Skiing nearby; 12 May be booked through travel agent.

The Inn at 410

410 N. Leroux Street, 86001
(520) 774-0088; (800) 774-2008;
FAX (520) 774-6354

Explore the Grand Canyon, Indian ruins, and Sedona, then relax at "the Place with the Personal Touch." The Inn at 410 offers award-winning hospitality in a charming 1907 Craftsman home. Scrumptious gourmet breakfasts and fresh-baked cookies recently featured on PBS-TV. Nine distinctive guest rooms with private baths, some with fireplaces or oversize Jacuzzi tubs. Walk two blocks to shops in historic downtown Flagstaff. Hike, bike, or ski the San Francisco Peaks.

Hosts: Howard and Sally Krueger
Rooms: 9 (PB) $125-165
Full Breakfast
Credit Cards: A, B
Notes: 2, 5, 7, 10, 11, 12

Jeanette's Bed and Breakfast

Jeanette's Bed and Breakfast

3380 E. Lockett Road, 86004-4043
(520) 527-1912; (800) 752-1912;
FAX (520) 527-1713
Web site: http://www.bbonline.com/AZ/JBB

Relax and enjoy while you step back in time. Architecture of the post-Victorian era recalls Arizona's first statehood days. Experience Jeanette's four rooms filled with signs of the time. Private baths reflect the style of the era and a "breakfast so divine" is served with the flair and detail of a fine Sunday dinner. Flagstaff is the place to be for sights, sounds, and the smell of cool, clean, pine-scented mountain air.

Hosts: Jeanette and Ray West
Rooms: 4 (PB) $95-125
Full Breakfast
Credit Cards: A, B
Notes: 2, 5, 7 (over 7), 8, 9, 10, 11, 12

GLOBE

Cedar Hill B&B

175 E. Cedar, 85501
(520) 425-7530

Cedar Hill B&B was built in 1903 by the Trojonavich family. They were owners of a lumber company, which accounts for the wainscoting walls in the kitchen and rear porch. The property has many fruit trees, flower beds, and a grape arbor for the enjoyment of our guests. Guests may enjoy both a front porch with swings and our back patio with shade trees. The backyard is fenced for the protection of children and pets you may wish to bring! Cable TV and VCR are available in the living room. Within driving distance of both

Cedar Hill Bed and Breakfast

NOTES: Credit cards accepted: A Master Card; B Visa; C American Express; D Discover; E Diners Club; F Other; 2 Personal checks accepted; 3 Lunch available; 4 Dinner available; 5 Open all year; 6 Pets

Tucson and Phoenix. Discounts for seniors and for stays longer than overnight.

Hostess: Helen Gross
Rooms: 2 (SB) $40-50
Full Breakfast
Credit Cards: none
Notes: 2, 5, 6, 7, 9

GREER

White Mountain Lodge

140 Main St.; PO Box 143, 85927
(520) 735-7568; FAX (520) 735-7498

This 1892 country home was remodeled in 1996. Each bedroom is individually decorated in attractive southwestern, country style with private baths. The common rooms reflect the home's southwestern country heritage with period antiques, regional art, and mission-style furniture. Overlooking a beautiful meadow and the Little Colorado River, surrounded by pine- and aspen-covered hills, the lodge affords guests spectacular scenery, country hospitality, and extraordinary full breakfasts. The cabins have fireplaces, full kitchens, and whirlpool tubs.

Hosts: Charles and Mary Bast
Rooms: 7 + 4 cabins (PB) $79-145
Full Breakfast
Credit Cards: A, B, D
Notes: 2, 3, 5, 6 (restrictions), 7, 11, 12

PHOENIX

Harmony House B&B Inn

7202 N. 7th Avenue, 85021
(602) 331-9554; FAX (602) 395-0528
E-mail: jfontaine@sprintmail.com

Built in 1934, the Harmony House currently has five rooms, each with a private bathroom. The interior is country/Victorian; architecture is European, Tudor-style. A full family-style breakfast is served. The house is close to the airport, downtown, freeway, and great shopping.

Hosts: Mike and Jennifer Fontaine
Rooms: 5 (PB) $75-115
Full Breakfast
Credit Cards: A, B, C
Notes: 2, 5, 7, 10

The Villa on Alvarado

2031 N. Alvarado Road, 85004
(602) 253-9352
E-mail: CKing24968@aol.com
Web site: http://www.rumford.com/King.html

Located in a quiet, historic neighborhood, the villa features a spacious guest house with two bedrooms, two baths, and a kitchenette. The deck overlooks the manicured gardens and a sparkling pool. If royalty is your preference, our English tower will be perfect for you. It has a private entrance, sitting room, curved stairway that leads to a magnificent, canopied king-size bed, private bath, and balcony.

Hosts: Kay and Chris King
Rooms: 3 (PB) $80-125
Continental Breakfast
Credit Cards: none
Notes: 5, 8, 9, 10

PRESCOTT

Hotel Vendome

230 S. Cortez Street, 86303
(520) 776-0900; (888) 468-3583
Web site: http://www.vendomehotel.com

Hotel Vendome is a historic landmark in the heart of Prescott. Built in 1917, the inn is fully refurbished to an immaculate condition. Very distinguished, with an aura of history and tradition. A cozy, intimate bar, warm, comfortable lobby, and inviting guest room all create unique ambience. Perfect for both leisure and corporate travel. Walking distance to downtown. Special romantic packages on request.

Hosts: Amrish and Rama Patel
Rooms: 20 (PB) $79-129
European-Style Breakfast Buffet
Credit Cards: A, B, C, D, E, F
Notes: 5, 7, 8, 9, 10, 12

Mount Vernon Inn

204 N. Mt. Vernon Avenue, 86301
(520) 778-0886; FAX (520) 778-7305
E-mail: mtvrnon@primenet.com
Web site: http://prescottlink.com/mtvrnon/index.html

Built in 1900 and listed on the National Register of Historic Places, the Mount Vernon Inn is one of Prescott's "Victorian Treasures." The four spacious guest rooms with private baths and three beautiful country cottages offer charming alternatives to conventional lodging and are designed for your comfort and relaxation. Breakfast is served in our dining room. The inn is just a few blocks from the town square. Come and enjoy the hospitality!

Mount Vernon Inn

Hosts: Michele and Jerry Neumann
Rooms: 7 (PB) $95-125
Full Breakfast
Credit Cards: A, B, D
Notes: 2, 5, 8, 9, 10, 12

SCOTTSDALE

La Paz in Desert Springs

6309 E. Ludlow Drive, 85254
(602) 922-5379; (888) 922-0963;
FAX (602) 905-0085

Enjoy peace and comfort in this freshly decorated, three-room suite with southwestern decor. Full bath, private entrance suite. The large master bedroom has a king bed and room for a rollaway crib. The living room has a queen sofa bed and entertainment center with cable television. A kitchenette is equipped with dishes, coffeemaker, microwave, and refrigerator. La Paz is ideally located close to Old Scottsdale, WestWorld, Rawhide, and other attractions. Great restaurants, golf, and shopping malls. Near the desert, hiking, rafting, and horseback riding. Within a day's travel of Sedona, Petrified Forest, Painted Desert, Meteor and Sunset craters, and Grand Canyon. Open October through April; limited summer schedule. Reservations required. No smoking.

Hosts: Luis and Susan Cuevas
Rooms: 3-room suite (PB) $95-135
Continental Plus Breakfast
Credit Cards: none
Notes: 2, 7, 8, 9, 10, 11, 12

Valley O' the Sun Bed and Breakfast

PO Box 2214, 85252
(602) 941-1281; (800) 689-1281 (voice and FAX)

"*Cead Mile Failte*" is the slogan in Gaelic on the doormat of the Valley O' the Sun Bed and Breakfast. It means "100,000 welcomes." This bed and breakfast is more than just a place to stay. Kathleen wants to make your visit to the great Southwest a memorable one. Ideally located in the college area of Tempe, but still close enough to Scottsdale to enjoy the glamour of its shops, restaurants, and theaters. Two guest rooms can comfortably accommodate four people. One bedroom has a full-size bed and the other has twin beds. Each room has its own TV. Within minutes of golf, horseback riding, picnic area, swimming, bicycling, shopping, and tennis. Within walking distance of Arizona State University.

Hostess: Kathleen Kennedy Curtis
Rooms: 2 (SB) $40
Continental Breakfast
Credit Cards: none
Notes: 2 (restricted), 5, 7 (over 10), 8, 9, 10, 11, 12

SEDONA

Adobe Village & Graham Inn

150 Canyon Circle Drive, 86351
(520) 284-1425; (800) 228-1425;
FAX (520) 284-0767
E-mail: graham@sedona.net
Web site: http://www.sedonasfinest.com

An award-winning inn with six unique theme rooms and four new luxury casitas with waterfall showers and bath fireplaces.

Adobe Village & Graham Inn

Rates include use of pool, hot tub, bicycles, CDs, and videos. Rooms have fireplaces, Jacuzzi tubs, TV/VCRs, and private balconies or decks with red rock views. AAA four diamonds; Mobil four stars.

Hosts: Carol and Roger Redenbaugh
Rooms: 6 + 4 casitas (PB) $119-369
Full Breakfast
Credit Cards: A, B, C, D
Notes: 2, 5, 7, 8, 9, 10, 12 (no fee)

Apple Orchard Inn

656 Jordan Road, 86336
(520) 282-5328; (800) 663-6968;
FAX (520) 204-0044
E-mail: appleorc@sedona.net
Web site: http://www.appleorchardbb.com

Nestled in the heart of Sedona, on the site of the historic Jordan Apple Orchard. Secluded on nearly 2 acres of wooded property. Our unparalleled location allows easy access to "uptown" galleries, shops, and trails. The inn features king beds, whirlpool tubs, TV/VCRs, private patios, fireplaces, and a massage room. Smoke-free environment. Walk to shops and Sedona Heritage Museum. Enjoy spectacular views of Sedona's red rocks, with hiking off the property.

Hosts: Bob and Paula Glass
Rooms: 7 (PB) $135-225
Full Gourmet Breakfast
Credit Cards: A, B, C
Notes: 2, 5, 7 (10 and older), 8, 9, 10, 11, 12

The Lodge at Sedona

125 Kallof Place, 86336
(520) 204-1942; (800) 619-4467;
FAX (520) 204-2128
E-mail: lodge@sedona.net
Web site: www.lodgeatsedona.com

Elegantly rustic, The Lodge at Sedona offers secluded privacy on 2½ acres. Our thirteen guest rooms and large, elegant common rooms with country pine antiques provide a comfortable, nurturing ambience. Some rooms have private decks, fireplaces, and Jacuzzi tubs. A full gourmet breakfast is served on the morning porch. Refreshments are served afternoons and evenings.

Hosts: Barb and Mark Dinunzio
Rooms: 13 (PB) $120-250
Full Breakfast
Credit Cards: A, B, C, D
Notes: 2, 3 and 4 (on request), 5, 7, 9, 10, 12

Territorial House: An Old West Bed and Breakfast

65 Piki Drive, 86336
(520) 204-2737; (800) 801-2737;
FAX (520) 204-2230
E-mail: oldwest@sedona.net
Web site: http://oldwestbb.sedona.net

Our large stone and cedar house has been tastefully decorated to depict Arizona's territorial era. Each room recalls different stages of Sedona's early history. Some rooms have private balcony, Jacuzzi tub, or fireplace. An enormous stone fireplace graces the living room and a covered veranda welcomes guests at the end of a day of sight-seeing. Relax in our outdoor hot tub. A full, hearty breakfast is served at the harvest table each morning. All of this is served with western hospitality.

Hosts: John and Linda Steele
Rooms: 4 (PB) $109-159
Full Breakfast
Credit Cards: A, B, C, D
Notes: 2, 5, 7, 8, 9, 10, 11, 12

TOMBSTONE

Priscilla's Bed and Breakfast

101 N. 3rd Street, 85638
(520) 457-3844
E-mail: prisc@theriver.com
Web site: http://www.tombstone1880.com/priscilla/index.htm

Priscilla's Bed and Breakfast is the only remaining two-story clapboard, country Victorian house in Tombstone. The house was built by an affluent attorney in 1904. It is painted in the authentic Victorian colors and is surrounded by the original picket fence. It is listed on the National Historic Register of Homes. The house has been restored to perfection by its owner; it still retains the original wood and some of the original gas light fixtures.

Hosts: Barbara and Larry Gray
Rooms: 4 (1PB; 3SB) $55-69
Full Breakfast
Credit Cards: A, B, C
Notes: 5, 6, 7

Casa Alegre Bed and Breakfast

TUCSON

Casa Alegre Bed and Breakfast

316 E. Speedway Boulevard, 85705
(520) 628-1800; (800) 628-5654;
FAX (520) 792-1880
E-mail: alegre123@aol.com

Casa Alegre B&B is a charming 1915 Craftsman-style bungalow featuring mahogany, leaded glass, built-in cabinetry, and hardwood floors. The serene gardens, pool, and hot tub make an oasis of comfort in central Tucson, just minutes from the University of Arizona. A scrumptious full breakfast is served. Private baths. AAA- and Mobil-rated.

Hostess: Phyllis Florek
Rooms: 5 (PB) $60-105
Full Breakfast
Credit Cards: A, B, C, D
Notes: 2, 5, 8, 9, 10, 11, 12

El Presidio Bed and Breakfast Inn

297 N. Main Avenue, 85701
(520) 623-6151; (800) 349-6151;
FAX (520) 623-3860

Experience southwestern charm in a desert oasis with the romance of a country inn. Garden courtyards with the Old Mexico ambience of lush, floral displays, fountains, and cobblestone surround a richly appointed guest house and suites. You will enjoy the antique decor, robes, complimentary beverages, fruit, snacks, TVs, and telephones. The 1880s Victorian adobe mansion has been featured in numerous magazines and in the book *The Desert Southwest*. The inn is located in a historic district. You can walk to fine restaurants, museums, shops, and the arts district. El Presidio is located close to downtown. Mobil and AAA three-star rated.

Hostess: Patti Toci
Rooms: 3 suites (PB) $95-115
Full Breakfast
Credit Cards: none
Notes: 2, 5, 8, 9, 10, 12

Ford's Affordable Bed and Breakfast

1202 N. Avenida Marlene, 85715
(520) 885-1202

A warm welcome awaits you at our nonsmoking home located in a residential cul-de-sac on Tucson's northeast side. Your English-born hostess has enjoyed living in Tucson many years and knows the area well. Guests enjoy a birds-eye view of the mountains from their private patio. A small sitting room with TV, frige, and microwave oven. Private entrance. Close to Saguaro National Park, Sabino Canyon, Colossal Cave; take scenic drives to other places of interest.

Hosts: Sheila and Tom Ford
Rooms: 2 (PB) $60
Full Breakfast
Credit Cards: none
Notes: 2

welcome; 7 Children welcome; 8 Tennis nearby; 9 Swimming nearby; 10 Golf nearby; 11 Skiing nearby; 12 May be booked through travel agent.

Hacienda Bed and Breakfast

5704 E. Grant Road, 85712
(520) 290-2224; (888) 236-4421;
FAX (520) 721-9066
E-mail: Hacienda97@aol.com
Web site: http://members.aol.com/Hacienda97/index.html

Four quiet, air-conditioned rooms with private baths. Two have TV/VCRs and private entrances; one offers handicap access and has a refrigerator, coffeemaker, and full hide-a-bed. Two bedrooms share a sitting room with television/VCR and table and chairs. Guests may use the private courtyard, barbecue, pool and spa, exercise room, computer, FAX, copier, fireproof file for valuables. There is lots of hiking, biking, and bird-watching in the area. Smoke-free. No pets. Supervised children welcome. AAA-rated; member of Tucson Convention Bureau and Chamber of Commerce, and of AABBI.

Hosts: Barbara and Fred Shamseldin
Rooms: 4 (PB) $85-105
Full Breakfast
Credit Cards: A, B, C, D
Notes: 2 (traveler's checks), 5, 10, 11 (short season), 12

Jeremiah Inn Bed and Breakfast

10921 E. Snyder Road, 85749-9066
(520) 749-3072; (888) 750-3072

For centuries, travelers have paused at quiet inns to refresh themselves before continuing life's journey. The Jeremiah Inn is one such place (Jeremiah 9:2). Santa Fe style with spacious contemporary comforts are offered in this 1995-constructed inn, a 3 1/3-acre desert retreat in the shadows of the Catalina Mountains. Birding, stargazing, hiking, swimming, queen-size beds, afternoon cookies, and smoke-free premises are offered.

Hosts: Bob and Beth Miner
Rooms: 3 (PB) $70-110
Full Breakfast
Credit Cards: A, B, C
Notes: 2, 5, 7, 8, 9, 10, 11, 12

June's Bed and Breakfast

3212-W Holladay Street, 85746
(520) 578-0857

Mountainside home with pool. Majestic, towering mountains. Hiking in the desert. Sparkling city lights. Beautiful rear yard and patio. Suitable for receptions.

Hostess: June Henderson
Rooms: 3 (1PB; 2SB) $45-55
Continental Breakfast
Credit Cards: none
Notes: 2, 8, 9, 10, 11

La Posada del Valle

1640 N. Campbell Avenue, 85719
(520) 795-3840 (voice and FAX)
Web site: http://www.arizonaguide.com/visitpremier

La Posada del Valle, surrounded by orange trees and lush gardens, is an elegant inn built in 1929. Five guest rooms with private baths and private entrances are furnished with antiques from the 1920s and '30s. Breakfast is served in the dining room with its glorious Catalina Mountain views. Guests gather for afternoon tea. The University of Arizona, University Medical Center, shops, restaurants, etc., are all within walking distance. *Wir sprechen*

Deutsch. La Posada del Valle is AAA three-diamond-rated. All rooms have TVs and three rooms have phones. Private, off-street parking.

Rooms: 5 (PB) $90-135
Full Breakfast
Credit Cards: A, B
Notes: 2, 5, 7, 8, 9, 10, 11, 12

Natural Bed and Breakfast

3150 E. Presidio Road, 85716
(520) 881-4582; FAX (520) 326-1385
E-mail: Bluefive@dakotacom.net
Web site: http://www.tbliz.com/naturalbb.htm

Come to the Natural Bed and Breakfast for the whole foods served in a homelike atmosphere. You will find a safe, nontoxic environment—good for guests with allergies and environmental illnesses. We use no chemicals in maintaining the guest rooms. A special amenity is the wonderful, professional, therapeutic massage after your travels.

Host: Marc Haberman
Rooms: 4 (2PB; 2SB) $65-75
Full Breakfast
Credit Cards: none
Notes: 2, 3, 5, 7, 8, 9, 10, 11, 12

Rincon Valley Bed and Breakfast

7080 S. Camino Loma Alta, 85747
(520) 647-3335
E-mail: valleyretreat@theriver.com
Web site: http://www.personal.riverusers.com/~valleyretreat

Retreat to our 2½ acres where the stars at night are unbelievably vivid and the howl of coyotes can be heard on the rise. Then greet the morning with the tunes of wonderful birds of many types. Enjoy the sight of our abundant wildlife, where even an occasional bobcat can add extra spice to your stay. Hearty breakfasts are served with your good health in mind. Sharon cooks with organic produce, whole grains, and eggs from cage-free chickens. Homemade treats with coffee or tea are served in the afternoon.

Hosts: Larry and Sharon Wilson
Rooms: 2 (PB) $85-95
Full Breakfast
Credit Cards: A, B
Notes: 2, 3 and 4 (picnic baskets, on request), 5, 7

Shadow Mountain Ranch Bed and Breakfast Inn

8855 N. Scenic Drive, 85743
(520) 744-7551; (888) 9-SHADOW
E-mail: shadmtn@aol.com
Web site: http://members.aol.com/shadmtn/

Enjoy a paradise in the desert, nestled in the Tucson Mountains (NW). The U-shaped hacienda offers a poolside villa, perfect for families and couples; two bedrooms, two baths, a full kitchen, 1,200 square feet. The main house has a luxury king suite and queen rooms. Shadow Mountain Ranch is a nature and outdoor lover's dream vacation. The hostess and her two loveable indoor cats, Benson and Patches, will lovingly share God's paradise of peace.

Hostess: Lyn Nelson
Rooms: 5 (4PB; 1SB) $75-175
Continental Breakfast
Credit Cards: none
Notes: 2, 6 (in villa), 7, 10, 12

ARKANSAS

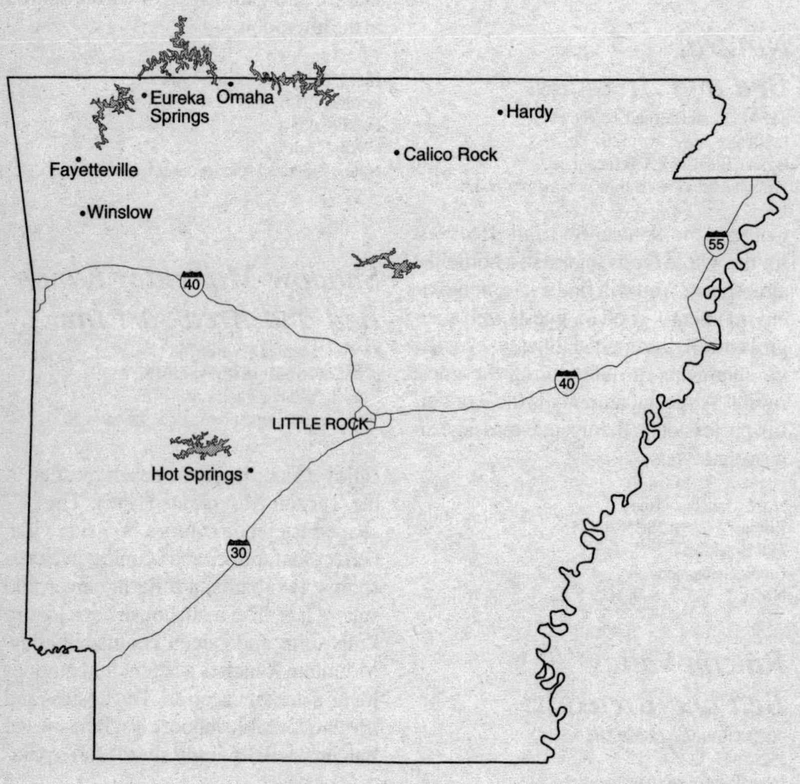

Eureka
Springs
Omaha
Hardy
Calico Rock
Fayetteville
Winslow
55
40
40
LITTLE ROCK
Hot Springs
30

Arkansas

CALICO ROCK

Happy Lonesome Log Cabins

HC 61, Box 72, 72519
(870) 297-8764
E-mail: hlcabins@centuryinter.net
Web site: http://www.bbonline.com/ar/hlcabins

Happy Lonesome offers secluded comfort and charm. Enjoy our natural, relaxing location surrounded by the Ozark National Forest. The cabins are unhosted but are provided with milk, juice, coffee, cereal, and homemade bread. They are decorated with the past in mind while providing modern comforts. Each cabin has a comfortable sleeping loft, kitchenette including microwave, downstairs living area, bath, hide-a-bed, woodstove, and AC. Outside is a covered porch with swing or double rocker; an outdoor grill is nearby. Enjoy a breathtaking view of the White River from the 200-foot bluff. Relax on the porch and delight in the panoramic river valley, forest, and wildlife.

Hosts: Christian and Carolyn Eck
Rooms: 4 (2PB; 2SB) $55-65 (7th night free)
Continental Breakfast
Credit Cards: A, B, C, D
Notes: 2, 7, 8, 9, 10

1881 Crescent Cottage Inn

EUREKA SPRINGS

1881 Crescent Cottage Inn

211 Spring Street, 72632
(501) 253-6022; (800) 223-3246;
FAX (501) 253-6234
E-mail: raphael@ipa.net
Web site: http://www.eureka-usa.com/crescott

Famous 1881 Victorian on National Register of Historic Places. The oldest, most historic and photographed bed and breakfast. Special features include a great arch, antiques, hand-painted ceiling decorations, and crystal chandeliers such as those that were in the home of the first governor of

---

NOTES: Credit cards accepted: A Master Card; B Visa; C American Express; D Discover; E Diners Club; F Other; 2 Personal checks accepted; 3 Lunch available; 4 Dinner available; 5 Open all year; 6 Pets welcome; 7 Children welcome; 8 Tennis nearby; 9 Swimming nearby; 10 Golf nearby; 11 Skiing nearby; 12 May be booked through travel agent.

Arkansas after the Civil War. Towers and sunbursts grace this Queen Anne home. All rooms have private Jacuzzis, baths, queen beds, TV/VCRs, and FM-AM radios. Beautiful view of the mountains and forests. It's only a short walk or trolley ride to downtown.

Hosts: Ralph and Phyllis Becker
Rooms: 4 (PB) $93-135
Full Breakfast
Credit Cards: A, B, D
Notes: 2, 5, 9, 10, 12

Angel at Rose Hall

56 Hillside, 72632
(501) 253-5405 (voice and FAX); (800) 828-4255
E-mail: rosehall@ipa.net
Web site: http://www.the-angel.com

Step back into time and enjoy the romantic ambience of breathtaking Victorian furnishings, grand fireplaces, and Jacuzzis for two. Twenty-eight century-old stained glass windows invite glorious streams of light into the Angel at Rose Hall, where rich fabrics, designer linens, and fresh flowers splash vibrant colors into rooms. Specializing in Victorian weddings, receptions, honeymoon suites, anniversaries, and special getaways. Adults only. No smoking.

Host: Sandy Latimer
Rooms: 5 (PB) $125-150
Full Breakfast
Credit Cards: A, B, C, D
Notes: 2, 5, 9, 10, 12

Beaver Lake Bed and Breakfast

1234 County Road 120, 72631
(501) 253-9210; (888) 253-9210
Web site: http://www.bbonline.com/ar/beaverlake

Beaver Lake Bed and Breakfast

Our comfortable country home has an awe-inspiring view of Beaver Lake and the surrounding Ozark Mountains from every room! Experience peace and beauty away from the crowds and the stress of your daily life. Swim or fish from our new boat dock. Hike the nature trails or just relax on the wraparound porch and let gracious hosts pamper you—the perfect place to renew your spirit. Nonsmoking adults only. Y'all come soon!

Hosts: David and Elaine Reppel
Rooms: 4 (PB) $65-95
Full Gourmet Breakfast
Credit Cards: A, B, D
Notes: 2, 5, 9, 10, 12

Bonnybrooke Farm Atop Misty Mountain

Route 2, Box 335A, 72631
(501) 253-6903
Web site: http://www.rosemart.com/bonnybrooke

If your heart's in the country—or longs to be—we invite you to share the sweet quiet and serenity that await you in your place to come home to. Five cottages, distinctly different in their pleasure to tempt you. Fireplace and Jacuzzi for two, full glass fronts and mountaintop views, shower under the stars, wicker porch swing in front of the fireplace. . .you're gonna love it! In order to preserve privacy, the location is given to registered guests only. Bonnybrooke Farm was featured as the most romantic accommodation in Arkansas (*Country Heart Magazine*).

Hosts: Bonny and Joshua Pierson
Rooms: 5 cottages (PB) starting at $95
Continental Breakfast
Credit Cards: none
Notes: 2, 5, 9, 12

Bridgeford House

263 Spring Street, 72632
(501) 253-7853; (888) 567-2422;
FAX (501) 253-5497
E-mail: bridgefordbb@earthlink.net
Web site: http://www.bridgefordhouse.com

Enjoy. Escape. Experience this 1884 Victorian delight! A beautiful example of Queen Anne/Eastlake architecture nestled in the heart of the historic district. Short, relaxing stroll to shops/restaurants. The antique-filled rooms have private baths, Jacuzzis/fireplaces, cable, queen beds. Horse-drawn carriage/trolley car route. Full gourmet southern breakfast. Our "Secret Garden" was honored as Eureka Springs' "Garden of the Season." Southern hospitality, Victorian charm!

Hosts: Linda and Henry Thornton
Rooms: 4 (PB) $85-145
Full Breakfast
Credit Cards: A, B, C, D
Notes: 2, 5, 7, 8, 9, 10, 12

Bridgeford House

The Brownstone Inn

75 Hillside Avenue, 72632
(501) 253-7505; (800) 973-7505
Web site: http://www.eureka-usa.com/brownstone

A present part of Eureka's past is this historic limestone building, located on the trolley route to historic downtown and an easy, short drive to the Great Passion Play. Victorian accommodations, private outside entrances, private baths, and gourmet breakfasts with coffee, tea, or juice at your doorstep before breakfast. Featured in *Best Places to Stay in the South.* Closed January and February.

Hosts: Marvin and Donna Shepard
Rooms: 4 (PB) $90-105
Full Breakfast
Credit Cards: A, B, D
Notes: 2, 5, 10, 12

Candlestick Cottage Inn Bed and Breakfast

6 Douglas Street, 72632
(501) 253-6813; (800) 835-5184
E-mail: candlecl@ipa.net
Web site: http://www.eureka-usa.com/candlecl

This restored Victorian home has six guest rooms, each with private bath; suites have two-person Jacuzzis, private entrances, color cable television, coffeepots, and refrigerators. A full breakfast is served on the treetop porch. No facilities for children or pets; no smoking. Small weddings arranged. Non-Jacuzzi unit available. Off-street parking. The quiet country setting is only 1 block from the downtown historic shopping district.

Hosts: Bill and Patsy Brooks
Rooms: 6 (PB) $65-109
Full Breakfast
Credit Cards: A, B, C, D
Notes: 2, 5, 12

Enchanted Cottages

18 Nut Street, 72632
(501) 253-6790; (800) 862-2788

Romantic, storybook cottages hidden in the historic district of Eureka Springs. Jacuzzi for two or private outdoor hot tub, cozy fireplaces, queen- or king-size beds, cable TV, kitchen, and patios with grills. These cottages have been featured on Eureka Springs' Homes Tour. Special honeymoon and anniversary packages.

Hosts: Barbara Kellogg and David Pettit
Rooms: 1 + 3 cottages (PB) $79-139
Continental Breakfast Optional
Credit Cards: A, B
Notes: 5, 9, 10, 12

Gardeners Cottage

c/o 11 Singleton, 72632
(501) 253-9111; (800) 833-3394
Web site: http://www.usa-eagle.com/singleton.htm

Tucked in a private, wooded historic district, the delightful Gardeners Cottage features charming country decor with romantic touches, cathedral ceilings, skylight, full kitchen, and Jacuzzi for two. The spacious porch with its swing and hammock is perfect for lounging. Great for honeymoons or a long, peaceful stay. Optional breakfast in a basket. Closed January–March.

Hostess: Barbara Gavron
Rooms: 1 cottage (PB) $95-125
Breakfast Optional
Credit Cards: A, B, C, D
Notes: 2, 9, 10, 12

Harvest House

104 Wall Street, 72632
(501) 253-9363; (800) 293-5665
E-mail: harvest@ipa.net
Web site: http://www.eureka-usa.com/harvest

Vintage Victorian filled with lovely antiques, collectibles, and family favorites. Guest rooms have private entrances and private baths. A full breakfast is served in the dining room each morning or, weather permitting, on the screened porch with its gazebo. Your host Bill, a native Arkansan, knows all the hidden treasures to be uncovered in the Eureka Springs area. Patt is a shopper with special interests in antiques and local artisans.

Hosts: Bill and Patt Carmichael
Rooms: 4 (PB) $89-129
Full Breakfast
Credit Cards: A, B, D
Notes: 2, 5, 6, 7 (over 12), 12

The Heartstone Inn and Cottages

35 Kings Highway, 72632
(501) 253-8916; (800) 494-4921;
FAX (501) 253-6821
E-mail: billiris@ipa.net
Web site: http://www.eureka-springs-usa.com/heartstone

An award-winning inn with all private baths, private entrances, and cable TV. King and queen beds. Antiques galore. Renowned gourmet breakfasts. In-house massage therapy studio. Golf privileges. Large decks and gazebo under the trees; great for bird-watching. Recommended by: *The New York Times, Country Home Magazine, America's Wonderful Little Hotels and Inns, Recommended Inns of the South*, and many more. Closed Christmas through January.

Hosts: Iris and Bill Simantel
Rooms: 10 + a 1-bedroom cottage and a 2-bedroom cottage (PB) $68-125
Full Gourmet Breakfast
Credit Cards: A, B, C, D
Notes: 2, 9, 10, 12

NOTES: Credit cards accepted: A Master Card; B Visa; C American Express; D Discover; E Diners Club; F Other; 2 Personal checks accepted; 3 Lunch available; 4 Dinner available; 5 Open all year; 6 Pets

Piedmont House B&B

165 Spring Street, 72632
(501) 253-9258; (800) 253-9258
Web site: http://www.eureka-usa.com/piedmont

Built as travelers' lodging in 1880, Piedmont House is located in the heart of the Victorian historic district. Each room has private bath, air-conditioning, ceiling fan, and private entrance from the wraparound porches. Excellent mountain views. Just a short walk to historic downtown shopping and great restaurants. A home away from home with the warmest hospitality you could ever find. Delicious full breakfasts served each morning.

Hosts: Sheri and Ron Morrill
Rooms: 8 (PB) $79-119
Full Breakfast
Credit Cards: A, B, C, D
Notes: 2, 5, 7 (over 12), 10

Ridgeway House B&B

Ridgeway House B&B

28 Ridgeway, 72632
(501) 253-6618; (800) 477-6618
E-mail: rheureka@ipa.net
Web site: http://www.eureka-usa.com/ridgeway

Prepare to be pampered! Sumptuous breakfasts, luxurious rooms, antiques, desserts, quiet street within walking distance of eight churches, 5-minute walk to historic downtown, trolley just 1 block away. Porches, decks, private Jacuzzi suites for anniversaries/honeymoons. All of our guests are VIPs! Open all year.

Hosts: Becky and "Sony" Taylor
Rooms: 5 (PB) $79-149
Full Breakfast
Credit Cards: A, B, D
Notes: 2, 5, 7, 12

Singleton House Bed and Breakfast

Singleton House Bed and Breakfast

11 Singleton, 72632
(501) 253-9111; (800) 833-3394
Web site: http://www.usa-eagle.com/singleton.htm

This old-fashioned Victorian house with a touch of magic is whimsically decorated and has an eclectic collection of treasures and antiques. Breakfast is served each morning on the balcony overlooking a wildflower garden and fishpond. You can walk 1 block to the historic district, shops, and cafés. Passion Play and Holy Land tour reservations can be arranged. A guest cottage with a Jacuzzi is available at a separate location. A hands-on apprenticeship program also is available! The Singleton House Bed and Breakfast has been featured in more than fifteen bed and breakfast guidebooks. We currently are celebrating our fifteenth year of operation! Closed January–February.

Hostess: Barbara Gavron
Rooms: 5 (PB) $60-95; cottage $65-105
Full Breakfast
Credit Cards: A, B, C, D
Notes: 2, 5, 7, 9, 10, 12

FAYETTEVILLE

Hill Avenue Bed and Breakfast

131 Hill Avenue, 72701
(501) 444-0865

This century-old inn is located in a residential neighborhood near the University of Arkansas, Walton Art Center, and the Bud Walton Arena. The accommodations are smoke-free and feature king beds and private baths.

Hosts: Dale and Cecelia Thompson
Rooms: 3 (PB) $60
Continental Breakfast
Credit Cards: none
Notes: 2, 5

HARDY

Hideaway Inn

Route 1, Box 199, 72542
(870) 966-4770; (888) 966-4770
Web site: http://www.bbonline.com/ar/hideaway

Hideaway Inn is a modern bed and breakfast on 376 acres. It offers three guest rooms with queen beds and central air. Gourmet breakfast and evening snack served. TV/VCR in common area. Beautiful setting, picnic sites, and outdoor pool. Children welcome. Log cabin with two bedrooms, two baths, living/dining/kitchenette combo. Located 10 miles from Hardy and Spring River.

Hostess: Julia Baldridge
Rooms: 5 (3PB; 2SB) $55-95
Full Breakfast
Credit Cards: A, B, C, D
Notes: 2, 5, 7, 9, 10, 12

Olde Stonehouse Bed and Breakfast Inn

511 Main Street, 72542
(870) 856-2983; (800) 514-2983;
FAX (870) 856-4036
E-mail: oldestonehouse@centuryinter.net
Web site: http://www.bbonline.com/ar/stonehouse

This native stone house is located in the historic district, 1 block from the Spring River and Old Hardy Town's quaint antique and craft shops. Guests enjoy the antiques, queen beds, private baths, central heat/air, ceiling fans, unusual stone fireplace with "Arkansas Diamonds," and player piano. A full breakfast is served family-style each morning. You may choose the separate 1904 cottage with opulent Victorian-inspired suites. Nearby you will find the Country Music-Comedy Theater with outdoor musicals, antique car and veterans museums, golfing, canoeing, trail rides, and Mammoth Springs and Grand Gulf state parks.

Hostess: Peggy Volland
Rooms: 7 (PB) $65-99
Full Breakfast
Credit Cards: A, B, C, D
Notes: 2, 3, 5, 8, 9, 10, 12

NOTES: Credit cards accepted: A Master Card; B Visa; C American Express; D Discover; E Diners Club; F Other; 2 Personal checks accepted; 3 Lunch available; 4 Dinner available; 5 Open all year; 6 Pets

HOT SPRINGS

Vintage Comfort Bed and Breakfast

303 Quapaw, 71901
(501) 623-3258; (800) 608-4682

Situated on a tree-lined street, a short walk from Hot Springs' historic Bath House Row, art galleries, restaurants, and shopping. Guests enjoy a comfortably restored Queen Anne house built in 1907. Four spacious rooms are available upstairs, each with private bath, ceiling fan, and period furnishings. A delicious full breakfast is served each morning in the dining room. Vintage Comfort B&B is known for its comfort and gracious southern hospitality.

Hostess: Helen Bartlett
Rooms: 4 (PB) $65-90
Full Breakfast
Credit Cards: A, B, C
Notes: 2, 5, 7 (over 6 years), 8, 9, 10, 12

OMAHA

Aunt Shirley's Sleeping Loft Bed and Breakfast

7250 Shirley Lane N., 72662
(870) 426-5408

Quiet, relaxed atmosphere. Rustic country setting with the convenience of home. Air-conditioning, private bath, clean. Beautiful view with walkways, patio. Gas grill, campfires available. Swings under the trees. *Big* country breakfast, lots of southern hospitality. Children welcome. Located 10 miles north of Harrison, 24 miles south of Branson, Missouri. Near Eureka Springs, Buffalo River, Tablerock Lake, Bull Shoals Lake. Member of Harrison Chamber of Commerce.

Hostess: Shirley LeBleu
Rooms: 2 + cabin (PB) $50-60
Full Breakfast
Credit Cards: A, B
Notes: 2, 5, 6, 7, 9, 10

WINSLOW

Sky-Vue Lodge

22822 N. Highway 71, 72959
(501) 634-2003; (800) 782-2003

Located on Scenic 71 near Fayetteville, Sky-Vue Lodge offers a 25-mile view of the Ozarks. Enjoy the spectacular view from the porch of your charming cabin, which has heating and air-conditioning for year-round comfort. Hike our 83 acres, or enjoy activities at two nearby state parks. Family-oriented, alcohol-free. Ideal for retreats, conferences, reunions, and weddings. Full breakfast included; other meals available.

Hosts: Glenn and Janice Jorgenson
Rooms: 7 cabins (PB) $45-55
Full Breakfast
Credit Cards: A, B, C, D
Notes: 2, 4, 5, 7, 8, 9

CALIFORNIA (NORTHERN)

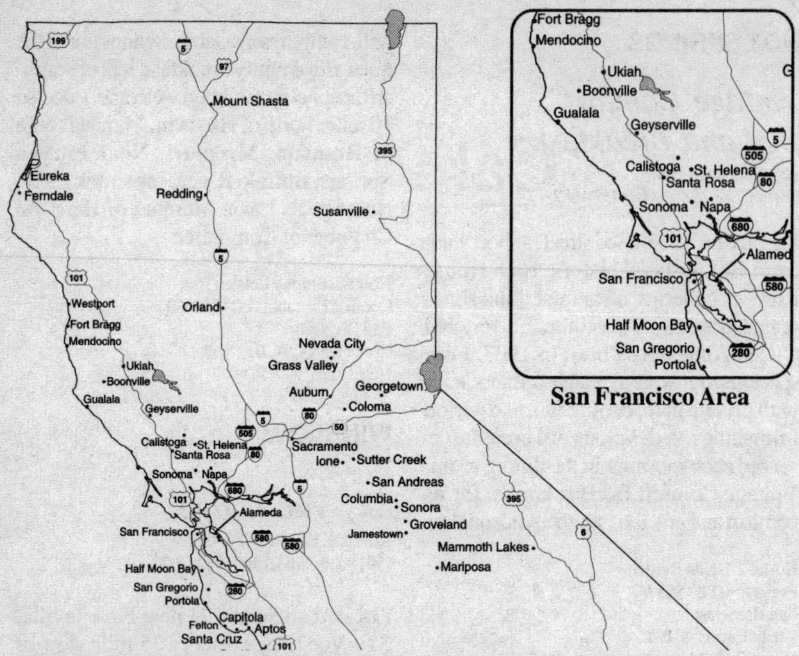

199
5
97
Mount Shasta
395
Eureka
Ferndale
Redding
Susanville
5
101
Westport
Fort Bragg
Mendocino
Orland
Nevada City
Grass Valley
Ukiah
Boonville
Gualala
Auburn
Georgetown
Coloma
Geyserville
5
505
80
50
Calistoga
St. Helena
Santa Rosa
80
Sacramento
Ione
Sutter Creek
Sonoma
Napa
680
5
San Andreas
101
Columbia
Sonora
Alameda
395
San Francisco
580
580
Groveland
Jamestown
6
Mammoth Lakes
Mariposa
Half Moon Bay
San Gregorio
280
Portola
Felton
Capitola
Aptos
Santa Cruz
101

Fort Bragg
Mendocino
Ukiah
Boonville
Gualala
Geyserville
5
505
Calistoga
St. Helena
Santa Rosa
80
Sonoma
Napa
680
101
Alamed
San Francisco
580
Half Moon Bay
San Gregorio
280
Portola

San Francisco Area

CALIFORNIA (SOUTHERN)

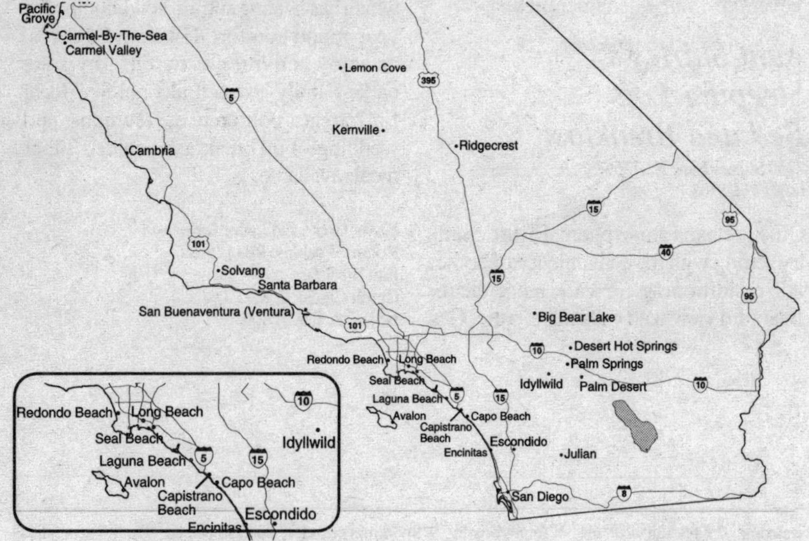

Los Angeles Area

California

ALAMEDA

Garratt Mansion

900 Union, 94501
(510) 521-4779; FAX (510) 521-6796
E-mail: garrattm@pacbell.net

Fifteen minutes from San Francisco, the quiet island of Alameda is convenient and unique. We can offer touring ideas or privacy to regroup. Whether you're on business or vacation, we love to anticipate and meet your needs. Fresh flowers, down comforters, afternoon cookies, fresh orange juice, direct-line phones, 24-hour beverages, and other amenities.

Hosts: Royce and Betty Gladden
Rooms: 7 (5PB; 2SB) $80-130
Full Breakfast
Credit Cards: A, B, C, E
Notes: 2, 5, 8, 9, 10

Garratt Mansion

APTOS

The Bayview Hotel

8041 Soquel Drive, 95003
(408) 688-8654; (800) 422-9843;
FAX (408) 688-5128
E-mail: lodging@bayviewhotel.com
Web site: http://www.bayviewhotel.com

Built in 1878, this three-story Victorian structure has been attractively renovated with lovely antiques and simple period furnishings that blend beautifully with its 10-foot ceilings. The guest rooms (including a two-room suite) all have private baths; some have two-person spas and fireplaces. The Bayview Hotel is located near a bevy of small antique stores, shops, and restaurants, and is just across Highway 1 from fine California beaches. The natural splendor of the Redwood Forest, with its miles of hiking, biking, and equestrian trails, lies literally just outside the front door of the hotel.

Host: Dan Floyd
Rooms: 11 (PB) $90-150
Continental Breakfast
Credit Cards: A, B, C
Notes: 3 and 4 (restaurant in building), 5, 9 (ocean), 10, 12

NOTES: Credit cards accepted: A Master Card; B Visa; C American Express; D Discover; E Diners Club; F Other; 2 Personal checks accepted; 3 Lunch available; 4 Dinner available; 5 Open all year; 6 Pets welcome; 7 Children welcome; 8 Tennis nearby; 9 Swimming nearby; 10 Golf nearby; 11 Skiing nearby; 12 May be booked through travel agent.

Marvista Bed and Breakfast

212 Martin Drive, 95003
(408) 684-9311; FAX (408) 684-9060
E-mail: innkeeper@2marvista.com
Web site: http://www.2marvista.com

Marvista is a luxury bed and breakfast on an acre of lovely gardens with panoramic views of the north crest of the Monterey Bay. It is an ideal location for a romantic getaway, quiet weekend, or refreshing retreat. The house was renovated in 1995 and is decorated in the Arts and Crafts period style. There are lovely gardens, a rolling lawn, and quiet deck areas to enjoy. The living room, with a massive stone fireplace, has comfortable seating for reading, playing games, or watching the surf. Guests have exceptional privacy. Each room has a white-water ocean view, cozy gas fireplace, king/feather bed, sitting area, and outside deck. Robes and slippers are in the closet. Rooms are equipped with phone, TV/VCR, clock-radio, and stocked refrigerator.

Hostess: Amy Bowles
Rooms: 2 (PB) $135-225
Full Breakfast
Credit Cards: A, B, C, D
Notes: 2, 5, 8, 9, 10, 12

AUBURN

Power's Mansion Inn

164 Cleveland Avenue, 95603
(530) 885-1166; FAX (530) 885-1386
E-mail: powerinn@westsierra.net
Web site: http://www.vfr.net/~powerinn

Power's Mansion Inn, a Victorian mansion built in 1898, has been restored to its original splendor and opened to guests. The beautiful old house has bay windows with lace curtains, an oak staircase, and period furnishings. It is well known for the numerous happy occasions, including weddings and parties, that have been enjoyed here. For the comfort and pleasure of our guests, all our rooms have queen-size beds, private baths, televisions, direct-dial phones, and individual temperature controls. There are two extra large suites and a family room.

Power's Mansion Inn

Hosts: Arno and Jean Lejniers
Rooms: 13 (PB) $79-149
Full Breakfast
Credit Cards: A, B, C
Notes: 2, 5, 8, 9, 10, 11, 12

AVALON

Zane Grey Pueblo Hotel

199 Chimes Tower Road; PO Box 216, 90704
(310) 510-0966; (800) 378-3256

Enjoy the best view of Avalon, the bay, and the mountains; freshwater pool surrounded by graceful gardens; ocean view and mountain view sunning decks; original living room with grand piano, fireplace, and television; complimentary coffee, tea, and morning toast. Courtesy taxi on arrival from boat dock, and scheduled taxis

NOTES: Credit cards accepted: A Master Card; B Visa; C American Express; D Discover; E Diners Club; F Other; 2 Personal checks accepted; 3 Lunch available; 4 Dinner available; 5 Open all year; 6 Pets

to and from downtown daily. Outside smoking areas provided.

Hostess: Karen Baker
Rooms: 17 (PB) $85-155
Continental Breakfast
Credit Cards: A, B, C
Notes: 2, 5, 7, 8, 9, 10, 12

BIG BEAR LAKE

Truffles Bed and Breakfast

43591 Bow Canyon Road; PO Box 130649, 92315
(909) 585-2772 (voice and FAX; call before FAXing)
Web site: http://www.bigbear.com/truffles

Gracious hospitality in peaceful surroundings describe this elegant country manor inn nestled on ¾ acre at a 7,000-foot-high mountain resort. Skiing, golf, hiking, and lake close by. Five guest rooms are individually appointed with private baths and feathertop beds. Full breakfasts, afternoon appetizers, and evening desserts topped off with truffles on bedtime pillows make for a memorable stay. This spacious lodging includes comfortable traditional and antique furnishings, with attention to detail. No smoking.

Hosts: Marilyn Kane and Carol Bracey
Rooms: 5 (PB) $115-150
Full Breakfast
Credit Cards: A, B, C, D
Notes: 2, 5, 7 (over 12), 10, 11

BOONVILLE

Anderson Creek Inn

12050 Anderson Valley Way; PO Box 217, 95415
(707) 895-3091; (800) 552-6202;
FAX (707) 895-9466
E-mail: innkeeper@andersoncreekinn.com
Web site: http://www.andersoncreekinn.com

Delightfully blending elegance with rustic, this lovely inn is spacious and quiet, surrounded by spectacular valley views and rolling pastures full of friendly farm animals. There are five gracious guest rooms with king beds and private baths. Prices include wine, hors d'oeuvres, and a full gourmet breakfast. Some rooms have fireplaces; all have wonderful views and plenty of privacy.

Hosts: Rod and Nancy Graham
Rooms: 5 (PB) $110-170
Full Breakfast
Credit Cards: A, B
Notes: 2, 5, 6 (prior approval), 7, 8, 9 (pool)

CALISTOGA

Foothill House

3037 Foothill Boulevard, 94515
(707) 942-6933; (800) 942-6933;
FAX (707) 942-5692
E-mail: GusGus@aol.com
Web site: http://www.foothillhouse.com

"The romantic inn of the Napa Valley," according to the *Chicago Tribune* travel editor. In the western foothills just north of Calistoga, the Foothill House offers spacious suites individually decorated with antiques. All suites have private baths and entrances, fireplaces, small refrigerators, and AC. Some suites have Jacuzzis. A luxurious cottage is also available. A gourmet breakfast is served each morning, appetizers and refreshments each evening. Foothill House received the American Bed & Breakfast Association's highest award for 1997 and 1998 (four crowns—placing it in the top 5 percent in U.S.). Spas, restaurants, wineries nearby.

Hosts: Doris and Gus Beckert
Rooms: 3 suites + 1 cottage (PB) $150-300
Full Breakfast
Credit Cards: A, B, C, D
Notes: 2, 5, 8, 9, 10, 12

Hillcrest Bed and Breakfast

3225 Lake County Highway, 94515
(707) 942-6334

Secluded hilltop country home with breathtaking views of the lush Napa Valley. Swimming, hiking, and fishing on 40 acres. The property has been in the family since 1860. The home is filled with antique furnishings. Rooms have balconies and offer HBO. Large pool and outdoor Jacuzzi for guests.

Hostess: Debbie O'Gorman
Rooms: 6 (4PB; 2SB) $50-98
Continental Breakfast
Credit Cards: none
Notes: 2, 5, 6, 8, 9, 10, 11 (water), 12

CAMBRIA

The Pickford House Bed and Breakfast

2555 MacLeod Way, 93428
(805) 927-8619

Eight large rooms are done in antiques. All have private baths with claw-foot tubs and showers. The front three rooms have fireplaces and a view of the mountains and valley. All rooms have a TV and king- or queen-size bed. Wine and fruitbreads are served at 5 PM. The Pickford House is located near beaches and wineries, only 7 miles from the Hearst Castle. Third person can stay for only $20. A full breakfast is served from 8 to 9 AM in our antique dining room with its cozy fireplace and 1860 antique bar. Gift certificates are offered. Abundant parking space is available for guests. Check in after 3 PM; check out at 11 AM.

Hostess: Anna Larsen
Rooms: 8 (PB) $89-140
Full Breakfast
Credit Cards: A, B
Notes: 2, 5, 7, 8, 9, 10

CAPISTRANO BEACH

Capistrano Seaside Inn

34862 Pacific Coast Highway, 92624
(949) 496-1399; (800) 252-3224;
FAX (949) 240-8977
E-mail: seaside-inn@home.com
Web site: http://www.seaside-inn.com

Enjoy Capistrano State Beach, the "Riviera of California," located directly across the street from the Seaside Inn. Our rooms offer views of the ocean and have private patios. Most rooms have a wood-burning fireplace, in-room coffee, and refrigerator. We have an outdoor Jacuzzi for your comfort and serve you with a friendly and efficient staff.

Host: Thad Anders
Rooms: 29 (PB) $49-129
Continental Breakfast
Credit Cards: A, B, C
Notes: 5, 7, 9, 10, 12

CAPITOLA-BY-THE-SEA

Inn at Depot Hill

250 Monterey Avenue, 95010
(408) 462-3376; (800) 572-2632;
FAX (408) 462-3697
E-mail: lodging@innatdepothill
Web site: http://www.innatdepothill.com

Near a sandy beach in a Mediterranean-style resort, this award-winning inn was named one of the top ten inns in the country. A decorator's delight. Upscale rooms resemble different parts of the world: Cote d' Azur, a chic auberge in St. Tropez; Paris, a romantic French hideaway; Portofino, an Italian coastal villa; Kyoto, classic Japanese; Sissinghurst, a traditional English garden room, etc. Fireplaces, TV/VCRs, stereos, phones and modern connections, robes, feather beds, and flowers. Most rooms have hot tubs in private garden patios. Mobil four-star.

Hosts: Suzie Lankes and Dan Floyd
Rooms: 12 (PB) $190-275
Full Breakfast
Credit Cards: A, B, C, D
Notes: 2, 5, 8, 9, 10, 12

CARMEL

Stonehouse Inn

PO Box 2517, 93921
(831) 624-4569; (800) 748-6618

A touch of old Carmel. Experience this luxurious country house in a quiet neighborhood setting. The Stonehouse Inn offers restful bedrooms that are light and airy; some have a view of the ocean through the trees. Each room is decorated in soft colors featuring antiques, cozy comforters, fresh flowers, and special touches for guests' comfort. A generous breakfast is served in the sunny dining room. Come join us at the Stonehouse Inn for a special, warm, memorable experience.

Stonehouse Inn

Hosts: Kevin Navaille and Terri Navaille
Rooms: 6 $109-199
Full Breakfast
Credit Cards: A, B, C
Notes: 5, 8

Sunset House

PO Box 1925, 93921
(408) 624-4884 (voice and FAX)
E-mail: sunsetbb@redshift.com
Web site: http://www.sunset-carmel.com

A romantic inn located on a quiet residential street, only 3 short blocks from the beach and 2 blocks from the quaint shops and galleries that make Carmel famous. Each guest room is uniquely decorated with antiques and designer touches to ensure an enjoyable stay. A special breakfast is brought to the room, allowing each guest to enjoy the glow from the woodburning fireplace and the lovely view. Cobblestone patios invite guests to relax in the sun or sea-misted air.

Hosts: Dennis and Camille Fike
Rooms: 4 (PB) $150-190
Continental Breakfast
Credit Cards: A, B
Notes: 2, 5, 6, 7, 8, 9, 10

CARMEL VALLEY

Carmel Valley Lodge

Carmel Valley Road & Ford Road, 93924-0093
(831) 659-2261; (800) 641-4646;
FAX (831) 659-4558

A warm Carmel Valley welcome awaits the two of you, a few of you, or a small conference. Relax in a garden patio room or a cozy one- or two-bedroom cottage with a fireplace and kitchen. In the morning, enjoy a sumptuous continental breakfast, our heated pool, the sauna, a hot spa, and the fitness center. Tennis and golf facilities are available nearby. You can walk to fine restaurants and quaint shops in Carmel Valley village, or just listen to your beard grow.

Hosts: Peter and Sherry Coakley
Rooms: 31 (PB) $119-279
Expanded Continental Breakfast
Credit Cards: A, B, C
Notes: 2, 5, 6 ($10 fee), 7, 8, 9 (onsite), 10, 12

COLOMA

The Coloma Country Inn

345 High Street; PO Box 502, 95613
(530) 622-6919; FAX (530) 622-1795

Built in 1852, this country Victorian farmhouse is surrounded by 5 acres of private gardens amid a 300-acre state park. The main house has five guest rooms and the carriage house has two suites. All guest rooms feature country decor, including quilts, stenciling, American antiques, and fresh flowers. You can enjoy hot-air balloon rides with your host from the backyard meadow or white-water rafting from the South Fork American River, 1 block from the inn.

Hosts: Alan and Cindi Ehrgott
Rooms: 5 + 2 suites (5PB; 2SB) $95-145
Full Breakfast
Credit Cards: none
Notes: 2, 5, 7, 9, 12

Fallon Hotel

COLUMBIA

Fallon Hotel

PO Box 1870, 95310
(209) 532-1470; (800) 532-1479;
FAX (209) 532-7027
E-mail: info@cityhotel.com
Web site: http://www.cityhotel.com

Fallon Hotel B&B has been authentically restored to its Victorian grandeur. Located in Columbia State Historic Park. Many of its antiques and furnishings are original to the hotel. Dine at nearby City Hotel. Come for a getaway weekend and enjoy our lodging/dinner theater package.

Host: Tom Bender
Rooms: 14 (1PB; 13SB) $50-105
Continental Breakfast
Credit Cards: A, B, C, D
Notes: 2, 4, 5, 7, 8, 9, 10, 11, 12

DESERT HOT SPRINGS

Traveller's Repose B&B

PO Box 655, 92240
(760) 329-9584

Bay windows, gingerbread trim, stained glass, and a white picket fence decorate this two-story Victorian home. Guest rooms are individually decorated: a rose room with antiques and lace accessories, a blue and white room with a heart motif, and a green room with handcrafted pine furniture. Tea is served midafternoon in the guest parlor. Located only 12 miles north of Palm Springs.

Hostess: Marian Relkoff
Rooms: 3 (PB) $65-85
Continental Breakfast
Credit Cards: none
Notes: 2, 8, 9, 10, 12

Traveller's Repose Bed and Breakfast

ELK

Elk Cove Inn

PO Box 367, 95432
(707) 877-3321; (800) 275-2967;
FAX (707) 877-1808
E-mail: elkcove@mcn.org
Web site: http://www.elkcoveinn.com

A uniquely romantic bed and breakfast with dramatic ocean views, located in the town of Elk just an easy 5-minute walk from the sandy beach. All rooms are provided with complimentary port wine and chocolates, fluffy robes, coffeemakers, feather beds, and down comforters. Our suites have separate living and bedroom areas, fireplaces, large baths with spa tubs, and balconies.

Hostess: Elaine Bryant
Rooms: 15 (PB) $98-278
Full Breakfast
Credit Cards: A, B, C
Notes: 2, 4, 5, 10, 12

ESCONDIDO

The Parsonage B&B

239 S. Maple Street, 92025
(760) 741-9160; FAX (760) 741-2630
E-mail: Parsonage5@juno.com

Built in 1910 as the parsonage of the First Congregational Church, this home has been restored to its original glory. Relax in a claw-foot tub, sleep on queen-size beds (down comforters and feather beds are available on request), and enjoy dessert every evening on the front porch. The Parsonage is within 30 minutes of all San Diego attractions and within walking distance of the California Center for the Arts, fine restaurants, and antique stores.

Hosts: Bob and Ann McQuead
Rooms: 3 (1PB; 2SB) $75-95
Full Breakfast
Credit Cards: none
Notes: 2, 5, 7 (over 12), 8, 9, 10

The Parsonage Bed and Breakfast

EUREKA

Abigail's "Elegant Victorian Mansion" B&B Lodging Accommodations

1406 "C" Street, 95501
(707) 444-3144
Web sites: http://www.bbonline.com/ca/abigails
http://www.bnbcity.com/inns/20016

An award-winning 1888 national historic landmark of opulence, grace, and grandeur. It features spectacular gingerbread exteriors, Victorian interiors, antique furnishings, and an acclaimed French gourmet breakfast. Available exclusively for the nonsmoking traveler, this is a "living history house-museum" for the discriminating connoisseur of authentic Victorian decor who also has a passion for quality, service, and the extraordinary. Breathtakingly authentic, with all the nostalgic trimmings of a century ago, this meticulously restored Victorian masterpiece offers both history and hospitality, combined with romance and pampering. Enjoy the regal splendor of this spectacular state historic site, and indulge in four-star luxury. With complimentary horseless carriage rides, bicycles, sauna, and laundry service, the inn is recommended by AAA, Mobil, *Fodor's*, and more. Arthur Frommer calls it "the very best that California has to offer—not to be missed."

Hosts: Doug and Lily Vierra
Rooms: 4 (2PB; 2SB) $75-185
Full Breakfast
Credit Cards: A, B
Notes: 5, 8, 9, 10, 11, 12

FELTON

The Inn at Felton Crest

780 El Solyo Heights Drive, 95018
(408) 335-4011 (voice and FAX); (800) 474-4011
Web site: http://www.Feltoncrestinn.com

Felton Crest, set in the majestic redwoods, is a wonderfully romantic getaway. Each accommodation is on a separate floor, ensuring privacy. Here you will find ingredients for a perfect romantic weekend or a special birthday, anniversary, or honeymoon celebration. Champagne/Martinelli's sparkling cider and a fruit and cheese tray are served on arrival. Rooms have fireplaces, TVs, Jacuzzis, VCRs, and phones. An expanded continental breakfast is prepared for you in the morning.

Hostess: Hanna Peters
Rooms: 4 (PB) $175-245
Continental Breakfast
Credit Cards: A, B, C
Notes: 2, 5

FERNDALE

The Gingerbread Mansion Inn

400 Berding Street, 95536
(707) 786-4000; (800) 952-4136;
FAX (707) 786-4381
E-mail: kenn@humboldt1.com
Web site: http://www.gingerbread-mansion.com

Nestled between giant redwoods and the rugged Pacific Coast is one of California's best-kept secrets: the Victorian village of Ferndale. A state historic landmark listed on the National Historic Register, Ferndale is a community frozen in time, with Victorian homes and shops relatively unchanged

NOTES: Credit cards accepted: A Master Card; B Visa; C American Express; D Discover; E Diners Club; F Other; 2 Personal checks accepted; 3 Lunch available; 4 Dinner available; 5 Open all year; 6 Pets

since their construction in the mid-to-late 1800s. One of Ferndale's best-known homes is the Gingerbread Mansion Inn. Decorated with antiques, the romantic guest rooms offer private baths, some with old-fashioned claw-foot tubs, and fireplaces. Also included is a full breakfast, high tea, four parlors, and formal English gardens. Rated four diamonds by AAA.

Host: Ken Torbert
Rooms: 10 (PB) $140-350
Full Breakfast
Credit Cards: A, B, C
Notes: 2, 5, 10, 12

FORT BRAGG

Grey Whale Inn

615 N. Main Street, 95437
(707) 964-0640; (800) 382-7244;
FAX (707) 964-4408
E-mail: stay@greywhaleinn.com
Web site: http://www.greywhaleinn.com

Handsome four-story Mendocino Coast landmark since 1915. Cozy to expansive. All rooms have private baths, TVs, phones, ocean, garden, hill, or town views. Some rooms have fireplaces; one has a Jacuzzi tub. Recreation area with pool table/library, fireside lounge, and TV/VCR room. Sixteen-person conference room. Full buffet breakfast features blue-ribbon coffee cakes. Friendly, helpful staff. Relaxed seaside charm, situated 6 blocks from the beach. Celebrate your special occasion on the fabled Mendocino Coast!

Hosts: Colette and John Bailey
Rooms: 14 (PB) $90-180
Full Breakfast
Credit Cards: A, B, C, D, F
Notes: 2, 5, 7, 8, 9, 10, 12

Ocean Breeze Lodge

212 S. Main Street, 95437
(707) 961-1177; (800) 864-7138

A small, cozy motel with a beautiful garden setting. Wonderfully comfortable beds in charming rooms that are sparkling with cleanliness. Color television plus HBO, in-room coffee, and private telephone. Centrally located in the town of Fort Bragg, Ocean Breeze Lodge is only minutes away from the Pacific Ocean, sandy beaches, sport fishing, whale-watching, and the beautiful redwoods.

Hostess: Linda Tarantino
Rooms: 10 (PB) $55-95
Credit Cards: A, B
Notes: 5

GEORGETOWN

American River Inn

Orleans and Main; PO Box 43, 95634-0043
(530) 333-4499; (800) 245-6566;
FAX (530) 333-9253
E-mail: ari@pcweb.net
Web site: http://www.pcweb.net/ari

The innkeepers carry on the century-old tradition of graciousness in a setting far removed from the fast pace of modern living. Cool off in a beautiful mountain pool or relax in the spa. Choose a day of bicycling amid the colorful, breathtaking daffodils, irises, and yellow-gold scotch broom; bicycles are provided. The historic Queen Anne inn specializes in ladies' and couples' retreats, and seminars and corporate meetings of fifteen to forty people.

Hosts: Will and Maria Collin
Rooms: 18 (12PB; 6SB) $85-115
Full Gourmet Breakfast
Credit Cards: A, B, C, D, E, F
Notes: 2, 3, 5, 7, 8, 9, 10, 11, 12

Campbell Ranch Inn

GEYSERVILLE

Campbell Ranch Inn

1475 Canyon Road, 95441
(707) 857-3476; (800) 959-3878;
FAX (707) 857-3239
Web site: http://www.campbellranchinn.com

A 35-acre country setting in the heart of the Sonoma County wine country between the Alexander Valley and Dry Creek Valley wine regions. Spectacular view, beautiful gardens, tennis court, swimming pool, bicycles. The cottage has a fireplace and a private hot tub on the deck overlooking the vineyards. The inn has four spacious rooms and a private cottage, private baths, king beds, and balconies. Quiet and peaceful. Breakfast served on the terrace; evening dessert is offered. Visit wineries and Lake Sonoma for water sports, fishing, and hiking. Color brochure.

Hosts: Mary Jane and Jerry Campbell
Rooms: 5 (PB) $125-225
Full Breakfast
Credit Cards: A, B, C
Notes: 2, 5, 10, 12

GRASS VALLEY

Elam Biggs Bed and Breakfast

220 Colfax Avenue, 95945
(530) 477-0906
Web site: http://www.virtualcities.com/ons/ca/g/cag1601.htm

This beautiful 1892 Queen Anne Victorian is set amidst a large yard surrounded by grand shade trees and a rose-covered picket fence. It's just a short stroll from historic downtown Grass Valley. In the

Elam Biggs Bed and Breakfast

NOTES: Credit cards accepted: A Master Card; B Visa; C American Express; D Discover; E Diners Club; F Other; 2 Personal checks accepted; 3 Lunch available; 4 Dinner available; 5 Open all year; 6 Pets

morning, enjoy brewed coffee and a hearty breakfast served in the lovely dining room or outside on the private porch.

Hosts: Peter and Barbara Franchino
Rooms: 5 (PB); $75-110
Full Breakfast
Credit Cards: A, B
Notes: 2, 5, 7, 8, 9, 10, 11, 12

Murphy's Inn

318 Neal Street, 95945
(530) 273-6873 (voice and FAX); (800) 895-2488
Web site: http://www.murphysinn.com

Murphy's Inn offers the discriminating traveler a return to the splendor of the Victorian era. Your first glimpse of the inn is the giant sequoia tree standing amidst well-kept grounds, and the ivy baskets surrounding the veranda. Eight bedrooms with lace curtains, antiques, and private baths make your stay comfortable. A full breakfast is included. Chocolate chip cookies and soft drinks always available.

Hosts: Ted and Nancy Daus, Linda Jones
Rooms: 8 (PB) $100-155
Full Breakfast
Credit Cards: A, B, C
Notes: 5, 7, 8, 9, 10, 11, 12

GUALALA

North Coast Country Inn

34591 S. Highway 1, 95445
(707) 884-4537; (800) 959-4537

Picturesque redwood buildings on a forested hillside overlooking the Pacific Ocean. The large guest rooms feature fireplaces, private baths, queen beds, decks, and minikitchens and are furnished with antiques. Two penthouse guest rooms, added in 1997, are surrounded by the hillside forest of pine, redwood, and fir; the rooms are wood-paneled with high ceilings and picture windows, fireplaces, private bathrooms, whirlpool tubs, king beds, and private decks. Breakfast and evening sherry are served in the common room by the fireplace. A TV and VCR are available. Enjoy a beautiful hilltop gazebo garden and romantic hot tub under the pines.

Hosts: Loren and Nancy Flanagan
Rooms: 6 (PB) $150-195
Full Breakfast
Credit Cards: A, B, C
Notes: 2, 5, 8, 10, 12

HALF MOON BAY

Cypress Inn on Miramar Beach

407 Mirada Road, 94019
(650) 726-6002; (800) 83-BEACH;
FAX (650) 712-0380
E-mail: lodging@cypressinn.com
Web site: www.cypressinn.com

A twelve-room contemporary beach house just 10 steps from the sand. Each room has a fireplace and private deck. Most have an unobstructed view of the ocean. Natural pine and wicker furniture; sky lights; a palette of nature's colors from the sea, sky, and earth; and colorful folk art capture the essence of California beachside living. Some rooms with deep two-person Jacuzzi tubs. Complimentary breakfast, wine, hors d' oeuvres, and dessert. In-house massage therapist. Conference facilities available.

Hosts: Dan Floyd and Suzie Lankes
Rooms: 12 (PB) $170-275
Full Breakfast
Credit Cards: A, B, C, D
Notes: 2, 5, 9, 10, 12

IDYLLWILD

The Pine Cove Inn

23481 Highway 243; PO Box 2181, 92549
(909) 659-5033; (888) 659-5033;
FAX (909) 659-5034
Web site: http://www.idyllwild.com

Enjoy clean air with great views of Mt. San Jacinto and Mt. Tahquitz. Our guest units are spacious and tastefully appointed in a variety of styles. Relax, read a book, or hike on 75 miles of marked trails in the San Jacinto wilderness area. New apartment unit above the lodge has a full kitchen, television, and fireplace. Come, get acquainted with paradise.

Hosts: Bob and Michelle Bollmann
Rooms: 10 (PB) $70-100 weekend;
discount Sunday-Thursday
Full Breakfast
Credit Cards: A, B, C, D
Notes: 2, 5, 7, 10, 11, 12

Strawberry Creek Inn

26370 Highway 243; PO Box 1818, 92549
(909) 659-3202; (800) 262-8969;
FAX (909) 659-4707

The "Essence of Idyllwild." This award-winning bed and breakfast inn is located in a rambling home and courtyard wing in the San Jacinto Mountains. Its cedar-shingled exterior blends quietly with the surrounding pines and oaks. Comfort mixes with nostalgia in the glassed-in porch where guests enjoy a full breakfast, the specially decorated bedrooms, the spacious living room with fireplace, and the inviting outdoor decks and hammocks.

Strawberry Creek Inn

Hosts: Diana and Jim Goff
Rooms: 9 + 1 cottage (PB) $89-150
Full Breakfast
Credit Cards: A, B, D
Notes: 2, 5

The Heirloom

IONE

The Heirloom

214 Shakeley Lane, 95640
(209) 274-4468; (888) 628-7896
Web site: http://www.theheirloominn.com

Travel down a country lane to a spacious, romantic English garden and a petite colonial mansion built circa 1863. The house features balconies, fireplaces, and heirloom antiques, along with gourmet breakfasts and gracious hospitality. The Heirloom is located in the historic Gold Country, close

NOTES: Credit cards accepted: A Master Card; B Visa; C American Express; D Discover; E Diners Club; F Other; 2 Personal checks accepted; 3 Lunch available; 4 Dinner available; 5 Open all year; 6 Pets

to all major northern California cities. The area abounds with antiques, wineries, and historic sites. Located within walking distance of a golf course. The Heirloom is closed Thanksgiving and Christmas.

Hostesses: Melisande Hubbs and Patricia Cross
Rooms: 6 (4 PB; 2 SB); $60-92
Full Breakfast
Credit Cards: A, B, C
Notes: 2, 5, 8, 9, 10

JAMESTOWN

Palm Hotel Bed & Breakfast

10382 Willow Street, 95327
(209) 984-3429; (888) 551-1852;
FAX (209) 984-4929
E-mail: innkeeper@palmhotel.com
Web site: http://www.palmhotel.com

More home than hotel, this Gold Country Victorian offers eight guest rooms with private bath, lacy curtains, fresh flowers, claw-foot tubs, marble showers, and robes. Air-conditioning, in-room TV, and disabled access. A full breakfast along with the Palm's special blend of coffee is served daily in the parlor. The Palm is located 2½ hours from San Francisco and about 1 hour from Yosemite Park's northern entrance, and is within walking distance of Main Street shops and restaurants and Railtown State Park. Guest comment: "The simple elegance of our room and ambience of the Palm in general was a balm for our souls."

Hosts: Rick and Sandy Allen
Rooms: 8 (PB) $85-145
Full Breakfast
Credit Cards: A, B, C
Notes: 5, 7, 10, 11, 12

JULIAN

Butterfield Bed and Breakfast

Box 1115, 2284 Sunset Drive, 92036
(760) 765-2179; (800) 379-4262;
FAX (760) 765-1229
E-mail: butterfield@abac.com
Web site: http://www.butterfieldbandb.com

From fluffy feather beds and private baths to crackling fireplaces and country views, our five beautifully decorated rooms offer country comfort and hospitality at its best. In the morning, you will be treated to a delicious gourmet breakfast served in the wedding gazebo during the warmth of summer, or by a crackling fireplace once winter sets in. Bedtime "sweet treats" are always at hand in the parlor, along with an assortment of intriguing teas, ciders, coffee, and cocoa.

Hosts: Ray and Mary Trimmins
Rooms: 5 (PB) $110-149
Full Breakfast
Credit Cards: A, B, C, D
Notes: 2, 4, 5, 7, 10, 12

Eden Creek Orchard Bed and Breakfast

1052 Julian Orchards Drive, 92036
(760) 765-2102; FAX (760) 943-7959
E-mail: eden_bb@ramonamall.com
Web site: http://www.ramonamall.com/eden_bb.html

Indulge yourself in romance on our 10-acre apple orchard with lovely mountain views. Eden Creek Orchard offers two private cottage suites with private patios; fireplaces; kitchenette; swings; and cozy, antique, overstuffed furniture. One suite has

welcome; 7 Children welcome; 8 Tennis nearby; 9 Swimming nearby; 10 Golf nearby; 11 Skiing nearby; 12 May be booked through travel agent.

two bedrooms with two private patios and fountain. Jacuzzi overlooks mountains. Adjacent winery. Great hiking. Walk to historical downtown Julian and pan for gold. Picnic in our orchard. Play horseshoes or bocci ball. You'll love it!

Hosts: Gary and Lee Simons
Rooms: 2 (PB) $95-110, $20/extra person
Full or Continental Breakfast
Credit Cards: A, B, C, D
Notes: 2, 5, 7, 10 (20 minutes), 12

KERNVILLE

Kern River Inn Bed and Breakfast

119 Kern River Drive; PO Box 1725, 93238
(760) 376-6750; (800) 986-4382;
FAX (760) 376-6643
E-mail: kernriverinn@lightspeed.net

A charming, classic country riverfront bed and breakfast located on the wild and scenic Kern River in the quaint little town of Kernville within the Sequoia National Forest in the southern Sierra Mountains. We specialize in romantic getaways. All guest rooms have private baths and feature river views; some have fireplaces and whirlpool tubs. A full breakfast is served. You can walk to restaurants, shops, parks, and the museum. It's only a short drive to giant redwood trees. This is an all-year vacation area with white-water rafting, hiking, fishing, biking, skiing, and Lake Isabella water activities.

Hosts: Jack and Carita Prestwich
Rooms: 6 (PB) $79-99
Full Breakfast
Credit Cards: A, B, C
Notes: 2, 5, 7, 9, 10, 11, 12

LAGUNA BEACH

Eiler's Inn Bed and Breakfast by the Sea

741 S. Coast Highway, 92651
(949) 494-3004 (voice and FAX)

Twelve rooms with private baths and a courtyard with gurgling fountain and colorful blooming plants are within walking distance of town and most restaurants; half a block from the beach.

Host: Nico, Diana, Cynthia, and Tracey Wirtz
Rooms: 12 (PB) $85-195
Full Breakfast
Credit Cards: A, B, C, D
Notes: 2, 5, 8, 9, 10, 12

LEUCADIA

Leucadia Inn by the Sea

960 N. Coast Highway 101, 92024
(760) 942-1668; (888) 942-1668;
FAX (760) 942-1065
E-mail: leucadia@abac.com
Web site: http://www.leucadiainn.com

Our "Theme Room Inn," just 1 block from the beach, is located on the Historic Scenic Coast Highway 101. The Africa, New Orleans, Hollywood, Fiesta, Nantucket,

Leucadia Inn by the Sea

NOTES: Credit cards accepted: A Master Card; B Visa; C American Express; D Discover; E Diners Club; F Other; 2 Personal checks accepted; 3 Lunch available; 4 Dinner available; 5 Open all year; 6 Pets

or Tropical Room with Jacuzzi have queen-size beds and private baths. Amenities include cable TV, "inn-room" coffee, free parking and local phone calls, minifrige, and microwave. Some of California's finest golf courses are nearby, along with other San Diego attractions. Close to the Amtrak and Coaster Train Stations. Leucadia is one of the oldest beach communities. Walk sandy beaches, watch an evening sunset, or try surfing.

Hosts: Ray and Mary Trimmins
Rooms: 7 (PB) $69-139
Continental Breakfast
Credit Cards: A, B, D
Notes: 9, 10

LONG BEACH

Lord Mayor's Bed and Breakfast Inn

435 Cedar Avenue, 90802
(562) 436-0324 (voice and FAX)
E-mail: innkeepers@lordmayors.com
Web site: http://www.lordmayors.com

A 1904 award-winning historic landmark with meticulously restored rooms, private baths, and sundeck access. Two recently restored 1906 cottages provide twelve rooms in the Lord Mayor's Bed and Breakfast Collection. You'll find warm hospitality enhanced by home-cooked specialty breakfasts. Within walking distance of the new Aquarium of the Pacific and tall ships. A gateway to the Catalina Island by ferry.

Hosts: Laura and Reuben Brasser
Rooms: 12 (10PB; 2SB) $85-125
Full Breakfast
Credit Cards: A, B, C, D, E
Notes: 2, 5, 7, 9, 10, 12

MAMMOTH LAKES

Snow Goose Inn Bed and Breakfast

57 Forest Trail; PO Box 387, 93546
E-mail: snowgoose@qnet.com
Web site: http://mammothweb.com/lodging/snowgoose/snowgoose.html

Mammoth's first bed and breakfast. No one is a guest; everyone is a friend. Many antiques and signature quilts. Full breakfast, evening appetizers, private bath, telephone, and TV. Outside hot tubs. Located close to restaurants, shops, hiking, fishing, bike riding, snowmobiling, skiing, snowboarding, etc.

Hosts: Scott and Denise Robertson
Rooms: 19 (PB) $68-98 (seasonal)
Full Breakfast
Credit Cards: A, B, C, D
Notes: 2, 5, 7, 8, 9, 10, 11, 12

MARIPOSA (GOLD COUNTRY AND YOSEMITE NATIONAL PARK)

Finch Haven Bed and Breakfast

4605 Triangle Road, 95338
(209) 966-4738
E-mail: finchams@yosemite.net

A quiet country home on 9 acres with panoramic mountain views. Birds, deer, and other abundant wildlife. Two rooms with private bath and private deck. Queen and twin beds. Nutritious breakfast. In the heart of the California Gold Rush country near historic attractions. Convenient access to the spectacular Yosemite Valley and Yosemite National Park. A restful

welcome; 7 Children welcome; 8 Tennis nearby; 9 Swimming nearby; 10 Golf nearby; 11 Skiing nearby; 12 May be booked through travel agent.

place to practice Mark 6:31 and to enjoy Christian hospitality.

Hosts: Bruce and Carol Fincham
Rooms: 2 (PB) $75
Full Breakfast
Credit Cards: none
Notes: 2, 5, 7, 8, 9, 11, 12

Shiloh Bed and Breakfast (Guest House)

Shiloh Bed and Breakfast

3265 Triangle Park Road, 95338
(209) 742-7200
Web site: http://www.sierranet.net/web/shiloh

An old, peaceful farmhouse with a private guest house nestled among Ponderosa pines in the foothills of Yosemite National Park. Two quaint, knotty-pine bedrooms in the main house share a private bath. The pleasantly decorated guest house sleeps five or six and has a full kitchen, living room, and deck. Playground for children, plus swimming pool and horseshoe pits. Historic Gold Rush country and Yosemite to explore. Christian hospitality.

Hosts: Ron and Joan Smith
Rooms: 3 (1PB; 2SB) $55-95
Expanded Continental Breakfast
Credit Cards: A, B, C, D
Notes: 2, 5, 7, 9, 10

MENDOCINO

Antioch Ranch

39451 Comptche Road, 95460
(707) 937-5570; FAX (707) 937-1757
E-mail: aranch@juno.com

Antioch Ranch, providing a Christian atmosphere of peace, is a place for refreshment and renewal. Located just 5½ miles inland from the picturesque town of Mendocino, the ranch features four guest cottages on 20 acres of rolling hills, redwoods, and apple orchards. Each cottage has its own style and ambience. Rustic, yet comfortable, each cottage features woodstoves, complete kitchen with microwave, two bedrooms, bath, and open living/dining room.

Hosts: Jerry and Pat Westfall
Rooms: 4 two-bedroom cottages (PB) $65-85
Breakfast on Request
Credit Cards: none
Notes: 2, 5, 7, 8, 9 (beach), 10

MT. SHASTA

Mt. Shasta Ranch Bed and Breakfast

1008 W. A. Barr Road, 96067
(530) 926-3870; FAX (530) 926-6882
E-mail: alpinere@snowcrest.net
Web site: http://travelassist.com/reg/cal21s.html

The inn is situated in a rural setting with a majestic view of Mt. Shasta and features a main lodge, carriage house, and cottage. Group accommodations are available. Our breakfast room is ideally suited for seminars and retreats, with large seating capacity. The game room includes piano,

Ping-Pong, pool table, and board games. Guests also enjoy an outdoor Jacuzzi. Nearby recreational facilities include Alpine and Nordic skiing, fishing, hiking, mountain bike rentals, surrey rides, and museums. Call for pastor's discount.

Hosts: Bill and Mary Larsen
Rooms: 9 + 1 cabin (5PB; 5SB) $55-95
Full Breakfast
Credit Cards: A, B, C, D
Notes: 2, 5, 7, 8, 9, 10, 11, 12

NAPA

La Belle Epoque

1386 Calistoga Avenue, 94559
(707) 257-2161; (800) 238-8070;
FAX (707) 226-6314

Elaborate Queen Anne architecture and extensive use of stained glass are complemented by elegant period furnishings. This century-old Victorian boasts six tastefully decorated guest rooms, each with private bath and two with fireplaces. A generous gourmet breakfast is offered each morning, either by fireside in the formal dining room or in the more relaxed atmosphere of the inn's plant-filled sunroom. Complimentary evening wine and appetizers on the premises. Wine tasting room/cellar. Walk to Old Town, Wine Train, and the Opera House. On-grounds parking. Air-conditioned throughout.

Hostess: Georgia Jump
Rooms: 6 (PB) $149-209
Full Gourmet Breakfast
Credit Cards: A, B, C, D
Notes: 2, 5, 8, 9, 10, 12

The Old World Inn

The Old World Inn

1301 Jefferson Street, 94559
(707) 257-0112; (800) 966-6624;
FAX (707) 257-0118
Web site: http://www.napavalley.com/oldworld

The Old World Inn was built in 1906 by contractor E.W. Doughty for his private town residence. The home is an eclectic combination of architectural styles detailed with wood shingles; wide, shady porches; clinker brick; and leaded and beveled glass. The inn is furnished throughout with painted antique furniture. Its eight guest rooms have been decorated individually with coordinated linens and fabrics. All the guest facilities have private bathrooms, most of them complete with Victorian claw-foot tubs and showers; one has a private spa tub. Bright, fresh Scandinavian colors abound. A complimentary carafe of Napa Valley wine awaits in your room. Satisfy your urge for a midafternoon snack and join us for tea and an assortment of homemade cookies. The inn is air-conditioned. A large, custom Jacuzzi is available for guests outside.

Host: Sam Van Hoeve
Rooms: 8 + cottage (PB) $110-160
Full Breakfast
Credit Cards: A, B, C, D
Notes: 2, 5, 8, 9, 10, 12

welcome; 7 Children welcome; 8 Tennis nearby; 9 Swimming nearby; 10 Golf nearby; 11 Skiing nearby; 12 May be booked through travel agent.

Deer Creek Inn

NEVADA CITY

Deer Creek Inn

116 Nevada Street, 95959
(530) 265-0363; (800) 655-0363;
FAX (530) 265-0980
E-mail: deercreek@gv.net
Web site: http://www.gv.net/~histinns/deer.htm

Romance and elegance abound as you wander through this lovely three-story Queen Anne Victorian. It sits high above the gardens, tastefully appointed with fountain, stone benches, and tiered rose gardens. All this—and beautiful Deer Creek to lullaby you to sleep. A gourmet, waddle-away-from-the-table breakfast starts your day. Nevada City is steps away.

Hosts: Elaine and Chuck Matroni
Rooms: 5 (PB) $90-145
Full Breakfast
Credit Cards: A, B, C
Notes: 2, 5, 8, 9, 10, 11, 12

The Parsonage

427 Broad Street, 95959
(530) 265-9478; FAX (530) 265-8147
Web sites: http://www.virtualcities.com/ons/ca/g/cag9504.htm
http://www.go-native.com

History comes alive in this 125-year-old home in Nevada City's historic district. The cozy guest rooms, parlor, and dining and family rooms are lovingly furnished with the innkeeper's pioneer family antiques. Breakfast is served on the veranda or in the formal dining room each morning. You may enjoy lunch or dinner at one of the twenty-six restaurants within the four-block area.

Hostess: Deborah Dane
Rooms: 6 (PB) $70-135
Full Breakfast
Credit Cards: A, B
Notes: 2, 4, 5, 7, 11, 12

ORLAND

The Inn at Shallow Creek Farm

4712 Road DD, 95963
(530) 865-4093 (voice and FAX); (800) 865-4093

The inn offers bed and breakfast at a working farm and orange orchard. Our two-story farmhouse has spacious rooms furnished with antiques, creating a blend of nostalgia and comfortable country living. Our breakfasts feature home-baked breads and an assortment of fruit and juice from our own trees. Delicious homemade jams and jellies complement our farm breakfasts. Nearby Black Butte Lake and the Sacramento National Wildlife Refuge offer outdoor recreational activities. French, German, and Spanish are spoken at the inn.

Hosts: Mary and Kurt Glaeseman
Rooms: 4 (2PB; 2SB) $65-85
Full Breakfast
Credit Cards: A, B
Notes: 2, 5, 9, 10, 12

Gatehouse Inn

PACIFIC GROVE

Gatehouse Inn

225 Central Avenue, 93950
(408) 649-8436; (800) 753-1881
E-mail: lew@redshift.com
Web site: http://www.sueandlewinns.com

Built in 1884 as a summer retreat for Sen. Langford, the inn features nine thematic guest rooms. Journey through the past in rooms such as the Steinbeck, Langford, or Victorian, all with Victorian elegance. For a different feel, try the Cannery Row, Turkish, or Italian rooms. Sumptuous food, breathtaking views, romantic elegance.

Hostess: Lois DeFord
Rooms: 9 (PB) $110-165
Full Breakfast
Credit Cards: A, B, C, D
Notes: 2, 5, 7 (8 and older), 8, 9, 10, 12

The Old St. Angela Inn

321 Central Avenue, 93950
(408) 372-3246; (800) 748-6306;
FAX (408) 372-8560
E-mail: lew@redshift.com
Web site: http://www.sueandlewinns.com

Built in 1910, the inn reminds you of a day on Cape Cod. Guest rooms are decorated in antiques. Ocean views, Jacuzzis, fireplaces, cast iron stoves. Add New England hospitality, a garden hot tub spa, and a warm, homey feeling, and you have our inn. Bring your appetites!

Hosts: Lewis Shaefer and Susan Kuslis
Rooms: 8 (PB) $110-165
Full Breakfast
Credit Cards: A, B, D
Notes: 2, 5, 6, 7, 8, 9, 10, 12

The Old St. Angela Inn

Seven Gables Inn and Grand View Inn

555 Ocean View Boulevard, 93950
(408) 372-6647; FAX (408) 372-2544

Crashing waves, rocky shorelines, sea otters, whales, and beautiful sunsets are seen from each guest room at century-old Seven Gables Inn. Such a romantic setting on the edge of Monterey Bay is enhanced by a dazzling display of fine European antiques, a sumptuous breakfast, afternoon tea, the comfort of all-private baths, and excellent service. Nearby attractions include the Monterey Bay Aquarium, Pebble Beach, Carmel, and Big Sur. Seven Gables Inn is Mobil Travel Guide four-star rated.

Hosts: Susan Flatley and Ed Flatley
Rooms: 14 (PB) $155-350
Full Breakfast
Credit Cards: A, B
Notes: 2, 5, 7 (over 12), 8, 9, 10, 12

Tres Palmas Bed and Breakfast

PALM DESERT

Tres Palmas Bed and Breakfast

73135 Tumbleweed Lane, 92260
(760) 773-9858; (800) 770-9858;
FAX (760) 776-9159
Web site: http://information.com/ca/trespalmas

Tres Palmas Bed and Breakfast is located just 1 block south of El Paseo, the "Rodeo Drive of the Desert," where you will find boutiques, art galleries, and many restaurants. Or you may choose to stay "home" and enjoy the desert sun in and around the pool and spa. The guest rooms feature queen- or king-size beds, climate controls, ceiling fans, and color televisions. The rooms are uniquely decorated in southwestern style. Lemonade and iced tea are always available for guests. Snacks are served in the late afternoons. Tres Palmas is AAA three-diamond rated; ABBA-rated A+.

Hosts: Karen and Terry Bennett
Rooms: 4 (PB) $70-185
Continental Breakfast
Credit Cards: A, B, C
Notes: 2, 5, 8, 9, 10, 12

PALM SPRINGS

Casa Cody B&B Country Inn

175 S. Cahuilla Road, 92262
(760) 320-9346; (800) 231-2639;
FAX (760) 325-8610

A romantic, historic hideaway is nestled against the spectacular San Jacinto Mountains in the heart of Palm Springs Village. Completely redecorated in Santa Fe decor, it has twenty-three ground-level units consisting of hotel rooms, studio suites, and one- and two-bedroom suites with private patios, fireplaces, and full kitchens. Cable TVs and private phones; two pools; secluded, tree-shaded whirlpool spa.

Hosts: Therese Hayes, Frank Tysen, and Elissa Goforth
Rooms: 23 (PB) $49-199
Continental Breakfast
Credit Cards: A, B, C
Notes: 2, 5, 6 and 7 (limited), 8, 9, 10, 11

PORTOLA

Pullman House Inn

256 Commercial Street, 96122
(530) 832-0107

This 1910 inn reflects Portola's history with a railroad theme. Enjoy a casual, hometown atmosphere. A full breakfast is served. Located within 10 minutes of all the recreation enjoyed in the mountains. Golf, railroad museum, shops, and restaurants are nearby.

Hosts: Jan and George Breitwieser
Rooms: 6 (PB) $58.50-80
Full Breakfast
Credit Cards: A, B, C, D
Notes: 2, 5, 8, 9, 10, 11, 12

REDDING

Palisades Paradise Bed and Breakfast

1200 Palisades Avenue, 96003
(530) 223-5305; FAX (530) 223-1200

Enjoy a breathtaking view of the Sacramento River, city, and mountains from this beautiful contemporary home with its garden spa, fireplace, wide-screen TV/VCR, and homelike atmosphere. You are always made to feel "special" here. Travelers and businesspeople alike seek out the comfort and relaxed atmosphere in this quiet, peaceful neighborhood. Palisades Paradise is a serene setting for a quiet hideaway, yet is conveniently located 1 mile from shopping and I–5, with water-skiing and river rafting nearby. Moderately priced. Major credit cards are accepted. Advance reservations desired; five-day cancellation policy.

Hostess: Gail Goetz
Rooms: 2 (SB) $70-100
Expanded Continental Breakfast
Credit Cards: A, B, C
Notes: 2, 5, 6, 7, 8, 9, 10, 11, 12

REDONDO BEACH

Breeze Inn

122 S. Juanita Avenue, 90277
(213) 316-5123

Located in a quiet, A-1 neighborhood. Large suite with private entrance, private bath with spa. Oriental carpet, California king bed. Breakfast area with microwave, toaster oven, and stocked refrigerator for a continental breakfast. Adjustable skylight and ceiling fan. Cable television. One of the rooms has twin beds and private bath. Brochure available with map. Located near Los Angeles, Disneyland, Universal City. Approximately 5 blocks from the pier and beach.

Hostess: Betty Binding
Rooms: 2 (PB) $45-65 (2-night minimum)
Continental Breakfast (extra charge for Full)
Credit Cards: none
Notes: 2, 5, 7 (over 5), 8, 9, 10

RIDGECREST

BevLen Haus Bed and Breakfast

809 N. Sanders Street, 93555
(760) 375-1988; (800) 375-1989;
FAX (760) 375-6871
E-mail: BLH_B&B@iwvisp.com

"Once a guest, always a friend." Gracious, quiet, safe, and comfortable; your "secret high desert hideaway." Nearly 2,000 square feet, furnished with antiques, handmade quilts, and comforters in winter! Paved parking. Cooling air in summer. Old-fashioned kitchen has antique cast-iron cookstove, hand-hammered copper sink. Year-round hot tub spa. In full-service community. Close to Sierra Nevada, Death Valley, Naval Air Warfare Center, China Lake, ghost towns, movie sites, and ancient Indian cultural sites. Wildflowers in spring. No smoking.

Hosts: Beverly and Leonard de Geus
Rooms: 3 (PB) $45-65
Full Breakfast
Credit Cards: A, B, C, D
Notes: 2, 5, 8, 9, 10, 12

ST. HELENA

La Fleur Bed and Breakfast

1475 Inglewood Avenue, 94574
(707) 963-0233 (voice and FAX)
Web site: http://www.lafleurinn.com

A charming 1882 Queen Anne Victorian nestled in the heart of Napa Valley's collection of fine wineries. Spacious, beautifully appointed rooms featuring old-world charm, private baths, spectacular views, and fireplaces will provide a most comfortable visit. Our breakfast of gourmet delights is elegantly served in the solarium while hot-air balloons drift above the adjacent vineyards. Your stay at La Fleur will include a private tour of neighboring Villa Helena Winery and an introduction to award-winning winemaker Don McGrath. Join us for such special events and classes as winemaking and wine appreciation.

Hosts: Kay Murphy and Staff
Rooms: 7 (PB) $150
Expanded Continental Breakfast
Credit Cards: none
Notes: 2, 5, 8, 9, 10, 12

SAN ANDREAS

The Robin's Nest

247 W. St. Charles Street, 95249-1916
(209) 754-1076; (888) 214-9202;
FAX (209) 754-3975
Web site: http://touristguide.com/b&b/ca/robinsnest

A traditional yet informal Victorian bed and breakfast country inn in the heart of the Gold Country. Eight hundred square feet of interior common space—ideal for group gatherings. One and one-third acres of gardens and fruit orchards with several seating areas. Central heat and air, hot spa, and five-course gourmet breakfast.

Hosts: Karen and William Konietzny
Rooms: 9 (7PB; 2SB) $60-125
Full Breakfast
Credit Cards: A, B, C, D
Notes: 4 (with reservations, minimum 4 people), 5, 7, 8, 9, 10, 11, 12

Carole's Bed and Breakfast

SAN DIEGO

Carole's Bed and Breakfast

3227 Grim Avenue, 92104
(619) 280-5258; (800) 975-5521

Built in 1904 by Mayor Frary, this historic site has the handsome style and craftsmanship of its time. It has been restored by the present owners, who live onsite, giving it constant loving care. The decor is of its period, with antiques and comfort as the focus. Amenities include a spa, black-bottom pool, and rose garden. Carole's Bed and Breakfast is within walking distance of Balboa Park, an assortment of small shops, and restaurants.

Hosts: Carole Dugdale and Michael O'Brien
Rooms: 10 (4PB; 6SB) $65-150
Continental Plus Breakfast
Credit Cards: A, B, C, D
Notes: 4, 5, 7, 8, 9 (on premises), 10, 12

Heritage Park Bed and Breakfast Inn

Heritage Park Bed and Breakfast Inn

2470 Heritage Park Row, 92110
(619) 299-6832; (800) 995-2470;
FAX (619) 299-9465
E-mail: innkeeper@heritageparkinn.com
Web site: http://www.heritageparkinn.com

Heritage Park Bed and Breakfast Inn, unique lodging for discriminating travelers, is far from ordinary yet central to everything in the area. Nestled in a quiet Victorian park lined with cobblestone walkways in the heart of historic Old Town, the award-winning Queen Anne mansion is only minutes from the San Diego Zoo, shops, beaches, and restaurants. Come for a glimpse of California's past. Stay and be pampered with feather beds; claw-foot tubs; Jacuzzi suites; full gourmet, candlelit breakfasts; and afternoon tea served on the veranda.

Hosts: Charles and Nancy Helsper
Rooms: 12 (PB) $90-225
Full Breakfast
Credit Cards: A, B, C, D, E
Notes: 2, 5, 7, 8, 9, 10, 12

SAN FRANCISCO

The Grove Inn

890 Grove St., 94117
(415) 929-0780; (800) 829-0780;
FAX (415) 929-1037
Web site: http://www.sftravel.com/grove.html

Victorian boardinghouse at Alamo Square historic site, close to the civic center and Golden Gate Park. The Grove Inn has been in business since 1983. Amenities include telephone, television, concierge, laundry service, car rental, vacation planning, and excursions.

Hosts: Klaus and Rosetta Zimmermann
Rooms: 19 (12PB; 7SB) $85-125
Continental Breakfast
Credit Cards: A, B, C
Notes: 7, 8, 9, 10

The Monte Cristo

The Monte Cristo

600 Presidio Avenue, 94115
(415) 931-1875; FAX (415) 931-6005

The Monte Cristo has been part of San Francisco since 1875, located 2 blocks from elegantly restored Victorian shops, restaurants, and antique stores on Sacramento Street. Convenient transportation to downtown San Francisco and to the financial district. Each room is elegantly furnished with authentic period pieces.

Host: George Yuan
Rooms: 14 (11PB; 3SB) $63-108
Continental Plus Breakfast
Credit Cards: A, B, C, D, E
Notes: 5, 7

Nob Hill Inn

1000 Pine Street, 94109
(415) 673-6080; (888) 982-2632;
FAX (415) 673-6098
E-mail: travelinfo@iname.com
Web site: http://www.citysearch.com/sfo/accommodations

Built in 1907 as a private home, the inn has been lovingly restored to maintain the ambience of a turn-of-the-century town house. Its guest rooms and suites are furnished with hand-picked antiques—beautifully carved chairs, armoires inlaid with exotic woods, graceful four-poster or brass beds. Modern conveniences such as direct-dial phones, electric heaters, and remote-control TVs have been discreetly added for the maximum in guest comfort.

Hostess: Sandra Miller
Rooms: 21 (PB) $99-134
Continental Breakfast
Credit Cards: A, B, C, E, F
Notes: 2, 5, 8, 9, 10, 12

The Red Victorian

1665 Haight Street, 94117
(415) 864-1978; FAX (415) 863-3293
E-mail: redvic@linex.com
Web site: http://www.redvic.com

The Red Victorian is dedicated to a peaceful world. In the geographic heart of San Francisco, on famous Haight Street, near Golden Gate Park, it welcomes creative people from everywhere. Breakfast is served family-style around a big table. The Red Victorian is beloved for its eighteen lighthearted and fanciful guest rooms—some meditative, like the Japanese Tea Garden Room and the Redwood Forest Room; some funny, like the Playground or Friends; some romantic; some historic. All the guest rooms celebrate the "Summer of Love" (the 1967 peace and ecology movement) and Golden Gate Park. The Red Victorian is a friendly, small hotel. Plan to stay a while.

Hostess: Sami Sunchild and Rosie Nguyen
Rooms: 18 (6PB; 12SB) $86-200
Continental Breakfast
Credit Cards: A, B, C
Notes: 4, 5, 8, 12

Wamsley Art Center Bed and Breakfast

1902 Filbert Street (corner Laguna), 94123
(415) 567-1526

In 1857, this B&B was located on the shores of Washer Woman's Cove here on Laguna 8-Filbert. This was then a most exciting location. The wide expanse of the bay at the foot of the street still exists, providing the marina green with a fine exercise course all the way to the exploratorium and yacht harbor by the Golden Gate Bridge. We are a five-room venue in a quiet, residential area.

Hostess: Helvi Wamsley
Rooms: 5 (PB) $105-145
Continental Breakfast
Credit Cards: A, B, C
Notes: 5, 7, 8, 10, 12

NOTES: Credit cards accepted: A Master Card; B Visa; C American Express; D Discover; E Diners Club; F Other; 2 Personal checks accepted; 3 Lunch available; 4 Dinner available; 5 Open all year; 6 Pets

Rancho San Gregorio

SAN GREGORIO

Rancho San Gregorio

Route 1, Box 54, 94074
(650) 747-0810; FAX (650) 747-0184
E-mail: rsgleebud@aol.com
Web site: http://www.seruznet.com/~prankstr/rancho/home.html

Five miles inland from the Pacific Ocean is an idyllic rural valley where Rancho San Gregorio welcomes travelers to relax. Picnic, hike, or bike in wooded parks or on ocean beaches. Our country breakfast features local specialties. Forty-five minutes from San Francisco, Santa Cruz, and the Bay area. Smoking outdoors only.

Hosts: Bud and Lee Raynor
Rooms: 4 (PB) $90-150
Full Breakfast
Credit Cards: A, B, C, D, E
Notes: 2, 5, 7, 9, 10, 12 (10%)

SANTA BARBARA

Long's Seaview B&B

317 Piedmont Road, 93105
(805) 687-2947

Overlooking the ocean and Channel Islands. Quiet neighborhood with lovely homes. Breakfast usually served on huge patio. Large bedroom with king-size bed. Private entrance, private bath. Convenient to all attractions and Solvang. Local information and maps. Great patio views.

Hostess: LaVerne Long
Rooms: 1 (PB) $80
Full Breakfast
Credit Cards: B
Notes: 2, 5, 8, 9, 10, 12

The Mary May Inn

111 W. Valerio Street, 93101
(805) 569-3398
Web site: http://www.silcom.com/~ricky/mary.htm

Perhaps Santa Barbara's best-kept secret! Situated in a residential neighborhood 16 blocks from the beach, two historical properties dating to the 1800s have been restored to their original elegance. The interiors are reminiscent of a time when life was slower. Each of the Mary May rooms shares a distinctive ambience. The inn is a showcase for extraordinary furnishings. Some rooms have canopied beds, wood-burning fireplaces, or Jacuzzi tubs. Queen beds and private baths.

Hosts: Kathleen M. Pohring and Mark S. Cronin
Rooms: 12 (PB) $85-180
Full and Continental Breakfast
Credit Cards: A, B, C, D
Notes: 2, 5, 6 (owner's discretion), 7, 8, 9, 10, 12

Montecito Bed and Breakfast

167 Olive Mill Road, 93108
(805) 969-7992 (voice and FAX)

Enjoy a spacious room with private bath, private entrance, TV, phone, desk, and eating area. Patio Jacuzzi is available for your use. Includes homemade continental breakfast and coffee. Room has garden atmosphere and looks out on a vista of trees and mountains. Located close to Westmont College and just above coastal village shopping and restaurants. Approximately ½ mile from the beach.

Hosts: Linda and Rick Ryan
Rooms: 1 (PB) $60-65
Continental Breakfast
Credit Cards: none
Notes: 2, 5, 7, 8, 9, 10, 12

Simpson House Inn

121 E. Arrellaga Street, 93101
(805) 963-7067; (800) 676-1280;
FAX (805) 564-4811
E-mail: SimpsonHouse@compuserve.com
Web site: http://www.SimpsonHouseInn.com

This elegantly restored 1874 landmark Victorian estate is a AAA five-diamond bed and breakfast. The inn is secluded in 1 acre of beautiful, peaceful English gardens, yet is just a 5-minute stroll from the historic center of Santa Barbara. The inn offers a delicious full breakfast served on private garden patios, evening wine and Mediterranean hors d'oeuvre buffet, afternoon refreshments, bicycling, spa services, wood fireplaces, and spa tubs.

Hosts: Linda and Glyn Davies
Rooms: 14 (PB) $175-425
Full Breakfast
Credit Cards: A, B, C, D
Notes: 2, 5, 8, 9, 10, 12

The Upham Hotel

1404 De la Vina Street, 93101
(805) 962-0058; (800) 727-0876;
FAX (805) 963-2825

Established in 1871, the beautifully restored hotel uniquely combines the quaint ambience of a bed and breakfast with the professionalism of a full-service hotel. Seven buildings surround 1 acre of lovely gardens and house fifty guest rooms and suites, some with fireplaces and private patios or porches. Located in the heart of downtown within walking distance of museums, theaters, shopping, and restaurants.

Hostess: Jan Martin Winn
Rooms: 50 (PB) $130-375
Continental Breakfast
Credit Cards: A, B, C, D, E
Notes: 3, 4, 5, 7, 8, 9, 10, 12

Apple Lane Inn

SANTA CRUZ

Apple Lane Inn

6265 Soquel Drive, **Aptos,** 95003
(408) 475-6868; (800) 649-8988;
FAX (408) 464-5790
E-mail: ali@cruzio.com
Web site: http://www.applelaneinn.com

Apple Lane Inn is a historic Victorian farmhouse restored to the charm and tranquillity of an earlier age. The house and barn were built in the 1870s with 3 acres of fields and apple orchards. Located just minutes south of Santa Cruz. The quiet country feeling has been crowned with a Victorian gazebo perched amid trim lawns and flowering gardens.

Hosts: Doug and Diana Groom
Rooms: 5 (PB) $95-150
Full Breakfast
Credit Cards: A, B, C, D
Notes: 2, 5, 6, 7, 8, 9, 10, 12

Chateau Victorian

118 First Street, 95060
(408) 458-9458
Web site: http://www.choice-guide.com/ca/victorian

Chateau Victorian was turned into an elegant B&B with a warm, friendly atmosphere in 1983. Built around 1885, the inn is only a block from the beach. All seven rooms have a queen-size bed; a private, tiled bathroom (one with a clawfoot tub and overhead shower); and a fireplace, with fire logs provided. Each room has its own heating system, controlled by the guest. Rooms are decorated and furnished individually. Wine and cheeses are available in the late afternoon. Within walking distance of downtown, Municipal Wharf, Boardwalk Amusement Park, and fine or casual dining.

Hostess: Alice June
Rooms: 7 (PB) $110-140
Expanded Continental Breakfast
Credit Cards: A, B, C
Notes: 2, 5, 8, 9, 10, 12 (no commissions)

Pleasure Point Inn

2-3665 E. Cliff Drive, 95062
(408) 475-4657; (800) 872-3029;
FAX (408) 464-3045
Web site: http://www.mcn.org/b&b/b&b.html

Pleasure Point Inn is situated on the water overlooking the beautiful Monterey Bay. Fantastic views from three of our rooms. Fireplaces and whirlpool tubs. Boat charters are underway daily for fishing or cruising. Your host is an accomplished captain of the *Margaret Mary* and your hostess is more than willing to arrange dinner reservations at a fine, local restaurant or point you to historic landmarks in the area. Located within walking distance of the beaches and shopping villages.

Hosts: Margaret and Sal Margo
Rooms: 4 (PB) $125-155
Continental Breakfast
Credit Cards: A, B
Notes: 5, 7, 8, 9, 10, 12

SANTA ROSA (WINE COUNTRY)

The Gables

4257 Petaluma Hill Road, 95404
(707) 585-7777; (800) GABLESN
E-mail: innkeeper@thegablesinn.com
Web site: http://www.thegablesinn.com

The Gables is a beautifully restored Victorian mansion in the center of Sonoma Wine Country. Elegant guest rooms feature fluffy goose down comforters, antiques, and private baths. A separate creekside cottage features a whirlpool tub for two. Guests are treated to a sumptuous, four-course gourmet breakfast. The Gables provides easy access to 165 premium wineries, the giant redwoods, the Russian River Resort, and the coastline and is just 1 hour north of San Francisco.

Hosts: Michael and Judy Ogne
Rooms: 8 (PB) $135-225
Full Breakfast
Credit Cards: A, B, C, D, E
Notes: 2, 5, 8, 9, 10, 12

Pygmalion House Bed and Breakfast

Pygmalion House B&B

331 Orange Street, 95401-6226
(707) 526-3407 (voice and FAX)

A lovely Victorian (1880s) furnished with many of Gypsy Rose Lee's antiques and memorabilia. All the spacious guest rooms are sound-proof and nicely decorated; all have private baths with tubs and showers, queen or king beds, and AC. The double parlor has a beautiful fireplace and a sitting room with octagonal windows. Off-street parking in rear. Secluded gardens.

Hostess: Carolyn E. Berry
Rooms: 6 (PB) $65-95 (seasonal; midweek discounts)
Full Country Breakfast
Credit Cards: A, B
Notes: 2, 5, 8, 9, 10

SEAL BEACH

The Seal Beach Inn and Gardens

212 5th Street, 90746
(562) 493-2416; (800) HIDEAWAY;
FAX (562) 799-0483
E-mail: hideaway@sealbeachinn.com
Web site: http://www.sealbeachinn.com

Elegant, historic Southern California inn, 1 block from the ocean beach in a charming, prestigious, seaside town next to Long Beach. Lush gardens, lovely estate appearance. The rooms and suites are exquisite. Pool, library, and kitchens are available. Free full breakfast/social hour. Modern amenities. Short walk to restaurants, shops, and beach pier. Three freeways close by. Easy drive to Disneyland and other major Los Angeles attractions and business centers. Meeting rooms available (twenty-four maximum). Convenient to LAX, Long Beach, and Orange County airports.

Hosts: Marjorie and Harty Schmaehl
Rooms: 23 (PB) $125-195
Full Breakfast
Credit Cards: A, B, C, D, E, F
Notes: 3, 4, 5, 8, 9, 10, 12

The Seal Beach Inn and Gardens

SEQUOIA NATIONAL PARK

Mesa Verde Plantation

33038 Sierra Highway 198, **Lemon Cove,** 93244
(209) 597-2555; (800) 240-1466;
FAX (209) 597-2551
E-mail: relax@plantationbnb.com
Web site: http://www.plantationbnb.com

Nestled among the peaceful foothills of the Sierra Nevada Mountains among acres of orange groves. The rooms are named after characters from *Gone With the Wind*

NOTES: Credit cards accepted: A Master Card; B Visa; C American Express; D Discover; E Diners Club; F Other; 2 Personal checks accepted; 3 Lunch available; 4 Dinner available; 5 Open all year; 6 Pets

and decorated accordingly. Located only 16 miles from Sequoia National Park. Heated swimming pool open all year, along with hot tub located in the orchard. Fireplaces, whirlpool tub, verandas, gazebos.

Hosts: Scott and Marie Munger
Rooms: 8 (6PB; 2SB) $70-125
Full Breakfast
Credit Cards: A, B, C, D, E
Notes: 2, 5, 9, 10, 11, 12

The Alisal Guest Ranch and Resort

SOLVANG

The Alisal Guest Ranch and Resort

1054 Alisal Road, 93463
(805) 688-6411; (800) 425-4725;
FAX (805) 688-2510
E-mail: sales@alisal.com
Web site: http://www.alisal.com

A working cattle ranch and full-service resort that has been privately owned and operated since 1946. The 10,000-acre ranch with its guest cottages offers a high level of accommodation. Facilities include two championship golf courses, seven tennis courts, a 96-acre fishing/boating lake, miles of scenic horseback riding, heated swimming pool, children's activities, rodeos, barbecues, winemaker dinners, and meeting facilities for two hundred delegates. Approximately 2 hours from Los Angeles and 40 minutes from Santa Barbara. Dinner included in room rate.

Host: David S. Lautensack
Rooms: 73 cottages (PB) 1998, $350-425
Full or Continental Breakfast
Credit Cards: A, B, C
Notes: 2, 3, 4, 5, 7, 8, 9, 10 (on premises), 12

SONOMA

Sonoma Hotel

110 W. Spain Street, 95476
(707) 996-2996; (800) 468-6016;
FAX (707) 996-7014

Sonoma Hotel is 1 hour's drive from San Francisco but 100 years away. On Sonoma's tree-lined plaza, this vintage hotel offers accommodations and dining to the discriminating guest. An evening here is a step back to a romantic period in history. Each antique-furnished room evokes a distinct feel of early California; the emphasis on comfort is decidedly European. Short walks to wineries, historic landmarks, art galleries, and unique shops.

Hosts: John and Dorene Musilli
Rooms: 17 (5PB; 12SB) $75-125
Continental Breakfast
Credit Cards: A, B, C
Notes: 2, 3, 4, 5, 7, 10, 12

Sparrow's Nest Inn

424 Denmark Street, 95476
(707) 996-3750; FAX (707) 938-5569
E-mail: SprrwsN@aol.com
Web site: http://www.innsandouts.com

Historic Sonoma is only 1 mile from this delightful cottage. It's just right for rest or romance. Pretty English country decor, fresh flowers, chocolates, cozy bed, scrumptious breakfast, privacy, garden, and courtyard for sunning and reading. The "Nest" is complete with bedroom, bath, small kitchen fully equipped, living room (including sofa bed), phone, cable TV/VCR, and air-conditioning. Within 3 miles are five wineries, historic sites, wonderful restaurants, and little shops.

Hosts: Thomas and Kathleen Anderson
Rooms: 1 private cottage (PB) $85-125
Full or Continental Breakfast
Credit Cards: A, B, C, D
Notes: 2, 5, 6, 7, 8, 10

SONORA

Barretta Gardens Bed and Breakfast Inn

700 S. Barretta Street, 95370
(209) 532-6039; (800) 206-3333;
FAX (209) 532-8257
E-mail: Barretta@mlode.com
Web site: http://www.barrettagarden.com

The inn is an elegantly restored Victorian home, fully air-conditioned, well known for its special warm atmosphere and Gold Country charm. Guests enjoy relaxing on our three open-air porches, plant-filled solarium, living room with fireplace, formal dining room, first- and second-floor parlors, and cheery breakfast room. Barretta Gardens offers a hilltop acre of gardens and lawns overlooking the town. Beautiful sunsets. "Best of Gold Country" and Mobil travel guide. It also has been rated "Most Kissable."

Hostess: Nancy Brandt
Rooms: 5 (PB) $95-105
Full Breakfast
Credit Cards: A, B, C
Notes: 2, 5, 7, 9, 10, 11, 12

Lavender Hill B&B

683 S. Barretta Street, 95370
(209) 532-9024; (800) 446-1333, Ext. 290
E-mail: lavender@sonnett.com
Web site: http://www.lavenderhill.com

Come home. . .to a 1900s Victorian home overlooking the historic gold rush town of Sonora. At sunset you can watch the world from a wraparound porch, enjoy a country walk through year-round flower gardens, and relax on a covered patio (ideal for a small wedding). In the morning, you wake to a home-cooked breakfast and listen and share experiences with others, perhaps planning your day to include hiking in Yosemite, fishing, biking, river rafting, or even a scenic steam train ride. Afternoons and evenings could include a stroll to downtown antique shops and boutiques, fine dining, and a performance at one of the professional repertory theaters. We will be glad to plan a dinner-theater package for your stay. Gift certificates are available. One visit will have you longing to return "home."

Hosts: Jean and Charlie Marinelli
Rooms: 4 (PB) $75-95
Full Breakfast
Credit Cards: A, B, C
Notes: 2, 5, 7, 8, 9, 10, 11, 12

Mountain View B&B

12980 Mountain View Road, 95370
(209) 533-0628; FAX (209) 533-1461
E-mail: disbrow@mlode.com
Web site: http://www.mtvu.com

This country home B&B is surrounded by majestic blue oaks in the midst of California's historic gold rush region. The inn is on a quiet, winding road that feels remote, but is just minutes from Jamestown and Sonora. After a day in

NOTES: Credit cards accepted: A Master Card; B Visa; C American Express; D Discover; E Diners Club; F Other; 2 Personal checks accepted; 3 Lunch available; 4 Dinner available; 5 Open all year; 6 Pets

Yosemite or exploring historic sites, enjoy a dip in the pool, or engineer the garden railroad. Close to theaters, caverns, river rafting, antique shops.

Hosts: Doris and Carl Disbrow
Rooms: 4 (2PB; 2SB) $60-80
Full Breakfast
Credit Cards: A, B, D
Notes: 5, 6 (arranged), 7, 9 (onsite), 10, 11, 12

SUSANVILLE

The Roseberry House

609 North Street, 96130
(530) 257-5675

The Roseberry House lives up to its name, with roses in profusion in the carpets, wallpapers, and vases. It features an unusual collection of antiques, with each guest room distinctly different. Enjoy a tastefully prepared full breakfast in the formal dining room. This is our home, and we want you to be comfortable here. Located just 2 blocks from Main Street in historic uptown Susanville and near a variety of Northern California recreational activities.

Hosts: Bill and Maxine Ashmore
Rooms: 4 (PB) $55-85
Full Breakfast
Credit Cards: A, B
Notes: 2, 5, 8, 9, 10, 11

SUTTER CREEK

Foxes in Sutter Creek

77 Main Street; PO Box 159, 95685
(209) 267-5882; (800) 957-3344;
FAX (209) 267-0712
E-mail: foxes@cdepot.net
Web site: http://www.foxesinn.com

Foxes in Sutter Creek, formerly known as "The Brinn House," originated in 1857 during the California gold rush. Since then, it has undergone substantial changes and now features seven beautiful guest accommodations. Sutter Creek is known as "the nicest town in the Mother Lode." Within walking distance, you'll find many interesting antique shops, restaurants, specialty shops, and art galleries. The local countryside abounds with interesting sights and exciting activities. Explore the many shops in quaint villages nearby.

Hosts: Min and Pete Fox
Rooms: 7 (PB) $125-180
Full Breakfast
Credit Cards: A, B, D
Notes: 2, 5, 8, 10, 12

The Hanford House

The Hanford House

Highway 49; 61 Hanford Street; PO Box 1450, 29685
(209) 267-0747; (800) 871-5839;
FAX (209) 267-1825
E-mail: bobkat@hanfordhouse.com
Web site: http://www.hanfordhouse.com

Located on a quiet corner of Sutter Creek's Main Street, The Hanford House is a classic, ivy-covered red brick building. Guests say it is filled with light, laughter, great food, personal attention, and thoughtful friends. With ten large rooms, a full-service guest pantry open 24 hours, and an 850-square-foot conference center onsite, it is the perfect getaway for both personal and business needs. All rooms have AC; some have marble fireplaces and Jacuzzi tubs; one is handicap-accessible. Guests are served a full gourmet breakfast, either in the charming breakfast room where prior guests have left their signatures and kudos about the inn, or in their rooms (by arrangement). Come, let your cares melt away as you rest, relax, and recharge in style! Gift certificates available.

Hosts: Bob and Karen Tierno
Rooms: 10 (PB) $89-149
Full Breakfast
Credit Cards: A, B, D
Notes: 2, 5, 7 (well-behaved), 8, 9, 10, 11 (90 minutes), 12

Sutter Creek Inn

75 Main Street; PO Box 385, 95685
(209) 267-5606; FAX (209) 267-9287
E-mail: info@suttercreekinn.com
Web site: http://www.suttercreekinn.com

Built in 1859, the inn is surrounded by tree-shaded lawns and gardens. It is within walking distance of shopping and dining in the historic gold rush town of Sutter Creek. The inn features seventeen rooms, all with private baths. Many rooms offer fireplaces or private patios. Enjoy the peace and quiet of our hammocks and chaise lounges during the summer, or the patter of rain on our tin roofs in the winter while enjoying our fireplaces. A full country breakfast is served family-style in our dining room each morning. Wineries, golf, hiking, biking, gold panning, and historical sites are nearby. Massages are available by appointment.

Hostess: Jane Way
Rooms: 17 (PB) $65-175
Full Breakfast
Credit Cards: A, B
Notes: 2, 5, 8, 9, 10, 11, 12

UKIAH

Vichy Hot Springs Resort and Inn

2605 Vichy Springs Road, 95482-3507
(707) 462-9515
E-mail: vichy@pacific.net
Web site: http://www.vichysprings.com

Vichy Springs is a delightful 2-hour drive north of San Francisco. Historic cottages and rooms await you with delightful vistas from all locations. Vichy Hot Springs features naturally sparkling, 90-degree mineral baths, a communal 104-degree pool, and an Olympic-size swimming pool. Guests can explore 700 private acres with trails and roads for hiking, jogging, picnicking, and mountain bicycling. Vichy's idyllic setting provides a quiet, healing environment for travelers. This is California State Landmark #980.

Hosts: Gilbert and Marjorie Ashoff
Rooms: 20 (PB) $135-205
Full Breakfast
Credit Cards: A, B, C, D, E, F
Notes: 2, 3, 4, 5, 7, 8, 9, 10, 12

VENTURA

La Mer Bed and Breakfast

411 Poli Street, 93001
(805) 643-3600; FAX (805) 653-7329
Web site: http://www.vcol.net/lamer

Built in 1890, this is a romantic European getaway in a Victorian Cape Cod home, a historic landmark nestled on a green hillside overlooking the spectacular California coastline. The distinctive guest rooms, all with private entrances and baths, are each a European adventure, furnished in European antiques to capture the feeling of a specific country. Bavarian buffet-style breakfast and complimentary refreshments; midweek packages; horse-drawn antique carriage rides. La Mer is both AAA- and Mobil-approved.

Hosts: Mike and Gisela Baida
Rooms: 5 (PB) $80-155
Full Breakfast
Credit Cards: A, B, C
Notes: 2, 5, 8, 9, 10, 12

Howard Creek Ranch

WESTPORT

Howard Creek Ranch

40501 N. Highway One; PO Box 121, 95488
(707) 964-6725, FAX (707) 964-1603
Web site: http://www.howardcreekranch.com

Howard Creek Ranch is a historic, 4,000-acre, oceanfront farm dating to 1867, bordered by miles of beach and mountains in a wilderness area. Award-winning flower gardens, antiques, fireplaces, redwoods, a 75-foot swinging footbridge over Howard Creek, cabins, comfortable beds, hot tub, sauna, pool, nearby horseback riding, and excellent restaurants are combined with hospitality and a full ranch breakfast. Termed "one of the most romantic places to stay on the planet" by the *San Francisco Examiner*.

Hostess: Sally Grigg
Rooms: 11 (9PB; 2SB) $75-160
Full Breakfast
Credit Cards: A, B, C
Notes: 2, 5, 6 and 7 (by prior arrangement)

YOSEMITE NATIONAL PARK

Yosemite River Resort (Formerly Lee's Middle Fork Resort)

11399 Cherry Lake Road, **Groveland,** 95321
(209) 962-7408; (800) 626-7408;
FAX (209) 962-7400
E-mail: LMR@sonnet.com
Web site: http://www.sonnet.com/usr/yosemite

Conveniently located 11 miles from Big Oak Flat entrance to Yosemite National Park, the resort is the perfect place for scenic landscapes while you vacation or simply pass through the charming Yosemite area. Relax, enjoy the restful atmosphere, and discover why Yosemite is so acclaimed for its beauty. You can gaze upon some of the most amazing rock formations and the most stunning waterfalls, or enjoy an afternoon of activities which include hiking, fishing in a well-stocked river, swimming, or white-water rafting. For winter guests there is downhill and cross-country skiing. A new ten-room B&B house will be finished soon. All rooms have private baths, some spas and hot tubs.

Hosts: Roland and Robin Hilarides
Rooms: 30 (PB) $59-200
Full or Continental Breakfast
Credit Cards: A, B, C, D, E
Notes: 3, 4, 5, 6, 7, 8, 9, 10, 11

COLORADO

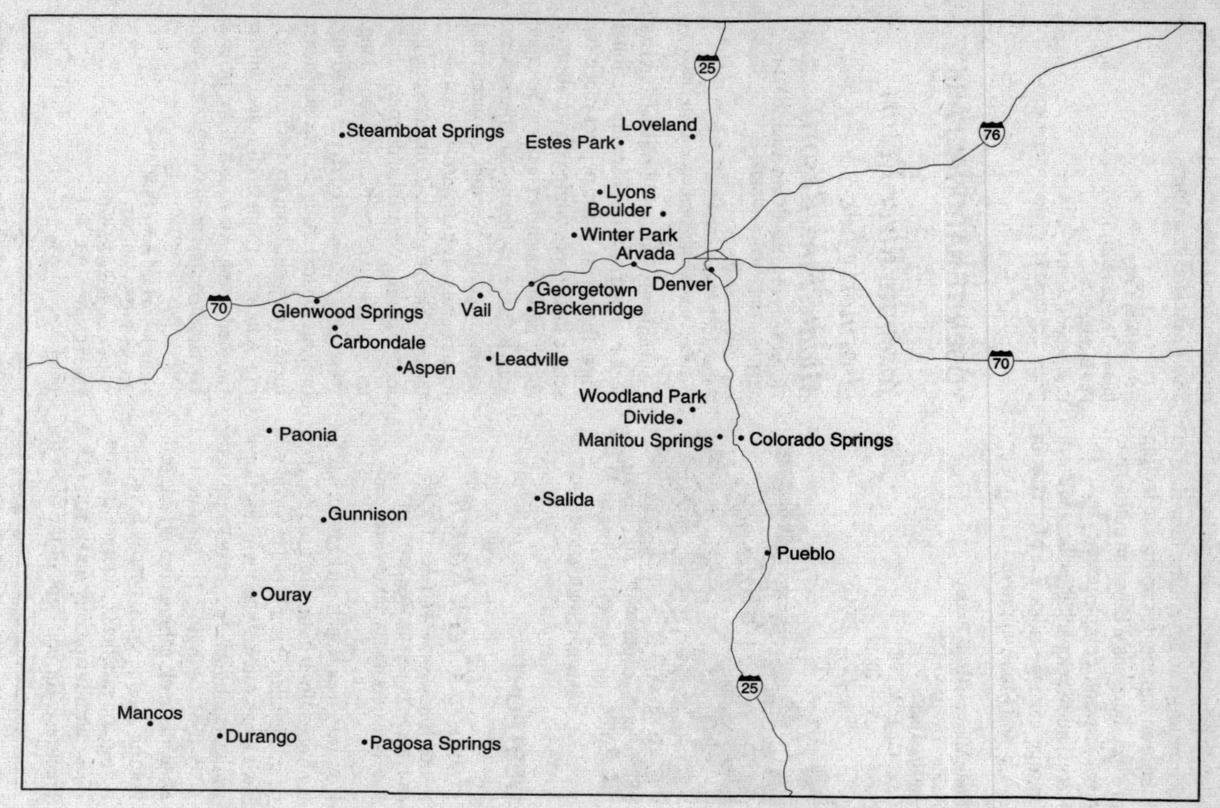

25
76
70
70
25
Steamboat Springs
Estes Park
Loveland
Lyons
Boulder
Winter Park
Arvada
Denver
Georgetown
Breckenridge
Vail
Glenwood Springs
Carbondale
Aspen
Leadville
Woodland Park
Divide
Manitou Springs
Colorado Springs
Paonia
Salida
Gunnison
Pueblo
Ouray
Mancos
Durango
Pagosa Springs

Colorado

ARVADA

On Golden Pond Bed and Breakfast

7831 Eldridge, 80005
(303) 424-2296; (800) 682-0193;
FAX (303) 431-6580
Web site: http://www.bbonline.com/co/ongoldenpond

For European hospitality and a relaxing blend of country comfort, join us at our secluded, 10-acre retreat located only 15 miles west of downtown Denver. Our guests enjoy dramatic views of the mountains, prairies, and pond with gazebo. A full breakfast is served indoors or on our decks. Each guest room has a large sliding door that opens to a private deck or patio. Three of the suites have a large Jacuzzi or hot tub. Horseback riding, golf, tennis, bicycles, and walking paths are nearby attractions. Enjoy our outdoor pool and hot tub.

Hostess: Kathy Kula
Rooms: 5 (PB) $60-130
Full Breakfast
Credit Cards: A, B, C, D, E
Notes: 2, 5, 6 (1 room only), 7 (1 room only), 8, 9, 10, 11 (1 hour), 12

Christmas Inn

ASPEN

Christmas Inn

232 W. Main Street, 81611
(970) 925-3822; (800) 625-5581;
FAX (970) 925-3328

This comfortable inn features attractive rooms with private baths, direct-dial phones, cable TVs, sundeck, off-street parking. Amenities include whirlpool and sauna (winter), daily housekeeping, complimentary breakfast, and afternoon refreshments. Walk to the quaint shops and restaurants of Aspen or use the free shuttle service to the Music Tent (summer), to four ski mountains, and around town.

Host: David Schlesinger
Rooms: 24 (PB) $56-110
Full Breakfast
Credit Cards: A, B, C
Notes: 5, 7, 8, 9, 10, 11, 12

NOTES: Credit cards accepted: A Master Card; B Visa; C American Express; D Discover; E Diners Club; F Other; 2 Personal checks accepted; 3 Lunch available; 4 Dinner available; 5 Open all year; 6 Pets welcome; 7 Children welcome; 8 Tennis nearby; 9 Swimming nearby; 10 Golf nearby; 11 Skiing nearby; 12 May be booked through travel agent.

Briar Rose Bed and Breakfast

BOULDER

Briar Rose Bed and Breakfast

2151 Arapahoe Avenue, 80302
(303) 442-3007; FAX (303) 786-8440
E-mail: brbbx@aol.com
Web site: http://www.globalmall.com/brose

When you enter the Briar Rose B&B, it's like entering a past era when hospitality was an art. This English country cottage is located near the University of Colorado and downtown Boulder. The nine unique guest rooms offer feather bed comforters, telephones, period antiques, fresh flowers, and good books. The innkeepers' friendly, attentive service includes afternoon and evening tea with our homemade shortbread cookies. A hearty, home-baked breakfast is served each morning in the dining room or on the sunporch. Groups and families may schedule ten- to fifteen-person retreats for the winter months.

Hosts: Margaret and Bob Weisenbach
Rooms: 9 (PB) $114-159
Continental Breakfast
Credit Cards: A, B, C, E
Notes: 2, 5, 7, 8, 9, 10, 11, 12

BRECKENRIDGE

Allaire Timbers Inn

9511 Highway 9; PO Box 4653, 80424
(970) 453-7530; (800) 624-4904;
FAX (970) 453-8699
E-mail: allairetimbers@worldnet.att.net
Web site: http://www.allairetimbers.com

This award-winning log bed and breakfast offers ten individually decorated guest rooms with private baths and decks, telephones, and televisions. Two elegant suites boast private hot tub and river rock fireplace. Great room with fireplace, sunroom, and loft provide cozy spaces to relax. You can unwind in the outdoor spa with spectacular mountain views. A hearty breakfast and afternoon refreshments are served daily. Breckenridge is Colorado's oldest Victorian town, offering an abundance of year-round activities.

Hosts: Jack and Kathy Gumph
Rooms: 10 (PB) $135-300
Full Breakfast
Credit Cards: A, B, C, D
Notes: 2, 5, 10, 11, 12

Muggins Gulch Inn

4023 Tiger Road; PO Box 3756, 80424
(970) 453-7414; (800) 275-8304;
FAX (970) 453-2711
E-mail: muginn@imageline.com
Web site: http://www.colorado-bnb.com/muginn

Spectacular vaulted post-and-beam inn. Beautiful antiques and appointments. Secluded on 160 acres, 10 minutes from Breckenridge. Three suites with fireplaces. Two charming rooms, private baths, skylights, hot tub, TV/video area. Gourmet breakfast, afternoon snack. In winter, enjoy onsite cross-country skiing and snowshoeing. In summer: llama treks, weddings and private parties, hiking, biking. Warm hospitality in a peaceful mountain setting.

Hosts: Bethanne and Tom Hossley
Rooms: 2 + 3 suites (PB) $85-150
Full Breakfast
Credit Cards: A, B
Notes: 2, 5, 7 (12 and older), 10, 11, 12

CARBONDALE

Ambiance Inn

66 N. 2nd Street, 81623
(970) 963-3597; (800) 350-1515;
FAX (970) 963-3130
E-mail: ambiance@compuserve.com

Enjoy Aspen, Glenwood Springs, and the beautiful Crystal Valley from this spacious chalet-style home featuring vaulted ceilings throughout. The 1950s ski lodge decor of the very large Aspen Suite or the Victorian elegance of the Sonoma Room, featuring a romantic four-poster bed, are ideal for getaways. The Santa Fe Room is alive with the warmth of the Southwest. All guest rooms adjoin the library/sitting room on the balcony. The Kauai Room features special atmosphere and a two-person Jacuzzi.

Hosts: Norma and Robert Morris
Rooms: 4 (PB) $60-90
Full Breakfast
Credit Cards: A, B
Notes: 2, 5, 8, 9, 10, 11, 12

Mt. Sopris Inn

0165 Mt. Sopris Ranch Road; PO Box 126, 81623
(970) 963-2209; (800) 437-8675;
FAX (970) 963-8975
E-mail: mt.soprisinn@juno.com
Web site: http://colorado-bnb.com/mtsopris

At Mt. Sopris Inn, country elegance surrounds the visitor who appreciates our extraordinary property. Central to Aspen, Redstone, and Glenwood Springs, the inn offers fifteen private rooms and baths, professionally decorated. All rooms have king- or queen-size bed, TV, and telephone; some have fireplaces, Jacuzzis, and steam baths. Guests may use the swimming pool, whirlpool, pool table, library, great rooms, and 7-foot grand piano. The inn is open to all.

Hostess: Barbara Fasching
Rooms: 14 (PB) $ 85-175
Full Breakfast
Credit Cards: A, B
Notes: 5, 9, 10, 11, 12

COLORADO SPRINGS

Holden House—1902 Bed and Breakfast Inn

1102 W. Pikes Peak Avenue, 80904
(719) 471-3980; FAX (719) 471-4740
E-mail: HoldenHouse@worldnet.att.net
Web site: http://www.bbonline.com/co/holden

Discover a Pikes Peak treasure! These 1902 storybook Victorians are filled with antiques and family heirlooms. Each guest suite boasts feather pillows, period furnishings, queen bed, in-room fireplace, and oversize bubble bath "tub for two." Centrally located in a residential area near historic Old Colorado City. You can enjoy shopping, restaurants, and attractions nearby. Experience "the romance of the past with the comforts of today." Inn cats "Mingtoy" and "Muffin" are in residence. AAA/Mobil-rated.

Hosts: Sallie and Welling Clark
Rooms: 5 suites (PB) $120-135
Full Gourmet Breakfast
Credit Cards: A, B, C, D, E
Notes: 5, 8, 9, 10, 12

Room at the Inn

618 N. Nevada Avenue, 80903
(719) 442-1896; (800) 579-4621;
FAX (719) 442-6802
E-mail: roomatinn@pcisys.net
Web site: http://www.colorado-bnb.com/roomattheinn

Experience a peek at the past in this elegant Victorian. Enjoy the charm of a classic, three-story, turreted, antique-filled Queen Anne featuring original wall murals, oak staircase, and pocket doors. Experience the romance of fireplaces, plush robes, and whirlpool tubs for two. Gracious hospitality includes full breakfast, afternoon tea, and turn-down service. AC, a hot tub, and off-street parking are available for guests. Ten-percent discount offered to full-time Christian staff. Mobil three-star-rated.

Hosts: Chick and Jan McCormick
Rooms: 7 (PB) $85-135
Full Breakfast
Credit Cards: A, B, C, D, E
Notes: 2, 5, 8, 9, 10, 12

Serenity Pines Guesthouse

11910 Windmill Road, 80908
(719) 495-7141 (voice and FAX)
E-mail: serenpines@aol.com
Web site: http://colorado-bnb.com/serenpines

A true getaway on acres of pines. Twelve-hundred-square-foot guesthouse rented by one visiting party at a time. Sleeps up to six. Full-size stocked/equipped kitchen. New appliances (dishwasher). Continental breakfast served; cook your own, stocked. Like walking into someone's home. B&B-style pampering. Private sundeck, picnic, barbecue area. Parklike setting. Cable, video library, phone, answering machine, crib. Fifteen minutes from Focus on the Family and city. Families, honeymooners, business travelers.

Hosts: Kathy and Bob Benjamin
Rooms: 2 (PB) $99 couple, $129 family up to 6
Continental Breakfast
Credit Cards: A, B, C
Notes: 2, 5, 7, 9, 10, 11, 12

Capitol Hill Mansion

DENVER

Capitol Hill Mansion

1207 Pennsylvania Street, 80203
(303) 839-5221; (800) 839-9329;
FAX (303) 839-9046
Web site: http://www.capitolhillmansion.com

Award-winning 1891 Victorian mansion with eight individually decorated guest rooms. It features antiques mixed with modern amenities such as cable television, refrigerators, complimentary beverages, hair dryers, telephones, desks, private baths, off-street parking, and breakfast. Whirlpool tubs, fireplaces, and balconies are available. A short walk to downtown, government offices, museums, galleries, shops, and restaurants; a short drive to major sports venues and the Rocky Mountains. Perfect for business or romance.

Hostess: Kathy Robbins
Rooms: 8 (PB) $90-165
Full Breakfast
Credit Cards: A, B, C, D
Notes: 2 (with ID), 5, 7, 8, 9, 10, 11, 12

Castle Marne—A Luxury Urban Inn

1572 Race Street, 80206
(303) 331-0621; (800) 92 MARNE (926-2763);
FAX (303) 331-0623
E-mail: themarne@ix.netcom.com
Web site: http://www.castlemarne.com

Chosen by *Country Inns Magazine* as one of the "Top 12 Inns in North America." Fall under the spell of one of Denver's grandest historic mansions. Your stay here combines Old World elegance with modern convenience and comfort. Each guest room is a unique experience in pampered luxury. All rooms have private baths. Two suites have Jacuzzis for two. Three rooms have private balconies and hot tubs. Afternoon tea and a full gourmet breakfast are served in the cherry-paneled dining room. Castle Marne is a certified Denver Landmark and is on the National Register of Historic Structures.

Hosts: Diane and Jim Peiker
Rooms: 9 (PB) $85-220
Full Breakfast
Credit Cards: B, C, D, E
Notes: 2, 3, 4, 5, 7 (over 10), 8, 9, 10, 11, 12

Queen Anne B&B Inn

2147 Tremont Place, 80205
(800) 432-INNS (4667); FAX (303) 296-2151
E-mail: queenanne@worldnet.att.net

Facing quiet Benedict Fountain Park in downtown Denver are two side-by-side National Register Victorian homes with fourteen guest rooms, including four gallery suites. Flowers, chamber music, phones, period antiques, and private baths are in all rooms. Six rooms have special tubs; one has a fireplace. AC, free parking. Within walking distance of the state capitol, 16th Street Pedestrian Mall, Convention Center, Larimer Square, shops, restaurants, and museums. Among its many awards: Best 12 B&Bs Nationally, 10 Most Romantic, Best of Denver, and Best 105 in Great American Cities. Now in its twelfth year, it is inspected and approved by major auto clubs and *Distinctive Inns of Colorado.*

Hosts: The King Family
Rooms: 14 (PB) $75-175
Full Breakfast
Credit Cards: A, B, C, D, E, F
Notes: 2, 5, 7, 8, 9, 10, 11, 12

Silver Wood Bed and Breakfast

DIVIDE

Silver Wood B&B

463 County Road 512, 80814
(719) 687-6784; (800) 753-5592;
FAX (719) 687-1007
E-mail: silver1007@aol.com
Web site: http://www.silverwoodinn.com

Silver Wood is a newly constructed, contemporary home located in rural Colorado near Divide. Your drive to Silver Wood winds through strands of aspen, open meadows, pine trees, and fantastic views of mountains. Only 22 miles from Cripple Creek, 30 miles from Colorado Springs, 7 miles from Mueller State Park. Silver Wood offers many sight-seeing opportunities in the Pikes Peak area, with country quiet. No smoking.

Hosts: Larry and Bess Oliver
Rooms: 2 (PB) $69-89
Full Breakfast
Credit Cards: A, B, C, D
Notes: 2, 5, 7, 12

DURANGO

Lightner Creek Inn

999 CR 207, 81301
(970) 259-1226; (800) 268-9804;
FAX (970) 259-9526
E-mail: lci@frontier.net
Web site: http://www.lightnercreekinn.com

Discover French countryside elegance in the Rockies. Lightner Creek Inn, just 4 miles from Durango, combines charming Victorian detail with antique furnishings and cozy fireplaces. Enjoy the tranquillity of the pond, stream, and views. Gazebo, queen and king beds, down comforters, private baths. Full breakfast. Baby grand piano, beautifully landscaped grounds. Wildlife refuge, Mesa Verde National Park, and the Durango-Silverton narrow-gauge train are close by. Let us make arrangements for dinner sleigh rides, snowmobiling, river rafting, and ski packages for you.

Hosts: Julie and Richard Houston
Rooms: 8 (PB) $85-160
Full Breakfast
Credit Cards: A, B, C, D, E
Notes: 2, 5, 7, 10, 11, 12

Logwood Bed and Breakfast Lodge

Logwood B&B

35060 U.S. Highway 550 N., 81301
(970) 259-4396; (800) 369-4082;
FAX (970) 259-7812
E-mail: logwood@frontier.net
Web site: http://www.fsnw.com/logwood

Built in 1988, this large cedar log home is on 15 acres amid the beautiful San Juan Mountains beside the Animas River. Guest rooms are decorated with a southwestern flair. Homemade country quilts adorn country-made, queen beds. Private baths in all guest rooms. A large, river rock fireplace warms the elegant living and dining areas in winter. Award-winning desserts are served in the evening. The entire lodge may be rented, with full kitchen. Pamper yourselves. Come home to Logwood.

Hosts: Debby and Greg Verheyden
Rooms: 8 (PB) $65-125
Full Breakfast
Credit Cards: A, B
Notes: 2, 5, 7 (over 8), 9, 10, 11, 12

Scrubby Oaks Bed and Breakfast Inn

PO Box 1047, 81302
(970) 247-2176
Web site: http://www.southwesterninns.com/scrubby.htm

Set on 10 acres overlooking the Animas River Valley, this sprawling ranch-style inn

NOTES: Credit cards accepted: A Master Card; B Visa; C American Express; D Discover; E Diners Club; F Other; 2 Personal checks accepted; 3 Lunch available; 4 Dinner available; 5 Open all year; 6 Pets

has a quiet country feel with the convenience of being 3 miles from downtown Durango. Scrubby Oaks is beautifully furnished with family antiques, artworks, and fine books. Lovely gardens and patios frame the outside, where guests can relax after a day of sight-seeing around the Four Corners area. Snacks are offered in the afternoons, and a full country breakfast is served each morning. Open from the end of April to the end of October.

Hostess: Mary Ann Craig
Rooms: 7 (3PB; 4SB) $70-80
Full Breakfast
Credit Cards: none
Notes: 2, 7, 8, 9, 10, 12

ESTES PARK

Quilt House Bed and Breakfast

PO Box 339, 80517
(970) 586-0427
E-mail: Hgraetzer@aol.com

A beautiful view can be enjoyed from every window of this sturdy mountain home. It is just a 15-minute walk from downtown Estes Park and only 4 miles from the entrance of Rocky Mountain National Park. There are three bedrooms upstairs, plus a lounge where guests can read, look at the mountains, and have a cup of coffee or tea. A guest house beside the main house has a kitchenette. The hosts gladly help with information concerning hiking trails, car drives, wildlife viewing, shopping, etc. No smoking.

Hosts: Hans and Miriam Graetzer
Rooms: 4 (PB) $60-75
Full Breakfast
Credit Cards: none
Notes: 2, 5, 8, 9, 10, 11

Romantic River Song Inn

Romantic River Song Inn

PO Box 1910, 80517
(970) 586-4666; FAX (970) 577-0699
E-mail: riversng@frii.com
Web site: http://www.starsend.com/getaway/rivers~1/rspge1.htm

This stunning Craftsman-style inn is secluded at the end of a country road on 27 wooded acres. All nine guest rooms are creatively designed with fireplaces and private baths featuring waterfall showers. Fireside dinners and backpack picnic lunches are available for your Rocky Mountain National Park excursions. Snowshoe weddings can be conducted by the innkeeper-minister.

Hosts: Gary and Sue Mansfield
Rooms: 9 (PB) $135-250
Continental Breakfast
Credit Cards: A, B
Notes: 4, 5, 10, 11, 12

GEORGETOWN

Hardy House Bed and Breakfast

605 Brownell; PO Box 156, 80444
(303) 569-3388; (800) 490-4802
E-mail: hhousebb@aol.com

With its late 19th-century charm, the Hardy House invites you to relax in the parlor by

Hardy House Bed and Breakfast

the potbelly stove, sleep under feather comforters, and enjoy a candlelight breakfast. Georgetown is only 55 minutes from Denver and the airport. Surrounded by mountains, it boasts unique shopping, wonderful restaurants, and close proximity to seven ski areas.

Hosts: Carla and Mike Wagner
Rooms: 4-5 (PB) $80-95
Full Breakfast
Credit Cards: A, B
Notes: 2, 5, 7 (over 12), 8, 10, 11, 12

GLENWOOD SPRINGS

Back in Time B&B

927 Cooper Avenue, 81601
(970) 945-6183; (888) 854-7733
E-mail: bitbnb@sprynet.com

A spacious Victorian home built in 1903 and filled with antiques, family quilts, and clocks. A full breakfast is served in the dining room: a hot dish accompanied by fresh hot muffins, fruit, and a specialty of June's mouth-watering cinnamon rolls.

Hosts: June and Ron Robinson
Rooms: 3 (PB) $85
Full Breakfast
Credit Cards: A, B, C, D
Notes: 2, 5, 8, 9, 10, 11, 12

GUNNISON

The Eagle's Nest

206 N. Colorado, 81230
(970) 641-4457

Wonderful accommodations for two people—three possible. Very large bedroom, bath, hallway, outside entrance, and sitting room—the entire upstairs of our house. Special breakfast after 9 AM; continental before then. No smoking.

Hosts: Jane and Hugh McGee
Rooms: 1 (PB) $45
Continental and Special Breakfast
Credit Cards: only for reservations
Notes: 2, 5, 10, 11

LEADVILLE

The Apple Blossom Inn

120 W. 4th Street, 80461
(719) 486-2141; (800) 982-9279;
FAX (719) 486-0994
E-mail: applebb@rmi.net
Web site: http://www.colorado-bnb.com/abi

This beautiful 1879 banker's home has been featured on two Victorian home tours and is the recipient of a 1998 Award of Excellence. Decorated with antiques, charm, and a flair for comfortable spaces.

The Apple Blossom Inn

NOTES: Credit cards accepted: A Master Card; B Visa; C American Express; D Discover; E Diners Club; F Other; 2 Personal checks accepted; 3 Lunch available; 4 Dinner available; 5 Open all year; 6 Pets

Breakfast is fully delicious. Free recreation center passes. Feather beds, fireplaces, and home-baked goodies make your stay here most memorable.

Hostess: Maggie Senn
Rooms: 5 (PB) $89-128
Full Breakfast
Credit Cards: A, B, C, D, E
Notes: 2, 5, 7, 8, 9, 10, 11, 12

The Ice Palace Inn

813 Spruce Street, 80461
(719) 486-8272; (800) 754-2840;
FAX (719) 486-0345
E-mail: ipalace@sni.net
Web site: http://colorado-bnb.com/icepalace

This gracious Victorian inn was built at the turn of the century, using lumber from the famous Leadville Ice Palace. Romantic guest rooms, elegantly decorated with antiques, feather beds, and quilts. Each has an exquisite private bath and is named after an original room of the Ice Palace. Begin your day with a delicious gourmet breakfast served at individual tables in this historic inn. Afternoon teas and goodies are available every day. Turn-down service in the evening. Hot tub.

Hosts: Giles and Kami Kolakowski
Rooms: 6 (PB) $79-139
Full Gourmet Breakfast
Credit Cards: A, B, C, D
Notes: 2, 5, 7, 8, 9, 10, 11, 12

Wood Haven Manor

809 Spruce; PO Box 1291, 80461
(719) 486-0109; (800) 748-2570 (voice and FAX)
Web site: http://colorado-bnb.com/woodhavn

Enjoy the taste and style of Victorian Leadville by stepping back 100 years in this beautiful home located on "Banker's Row." Each room is distinctively decorated

Wood Haven Manor

in Victorian style and offers a private bath. Two of the suites have whirlpools and one includes a fireplace. Spacious dining room; comfortable living room with fireplace. Snacks and goodies all day. Historic city with a backdrop of Colorado's highest mountains. Snowmobiling, skiing, hiking, and more.

Hosts: Bobby and Jolene Wood
Rooms: 8 (PB) $79-139
Full Breakfast
Credit Cards: A, B, C, D
Notes: 2, 3, 4, 5, 7, 8, 9, 10, 11, 12

LOVELAND

Derby Hill Inn

2502 Courtney Drive, 80537
(970) 667-3193 (voice and FAX); (800) 498-8086
E-mail: DMcCue31@aol.com
Web site: http://www.guestinns.com/derbyhill

Semifinalists for "1997 Inn of the Year" in small new inn category. Located in a quiet residential neighborhood close to retail and antique shops, art galleries, four-star golf courses, Rocky Mountain National Park. Friendly hospitality welcomes the casual and business traveler to enjoy the well-decorated, comfortable rooms with private baths, queen beds, in-room phones,

welcome; 7 Children welcome; 8 Tennis nearby; 9 Swimming nearby; 10 Golf nearby; 11 Skiing nearby; 12 May be booked through travel agent.

desks, televisions, and robes. A delectable home-cooked breakfast is served. Our homelike atmosphere is enhanced with art and antiques. Computer and FAX available.

Hosts: Dale and Bev McCue
Rooms: 2 (PB) $75-85
Full Breakfast
Credit Cards: A, B, C, E
Notes: 2, 5, 8, 9, 10, 12

LYONS

Inn at Rock 'n River

16858 N. St. Vrain Drive, 80540
(303) 443-4611; (800) 448-4611
E-mail: rocknriver@estes-park.com
Web site: http://www.estes-park.com/rocknriver

Scenic inn (featured in *Country Magazine*, October 1991) on the river in the mountains, surrounded by ponds, waterfalls, covered bridges, waterwheel, and flowers. Stocked trout ponds are available for fishing (bait, license, and cleaning provided). Awesome nearby open-space hiking, fantastic bird-watching. All rooms have king beds, private baths and entrances; some have kitchens. Outdoor grills.

Hosts: Marshall and Barbara McCrummen
Rooms: 9 (PB) $89
Full Breakfast
Credit Cards: A, B, C, D
Notes: 7, 12

MANCOS

Riversbend B&B

42505 Highway 160, 81328
(970) 533-7353; (800) 699-8994;
FAX (970) 533-1221
E-mail: riversbn@fone.net
Web site: http://www.riversbend.com

Riversbend Bed and Breakfast is located on the San Juan Skyway (Mesa Verde: 7 miles; Durango: 25 miles). Riversbend serves as a hub for the many area activities and will be your haven for rest and relaxation when the day is over. In the two-story log inn located on the Mancos River, you are welcomed by the charm of yesteryear as you are engulfed by the soft glow of the overhead hurricane lamps, the hominess and warmth of the log walls and antiques, the crisp white priscillas. Guests drift off to sleep between cool white sheets that smell of Colorado sunshine, and awaken to the tantalizing scent of a scrumptious gourmet breakfast. Take your morning glass of juice to the hot tub. Enjoy an invigorating warm massage as you listen to the sound of the gently rushing river and watch the day unfold. Count the brilliant stars at night after a day of horseback riding, exploring Mesa Verde, or riding the narrow-gauge train. Riversbend is close to something for everyone!

Hosts: Gaye and Jack Curran
Rooms: 5 (PB) $75-125
Full Breakfast
Credit Cards: A, B, C, D
Notes: 2, 10, 11, 12

MANITOU SPRINGS

Spring Cottage

113 Pawnee Avenue, 80829
(719) 685-9395 (voice and FAX); (888) 588-9395
E-mail: lancaster@springcottage.com
Web site: http://www.springcottage.com

Relax in your own 1885, separate, private cottage. Spring Cottage, a five-room retreat, welcomes families with children of all ages or couples looking for a warm, intimate setting located centrally to the many attractions in this mountain vacationland. The second cottage—Spring Cottage, Too—is for your personal holiday, honeymoon, or anniversary. You will step into an intimate rose garden setting of 100-year-old wicker, Battenburg lace, and roses on your bed. Breakfast is served privately. Smoking outdoors only.

Hosts: Ron and Judy Lancaster
Rooms: 2 cottages (PB) $85 single
Full Breakfast
Credit Cards: A, B
Notes: 2, 5, 6, 7, 8, 9, 10, 11, 12

The Damn Yankee Country Inn

OURAY

The Damn Yankee Country Inn

PO Box 410, 100 Sixth Avenue, 81427
(970) 325-4219; (800) 845-7512;
FAX (970) 325-4339
E-mail: damnyankee@montrose.net
Web site: http://www.montrose.net/users/damnyank

Luxurious B&B located in the midst of the beautiful San Juan Mountains. All rooms have private bath, television, and telephone; some have king bed, Jacuzzi tub, VCR, and fireplace.

Hosts: Matt and Julie Croce
Rooms: 10 (PB) $74-195
Full Breakfast
Credit Cards: A, B, D
Notes: 2, 5, 9, 11

Ouray 1898 House

322 Main Street, 81427-0641
(970) 325-4871
E-mail: bates@netzone.com
Web site: http://colorado-bnb.com/mainst

This 100-year-old house has been carefully renovated and combines the old with the comfortable amenities of today. Each room features antique furnishings, cable TV, and a private bath. From the deck off each guest room is a spectacular view of the San Juan Mountains—or enjoy this view from the unique Victorian gazebo and soothing spa. A full breakfast is served with a "variety for every appetite." Ouray is known as the "Jeep Capital of the World" and also is known for its natural hot springs and marvelous hiking trails.

Hosts: Lee and Kathy Bates
Rooms: 4 (PB) $68-95
Full Breakfast
Credit Cards: A, B, C
Notes: 2, 8, 9, 10

PAGOSA SPRINGS

Be Our Guest— A B&B Guesthouse

19 Swiss Village Drive, 81147
(970) 264-6814; FAX (970) 264-6953 (call first)

Welcome to your place in Colorado. The warm, inviting atmosphere of this lodgelike home greets you as you pull off Highway 160, 6 miles east of town. Ample parking. Views, San Juan River and national forest. Each theme room offers comfort. Lower level provides family or group privacy, kitchen, and three baths (one with Jacuzzi). Great common areas have satellite, VCRs, games, warm fires, awesome views. Delightful breakfast with most accommodations. Take a room or the whole house. Great group rates. Well-behaved children welcome. Small fee for pets.

Hosts: Tom and Pam Schoemig
Rooms: 5 (3PB; 2SB) $47-85
Full Breakfast
Credit Cards: none
Notes: 2, 5, 6 (by prior arrangement), 9, 10, 11

Davidson's Country Inn

PO Box 87, 81147
(970) 264-5863; FAX (970) 264-5492

Davidson's Country Inn is a three-story log house located at the foot of the Rocky Mountains on 32 acres. The inn provides a library, playroom, game room, and outdoor activities. A two-bedroom cabin is also available. The inn is tastefully decorated with family heirlooms and antiques, with a warm country touch to make you feel at home. Located 2 miles east of Highway 160. Hot tub. We are available to host family reunions on request.

Hosts: Nancy and Gilbert Davidson
Rooms: 8 (3PB; 5SB) $59-95
Full Breakfast
Credit Cards: A, B, C, D
Notes: 2, 5, 6 (by arrangement), 7, 8, 9, 10, 11, 12

PAONIA

Pitkin Mesa Bed and Breakfast

3954 "P" Road, 81428
(970) 527-7576

Pitkin Mesa Bed and Breakfast is in the mild climate of Paonia's fruit-growing area. Guests enjoy restful views of the North Fork of Gunnison Valley and nearby mountains. They can hike or bike to shops and restaurants. This is a newer home in a semirural area with an indoor, heated swimming pool and spa. From the porch swing on our spacious deck you can view Mt. Lamborn (Romans 5:12). Close to Black Canyon, scenic byways, and Grand Mesa's lakes. Tobacco- and alcohol-free. Children under 14 by special arrangement only. Open June–October.

Hosts: Dale and Barbara Soucek
Rooms: 3 (1PB; 2SB) $55-65
Full Breakfast
Credit Cards: A, B
Notes: 2, 8, 9

PUEBLO

Abriendo Inn

300 W. Abriendo Avenue, 81004
(719) 542-6544; FAX (719) 542-6544
E-mail: abriendo@vmi.net

Experience the elegance of an estate home as you delight in the pleasure of personal attention and hospitality. Get away to yesterday with the conveniences you expect of today. Breakfast is always hearty, home-baked, and served in the oak-wainscoted dining room or on one of the picturesque porches. The inn is located within walking distance of restaurants, shops, and galleries—all in the heart of Pueblo. All rooms have air-conditioning, king/queen beds, TVs, and telephones; some have whirlpool tubs.

Hostess: Kerrelyn M. Trent
Rooms: 10 (PB) $59-115
Full Breakfast
Credit Cards: A, B, C, E
Notes: 2, 5, 8, 9, 10, 12

The Tudor Rose

SALIDA

The Tudor Rose

6720 County Road 104; PO Box 89, 81201
(719) 539-2002; (800) 379-0889;
FAX (719) 530-0345
E-mail: tudorose@amigo.net
Web site: http://www.bbonline.com/co/tudorose

Stately elegance and homelike comfort are combined tastefully at this majestic country manor. Nestled in pinon pines on 37 acres and surrounded by three mountain ranges, the inn commands views of the Rocky Mountains by day and starry skies by night. Overly large guest rooms, spacious common areas. Wildlife, native landscape, sunken hot tub, and a hiking trail enrich the surrounding grounds.

Hosts: Jon and Terré Terrell
Rooms: 6 (4PB; 2SB) $50-120
Full Breakfast
Credit Cards: A, B, D
Notes: 2, 3, 5, 6, 7, 8, 9, 10, 11, 12

STEAMBOAT SPRINGS

The Iron Horse Inn

333 S. Lincoln Avenue; PO Box 771873, 81477
(970) 879-6505; (800) 856-6505;
FAX (970) 879-6129
Web site: http://www.ironhorseresort.com

Warm hospitality and western charm overlooking the Yampa River. If you long for a feeling of comfort and familiarity while you are away from home, The Iron Horse Inn is for you. Available for your comfort are twenty-four kitchenettes, two suites, and twenty-six new rooms with excellent views of the Yampa Valley. We offer a relaxing indoor hot tub and sauna to soothe the traveler. The Iron Horse Inn abuts the 9-mile river walk, just blocks from downtown Steamboat's shopping, dining, and hot spring pool.

Hostess: Suzie Hawkins
Rooms: 52 (PB) $49-122
Continental Breakfast
Credit Cards: A, B, C, E
Notes: 5, 7, 8, 9, 10, 11, 12

VAIL

Bed and Breakfast Reservations @ Vail/Colorado

2488 Garmisch Drive, 81657
(970) 476-0792; (800) 748-2666;
FAX (970) 476-0711
E-mail: bbresser@vail.net
Web site: http://www.vail.net/lodging/bnb/bbres

A bed and breakfast reservation agency representing Vail and all resort areas. We offer private homestays, inns, and cabins to meet the needs of the traveler who enjoys the unique adventure. From the excitement of the winter and summer resorts to the serenity of nature's wonders, we have the perfect place for you.

Owners: Beverly Miller and Narda Reigel
Full and Continental Breakfast
Credit Cards: A, B, C, D, E
Notes: 2

WINTER PARK

Candlelight Mountain Inn

PO Box 600, 80482
(970) 887-2877; (800) KIM-4-TIM (546-4846)
E-mail: kim-4-tim@juno.com
Web site: http://www.cism.com/candlelight.html

Nestled on a mountainside among pine and aspen trees, the Candlelight Mountain Inn is located in Colorado's beautiful Fraser Valley. Married couples, retired folks, and families will enjoy the comfortable beds, full breakfasts, candlelit lane, game and toy room, hot tub under the stars, glider swings around the campfire, beautiful view, and other surprises. Our inn is situated in the heart of a vacation paradise; it's just 15 minutes to the ski slopes, 30 minutes to Rocky Mountain National Park, and only 3 minutes to the Pole Creek Golf Course and the YMCA of the Rockies. You may rent our inn as your private vacation home during certain times of the year.

Hosts: Kim and Tim Onnen
Rooms: 3 (PB) $65-90
Full Breakfast
Credit Cards: none
Notes: 2, 5, 7, 8, 9, 10, 11

WOODLAND PARK

Pikes Peak Paradise

236 Pinecrest Road, 80863
(719) 687-6656; (800) 728-8282;
FAX (719) 687-9008
E-mail: ppp@cyber-bbs.com
Web site: http://www.cyber-bbs.com/ppp

Luxury accommodations, in-room hot tubs and fireplaces, romance, peace, privacy. All rooms include incredible Pikes Peak views, complimentary beverages and snacks, private attached bath, full use of outdoor hot tub, and gourmet breakfast. Smoke-free environment. Northwest of Colorado Springs.

Hostess: Priscilla Arthur
Rooms: 6 (PB) $135-220
Full Breakfast
Credit Cards: A, B, C, D
Notes: 2, 5, 10, 12

Woodland Inn Bed and Breakfast

159 Trull Road, 80863
(719) 687-8209; (800) 226-9565;
FAX (719) 687-3112
E-mail: woodlandbb@aol.com
Web site: http://www.bbonline.com/co/woodland

Guests enjoy the relaxing, homelike atmosphere and fantastic views of Pikes Peak from this cozy country inn in the heart of the Rocky Mountains. Peacefully secluded on 12 private acres of woodlands, the Woodland Inn is convenient to varied attractions, some of which include limited-stakes gambling in Cripple Creek, Pikes Peak, the Cog Railway and highway, hiking, biking, golf, trail riding, and cross-country skiing. Hot-air ballooning with the host is also available! We welcome small wedding retreats and seminars; the Woodland Inn can accommodate fifteen to twenty overnight guests and up to fifty people at gatherings. (Note: We have a cat in residence.)

Hosts: Frank and Nancy O'Neil
Rooms: 7 (PB) $70-100
Full Breakfast
Credit Cards: A, B, C, D
Notes: 2, 5, 7, 8, 10, 11, 12

Connecticut

Bed and Breakfast, Ltd.

PO Box 216, **New Haven,** 06513
(203) 469-3260
E-mail: BandBLtd@aol.com

Bed and Breakfast, Ltd., offers more than 125 listings of private homes and small inns throughout **Connecticut** (with additional locations in **Massachusetts** and **Rhode Island**)—from elegantly simple to simply elegant. Affordable and varied. A quick phone call assures up-to-the-minute descriptions and availability.

Director: Jack M. Argenio
Rooms: 125+ (75PB; 50SB) $60-149
Full and Continental Breakfast
Credit Cards: (at some) A, B
Notes: (at some) 2, 4, 5, 6, 7, 8, 9, 10, 11

CLINTON

Captain Dibbell House Bed and Breakfast

21 Commerce Street, 06413
(860) 669-1646; FAX (860) 669-2300
Web site: http://clintonct.com/dibbell

Our 1886 Victorian, just 2 blocks from the shore, features a wisteria-covered, century-old footbridge and gazebo on our ½ acre of lawn and gardens. Spacious living rooms and bedrooms are comfortably furnished with antiques and family heirlooms, fresh flowers, fruit baskets, and home-baked treats. There are bicycles, nearby beaches, and marinas to enjoy.

Hosts: Helen and Ellis Adams
Rooms: 4 (PB) $75-105
Full Breakfast
Credit Cards: A, B
Notes: 2, 8, 9, 10, 12

Butternut Farm

GLASTONBURY

Butternut Farm

1654 Main Street, 06033
(860) 633-7197; FAX (860) 659-1758

This 18th-century architectural jewel is furnished in period antiques. Prize-winning dairy goats, pigeons, and chickens roam in an estate setting with trees and herb gardens. Enjoy fresh eggs for breakfast.

---

welcome; 7 Children welcome; 8 Tennis nearby; 9 Swimming nearby; 10 Golf nearby; 11 Skiing nearby; 12 May be booked through travel agent.

CONNECTICUT

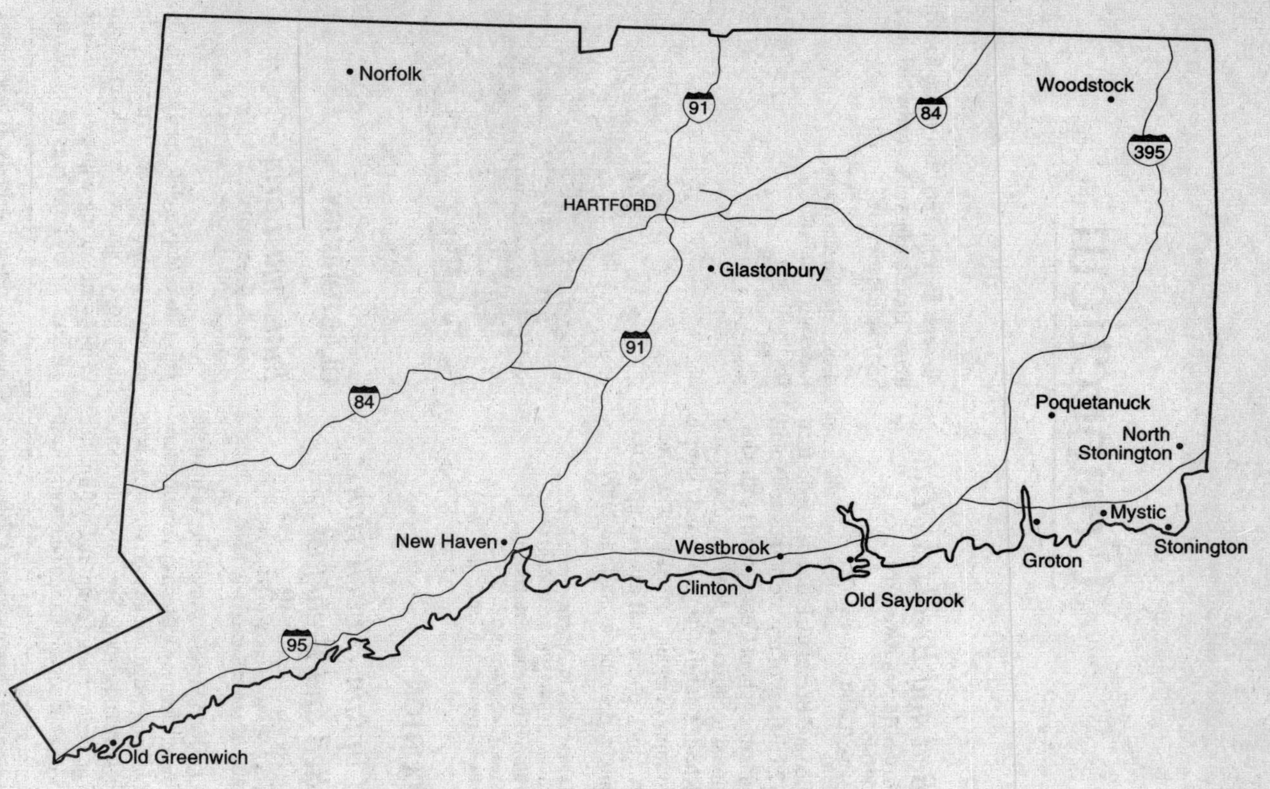

Ten minutes from Hartford by expressway; 1½ hours from any place in Connecticut. No pets, no smoking.

Host: Don Reid
Rooms: 3 + suite and apartment (PB) $70-90
Full Breakfast
Credit Cards: C
Notes: 2, 5, 7, 8, 9, 10, 11

GROTON

Bluff Point B&B

26 Fort Hill Road, 06340
(860) 445-1314
Web site: http://www.visitmystic.com/bluffpoint

A restored colonial bed and breakfast (circa 1850) located on U.S. Route 1 and adjacent to Bluff Point State Park Coastal Preserve. Conveniently located 4 miles from Mystic Seaport Museum. Large common area with shared TV is available for our guests. Our home is equipped with a central fire sprinkler system. No smoking or pets. Warm, friendly service.

Hosts: Walter and Edna Parfitt
Rooms: 3 (PB) $85-95
Continental Breakfast
Credit Cards: A, B, C
Notes: 2, 5, 8, 9, 10

MYSTIC

The Adams House of Mystic

382 Cow Hill Road, 06355
(860) 572-9551
E-mail: adamshse@aol.com
Web site: http://www.visitmystic.com/adamshouse

Historic 1749 colonial home close to Mystic Seaport and Mystic Aquarium.

The Adams House of Mystic

Seven rooms with queen beds, private baths, and AC. Hearty breakfast included. Children welcome. Large yard with gardens and patio. Smoke-free.

Hosts: Mary Lou and Gregory Peck
Rooms: 7 (PB) $95-175
Full Breakfast
Credit Cards: A, B, C, D
Notes: 2, 5, 7, 9, 10

The Harbour Inne and Cottage

15 Edgemont Street, 06355
(860) 572-9253
Web site: http://www.visitmystic.com/harbourinne

The Harbour Inne and Cottage is located on the Mystic River, 2 blocks from historic downtown Mystic. Six rooms and a cottage. The three-room cottage has a fireplace and two double beds in the bedroom. A sleeper sofa and color TV are in the living room, with glider doors opening onto a deck with a hot tub spa. Shower/lavatory facilities, kitchen and dining area. The guest house has five rooms, each with double bed, color TV, shower or bath, and

NOTES: Credit cards accepted: A Master Card; B Visa; C American Express; D Discover; E Diners Club; F Other; 2 Personal checks accepted; 3 Lunch available; 4 Dinner available; 5 Open all year; 6 Pets welcome; 7 Children welcome; 8 Tennis nearby; 9 Swimming nearby; 10 Golf nearby; 11 Skiing nearby; 12 May be booked through travel agent.

air-conditioning. Guests have an equipped galley and dining area, as well as a social area with fireplace and antique piano.

Host: Charles Lecouras, Jr.
Rooms: 6 + cottage (PB) $75-250
Self-Catered Breakfast
Credit Cards: none
Notes: 5, 6, 7, 8, 9, 10

Red Brook Inn

PO Box 237, 06372
(860) 572-0349; (800) 290-5619
E-mail: RKeyes1667@aol.com

Nestled on 7 acres of old New England wooded countryside, your lodging is provided in two historic buildings. The Haley Tavern, circa 1770, is a colonial built by sea captain Nathaniel Crary. Each room is appointed with period furnishings, including canopy beds. There are many working fireplaces throughout the inn and guest rooms. A hearty breakfast is served family-style in the ancient keeping room. Enjoy a quiet atmosphere near Mystic Seaport Museum, antique shops, Foxwoods Casino, and Aquarium. Colonial dinner weekends available November–December. No smoking.

Hostess: Ruth Keyes
Rooms: 10 (PB) $95-189
Full Breakfast
Credit Cards: A, B, C, D
Notes: 2, 5, 7, 8, 9, 10

Steamboat Inn

73 Steamboat Wharf, 06355
(860) 536-8300; FAX (860) 536-1379
E-mail: sbwharf@aol.com
Web site: http://www.visitmystic.com/steamboat

Elegant and intimate. Steamboat Inn is situated directly on the Mystic River in historic downtown Mystic. Restaurants are within walking distance of the inn. Enjoy the fireplaces, whirlpool baths, and river views. Guests have individual HVAC controls. Telephones and televisions are in all guest rooms.

Hostess: Diana Stadt Miller
Rooms: 10 (PB) $110-275
Continental Breakfast
Credit Cards: A, B, C, D
Notes: 2, 5, 12

Three Chimneys Inn at Yale University

NEW HAVEN

Three Chimneys Inn at Yale University

1201 Chapel Street, 06511
(203) 789-1201; (800) 443-1554;
FAX (203) 776-7363
E-mail: chimneysnh@aol.com
Web site: http://www.ultranet.com/~chimney3

Three Chimneys Inn is a lovely Queen Anne–style mansion located ½ block from the Yale University campus, restaurants, and museums. The ten distinctive guest rooms have private full baths, Georgian

NOTES: Credit cards accepted: A Master Card; B Visa; C American Express; D Discover; E Diners Club; F Other; 2 Personal checks accepted; 3 Lunch available; 4 Dinner available; 5 Open all year; 6 Pets

and Federal period furnishings, four-poster king- and queen-size beds, inlaid parquet floors, Oriental rugs, full-size desks, color televisions, and telephones with data ports. The grand staircase and the two parlors with their four fireplaces reflect the fine oak millwork detail prevalent during the 1870s.

Host: Michael Marra
Rooms: 10 (PB) $160
Full Breakfast
Credit Cards: A, B, C, D
Notes: 2, 5

NORFOLK

Greenwoods Gate Bed and Breakfast

105 Greenwoods Road E.; PO Box 491, 06058
(860) 542-5439
Web site: http://www.greenwoodsgate.com

Warm hospitality greets you in this beautifully restored 1797 Colonial home. Greenwood Gate is small and elegant, with four exquisitely appointed guest suites, each with private bath (one with a Jacuzzi tub). Fine antiques, fireplaces, and sumptuous breakfasts indulge you. Afternoon tea and refreshments are served before you go out to dinner. *Yankee Magazine* has called this "New England's most romantic bed and breakfast." *Country Inns Bed and Breakfast Magazine* termed it "a Connecticut jewel." Come, join us at the home of Yale University's renowned summer music festival.

Host: George E. Schumaker
Rooms: 4 suites (PB) $175-245
Gourmet Breakfast
Credit Cards: none
Notes: 5, 7, 8, 9, 11, 12

Antiques and Accommodations

NORTH STONINGTON

Antiques and Accommodations

32 Main Street, 06359
(860) 535-1736; (800) 554-7829;
FAX (860) 535-2613

Stroll through our well-tended gardens filled with edible flowers and herbs. Relax on our porches and patios. Our country retreat is located 2.5 miles from I–95, minutes from Mystic Seaport, Aquarium, and superb beaches. Gracious hospitality awaits you at our lovingly restored homes: antiques, canopy beds, fireplaces, private baths, air-conditioned rooms, and cable TV. Greet the day with our acclaimed four-course candlelight breakfast. Always an abundance of flowers. We welcome children who appreciate antiques.

Hosts: Ann and Tom Gray
Rooms: 5 + a 3-bedroom suite (PB) $99-229
Full Breakfast
Credit Cards: A, B
Notes: 2, 5, 7, 8, 9, 10, 12

OLD GREENWICH

Harbor House Inn

165 Shore Road, 06870
(203) 637-0145; FAX (203) 698-0943
Web site: http://www.HHInn.com

Located in Old Greenwich, surrounded by charm that speaks of times long ago, a short stroll to the beach and the lovely park that adjoins it—and yet, only minutes away from restaurants, stores, the train station and I–95, and a mere 45 minutes from New York City. No smoking.

Hostesses: Dolly Stuttig and Dawn Browne
Rooms: 23 (17PB; 6SB) $89-149
Continental Breakfast
Credit Cards: A, B, C
Notes: 2, 5, 7, 8, 9, 10, 12

OLD SAYBROOK

Deacon Timothy Pratt Bed and Breakfast

325 Main Street, 06475
(860) 395-1229; FAX (860) 395-4748
E-mail: shelley.nobile@snet.net
Web site: http://www.virtualcities.com/ct/pratthouse.htm

Step back in time and enjoy the splendor of this magnificent center-chimney Colonial, which is listed on the National Historic Register. Guest rooms are romantically furnished in period style with working fireplaces, four-poster canopy beds, and Jacuzzis. A full breakfast is served in the elegant dining room on fine china by candlelight. Located in Old Saybrook, where the Connecticut River meets Long Island Sound, the Pratt House is conveniently located in the historic and shopping district. Walk to shops, restaurants, theaters, town green, and Saybrook Point. The home is located near beaches, antique shops, museums, Mystic Seaport and Aquarium, Foxwoods and Mohegan Sun Casinos, Goodspeed musicals, factory outlet malls, Essex Steam Train, CT River and Long Island Sound cruises, Gillette Castle State Park, and lots more!

Deacon Timothy Pratt Bed and Breakfast

Hostess: Shelley C. Nobile
Rooms: 3 (PB) $95-140
Full Breakfast
Credit Cards: A, B, C
Notes: 2, 3, 5, 7, 8, 9, 10, 11, 12

POQUETANUCK

1754 Captain Grant's

109 Route 2A, 06365
(860) 887-7589; (800) 982-1772;
FAX (860) 892-9151
Web site: http://www.bbonline.com/ct/captaingrants

Captain Grant's, 1754, is nestled in a national historic district. Built in 1754, it has open-beamed ceilings, wide board floors, and canopy beds, adding charm and romance to your stay. A library, keeping room, dining room, and kitchenette are for guests' exclusive use. Complimentary wine is served each evening; a full country breakfast starts your day. Each room boasts a modern bath and color cable TV. Area maps are furnished upon arrival.

Hosts: Carol and Ted
Rooms: 4 (PB) $80-135
Full Breakfast
Credit Cards: A, B, C, D, F
Notes: 5, 7, 8, 9, 10, 12

WESTBROOK

Welcome Inn Bed and Breakfast

433 Essex Road, 06498
(860) 399-2500; FAX (860) 399-1840
E-mail: r.bambino@snet.net

The Welcome Inn Bed and Breakfast, originally a strawberry farm, was built in 1896 and retains its country charm. It is conveniently located to everything the Connecticut Shoreline and River Valley have to offer. The three lovely guest rooms and house are decorated with antiques, fine reproductions, and family heirlooms. Robert, your host, is an antique restorer and cabinetmaker who has built or restored many pieces in the inn. Alison, your hostess, is an illustrator and graphic artist. A complimentary full, sumptuous breakfast is served daily, including our special house-blend coffee. You can relax in the parlor with a crackling fire, glass of sherry, and good book, or in the garden (weather permitting). We help guests arrange dinner reservations, tours, or other activities.

Hosts: Robert and Alison Bambino
Rooms: 3 (1PB; 2 SB) $80-125
Full Breakfast
Credit Cards: A, B
Notes: 2, 5, 8, 9, 10, 12

Taylor's Corner Bed and Breakfast

WOODSTOCK

Taylor's Corner Bed and Breakfast

880 Route 171, 06281-2930
(860) 974-0490; (888) 503-9057;
FAX (860) 974-0498
E-mail: taylors@neca.com
Web site: http://www.neguide.com/taylors

Taylor's Corner Bed and Breakfast—a romantic, 18th-century Colonial home with eight working fireplaces—is on the National Register of Historic Places. Common areas and air-conditioned guest rooms with phones and private baths are furnished with antiques. Originally a farmhouse, Taylor's Corner maintains its pastoral setting, surrounded by gardens and towering trees. Breakfast is served on fine Danish porcelain. The home is located just off Scenic Route 169 in Connecticut's "Quiet Corner." We're only 5 minutes from terrific antiquing in Putnam and 20 minutes from Old Sturbridge Village.

Hosts: Peggy and Doug
Rooms: 3 (PB) $80-125
Full Breakfast, weekend; Continental, weekday
Credit cards: none
Notes: 2, 5, 7 (over 12), 9, 10, 11 (cross-country), 12

DELAWARE

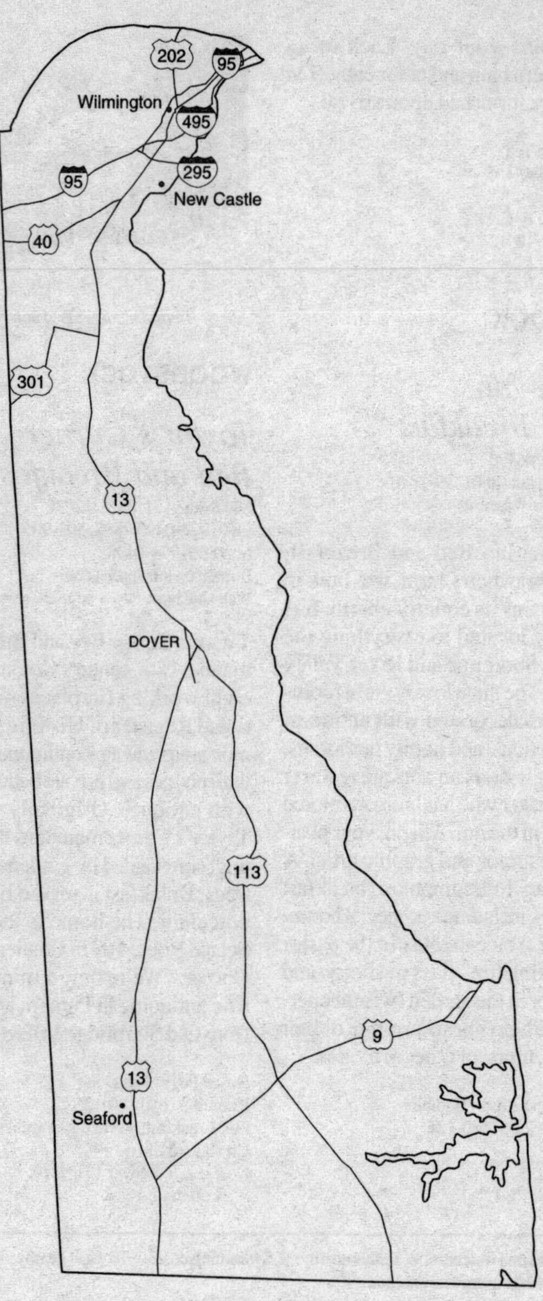

202
95
Wilmington
495
95
295
New Castle
40
301
13
DOVER
113
9
13
Seaford

Delaware

Bed and Breakfast of Delaware

2701 Landon Drive, **Wilmington,** 19810-2211
(302) 479-9500; FAX (302) 478-1437
Web site: http://home.travel.bbww.service/bb.of.de

A bed and breakfast reservation service. We will make reservations for you in historic inns, farms, estates, private homes, mini-efficiencies, and spacious manors. Venues located in **Delaware, Pennsylvania, Maryland,** and **Virginia** serve full or continental breakfast and may accept MasterCard, Visa, American Express, and Discover cards, as well as checks. Year-round availabilities with nearby activities such as tennis, swimming, and golf. Children welcome. May be booked by a travel agent. Millie Alford, coordinator.

NEW CASTLE

Armitage Inn

2 The Strand, 19720
(302) 328-6618; FAX (302) 324-1163
E-mail: armitageinn@earthlink.net

Built in 1732, the Armitage Inn is beautifully situated on the bank of the Delaware River in historic New Castle. Elegantly furnished, air-conditioned guest rooms, all with private baths and most with whirlpool tubs, overlook the picturesque vistas of the grand Delaware River, the acres of parkland surrounding the inn, and a peaceful walled garden. A gourmet buffet breakfast is served in the grand dining room or in the garden each morning. The inn is conveniently located in the heart of this historic town. New Castle was established in 1651 and functions today as a living museum, with buildings dating back to its founding years. New Castle is situated in the heart of the Brandywine Valley, a region noted for its many museums and attractions.

Hosts: Stephen and Rina Marks
Rooms: 5 (PB) $105-150
Full Breakfast
Credit Cards: A, B, C, D
Notes: 5, 8, 10, 12

William Penn Guest House

206 Delaware Street, 19720
(302) 328-7736

Visit historic New Castle and stay in a charmingly restored home, circa 1682,

NOTES: Credit cards accepted: A Master Card; B Visa; C American Express; D Discover; E Diners Club; F Other; 2 Personal checks accepted; 3 Lunch available; 4 Dinner available; 5 Open all year; 6 Pets welcome; 7 Children welcome; 8 Tennis nearby; 9 Swimming nearby; 10 Golf nearby; 11 Skiing nearby; 12 May be booked through travel agent.

close to museums and major highways. Rates are $60 for shared baths and $85 for private baths.

Hosts: Irma and Richard Burwell
Rooms: 4 (2PB; 2SB) $60-85
Continental Breakfast
Credit Cards: A, B, C, D
Notes: 2, 5, 8

SEAFORD

Nanticoke House Bed and Breakfast

121 S. Conwell Street, 19973
(302) 628-1331
E-mail: bds@shore.intercom.net

Nanticoke House is a 100-year-old home located on the Nanticoke River in the central Delmarva Peninsula. It is convenient to ocean beaches, the Delaware and Chesapeake Bays, Cape May-Lewis Ferry, and the barrier islands of Assateague and Chincoteague. There are many historical points of interest, antique shops, and outlet stores. Guests enjoy the river view, flower gardens, and relaxing, congenial atmosphere. Plenty of good food, fun, and fellowship. Nonsmoking residence. Nanticoke House is a God-given home we enjoy sharing (Hebrews 13:2).

Hosts: Bob and Dianne Seiler
Rooms: 3 (1PB; 2SB) $55-65
Full Breakfast
Credit Cards: none
Notes: 2, 5, 7, 9, 10

WILMINGTON

The Boulevard B&B

1909 Baynard Boulevard, 19802
(302) 656-9700; FAX (302) 656-9701
E-mail: blvdbb@wserv.com

This beautifully restored city mansion was built in 1913. An impressive foyer and magnificent staircase lead to a landing that features a window seat and large leaded-glass windows flanked by 15-foot columns. Central AC. A full breakfast is served on the screened porch or in the formal dining room. Bedrooms are furnished with antiques and family heirlooms. Located near the business district and area attractions.

Hosts: Judy and Charles Powell
Rooms: 6 (4PB; 2SB) $70-85
Full Breakfast
Credit Cards: A, B, C
Notes: 2, 5, 7, 8, 10

NOTES: Credit cards accepted: A Master Card; B Visa; C American Express; D Discover; E Diners Club; F Other; 2 Personal checks accepted; 3 Lunch available; 4 Dinner available; 5 Open all year; 6 Pets

District of Columbia

ALSO SEE LISTINGS UNDER MARYLAND AND VIRGINIA.

Adams Inn

1744 Lanier Place NW, 20009
(202) 745-3600; (800) 578-6807;
FAX (202) 319-7958
E-mail: adamsinn@adamsinn
Web site: http://www.adamsinn.com

This turn-of-the-century town house is in the Adams-Morgan neighborhood with more than forty ethnic restaurants. It offers clean, comfortable, home-style furnishings. Adams Inn, located north of the White House and near the National Zoo, is convenient to transportation (Woodley Park Zoo Metro), convention sites, government buildings, and tourist attractions.

Hosts: Gene and Nancy Thompson
Rooms: 25 (14PB; 11SB) $45-90
Expanded Continental Breakfast
Credit Cards: A, B, C, D, E
Notes: 2, 5, 7, 12

Kalorama Guest House at Kalorama Park

1854 Mintwood Place NW, 20009
(202) 667-6369; FAX (202) 319-1262
Web site: http://www.WashingtonPost.com/yp/KGH

Enjoy Washington, DC, the right way! Try bed and breakfast in a charming Victorian

Kalorama Guest House at Kalorama Park

town house. Lodge downtown, within an easy walk of the restaurants, clubs, and nightlife of Adams Morgan and Dupont Circle. Walk to the Metro (subway). Allow us to provide you with a complimentary continental breakfast when you awake, and an evening aperitif when you return to your "home away from home." Most of the famous tourist attractions are only 10 minutes away.

Hosts: Michael, Stephen, and Jessica
Rooms: 24 + 4 suites + 1 apartment (15PB; 14SB) $55-125
Continental Breakfast
Credit Cards: A, B, C, D, E
Notes: 5, 7, 8, 12

---

welcome; 7 Children welcome; 8 Tennis nearby; 9 Swimming nearby; 10 Golf nearby; 11 Skiing nearby; 12 May be booked through travel agent.

DISTRICT OF COLUMBIA

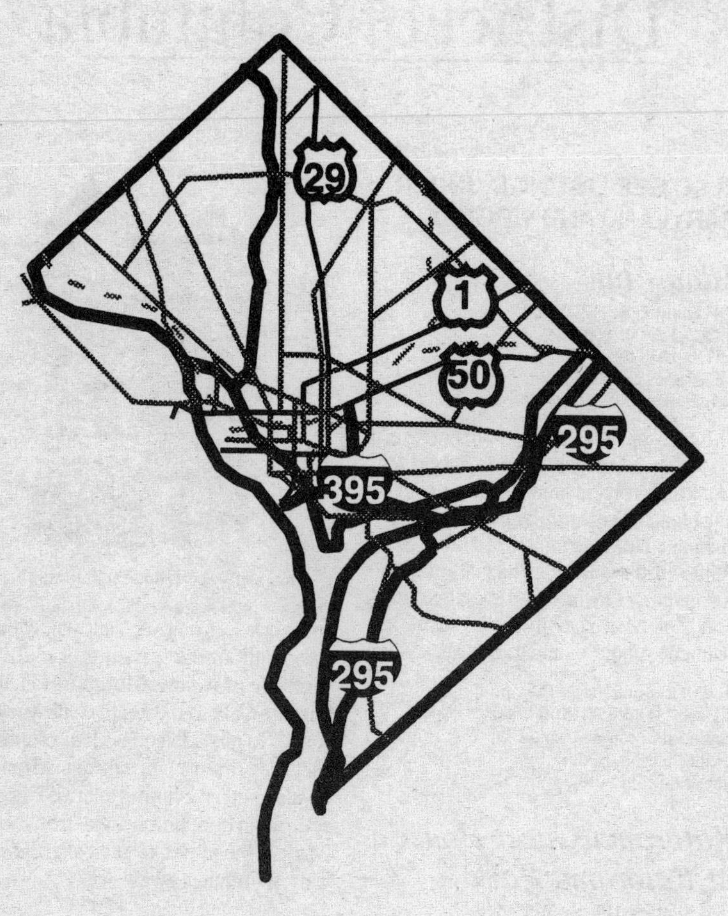

Kalorama Guest House at Woodley Park

2700 Cathedral Avenue NW, 20008
(202) 328-0860; FAX (202) 328-8730
Web site: http://www.WashingtonPost.com/yp/KGH

This charming Victorian inn offers visitors to Washington, DC, a cozy home away from home. Located on a quiet street in a lovely downtown residential neighborhood, the guest house is only a stroll from the Metro (subway), neighborhood restaurants, and various shops. The guest rooms at Kalorama are tastefully decorated in period style. You may enjoy your breakfast in a sun-filled room and relax with an aperitif at day's end. Our hospitality and personal service are nationally known. You'll find most of the popular tourist attractions in the nation's capital only ten minutes away.

Hosts: Carlotta, MaryAnn, and Angie
Rooms: 19 (12PB; 7SB) $50-105
Continental Breakfast
Credit Cards: A, B, C, D, E
Notes: 5, 12

The Swiss Inn

1204 Massachusetts Avenue NW, 20005
(202) 371-1816; (800) 955-7947;
FAX (202) 371-1138
E-mail: SwissInnDC@aol.com
Web site: http://www.theswissinn.com

The Swiss Inn is a charming turn-of-the-century Victorian town house located in Washington, DC. Amenities include bay windows, high ceilings, and fully equipped kitchenettes. The small, family-owned-and-operated inn is within walking distance of the White House, FBI, *National Geographic*, Chinatown, Convention Center, Smithsonian Museums, Ford's Theater, Women in the Arts Museum, subway, and many other attractions. We are also just 2 blocks from the main business district. Grocery stores are within walking distance, as are many noted churches, including St. Matthew's Cathedral.

Hosts: Ralph and Kelley
Rooms: 7 (PB) $59-109
Self-Prepared Breakfast
Credit Cards: A, B, C, D
Notes: 2, 5, 6, 7, 12

NOTES: Credit cards accepted: A Master Card; B Visa; C American Express; D Discover; E Diners Club; F Other; 2 Personal checks accepted; 3 Lunch available; 4 Dinner available; 5 Open all year; 6 Pets welcome; 7 Children welcome; 8 Tennis nearby; 9 Swimming nearby; 10 Golf nearby; 11 Skiing nearby; 12 May be booked through travel agent.

FLORIDA

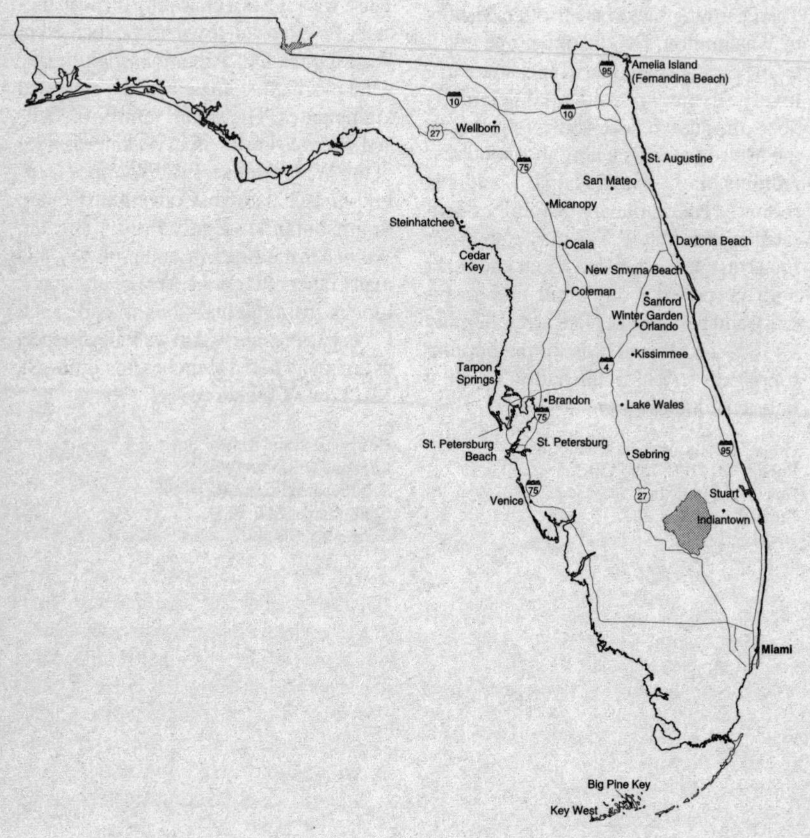

Amelia Island
(Fernandina Beach)
95
10
10
27
Wellborn
75
St. Augustine
San Mateo
Micanopy
Steinhatchee
Ocala
Daytona Beach
Cedar
Key
New Smyrna Beach
Coleman
Sanford
Winter Garden
Orlando
Kissimmee
4
Tarpon
Springs
Brandon
Lake Wales
75
St. Petersburg
Beach
St. Petersburg
Sebring
95
75
27
Stuart
Venice
Indiantown
Miami
Big Pine Key
Key West

Florida

Bailey House

AMELIA ISLAND/ FERNANDINA BEACH

Bailey House

28 S. 7th Street, **Amelia Island,** 32034
(904) 261-5390; (800) 251-5390;
FAX (904) 321-0103
E-mail: Bailey@net-magic.com
Web site: http://www.Bailey-house.com

Visit an elegant Queen Anne home furnished in Victorian decor. The beautiful home, with its magnificent stained-glass windows, turrets, and wraparound porch, was built in 1895 and is on the National Register of Historic Places. The recently renovated home offers the comforts of air-conditioning and private baths. The location in Fernandina's historic district is within walking distance of excellent restaurants, antique shopping, and many historic churches. No smoking or pets, please.

Hosts: Tom and Jenny Bishop
Rooms: 9 (PB) $95-150
Full Breakfast
Credit cards: A, B, C
Notes: 2, 5, 8, 9, 10, 12

AMELIA ISLAND

Elizabeth Pointe Lodge

98 S. Fletcher Avenue, 32034
(904) 277-4851; (800) 772-3359;
FAX (904) 277-6500
Web site: http://www.Elizabethpointelodge.com

The main house is constructed in an 1890s Nantucket shingle style with a strong maritime theme, broad porches, rockers, sunshine, and lemonade. Located prominently on the Atlantic Ocean, the lodge is only steps from often-deserted beaches. Suites are available for families. A newspaper is delivered to your room in the morning, and breakfast is served overlooking the ocean.

Hosts: David and Susan Caples
Rooms: 25 (PB) $130-225
Full Breakfast
Credit Cards: A, B, C, D
Notes: 2, 3, 5, 7, 8, 9, 10, 12

NOTES: Credit cards accepted: A Master Card; B Visa; C American Express; D Discover; E Diners Club; F Other; 2 Personal checks accepted; 3 Lunch available; 4 Dinner available; 5 Open all year; 6 Pets welcome; 7 Children welcome; 8 Tennis nearby; 9 Swimming nearby; 10 Golf nearby; 11 Skiing nearby; 12 May be booked through travel agent.

BIG PINE KEY

Deer Run

PO Box 431, 33043
(305) 872-2800; FAX (305) 872-2842
E-mail: deerrunbb@aol.com
Web site: www.latitude24.com

A Florida Cracker-style home nestled in lush native trees on the oceanfront on Big Pine Key. It is furnished with antiques, wicker, and rattan. Upstairs rooms have high ceilings, Bahama fans, and French doors. Air-conditioned. Breakfast is served on the big veranda overlooking the ocean. You can dive Looe Key, fish the flats, or charter a boat to fish the Gulf Stream. Bahia Honda State Park, only minutes away, is regarded as one of the most beautiful beaches in Florida. Large, oceanfront rooms with king beds. Full breakfast with local fruits, homemade jams and syrups, hot entrées. The house is 75 feet from the ocean, with beautiful views. Hot tub, bikes, canoe, grill. Two miles off the highway. Watch key deer on the beach! Great birding!

Hostess: Sue Abbott
Rooms: 3 (PB) $95-150
Full Breakfast
Credit Cards: none
Notes: 5

BRANDON

Behind the Fence Bed and Breakfast Inn

1400 Viola Drive, 33511
(813) 685-8201; (800) 44-TAMPA (448-2672)

Retreat into the simplicity and tranquillity of a bygone era with the conveniences of today's world. Choose your accommodations, from a cottage by our pool to a private room in our antique-filled New England saltbox house. Nearby parks and river canoeing offer lots of opportunities for family activities. Homemade Amish sweet rolls are featured, and "relaxing" is the word most guests use to refer to their stay "behind the fence." Country furniture is for sale. Tours are available upon request. AAA, three-star approved.

Hosts: Larry and Carolyn Yoss
Rooms: 5 (3PB; 2SB) $69-79
Expanded Continental Breakfast
Credit Cards: none
Notes: 2, 5, 6 (some), 7, 8, 9, 10

Island Hotel

CEDAR KEY

Island Hotel

PO Box 460; 373 2nd Street, 32625
(352) 543-5111; (800) 432-4640;
FAX (352) 543-6949
E-mail: ishotel@islandhotel-cedarkey.com
Web site: http://www.islandhotel-cedarkey.com

Built in 1859, this country inn is on the National Register of Historic Places. Constructed from seashell tabby with oak supports, with its sloping wood floors. Sit on a rocker on the long balcony, or relax in our cozy lounge bar painted with murals of Cedar Key from the 1940s. Dine in our gourmet restaurant, which serves a distinctively Cedar Key menu.

Hosts: Dawn and Tony Cousins
Rooms: 13 (11PB; 2SB) $75-110
Full Breakfast
Credit Cards: A, B, D
Notes: 4, 5, 7, 9, 12

The Son's Shady Brook Bed and Breakfast

COLEMAN

The Son's Shady Brook Bed and Breakfast

PO Box 551, 33521
(352) PIT-STOP (748-7867)

Here is a refreshing change for all who seek solitude and tranquillity in a therapeutic, scenic setting. Escape the humdrum of everyday life. Exclude the ordinary and enjoy the beautiful wooded area with a rapidly flowing creek. Atmosphere conducive to reading, writing, table games, or just relaxing. Comfortable beds, delicious breakfasts, many interesting amenities. Central Florida attractions about 50 miles away. Brochures, gift certificates.

Hostess: Jean Lake Martin
Rooms: 4 (PB) $50-60
Full Breakfast
Credit Cards: A
Notes: 2, 5, 8, 9, 10, 12

DAYTONA BEACH

Live Oak Inn and Restaurant

444-448 S. Beach Street, 32114
(904) 252-4667; (800) 881-4667;
FAX (904) 239-0068

Live Oak Inn is the oldest house and stands where Mathias Day founded Daytona. Two carefully restored homes—both listed in the National Register of Historic Places (circa 1871 and 1881)—are rated among Florida's top ten historic inns and are the cornerstone of the Daytona historic district.

Hosts: Jessie and Del Glock
Rooms: 14 (PB) $80-200
Continental Breakfast
Credit Cards: A, B
Notes: 2, 3, 4, 5, 8, 9, 10, 12

INDIANTOWN

Seminole Country Inn

15885 SW Warfield Boulevard; PO Box 1818, 34956
(561) 597-3777; FAX (561) 597-2883

Built in 1926, our inn has the grandeur of an age gone by and southern hospitality that immediately puts you at ease. Cozy wood-burning fireplaces, beautiful hardwood floors, native gardens, intimate rooms with antiques and mosquito netting for added romance. Access to ecological activities that include hiking, bicycling, horseback riding, and watchable wildlife tours on our two large working cattle ranches, a short drive away. Get to know the real Florida at our gracious southern inn complete with every modern convenience. Located exactly halfway between West Palm Beach and Lake Okeechobee, we are a world away. Corporate meeting and retreat facilities available. Pool, gardens, and gym. Children welcome.

Hostess: Jonnie Williams
Rooms: 22 (PB) $65-95
Expanded Continental Breakfast
Credit Cards: A, B, C, D
Notes: 3, 4, 5, 7, 8, 9, 10, 12

KEY WEST

Center Court Historic Inn and Cottages

916 Center Street, 33040
(305) 296-9292; (800) 797-8787;
FAX (305) 294-4104
E-mail: kwinn@conch.net
Web site: http://www.centercourtkw.com

Center Court Historic Inn and Cottages offers affordable, elegant, Historic Preservation Award-winning accommodations nestled in quiet, tropical gardens just one-half block off Duval! We have sixteen rooms and cottages with queen and king beds, TVs, phones, air-conditioning, fans, private baths, and hair dryers. Enjoy breakfast each morning overlooking the heated pool, Jacuzzi, exercise pavilion, and fishpond with its waterfall. Be pampered in our secret paradise! Center Court Historic Inn and Cottages is three-diamond AAA-rated.

Hostess: Naomi Van Steelandt
Rooms: 16 (PB) $88-208
Expanded Continental Breakfast
Credit Cards: A, B, C, D
Notes: 2, 5, 6, 7, 8, 9, 10

Garden House

329 Elizabeth Street, 33040
(305) 296-5368; (800) 695-6453;
FAX (305) 292-1160

Quaint ten-room B&B in old town Key West. Extended continental breakfast and wine hour included. Situated by a small tropical pool fed by a waterfall. Enjoy the peacefulness of the unique guest house out back or swing in a hammock.

Host: John Montagen
Rooms: 10 (8PB; 2SB) $62-125 (seasonal)
Extended Continental Breakfast
Credit Cards: all major

Walden Guest House

717 Caroline Street (office: 223 Elizabeth Street), 33040
(305) 296-7161

The home is in the historic seaport district in Old Towne, downtown Key West. We are totally accessible to all Old Towne attractions, lower Duval Street, Sloppy Joe's Bar, restaurants, museums, boating, beaches, fishing, and night life. Let us be your vacation hosts for a getaway.

Host: Richard Jabour
Rooms: 6 (2PB; 4SB) $54-105
No Breakfast
Credit Cards: A, B, D
Notes: 5, 7, 8, 9, 10, 12

Whispers Bed and Breakfast

409 William Street, 33040
(305) 294-5969; (800) 856-7444;
FAX (305) 294-3899
E-mail: whispersbb@aol.com
Web site: http://www.whispersbb.com

Whispers sits in the heart of Olde Town Key West, within view of the Gulf Harbor

NOTES: Credit cards accepted: A Master Card; B Visa; C American Express; D Discover; E Diners Club; F Other; 2 Personal checks accepted; 3 Lunch available; 4 Dinner available; 5 Open all year; 6 Pets

Whispers Bed and Breakfast

and surrounded by a 30-block historic district of distinctive 19th-century homes. Ceiling fans whirl above rooms filled with antique furnishings. Guests enjoy the cool porches and lush garden. Take advantage of our complimentary membership in a local resort with private beach, pool, and health spa. Enjoy our tropical fish, birds, and gourmet breakfast creations. Come to paradise. Come home to Whispers.

Host: John Marburg
Rooms: 7 (PB) $80-175
Full Gourmet Breakfast
Credit Cards: A, B, C, D
Notes: 2, 5, 8, 9, 10, 12

LAKE WALES

Chalet Suzanne Country Inn/Restaurant

3800 Chalet Suzanne Drive, 33853
(941) 676-6011; (800) 433-6011;
FAX (941) 676-1814
E-mail: info@chaletsuzanne.com
Web site: http://www.chaletsuzanne.com

Listed on the National Register, Chalet Suzanne Country Inn/Restaurant has been family-owned and -operated since 1931 on 100 acres in a fairy tale setting. The thirty guest rooms have all the amenities. Our five-star restaurant serves breakfast, lunch, and dinner. We have gift shops, a ceramic studio, a swimming pool, a soup cannery, and a lighted airstrip. We are proud to say our soups accompanied Jim Irwin to the moon on Apollo 15. Inquire about our summer package.

Hosts: Vita and Carl Hinshaw
Rooms: 30 (PB) $159-219
Full Breakfast
Credit Cards: A, B, C, D, E, F
Notes: 2, 3, 4, 5, 7, 8, 9, 10, 12

MIAMI

Miami River Inn

118 SW South River Drive, 33130
(305) 325-0045; (800) HOTEL 89;
FAX (305) 325-9227
E-mail: miami100@ix.netcom.com
Web site: Travelbase or Expedia

Built between 1906 and 1910, the inn boasts four wooden cottages surrounding a pool and Jacuzzi in a lush tropical garden. The inn's forty rooms are individually decorated with antique furnishings, featuring cable television, touchtone phones, central air/heat, and private bathrooms. A quick walk to downtown offers shopping, dining, museums, and galleries. Office services are available free to business travelers. Beaches, airport, and Port of Miami are within a 15-minute drive.

Hosts: Jane Caporelli, Sallye Jude, and Raymond Hawkins
Rooms: 40 (39PB; 1SB) $59-125
Continental Breakfast
Credit Cards: A, B, C, D, E
Notes: 2, 5, 6, 7, 8, 9, 10, 12

Herlong Mansion

MICANOPY

Herlong Mansion

PO Box 667, 32667
(352) 466-3322 (voice and FAX); (800) HERLONG
Web site: http://www.afn.org/~herlong

"Easily Florida's most elegant bed and breakfast"—*Florida Trend*, November 1989. Located in historic Micanopy, 12 miles south of Gainesville, Herlong Mansion is a three-story, brick, Greek Revival historic house with four suites, six rooms, and two cottages.

Host: H.C. (Sonny) Howard, Jr.
Rooms: 12 (PB) $55-175
Full Breakfast
Credit Cards: A, B
Notes: 2, 4 (by reservation), 5, 7, 12

Shady Oak Bed and Breakfast

203 Cholokka Boulevard; PO Box 327, 32667
(352) 466-3476
E-mail: shadyoak@mindspring.com
Web site: http://www.shadyoak.com

The Shady Oak stands majestically in the center of historic downtown Micanopy. A marvelous canopy of live oaks, quiet streets, and many antique shops offers visitors a memorable connection to Florida's past. This three-story, 19th-century-style mansion features eight lovely, spacious rooms; private baths; porches; Jacuzzi; Florida room; and widow's walk. Several churches within walking distance. Local activities include antiquing, bicycling, canoeing, bird-watching, stained-glass workshops, and much more. "Playfully elegant accommodations, where stained glass, antiques, and innkeeping go together as kindly as warm hugs with old friends."

Host: Frank James
Rooms: 8 (PB) $75-150
Full Breakfast
Credit Cards: A, B, D
Notes: 2, 4, 5, 7

NEW SMYRNA BEACH

Indian River Inn and Conference Center

1210 S. Riverside Drive, 32168
(904) 428-2491; (800) 541-4529;
FAX (904) 426-2532
E-mail: indianriverinn@ucnsb.net
Web site: http://www.volusia.com/indianriverinn

Built in 1916, this inn is the oldest extant hotel in Volusia County. It has been lovingly restored and remodeled to meet all current standards of security, comfort, and convenience without sacrificing its charm and character. A gracious atmosphere of warmth and friendliness, unsurpassed in today's often frantic lifestyle, can be found here. We are located on the Atlantic Intracoastal Waterway, minutes from I–95 and I–4 between Daytona Beach and the

Kennedy Space Center. Church groups and buses welcomed.

Hosts: Ed and Donna Ruby
Rooms: 27 + 15 suites (PB) $50-115
Continental Breakfast
Credit Cards: A, B, D
Notes: 2, 3 and 4 (available Thanksgiving-Easter), 5, 7, 8, 9 (on premises), 10, 12

Night Swan Intracoastal

512 S. Riverside Drive, 32168-7345
(904) 423-4940; (800) 465-4261;
FAX (904) 427-2814
E-mail: NightSwanB@aol.com
Web site: http://www.NightSwan.com

Watch the pelicans, dolphins, sailboats, and yachts along the Intracoastal Waterway from our beautiful front room, wraparound porch, 140-foot dock—or your room. Our spacious, three-story home has kept its character and charm of 1906 in the historic district, with its central fireplace and its intricate natural wood in every room. We are located between Daytona Beach and Kennedy Space Center on the Indian River, just 2 miles from the beach. Some rooms have whirlpool tubs. Midweek special rates. AAA-approved.

Hosts: Martha and Chuck Nighswonger
Rooms: 15 (PB) $80-150
Full Breakfast
Credit Cards: A, B, C, D
Notes: 2, 5, 7, 8, 9, 10, 12

OCALA

Seven Sisters Inn

820 SE Fort King Street, 34471
(352) 867-1170; (800) 250-3496;
FAX (352) 867-5266
E-mail: sisterinn@aol.com

Chosen "Inn of the Month" by *Country Inns Bed and Breakfast Magazine,*

Seven Sisters Inn

Seven Sisters Inn is located in the heart of Ocala's historic district. Built in 1888, this Queen Anne–style Victorian house has been lovingly restored to its original stately elegance, with beautiful period furnishings. Each guest room has a private bath; carefully chosen, elegant decor; sitting room; fireplace; and much more. The owners, both airline pilots, have traveled all over the world, collecting superb recipes—no wonder their gourmet dishes are received with such enthusiasm! Triple-Crown ABBA-, AAA three-diamond-, and three-star Mobil-rated.

Hosts: Bonnie Morehardt and Ken Oden
Rooms: 8 (PB) $105-165
Full Breakfast
Credit Cards: A, B, C, D, E
Notes: 2, 4, 5, 7 (over 12), 8, 9, 10, 12

ORLANDO

Meadow Marsh B&B

940 Tildenville School Road, **Winter Garden,** 34787
(407) 656-2064; (888) 656-2064
Web site: http://www.bbonline.com

Peace and tranquillity surround you as God's beauty unfolds in 12 acres of ol'

Florida. Giant oaks, stately palms, and abundant wildlife make your stay at Meadow Marsh one for relaxing and renewing your spirit. The spacious lawn invites a romantic picnic or hand-in-hand walk through the meadow to the adjacent rails-to-trails path. Old-fashioned swings, croquet, and badminton add to the feeling of yesteryear. You'll enjoy the 1877 Victorian farmhouse where cozy fireplaces, hardwood floors, and lace curtains add to the warmth and beauty of this country estate. Suites offer two-person whirlpools, while the smaller bedrooms have antique tubs. Pamper yourselves for a moment in an atmosphere of a sweeter time that existed not so very long ago.

Hosts: Cavelle and John Pawlack
Rooms: 2 + 2 suites + 1 cottage (PB) $95-199
Full Three-Course Breakfast
Credit Cards: A, B, D
Notes: 3, 5, 8, 10, 12

PerriHouse Bed and Breakfast Inn

10417 Centurion Court, 32836
(407) 876-4830; (800) 780-4830;
FAX (407) 876-0241
E-mail: birds@perrihouse.com
Web site: http://www.perrihouse.com

PerriHouse is a quiet, country estate inn secluded on 3 acres of land adjacent to the popular Walt Disney World Resort. Surrounded by trees, grassy fields, and orange groves, the PerriHouse estate is a natural bird sanctuary; bird feeders and baths make viewing birds in their natural activities a delight. Five minutes to Disney Village, Pleasure Island, and EPCOT Center. Upscale continental breakfast, pool, hot tub. Eight guest "nests" with private baths, entrances. Four birdhouse cottages are planned, featuring king-size canopy beds and whirlpool tubs for two. Three-, five-, and seven-day vacation packages will be offered.

Hosts: Nick and Angi Perretti
Rooms: 8 (PB) $89-119
Continental Breakfast
Credit Cards: A, B, C, D, E
Notes: 2 (2 weeks ahead), 5, 7, 8, 9, 10, 12

The Unicorn Inn English Bed and Breakfast

The Unicorn Inn English Bed and Breakfast

8 S. Orlando Avenue, **Kissimmee,** 34741-5674
(407) 846-1200; (800) 865-7212;
FAX (407) 846-1773
E-mail: unicorn@gate.net
Web site: http://touristguide.com/b&b/florida/unicorn

The Unicorn—the only bed and breakfast in Kissimmee—is located in historic downtown off the Broadway. A safe, peaceful, relaxing district 300 yards from Lake Tohopekalegia (fishing boats and other boats can be rented), the Unicorn is situated close to golf courses, horseback riding, and other attractions like Disney World, Sea World, and Wet and Wild (a 15-minute drive). Orlando airport is only a 25-minute drive away. Amtrak and Greyhound stations are nearby. Guest rooms have TVs and air-conditioning. Kitchen facilities provide complimentary tea and coffee. Restored to its full grandeur, the inn has antique pottery, prints, and furniture. Many churches nearby. The inn is British-owned and run by Fran and Don Williamson of Yorkshire. Our only rule is: "Make Yourself at Home." Airport pickups available. The inn is AAA three-diamond-rated; Mobil two-star-rated. A member of the Inn Route of Florida.

Hosts: Don and Fran Williamson
Rooms: 8 (including a 2-room suite) (PB) $85-95
Full Five-Course Breakfast
Credit Cards: A, B
Notes: 2, 5, 7, 8, 9, 10, 12

ST. AUGUSTINE

Casa de la Paz Bayfront Inn

22 Avenida Menendez, 32084
(904) 829-2915; (800) 929-2915;
FAX (904) 824-6269
E-mail: delapaz@aug.com
Web site: http://www.casadelapaz.com

Upon arrival at Casa de la Paz, guests are immediately aware that this is a special place. A historic Mediterranean-style home, the inn was built as a private residence in 1915, during St. Augustine's opulent Flagler era. Only steps away from the spectacular Castillo de San Marcos, Bridge of Lions, and other famous sites of the nation's oldest city, through expansive windows, one enjoys breathtaking views of the scenic Matanzas Bayfront. The comfort of the home's interior is enhanced by antique furnishings, heart-of-pine floors, and richly upholstered sofas, arm chairs, and rockers. Lush plants, including the inn's namesake Peace Lily, thrive here.

Hosts: Bob and Donna Marriott
Rooms: 6 (PB) $89-189
Full Breakfast
Credit Cards: A, B, D

Castle Garden Bed and Breakfast

15 Shenandoah Street, 32084
(904) 829-3839; FAX (904) 829-9049
E-mail: castleg@aug.com

Stay at a castle and be treated like royalty! Relax and enjoy the peace, quiet, and "royal treatment" at our newly restored, 100-year-old castle of the Moorish Revival design. The only sounds you'll hear are the occasional roar of a cannon shot from the old fort 200 yards to the south, or the creak of solid wood floors. Awaken to the aroma of freshly baked goodies as we prepare a full, mouth-watering, country breakfast just like "Mom used to make." The unusual coquina stone exterior remains virtually untouched. The interior of the former Castle Warden Carriage House boasts three beautiful bridal rooms complete with soothing in-room Jacuzzis and sunken bedrooms! Amenities: complimentary wine, chocolates, bikes, and private parking. Packages and gift baskets are available. We believe every guest is a gift from God.

Hosts: Kimmy VanKooten Kloeckner and Bruce Kloeckner
Rooms: 7 (PB) $75-150
Full Breakfast
Credit Cards: A, B, C, D
Notes: 2, 5, 7, 8, 10, 12

The Cedar House Inn

79 Cedar Street, 32084
(904) 829-0079; (800) 233-2746;
FAX (904) 825-0916
E-mail: russ@aug.com
Web site: http://www.CedarHouseInn.com

Capture romantic moments at our 1893 Victorian home in the heart of the ancient city. Escape into your antique-filled bedroom with private whirlpool bath or clawfoot tub; enjoy the comfortable parlor with its fireplace, player piano, and antique Victrola; or sit on the shady veranda. Elegant full breakfast, evening snack, parking on premises, Jacuzzi spa, and bicycles. Walk to historical sites or bicycle to the beach. AAA-approved, three-diamond rated. Smoke-free home.

Hosts: Russ and Nina Thomas
Rooms: 5 + 1 suite (PB) $69-155
Full Breakfast
Credit Cards: A, B, C, D
Notes: 2, 3 (picnic), 4, 5, 7 (over 10), 8, 9, 10, 12

The Kenwood Inn

The Kenwood Inn

38 Marine Street, 32084
(904) 824-2116; FAX (904) 824-1689
Web site: http://www.oldcity.com/kenwood

Since 1886, the Kenwood Inn has been "a classic old Florida inn." After you experience the charm and romance of our nation's oldest city, continue your stroll through the past at the inn. Located in a quiet section of the historic waterfront district in walking distance of all attractions, the inn offers a pool, walled-in courtyard, and continental buffet breakfast featuring homemade breads, cakes, and muffins.

Hosts: Mark and Kerrianne Constant
Rooms: 14 (PB) $85-175
Continental Breakfast
Credit Cards: A, B, D
Notes: 2, 5, 7 (over 8), 8, 9, 10, 12

The Old Powder House

38 Cordova Street, 32084
(904) 824-4149; (800) 447-4149;
FAX (904) 825-0143
E-mail: ahowes@aug.com
Web site: http://www.oldcity.com/powderhouse

Escape to a romantic getaway in this charming, turn-of-the-century Victorian inn. Lace curtains and hardwood floors adorn antique-filled rooms. Towering pecan and oak trees shade verandas with rockers, from where you can watch the passing horse-drawn buggies. Or you may relax by the fountain in our courtyard. Amenities include a full gourmet breakfast, hors d'oeuvres, Jacuzzi, cable TV, parking on site, bicycles, special packages and weddings, and owner hospitality.

Hosts: Al and Eunice Howes
Rooms: 6 + 2 suites (PB) $79-165
Full Gourmet Breakfast
Credit Cards: A, B, D
Notes: 2, 5, 7, 8, 9, 10, 12

St. Francis Inn

279 St. George Street, 32084
(904) 824-6068; (800) 824-6062;
FAX (904) 810-5525
E-mail: innceasd@aug.com
Web site: http://www.stfrancisinn.com

Built in 1791, the St. Francis Inn is a beautiful Spanish Colonial building. The courtyard garden provides a peaceful setting for traditional hospitality. Our accommodations range from double rooms and suites to a five-room cottage—all with private bath, cable television, and central air/heat; many have fireplaces. The inn is centrally located in the historic district within easy walking distance of restaurants, shops, and sites.

Host: Joe Finnegan
Rooms: 14 (PB) $69-179
Full Breakfast
Credit Cards: A, B, C, D
Notes: 2, 5, 7 (limited), 8, 9 (onsite), 10, 12

The Westcott House Bed and Breakfast

146 Avenida Menendez, 32084
(904) 824-4301 (voice and FAX);
(800) 513-9814
E-mail: westcotth@aol.com
Web site: http://www.westcotthouse.com

Built in the late 1890s, this example of fine vernacular architecture tempts you to share in a fragment of St. Augustine's long history. This elegant bed and breakfast inn overlooks the Matanzas Bay and allows guests to step back to the turn of the century and enjoy a romantic setting. We are located in the historic district—perfect for leisurely strolling to historical sights, intriguing restaurants, and quaint shops. The exquisitely furnished rooms all offer king- or queen-size beds, private baths, telephones, television, and air-conditioning. We strive to make your stay in historic St. Augustine memorable.

Hosts: Janet and Tom Murray
Rooms: 9 (PB) $95-175
Continental Breakfast
Credit Cards: A, B, C, D

ST. PETE BEACH

Island's End Resort

1 Pass-A-Grille Way, 33706
(813) 360-5023; FAX (813) 367-7890

The compelling appeal of all that paradise can offer abounds at Island's End. Deep blue sky, turquoise waters, exotic sunrises and sunsets—all work in concert to entertain you. Island's End features six well-appointed guest homes (all with fully equipped kitchens), including a fantastic three-bedroom house with a private pool. Small private beach only a half block from our beautiful 5-mile beach.

Hosts: Jane and Millard Gamble
Rooms: 6 (PB) $68-175
Continental (Tuesday, Thursday, Saturday)
Credit Cards: A, B
Notes: 2, 5, 7, 8, 9, 10

ST. PETERSBURG

Mansion House B&B

105 Fifth Avenue NE, 33701
(813) 821-9391 (voice and FAX); (800) 274-7520
E-mail: mansion1@ix.netcom.com
Web site: http://www.mansionbandb.com

Mansion House, built in 1904 and beautifully restored, has five rooms with private baths in the main house. A sixth room, the Carriage House, has a cathedral ceiling, four-poster bed, phone, and TV. Common areas include a library/TV room with VCR, sun porch, living room, and patio. Guests have access to kitchen and 24-hour snacks. Antiques from around the world are dispersed throughout the house. Convenient to cultural and sports attractions, water, restaurants, and shopping. Private boat cruises are available on the bay or

welcome; 7 Children welcome; 8 Tennis nearby; 9 Swimming nearby; 10 Golf nearby; 11 Skiing nearby; 12 May be booked through travel agent.

gulf, with your host as captain. Portuguese spoken. ABBA 1998 Excellence Award, three crowns. AAA, three diamonds. Superior Small Lodging, St. Petersburg/ Clearwater Visitors and Convention Bureau. InnPoints travel incentives are awarded to guests. Mansion House offers travel agent commissions and online reservations through ASTRA Net, B&B Direct Worldcom/Places to Stay, and our Web site. Swimming pool, garden. King/ queen beds. Meeting/conference room. Weddings performed onsite. Boat cruises, receptions for up to 100 persons.

Hosts: Robert and Rose Marie Ray
Rooms: 11 (PB) $95-165
Full Breakfast
Credit Cards: A, B, C
Notes: 2, 5, 7, 8, 9, 10, 12

SAN MATEO

Ferncourt Bed and Breakfast

150 Central Avenue; PO Box 758, 32187
(904) 329-9755

This 1889 "painted lady" has been lovingly restored by your hosts. They delight in sharing this bit of Florida history with you. A full complimentary breakfast is served in the dining room each morning. Dee loves to cook, and the eggs provided by her own hens are always on the menu in some form. Located just a short drive from St. Augustine, Ferncourt offers a peaceful place to relax after a day of sightseeing and shopping.

Ferncourt Bed and Breakfast

Hosts: Jack and Dee Morgan
Rooms: 6 (5PB; 1SB) $55-85
Full Breakfast
Credit Cards: A, B, C, D
Notes: 2, 5, 10, 12

SANFORD

The Higgins House Victorian Bed and Breakfast

420 Oak Avenue, 32771
(407) 324-9238; (800) 584-0014;
FAX (407) 324-5060
E-mail: reservations@higginshouse.com
Web site: http://www.higginshouse.com

Enjoy the romance of a bygone era at this 104-year-old Queen Anne Victorian bed and breakfast. Three guest rooms and a cottage all have private baths. Enjoy the Victorian gardens and hot tub. The Higgins House Bed and Breakfast is located in historic Sanford near beautiful Lake Monroe and the St. Johns River. Antique shops are nearby.

Hosts: Walter and Roberta Padgett
Rooms: 3 + cottage (PB) $95-125
Continental Plus Breakfast
Credit Cards: A, B, C, D
Notes: 2, 5, 8, 10, 12

NOTES: Credit cards accepted: A Master Card; B Visa; C American Express; D Discover; E Diners Club; F Other; 2 Personal checks accepted; 3 Lunch available; 4 Dinner available; 5 Open all year; 6 Pets

STEINHATCHEE

Steinhatchee Landing Resort

PO Box 789, 32359
(352) 498-3513; (800) 584-1709;
FAX (352) 498-2346
E-mail: sli@4ez.com
Web site: http://www.SteinhatcheeLanding.com

Nestled on the banks of the Steinhatchee River, Steinhatchee Landing Resort offers all the advantages of modern resort-style living combined with untouched natural surroundings. Our guests stay in one of twenty fully furnished Victorian cottages, complete with modern kitchens, televisions, and VCRs. They can partake in any of a great variety of activities, such as swimming, tennis, fishing, canoeing, horseback riding, and bird-watching, just to name a few.

Host: Dean Fowler
Rooms: 20 (PB) $120-125
Credit Cards: A, B, D
Notes: 2, 3 (Sunday only), 4 (Thursday-Saturday), 5, 6, 7, 8, 9, 10 (45 minutes), 12

STUART

The Homeplace Bed and Breakfast

501 Akron Avenue, 34994
(561) 220-9148; (800) 251-5473;
FAX (561) 221-3265
E-mail: suzanne@homeplacebb.com
Web site: http://www.homeplacebb.com

The Homeplace, Stuart's premier bed and breakfast inn, was built in 1913 and lovingly restored in 1989. The inn is best

The Homeplace Bed and Breakfast

known for its romantic ambience, quality, and unequaled graciousness. The four guest rooms are air-conditioned and appointed comfortably with antiques. The "wickered" sunporch and century-old parlor create a Victorian setting in which to recall pleasurable reminiscences. The lush patio garden, swimming pool, and heated spa beckon you. Stroll or bike to the town's newly restored historic area for shopping and fine dining. The Homeplace Bed and Breakfast is located on 2½ acres bordering Frazier Creek.

Hosts: Suzanne and Michael Pescitelli
Rooms: 4 + garden suite (PB) $85-160
Full Breakfast
Credit Cards: A, B
Notes: 2, 5, 8, 9 (on site), 10, 12

TARPON SPRINGS

East Lake Bed and Breakfast

421 Old East Lake Road, 34689
(727) 937-5487
E-mail: LittleFlower@prodigy.com

East Lake Bed and Breakfast is a private home on 2½ acres, situated on a quiet road along Lake Tarpon, close to the Gulf of Mexico. The hosts are retired businesspeople who enjoy new friends and are well informed about the area. The room and adjoining bath are at the front of the house, away from the family quarters. The room has central air-conditioning, color television, and telephone. Breakfast includes fresh fruit, juice, entrée, and homemade breads and jams. Located close to many Florida attractions.

Hosts: Dick and Marie Fiorito
Rooms: 1 (PB) $35 single, $40 double
Full Home-Cooked Breakfast
Credit Cards: none
Notes: 2, 5, 8, 9, 10

VENICE

The Banyan House Bed and Breakfast

519 S. Harbor Drive, 34285
(941) 484-1385; FAX (941) 484-8032
Web site: http://www.banyan.qpg.com

Experience the Old World charm of one of Venice's historic Mediterranean homes, circa 1926, on the Gulf Coast. Relax in the peaceful atmosphere of our lovely courtyard dominated by a huge banyan tree. This provides an unusual setting for the garden patio, pool, and Jacuzzi. The Banyan House is central to shopping, beaches, restaurants, and golf. Complimentary bikes. No smoking. Minimum two-night stay on weekends.

Hosts: Chuck and Susan McCormick
Rooms: 9 (PB) $69-119
Credit Cards: A, B
Notes: 2, 5, 7 (over 12), 8, 9, 10

WELLBORN

1909 McLeran House Bed and Breakfast

12408 County Road 137, 32094
(904) 963-4603

A beautifully restored two-story Victorian home on 5 landscaped acres features a lovely garden area with gazebo, garden swing, deck area, goldfish pond, and an abundance of trees and shrubs. Guests enjoy a large, comfortable room with mini-refrigerator and cable TV. The private bath downstairs features a claw-foot tub with shower. Enjoy the many antiques throughout the house, relax in the garden, stroll the grounds, or visit the "collectibles" shop in the old barn. Additional charge for extra people. Many local attractions are nearby, including the Stephen Foster Folk Culture Center.

Hosts: Robert and Mary Ryals
Rooms: 2 (PB) $70-80
Full Breakfast
Credit Cards: none
Notes: 2, 5, 9, 10

Georgia

1906 Pathway Inn

AMERICUS

1906 Pathway Inn

501 S. Lee Street, 31709
(912) 928-2078; (800) 889-1466
E-mail: pathway@sowega.net
Web site: http://www.bestinns.net/usa/ga/pathway.html

Parlors, porches, whirlpools, down comforters, fireplaces, friends, muffins, and more await you at a 1906 English Colonial Revival-style inn with stained glass and extensive woodwork. Situated between Plains (home of President Carter) and Civil War Andersonville/National POW Museum. Habitat for Humanity headquarters, Providence Canyon. Candlelit English breakfast. On Sunday, attend church and hear President Carter teach Sunday school. Afternoon refreshments. We're here to spoil you! Three-star inn.

Hosts: David and Sheila Judah
Rooms: 5 (PB) $77-107
Full Breakfast
Credit Cards: A, B, C, D
Notes: 2, 5, 6, 7, 8, 10, 12

ATLANTA

Beverly Hills Inn

65 Sheridan Drive, 30305
(404) 233-8520; (800) 331-8520;
FAX (404) 233-8659
E-mail: info@beverlyhillsinn.com
Web site: http://www.beverlyhillsinn.com

This is a charming, European-style hotel with eighteen suites uniquely decorated with period furnishings. We offer fresh flowers, a continental breakfast, and the little things that count to a traveler. Within walking distance of first-class dining, shopping, and entertainment. The inn features hardwood floors, balconies, kitchens, loveseats, and private baths. Library, FAX, data port phones available. Breakfast served in the garden room.

Host: Mit Amin
Rooms: 18 (PB) $90-160
Continental Breakfast
Credit Cards: A, B, C, D, E
Notes: 2, 5, 6, 7, 12

---

welcome; 7 Children welcome; 8 Tennis nearby; 9 Swimming nearby; 10 Golf nearby; 11 Skiing nearby; 12 May be booked through travel agent.

GEORGIA

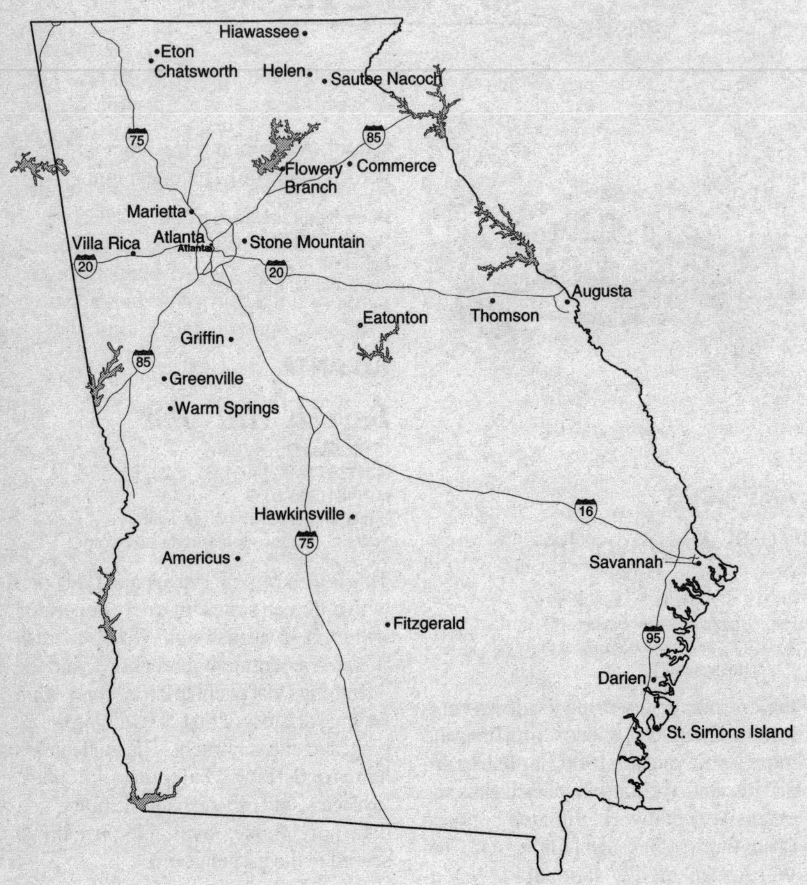

Hiawassee
Eton
Chatsworth
Helen
Sautee Nacoch
75
85
Flowery Branch
Commerce
Marietta
Villa Rica
Atlanta
Atlanta
Stone Mountain
20
20
Augusta
Eatonton
Thomson
Griffin
85
Greenville
Warm Springs
16
Hawkinsville
75
Americus
Savannah
Fitzgerald
95
Darien
St. Simons Island

Shellmont Bed and Breakfast Lodge

Shellmont Bed and Breakfast Lodge

821 Piedmont Avenue NE, 30308
(404) 872-9290; FAX (404) 872-5379

The Shellmont Bed and Breakfast Lodge is an impeccably restored 1891 National Register mansion located in midtown Atlanta's theater, restaurant, and cultural district. It is a virtual treasure chest of stained, leaded, and beveled glass; intricately carved woodwork; and hand-painted stenciling. Guest accommodations are furnished with antiques, Oriental rugs, and period wall treatments. Shellmont's wicker-laden verandas overlook beautifully manicured lawns and gardens—including a lovely Victorian fishpond. When you are visiting Atlanta, we believe you will find your experience at Shellmont to be unforgettable.

Hosts: Ed and Debbie McCord
Rooms: 5 (PB) $120-160
Full Breakfast
Credit Cards: A, B, C, D, E
Notes: 2, 5, 7 (limited), 8, 10, 12

The Woodruff Bed and Breakfast Inn

223 Ponce de Leon Avenue, 30308
(404) 875-9449; (800) 473-9449;
FAX (404) 870-0042
E-mail: rsvp@mindspring.com

Prepare yourself for southern charm, hospitality, and a full southern breakfast. The Woodruff Bed and Breakfast Inn is conveniently located in midtown Atlanta. It is a 1906 Victorian home built by a prominent Atlanta family, fully restored by the current owners. Each room has been meticulously decorated with antiques. The inn has a very colorful past, which lends to the charm and history of the building and city. Close to everything. Ya'll come!

Hosts: Douglas and Joan Jones
Rooms: 14 (10PB; 4SB) $89-149
Full Breakfast
Credit Cards: A, B, C, D
Notes: 2, 5, 7, 9, 12

AUGUSTA

Perrin Guest House Inn

208 LaFayette Drive, 30909
(706) 731-0920; (800) 668-8930;
FAX (706) 731-9009
E-mail: perrinplace@mindspring.com

The Perrin Place is an old cotton plantation home established in 1863. The plantation has long since become the Augusta National Golf Course, home of the Masters. The 3-acre homeplace remains a little spot of magnolia heaven surrounded by shopping, golfing, and fine dining. Our guest house has beautifully redecorated bedrooms that feature fireplaces, Jacuzzis, antiques, and comforters. Enjoy the privacy of your own fireplace in spacious accommodations, or share the pleasure of a front porch rocker, the comfort of a cozy parlor, or the cool of a scuppernong arbor with other guests. Weddings, receptions, and other social functions become treasured events when held at the Perrin. Available by reservation only.

Hosts: Ed and Audrey Peel
Rooms: 10 (PB), $75-125
Continental Breakfast
Credit Cards: A, B, C
Notes: 2, 5, 7, 8, 10, 12

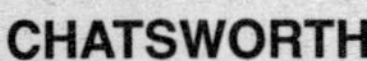

CHATSWORTH

Hearthstone Hall: A Bed and Breakfast

2755 Highway 282, 30705-6834
(706) 695-6515 (voice and FAX)
E-mail: hrsthall@ocsonline.com

Welcome to Hearthstone Hall, an authentic mountain log house. Nestled in the North Georgia mountains near Ellijay. Distinctive guest rooms with country antiques, spacious sitting areas, and private baths. Mornings bring a full, savory mountain breakfast and evenings an after-dinner refreshment or dessert. (Special diets are accommodated, with advance notice.) Enjoy the quiet and tranquillity of an unspoiled, natural mountain setting—yet, only minutes away from the many attractions the area has to offer. Call for a brochure.

Hosts: Ilia and Mack Cartwright
Rooms: 3 (PB) $75-85
Full Breakfast
Credit Cards: A, B
Notes: 2, 5, 9, 10, 11 (water), 12

The Pittman House Bed and Breakfast

COMMERCE

The Pittman House Bed and Breakfast

81 Homer Road, 30529
(706) 335-3823

The Pittman House Bed and Breakfast is located in the beautiful, rolling hill country of northeastern Georgia in the bustling town of historic Commerce. We invite you to come rock with us on the wraparound porch of our restored 1890s four-square Colonial house, which is furnished throughout with antiques that take you back to a quieter time and enhance the hominess of The Pittman House. Conveniently located within minutes of the University of Georgia, boating, historic Hurricane Shoals, shopping, vineyards, restaurants, and more. Only an hour from Atlanta. Three-diamond AAA rating. A 72-hour cancellation notice is required.

Hosts: Tom and Dot Tomberlin
Rooms: 4 (2PB; 2SB) $55-75
Full Breakfast
Credit Cards: A, B
Notes: 2, 5, 7, 8, 9, 10, 11, 12

NOTES: Credit cards accepted: A Master Card; B Visa; C American Express; D Discover; E Diners Club; F Other; 2 Personal checks accepted; 3 Lunch available; 4 Dinner available; 5 Open all year; 6 Pets

DARIEN

Open Gates

Vernon Square, National Historic District;
PO Box 1526, 31305
(912) 437-6985

Georgia's second-oldest town is just 2 miles east of I–95 exits 9 and 10. Environmentalist/hostess Carolyn Hodges encourages stays of two days to explore the Altamaha River (longest east of Mississippi) and its delta, the barrier birding islands, and remote beaches. Near Sapero Island departure area. Great for birding. Open Gates is filled with family quilts; has a lovely garden and pool. Rice plantation nearby. Many books inspired by the area. Tours by water, $35-65. Fishing nearby.

Hostess: Carolyn Hodges
Rooms: 5 (2PB; 3SB) $64-75.90
Full Breakfast
Credit Cards: none
Notes: 2, 5, 6 and 7 (inquire)

EATONTON

The Crockett House Bed and Breakfast

671 Madison Road, 31024
(706) 485-2248
Web site: http://www.bbonline.com/ga/crocketthouse

The Crockett House, circa 1895, is nestled among 100-year-old pecan, oak, pine, and magnolia trees, and is gracefully adorned by beautiful weeping willows. Experience a new adventure as you step back in time to luxurious accommodations, fine dining, and a slower pace at this historic Victorian home. "The Crockett House is the perfect place for a romantic rendezvous," said the *Atlanta Journal–Constitution* (February 4, 1996). Eleven fireplaces; large wraparound porch; antique-filled guest rooms with king, queen, or two double beds; claw-foot tubs beside working fireplaces. Enjoy refreshments on arrival and Christa's memorable gourmet breakfast served in elegant style each morning. The Crockett House is located on Georgia's historic antebellum trail, approximately 1¼ hours from Atlanta, 1½ hours from Augusta, 50 minutes from Athens, 40 minutes from Macon.

Hosts: Christa and Peter Crockett
Rooms: 6 (4PB; 2SB) $65-95
Full Breakfast
Credit Cards: A, B
Notes: 2, 5, 7 (over 10), 8, 9, 10, 12

ETON

Ivy Inn

245 Fifth Avenue E.; PO Box 406, 30724
(706) 517-0526 (voice and FAX)
Web site: http://www.bbonline.com/ga/ivyinn

Historic 1908 country home was one of the first homes built in Eton. Rocking chair porches offer a break from a busy day

Ivy Inn

shopping for antiques, clothes, or carpet—Eton is part of the carpet capital of the world. Hiking in Cohutta Wilderness or bicycling on the inn's bikes refreshes the weary soul. In-room air-control and TV. Day trips to Atlanta, Chattanooga, and Ocoee River. Horses/stabling next door to the inn. Restricted smoking.

Hosts: Gene and Juanita Twiggs
Rooms: 3 (PB) $75
Full Southern Breakfast
Credit Cards: A, B, C
Notes: 2, 5, 9, 10, 11 (water), 12

Dorminy-Massee House Bed and Breakfast

FITZGERALD

Dorminy-Massee House B&B

516 W. Central Avenue, 31750
(912) 423-3123; FAX (912) 423-2226

Located just 20 miles east of I–75, this beautiful family-owned 1915 Colonial home, designed by architect T. F. Lockwood, contains eight charmingly furnished, air-conditioned bedrooms with television, telephone, computer modem, and private bath. Guests especially enjoy the dining, living, and parlor areas. Spacious, beautifully landscaped grounds include fishpool, gazebo, smokehouse, carriage house, and private parking. Walk 3 blocks to the Blue-Gray Museum and learn Fitzgerald's history—the only town colonized by Union and Confederate veterans.

Hosts: Mark and Sherry Massee, Marion and Joyce Massee
Rooms: 8 (PB) $75-85
Continental Breakfast
Credit Cards: A, B
Notes: 2, 5, 7, 8, 10

FLOWERY BRANCH

Whitworth Inn

6593 McEver Road, 30542
(770) 967-2386; FAX (770) 967-2649
E-mail: visit@whitworthinn.com
Web site: http://www.whitworthinn.com

The Whitworth Inn is a contemporary country inn on 5 wooded acres offering a relaxing atmosphere. Ten uniquely decorated guest rooms have their own baths. Two guest living rooms are available. A full country breakfast is served in a large, sunlit dining room. Meeting/party space is available. The inn is located 30 minutes northeast of Atlanta at Lake Lanier. Nearby attractions and activities include boating, golf, beaches, and water parks. Close to Road Atlanta and Chateau Elen Winery/Golf Course. Easily accessible from major interstates. Three-diamond AAA rating.

Hosts: Ken and Christine Jonick
Rooms: 10 (PB) $65-85
Full Breakfast
Credit Cards: A, B, C
Notes: 2, 5, 7, 8, 9, 10, 12

Samples Plantation

GREENVILLE

Samples Plantation

15380 Roosevelt Highway; PO Box 649, 30222
(706) 672-4765
E-mail: samplesbb@mindspring.com
Web sites: http://www.virtualcities.com/ons/ga/p
http://www.georgia.org

Sample the South. Beautiful antebellum home with original cemetery, cookhouse, smokehouse, playhouse. Wonderful, full breakfast. Enjoy the feather beds, fireplace, and large porches with swing!

Hostess: Marjorie Samples
Rooms: 6 (PB) $130-200
Full Breakfast
Credit Cards: A, B, C, D
Notes: 2, 3, 5, 7 (14 years+), 8, 9, 10, 12

GRIFFIN

Double Cabins

3335 Jackson Road, 30223
(770) 227-6611

This National Register home was built in 1842 in the Greek Revival style characteristic of southern country homes. The large home features an original walnut staircase and gold leaf cornice boards in the living room, and numerous additional period accents. The doors throughout have original knobs and locks with brass keys. The property was part of the 1823–25 land purchase and lies on the McIntosh Trail. It included two cabinlike structures called "Double Cabins." Groups can tour the house, museum, and property.

Hostess: Mrs. Douglas Hollberg
Rooms: 3 (2PB; 1SB)
Full Breakfast
Credit Cards: none
Notes: 2, 5, 7

HELEN

Chattahoochee Ridge

PO Box 175, 30545
(706) 878-3144; (800) 476-8331
E-mail: rooms@stc.net
Web site: http://www.stc.net/~rooms

Alone on a woodsy mountain above a waterfall in Helen, the lodge has four new rooms and suites (kitchens and fireplaces) with private entrances, TV, AC, free phones, and Jacuzzis in all rooms. There is double insulation and back-up solar for stewards of the earth. In the lodge and cabins, you'll like the quiet seclusion, large windows, and deep-rock water. We'll help you plan great vacation days. Decor includes wide-board knotty pine, brass beds, full carpeting, and paddle fans.

Hosts: Bob and Mary Swift
Rooms: 4 + cabins (PB) $50-85 average
Credit Cards: A, B, C, D
Notes: 2, 5, 7, 8, 9, 10

Henson Cove Place Bed and Breakfast and Cabin

HIAWASSEE

Henson Cove Place B&B and Cabin

3840 Car Miles Road, 30546
(706) 896-6195; (800) 714-5542;
FAX (706) 896-5252
E-mail: nle@yhc.edu
Web site: http://www.yhc.edu/users/nle

Henson Cove Place Bed and Breakfast is a unique lodging in northeast Georgia near Hiawassee in the mountains. Guests can relax on the front porch swing or rockers and view Kelly Ridge or watch the cows nearby. A full breakfast is prepared on a 1929 Tappan gas range. A cabin in the woods is also available. Come and stay with us—we treat you like family.

Hosts: Bill and Nancy Leffingwell
Rooms: 2 (PB) $70
Full Breakfast
Credit Cards: A, B
Notes: 2, 5, 8, 9, 10, 11

MARIETTA

Sixty Polk Street

60 Polk Street, 30064
(770) 419-1688; (800) 845-7266
E-mail: JMertes@aol.com
Web site: http://www.waterspaniel.com/60polk/home.htm

Fully restored to its original glory, this French Regency Victorian home, built in 1872, features warm, inviting bedrooms. Delight in exquisite period antiques as you peruse the library, relax in the parlor, or savor afternoon sweets in the dining room. Wake to early coffee followed by a sumptuous southern breakfast before walking to the antique shops, restaurants, museums, or the theater on Marietta Square.

Hosts: Joe and Glenda Mertes
Rooms: 4 (PB) $95-175
Full Breakfast
Credit Cards: A, B, C
Notes: 2, 5, 8, 10, 12

PERRY

New Hope Guest House Ministry

115 Thunder Road, 31036
(912) 987-8096
E-mail: chris96@ibm.net

Come treat yourself to a relaxing stay in our country guest house just 10 minutes from I–75 and the Perry National Fairgrounds. This home is a labor of love specially designed for people with disabilities. Amenities include a full kitchen, living room, and two bedrooms beautifully decorated with magnolias and ivy. A large bath has a whirlpool and wheelchair-accessible shower. Private pool on-premises.

Hosts: Samuel and Christine Vines
Rooms: 2 (SB) $40 suggested donation
Continental Breakfast
Credit Cards: none
Notes: 2, 5, 6, 7, 9, 10

ST. SIMONS ISLAND

The Lodge on Little St. Simons Island

PO Box 21078, 31522
(912) 638-7472; (888) 733-5774;
FAX (912) 634-1811
E-mail: lssi@mindspring.com
Web site: http://www.pactel.com.au/lssi

Nature prevails on this pristine island paradise where 10,000 acres and 7 miles of secluded beaches are shared with no more than thirty overnight guests. Outdoor enthusiasts can enjoy endless recreational activities. Explore tidal creeks by boat, hike or bicycle on island trails, or enjoy swimming, shelling, and fishing. Creature comforts include thirteen gracious guest rooms (all with private baths) and gourmet cuisine. Rates include all activities, recreational equipment, and meals.

Hosts: Debbie and Kevin McIntyre
Rooms: 13 (PB) $300-540
Full Breakfast and All Meals
Credit Cards: A, B
Notes: 2 (and traveler's checks), 3 and 4 (included), 5, 7, 8, 9, 10, 12

SAUTEE

The Stovall House Country Inn and Restaurant

1526 Highway 255 N., 30571
(706) 878-3355
Web site: http://www.georgiamagazine.com/sh

Our 1837 Victorian farmhouse, restored in 1983, is listed on the National Register of Historic Places. Located on 26 acres in the historic Sautee Valley, the inn has views of the mountains in all directions. The recipient of several awards for its attentive restorations, the inn is furnished with family antiques and decorated with hand-stenciling. The restaurant, open to the public, features regional cuisine prepared with a fresh difference and served in an intimate yet informal setting. It's a country experience!

Host: Hamilton (Ham) Schwartz
Rooms: 5 (PB) $64-80
Continental Breakfast
Credit Cards: A, B
Notes: 2, 4, 5, 7, 8, 9, 10

SAVANNAH

Bed and Breakfast Inn

117 W. Gorden Street, 31401
(912) 238-0518; FAX (912) 233-2537
E-mail: bnbinn@email.msn.com
Web site: http://www.travelbase.com/destinations/savannah/bed-breakfast

Elegant 19th-century home nestled among magnificent moss-draped live oaks in the heart of Savannah's historic district. Antiques, original artwork, and oriental carpets. Most guest rooms have queen beds and private baths. Enjoy our full, hearty breakfast and freshly baked breads while seated on the deck overlooking our garden courtyard with its colorful, fragrant flowers. Then stroll Savannah's streets and squares to the many shops and restaurants, all within an easy walk of our inn.

Rooms: 15 (PB) $80-110
Full Breakfast
Credit Cards: A, B, C, D
Notes: 2, 5, 7, 8, 10, 12

Eliza Thompson House

5 W. Jones Street, 31401
(912) 236-3620; (800) 348-9378;
FAX (912) 238-1920
E-mail: ElizaTh@aol.com
Web site: http://www.bbonline.com/ca/savannah/elizathompson/index.html

Southern Living calls "Jones" the most beautiful cobblestone street in Savannah. Our Federal-style mansion is located in the heart of Savannah's historic district. It has twenty-three guest rooms, private baths, period antiques, fireplaces, and fine linens. Magnificent fountains are in our beautiful courtyard. Full breakfast, wine and cheese reception, dessert and coffee.

Host: Carol L. Day
Rooms: 25 (PB) $89-199
Full Breakfast
Credit Cards: A, B
Notes: 2, 5, 7, 9, 10, 12

Lion's Head Inn

120 E. Gaston Street, 31401
(912) 232-4580; (800) 355-5466;
FAX (912) 232-7422
E-mail: lionshead@sys.conn.com
Web site: http://www.choice-guide.com/ga/lionshead

The stately 19th-century mansion is in a quiet neighborhood just north of picturesque Forsyth Park. This lovely, 9,200-square-foot home is exquisitely appointed with four-poster beds, private baths, period furnishings, fireplaces, televisions, and phones. Each morning, enjoy a deluxe continental breakfast. Each evening, have wine and cheese on the veranda overlooking the marbled courtyard.

Lion's Head Inn

Hostess: Christy Dell'Orco
Rooms: 6 (PB) $95-220
Continental Breakfast
Credit Cards: A, B, C, D
Notes: 2, 5, 7, 8, 9, 10, 12

Magnolia Place Inn

503 Whitaker Street, 31401
(912) 236-7674; (800) 238-7674;
FAX (912) 236-1145
E-mail: b.b.magnolia@me12000.com
Web site: http://www.MagnoliaPlaceInn.com

Magnolia Place Inn is the "Grand Inn of Savannah." This 1878 Victorian structure overlooks beautiful Forsyth Park. It has fifteen rooms with private baths, fourteen fireplaces, and seven Jacuzzi tubs. Continental breakfast is served in the parlor, veranda, or garden or is brought to your room. Afternoon wine and tea, evening

NOTES: Credit cards accepted: A Master Card; B Visa; C American Express; D Discover; E Diners Club; F Other; 2 Personal checks accepted; 3 Lunch available; 4 Dinner available; 5 Open all year; 6 Pets

sweets and coffee, late-evening turndown service, cordials and pralines. The inn is beautifully decorated with English antiques, Oriental porcelains, and original prints.

Hosts: Kathy Medlock, Rob and Jane Sales
Rooms: 15 (PB) $145-250
Continental Breakfast
Credit Cards: A, B, C, D, E
Notes: 5, 8, 9, 10, 12

The Village Inn Bed and Breakfast

STONE MOUNTAIN

The Village Inn Bed and Breakfast

992 Ridge Avenue, 30083
(770) 469-3459; (800) 214-8385;
FAX (770) 469-1051

Come experience southern hospitality and classic antebellum charm. Built circa 1850, this home served as a hospital during the Civil War. Less than 1 mile from Stone Mountain Park, convenient to Atlanta. Six guest rooms, whirlpool tubs, fireplaces, telephones, television/VCR. Great view of Stone Mountain from our second-floor veranda. Full southern breakfast served each morning. Business travelers welcome! Special packages available. Golfing, tennis, fishing, and swimming nearby. Available for weddings!

Hosts: Earl and Christy Collins
Rooms: 6 (PB) $95-125
Full Breakfast
Credit Cards: A, B, C, D
Notes: 2, 7, 8, 9, 10, 12

THOMSON

1810 West Inn

254 N. Seymour Drive, 30824
(706) 595-3156; (800) 515-1810;
FAX (706) 595-3155
Web site: http://www.bbonline.com/ga/1810west

The property includes a historic, restored farmhouse, circa 1810, and accompanying renovated country houses on 12 landscaped acres. All rooms have central air and heat, antique furnishings, and fireplaces. Enjoy the country kitchen, screened veranda, strolling peacocks, and nature trails. The inn is ideal for business retreats. It has been featured in *Country Inns Magazine* and was named a "Great Inn of Georgia." Convenient to I–20 and Augusta; 2 hours from Atlanta.

Hostess: Virginia White
Rooms: 10 (PB) $60-79
Extended Continental Breakfast
Credit Cards: A, B, C, D
Notes: 2, 5, 7 (10 and over), 8, 9, 10, 12

1810 West Inn

VILLA RICA

Twin Oaks Bed and Breakfast Cottages

9565 E. Liberty Road, 30180
(770) 459-4374 (voice and FAX)
Web site: http://www.bbonline.com/ga/twinoaks

A uniquely intimate bed and breakfast located on a 23-acre farm only 30 minutes from Atlanta. The two exquisite guest cottages are ideal for honeymoons or celebrating anniversaries. The cottages have CD/tape players; we furnish blues and jazz CDs. There are also two private suites on the property. All accommodations have hot tubs or Jacuzzis, fireplaces, private bathrooms, queen-size beds, televisions, VCRs, refrigerators, microwaves, and coffeemakers. Enjoy the swimming pool, walking trails, horseback riding, and exotic animals for feeding and viewing. (Our pet pig "Elmer Leroy" enjoys scraps from supper!) Located near Six Flags Over Georgia and the projected *Gone With the Wind* theme park.

Hosts: Earl and Carol Turner
Rooms: 2 suites + 2 cottages (PB) $115-155
Full Breakfast
Credit Cards: A, B, C, D
Notes: 2, 5, 9, 10, 12

WARM SPRINGS

Hotel Warm Springs Bed and Breakfast Inn

PO Box 351, 31830
(706) 655-2114; (800) 366-7616;
FAX (706) 655-2406

"Presidents, passion, and the past." Relive history and the Roosevelt era in our 1907 hotel, ice cream parlor, and gift shops. Authentically restored and beautifully decorated with Roosevelt furniture and family antiques. Featuring our cozy honeymoon suite with king bed, suspended canopy, Victorian antiques, red heart tub, gold fixtures, breakfast in bed, flowers, champagne, and chocolates. Our large living room and dining room with Queen Anne furniture, Oriental rugs, and crystal teardrop chandelier are ideal for group meetings. Nestled in quaint Warm Springs Village—a shopper's paradise, home of FDR's Little White House, 14 miles from Callaway Gardens, and 1 hour from Atlanta. Award-winning cheese grits and homemade peach ice cream.

Hostess: Gerrie Thompson
Rooms: 14 (PB) $45-170
Full Breakfast
Credit Cards: A, B, C, D
Notes: 2, 5, 7, 8, 9, 10, 12

NOTES: Credit cards accepted: A Master Card; B Visa; C American Express; D Discover; E Diners Club; F Other; 2 Personal checks accepted; 3 Lunch available; 4 Dinner available; 5 Open all year; 6 Pets

Hawaii

HAWAII—HILO

Hale Kai Bjornen

111 Honolii Pali, 96720
(808) 935-6330; FAX (808) 935-8439

Beautiful four-star bed and breakfast on the ocean bluff facing Hilo Bay and Honolii surfing beach. All rooms face the ocean and have private baths. There are fresh flowers in all rooms and bathrooms. A full gourmet breakfast is served, with such items as macadamia nut waffles, sausage, huge fruit platters, local juices, and kona coffee. Swimming pool and hot tub. Two miles from downtown. Very quiet area. Hosts help with directions, restaurants. Friendly Christians. We also have a two-bedroom, two-and-a-half-bath condo available on the ocean in Hilo for weekly or monthly rental.

Hosts: Evonne Bjornen and Paul Tallett
Rooms: 5 (PB) $85-105
Full Gourmet Breakfast
Credit Cards: none
Notes: 2, 5, 7, 8, 9, 10, 11, 12

HAWAII—KAMUELA

Kamuela Inn

PO Box 1994, 96743
(808) 885-4243; (800) 555-8968;
FAX (808) 885-8857
E-mail: kaminn@aloha.net
Web site: http://www.hawaii-bnb.com/kamuela.html

The Kamuela Inn offers comfortable, cozy rooms and suites with private baths, with or without kitchenettes, all with cable, color television. A complimentary continental breakfast is served in our coffee lanai each morning. The inn is situated in a quiet, peaceful setting just off Highway 19. It is conveniently located near shops, retail outlets, banks, theaters, parks, tennis courts, museums, restaurants, and the post office. The big island's famous white sand beaches, golf courses, horseback rides, and valley and mountain tours are only minutes away.

Hostess: Carolyn Cascavilla
Rooms: 32 (PB) $54
Continental Breakfast
Credit Cards: A, B, C, D, E, F
Notes: 2, 5, 7, 8, 9, 10, 11, 12

---

welcome; 7 Children welcome; 8 Tennis nearby; 9 Swimming nearby; 10 Golf nearby; 11 Skiing nearby; 12 May be booked through travel agent.

HAWAII

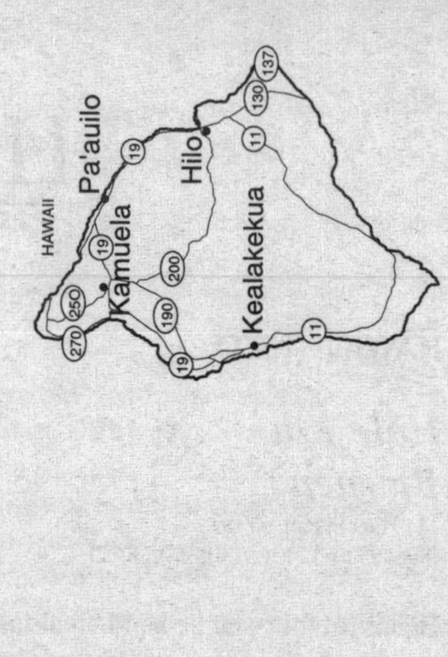

HAWAII
Pa'auilo
Hilo
Kamuela
Kealakekua
19
137
130
11
200
250
270
190

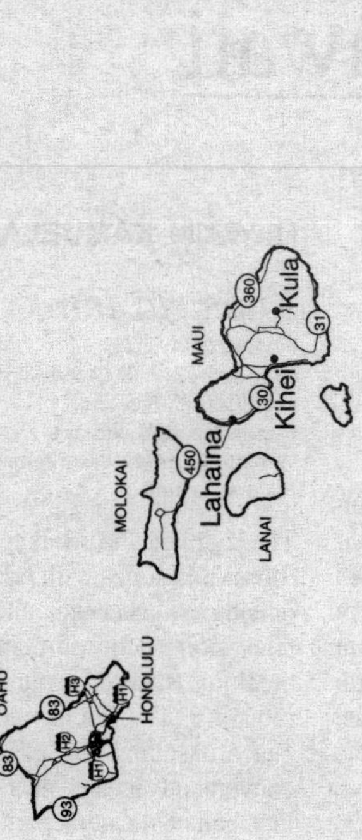

MAUI
Kula
Kihei
Lahaina
MOLOKAI
LANAI
360
31
30
450
OAHU
HONOLULU
83
93
H1
H2
H3

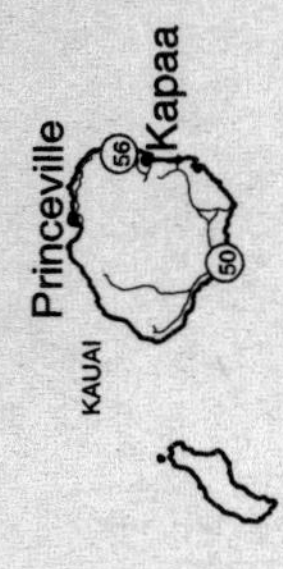

KAUAI
Princeville
Kapaa
56
50

HAWAII—PA'AUILO

Suds Acres Bed and Breakfast

43-1973 Paauilo Mauka Road, 96776
(808) 776-1611 (voice and FAX); (800) 735-3262

Our cozy, two-bedroom cottage, with its complete kitchen and microwave oven, comfortably sleeps a family of five. It is situated on a macadamia nut farm at an elevation of 1,800 feet on the slopes of Mauna Kea. In our main house we have additional guest accommodations and provide wheelchair access. Suds Acres is located 40 miles north of Hilo airport, 20 miles from Waimea, and 30 miles from some of Hawaii's best beaches.

Hosts: "Suds" and Anita Suderman
Rooms: 3 (PB) $65
Continental Breakfast
Credit Cards: A, B, D, E, F
Notes: 5, 7, 9, 10, 12

HAWAII—WAIKIKI

Aston Waikiki Beachside Hotel

2452 Kalakaua Avenue, 96815
(808) 931-2100; (800) 922-7866;
FAX (808) 931-2129
E-mail: ruthuy@aston-hotels.com
Web site: http://www.aston-hotels.com

Situated within the grounds of "Pualeilani," the former estate of Prince Jonah Kuhio Kalanianaole, this elegant, boutique hotel overlooking Waikiki Beach is a re-creation of the subtle opulence exhibited in lavish Hawaiian homes at the turn of the century. An excellent location, exquisite appointments, and exceptional service in an exclusive environment will make anyone feel pampered and envied. Ask for the "Bed & Breakfast" rate for a very deep discount!

General Manager: Donna Wheeler
Rooms: 79 (PB)
Continental Breakfast
Credit Cards: A, B, C, D, E, F
Notes: 2, 5, 8, 9, 12

KAUAI—KAPAA

Aloha Country Bed and Breakfast

505 Kamalu Road, 96746
(808) 822-0166; FAX (808) 822-2708
E-mail: wery@aloha.net

Luxury bed and breakfast estate in peaceful country setting. Two acres of yard, fruit trees. Tropical flowers, spacious suites, studios, and cottages. Centrally located close to everything. Homemade breads and jams and an array of fresh fruits every morning. Honeymoon suite has Jacuzzi room. Feel right at home with the warm aloha of the owner's hospitality.

Hostess: Theresa Wery
Rooms: 5 + 4-room honeymoon suite (PB)
$55-300
Continental Breakfast
Credit Cards: A, B, F
Notes: 5, 7, 8, 9, 10, 12

NOTES: Credit cards accepted: A Master Card; B Visa; C American Express; D Discover; E Diners Club; F Other; 2 Personal checks accepted; 3 Lunch available; 4 Dinner available; 5 Open all year; 6 Pets welcome; 7 Children welcome; 8 Tennis nearby; 9 Swimming nearby; 10 Golf nearby; 11 Skiing nearby; 12 May be booked through travel agent.

KAUAI—PRINCEVILLE

Hale 'Aha— "House of Gathering"

3875 Kamehameha Drive; PO Box 3370, 96722
(808) 826-6733; (800) 826-6733;
FAX (808) 826-9052
E-mail: kauai@pixi.com
Web site: http://wwwpixi.com/~kauai

Vacation, honeymoon, or retreat in this peaceful resort setting on the golf course, overlooking the ocean and majestic mountains of the Garden Isle. On one side enjoy Hanalei, where *South Pacific* was filmed, with one beach after another leading you to the famous, lush, Napoli Coast hiking trails. Hale 'Aha has been written about in many books and magazines, but only a brochure can tell it all. Enjoy bananas, papayas, and pineapple from the Hale 'Aha garden.

Hostess: Ruth Bockelman
Rooms: 2 + 2 suites (PB) $88-220
"More Than" Continental Breakfast
Credit Cards: A, B
Notes: 2, 5, 8, 9, 10, 12

KONA—KEALAKEKUA

Merryman's Bed and Breakfast

PO Box 474, 96750
(808) 323-2276; FAX (808) 323-3749
E-mail: merryman@ilhawaii.net
Web site: http://www.lavazone2.com/merrymans

Beautiful and quiet ocean view upcountry estate in Kealakekua/Captain Cook, minutes from the best snorkeling, historical sites, activities. Enjoy spacious, charming rooms; pretty linens; fresh flowers; and cable TV. Complementary Hawaiian breakfast, Jacuzzi. AAA, three diamonds.

Hosts: Don and Penny Merryman
Rooms: 4 (2PB; 2SB) $75-125
Full Breakfast
Credit Cards: A, B, D
Notes: 2, 5, 8, 9, 10, 12

MAUI—KIHEI

Anuhea Bed and Breakfast

3164 Mapu Pl., 96753
(808) 874-1490; (800) 206-4441;
FAX (808) 874-8587
E-mail: anuhea@maui.net
Web site: http://www.maui.net/~anuhea

Wonderfully appointed six-bedroom home near beautiful beaches with partial ocean view and hot tub. Sleeps twelve. Excellent for groups and families. Full breakfast. Whole house rentals. True Aloha spirit will be found here at Anuhea.

Hosts: Cherie and Russell Kolbo
Rooms: 6 (4PB; 2SB) $65-110 (summer rates available)
Continental Breakfast
Credit Cards: A, B, D
Notes: 2, 5, 9, 10

MAUI—KULA

Elaine's Upcountry Guest Rooms

2112 Noalae Road, 96790
(808) 878-6623; FAX (808) 878-2619

Located in a quiet country setting with splendid ocean and mountain views. All

NOTES: Credit cards accepted: A Master Card; B Visa; C American Express; D Discover; E Diners Club; F Other; 2 Personal checks accepted; 3 Lunch available; 4 Dinner available; 5 Open all year; 6 Pets

rooms have private baths, full kitchens, and sitting room privileges. Guests are welcome to cook breakfast or whatever meals they like. Next to our main house is a delightful cottage made to order for a family; it has one bedroom with queen-size bed and twin beds in the loft. Large kitchen. We ask that our guests do not smoke or drink. For three or more nights, $60 for rooms and $100 for cottage with four people.

Hosts: Elaine and Murray Gildersleeve
Rooms: 3 + cottage (PB) $60-125
No Breakfast
Credit Cards: none
Notes: 2, 5, 7, 9, 10, 12

MAUI—LAHAINA

The Guesthouse

1620 Ainakea Road, 96761
(808) 661-8085; (800) 621-8942;
FAX (808) 661-1896
E-mail: guesthouse@compuserve.com
Web site: http://ourworld.compuserve.com/homepages/guesthouse

Located between the historic whaling town of Lahaina and the beach resorts of Kaanapali, The Guesthouse is nestled in a quiet residential neighborhood. All rooms have air-conditioning, private phones, refrigerators, TVs, and VCRs. Our suites also have private baths and Jacuzzis! Full kitchen and laundry facilities. Relax at poolside or take a short stroll to the beach. Receive discounts on rental cars and all island activities.

Host: c/o Trinity Tours; Tanna Swanson
Rooms: 4 (3PB; 1SB) $65-95
Full Breakfast
Credit Cards: A, B, C, D
Notes: 2, 5, 7 (over 12), 8, 9, 10, 12

Old Lahaina House Bed and Breakfast

PO Box 10355, 96761
(808) 667-4663; (800) 847-0761;
FAX (808) 667-5615
Web site: http://www.mauiweb.com/maui/olhouse

We are located on the outskirts of Lahaina, just 1 minute from the beach. The home offers two guest rooms with king-size beds, two rooms with two twin beds each. All rooms are air-conditioned and have television, phone, and private bath. A swimming pool and tropical courtyard will add to the enchantment of your stay.

Hosts: John and Sherry Barbier
Rooms: 4 (PB) $69-95
Continental Breakfast
Credit Cards: A, B, C, D
Notes: 2, 5, 7, 8, 9, 10, 12

The Walkus House Bed and Breakfast

1620 Ainakea Road, 96761
(808) 661-8085; (800) 621-8942;
FAX (808) 661-1896

Visit Maui. . .from home to home. Have the privacy of this new four-bedroom, three-bath home (the den can be used as a fifth bedroom). Sunbathe at poolside, relax in the Jacuzzi, or take a short stroll to "Baby Beach" right in Lahaina. With central air-conditioning, modern laundry facilities, and a kitchen that lacks nothing, you'll be right at home. Great for families or small groups.

Host: c/o Trinity Tours
Rooms: 4 + den (1PB; 4SB) $295
Self-Serve Breakfast
Credit Cards: A, B, C, D
Notes: 2, 5, 7, 8, 9, 10

IDAHO

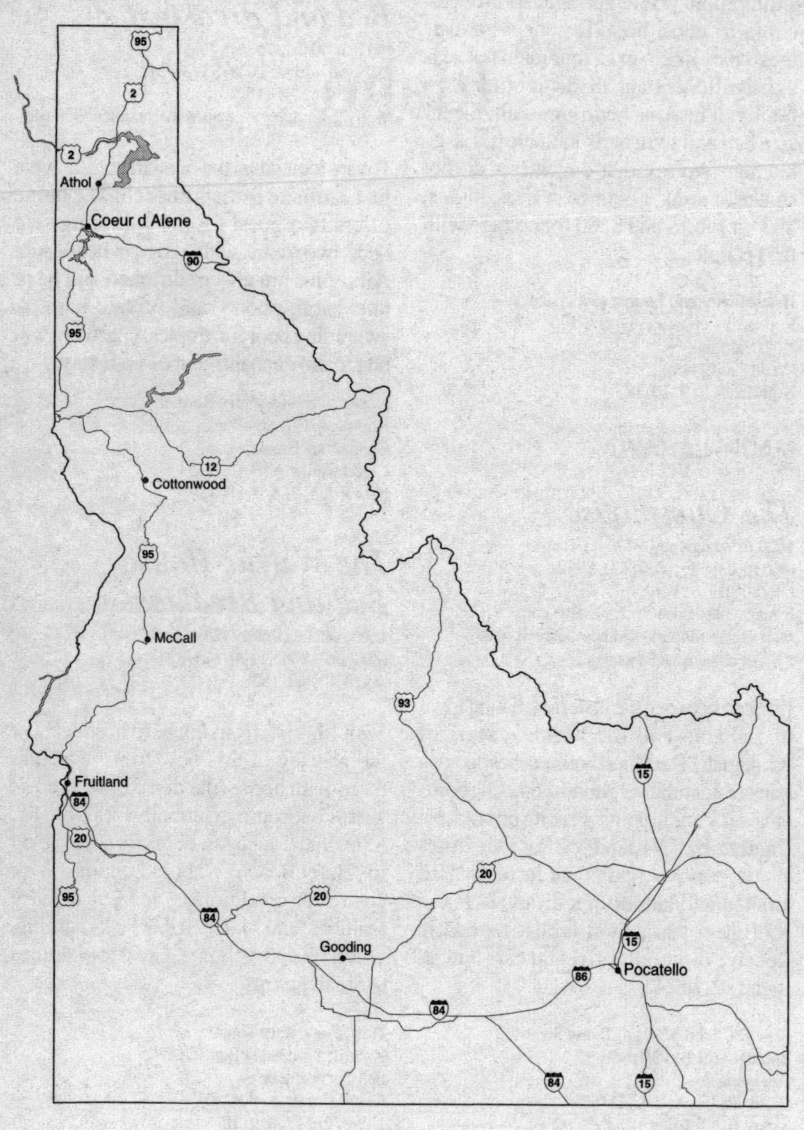

95
2
2
Athol
Coeur d Alene
90
95
12
Cottonwood
95
McCall
93
15
Fruitland
84
20
20
20
95
84
15
Gooding
86
Pocatello
84
84
15

Idaho

ATHOL

The Ponderosa

2555 Brunner Road, 83801
(208) 683-2251; (888) 683-2251;
FAX (208) 683-5112
E-mail: ponderosa@ior.com
Web site: www.onlinenow.com/theponderosa

A breathtaking log home located on a 10-acre wooded estate just minutes north of Coeur d'Alene, near Silverwood Theme Park. Queen-size log beds, private baths. Tasting in our 2,000-bottle wine cellar. Full breakfast. Enclosed spa. Many sports activities nearby. Ask about children. Guests receive free passes to Silverwood.

Hosts: Jack and Betty Bonzey
Rooms: 4 (PB) $85-125
Full Breakfast
Credit Cards: A, B
Notes: 2, 5, 7 (inquire), 8, 9, 10, 11

COEUR D'ALENE

Gregory's McFarland House Bed and Breakfast

601 Foster Avenue, 83814
(208) 667-1232; (800) 335-1232
Web site: http://www.bbhost.com/mcfarlandhouse

Surrender to the elegance of this award-winning historical home, circa 1905. The full breakfast is gourmet to the last crumb. Guests will be delighted by an ideal blending of beauty, comfort, and clean surroundings. Jerry Hulse, travel editor for *The Los Angeles Times*, wrote, "Entering Gregory's McFarland House is like stepping back 100 years to an unhurried time when four posters were in fashion and lace curtains fluttered at the windows." Our guest accommodations offer private baths and are air-conditioned. This is a nonsmoking house. If you're planning a wedding, our resident minister and professional photographer are available to make your special day beautiful.

Gregory's McFarland House Bed and Breakfast

Hosts: Winifred, Carol, and Stephen Gregory
Rooms: 5 (PB) $85-135
Full Gourmet Breakfast
Credit Cards: A, B, D
Notes: 2, 5, 8, 9, 10, 11, 12

NOTES: Credit cards accepted: A Master Card; B Visa; C American Express; D Discover; E Diners Club; F Other; 2 Personal checks accepted; 3 Lunch available; 4 Dinner available; 5 Open all year; 6 Pets welcome; 7 Children welcome; 8 Tennis nearby; 9 Swimming nearby; 10 Golf nearby; 11 Skiing nearby; 12 May be booked through travel agent.

COTTONWOOD

Mariel's B&B

RR 1, Box 207, 83522
(208) 962-5927

Experience the peace and quiet of rural Idaho in this big, comfortable home on a dryland wheat farm. From the windows of the seven spacious bedrooms, view the Camas Prairie, with its rolling hills surrounded by canyons and framed by mountains. Enjoy walking along quiet country roads, then relax in our indoor hot tub. Five bedrooms have private baths, queen or twin beds. Guests are served a full country breakfast in the family dining room.

Hostess: Mariel H. Arnzen
Rooms: 7 (5PB; 2SB) $46
Full Breakfast
Credit Cards: D
Notes: 2, 5, 10

FRUITLAND

Elm Hollow

4900 Highway 95, 83619
(208) 452-6491

A quiet country setting with a panoramic view and warm Christian hospitality awaits guests at Elm Hollow Bed and Breakfast. Guests are welcome to take walks, relax or picnic in the arbor, and visit the animals. A full breakfast is served family-style in the dining room or guest house. Children welcome. Rooms have private baths.

Hosts: Delores and Florence Koehn
Rooms: 2 (PB) $45-60
Full Breakfast
Credit Cards: none
Notes: 2, 5, 6, 7

GOODING

The Gooding Hotel Bed and Breakfast

112 Main Street, 83330
(208) 934-4374; (888) 260-6656

"Just like Grandma's house." "Home-away-from-home atmosphere." These are comments we frequently hear to describe The Gooding Hotel, circa 1906, which is listed on the National Historic Register of Historic Places. Seven comfy, individually decorated guest rooms; an upstairs sitting/reading room and outdoor balcony; main floor family room with TV and kitchen. Breakfast features one of our special entrées, fruit, juice, and coffee in our charming breakfast room. Families and groups welcome.

Hosts: Dean and Juddee Gooding
Rooms: 7 (1PB; 6SB) $49-59
Full Breakfast
Credit Cards: A, B, C
Notes: 5, 6 (with approval and deposit), 7, 10, 11, 12

HELLS CANYON

Hells Canyon Adventures/ S. Hells Canyon Lodge

PO Box 159, **Oxbow, OR,** 97840
(541) 785-3352; (800) 422-3568;
FAX (541) 785-3353
E-mail: jeatboat@pdx.oneworld.com
Web site: http://www.hellscanyonadventures.com

Located along a private road into the southern part of the Hells Canyon Recreation area, overlooking the Hells Canyon Reservoir. Accessible through eastern Oregon on Highway 86 and southwest-

NOTES: Credit cards accepted: A Master Card; B Visa; C American Express; D Discover; E Diners Club; F Other; 2 Personal checks accepted; 3 Lunch available; 4 Dinner available; 5 Open all year; 6 Pets

ern Idaho by Highway 71. Minutes from White Water Jetboat Tours and Rafting, fishing, hiking, snowmobiling, and cross-country skiing. The lodge has three very spacious guest rooms, two with private baths. All rooms offer comfort to stretch out and relax. The lodge also works well for small corporate meetings. We surprise you each morning with our full country breakfast, fresh-baked goodies, juice, and all the trimmings. We speak German.

Hosts: Doris and Bret Armacost
Rooms: 3 (2PB; 1SB) $150+
Full Breakfast
Credit Cards: A, B, D
Notes: 2, 3, 4, 5, 9 (river), 11 (cross-country)

MCCALL

Meadowood Lodge

3580 Meadowood Lane, 83638
(208) 634-3330
E-mail: mwlodge@micron.net

Located in the central Idaho mountains on 10 acres, surrounded by national forest. Lodge atmosphere, grand log staircase, and river rock-surrounded living area. Panoramic view of mountains, meadow, and pond. Varied wildlife are frequent visitors. Breakfast: traditional home cooking. Afternoon tea/coffee with fresh-baked goodies served daily. Can accommodate small groups, retreats, families. Snowmobile parking. Cross-country skiing; downhill skiing within 4 miles. Hiking, biking, fishing, boating, and hot springs close by. Inquire about our ministerial discounts.

Hosts: Randy and Lois Hamilton
Rooms: 4 (3PB; 1SB) $45-75
Full Breakfast
Credit Cards: A, B, D
Notes: 2, 5, 7, 8, 9, 10, 11

Northwest Passage B&B

PO Box 4208, 83638
(208) 634-5349; (800) 597-6658;
FAX (208) 634-4977

Nestled among the tall Ponderosa pines, the Northwest Passage B&B has been an integral part of McCall's history. It was built by MGM Studios to house the cast of the 1938 movie *Northwest Passage* (Spencer Tracy and Robert Young). Our four-season resort has something for everyone to enjoy. Gourmet breakfast, complimentary wines. Gift certificates—ask about business rates. Small retreats.

Hosts: Barbara and Steve Schott
Rooms: 6 (3PB; 3SB) $65-85
Full Gourmet Breakfast
Credit Cards: A, B, C
Notes: 2, 5, 6, 11

POCATELLO

Back o' Beyond

404 S. Garfield Avenue; 83204
(888) 232-3820; FAX (208) 232-2771
E-mail: backbeyond@gemstate.net
Web site: http://gemstate.net/backbeyond

An 1893 Victorian home restored with lovely antiques. "Your home along the Oregon Trail" features comfortable rooms with private baths and a pioneer patio to hear the author discuss his book about the trail. The old-fashioned front porch beckons guests to linger with cookies, tea, or lemonade. Country breakfast is served in the old dining room. Near downtown Old Pocatello, skiing, the Fort Hall Replica.

Hosts: Jay and Sherrie Mennenga
Rooms: 3 (PB) $65
Full Country Breakfast
Credit Cards: A, B, C, D
Notes: 2, 3, 4, 5, 7, 8, 9, 10, 11, 12

ILLINOIS

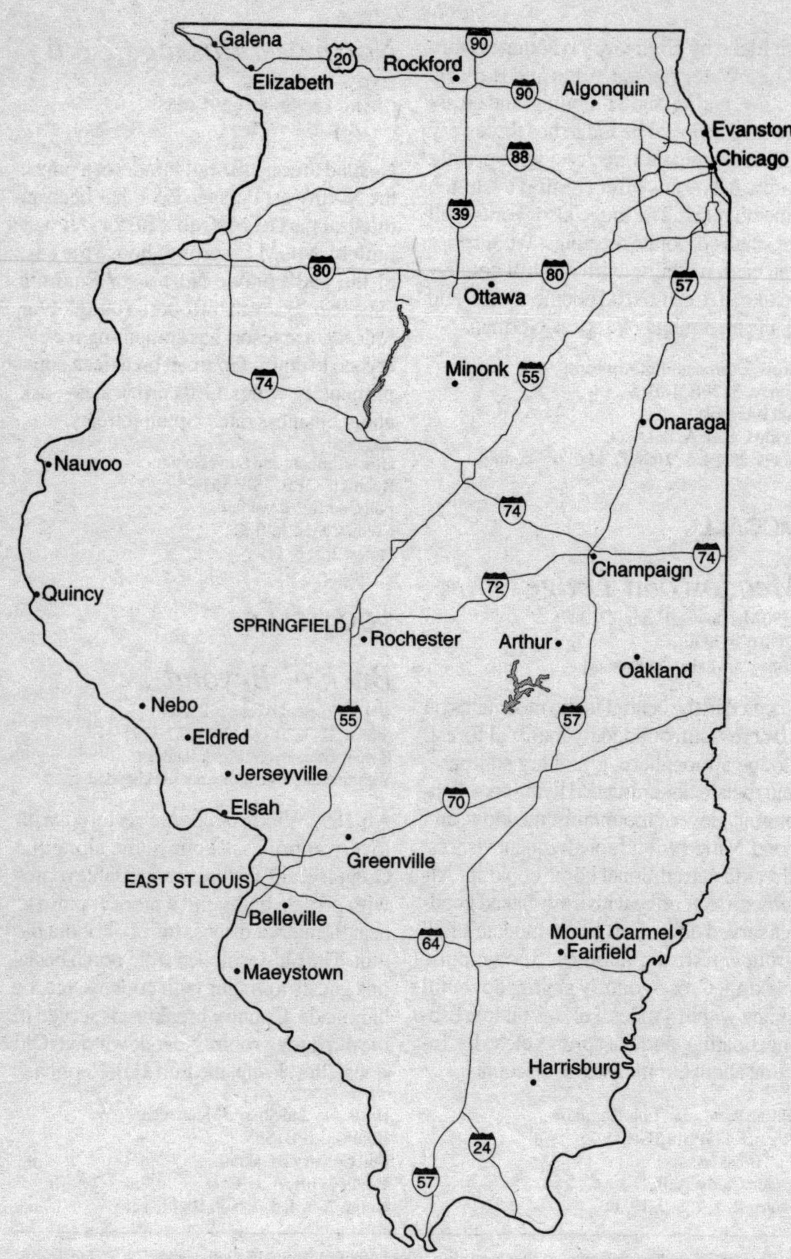

Galena
20
90
Rockford
Elizabeth
90
Algonquin
Evanston
Chicago
88
39
80
80
Ottawa
57
Minonk
55
74
Onaraga
Nauvoo
74
74
Champaign
72
Quincy
SPRINGFIELD
Rochester
Arthur
Oakland
Nebo
55
57
Eldred
Jerseyville
70
Elsah
Greenville
EAST ST LOUIS
Belleville
64
Mount Carmel
Fairfield
Maeystown
Harrisburg
24
57

Illinois

ALGONQUIN

Victorian Rose Garden

314 Washington Street, 60102
(847) 854-9667; (888) 854-9667;
FAX (847) 854-3236
Web site: http://www.7comm.com/rosegarden

Built in 1886, the Victorian Rose Garden invites guests to relax on its wraparound porch, read by the fireplace, play the baby grand piano, and enjoy the old-fashioned barber corner. Bedrooms are individually decorated with antiques and collectibles. A delicious breakfast is served formally in the dining room each morning. Nearby you will find golf courses, antiques, a bike trail, restaurants, and a dinner boat. Chicago is only 1 hour away. The Victorian Rose Garden is a nonsmoking, nonalcoholic, animal-free residence. Special guest packages are available. Come and let us pamper you!

Hosts: Don and Sherry Brewer
Rooms: 4 (PB) $65-139
Full Breakfast
Credit Cards: A, B, C
Notes: 2, 5, 7 (over 12), 10, 12

ARTHUR

Heart and Home Bed and Breakfast

137 E. Illinois Street, 61911
(217) 543-2910

Located in the heart of Illinois Amish country. Constructed in 1911, Heart and Home is a Victorian bed and breakfast filled with the warmth of oak floors and stained-glass windows. A large front porch and second-story sunporch await guests for their relaxation. Choose from three nice guest rooms, one with a pull-out Murphy bed—ideal for an additional guest. All guest rooms are upstairs (not handicap-accessible). Heart and Home is a smoke- and alcohol-free lodging. Situated only two blocks from downtown. We have central air-conditioning. Open Thursdays–Saturdays, April–October.

Hosts: Don and Amanda Miller
Rooms: 3 (1PB; 2SB) $50-60
Full Breakfast
Credit Cards: none
Notes: 2, 8

NOTES: Credit cards accepted: A Master Card; B Visa; C American Express; D Discover; E Diners Club; F Other; 2 Personal checks accepted; 3 Lunch available; 4 Dinner available; 5 Open all year; 6 Pets welcome; 7 Children welcome; 8 Tennis nearby; 9 Swimming nearby; 10 Golf nearby; 11 Skiing nearby; 12 May be booked through travel agent.

Swans Court Bed and Breakfast

BELLEVILLE

Swans Court B&B

421 Court Street, 62220
(618) 233-0779; (800) 840-1058;
FAX (618) 277-3150
E-mail: mdixon@isbe.accessus.net
Web sites: http://www.innsite.com
http://www.innsandout.com

Swans Court is located in a federal historic district. Built in 1883, the house was restored in 1995. Furnished in period antiques, it reflects the gracious lifestyle of an earlier time without sacrificing modern amenities. Walk to shops, restaurants, and historic houses. Many nearby attractions of southwestern Illinois; an easy 20-minute drive to downtown St. Louis.

Host: Monty Dixon
Rooms: 4 (2PB; 2SB) $65-80
Full Breakfast
Credit Cards: A, B, C, D
Notes: 2, 5, 10, 12

Victory Inn

712 S. Jackson Street, 62220
(618) 277-1538; (800) 277-8586;
FAX (618) 277-1576
E-mail: jo@victoryinn.com
Web site: http://www.victoryinn.com

This stately brick home was built in 1877 and offers an exciting picture from first sight. From the huge entry to the individual sleeping accommodations, guests will feel transformed in time while enjoying comfortable, convenient living space. Relax in the comfort of several sitting areas and the company of a family pet, or secret away to the quiet of your room. The Victory Inn offers two guest suites with private Jacuzzis and hospitality that is sure to warm the weary traveler.

Hosts: Tom and Jo Brannan
Rooms: 3/4 (one can be divided) (3PB) $60-125
Expanded Continental Breakfast
Credit Cards: A, B, C
Notes: 2, 5, 7 (inquire), 8, 10, 12

CHAMPAIGN

Grandma Joan's Homestay

2204 Brett Drive, 61821
(217) 356-5828
E-mail: jge@uiuc.edu
Web site: (see Illinois B&B Association site)

This comfortable, contemporary home features multilevel decks, outdoor spa, screened-in porch, two fireplaces, and a collection of both modern and folk art. Grandma pampers you with cookies and milk at bedtime and a healthy breakfast in the morning. Ten minutes from the University of Illinois and several parks and recreational options. Let this be your home away from home.

Hostess: Joan Erickson
Rooms: 3 (1PB; 2SB) $50-80
Full Breakfast
Credit Cards: none
Notes: 2, 5, 8, 9, 10

CHICAGO

Amber Creek's Chicago Connection

10 W. Elm Street, **Chicago,** 60610;
Mail: 122 S. Bench Street, **Galena,** 61036
(815) 777-8400; FAX (815) 777-8446

Attractive apartment on Chicago's Gold Coast. Walk to restaurants, night life, Michigan Avenue shopping, Water Tower Place, and Lake Michigan. Spacious living room with lake and city views, antique decor, fully equipped kitchen, bath with tub and shower. Romantic master bedroom with queen bed, second bedroom with double bed. One block to airport limousine and public transportation. Parking garage across the street. Ideal for one or two couples or small family.

Hosts: Doug and Kate Freeman
Apartment: 1 (PB) $109-169
Continental Breakfast
Credit Cards: A, B, C, D, E
Notes: 2, 3, 5, 7, 9, 12

Bed and Breakfast Chicago, Incorporated

607 W. Deming Place, 60614
(773) 248-0005; (800) 375-7084;
FAX (773) 248-7090
E-mail: BnBChicago@aol.com

A reservation service providing comfortable, reasonably priced lodging in private homes; furnished, "self-catering" apartments; and guest houses. Most are in the center of Chicago or close to it.

Hosts: Mary and Andy Shaw
Rooms: 150 (99 percent PB) $85-185
Continental Breakfast
Credit Cards: A, B, C, D
Notes: 2, 5, 7

Bluffdale Vacation Farm

ELDRED

Bluffdale Vacation Farm

Route 1, Box 145, 62027
(217) 983-2854

Our new hideaway cottage in the woods is secluded and luxurious. Soak in the whirlpool while you watch the sun set or gaze at the stars, then pop on a robe and enter your room where the fireplace is blazing. From the base of the bluffs, you'll have 200 acres of woodlands to explore by foot or horse. Whatever your recreational and culinary desires, you'll find them in our warmth and hospitality.

Hosts: Bill and Lindy Hobson
Rooms: 2 (PB) $90
Full Breakfast
Credit Cards: none
Notes: 2, 3, 4, 5, 7, 9, 10, 12

ELSAH

Maple Leaf Cottages

PO Box 156, 62028
(618) 374-1684

Fifty years as a midwestern B&B. We offer the tradition of the past with today's

Maple Leaf Cottages

quality hospitality. Fine food and lodging in a retreat garden setting. All accommodations have private full bath, bedroom, and sitting area. Breakfast is brought to your room. Come share in our jubilee year. Your "somewhere inn time" is now.

Hostess: Mrs. Patricia J. Taetz
Rooms: 5 (PB) $89-100
Full Breakfast
Credit Cards: none
Notes: 2, 5, 8, 9, 10

ELIZABETH

Brookside B&B

1298 E. Menzemer Road, 61028
(815) 845-2251

Situated between scenic lakes, a dramatic waterfall, picturesque golf courses, and a rustic lakeside restaurant/lounge in two beautiful resort developments, Brookside invites you to share the fun and spectacular views. Special accommodations are offered by our modern chateau, lodged above a stream in a secluded valley.

Hosts: Mariann and Bob Fitzgerald
Rooms: 3 (PB) $55-85
Full Breakfast
Credit Cards: A, B
Notes: 2, 5, 7 (older), 9, 10, 11

EVANSTON

The Margarita European Inn

1566 Oak Avenue, 60201
(847) 869-2273; FAX (847) 869-2353

The romantic at heart truly will enjoy this charming European-style inn located near Chicago in Evanston—the home of Northwestern University. You can relax in the inn's grand parlor with breakfast and the morning newspaper, and in the roof garden at sunset. You will love exploring the numerous antique and specialty shops nearby in Evanston. On rainy days, you may want to curl up with a novel from the wood-paneled English library, or indulge in a delightful culinary creation from our award-winning regional Italian ristorante, Va Pensiero. The Margarita European Inn offers facilities for weddings; special arrangements for business meetings also can be made.

Hosts: Barbara and Tim Gorham
Rooms: 44 (20PB; 24SB) $75-145
Continental Breakfast
Credit Cards: A, B, C, E
Notes: 3, 4, 5, 7, 8, 9, 10, 12

FAIRFIELD

Glass Door Inn

RR3, Box 101, 62837
(618) 847-4512
E-mail: gdinn@midwest.net
Web site: http://www.flinthills.com/~atway/il/glassdr.html

Nestled in a serene, rural setting, the inn is complete with televisions, telephones, VCRs, data ports, onsite computer, and FAX. Uniquely decorated rooms are located on the second floor surrounding a library/sitting area and a spacious porch. Outdoor spa, meeting room, and fishing on site. Private guest entrance.

Hosts: Linda and Richard Merrick
Rooms: 4 (PB) $53-65
Full Breakfast
Credit Cards: A, B, D
Notes: 5, 8, 9, 10, 12

GALENA

Accommodations and Reservations in and Around Galena

122 S. Bench Street, 61036
(815) 777-8400; FAX (815) 777-8446
E-mail: lodgings@galenareservations.com

This free service books many types of accommodations in Galena and the surrounding countryside: bed and breakfasts, country inns, historic properties, facilities for family reunions and retreats, cottages, apartments, and private vacation homes. Amenities and prices vary. Some locations welcome pets. Special attention is paid to match callers with just the accommodations they are looking for.

Avery Guest House

Avery Guest House

606 S. Prospect Street, 61036
(815) 777-3883
E-mail: avery@galenalink.com
Web site: http://www.worksweb.com/avery

This pre-Civil War home located near Galena's main shopping and historic buildings is a homey refuge after a day of exploring. Enjoy the view from our porch swing, feel free to watch TV, or join a table game. Sleep soundly on comfortable queen beds. Our delicious full breakfast is served in our sunny dining room with a bay window overlooking the valley. Mississippi riverboats nearby.

Hosts: Gerry and Armon Lamparelli
Rooms: 3 (1PB; 2SB) $65-90
Full Breakfast
Credit Cards: A, B, D
Notes: 2, 5, 8, 9, 10, 11

Belle Aire Mansion Guest House

11410 Route 20 W., 61036
(815) 777-0893
E-mail: belleair@galenalink.com
Web site: http://www.galena-bnb.com/belleaire

Belle Aire Mansion Guest House is a pre-Civil War Federal home surrounded by

11 well-groomed acres that include extensive lawns, flowers, and a block-long, tree-lined driveway. Whirlpool and fireplace suites are available. We do our best to make guests feel like special friends.

Hosts: Jan and Lorraine Svec
Rooms: 5 (PB) $70-155
Full Breakfast
Credit Cards: A, B, D
Notes: 2, 7, 8, 10, 12

Brierwreath Manor Bed and Breakfast

216 N. Bench Street, 61036
(815) 777-0608
Web site: http://www.galena-bnb.com

Brierwreath Manor, circa 1884, is just one block from Galena's Main Street and has a dramatic, inviting wraparound porch that beckons after a hard day. The house is furnished in an eclectic blend of antique and early American. You'll not only relax but feel right at home. Two suites offer gas log fireplaces; the third one has an extra twin-size bed. Central AC, ceiling fans, and cable TV add to your enjoyment.

Hosts: Mike and Lyn Cook
Rooms: 3 suites (PB) $85-105
Full Breakfast
Credit Cards: none
Notes: 2, 5, 8, 9, 10, 11

Captain Harris Guest House

713 S. Bench Street, 61036
(815) 777-4713; fax (815) 777-4723
Web site: http://www.galena-bnb.com

Circa-1836 home built by riverboat captain. Lovingly restored in 1920 with leaded-glass windows and doors by associate of F. Lloyd Wright, four guest rooms with private baths and cable TVs. Separate honeymoon cottage on property. Full formal breakfast. One block from Main Street shops and restaurants.

Hosts: Judy Dixon and Ed Schmit
Rooms: 4 (PB) $90-125
Full Breakfast
Credit Cards: A, B, D

Eagle's Nest

410 S. High Street, 61036
(815) 777-8400; FAX (815) 777-8446

Charming 1842 Federal brick cottage tucked into a wooded hillside in the historic district. Walking distance to shops, restaurants, most of Galena. Faithfully restored, furnished with period antiques. Living room with fireplace, master bedroom with queen bed, second bedroom with double bed. Full kitchen, bath with two-person tub, air-conditioning, television, VCR, stereo, phone. Landscaped yard, patio, grill, and small garden with fountain. Ideal for one couple; will comfortably accommodate two couples or a small family.

Hosts: Kate and Doug Freeman
Rooms: 1 cottage (PB) $99-169
Credit Cards: A, B, C, D, E
Notes: 2, 3, 4, 5, 6, 7, 8, 9, 10, 11, 12

Forget-Me-Not B&B

1467 N. Elizabeth Scales Mound Road, **Elizabeth,** 61028
(815) 858-3744 (voice and FAX, call first)
E-mail: forget-me-not@juno.com
Web site: http://www.flinthills.com/~atway/il/forgtnot.html

Enjoy peace, tranquillity, and natural beauty high on a ridge that overlooks a

Forget-Me-Not Bed and Breakfast

spectacular forest valley and panoramic countryside. Located on the eastern edge of Eagle Ridge Territory. Relax in the comforts of spacious rooms that will suit any occasion: romantic retreats, anniversaries, honeymoons, etc. Each guest room features a private bath, private entrance, queen bed, air-conditioning, and heat control. A hearty full breakfast is served daily. Songbirds greet you with each new day. Discover living nature on 23 acres of natural rolling forest trails, or just unwind on our deck, screened porch, or your private patio. Relax in a comfortable great room with large TV, imported furnishings, and rustic fireplace.

Hosts: Christa and Richard Grunert
Rooms: 3 (PB) $75-95
Full Breakfast
Credit Cards: A, B, D
Notes: 2, 5, 7 (12 and older), 8, 9, 10, 11

Hawk Valley Retreat

2752 W. Cording Road, 61036
(815) 777-4100 (voice and FAX)

French country-appointed home on 10 secluded acres, just 10 minutes from Galena off historic Stagecoach Trail. Three guest rooms (one handicap-equipped), each with private entrance, TV/VCR, and private bath. Panoramic views from every room. A wraparound deck provides the opportunity to watch the beauty of nature. Antique fireplaces in living room, book and video library, central air-conditioning, gardens, fishing pond, badminton, croquet, porch swing, picnic area. Hearty full breakfast. Limited one-night stays available. Packages and gift certificates. Off-season and multiple-night discounts.

Hosts: Fritz and Jane Fuchs
Rooms: 3 (PB) $85-95
Full Breakfast
Credit Cards: A, B, D
Notes: 2, 5, 7 (by arrangement), 8, 9, 10, 11

Hellman Guest House

Hellman Guest House

318 Hill Street, 61036
(815) 777-3638; FAX (815) 777-3658
E-mail: hellman@galenalink.com
Web site: http://www.galena.com/hellman

An 1859 Queen Anne Victorian with wraparound porch overlooking downtown and countryside, the Hellman Guest House has stained- and beveled-glass windows, original woodwork, pocket doors, and period decor. For guests' comfort and convenience, there are queen beds, private baths, central AC, parlor fireplaces, complimentary early morning coffee and tea, a full breakfast, and afternoon beverages for our guests.

Hostess: Merilyn Tommaro
Rooms: 4 (PB) $99-159
Full Breakfast
Credit Cards: A, B, D
Notes: 2, 5, 7 (over 10), 8, 9, 10, 11

Park Avenue Guest House

208 Park Avenue, 61036
(815) 777-1075
E-mail: parkave@galenalink.com
Web site: http://www.galena.com/parkave

This is an 1893 Queen Anne "painted lady." Wraparound, screened porch, gardens, and gazebo for summer. Fireplace and opulent Victorian Christmas in winter. One suite sleeps three, and there are three antique-filled guest rooms, all with queen-size beds and fireplaces. Located in a quiet residential area. Only a short walk to Grant Park or across a footbridge to Main Street shopping and restaurants.

Hosts: John and Sharon Fallbacher
Rooms: 4 (PB) $70-105
Full Breakfast
Credit Cards: A, B, D
Notes: 2, 5, 7, 8, 9, 10, 11

Snoop Sisters Inn

1000 Third Street, 61036
(815) 777-3062 (voice and FAX)

The Snoop Sisters Inn, located in beautiful, historic Galena, was built in 1858 and retains the charm of that bygone era. Whether you're here for a relaxed getaway, an adventure, or spending time with the family, many delights await you in the Galena area. The Snoop Sisters Inn is centrally located, providing easy access to the many activities and sights to enjoy. Our guest rooms are elegant while still maintaining the comfort you demand.

Hosts: Fran and Elouise
Rooms: 3 (PB) $75-95
Full Breakfast
Credit Cards: A, B
Notes: 2, 5, 7, 8, 9, 10, 11

GREENVILLE

Green Pastures

RR 1, Box 171, Hillsboro Road, 62246
(618) 664-4006
E-mail: robertlm@accessUS.net

Nestled on 52 rolling acres between two picturesque lakes lies a classic turn-of-the-century farm home. Newly remodeled in elegant country decor, each room is exquisite with antique chandeliers, custom drapes and bedspreads. Choose from among five romantic bedrooms with antique sleigh bed, high poster brass beds, Queen Anne cherry wood, cozy country farmhouse, or magnificent oak reproduction. In the morning, awaken to the aroma of fresh-brewed coffee, home-baked cinnamon rolls, sausage gravy, and biscuits.

Hosts: Pastors Robert and Dareda Mueller
Rooms: 5 (1PB; 4SB) $69-79
Full or Continental Breakfast
Credit Cards: A, B
Notes: 2, 4, 5, 8, 9, 10

HARRISBURG

House of Nahum

90 Sally Holler Lane, 62946
(618) 252-1414

New country home on 5 secluded acres neighboring Shawnee National Forest.

NOTES: Credit cards accepted: A Master Card; B Visa; C American Express; D Discover; E Diners Club; F Other; 2 Personal checks accepted; 3 Lunch available; 4 Dinner available; 5 Open all year; 6 Pets

Country-antique decor. Relax on the old-fashioned veranda. Enjoy a charming room with views of forest, creek, and flowers. Nestle before a fire or bask in a whirlpool for two in a beautiful suite. A bountiful breakfast is served on a deck overlooking the flower garden, or in the charming dining room.

Hostess: Sona Thomas
Rooms: 4 + 1 suite (PB) $73-120
Full Breakfast
Credit Cards: A, B (on request)
Notes: 2, 5, 8, 9, 10

JERSEYVILLE

The Homeridge Bed and Breakfast

1470 N. State Street, 62052
(618) 498-3442 (voice and FAX); (888) 368-6588
Web site: http://www.chioce-guide.com/il/homeridge

The Homeridge Bed and Breakfast is a beautiful, warm, brick 1867 Italianate Victorian private home on 18 acres in a comfortable country atmosphere. Drive through stately iron gates and a pine-lined driveway to the fourteen-room historic estate of Sen. Theodore Chapman. Expansive, pillared front porch; hand-carved, curved stairway to the spacious guest rooms. Large swimming pool. Central AC. Located between Springfield, Illinois, and St. Louis, Missouri.

Hosts: Sue and Howard Landon
Rooms: 4 (PB) $75-85
Full Breakfast
Credit Cards: A, B, C
Notes: 2, 5, 7 (over 14), 8, 9 (on grounds), 10

MAEYSTOWN

Corner George Inn

1101 Main Street, 62256
(618) 458-6660; (800) 458-6020;
FAX (618) 458-7770
E-mail: cornrgeo@htc.net
Web site: http://www.rivervalleyinns.com

A frontier Victorian structure built in 1884, when it was known as the Maeystown Hotel and Saloon, the Corner George Inn has been painstakingly restored. In addition to the seven antique-filled guest rooms, there are two sitting rooms and an elegant ballroom, where David and Marcia serve breakfast. Maeystown is a quaint 19th-century village; guests can tour it on a bicycle built for two or aboard a horse-drawn carriage. Nearby are St. Louis, Fort de Chartres, Fort Kaskaskia, and the scenic Mississippi bluff road.

Hosts: David and Marcia Braswell
Rooms: 7 (PB) $67-149
Full Breakfast
Credit Cards: A, B, C, D
Notes: 2, 5, 7 (with parental supervision), 10, 12

MINONK

Victorian Oaks Bed & Breakfast

435 Locust Street, 61760-1338
(309) 432-2771; FAX (309) 432-3309
E-mail: locust@davesworld.net
Web site: http://www.angelfire.com/biz/victorianoaks/index.html

One of the few B&Bs that will let you choose what you want for breakfast and will serve it at the time you choose. Your stay is customized around your wishes and your schedule. We are centrally located so that our guests can plan a variety of day trips.

Hostess: Sharon Kimzey
Rooms: 5 (up to 3 PB; 4 SB) $75-100 (seasonal)
Full Breakfast
Credit Cards: A, B, D
Notes: 3, 4, 5, 6, 7, 8, 9, 10, 12

MOUNT CARMEL

The Poor Farm B&B

Poor Farm Road, 62863-9803
(618) 262-HOME (4663);
(800) 646-FARM (3276); FAX (618) 262-8199
E-mail: poorfarm@midwest.net

From 1857 to 1949, the Wabash Country Poor Farm served as a home for the homeless. Today the Poor Farm B&B is a home for the traveler who enjoys a warm, friendly atmosphere and a gracious glimpse of yesteryear. Located next to a 25-acre park with a well-stocked lake; within walking distance of perhaps the finest eighteen-hole municipal golf course in Illinois. A 15-minute drive lands you in the spectacular 640-acre Beall Woods Conservation Area and Nature Preserve!

Hosts: Liz and John Stelzer
Rooms: 5 (2 suites and 3 doubles) (PB) $49-89
Full Country Breakfast
Credit Cards: A, B, C, D
Notes: 2, 3 and 4 (for groups of 10-30), 5, 7, 8, 9, 10, 12

NAUVOO

Mississippi Memories

1 Riverview Terrace, 62354
(217) 453-2771

Located on the banks of the Mississippi, this gracious home offers peaceful lodging and an elegantly served, all-homemade, full breakfast. Each room features fresh fruit and flowers. In quiet, wooded surroundings, it's just 2 miles from historic Nauvoo with thirty restored Mormon-era homes and shops. Two decks offer spectacular sunsets, drifting barges, bald eagle watching, a grand piano, two fireplaces, and a library. Inspected by two motor clubs. No smoking, alcohol, or pets will interrupt your stay.

Hosts: Marge and Dean Starr
Rooms: 4 (2PB; 2SB) $49-95
Full Breakfast
Credit Cards: A, B
Notes: 2, 5, 10

NEBO

Harpole's Heartland Lodge

RR 1, Box 8A, 62355
(217) 222-0899; (800) 717-4868;
FAX (217) 222-6361
E-mail: hartland@bcl.net
Web site: http://www.bcl.net/~hartland

This rustic but luxurious, fully accommodated oak lodge (from feather pillows to Ralph Lauren towels) is the Midwest's best-kept secret. Prices include beautifully decorated rooms with private baths, two

NOTES: Credit cards accepted: A Master Card; B Visa; C American Express; D Discover; E Diners Club; F Other; 2 Personal checks accepted; 3 Lunch available; 4 Dinner available; 5 Open all year; 6 Pets

made-from-scratch meals for each guest, recreation and great rooms, hayrides, hiking, fishing, bird-watching, and equestrian stables. Suite: king bed with Jacuzzi. Family room: queen bed with bunk beds. Mark Twain, Abraham Lincoln, and St. Louis attractions. Reservations required.

Hosts: Wanda Harpole and Gary D. Harpole II
Rooms: 28 (13 PB) $125-175
Two Full Meals per Guest (dinner/brunch)
Credit Cards: A, B, C, D
Notes: 2, 4, 5, 7, 8, 9, 12

OAKLAND

Inn on the Square

3 Montgomery Street, 61943
(217) 346-2289

Located 20 minutes from Eastern Illinois University, the inn specializes in fine food and friendly atmosphere. Best of all is the return of bed and breakfast tourism. Blending the old with the new, we offer warm hospitality and simple country pleasures, as well as historical sites, recreational activities, shopping, and plain old sittin' and rockin'. Three upstairs bedrooms are comfortably furnished for country living, each with a private bath.

Hosts: Gary and Linda Miller
Rooms: 3 (PB) $55-60
Full Breakfast
Credit Cards: A, B
Notes: 2, 3 (Monday-Saturday), 4 (Friday-Sunday), 5, 7, 9, 10, 12

Johnson's Country Home

109 E. Main Street, 61943
(217) 346-3274

This two-story brick Italianate-style home was built in 1874 by L.S. Cash. It has been home to the Johnson family for more than 25 years. After extensive renovations, the home today is restored to its original grandeur, decorated with period furnishings to accentuate its rich history. The Johnsons lovingly share their home. Two blocks east of the town square on Main Street. Open April 15–October 15.

Hosts: Reece and June Johnson
Rooms: 2 (SB) $40-50
Continental Breakfast
Credit Cards: none
Notes: 2, 6, 7, 8, 9, 10

ONARGA

Dairy on the Prairie

1437 N. State Route 49, 60955
(815) 683-2774

Situated among miles of corn and soybean fields on God's prairie is this recently remodeled homestead that has been "in the family" since 1892. Three tall silos and Holstein cows await you at the modern dairy/grain family farm. Enjoy the piano, organ, or keyboard along with hearty food, "down on the farm" hospitality, and a Christian atmosphere.

Hosts: Ken and Martha Redeker
Rooms: 3 (SB) $40-60
Full Breakfast (Continental on request)
Credit Cards: none
Notes: 2, 5, 7, 8, 9, 10

OTTAWA

Prairie Rivers B&B

121 E. Prospect Avenue, 61350
(815) 434-3226; (888) 288-2659 (pin 5918)

A comfortable, friendly, private place where you are free to come and go as you would in your own home. Spacious 1890 New England Queen Anne with great views of the Illinois and Fox Rivers. Gateway to four state parks, historic I&M canal, golf, hiking, canoeing. A "knife and fork" breakfast is served with fresh fruit in season. Gardens, porch, patio, and grill.

Hosts: Carole and Ed Mayer
Rooms: 3 (PB) $80-125
Full Breakfast
Credit Cards: A, B
Notes: 2, 5, 7, 8, 10, 11 (cross-country)

QUINCY

The Kaufmann House

1641 Hampshire Street, 62301
(217) 223-2502

Nestled among majestic trees and lush gardens, our eclectic Queen Anne is in the heart of the historic district. We have lovingly restored it and filled it with abundant antiques. Your comfort and pleasure are of utmost importance. You'll delight in your breakfast of fresh pastries and fruit and our special blend of piping-hot coffee. Relax and prepare to be pampered.

Hosts: Emery and Bettie Kaufmann
Rooms: 3 (PB) $70
Gourmet Continental Breakfast
Credit Cards: F
Notes: 2, 5, 7, 8, 9, 10

ROCKFORD

The Barn of Rockford

6786 Guilford Road, 61107
(815) 395-8535; (888) 378-1729

Experience country living within the city limits of Illinois's second-largest city. Just minutes from a wide variety of shopping, fine dining, and one of the Midwest's best selections of antiques. Relax and explore our 110-year-old restored and converted barn. Walk through perennial gardens or swim in the indoor pool. Then start your day with a sure-to-delight breakfast!

Hosts: Ken and Karen Sharp
Rooms: 4 (1PB; 3SB) $65-95
Full Breakfast
Credit Cards: A, B, D
Notes: 2, 5, 8, 9, 10, 11

SPRINGFIELD

Country Dreams B&B

3410 Park Lane, **Rochester,** 62563
(217) 498-9210; FAX (214) 498-8178
E-mail: host@countrydreams.com
Web site: http://www.countrydreams.com

After spending an enjoyable but busy day visiting the Lincoln sites or just needing a break from the children, pamper yourself and your special one at a relaxing country retreat, a safe and quiet rural setting only 10 minutes from downtown Springfield. Country Dreams welcomes you to a homey getaway—a romantic suite, complete with a cozy fireplace, whirlpool tub, and sumptuously delicious homemade breakfast, served graciously by your hosts.

Hosts: Ralph and Kay Muhs
Rooms: 4 (PB) $75-125
Full Breakfast weekends, Continental weekdays
Credit Cards: A, B, C
Notes: 2, 4, 5 (sometimes), 8, 9, 10, 12

Country Dreams Bed and Breakfast

NOTES: Credit cards accepted: A Master Card; B Visa; C American Express; D Discover; E Diners Club; F Other; 2 Personal checks accepted; 3 Lunch available; 4 Dinner available; 5 Open all year; 6 Pets

Indiana

ALEXANDRIA

Country Gazebo Inn

13867 N. 100 W., 46001
(765) 754-8783 (voice and FAX)
E-mail: ccunningham@iquest.net
Web site: http://www.innsite.com
(push "Browse," then "Indiana")

The inn is a lovely 40-year-old white, maroon-trimmed farmhouse surrounded by 15 rolling acres, 3 miles northwest of Alexandria. A 1,000-foot brick addition was added in 1997. Accommodations include a central bath, whirlpool tub, private phone, and new TV in each newly decorated, spacious room. Rooms have one bed each—king, queen, or regular. A roll-away may be provided for $15 in three rooms, which includes breakfast.

Hostess: Carolyn Cunningham
Rooms: 6 (3PB; 3SB) $45-70
Full Breakfast
Credit Cards: none
Notes: 2, 5, 6 (limited), 7, 8, 9, 10, 12

BEVERLY SHORES

Dunes Shore Inn

33 Lakeshore County Road, 46301-0807
(219) 879-9029

The Dunes Shore Inn is a quiet, informal B&B 1 block from Lake Michigan. We are surrounded by the Indiana Dunes, yet are only 1 hour from Chicago. Miles of wooded trails and beaches await you.

Hosts: Rosemary and Fred Braun
Rooms: 10 (PB) $60
Continental Breakfast
Credit Cards: none
Notes: 2, 7, 8, 9, 10

BLUFFTON

Washington Street Inn

220 E. Washington Street, 46714
(219) 824-9070
E-mail: schaffer@ssi.parlorcity.com
Web site: http://www.bbonline.com/in/washington/index.html

For those who desire to stay "somewhere else," we invite you to spend time with us

Washington Street Inn

---

welcome; 7 Children welcome; 8 Tennis nearby; 9 Swimming nearby; 10 Golf nearby; 11 Skiing nearby; 12 May be booked through travel agent.

INDIANA

Beverly Shores
94
80
80
Shipshewana
Middlebury
Valparaiso
Goshen
Millersburg
Schererville
Walkerton
Nappanee
Tippecanoe
Silver Lake
Huntington
65
Monticello
Peru
Bluffton
Hartford
City
Alexandria
69
Muncie
Covington
Middletown
74
Shirley
70
Indianapolis
Knightstown
Richmond
Rushville
70
74
Nashville
Osgood
65
Madison
Vevay
West Baden Springs
New Albany
64
64
Corydon
164

in our century-old home. The inn is decorated in a "comfortable Victorian" atmosphere. The art of master woodworkers is evident throughout. Two cherry fireplaces grace the first floor. A small guest kitchen with a refrigerator and microwave is available for guests' use. Business travelers welcome.

Hosts: Tammy and Tim Schaffer
Rooms: 4 (SB) $60
Full Breakfast weekends, Continental weekdays
Credit Cards: A, B
Notes: 2, 5, 9, 10, 12

CORYDON

The Kintner House Inn Bed and Breakfast

101 S. Capital Avenue, 47112
(812) 738-2020; FAX (812) 738-7430

This historic bed and breakfast was built in 1873, restored in 1986. Fifteen elegant guest rooms all have private baths and televisions; five have fireplaces, and eight have VCRs. Antique furnishings are in all the rooms. It is a nonsmoking facility. The home is open year-round. The first floor is handicap-accessible. Listed on the National Register of Historic Places and featured on two 1991 Hallmark™ Christmas cards. A hideaway for romantics, the inn is located in historic downtown Corydon, Indiana's first state capital.

Hostess: Dee Windell
Rooms: 15 (PB) $49-99
Full Breakfast
Credit Cards: A, B, C, D

COVINGTON

Green Gables Bed and Breakfast

504 Fancy Street, 47932
(765) 793-7164

Covington's first bed and breakfast offers three guest rooms, each with a private bath, including the spacious loft with its two queen-size beds. Each guest room has a television. New air-conditioning is available throughout the house. Home-cooked breakfasts are served beside the private, in-ground pool or beside one of two fireplaces. This hilltop home is located near I–74 in western Indiana, only 5 miles from Indiana's finest steakhouse. ArtFest in May and AppleFest in October, both on the courthouse lawn.

Hosts: Bill and Marsha Wilkinson
Rooms: 3 (PB) $70
Full Breakfast
Credit Cards: A, B, C
Notes: 2, 5, 8, 9, 10

Indian Creek Bed and Breakfast

GOSHEN

Indian Creek B&B

20300 County Road 18, 46528-9513
(219) 875-6606; FAX (219) 875-3968
E-mail: 71224.1462@compuserve.com
Web site: http://www.bestinns.net/usa/in/IndianCreek.html

Come and enjoy our newly built country Victorian home in the middle of Amish country. It is decorated with family antiques. Walk back to the woods or sit on the deck to watch for deer. Also enjoy the great room, game room, and family room. Full breakfast. Children welcome. Handicap-accessible.

Hosts: Shirley and Herman Hochstetler
Rooms: 5 (PB) $79
Full Breakfast
Credit Cards: A, B, C, D
Notes: 2, 5, 7, 8, 9, 10, 12

Prairie Manor B&B

66398 U.S. 33 S., 46526
(219) 642-4761; (800) 791-3952;
FAX (219) 642-4762
E-mail: jeston@npcc.net
Web site: http://www.prairiemanor.com

Prairie Manor, our historic English country manor–style home, is situated on 12 acres. The living room replicates the builder's favorite painting at the Metropolitan Museum of Art: an English baronial hall. The house has many interesting architectural details such as arched doorways, wainscoting, and hidden compartments. A variety of activities include antiquing, the famous Shipshewana auction and flea market, and other attractions in northern Indiana Amish country.

Hosts: Jean and Hesston Lauver
Rooms: 4 (PB) $70-95
Full Breakfast
Credit Cards: A, B, D
Notes: 2, 5, 7, 9, 10, 12

Prairie Manor Bed and Breakfast

Spring View Bed and Breakfast

63189 County Road 31, 46528
(219) 642-3997; FAX (219) 642-2697

Specializing in country hospitality, this new bed and breakfast is located in the heart of Amish country. Relax as you stroll around our waterfront or rest in the gentle breeze of the screened lakeside sitting room. Walk the quiet trail on our spacious 48 acres. Enjoy a luxurious steam bath or whirlpool tub in the privacy of your own room. Two-bedroom suite available.

NOTES: Credit cards accepted: A Master Card; B Visa; C American Express; D Discover; E Diners Club; F Other; 2 Personal checks accepted; 3 Lunch available; 4 Dinner available; 5 Open all year; 6 Pets

Amish neighbors, Amish buggy rides available. Fishing and paddleboating.

Hosts: Phil and Roz Slabaugh
Rooms: 6 (5PB; 1SB) $59-79
Full Breakfast
Credit Cards: A, B, C, D
Notes: 2, 5, 10

De'Coy's Bed and Breakfast

HARTFORD CITY

De'Coy's Bed and Breakfast

1546 W. 100 N., 47348
(765) 348-2164 (voice and FAX)

Situated just west of Hartford City, De'Coy's Bed and Breakfast is conveniently located near Taylor University, Ball State University, and Indiana Wesleyan College. This charming country home offers its guests extraordinarily attractive accommodations with many extra special Hoosier touches. Visitors can relax in the quiet rural atmosphere of this old, restored home, enriched with many amenities not customary to the typical motel or hotel setting. Each room demonstrates its own character with antique furnishings and comfortable arrangements.

Hosts: Chris and Tiann Coy
Rooms: 5 (3PB, 2SB) $52-75
Full Breakfast
Credit Cards: none
Notes: 2, 5, 7, 12

HUNTINGTON

Purviance House B&B

326 S. Jefferson Street, 46750
(219) 356-9215

Built in 1859, this beautiful home is on the National Register of Historic Places. It features a winding staircase, ornate ceilings, unique fireplaces, and parquet floors. It has been lovingly restored and decorated with antiques and period furnishings. Amenities include TVs in the guest rooms, snacks, beverages, kitchen privileges, and library. Purviance House Bed and Breakfast is located near recreational areas with swimming, boating, hiking, bicycling. Historic tours. One-half hour from Fort Wayne, 2 hours from Indianapolis.

Hosts: Robert and Jean Gernand
Rooms: 5 (2PB; 3SB) $50-65
Full Breakfast
Credit Cards: A, B, D
Notes: 2, 5, 7, 8, 9, 10, 12

INDIANAPOLIS

Friendliness With a Flair

5214 E. 20th Place, 46218
(317) 356-3149

Two beautifully furnished rooms in a residential section of the city, about 12-15 minutes from the heart of the city. Driveway parking available. A bountiful breakfast is served—weather permitting, in an outside, glassed-in Florida-type dining area. As private as you wish.

Hostess: Loretta Whitten
Rooms: 2 (PB) $55
Full Breakfast
Credit Cards: none
Notes: 2, 5, 10

The Old Northside Bed and Breakfast

The Old Northside Bed and Breakfast

1340 N. Alabama Street, 46202
(317) 635-9123; (800) 635-9123 (reservations only); FAX (317) 635-9243
E-mail: oldnorth@indy.net
Web site: http://www.hofmeister.com/b&b.htm

The Old Northside Bed and Breakfast is an 1885 luxurious Victorian mansion located in the historic downtown, convenient to I–65, I–70, and city attractions. It represents the city's finest example of Romanesque Revival architecture with elegant European turn-of-the-century decor. The home features themed rooms with Jacuzzi tubs in private baths—two with fireplaces. Guests may use the exercise room, conference room, and corporate services. A personal coffee service is delivered to your room before your full gourmet breakfast each morning. Complimentary snack and exceptional service.

Hostess: Susan Berry
Rooms: 6 (PB) $95-165
Full Breakfast weekends, Continental weekdays
Credit Cards: A, B, C, D
Notes: 2 (10 days in advance), 5, 8, 9, 10, 12

Our Country Home Bed, Breakfast, Stables & Carriage Co.

PO Box 51762, 46251
(765) 794-3139

Enjoy the beautiful sunrises, colorful sunsets, and canopy of stars that make the country so relaxing. Listen to the chirp of the birds, the babble of the creek, or the clip-clop of the horse as you ride through the countryside in a carriage. Horseback riding, a hot tub, swimming, a telescope, and a bicycle built for two will add to your memories. In the winter you can curl up by the fireplace or go for a sleigh ride. Private candlelight dinners, hearty country breakfasts and a generous share of Hoosier hospitality will make your country getaway special. All this and more awaits you at Our Country Home, where you come as a guest and leave as a friend!

Hosts: The Smith Family
Rooms: 3+ (SB) $75-130
Full Breakfast
Credit Cards: A, B, C, D
Notes: 2, 3, 4, 5, 7, 9, 10, 12

KNIGHTSTOWN

Old Hoosier House Bed and Breakfast

7601 S. Greensboro Pike, 46148
(765) 345-2969; (800) 775-5315

Central Indiana's first and favorite country bed and breakfast, located in historic Knightstown, midway between Indianapolis and Richmond. The Old Hoosier

House is ideally situated for sight-seeing and shopping in Indiana's "Antique Alley." Our guests may enjoy golf on the adjoining eighteen-hole Royal Highlands golf course; a golf package is available. The bed and breakfast is handicap-accessible. It is a member of the Indiana Bed and Breakfast Association and the American Historic Inn, Inc.

Hosts: Tom Lewis and Jean Lewis
Rooms: 4 (PB) $60-70
Full Breakfast
Credit Cards: none
Notes: 2, 5, 7, 8, 9, 10, 12

Schussler House Bed and Breakfast

MADISON

Schussler House Bed and Breakfast

514 Jefferson Street, 47250
(812) 273-2068; (800) 392-1931

Experience the quiet elegance of a circa-1849 Federal/Greek Revival home tastefully combined with today's modern amenities. Located in Madison's historic district, where antique shops, historic sites, restaurants, and churches are within a pleasant walking distance. This gracious home offers spacious rooms decorated with antiques and reproductions and carefully selected fabrics and wall coverings. A sumptuous breakfast in the sun-filled dining room begins your day.

Hosts: Judy and Bill Gilbert
Rooms: 3 (PB) $99
Full Breakfast
Credit Cards: A, B, D
Notes: 2, 5, 8, 9, 10, 12

MIDDLEBURY

Auer House

11584 County Road 14, 46540
(219) 825-5366
E-mail: auerbnb@juno.com
Web site: http://www.auerhouse.com

"Auer" beautiful old renovated farmhouse is located just 1 mile north of Middlebury and 5 miles west of Shipshewana. Auer House offers a tranquil country setting with acres of farmland surrounding our home. Come and relax in "Auer" large gazebo beside the flower/rock garden or the in-ground pool after attending the flea market or visiting the Amish country sights.

Hosts: John and Carol Auer
Rooms: 5 (4PB; 1SB) $65-70
Full Breakfast
Credit Cards: none
Notes: 2, 5, 7, 8, 9, 10

Bee Hive Bed and Breakfast

Box 1191, 46540
(219) 825-5023

Come visit Amish country and enjoy our Hoosier hospitality. The Bee Hive Bed and

Breakfast is a two-story, open-floor plan with exposed, hand-sawn, red oak beams and a loft. Enjoy our collection of antique farm machinery and other collectibles. Snuggle under handmade quilts and wake in the morning to the smell of freshly baked muffins. A guest cottage is available. Be one of our many return guests, and become a friend.

Hosts: Herb and Treva Swarm
Rooms: 4 (1PB; 3SB) $52-70
Full Breakfast
Credit Cards: A, B
Notes: 2, 5, 7, 8, 9, 10, 11

Bee Hive Bed and Breakfast

Bontreger Guest Rooms

10766 County Road 16, 46540
(219) 825-2647

Located between Middlebury and Shipshewana on a county road in an Amish neighborhood. Cozy rooms and common room located away from family space. Continental breakfast in sunroom. Private bath. Smoke-free.

Hosts: Tom and Ruby Bontreger
Rooms: 2 (PB) $50
Continental Plus Breakfast
Credit Cards: none
Notes: 2, 7, 9, 10

Country Victorian Bed and Breakfast

435 S. Main Street, 46540
(219) 825-2568; (800) BNB-STAY (262-7829);
FAX (219) 825-3411
E-mail: stay@countryvictorian.com
Web site: http://www.countryvictorian.com

Come celebrate 100 years of lovely Victorian living. Our large home is a fully updated Victorian with lots of charm and original style, located in the heart of Amish country. Relax on the front porch and watch buggies drive by. In colder months, sit by the fireplace to chat or curl up with a good book. Get pampered and experience the loving family atmosphere where children are a pleasure! Honeymoon suite with Jacuzzi. Bicycle rental. Special packages available. Very accessible to Indiana's toll road (I–80/90) and close to Shipshewana. Other attractions include Amish-style restaurants and crafters, community festivals, University of Notre Dame, and Goshen College.

Hosts: Mark and Becky Potterbaum
Rooms: 5 (PB) $69-109
Full Breakfast
Credit Cards: A, B, C, D
Notes: 2, 5, 7, 8, 10, 11, 12

Essenhaus Country Inn

240 U.S. 20, 46540
(219) 825-9471; (800) 455-9471;
FAX (219) 825-1303
Web site: http://www.essenhaus.com

Essenhaus Country Inn is your home away from home. It's a place where you can relax and be yourself. You will be delighted with your elegant country-style room, our spacious atrium lobby, and our friendly Amish hospitality. Take a stroll through the

Essenhaus Country Inn

old-fashioned flower gardens or steal a snooze beneath one of our colorful, hand-stitched quilts. "You'll be right at home in Amish Country." Call us today; we're waiting to be your hosts.

Hosts: Wilbur and Rosalie Bontrager
Rooms: 40 (PB)
Credit Cards: A, B, D
Notes: 3, 4, 5, 7, 9, 10, 11, 12

A Laber of Love —B&B by Lori

11030 County Road 10, 46540
(219) 825-7877
E-mail: Laberelm@juno.com

This Cape Cod home is located in northern Indiana Amish farm country on 3 acres, 2 of which are wooded. A screened-in gazebo in the woods is ideal for quiet time or just relaxing. Guest quarters offer queen-size beds and private baths. A common game/sitting room is available for guests. Air-conditioned for year-round comfort. (Guest rooms are located upstairs.) A Laber of Love is situated close to a large flea market, open from May to October on Tuesdays and Wednesdays. Visitors will find lots of shopping in Middlebury and Shipshewana. Home-baked cinnamon rolls highlight breakfast each morning. This is a smoke-free B&B.

Hostess: Lori Laber
Rooms: 2 (PB) $55
Continental Breakfast
Credit Cards: none
Notes: 2, 5, 10, 12

Meadows Inn Bed and Breakfast

Meadows Inn B&B

12013 U.S. 20, 46540
(219) 825-3913; (888) 868-3913;
FAX (219) 768-7174

Located in the heart of Indiana Amish country where quilts, furniture, shops, and restaurants are plentiful. A restored Amish farmstead, Meadows Inn is the warm, comfortable home away from home for any traveler. Situated by the Spring Meadow Golf Club, an award-winning course. Hosted by a Mennonite couple who can share the Amish and Mennonite lifestyle with you. All beds are queen or king with large sitting room; dining area and deck overlooking the golf course. We look forward to your visit!

Hosts: Beth and Ryan Hershberger
Rooms: 5 (PB) $69-99
Continental Breakfast
Credit Cards: A, B
Notes: 2, 5, 8, 9, 10

The Patchwork Quilt Country Inn

11748 County Road 2, 46540
(219) 825-2417; FAX (219) 825-5172
E-mail: rgminn@aol.com

Relax and enjoy the simple grace and charm of our 100-year-old farmhouse. Sample our country cooking with homemade breads and desserts. Complete your visit with one of our 4-hour guided Amish back-road tours. Our knowledgeable guides will drive you along little-known byways deep in the heart of Amish country near our inn. Visit our Amish handmade quilt and wall-hanging shop. Inquire about our hands-on quilt and craft projects. Smoke-free, charming rooms.

Hosts: Ray and Rosetta Miller
Rooms: 15 (PB) $70-100
Full Breakfast
Credit Cards: A, B
Notes: 2, 3, 4, 8, 10, 11, 12

That Pretty Place Bed and Breakfast Inn

212 U.S. 20, 46540
(219) 825-3021
E-mail: inbasket@thatprettyplace.com
Web site: http://www.thatprettyplace.com

Enjoy the seclusion of a country setting within the heart of Amish country. All rooms with private baths; one is a honeymoon suite with heart-shaped whirlpool tub. Close to Shipshewana flea market. All rooms have TV, central air. Hot, full breakfast is served and can be eaten in our dining room or out on the deck—both overlook our own private pond. Member of the Indiana Bed and Breakfast Association and the 4-Seasons Bed and Breakfast Association.

Hosts: Regina and Steve Troyer
Rooms: 4 + honeymoon suite (PB) $70-90
Full Breakfast
Credit Cards: A, B, D
Notes: 2, 5, 10

Yoder's Zimmer Mit Frühstück Haus

PO Box 1396, 46540
(219) 825-2378

We enjoy sharing our Amish-Mennonite heritage in our spacious Crystal Valley home. The rooms feature handmade quilts and antiques. Antiques and collectibles can be seen throughout the home. Three of our rooms can accommodate families. Several common rooms are available for relaxing, reading, television, games, or socializing. Facilities are also available for pastor-elder retreats. Air-conditioning, playground, swimming pool.

Hosts: Wilbur and Evelyn Yoder
Rooms: 5 (SB) $52.50
Full Breakfast
Credit Cards: A, B
Notes: 2, 5, 7, 8, 9, 10, 11, 12

MIDDLETOWN

The Cornerstone Guest House

705 High Street, 47356
(765) 354-6004; (800) 792-6004

Situated in the small, quiet town of Middletown, The Cornerstone Guest House is an elegant place to stay. The 90-year-old prairie-style home has original oak woodwork and flooring and is decorated tastefully in period styles. Coffee is brought to your room an hour before breakfast, and a full breakfast is served in the formal dining room. Cornerstone Guest House is 10 minutes from Interstate 69 and 40 minutes northeast of Indianapolis.

Hosts: Dave and Debbie Lively
Rooms: 2 + 1 suite (PB) $75-95
Full Breakfast
Credit Cards: A, B
Notes: 2, 5, 10

Country Rose Bed and Breakfast

5098 N. Mechanicsburg Road, 47356
(765) 779-4501; (800) 395-6449

A small-town bed and breakfast looking out on berry patches and a flower garden. Awake early or late to a delicious full breakfast. Only 50 minutes from Indianapolis, 20 minutes from Anderson and Ball State universities.

Hosts: Rose and Jack Lewis
Rooms: 2 (1 suite, 1SB) $55-75
Full Breakfast
Credit Cards: none
Notes: 2, 5, 7, 8, 10

MILLERSBURG

Big House in the Little Woods

4245 S. 1000 W., 46543
(219) 593-9076

Situated along a quiet country road in the heart of the Amish and Mennonite community, located in a small woods which isolates it from the surrounding countryside. The 4,000-square-foot home was newly built in 1993–1994. The bedrooms are located upstairs; each is uniquely decorated with both antiques and new furniture. Each room has a TV and central air. King or queen beds.

Hosts: Sarah and Jacob Stolzfus
Rooms: 4 (PB) $65-85
Full Breakfast
Credit Cards: A, B, D
Notes: 2, 5

MONTICELLO

Quiet Water Bed and Breakfast

4794 E. Harbor Court, 47960-1256
(219) 583-6023; FAX (219) 583-5981
E-mail: QuietBnB@aol.com
Web site: http://members.aol.com/QuietBnB/index.html

Within walking distance of famous Indiana Beach Amusement Park. Our four new guest rooms await your arrival. Relax in the Ivy, Quilt, or Paisly Rooms, or the large Southwest Room with its own Jacuzzi tub. Enjoy breakfast on the spacious deck overlooking beautiful Lake Shafer. Visit the antique and specialty shops in town. Golf on one of the three local courses, and take pleasure in the fine or casual dining Monticello has to offer. Cable TV and central air are in each room. The cookie jar is always open. All four rooms are handicap-accessible.

Hostess: Ola Bergdall
Rooms: 4 (PB) $50-80
Full or Continental Breakfast
Credit Cards: A, B, D
Notes: 2, 5, 6, 7, 8, 9, 10, 12

MUNCIE

Ole Ball Inn Bed and Breakfast

1000 W. Wayne Street, 47303
(765) 281-0466; (800) 252-0262;
FAX (765) 281-6439

Coming through Muncie for business or a university visit? You have a welcome awaiting you at the Ole Ball Inn! Queen-size beds, TV, local phone in each room, plus a full breakfast. Three blocks from campus and close to the restaurant strip.

Manager: Helen Kreps
Rooms: 3 + 1 suite (PB) $55-95
Full Breakfast
Credit Cards: A, B
Notes: 2, 5, 7, 12

NAPPANEE

Olde Buffalo Inn Bed and Breakfast

1061 Parkwood Drive, 46550
(219) 773-2223; (888) 773-2223;
FAX (219) 773-4275

Step back in time to an era that was peaceful and serene. The Olde Buffalo Inn has all of today's amenities and lots of 19th-century charm. The inn is surrounded by a white picket fence and a restored red barn, traditional windmill, carriage house, brick sidewalk, and east patio. The inn is set on 2½ acres with a beautiful view of the golf course.

Hosts: The Lakins
Rooms: 6 (PB) $79-109
Full Breakfast
Credit Cards: A, B, D
Notes: 2, 5, 8, 9, 10, 12

Victorian Guest House

302 E. Market Street, 46542
(219) 773-4383

Antiques, stained-glass windows, and pocket doors highlight this 1887 Historical Register mansion. Nestled amongst the Amish countryside where antique shops abound. A warm welcome awaits as you return to gracious living with all the ambience of the 1800s. Everything has been designed to make your bed and breakfast stay a memorable one. Close to Notre Dame and Shipshewana. Two hours from Chicago. Complimentary evening tea and sweets. "Prepare for a memory."

Hosts: Bruce and Vickie Hunsberger
Rooms: 6 (PB) $49-119
Full Breakfast
Credit Cards: A, B, D
Notes: 2, 5, 8, 9, 10

NASHVILLE

Day Star Inn

Box 361, 47448
(812) 988-0430

A friendly, homey atmosphere awaits as you retreat to the heart of Nashville's unique downtown shopping area. Short drive to Brown County State Park, golf courses, and other recreational areas. Five clean rooms can accommodate up to twenty-two guests (including children, if well-supervised). AC, cable television, private bath, and parking for guests. No smoking, alcohol, or pets, please.

Host: Edwin K. Taggart
Rooms: 5 (PB) $80-95
Continental Breakfast
Credit Cards: A, B, D
Notes: 2, 5, 7, 8, 9, 10, 11, 12

NOTES: Credit cards accepted: A Master Card; B Visa; C American Express; D Discover; E Diners Club; F Other; 2 Personal checks accepted; 3 Lunch available; 4 Dinner available; 5 Open all year; 6 Pets

NEW ALBANY

Honeymoon Mansion Bed and Breakfast Inn and Wedding Chapel

1014 E. Main Street, 47150
(812) 945-0312; (800) 759-7270
E-mail: honeymoonmansion@juno.com
Web site: http://www.bbonline.com/indiana/honeymoon

Honeymoon Mansion has six lovely suites with private baths, marble Jacuzzis, and 8-foot-high marble columns. Our guests will enjoy queen-size, hand-carved cherry beds with lace-covered canopies. Stained-glass windows, grand staircase. Our wedding chapel seats seventy and has an ordained minister on staff; guests can marry or renew their vows. The mansion, built in 1850, is on the National Register of Historic Homes. A 10-percent discount is offered Sunday through Thursday. Senior citizens' discount.

Hosts: Franklin and Beverly Dennis
Rooms: 6 (PB) $70-140
Full Breakfast
Credit Cards: A, B, C, D
Notes: 2, 5, 8, 9, 10, 11, 12

OSGOOD

Victorian Garden Bed and Breakfast

243 N. Walnut Street, 47037
(812) 689-4469

The Victorian Garden is a beautiful 1895 Victorian home. It features golden oak woodwork, gingerbread, and pocket doors. The bedrooms are all comfortably furnished, clean and cheerful, and have air-conditioning. Awaken to an abundant breakfast served in the dining room. Guests are encouraged to feel at home on the wraparound porch, enjoy the garden gazebo, or sit and bird-watch on our patio.

Hosts: Paul and Linda Krinop
Rooms: 3 (2PB; 1SB) $75-85
Full Breakfast
Credit Cards: A, B
Notes: 5, 7, 9, 10

Rosewood Mansion Inn

PERU

Rosewood Mansion Inn

54 N. Hood Street, 46970
(765) 472-7151; FAX (765) 472-5575
E-mail: rosewood@netusa1.net
Web site: http://www.netusa1.net/~rosewood

The Rosewood Mansion Inn, built in 1872 by Elbert Shirk, consists of a lovely Victorian home and carriage house situated near the downtown area of Peru, Indiana. The mansion has nineteen rooms, including ten guest rooms, each with private bath. The carriage house has one guest room with a private bath.

Hosts: David and Lynn Hausner
Rooms: 11 (PB) $70-90
Full Breakfast
Credit Cards: A, B, C, D
Notes: 2, 5, 7, 8, 9, 10

Philip W. Smith Bed and Breakfast

RICHMOND

Philip W. Smith B&B

2039 E. Main Street, 47374
(765) 966-8972; (800) 966-8972

Elegant Queen Anne Victorian family home located in East Main-Glen Miller Park Historic District, right on the Indiana-Ohio border off I–70. Built in 1890 by Philip W. Smith, the two-and-a-half-story brick home has Romanesque details and features stained-glass windows and ornate-carved wood. Four distinctive guest rooms: two with full-size beds, two with queen-size beds. Unwind in the evening with homemade snacks, coffee, and tea. Awaken to a breakfast highlighting fresh, regional ingredients. Stroll through historic districts, listen to outdoor concerts in the park, hike Whitewater River Gorge, relax in the garden, and shop in Richmond and "Antique Alley." AAA-approved.

Hosts: Chip and Chartley Bondurant
Rooms: 4 (PB) $65-75
Full Breakfast
Credit Cards: A, B, C
Notes: 2, 5, 7, 8, 10, 11, 12

RUSHVILLE

The Greystone Inn

525 N. Main Street, 46173
(888) 272-0022; FAX (765) 932-2192
E-mail: rngrady@comsys.net
Web site: http://www.thegreystoneinn.com

The Greystone Inn bed and breakfast is dedicated to providing a charming, unique place of hospitality where visitors can find the time to be refreshed, spiritually and physically. It is an inn of conservative eloquence, and those who share that particular lifestyle will find it a haven to nourish their souls. "It is dedicated to Jesus Christ." The inn was Jasper Case's mansion, built in 1918. Ranny and Denise Grady invite you to step back in time as you enter the door of this stately, twenty-five-room stone mansion. You will be greeted and enchanted by the eight beautiful Rookwood Pottery tiled fireplaces, the recreation/fitness room (in the basement), and the six elegant guest rooms, each named after a flower and decorated with antiques that have been chosen specifically to reflect its unique name.

Hosts: Ranny and Denise Grady
Rooms: 25
Full Breakfast
Credit Cards: A, B
Notes: 2, 5, 8, 9, 10

SCHERERVILLE

Sunset Pines Bed and Breakfast

862 Sunset Drive, 46375
(219) 322-3322; (800) 458-0919-19

Sunset Pines Bed and Breakfast is hidden away on the edge of a 50-acre forest. Our guests enjoy a country setting while still in the heart of town. We serve a generous continental or full-service breakfast. Our nonsmoking rooms offer every comfort at prices ranging from $55 to 95 per night. Rooms have private baths, queen-size beds, whirlpool tubs. Our outdoor pool is open during the summer. We are recommended by the Lake County Indiana Visitors Center. Cash only.

Hosts: Clay and Nikki Foster
Rooms: 2 (PB) $55-95
Full or Continental Breakfast
Credit Cards: none
Notes: 5, 7, 8, 9, 10

SHIPSHEWANA

Morton Street Bed and Breakfast

140 Morton Street; PO Box 775, 46565
(219) 768-4391; (800) 447-6475
E-mail: mortonst@ligtel.com
Web site: http://www.shipshewana.com

Come to Shipshewana, relax, and enjoy our three restored homes nestled in the heart of Amish country. Decorated Victorian, country, or eclectic, our homes provide an escape from the everyday bustle of life. Sit on the porch and watch the buggies go by, or walk to more than fifty shops, restaurants, and the famous Shipshewana flea market. Special winter and weekend rates are available.

Hosts: David and Peggy Scherger
Rooms: 10 (PB) $50-100 (seasonal)
Full Breakfast
Credit Cards: A, B, C, D
Notes: 2, 4, 5, 7, 10, 11, 12

SHIRLEY

Sweet's Home Sweet Home

402 Center Street, 47384
(765) 737-6357; (800) 418-2076

This is a large, comfortable home specializing in small-town hospitality. It features a large yard with a rose garden and is within walking distance of Shirley's historic district. Sweet's Home Sweet Home is centrally located within an easy drive of several attractions. Each guest room is special. You can have Christmas year-round in the Christmas Room, see all the treasures in Papaw's Treasure Room, sleep in Grandma's antique feather bed, or lounge in bows and lace in the lovely Jo-lia-Reneé Room.

Hosts: Jeanie and Ray Sweet
Rooms: 4 (SB)
Continental Breakfast and Evening Snack
Credit Cards: none
Notes: 2, 4, 5, 7

SILVER LAKE

Rollin'-Acres Holsteins Bed and Breakfast

11434 S. 100 W., 46982
(219) 352-2725

Enjoy Hoosier hospitality as your Mennonite host family invites you to a working 310-acre dairy farm. Families welcome. Full breakfast served family-style in our dining room. Farm tours available, if desired. Close to Grace College, North Manchester College, Wagon Wheel Playhouse, antique stores, swimming, skiing, boating, and Shipshewana. Special rates and activities for scout and youth groups!

Hosts: Randy and Teresa Martin
Rooms: 2 (PB) $50
Full Breakfast
Credit Cards: none
Notes: 2, 5, 7, 8, 9, 10, 11

TIPPECANOE

Bessinger's Hillfarm Wildlife Refuge B&B

4588 State Road 110, 46570
(219) 223-3288

This cozy log home overlooks 265 acres of rolling hills, woods, pasture fields, and marsh with thirty-one islands. It is ideal for geese and deer year-round. The farm features hiking trails with beautiful views, picnic areas, and benches tucked away in a quiet area. Varied seasons make it possible to canoe, swim, fish, bird-watch, hike, and cross-country ski. Start with a country breakfast each morning—be ready for an unforgettable table experience.

Hosts: Wayne and Betty Bessinger
Rooms: 3 (PB) $69.90
Full Breakfast
Credit Cards: none
Notes: 2, 5, 9

VALPARAISO

Inn at Aberdeen, Ltd.

3158 S. State Road 2, 46385
(219) 465-3753; FAX (219) 465-9227
E-mail: innaberd@netnitco.net
Web site: http://www.valpomall.com/theinn

Travel back in time to the late 1800s, but relax in the splendor of your own spacious suite. Private bath, Jacuzzi, cable television, balcony, and a cozy fire—all for you. A library, solarium, and open kitchen offer quiet respite. An executive conference center is available for that important meeting—or lease the entire inn for a special occasion. Less than 1 hour from downtown Chicago. Championship golf, outdoor pool, walking paths, ponds, streams—on site. Gift certificates.

Hosts: Gary Atherton, Linda and John Johnson
Rooms: 11 (PB) $90-150
Full Gourmet Breakfast
Credit Cards: A, B, C, D, E
Notes: 5, 7, 8, 9, 10, 12

VEVAY

Rosemont Inn Bed and Breakfast

806 Market Street, 47043
(812) 427-3050

An elegant 1881 Victorian Italianate home located on the beautiful Ohio River on 2½ acres. Watch the Ohio River drift by from a seat on the wicker-filled front porch. Open grand entrance stairway with stained glass. Five bedrooms with private baths, terry cloth robes, and fireplaces. Grounds are planted in perennial and rose gardens. Full breakfast. Antiquing, historical sites, nature areas, and casinos are located within 25 miles. Only 1 hour from Cincinnati and Louisville.

Hosts: Dan and Rebecca Hoberland, Peggy Kinnetz
Rooms: 5 (PB) $75-95
Full Breakfast
Credit Cards: none
Notes: 2, 5, 9, 10

WALKERTON

Hesters Farm Log Home

71880 State Route 23, 46574
(219) 586-2105

An 1830 log home furnished with antiques, including a player piano and eight dish patterns. Huge brick and stone fireplace. Gas/candle/electric lighting. Oak table with twelve chairs. Wooded area. Herb garden. Peace, quiet. Retreat, family reunions, small weddings, and receptions. Ideal for couples. Horse-drawn equipment, antique tractors. Haflinger Horse Farm. Hay, sleigh, or surrey rides. Working Jersey dairy farm.

Hostess: Annette Hestors
Rooms: 3 (SB) $66/room, $125/entire home for family reunion or retreat
Full Breakfast
Credit Cards: none
Notes: 2, 3, 4, 5, 7, 9, 10

WEST BADEN SPRINGS

E.B. Rhodes House Bed and Breakfast

Box 7, Rhodes Avenue, 47469
(812) 936-7378; (800) 786-5176

Relax in the homey luxury of an 1890s Victorian home filled with beautiful carved wood and stained glass. Rock on one of the wraparound porches and enjoy the peaceful view of the town park. Hoosier hospitality with a home-grown breakfast. Opportunity abounds for historians, sports buffs, and antique enthusiasts. Carriage house available, with full bath and fireplace. Screened porch and garden view.

Hosts: Frank and Marlene Sipes
Rooms: 3 (PB) $45-85
Full Breakfast
Credit Cards: A, B, C, D
Notes: 5, 6 (housed separately), 7, 8, 9, 10, 11

welcome; 7 Children welcome; 8 Tennis nearby; 9 Swimming nearby; 10 Golf nearby; 11 Skiing nearby; 12 May be booked through travel agent.

IOWA

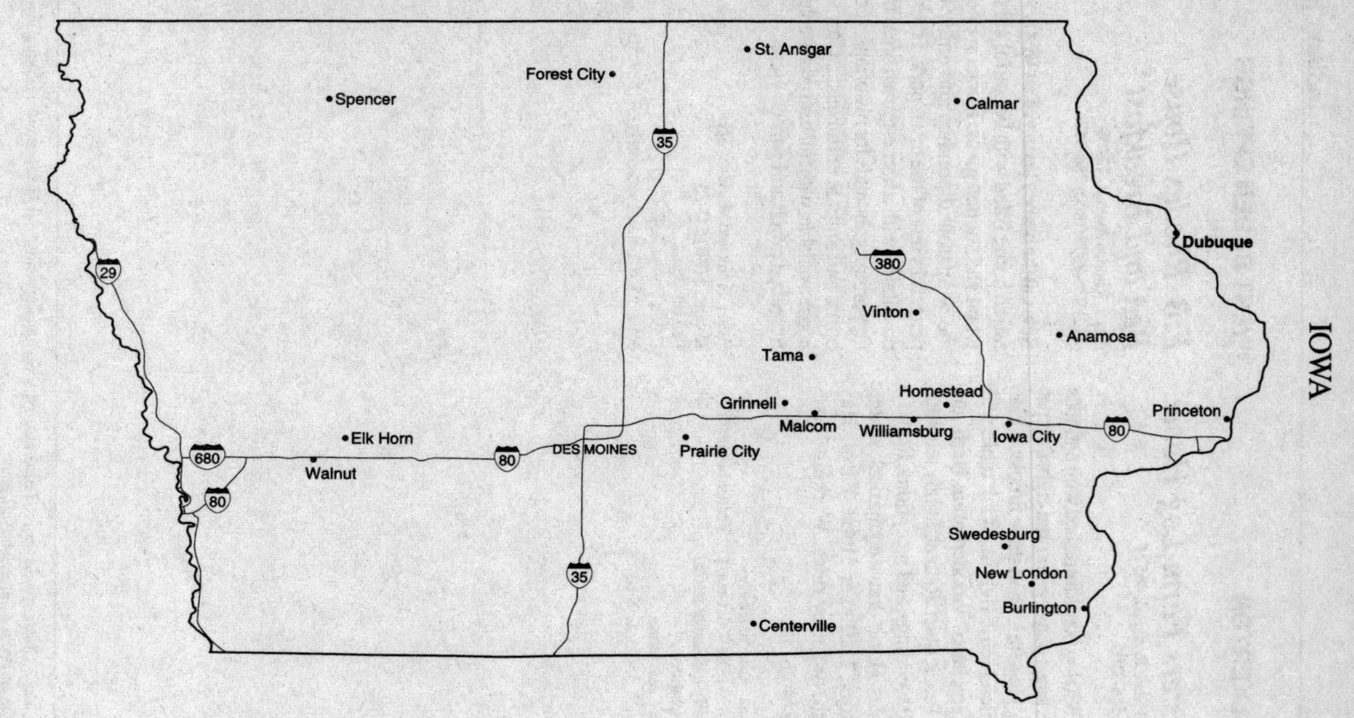
St. Ansgar
Forest City
Spencer
Calmar
35
Dubuque
29
380
Vinton
Anamosa
Tama
Homestead
Grinnell
Malcom
Williamsburg
Iowa City
80
Princeton
Elk Horn
680
Walnut
80
DES MOINES
Prairie City
80
Swedesburg
New London
35
Burlington
Centerville

Iowa

AMANA COLONIES

Die Heimat Country Inn

4430 V Street, **Homestead,** 52236
(319) 622-3937

Die Heimat, "the home place," has nineteen rooms furnished with Amana walnut and cherry furniture. Televisions and air-conditioning. Amana walnut canopy beds are the specialty of this, the oldest and largest bed and breakfast in the Colonies. A nature trail, wineries, woolen mills, and restaurants are all nearby.

Hosts: Jacki and Warren Lock
Rooms: 19 (PB) $49.95-69.95
Full Breakfast
Credit Cards: A, B, D
Notes: 2 (preferred), 5, 6, 7, 8, 9, 10

ANAMOSA

Shaw House Bed and Breakfast

509 S. Oak Street, 52205
(319) 462-4485

Enjoy a relaxing step back in time in this three-story 1870 Italianate mansion on a hilltop overlooking scenery immortalized in the paintings of native son Grant Wood. Special rooms include porch with panoramic countryside view, two-room tower suite, and ballroom. The mansion is on a 45-acre farm within easy walking distance of town. State park, antique shop, and canoeing are nearby.

Hosts: Connie and Andy McKean
Rooms: 4 (3PB; 1SB) $60-85
Full Breakfast
Credit Cards: none
Notes: 2, 5, 7, 8, 9, 10, 11

BURLINGTON

The Schramm House Bed and Breakfast

616 Columbia Street, 52601
(319) 754-0373 (voice and FAX);
(800) 683-7117
E-mail: shramhse@interl.net

Step into the past when you enter this restored 1870s Victorian in the heart of the Burlington historic district. Unique architecture and antique furnishings create the mood of an era past. Three guest rooms, all with private baths, offer queen-size or

---

NOTES: Credit cards accepted: A Master Card; B Visa; C American Express; D Discover; E Diners Club; F Other; 2 Personal checks accepted; 3 Lunch available; 4 Dinner available; 5 Open all year; 6 Pets welcome; 7 Children welcome; 8 Tennis nearby; 9 Swimming nearby; 10 Golf nearby; 11 Skiing nearby; 12 May be booked through travel agent.

The Schramm House Bed and Breakfast

twin beds, quilts, and more. Experience Burlington hospitality while having lemonade on the porch or tea by the fire with your hosts. Walk to the Mississippi River, antique shops, restaurants, etc.

Hosts: Sandy and Bruce Morrison
Rooms: 4 (PB) $65-85
Full Breakfast
Credit Cards: A, B, C, D
Notes: 2, 5, 7, 8, 9, 10, 12

CALMAR

Calmar Guesthouse

103 W. North Street, 52132
(319) 562-3851
E-mail: lbkruse@salamander.com

Beautiful restored Victorian home with antiques. Located in northeastern Iowa near Decorah, Luther College, N.I.C. College, Hand-Carved Bily Brother Clocks Museum, smallest church (Little Brown Church), Niagara Cave, Seed Sower Farm. Many parks, waterfalls. Nice area. B&B has warm hospitality, quiet elegance, good food.

Hostess: Lucille Kruse
Rooms: 5 $45-49.95
Full Breakfast
Credit Cards: A, B
Notes: 2, 7, 8, 9, 10, 11

CENTERVILLE

One of a Kind

314 W. State, 52544
(515) 437-4540 (voice and FAX)

One of a Kind is a stately, three-story brick home built in 1867. Situated in one of Iowa's delightful small communities. You'll be within walking distance of antique shops, the town square, city park with tennis courts, the swimming pool, etc. Twelve minutes to Lake Rathbun, Iowa's largest lake. Browse the gift shop filled with collectibles, original paintings, etc. Enjoy our special delicacies in the Tea Room.

Hosts: Jack and Joyce Stufflebeem
Rooms: 5 (2PB; 3SB) $35-60
Full Breakfast
Credit Cards: A, B, C, D
Notes: 2, 3, 4, 5, 8, 9, 10, 11, 12

DAVENPORT (PRINCETON)

The Woodlands B&B

PO Box 127, **Princeton,** 52768
(319) 289-3177; (800) 257-3177

The Woodlands Bed and Breakfast is a secluded woodland escape that can be as private or social as you wish. Nestled among pines on 26 acres of forest and meadows in a private wildlife refuge. Guests delight in an elegant breakfast by the swimming pool or by a cozy fireplace while viewing the outdoor wildlife activity. The Woodlands is the perfect setting for intimate weddings!

Hosts: The Wallace Family
Rooms: 2 (PB) $60-115
Full Breakfast
Credit Cards: none
Notes: 2, 3, 4, 5, 6 (limited), 7, 8, 9, 10, 11, 12

NOTES: Credit cards accepted: A Master Card; B Visa; C American Express; D Discover; E Diners Club; F Other; 2 Personal checks accepted; 3 Lunch available; 4 Dinner available; 5 Open all year; 6 Pets

DUBUQUE

Another World —Paradise Valley Inn

16338 Paradise Valley Road, 52001
(800) 388-0942
Web site: http://www.mall.mwci.net/aw

The "Inn With a Difference." Secluded country log inn, hilltop location with valley view. Wraparound deck. Three standard rooms. Fantasy suites with world-famous, heart-shaped bubble tubs, in-room waterfalls and pond, fireplace. Amenities including candlelight dessert. Gift shop on the premises. Within minutes of nature trail, riverboats, antique malls, excellent dining.

Hostess: Karen Parker
Rooms: 5 (PB) $75-150
Full Breakfast
Credit Cards: A, B, D
Notes: 2, 5, 8, 9, 10, 11, 12

The Hancock House

1105 Grove Terrace, 52001
(319) 557-8989

Located in Dubuque's 11th Street Historic District, this gracious Queen Anne creates a timeless romantic atmosphere. Fireplaces, antique-filled guest quarters, whirlpool baths, and an outstanding panoramic view combine to make your stay unforgettable. The home was featured in *Victorian Sampler* for its "warm hospitality, cloudlike feather beds, and a breakfast to ooh and aah over."

Hosts: Chuck and Susan Huntley
Rooms: 9 (PB) $80-175
Full Breakfast
Credit Cards: A, B, C, D
Notes: 2, 5, 7 (12 and older), 8, 9, 10, 11, 12

The Mandolin Inn

The Mandolin Inn

199 Loras Boulevard, 52001
(319) 556-0069; (800) 524-7996;
FAX (319) 556-0587
Web site: http://www.mandolininn.com

The Mandolin Inn is an Edwardian bed and breakfast dedicated to sharing the elegance and comfort of an earlier era with a few discerning guests. A perfect place to kindle romance. Gourmet breakfasts, queen-size beds, beautifully furnished rooms. Explore historic Dubuque, Galena, and other lovely towns nearby along the upper Mississippi River.

Hostess: Amy Boynton
Rooms: 7 (5PB; 2SB) $75-135
Full Breakfast
Credit Cards: A, B, C, D
Notes: 2, 5, 7, 8, 9, 10, 11

ELK HORN

Joy's Morning Glory

4308 Main Street, Box 12, 51531
(712) 764-5631; (888) 764-5631

Be special guests in our beautiful, refurbished 1912 home. As our guest, you will

Joy's Morning Glory Bed and Breakfast

be greeted by an abundant array of flowers that line our walkways. Inside, your choice of floral-decorated bedrooms awaits you. Breakfast is prepared on Joy's antique cookstove and served in the dining room, on the front porch, or in the flower-filled backyard. Elk Horn community is home of the largest rural Danish settlement in the United States. The town has a working windmill and is home of the National Danish Immigrant Museum.

Hosts: Merle and Joy Petersen
Rooms: 3 (SB) $35-50
Full Breakfast
Credit Cards: none
Notes: 2, 7 (over 10), 8, 9, 10

FOREST CITY

1897 Victorian House Bed and Breakfast

306 S. Clark Street, 50436
(515) 582-3613

As a guest in this turn-of-the-century Queen Anne Victorian home, you may choose from four beautifully decorated bedrooms, each with private bath. There is one luxurious carriage house suite with whirlpool bath. Beautiful, quiet, and very private. Breakfast, included in your rate, is served in our dining room, and we specialize in good, homemade food. A Victorian antique shop and tearoom are 2 blocks away. Play our 1923 baby grand player piano, play croquet, and relax in Forest City, a quiet yet progressive rural midwestern community.

Hosts: Richard and Doris Johnson
Rooms: 5 (PB) $60-135
Full Breakfast
Credit Cards: A, B
Notes: 2, 3 and 4 (by reservation), 5, 9, 10, 12

1897 Victorian House Bed and Breakfast

GRINNELL

Carriage House B&B Inn

1133 Broad Street, 50112
(515) 236-7520

Beautiful Queen Anne–style Victorian home with relaxing wicker furniture and a swing seat on the front porch. Several fireplaces to be enjoyed in the wintertime. Gourmet breakfast with fresh fruit, quiche, and Irish soda bread fresh from the griddle. Local shopping, nearby lake and hiking, excellent restaurants. One block from Grinnell College, 1 hour from Des Moines and Iowa City. Member of Iowa Bed and Breakfast Innkeepers Association, Iowa Lodging Association, and

NOTES: Credit cards accepted: A Master Card; B Visa; C American Express; D Discover; E Diners Club; F Other; 2 Personal checks accepted; 3 Lunch available; 4 Dinner available; 5 Open all year; 6 Pets

Grinnell Area Chamber of Commerce. State-licensed and -inspected. Gift certificates available.

Hosts: Ray and Dorothy Spriggs
Rooms: 5 (PB) $50-65
Full Breakfast
Credit Cards: A, B
Notes: 2, 5, 8, 9, 10, 11, 12

Clayton Farms Bed and Breakfast

Clayton Farms Bed and Breakfast

621 Newburg Road, 50112
(515) 236-3011

Clayton Farms Bed and Breakfast is an extra nice contemporary farm home on a 320-acre livestock and grain operation. Guests may enjoy fishing and boating on the farm pond, with a place for campfires in season. You may use the family room with fireplace, TV, VCR, library of movies, and kitchenette stocked with beverages and snacks. A family-style country breakfast is served. Group packages for pheasant hunters and hunters of antiques and collectibles. Located only 7 miles from Grinnell College; 1 hour from Des Moines, Iowa City, and Cedar Rapids; 45 minutes from the Amana Colonies; 20 miles from casinos. The accommodations are air-conditioned. Smoking is restricted to outdoors. The B&B is state-licensed and -inspected. Brochures are available—specify general, hunting, or antiquing; request a brochure for hunting rates.

Hosts: Ron and Judie Clayton
Rooms: 3 (1PB; 2SB) $57.75-63
Full Breakfast
Credit Cards: A, B, C
Notes: 2, 7, 8, 9, 10, 11

IOWA CITY

2 Bella Vista Place Bed and Breakfast

2 Bella Vista Place, 52245
(319) 338-4129

Daissy Owen has furnished her lovely, air-conditioned, 1920s home with antiques and artifacts she has acquired on her travels in Europe and Latin America. The home is conveniently located on the city's historic north side with a beautiful view of the Iowa River. The Hoover Library, the Amana Colonies, and the Amish center of Kalona are all nearby. A full breakfast, with Daissy's famous coffee, is served in the dining room's unique setting each morning. Daissy is fluent in Spanish and speaks some French. From I–80, take Dubuque Street Exit 244, turn left on Brown Street, then first left on Linn Street; it is 1 block to #2 Bella Vista Place Bed and Breakfast.

Hostess: Daissy P. Owen
Rooms: 4 (2PB; 2SB) $55-95
Full Breakfast
Credit Cards: none
Notes: 2, 5, 8, 9, 12

Haverkamps' Linn Street Homestay

Haverkamps' Linn Street Homestay

619 N. Linn Street, 52245-1934
(319) 337-4363; FAX (319) 354-7057
E-mail: havb-b@soli.inav.net

Enjoy the warmth and hospitality in our 1908 Edwardian home filled with heirlooms and collectibles. Only a short walk from downtown Iowa City and the University of Iowa main campus, and a short drive from the Hoover Library in West Branch, the Amish in Kalona, and seven Amana Colonies.

Hosts: Clarence and Dorothy Haverkamp
Rooms: 3 (SB) $35-45
Full Breakfast
Credit Cards: none
Notes: 2, 5, 7, 8, 9, 12

MALCOM

Pleasant Country Bed and Breakfast

4386 110th Street, 50157
(515) 528-4925
E-mail: pcbb@pcpartner.net

Eugene and Mary Lou Mann are a third-generation farm family living in their 1896 home. It is filled with antiques and country deco. The home is a working farm; tours are available. Enjoy a full country breakfast with homemade specialties. We have a pond for fishing, and pheasant hunting in season. Rest and relax in the quietness of the countryside.

Hosts: Eugene and Mary Lou Mann
Rooms: 4 (SB) $50-55
Full Breakfast
Credit Cards: none
Notes: 2, 5, 7, 8, 9, 10, 11, 12

Pleasant Country Bed and Breakfast

NEW LONDON

Old Brick Bed and Breakfast

2759 Old Highway 34, 52645
(319) 367-5403

This 1860s Italianate brick farmhouse, comfortably furnished with family pieces, beckons guests with welcome candles in each window. Our working grain farm offers an opportunity to view current farming techniques, equipment, and specialty crops. Enjoy peaceful surroundings, walk down a country road, visit area antique shops, sit on one of the porches, or relax in spacious guest rooms with queen-size

NOTES: Credit cards accepted: A Master Card; B Visa; C American Express; D Discover; E Diners Club; F Other; 2 Personal checks accepted; 3 Lunch available; 4 Dinner available; 5 Open all year; 6 Pets

Old Brick Bed and Breakfast

beds and private baths. A full breakfast and arrival refreshments are served.

Hosts: Jerry and Caroline Lehman
Rooms: 2 (PB) $55
Full Breakfast
Credit Cards: none
Notes: 2, 4, 5, 7, 8, 9, 10

PRAIRIE CITY

Country Connection Bed and Breakfast

9737 W. 93rd Street S., 50228-8306
(515) 994-2023

Experience the friendly atmosphere of a working farm community surrounded by the tranquillity of beautiful crop land. The Country Connection Bed and Breakfast is a turn-of-the-century farm home with period furnishings blended with privacy, charm, and hospitality. A hearty breakfast is served on the cheerful sunporch or in the formal dining room. Guests are treated to a complimentary bedtime snack, home-made ice cream, and cookies. Near Pella Tulip Time and Walnut Creek Wildlife Refuge, 20 miles east of Des Moines, 3½ miles southeast of Prairie City. The B&B is open May–November.

Country Connection Bed and Breakfast

Hostess: Jim and Alice Foreman
Rooms: 2 (SB); $50-60
Continental Breakfast
Credit Cards: A, B
Notes: 2, 7, 9, 10, 12

ST. ANSGAR

The Blue Belle Inn

513 W. Fourth Street; PO Box 205, 50472
(515) 736-2225; FAX (515) 736-4024
E-mail: bluebelle@deskmedia.com
Web site: http://deskmedia.com/~bluebelle

Rediscover the romance of the 1890s while enjoying the comfort and convenience of the 1990s in one of six distinctively decorated guest rooms at the Blue Belle Inn. The festive Victorian "painted lady" features air-conditioning, fireplaces, and Jacuzzis. Lofty tin ceilings, gleaming maple woodwork, stained glass, and crystal chandeliers in bay and curved window pockets create a shimmering interplay of light and color. Enjoy breakfast on the balcony or gourmet dining by candlelight.

Hostess: Sherrie C. Hansen
Rooms: 6 (5PB; 1SB) $50-130
Full Breakfast
Credit Cards: A, B, C, D
Notes: 2, 3, 4, 5, 7, 9, 10, 12

welcome; 7 Children welcome; 8 Tennis nearby; 9 Swimming nearby; 10 Golf nearby; 11 Skiing nearby; 12 May be booked through travel agent.

Hannah Marie Country Inn

SPENCER

Hannah Marie Country Inn

4070 Highway 71, 51301
(712) 262-1286; (800) 972-1286 (outside Iowa); FAX (712) 262-3294
Web site: http://www.nwiowabb.com/hannah.htm

The romance of the country awaits you at the Hannah Marie Country Inn. Our guests enjoy in-room double whirlpools, queen-size feather beds, a three-course candlelight breakfast, central air-conditioning, softened water, and an evening candlelight dessert. Come, walk the garden labyrinth. We are located near the Iowa Great Lakes. The Hannah Marie has been termed the "Best Iowa B&B" (*Des Moines Register* readers, '91) and "One of 50 Best B&Bs" (*Inn Times*, '95). The inn was selected by Lipton Tea Company for its 1997 promotion.

Hostess: Mary Nichols
Rooms: 6 (PB) $72-110
Full Breakfast
Credit Cards: A, B, D
Notes: 2, 3 and 4 (reservations), 5, 6 (outside), 7, 8, 9, 10, 12

SWEDESBURG

The Carlson House

105 Park Street; PO Box 86, 52652
(319) 254-2451; FAX (319) 254-8809
E-mail: r2009@se-iowa.net
Web sites: http://www.innsandouts.com/property/the_carlson_house.html
http://www.flinthills.com
http://www.travelguides.com

Experience a touch of Sweden in this stylish home in a Swedish-American country village. Guests enjoy comfortable rooms with queen-size beds and private baths (one with a whirlpool tub); a full Swedish breakfast; a cheerful sitting room for relaxation, reading, and television; and a new whirlpool hot tub on our deck. Favorite pastimes here include browsing in the books, chatting on the porches, strolling through the local Swedish immigrant villages, and visiting the nearby Swedish-American Museum.

Hosts: Ned and Ruth Ratekin
Rooms: 3 (2PB; 1SB) $50
Full Breakfast
Credit Cards: A, B

TAMA

Hummingbird Haven Bed and Breakfast

1201 Harding Street, 52339
(515) 484-2022

We hope you will join us at Hummingbird Haven and get a taste of Central Iowa's hospitality. The B&B offers two guest rooms with a large shared bath. Guests have use of the home. Laundry services are available. The home has central air and heat. Tama's central location makes our B&B a perfect home base for seeing many of Iowa's attractions. Ten minutes from Tama County Museum and Mesquaki Bingo and Casino; 30 minutes from Marshalltown, County Lake with water sports, Opera House in Brooklyn, and Grinnell College and Museum. One hour from many more attractions. Please, no pets or smoking.

Hostess: Bernita Thomsen
Rooms: 2 (SB) $38-50
Full Breakfast
Credit Cards: A, B
Notes: 2, 3, 4, 5, 7, 9, 10

VINTON

The Lion and the Lamb Bed and Breakfast

913 2nd Avenue, 52349
(319) 472-5086; (888) 390-LAMB (5262);
FAX (319) 472-9115
E-mail: LionLambBB@aol.com
Web site: http://members.aol.com/lionlambbb/bnb.htm

Located along the Cedar River, this small town whispers of a time gone by when Victorian opulence was at its peak. Vinton boasts many turn-of-the-century homes. Experience elegant accommodations in this 1892 Queen Anne mansion. Each guest room features a queen-size bed, TV, overhead fan, and AC. Call for a free color brochure and information on things to do in the area. Murder mystery dinners available, priced at $165-195 per couple.

Hosts: Richard and Rachel Waterbury
Rooms: 4 (2PB; 2SB) $65-95
Full Breakfast
Credit Cards: A, B, D
Notes: 2, 5, 7, 8, 9, 10, 11 (cross-country), 12

Antique City Inn

WALNUT

Antique City Inn

400 Antique City Drive; PO Box 584, 51577
(712) 784-3722

This 1911 Victorian home has been restored and furnished to its original state. Enjoy a nostalgic experience combining simplicity of life, the craftsmanship of yesterday, quiet living, and small-town hospitality. The inn is located 1 block from eight malls and stores with 250 antique dealerships. The home has beautiful woods, a dumbwaiter icebox, French doors, and a wraparound porch.

Hostess: Sylvia Reddie
Rooms: 6 (2PB; 4SB) $47.70-58.30
Full Breakfast
Credit Cards: A, B, C, D
Notes: 2, 3, 4, 5, 10, 12

Clark's Country Inn

701 Walnut Street; Box 533, 51577
(712) 784-3010 (voice and FAX)

Iowa's antique capital, just 1 mile south of I–80 between Omaha and Des Moines. Six malls, individual shops, more than 200 dealers. Open all year. Clark's Country Inn is a 1912 two-story home with oak interior, antiques, newly remodeled guest rooms, private baths, king and queen beds, and central AC. Mastercard/Visa deposit required. No smoking.

Host: Ron and Mary Lou Clark
Rooms: 3 (PB) $58
Full Breakfast
Credit Cards: A, B
Notes: 2, 5, 7 (over 12), 8, 9, 10, 12

WILLIAMSBURG

Lucille's Bett und Breakfast

2835 - 225th Street, 52361-8607
(319) 668-1185

Enjoy the charm of our scenic country Tudor home. Guests may want to relax in our spacious yard or grill on our patios. Croquet, anyone? Flowers and shrubs enhance the area. Enjoy the comfort of our air-conditioned home. Our cozy fireplace will warm any chilly, snowy evening. Care for popcorn? Piano and organ available for music lovers. Sheephead card game and cribbage instructions offered. We will request the songbirds to greet you in the morning. Watch the goldfinches at their feeders. Children welcome. Smoking outside only, please. No pets, please. A full refund is offered with 24 hours' notice. Member of the Iowa Bed and Breakfast Innkeepers Association and Iowa Lodging Association.

Hosts: Dale and Lucille Bell
Full Breakfast

Kansas

ELK FALLS

The Sherman House

Box 15, 67345
(316) 329-4425

A popular stop for passenger trains from 1879 to 1890, the Sherman House has been lovingly restored as a private guest house offering visitors a little unhurried time in this unusual rural community. Guests may visit in the studio of their hosts—professional potters—and explore waterfalls, floral gardens, unique restaurants, and historic churches, or just enjoy peace and quiet. Large, comfortable rooms. Perfect retreat for couples, families, small groups.

Hosts: Steve and Jane Fry
Rooms: 2 (PB) $40-53
Full Breakfast
Credit Cards: none
Notes: 2, 5, 7

EMPORIA

Plumb House B&B

628 Exchange, 66801
(316) 342-6881; (800) 288-6198
Web site: http://www.fhtc.kansas.net/~plumb

Your hostess will greet you with tea on the lovely front porch or hot chocolate by the fireplace. Wonderful breakfast smells will awaken you in the morning after a restful night for weary travelers or business visitors. Guest rooms are decorated with antiques, made comfortable with modern amenities and private bathrooms. The bird sanctuary and butterfly garden are eye-pleasing and restful, with a waterfall in the pond and a swing to rest in. Senior rates, corporate rates, weekly rates.

Hostess: Barbara Stoecklein
Rooms: 5 (4PB; 1PB) $69-79
Full Breakfast
Credit Cards: A, B, C, D
Notes: 2, 5, 7, 8, 9, 10, 12

GREAT BEND

Peaceful Acres Bed and Breakfast

Route 5, Box 153, 67530
(316) 793-7527

Enjoy a minifarm and sprawling, tree-shaded old farmhouse furnished with some antiques. If you like peace and quiet, chickens, calves, guineas, kittens in the springs, and old-fashioned hospitality, you need to come and visit us. Breakfast will be fixed from homegrown products. We are near historical areas—Sante Fe Trail,

---

welcome; 7 Children welcome; 8 Tennis nearby; 9 Swimming nearby; 10 Golf nearby; 11 Skiing nearby; 12 May be booked through travel agent.

KANSAS

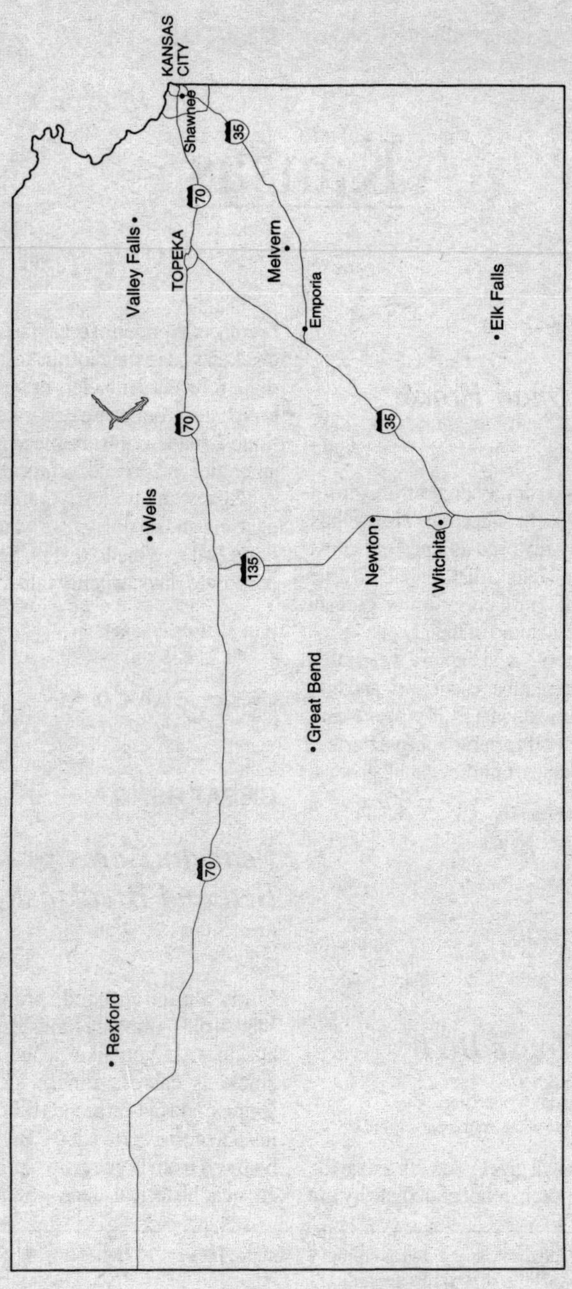

KANSAS CITY
Shawnee
35
70
Valley Falls
TOPEKA
Melvern
Emporia
Elk Falls
70
35
Wells
Newton
Witchita
135
Great Bend
70
Rexford

Ft. Larned, Cheyenne Bottoms—and to the zoo and tennis courts.

Hosts: Dale and Doris Nitzel
Rooms: 3 (1 PB; 2 SB) $30
Full Breakfast
Credit Cards: none
Notes: 2, 3, 4, 5, 7, 8, 9, 10, 12

MELVERN

Schoolhouse Inn

122 SE Beck, 66510
(785) 549-3473

The Schoolhouse Inn is a two-story, limestone building built in 1870. It sits on a 1½-acre lawn. In 1986 it was entered in "Kansas Historic Places." This inn is a place you need to visit. Three large bedrooms are upstairs with antique furniture. Enjoy this bed and breakfast for celebrating your anniversary or just a quiet getaway to our small town. Member of the Kansas B&B Association.

Hosts: Rudy and Alice White
Rooms: 3 (PB) $55-60
Full Breakfast
Credit Cards: A, B
Notes: 2, 5, 9

Schoolhouse Inn

NEWTON

The Old Parsonage B&B

330 E. Fourth Street, 67114
(316) 283-6808

Located in Newton's oldest neighborhood, this charming home once served as the parsonage for First Mennonite Church. It features a cozy yet spacious atmosphere filled with antiques and family heirlooms. The Old Parsonage is a short walk from the historical Warkentin House and Warkentin Mill, which are listed on the National Register of Historic Places. Two miles from Bethel College. Dine in one of Newton's fine ethnic eateries, or browse quaint antique and craft shops.

Hosts: Karl and Betty Friesen
Rooms: 3 (1PB; 2SB) $48
Continental Breakfast
Credit Cards: A, B
Notes: 2, 5, 7

REXFORD

Carousel Cottage

310 Kansas Street; PO Box 87, 67753
(913) 687-3600; FAX (817) 465-8016
E-mail: jdingw@flash.net
Web site: http://www.shepherdstaff.org

Enjoy the peace and quiet of northwestern Kansas in this quaint two-bedroom cottage filled with antiques and crystal chandeliers. The master bedroom has a king-size brass headboard and an antique floral carpet from a historic opera house. The living room is furnished with a television/VCR and plenty of good books to browse. Adjacent to the Shepherd's Staff

Conference Center, which offers accommodations for any size group. On Highway 83, 20 miles north of I–70.

Hostess: Nancy Dahl
Rooms: 2 (SB) $55-70
Continental Breakfast
Credit Cards: none
Notes: 2, 5, 7

VALLEY FALLS

The Barn Bed and Breakfast Inn

14910 Bluemound Road, 66088
(785) 945-3225; (800) 869-7717;
FAX (785) 945-3226
E-mail: thebarn@grasshoppernet.com

In the rolling hills of northeast Kansas, this 106-year-old barn has been converted into a bed and breakfast. Sitting high on a hill with a beautiful view, it has a large indoor heated pool, fitness room, three living rooms, and king or queen beds in all rooms. We serve you supper, as well as a full breakfast, and have three large meeting rooms available.

Hosts: Tom and Marcella Ryan, Patricia Miller
Rooms: 20 (PB) $86-96
Full Breakfast
Credit Cards: A, B, C, D
Notes: 2, 3, 4, 5, 7, 8, 9 (in house), 10, 12

WELLS

Traders Lodge

1392-210th Road, 67467
(785) 488-3930

Join us for "a taste of the wild west" and experience the history of the fur trade era in our lodge of fir and limestone, decorated with antiques, furs, and Indian artifacts. Choose from the Trapper's Room, Plains Indian Room, Southwest Room, or Renaissance Room, each with individual climate control and private bath. Fitness room and hot tub downstairs. Quiet country setting near a state lake. No alcohol or tobacco, please.

Hosts: Kay and Neal Kindall
Rooms: 4 (PB) $65-85
Full Breakfast
Credit Cards: A, B, C, D
Notes: 2, 3, 4, 5, 7

WICHITA

The Castle Inn Riverside

1155 N. River Boulevard, 67203
(316) 263-9300
E-mail: castle@gte.net
Web site: http://www.castleinnriverside.com

The Castle Inn Riverside, the historic Campbell Castle, was built in 1888 by Col. Burton Harvey Campbell from blueprints of an original Scottish castle. This small luxury inn features fourteen uniquely appointed guest rooms, each with a distinctive theme. Amenities include Jacuzzi tubs for two (six rooms), fireplaces (twelve rooms), full gourmet breakfast, complimentary wine and hors d'oeuvres, and an assortment of homemade desserts and gourmet coffees served each evening.

Hosts: Dr. Terry and Paula Lowry
Rooms: 14 (PB) $125-250
Full Breakfast
Credit Cards: A, B, D, E
Notes: 2, 5, 7 (over 10), 8, 10

NOTES: Credit cards accepted: A Master Card; B Visa; C American Express; D Discover; E Diners Club; F Other; 2 Personal checks accepted; 3 Lunch available; 4 Dinner available; 5 Open all year; 6 Pets

Kentucky

AUGUSTA

Augusta White House Inn Bed and Breakfast

307 Main Street, 41002
(606) 756-2004 (voice and FAX)
E-mail: awhibb@juno.com

A beautifully restored, two-story brick structure (c. 1830) retaining its early Victorian style and elegance, coupled with true southern hospitality. Comfortable rooms with flowered wallpaper and high crown molded ceilings as a reminder of yesteryear, but with modern convenience.

Hostess: Rebecca Spencer
Rooms: 1 suite (PB) $59-79
Full Breakfast
Credit Cards: A, B, C, D
Notes: 8, 9, 10

BARDSTOWN

Beautiful Dreamer Bed and Breakfast

440 E. Stephen Foster Avenue, 40004
(502) 348-4004; (800) 811-8312
Web site: http://www.bbonline.com/ky/dreamer

Beautiful Dreamer Bed and Breakfast is a Federal-design home in the historic district of Bardstown. Guest rooms are fully air-conditioned. The home features cherry furniture and antiques. All rooms are available with queen-size beds: Beautiful Dreamer (double Jacuzzi), Stephen Foster (handicap-accessible), and Captain's (fireplace, single Jacuzzi). Enjoy a hearty breakfast; then relax on our porches with a breathtaking view of my Old Kentucky Home. Come, and make your own beautiful dreams!

Hostess: Lynell Ginter
Rooms: 3 (PB) $89-109
Full Breakfast
Credit Cards: A, B, C, D
Notes: 2, 5, 7 (over 8), 8, 9, 10, 12

Bruntwood Inn

714 N. 3rd Street, 40004
(502) 348-8218

Bruntwood Inn was built in the 1830s by James Marshall Browne. This gracious old southern home is beautifully restored with a breathtaking, three-story oval, spiral staircase; 12- and 13-foot ceilings; wide plank yellow poplar and ash floors throughout; elegant chandeliers; antique furnishings; and a fireplace in every room. It is the type setting that moved Stephen Foster to write about his "Old Kentucky

---

welcome; 7 Children welcome; 8 Tennis nearby; 9 Swimming nearby; 10 Golf nearby; 11 Skiing nearby; 12 May be booked through travel agent.

KENTUCKY

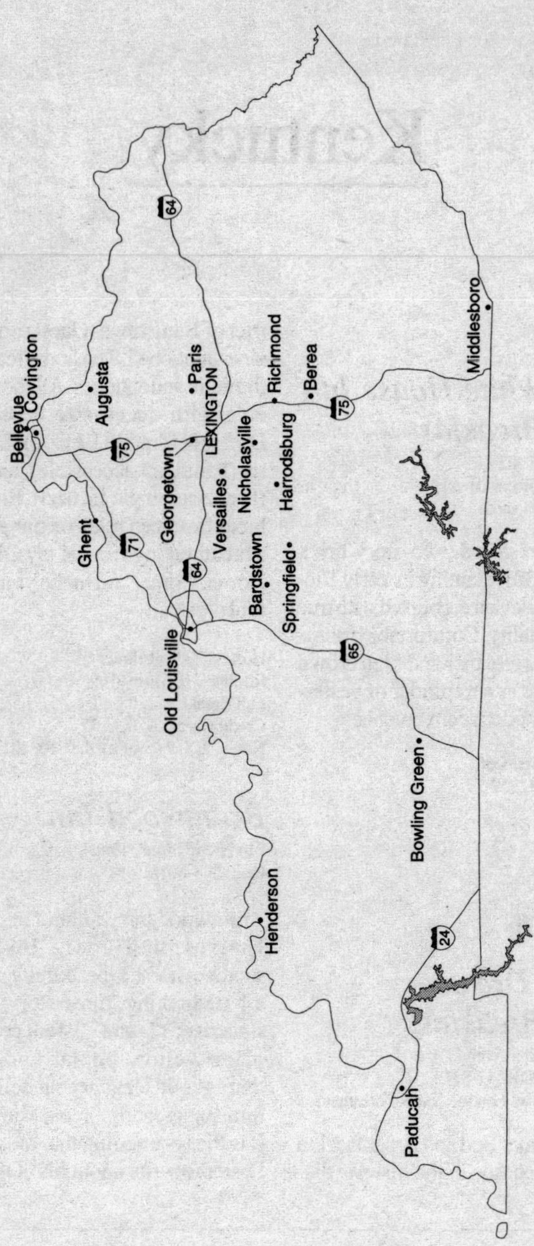

64
Middlesboro
Covington
Bellevue
Augusta
Paris
LEXINGTON
Richmond
Berea
75
75
Georgetown
Nicholasville
Harrodsburg
Versailles
Ghent
71
64
Bardstown
Springfield
Old Louisville
65
Bowling Green
Henderson
24
Paducah

Home." Seven spacious guest bedrooms from which to choose. A huge plantation breakfast is included.

Hosts: Susan and Zyg Danielak
Rooms: 7 (6PB; 1SB) $90-110
Full Breakfast
Notes: 2, 5, 7, 8, 9, 10, 12

Jailer's Inn

111 W. Stephen Foster Avenue, 40004
(502) 348-5551; (800) 948-5551
E-mail: paul@jailersinn.com
Web site: http://www.jailersinn.com

Iron bars on windows, 30-inch-thick stone walls, and a heavy steel door slamming behind you may not sound like the typical tourist accommodation—and Jailer's Inn is anything but typical. The Jailer's Inn, circa 1819, offers a unique and luxurious way to "do time." The inn is a place of wonderful, thought-provoking contrasts. Each guest room is beautifully decorated with antiques and heirlooms, located in the renovated front jail. All rooms have private baths; two have double Jacuzzis. The back jail, built in 1874, is basically unchanged; you get a chilling and sobering look at what conditions were like in the old Nelson County Jail. On spring and summer mornings, as you sip hot coffee and chat with other guests over a full breakfast in the courtyard, it's difficult to imagine the previous uses of the courtyard.

Host: Paul McCoy
Rooms: 6 (PB) $65-105
Full Breakfast
Credit Cards: A, B, C, D
Notes: 2, 7, 8, 9, 10, 12

Kenmore Farms Bed and Breakfast

Kenmore Farms Bed and Breakfast

1050 Bloomfield Road, 40004
(800) 831-6159
Web site: http://www.bbonline.com/ky/kenmorefarms

Drop your hurried ways and enjoy the charm and warmth of days gone by. This beautifully restored 1860s Victorian home features antiques, Oriental rugs, gleaming poplar floors, and a cherry stairway. The air-conditioned guest rooms are furnished with queen-size poster or Lincoln beds and lovely linens, including period pieces. They have large, private baths and spacious vanities. A hearty country breakfast is served—all home-cooked. The decor and our brand of hospitality create a relaxing and enjoyable atmosphere. Kenmore Farms is AAA-approved.

Hosts: Dorothy and Bernie Keene
Rooms: 4 (PB) $80-90
Full Breakfast
Credit Cards: none
Notes: 2, 5, 7 (over 12), 8, 9, 10

NOTES: Credit cards accepted: A Master Card; B Visa; C American Express; D Discover; E Diners Club; F Other; 2 Personal checks accepted; 3 Lunch available; 4 Dinner available; 5 Open all year; 6 Pets welcome; 7 Children welcome; 8 Tennis nearby; 9 Swimming nearby; 10 Golf nearby; 11 Skiing nearby; 12 May be booked through travel agent.

The Mansion Bed and Breakfast

1003 N. Third Street, 40004
(502) 348-2586; (800) 399-2586;
FAX (502) 349-6098
E-mail: ddowns@bardstown.com
Web site: http://www.bbonline.com/ky/mansion

An elegant B&B! The Mansion, an 1851 Greek Revival home, offers a rich history in elegant surroundings. Air-conditioned rooms feature period antiques, bedspreads crocheted by hand, dust ruffles, and shams. A seated gourmet breakfast is served at 8:30 AM in the dining room using our china, crystal, and silver.

Hosts: Joseph and Charmaine Downs
Rooms: 8 (PB) $75-125
Gourmet Breakfast
Credit Cards: A, B, C, D
Notes: 2, 5, 7 (10 or older), 8, 9, 10, 12

BELLEVUE

Christopher's Bed and Breakfast

604 Poplar Street, 41073
(606) 491-9354; (888) 585-7085;
FAX (513) 853-1360
Web site: http://www.bbonline.com/ky/christophers

This late 1800s church was transformed into Christopher's B&B in 1997. The unique establishment is located in Bellevue's historic district, Taylor's Daughter's. Christopher's, named after the patron saint of travelers, features two standard rooms and one suite. Guest rooms have stained-glass windows, private bathrooms with whirlpools. Located ½ mile south of downtown Cincinnati. Easily accessible from I–71, I–75, I–275, and I–471.

Hosts: Steve and Brenda Guidueli
Rooms: 3 (PB)
Continental Breakfast
Credit Cards: A, B
Notes: 2, 5, 7, 8, 9, 10, 12

BEREA

Berea Shady Lane

123 Mt. Vernon Road, 40403
(606) 986-9851 (voice and FAX)
E-mail: lrwebber@aol.com
Web site: http://www.bbonline.com/ky/shadylane

Shady Lane was so named because of the many beautiful trees on the property. It is a bird lover's paradise. It is in a secluded area of Berea, yet convenient to Berea College and to craft and antique shops. Our rooms are decorated with interesting artwork and artifacts with local artisan participation. Several areas are set aside for relaxation and bird watching. A hot tub is available for our guests. A day is twice blessed with the ambience of a restful night.

Hosts: Les and Clarine Webber
Rooms: 2 (PB) $50-65
Full Breakfast
Credit Cards: none
Notes: 2, 5, 8, 9, 10, 12

Cabin Fever

112 Adams Street, 40403
(606) 986-9075 (voice and FAX)
E-mail: jenrose@mis.net

Located in the folk arts and crafts capital of Kentucky, our home features hand-hewn log construction and hardwood floors. The Martin Room offers a queen bed and is docorated with family heirlooms

Cabin Fever

from near and far. The Gallery Room, with three twin beds, is decorated in a more modern style, with our own artwork. Behind the house is a small cabin, built in 1819 and furnished in period style. Guests can walk west to Old Town, where artisans are always at work, and east to historic the Berea College campus.

Hosts: Alfredo and Jennifer Rose Escobar
Rooms: 2 (PB) $65-75
Full Breakfast
Credit Cards: none
Notes: 2, 5, 6 (small), 7, 8, 9, 10

Cummins Country B&B

725 S. Dagwood Drive, 40403
(606) 986-7272 (voice and FAX)

Cummins Country Bed and Breakfast features private facilities in a country barn with a view of the Cumberland Mountains. Guests may stroll over well-groomed acres or take an extended rest by a shaded brook for a very comforting experience. Or sit in the shade by the lake—home to swan and exotic waterfowl.

Hosts: Ken and Mildred Cummins
Rooms: 3 (PB)
Full Breakfast
Credit Cards: none
Notes: 2, 5, 8, 9, 10, 12

BOWLING GREEN

Alpine Lodge

5310 Morgantown Road, 42101-8201
(502) 843-4846; (888) 444-3791, 6293

A spacious, Swiss chalet–style home with 6,000 square feet, situated on 12 acres. A full southern breakfast is served. There are lovely gardens and trails to stroll. We have a swimming pool, outdoor spa, gazebo, and deck. Close to Mammouth Cave, Nashville, Norse Cave, theater, and Corvette City.

Hosts: Dr. and Mrs. David Livingston
Rooms: 5 (3PB; 2SB) $45-65
Full Breakfast
Credit Cards: none
Notes: 2, 4, 5, 6, 7, 9, 10, 12

COVINGTON

Licking-Riverside Historic B&B

516 Garrard Street, 41011
(606) 291-0191; (800) 483-7822;
FAX (606) 291-0939
Email: freelyn@aol.com
Web site: http://www.bbonline.com/ky/riverside

This is a historic home in the historic district along the Licking River. Accommodations include Jacuzzi suites, river view, Victorian decor, fireplace, sitting area, TV/VCR, and deluxe queen rooms with private baths. A courtyard with decks overlooks a wooded area with river frontage. Enjoy a short walk to the Ohio River and get a marvelous view of the Cincinnati skyline. Many year-round activities are nearby, as well as our beautiful

welcome; 7 Children welcome; 8 Tennis nearby; 9 Swimming nearby; 10 Golf nearby; 11 Skiing nearby; 12 May be booked through travel agent.

riverfront. Packages include Reds, Bengals, and the Arts!

Hostess: Lynda L. Freeman
Rooms: 2 + 2 suites (PB) $99-149
Continental Breakfast
Credit Cards: A, B, D
Notes: 2, 5, 7, 8, 9, 10, 12

GEORGETOWN

Pineapple Inn

645 S. Broadway, 40324
(502) 868-5453 (voice and FAX)
Web site: http://www.GeorgetownKy.com

Located in beautiful, historic Georgetown, our inn—built in 1876—is on the Historic Register. Furnished with antiques and beautifully decorated. Three guest rooms are upstairs: the Country Room and Victorian Room, each with full bed, and the Americana Room, with two full beds and one twin bed. Our Derby Room is on the main floor with a queen-size canopy bed and hot tub in a private bath. A full breakfast is served each morning in our country French dining room. Relax in our large living room.

Hosts: Muriel and Les
Rooms: 4 (PB) $65-90
Full Breakfast
Credit Cards: A, B
Notes: 2, 5, 7, 8, 9, 10, 12

GHENT

Ghent House Bed and Breakfast

411 Main Street (U.S. 42); PO Box 478, 41045
(502) 347-5807
Web site: http://www.bbonline.com/ky/ghent

Ghent House is a gracious reminder of the antebellum days of the Old South. The home is Federal style with a beautiful fantail window, coach lights. Two slave walls, rose and English gardens, gazebo. Crystal chandeliers, fireplaces, whirlpool, and hot tub. One almost can visualize the

Ghent House Bed and Breakfast

NOTES: Credit cards accepted: A Master Card; B Visa; C American Express; D Discover; E Diners Club; F Other; 2 Personal checks accepted; 3 Lunch available; 4 Dinner available; 5 Open all year; 6 Pets

steamboats on the river. Step back in time. Come as a guest, leave as a friend!

Hosts: Wayne and Diane Young
Rooms: 3 (PB) $60-120
Full Breakfast
Credit Cards: A, B, C
Notes: 2, 5, 7, 8, 9, 10, 12

Bauer Haus Bed and Breakfast

HARRODSBURG

Bauer Haus B&B

362 N. College Street, 40330
(606) 734-6289
Web site: http://www.bbonline.com/ky/bauer

Savor the craftsmanship of the past in this 1880s Victorian home listed on the National Register and designated a Kentucky landmark. Nestle in the sitting room, sip tea or coffee in the dining room, repose in the parlor, or ascend the stairs to a private room for a relaxing visit. In Kentucky's oldest settlement, Bauer Haus is within walking distance of Old Fort Harrod State Park and historic Harrodsburg.

Hosts: Dick and Marian Bauer
Rooms: 4 (2PB; 2SB) $65-75
Full Breakfast
Credit Cards: A, B, C, D
Notes: 2, 5, 8, 10

Canaan Land Farm

700 Canaan Land Road, 40330
(606) 734-3984; (888) 734-3984
Web site: http://www.bbonline.com/ky/canaan

Step back in time to a house more than 200 years old. Canaan Land Farm features a historic home, c.1795. The rooms contain antiques, collectibles, and feather beds. Full breakfast included, with true southern hospitality. This is a working sheep farm with lambing in spring and fall. Large swimming pool and hot tub. Your host is a shepherd/attorney, and your hostess is a handspinner/artist. The farm is secluded and peaceful. Close to Shaker Village. A historic log cabin (c. 1815) has three additional rooms with private baths and two working fireplaces. This is a nonsmoking bed and breakfast.

Hosts: Theo and Fred Bee
Rooms: 7 (6PB; 1SB) $75-125
Full Breakfast
Credit Cards: none
Notes: 2, 5, 7 (by arrangement), 8, 9 (onsite), 10, 12

HENDERSON

L&N Bed and Breakfast

327 N. Main Street, 42420
(502) 831-1100; FAX (502) 826-0075
E-mail: LNBB@vaughnins.com
Web site: http://www.go-henderson.com/lnbb.htm

L&N is a two-story Victorian home featuring oaken floors and woodwork, stained glass, antique furnishings, and a convenient location in the heart of downtown Henderson, next door to a railroad overpass. Four bedrooms are available, each with private bath, direct-dial telephone, and cable TV. The John James Audubon

Park and Museum is only 3½ miles away and is open year-round. Your innkeepers reside next door.

Hosts: Norris and Mary Elizabeth Priest
Rooms: 4 (PB) $75
Continental Breakfast
Credit Cards: none
Notes: 2, 5, 7, 8, 9, 10

LEXINGTON

Swann's Nest at Cygnet Farm

3463 Rosalie Lane, 40510
(606) 226-0095; FAX (606) 252-4499

Southern Colonial home located on a thoroughbred horse farm, offering tranquillity and grace. Swann's Nest provides all the comforts of home.

Hosts: Rosalie Swann and Angie Swann
Rooms: 5 (2PB; 3SB) $75-150
Continental Breakfast
Credit Cards: A, B, C

LOUISVILLE

Ashton's Victorian Secret Bed and Breakfast

1132 S. First Street, 40203
(502) 581-1914

"Step inside and step back 100 years in time" at this three-story, Victorian brick mansion in historic Louisville. Restored to its former elegance, the 100-year-old structure features spacious accommodations, high ceilings, and original woodwork. The Louisville area, rich in historic homes, also will tempt railbirds and would-be jockeys to make a pilgrimage to the famous Churchill Downs, home of the annual Kentucky Derby.

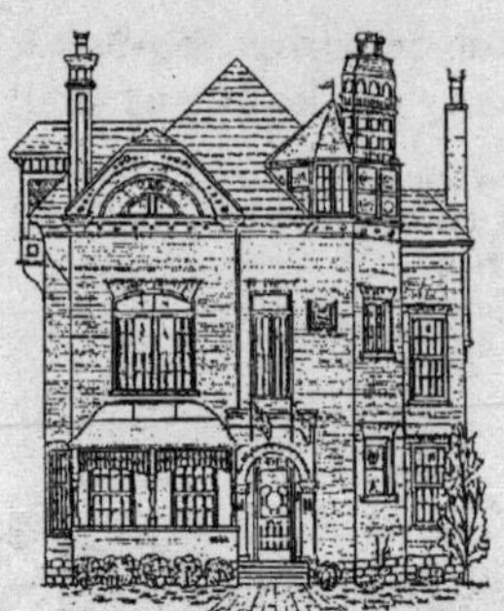
Ashton's Victorian Secret Bed and Breakfast

Hosts: Stephen and Nan Roosa
Rooms: 6 (2PB; 4SB) $58-89
Continental Breakfast
Credit Cards: none
Notes: 5, 7, 8, 9, 10, 11, 12

Pinecrest Cottage

2806 Newburg Road, 40205
(502) 454-3800
Web site: http://www.bbonline.com/ky/pinecrest

Situated on land deeded by forefather Patrick Henry, this century-old, fully renovated, 1,400-square-foot cottage near the Louisville Zoo and Kentucky Kingdom features a 6½-acre wooded "yard," perennial beds, gazebo, tennis court, and pool. The guest house has a king bedroom; separate living room with two sofas (one folds out into a double bed); large bath; and sunporch. TV, VCR, phone, gas log fireplace, kitchen stocked with breakfast and lunch goodies. Air-conditioned.

Hosts: Nancy and Allan Morris
Rooms: 1 (PB) $95-125
Continental Breakfast
Credit Cards: A, B, C
Notes: 2, 5, 7, 8 and 9 (on premises), 10

NOTES: Credit cards accepted: A Master Card; B Visa; C American Express; D Discover; E Diners Club; F Other; 2 Personal checks accepted; 3 Lunch available; 4 Dinner available; 5 Open all year; 6 Pets

The RidgeRunner Bed and Breakfast

MIDDLESBORO

The RidgeRunner Bed and Breakfast

208 Arthur Heights, 40965
(606) 248-4299
Web site: http://www.bbonline.com/ky/ridgerunner

An 1849 Victorian home. Two rooms with shared bath, two with private bath. Nestled in the Cumberland Mountains, overlooking downtown. Home-cooked breakfast in a friendly atmosphere. No smoking. No air-conditioning. Reservations required. Free brochure.

Hosts: Sue Richards and Irma Gall
Rooms: 4 (2PB; 2SB) $60-75
Full Breakfast
Credit Cards: none
Notes: 2, 5, 8, 9, 10, 12

NICHOLASVILLE

Cedar Haven Farm B&B

2380 Bethel Road, 40356
(606) 858-3849
E-mail: CedhvfmBB@compuserve.com
Web site: http://www.bbonline.com/ky/cedarhaven

Cedar Haven Farm is a working farm in central Kentucky, in the rolling bluegrass area. Our rooms are large, with double beds, TV, and phones, and are furnished in a relaxed manner. Our country breakfasts are served family-style and include homemade breads and jams and/or jelly. A retreat from the fast lane.

Hosts: Irene and Jim Smith
Rooms: 3 (1PB; 2SB) $40-50
Full Breakfast
Credit Cards: none
Notes: 2, 5, 6, 7

Sandusky House and O'Neal Log Cabin

1626 Delaney Ferry Road, 40356
(606) 223-4730
E-mail: humphlin@aol.com

A tree-lined drive to the Sandusky House is just a prelude to a wonderful visit to the bluegrass. A quiet, 10-acre country setting amid horse farms, yet close to Lexington, Horse Park, and Shakertown. The Greek Revival Sandusky House was built circa 1850 from bricks fired on the farm. A 1,000-acre land grant from Patrick Henry, governor of Virginia, in 1780 was given to soldiers who had fought in the American Revolution. In addition to the Sandusky House, we have an 1820s, reconstructed, two-story, two-bedroom log cabin with full kitchen and whirlpool bath. The cabin has a large stone fireplace and air-conditioning, and is located in a wooded area close to the main house. An ideal getaway for the entire family! Please call for a brochure.

Hosts: Linda and Jim Humphrey
Rooms: 3 (PB) $79 main house, $99 cabin
Full Breakfast (Continental Plus in cabin)
Credit Cards: A, B
Notes: 2, 5, 7 (over 12 in main house; all in cabin)

PADUCAH

The 1857's B&B

PO Box 7771, 42002-7771
(502) 444-3960; (800) 264-5607;
FAX (502) 444-6751

The 1857's Bed and Breakfast is in the center of Paducah's historic downtown on Market House Square. The three-story building was built in 1857 and is on the National Register of Historic Places. The first floor is Cynthia's Ristorante. Second-floor guest rooms have been renovated in Victorian style. Period furnishings abound. On the third floor, guests may enjoy the game room with a view of the Ohio River; the room features an elegant mahogany billiard table. A hot tub is on the second-floor outside deck. Reservations advised.

Hostess: Deborah Bohnert
Rooms: 3 (1PB; 2SB) $65-85
Continental Breakfast
Credit Cards: A, B
Notes: 2, 5, 8, 9, 10, 11, 12

1868 Bed and Breakfast

914 Jefferson, 42001
(502) 444-6801
E-mail: plmcgill@vci.net

Conveniently located to downtown Paducah, 1868 B&B offers a charming blend of old and new. On the National Register of Historic Places and the Lower Town Walking Tour of 19th-Century Homes. Walk to several fine restaurants, antique shops, the Museum of American Quilters Society, and the riverfront.

Hosts: Phil and Judy McGill
Rooms: 3 (1PB; 2SB) $55-65
Full Breakfast
Credit Cards: none
Notes: 2, 5

Ehrhardt's Bed and Breakfast

285 Springwell Lane, 42001
(502) 554-0644

Our brick Colonial ranch home is located just 1 mile off I–24, which is noted for its lovely scenery. We hope to make you feel at home in our antique-filled bedrooms and the cozy den with its fireplace. Nearby you'll enjoy the beautiful Kentucky and Barkley Lakes and the famous Land Between the Lakes area.

Hosts: Eileen and Phil Ehrhardt
Rooms: 2 (SB) $45
Full Breakfast
Credit Cards: none
Notes: 2, 7 (over 6), 8, 9, 10

Farley Place Bed and Breakfast

Farley Place Bed and Breakfast

166 Farley Place, 42003
(502) 442-2488 (voice and FAX)

Farley Place Bed and Breakfast is one of the finer Victorian homes in Paducah that dates back to the early to mid-1800s. Surrounded by a white picket fence, Farley Place dominates the block on a quiet side street. Farley Place is furnished in period

NOTES: Credit cards accepted: A Master Card; B Visa; C American Express; D Discover; E Diners Club; F Other; 2 Personal checks accepted; 3 Lunch available; 4 Dinner available; 5 Open all year; 6 Pets

antiques. It is on the National Register of Historic Homes and is located 1½ miles from downtown Paducah.

Hosts: Harold and Bernice Jones
Rooms: 3 (1PB; 2SB) $55-85
Full Breakfast
Credit Cards: A, B, C, D
Notes: 2, 5, 6, 7, 8, 9, 10, 12

Fisher Mansion Bed and Breakfast

901 Jefferson Street, 42001
(502) 443-0716

The stately Queen Anne mansion offers overnight guests Victorian elegance with today's luxuries. Beautifully appointed with antiques and reproductions. Located in the heart of Paducah's Historic Lower Town District, within walking distance of many attractions, museums, unique boutiques, antique shops, and outstanding restaurants.

Hosts: Richard and Patricia Mathis
Rooms: 4 (PB) $79-135
Full Breakfast
Credit Cards: A, B
Notes: 2

Trinity Hills Farm Bed and Breakfast Home —Stained-Glass Studio

10455 Old Lovelaceville Road, 42001
(502) 488-3999; (800) 488-3998
E-mail: trinity8@apex.net
Web site: http://www.bbonline.com/ky/trinityhills

Share the serenity of our peaceful 17-acre country retreat for romantic getaways, family gatherings, or a second home to travelers. Nonsmoking, handicap access, stained-glass creations, fireplaces, ceiling fans, whirlpools, spacious common areas. Private baths, queen beds, guest robes, hair dryers, toiletries, soft music and lighting, TV/VCRs. Candlelight desserts and breakfast feasts. Outdoors: hiking, birding, fishing lake, pedalboat, bonfires. Visit the farm animals and peacocks. Chauffered convertible available. Nearby attractions, shopping, recreation, dining.

Trinity Hills Farm Bed and Breakfast Home

Hosts: Mike and Ann Driver, Jim and Nancy Driver
Rooms: 1 + 4 suites (PB) $70-105
Full Breakfast
Credit Cards: A, B, D
Notes: 2, 5, 6 (with prior notice), 7, 12

PARIS

Rosedale Bed and Breakfast

1917 Cypress Street, 40361
(606) 987-1845; (800) 644-1862
Web sites: http://www.cre8IV.com/rosedale.html
http://www.parisky.com

Nestled on 3 secluded acres, complete with flower and herb gardens, benches, a hammock, and lawn games. The fourteen-room, 1862 Italianate brick home is furnished with comfortable antiques. Guests are welcome to peruse the shelves of the mahogany library with its cozy fireplace.

The screened porch, which overlooks some of the gardens, is a picturesque setting for breakfast, reading, and relaxing. Rosedale Bed and Breakfast is less than 20 miles from I–64 and I–75, 18 miles northeast of Lexington in the heart of bluegrass thoroughbred country. Paris and the surrounding area offer outstanding antique shopping and a number of specialty shops. The Kentucky Horse Park is 15 minutes away; Keeneland Race Course, Rupp Arena, and the University of Kentucky are less than 30 minutes away.

Hosts: Katie and Jim Haag
Rooms: 4 (2PB; 2SB) $65-90
Full Breakfast
Credit Cards: A, B
Notes: 2, 5, 7 (12 and up), 8, 10

RICHMOND

Riverhill Bed and Breakfast

661 River Hill Drive, 40475
(606) 624-3222; (800) 378-3877;
FAX (606) 625-5439
E-mail: riverhill@riverhill.net
Web site: http://www.riverhill.net

Located between Lexington and Richmond, the inn offers the best of both worlds: a scenic country setting with quick and easy access to two diverse cities. Enjoy a retreat to peace and quiet or a romantic getaway. The house is new, with a theme taken from the history of Fort Boonesborough. Our bountiful breakfasts are home-cooked and served cafe-style.

Hosts: Glenda and Terry Fields
Rooms: 4 (PB) $79-119
Full Breakfast
Credit Cards: A, B
Notes: 5, 7 (9 and older), 9, 10

SPRINGFIELD

Maple Hill Manor

2941 Perryville Road, 40069-9611
(606) 336-3075; (800) 886-7546

Listed on the National Register of Historic Places, Maple Hill Manor is surrounded by 14 tranquil acres in the scenic bluegrass region. It took 3 years to build, circa 1851, and has 10-foot doors, 13½-foot ceilings, 9-foot windows, a cherry spiral staircase, stenciling in the foyer, three brass and crystal chandeliers, and nine fireplaces. The honeymoon hideaway has a canopy bed and Jacuzzi. Ask about our murder mystery packages. Maple Hill is 1 hour from Louisville and Lexington. This is a no-smoking home.

Hosts: Bob and Kay Carroll
Rooms: 7 (PB) $65-90
Full Breakfast
Credit Cards: A, B
Notes: 2, 5, 7, 8, 9, 10, 12

VERSAILLES

Rose Hill Inn

233 Rose Hill, 40383
(606) 873-5957; (800) 307-0460;
FAX (606) 873-3063
E-mail: innkeepers@rosehillinn.com
Web site: http://www.rosehillinn.com

The 1823 historic Victorian home with its estatelike yard and romantic old trees is near downtown for antiquing and restaurants. Our home has been totally renovated. It offers four guest rooms, all with private baths. The library, parlor, veranda, and porch swing are ready for guests' use. The unique Cottage (summer kitchen) and Auntie's Apartment provide space that is well-suited for families or guests with well-behaved dogs. The full breakfast includes specialties such as banana-filled French toast and garden quiche.

Hosts: Sharon Amberg and Marianne Ruano
Rooms: 5 + cottage (PB) $85-125
Full Breakfast
Credit Cards: A, B, C
Notes: 2, 5, 6 (with approval), 7 (in cottage), 8, 9, 10, 12

WILMORE

Scott Station Inn

305 E. Main Street, 40390
(606) 858-0121

The Scott Station Inn, a late 1800s country farmhouse, was beautifully refurbished in 1990. The inn has kept the charm and gracious air of an old Kentucky home.

Scott Station Inn

Each room has its own decorative theme reflecting the beauty of the state. The green shutters and white picket fence add just the right finishing touch.

Hosts: Ruth and Ian Yorston
Rooms: 6 (4PB; 2SB) $39.95-49.95
Full Breakfast
Credit Cards: A, B, D
Notes: 2, 5, 7, 10, 12

welcome; 7 Children welcome; 8 Tennis nearby; 9 Swimming nearby; 10 Golf nearby; 11 Skiing nearby; 12 May be booked through travel agent.

LOUISIANA

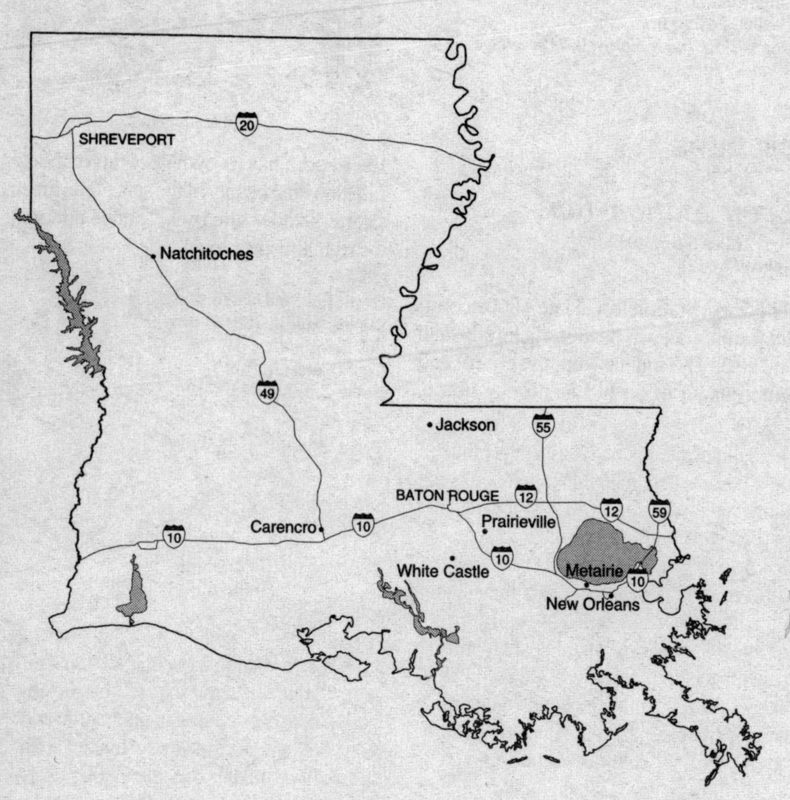

SHREVEPORT
20
Natchitoches
49
Jackson
55
BATON ROUGE
12
12
59
Prairieville
Carencro
10
10
10
White Castle
Metairie
10
New Orleans

Louisiana

CARENCRO/LAFAYETTE

La Maison de Compagne, Lafayette, Bed and Breakfast

825 Kidder Road, **Carencro,** 70520
(318) 896-6529; (800) 895-0235;
FAX (318) 896-1494

Lovely turn-of-the-century Victorian home. Inquire about Enchanting Evening™ and Covenant Marriage Renewal. Cajun country gourmet breakfast prepared by hostess/author of *Lache Pas la Patate* cookbook. Quiet, pastoral location in Cajun country. Cajun culture, music, festivals, and food abound. Near three of Lafayette's best Cajun restaurants: Prudhomme's, Prejean's, and Paul's Pirogue. Swamp tours, museums, gardens, water sports, and much more. Pool, antiques, privacy. Christian home.

Hosts: Joeann and Fred McLemore
Rooms: 4 (PB) $100-135
Full Breakfast
Credit Cards: A, B, D
Notes: 2, 5, 9 (on premises), 12

Milbank Historic House

JACKSON

Milbank Historic House

3045 Bank Street; PO Box 1000, 70748
(504) 634-5901; FAX (504) 634-5151

Located in the beautiful Felicianas of Louisiana, Milbank is a massive, romantic antebellum mansion. It has an interesting and varied history. Rooms are furnished with antique furniture of the late 1800s. Persian rugs, ormolu clocks, carved settees, poster beds, armoires, and much more. Upstairs galleries from which to enjoy the scenic backyard. Delicious breakfast.

NOTES: Credit cards accepted: A Master Card; B Visa; C American Express; D Discover; E Diners Club; F Other; 2 Personal checks accepted; 3 Lunch available; 4 Dinner available; 5 Open all year; 6 Pets welcome; 7 Children welcome; 8 Tennis nearby; 9 Swimming nearby; 10 Golf nearby; 11 Skiing nearby; 12 May be booked through travel agent.

Friendly hosts. The owners are Mr. and Mrs. M.L. Harvey.

Hostess: Marjorie Collamer
Rooms: 2 + 1 suite (PB) $75-100
Full Breakfast
Credit Cards: A, B, D
Notes: 2, 5, 7, 10, 12

NATCHITOCHES

The Levy-East House

358 Jefferson Street, 71457
(318) 352-0662; (800) 840-0662;
FAX (318) 352-9685
Web site: http://www.virtualcities.com/ons/la/z/laz8601.htm

A luxurious B&B located in the heart of the historic district. The beautiful Greek Revival house (circa 1838) has been restored and tastefully renovated to capture the spirit of an earlier time. Furnished with fine antiques that have been in the house for more than 100 years, the Levy-East House offers a gourmet breakfast, queen-size beds, private whirlpool baths, private parking, telephones, and televisions with VCRs in each room. Enjoy elegant rooms and luxurious leisure.

Hosts: Judy and Avery East
Rooms: 4 (PB) $105-200
Full Breakfast
Credit Cards: A, B
Notes: 2, 5, 8, 10, 11, 12

NEW ORLEANS

Bougainvillea House

841 Bourbon Street, 70116
(504) 525-3983

Antique ambience in the heart of the French Quarter—riverboats, gambling, antique stores, and famous restaurants. Central air/heat, private telephones, balconies, patios, cable TV. Walk to everything: aquarium, the Mississippi River, and more. Offstreet parking available.

Hosts: Flo Cairo, Pat and Greg Kohn
Rooms: 3 (PB) $90-250
Continental Breakfast
Credit Cards: B, C
Notes: 5, 10, 12

Essem's House

3660 Gentilly Boulevard, 70122
(504) 947-3401; (888) 240-0070;
FAX (504) 838-0140
E-mail: smb@neworleansbandb.com
Web site: http://www.neworleansbandb.com

Tree-shaded boulevards, direct transport to French Quarter (15–20 minutes), safe, convenient area of stable family homes. This ten-room brick home, "New Orleans' First Bed and Breakfast," has three bedrooms—one king with private bath, two doubles with a shared bath. Separate cottage efficiency (one king or two singles with private bath). Enjoy the solarium, living room, and back garden!

Hostess: Sarah Margaret Brown
Rooms: 4 (2PB; 2SB) $65-85
Continental Breakfast
Credit Cards: A, B, C, D
Notes: 5, 8, 9, 10

New Orleans B&B and Accommodations

671 Rosa Avenue, **Metairie,** 70005
(504) 838-0071; (888) 240-0070;
FAX (504) 838-0140
E-mail: info@neworleansbandb.com
Web site: http://www.neworleansbandb.com

If you appreciate the beauty of crystal chandeliers, hardwood floors, antiques,

NOTES: Credit cards accepted: A Master Card; B Visa; C American Express; D Discover; E Diners Club; F Other; 2 Personal checks accepted; 3 Lunch available; 4 Dinner available; 5 Open all year; 6 Pets

Oriental rugs, interesting architecture, or simple, traditional elegance, call us. If you want private hideaways, condominiums, private apartments, or cozy rooms in New Orleans neighborhoods, call us. Whatever your choice, you will find gracious hospitality and knowledgeable hosts who are concerned about your safety, comfort, and pleasure. We also are familiar with bed and breakfast plantations, homes, and cottages throughout Louisiana. Call us, too, for referrals to other states or England.

Owner: Sarah Margaret Brown
Rooms: 200 (some PB) $65-300
Continental Breakfast
Credit Cards: A, B, C, D
Notes: 5

St. Vincent's Guest House

1507 Magazine Street, 70130
(504) 566-1515; FAX (504) 566-1518
E-mail: PeterSchreiber@compuserve.com

A European-style guest house, St. Vincent's is an impressive structure of significant architectural, historical importance. Wrought iron lacework and wraparound balconies complement the softly aged red brick facade and imbue the old orphanage with a romantic, gracious air. Landscaped courtyard and swimming pool. The old-world ambience is continued inside with chintz, wicker, and antique furnishings; high ceilings; and original architectural moldings and pediments. Guests and visitors enjoy the traditional English tea room in which breakfast, lunch, and afternoon tea are served; the airy salon; the conference room; and the guest rooms, all individually and tastefully decorated. You'll find the comforts of the modern world and the charm of the old within a moderate budget. Accommodations and services compare to expensive downtown hotels at a fraction of the price.

Hosts: Peter and Sally Schreiber
Rooms: 75 (PB) $59-69
Full Breakfast
Credit Cards: A, B, C, D, E
Notes: 3, 5, 6, 7, 8, 9 (onsite), 10, 12

PRAIRIEVILLE

The Tree House in the Park

16520 Airport Drive, 70769
(225) 622-3885; (800) LE CABIN (532-2246)

A Cajun cabin in the swamp high among the trees and Spanish moss. There are three bed and breakfast accommodations with private entrance, private bath, queen-size waterbed, satellite TV, refrigerator, and private deck with hot tub. A Cajun supper is served the evening you arrive, as well as a full breakfast every morning. The Tree House is perfect for a honeymoon hideaway, birthday, or anniversary.

Hosts: Vic and Vikki Hotopp
Rooms: 3 (PB) $125-175
Full Breakfast
Credit Cards: A, B, C, D
Notes: 2, 3, 4 (included 1st night), 5, 9 (pool), 12

ST. FRANCISVILLE

Lake Rosemound Inn

10473 Lindsey Lane, 70775
(504) 635-3176; FAX (504) 635-2224

Lake Rosemound is one of the most picturesque areas in the heart of plantation country, just minutes from historic St. Francisville. All four guest rooms have a view of the lake and king- or queen-size beds, television, air-conditioning, and paddle fans. The Rosemound and Feliciana suites have Jacuzzi tubs for two. Start your day with a great country breakfast, then enjoy the hammocks, porch swings, canoe, paddleboat, and famous "help yourself" ice cream bar. The inn is handicap-accessible. Hiking, horseback riding nearby.

Hosts: Jeane and Jon Peters
Rooms: 4 (PB) $75-105
Full Breakfast
Credit Cards: A, B, C, D
Notes: 2, 5, 6, 7, 9, 10

WHITE CASTLE

Nottoway Plantation Restaurant and Inn

PO Box 160, 70788-0160
(504) 545-2730; FAX (504) 545-8632
E-mail: nottoway@worldnet.att.net
Web site: http://www.louisianatravel.com

Experience the grandeur and elegance of 19th-century southern living in the largest plantation home in the South. Known as the "White Castle of Louisiana," Nottoway was completed in 1859 and is listed on the National Register of Historic Places. Accommodations in the mansion, private baths, wake-up, full breakfast. Daily guided tours, 9 AM–5 PM. The restaurant serves Cajun and Creole cuisine, 11 AM–3 PM and 6–9 PM. Gift shop, pool.

Hostess: Cindy Hidalgo
Rooms: 13 (PB) $125-250
Full Breakfast
Credit Cards: A, B, C, D
Notes: 2, 3, 4, 5, 7, 8, 9, 10, 12

Maine

BAILEY ISLAND

Captain York House B&B

PO Box 298, 04003
(207) 833-6224
E-mail: athorn7286@aol.com
Web site: http://www.iwws.com/captainyork

Stay at a restored sea captain's house on Bailey Island. Spectacular view of the ocean, beautiful sunsets. Relax in a peaceful environment, yet close to Portland, Freeport, Brunswick, Bath, and Boothbay Harbor. Quiet island living in midcoast Maine. Quaint fishing villages nearby.

Hosts: Alan and Jean Thornton
Rooms: 5 (3PB; 2SB) $65-105
Full Breakfast
Credit Cards: A, B
Notes: 2, 5, 7 (over 12), 10, 12

BAR HARBOR

Atlantic Oakes By-the-Sea

119 Eden Street, 04609
(207) 288-5801; (800) 336-2463;
FAX (207) 288-8402
E mail: oakes@acadia.net
Web site: http://www.barharbor.com/oakes

We have restored the Sir Harry Oakes mansion/summer cottage on our grounds. This charming house was named "The Willows" after the willow trees on the entrance drive. About 200 summer cottages were built in Bar Harbor from 1880 to 1890. "The Willows" was built in 1913—one of the last estates built. The large wooden hotels (now gone) were built from 1865 to 1885. No matter how large and ostentatious the summer homes were, they always were called "cottages." "The Willows" is located on the ground of the Atlantic Oakes By-the-Sea. There are four tennis courts and indoor and outdoor pools available for use by B&B guests.

Hostess: Betty Cough
Rooms: 8 (PB) $133-245
Continental Breakfast
Credit Cards: A, B, C
Notes: 8 and 9 (on premises), 10, 12

Black Friar Inn

10 Summer Street, 04609-1424
(207) 288-5091; FAX (207) 288-4197
E-mail: blackfriar@acadia.net
Web site: http://www.blackfriar.com

Black Friar Inn is a completely rebuilt and restored inn incorporating beautiful woodwork, mantels, windows, and bookcases from old mansions and churches on Mount Desert Island. Gourmet breakfast may

---

welcome; 7 Children welcome; 8 Tennis nearby; 9 Swimming nearby; 10 Golf nearby; 11 Skiing nearby; 12 May be booked through travel agent.

MAINE

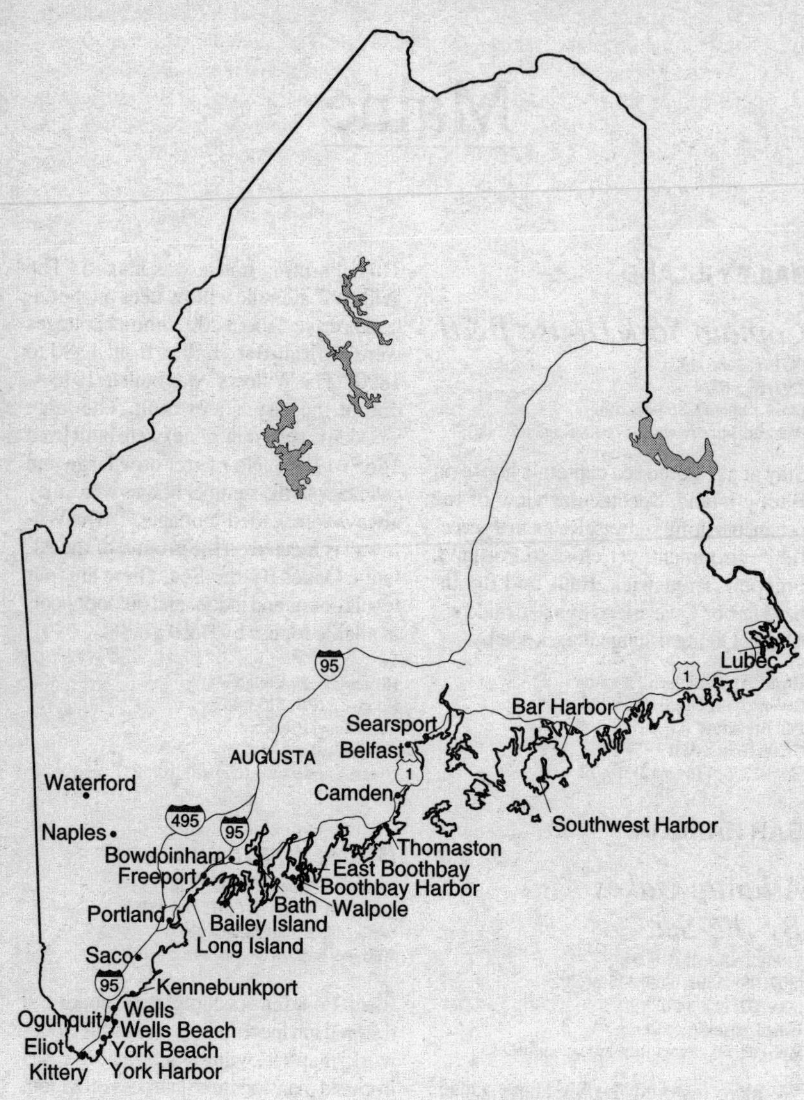

95
1
Lubec
Bar Harbor
Searsport
Belfast
AUGUSTA
1
Waterford
Camden
495
95
Naples
Southwest Harbor
Thomaston
Bowdoinham
East Boothbay
Freeport
Boothbay Harbor
Bath
Walpole
Portland
Bailey Island
Long Island
Saco
95
Kennebunkport
Wells
Ogunquit
Wells Beach
Eliot
York Beach
Kittery
York Harbor

include homemade breads, pastry, and muffins; fresh fruit; eggs *du jour*; etc. Afternoon refreshments are provided. All rooms have queen beds; the suite has a king bed. Within walking distance of the waterfront, restaurants, and shops, with ample parking available. Short drive to Acadia National Park.

Hosts: Perry and Sharon Risley and Falke
Rooms: 7 (PB) $95-150
Full Breakfast
Credit Cards: A, B, D
Notes: 2, 7 (over 11), 8, 9, 10, 11 (cross-country)

The Inn at Bay Ledge

The Inn at Bay Ledge

1385 Sand Point Road, 04609
(207) 288-4204; FAX (207) 288-5573
E-mail: bayledge@downeast.net
Web site: http://www.maineguide.com/barharbor/bayledge

Dramatic and peaceful, overlooking Frenchman's Bay. At the top of an 80-foot cliff with seventy-nine steps (and some benches along the way) leading to a private (Maine stone) beach. On 2 acres of tall pines. Five miles from town center, 2 miles from the Acadia National Park main entrance. Every room except one in the main house has an ocean view. Enjoy a dip in the pool, a sauna, a steam shower, or a book in the hammock overlooking the water. Eagles fly by. From the deck you watch seals and dolphins eating their breakfast. The "added to a million times" early 1900s house has welcoming fireplaces, Oriental rugs, and rooms with feather beds, antiques, designer linens, and down comforters.

Hosts: Jack and Jeani Ochtera
Rooms: 10 (PB) $75-265 (seasonal)
Full Breakfast
Credit Cards: A, B
Notes: 2, 8, 9 (onsite), 10

The Maples Inn

16 Roberts Avenue, 04609
(207) 288-3443; FAX (207) 288-0356
E-mail: maplesinn@acadia.net
Web site: http://www.acadia.net/maples

Built in the early 1900s, the Maples Inn is located on a quiet, tree-lined, residential street. Guests will be away from Bar Harbor traffic, yet within walking distance of intimate restaurants and the surrounding sea. Reserve the White Birch Suite with its fireplace or the Red Oak room with its treehouse. Palates will be treated to recipes featured in *Gourmet* and *Bon Appetit*

The Maples Inn

NOTES: Credit cards accepted: A Master Card; B Visa; C American Express; D Discover; E Diners Club; F Other; 2 Personal checks accepted; 3 Lunch available; 4 Dinner available; 5 Open all year; 6 Pets welcome; 7 Children welcome; 8 Tennis nearby; 9 Swimming nearby; 10 Golf nearby; 11 Skiing nearby; 12 May be booked through travel agent.

magazines. Classic tranquillity near Acadia National Park awaits you.

Hosts: Tom and Sue Palumbo
Rooms: 6 (PB) $60-150
Full Breakfast
Credit Cards: A, B, D
Notes: 2, 5, 8, 9, 10, 11

Stratford House Inn

45 Mt. Desert Street, 04609
(207) 288-5189
E-mail: inkeeper@agate.net
Web site: http://maine.com/people/stratford

Beautiful English Tudor inn styled after Shakespeare's birthplace at Stratford-Upon-Avon. Furnished with antiques of the Victorian and Jacobean periods. The beautiful music room has a restored grand piano and electronic organ. The inn is located within easy walking distance of the fine shops and restaurants of downtown Bar Harbor. Acadia National Park is but 8 minutes by car.

Hosts: Barbara C. and Norman W. Moulton
Rooms: 10 (8PB; 2SB) $90-150
Continental Breakfast
Credit Cards: A, B, C
Notes: 2, 7, 8, 9, 10, 12

BATH

Fairhaven Inn

RR 2, Box 85, N. Bath Road, 04530
(207) 443-4391; (888) 443-4391;
FAX (207) 443-6412
E-mail: fairhvn@gwi.net
Web site: http://www.mainecoast.com/fairhaveninn

Fairhaven Inn is a 1790 Colonial nestled on the hillside overlooking the Kennebec River. Guests have 20 acres of country sights and sounds to enjoy. Beaches, golf, and a maritime museum are nearby, plus cross-country ski trails and wood fire sites. A gourmet breakfast is served each morning, year-round. Special winter packages are available.

Hosts: Dave and Susie Reed
Rooms: 8 (6PB; 2SB) $80-120
Full Breakfast
Credit Cards: A, B, D
Notes: 4 (weekend package), 5, 7 (by arrangement), 8, 9, 10, 11 (cross-country)

BELFAST

Belhaven Inn B&B

14 John Street, 04915
(207) 338-5435
E-mail: belhaven@ime.net
Web site: http://www.ime.net/~belhaven

Stay with us in our circa-1861 Victorian home. A comfortable, *family*-oriented inn. A full three-course country breakfast makes lunch unnecessary. A circular staircase leads up to four bright and charmingly decorated guest rooms. Unwind in one of four parlors or the veranda. A fully equipped efficiency guest suite with private entrance and sundeck is available for longer stays.

Hosts: Anne and Paul Bartels
Rooms: 5 (3PB; 2SB) $65-95
Full Breakfast
Credit Cards: A, B
Notes: 2, 5, 6, 7, 8, 9, 10, 11 (cross-country)

The Jeweled Turret Inn

40 Pearl Street, 04915
(207) 338-2304; (800) 696-2304
Web sites: http://www.bbonline.com/me/jeweledturret/
http://www.maineguide.com/me/jeweledturret/

This grand representative of the Victorian era, constructed circa 1898, offers unique architectural features and is listed on the National Register of Historic Places. The inn is named for the grand staircase that winds up the turret, which is lighted by both stained- and leaded-glass panels with jewellike embellishments. Guests will find the rooms filled with Victoriana. Each guest room has its own bath. A gourmet breakfast is served each morning. Shops, restaurants, and the waterfront are just a pleasant stroll away.

Hosts: Carl and Cathy Heffentrager
Rooms: 7 (PB) $75-105
Full Breakfast
Credit Cards: A, B
Notes: 2, 5, 8, 9, 10, 11, 12

The White House at No. 1 Church Street

No. 1 Church Street, 04915
(207) 338-1901; (888) 290-1901;
FAX (207) 338-5161
E-mail: whitehouse@mainebb.com
Web site: http://www.mainebb.com

The White House is one of the most photographed homes along Maine's coast. Its unique design places it as one of the top Greek Revival homes in the state. The regal home is surrounded by a parklike triangle of beautiful grounds and gardens. Limited water views of picturesque Penobsot Bay. Located in a national historic district, a short walk from the harbor and downtown with its several fine restaurants and shops.

Hosts: Dianne Porter, Robert Hansen, Terry Prescott
Rooms: 6 (PB) $75-125 (seasonal)
Full Breakfast
Credit Cards: A, B, D
Notes: 2, 5, 7 (10 and older), 8, 9, 10, 11

1830 Admiral's Quarters Inn

BOOTHBAY HARBOR

1830 Admiral's Quarters Inn

71 Commercial Street, 04538
(207) 633-2474; FAX (207) 633-5904
E-mail: loon@admiralsquartersinn.com
Web site: http://www.admiralsquartersinn.com

The Admiral's Quarters Inn, a recently renovated sea captain's house, provides an eagle's-eye view of all that's going on at sea and on land. It's within easy walking distance of shops, restaurants, and piers. Built in 1830, the inn offers six tidy guest rooms (most two-room suites) equipped with private entrances, decks, baths, phones, and cable TVs. You can linger over your hearty homemade buffet breakfast in the new solarium, which overlooks the harbor and all the bustle of Commercial Street. On those occasional dreary Maine summer days, there's sure to be a fire in the wood stove. Settle down in the sliding swing on the beautifully manicured grounds, or stand sentry on your deck.

Hosts: Les and Deb Hallstrom
Rooms: 6 (PB) $75-145 (seasonal)
Full Hearty, Homemade Breakfast
Credit Cards: A, B, D
Notes: 2, 5, 8, 9, 10

---

welcome; 7 Children welcome; 8 Tennis nearby; 9 Swimming nearby; 10 Golf nearby; 11 Skiing nearby; 12 May be booked through travel agent.

Anchor Watch Bed and Breakfast

9 Eames Road, 04538
(207) 633-7565
E-mail: diane@lincoln.midcoast.com
Web site: http://www.maineguide.com/boothbay/anchorwatch

Our seaside captain's house welcomes you to Boothbay Harbor. It is a short walk to unique shops, fine dining, and scenic boat trips on your host's *Balmy Days Cruises*. A delicious breakfast is served each morning by the fireplace in the sunny breakfast nook by the sea. The comfortable guest rooms are decorated with quilts and stenciling and have private baths—one with a whirlpool tub, three with water-view balconies. You may enjoy late afternoon tea by the fire, watching the lobster boats returning, and beautiful sunsets from our private pier.

Hostess: Diane Campbell
Rooms: 5 (PB) $80-129
Full Breakfast
Credit Cards: A, B, D
Notes: 2, 5, 8, 9, 10, 12

Five Gables Inn

Murray Hill Road; PO Box 335, **East Boothbay,** 04544
(207) 633-4551; (800) 451-5048
E-mail: info@fivegablesinn.com
Web site: http://www.fivegablesinn.com

For more than a century, the Five Gables Inn has perched on a garden-framed hillside overlooking Linekin Bay. The inn still has a broad veranda with a hammock and plenty of comfortable chairs, with a view of lobster boats tugging at their moorings. Completely renovated and restored to its original Victorian charm. All the rooms afford spectacular views of the bay. Five rooms have working fireplaces.

Five Gables Inn

Hosts: Mike and De Kennedy
Rooms: 15 (PB) $90-160
Full Breakfast
Credit Cards: A, B
Notes: 2, 7 (above 8), 8, 9, 10, 12

Harbour Towne Inn on the Waterfront

71 Townsend Avenue, 04538
(207) 633-4300 (voice and FAX); (800) 722-4240
E-mail: maineo@gwi.net
Web site: http://www.acadia.net/harbortowneinn

Our refurbished Victorian inn retains turn-of-the-century ambience while providing all modern amenities. The colorful gardens and quiet, tree-shaded location slopes right to the edge of the beautiful New England harbor. Five-minute walk to all activities. Choose a room with outside deck for waterfront views. Our luxurious penthouse is a modern, spacious home that sleeps up to six in luxury and privacy. Stay just once and you will know why our guests return year after year. No smoking or pets.

Host: The Thomas Family
Rooms: 12 (PB) $55-250 (seasonal)
Deluxe Continental Breakfast
Credit Cards: A, B, C, D
Notes: 2, 5, 7 (well-behaved), 8, 9, 10, 11 (cross-country), 12

NOTES: Credit cards accepted: A Master Card; B Visa; C American Express; D Discover; E Diners Club; F Other; 2 Personal checks accepted; 3 Lunch available; 4 Dinner available; 5 Open all year; 6 Pets

Hodgdon Island Inn Bed and Breakfast

Box 492; Barter's Island Road, 04571
(207) 633-7474

An old, restored sea captain's home, circa 1810, overlooking a quiet little cove, just a 5-minute drive from downtown Boothbay Harbor. Perfect for joggers and bicyclists. Six tastefully furnished guest rooms all have private baths. A full breakfast is served, and a swimming pool is available for guests. Open most of the year. Reservations recommended. A warm welcome is assured.

Hosts: Joseph and Sydney Klenk
Rooms: 6 (PB) $70-102
Full Breakfast
Credit Cards: none
Notes: 2, 5 (most), 7 (over 12), 8, 9 (on premise), 10

The Howard House Bed and Breakfast

347 Townsend Avenue, 04538
(207) 633-3933; (800) 872-0721;
FAX (207) 633-6244

The unique, chalet-type design features beamed cathedral ceilings and sliding glass patio doors with private balconies. Each spacious room has cable TV; private bath; and plush, wall-to-wall carpeting. Early American–style furnishings and appointments combine with natural wood walls to provide luxurious accommodations with a decidedly country feeling.

Hosts: Ginny and Tim Farrin
Rooms: 14 (PB) $60-81
Full Breakfast
Credit Cards: none
Notes: 2, 8, 9, 10, 12

BOWDOINHAM

Trelights Bed and Breakfast

RR 2, Box 4503, 04008
(207) 666-3267

Our quiet country getaway is a spacious log home offering friendly hospitality. Convenient location only 25 minutes from Bowdoin College, Freeport Outlet Malls, theaters, and restaurants. Excellent area for hiking and bicycling. Beaches nearby. Full country breakfast with homemade breads and rolls. Extensive library. No smoking. Cat and dog in residence. Open May 1–October 31.

Hosts: Rodney and Beverly Chute
Rooms: 3 (1PB; 2SB) $40-60
Full Breakfast
Credit Cards: A, B
Notes: 2, 7, 9

CAMDEN

Castleview by the Sea

59 High Street, 04843
(207) 236-2344; (800) 272-VIEW (8439)

Castleview by the Sea. It's the setting that sets us apart. We're located on the water side of the oceanview section of Camden's historic district, with spectacular glass-walled views of Camden's only two castles and the sea, right from your bed! You can count the stars across the bay and wake up to bold Maine coast views. Bright and airy charm of classic 1856 cape architecture, wide pine floors, beams, claw-foot tubs, skylights, ceiling fans, and stained glass. A true Maine memory, with decks,

welcome; 7 Children welcome; 8 Tennis nearby; 9 Swimming nearby; 10 Golf nearby; 11 Skiing nearby; 12 May be booked through travel agent.

awnings, and library. Eight-minute walk to harbor restaurants.

Host: Bill Butler
Rooms: 3 (PB) $75-175
Full Breakfast
Credit Cards: A, B
Notes: 2, 8, 9, 10, 11, 12

Windward House B&B

6 High Street, 04843
(207) 236-9656; (207) 230-0433
E-mail: windward@coastalmaine.com
Web site: http://www.windwardhouse.com

Hebrews 13:2: "Do not forget to entertain strangers, for by so doing some have unwittingly entertained angels." A splendid example of Victorian architecture, the Windward House was built in 1854 by Elijah Glover, a prominent shipbuilder and lumberman. Our delightful bedchambers offer canopied beds, claw-foot soak tubs, fireplaces, CD players, romantic music, fluffy duvets, fine linens, and outstanding attention to detail. Indulge in our candlelit, full-service breakfast as reviewed in *Getaway for Gourmets*. Please accept our warm invitation to love and romance in our intimate inn. One block from the village.

Hosts: Tim and Sandy LaPlante
Rooms: 8 (PB) $90-195
Full Breakfast
Credit Cards: A, B
Notes: 2, 5, 10, 11, 12

DAMARISCOTTA (WALPOLE)

Brannon-Bunker Inn

349 State Route 129, **Walpole,** 04573
(207) 563-5941; (800) 563-9225

Brannon-Bunker Inn is an intimate and relaxed country bed and breakfast situated only minutes from a sandy beach, lighthouse, and historic fort in Maine's midcoastal region. Located in a 1920s Cape, converted barn, and carriage house, the guest rooms are furnished in themes that combine the charm of yesterday with the comforts of today. You'll find antique shops nearby.

Hosts: Jeanne and Joe Hovance
Rooms: 7 (5PB; 2SB) $50-75
Continental Breakfast
Credit Cards: A, B, C
Notes: 2, 5, 7, 8, 9, 10, 12

The Farmstead

ELIOT

Farmstead

379 Goodwin Road, 03903
(207) 748-3145

Lovely country inn on 3 acres. Warm, friendly atmosphere exemplifies farm life of the late 1800s. Each Victorian-style guest room has a minirefrigerator and microwave for snacks or special diets. Breakfast may include blueberry pancakes or French toast, homemade syrup, fruit, and juice. Limited handicap access. Minutes from Kittery Factory Outlets, York beaches, Portsmouth, historic sites. One hour from Boston.

Hosts: Meb and John Lippincott
Rooms: 6 (PB) $48-58
Full Breakfast
Credit Cards: A, B, D
Notes: 2, 5, 6, 7, 10, 12

NOTES: Credit cards accepted: A Master Card; B Visa; C American Express; D Discover; E Diners Club; F Other; 2 Personal checks accepted; 3 Lunch available; 4 Dinner available; 5 Open all year; 6 Pets

Captain Briggs House

FREEPORT

Captain Briggs House

8 Maple Avenue, 04032
(207) 865-1868; (800) 217-2477

Welcome to the Captain Briggs House B&B, your home away from home. The inn is located in the heart of the quaint village of Freeport, only 2 short blocks from L.L. Bean. It is a charming, informal, intimate 1853 Federal house, ideally situated. A sea captain and shipbuilder's home, the house has been lovingly restored, with modern amenities tastefully added. Comfortable, bright, cheerful rooms. AAA three-diamond rating. No smoking.

Hosts: The Frank Family
Rooms: 5 (PB) $66-106 (seasonal)
Full Breakfast
Credit Cards: A, B
Notes: 2, 5, 9, 10, 11, 12

Captain Josiah Mitchell House Bed and Breakfast

188 Main Street, 04032
(207) 865-3289

Two blocks from L.L. Bean, this house is a few minutes' walk past centuries-old sea captains' homes and shady trees to more than 120 factory discount shops. After exploring, relax on our beautiful, peaceful veranda with antique wicker furniture and swing. State-approved. Family-owned and -operated. AAA three-diamond.

Hosts: Loretta and Alan Bradley
Rooms: 7 (PB) $68-95
Full Breakfast
Credit Cards: A, B
Notes: 2, 5, 8, 9, 10, 11, 12

White Cedar Inn

178 Main Street, 04032
(207) 865-9099; (800) 853-1269
Web site: http://members.aol.com/bedandbrk/cedar

The White Cedar Inn is a historic inn just 2 blocks north of L.L. Bean and most of Freeport's luxury outlets. Our seven air-conditioned bedrooms are spacious and furnished with antiques. We serve a full country breakfast each morning overlooking our beautifully landscaped grounds. A common room with a television and library is available to our guests. This is a non-smoking inn. The White Cedar Inn has a AAA three-diamond rating.

Hosts: Phil and Carla Kerber
Rooms: 7 (PB) $70-130
Full Breakfast
Credit Cards: A, B, C, D
Notes: 5, 8, 9, 10, 11, 12

KENNEBUNKPORT

Captain Lord Mansion

PO Box 800, 04046-0800
(207) 967-3141; FAX (207) 967-3172
E-mail: captain@biddeford.com
Web site: http://www.captainlord.com

Enjoy an unforgettable romantic experience at the Captain Lord Mansion, where both your personal comfort and intimacy are assured by large, beautifully appointed guest rooms, luxurious amenities such as oversize four-poster beds, cozy gas fireplaces, heated marble/tile bathroom floors, several double Jacuzzis, as well as fresh flowers, full breakfasts, afternoon sweets, and personal attention. At the head of a sloping village green overlooking the Kennebunk River, the inn affords a picturesque, quiet, convenient location from which to explore historic Kennebunkport.

Hosts: Bev Davis and Rick Litchfield
Rooms: 16 (PB) $99-399
Full Breakfast
Credit Cards: A, B, D, E
Notes: 2, 5, 8, 9, 10, 12

Charrid House

2 Arlington Avenue, 04046
(207) 967-5695

Built in 1887, this charming cedar-shingled home started as a gambling casino for the Kennebunkport River Club. It went through incarnations as a tennis club house and a single-family home before becoming Charrid House in 1986. Located on a quiet residential street, it is 1 block from the stunning scenery of Ocean Avenue and the Colony Beach. Several restaurants and shops are within walking distance; the village is 1 mile south. Your hostess is a Maine native and world traveler who has hosted guests from nearly every state, Europe, and beyond. Her breakfasts, which vary daily, include traditional Maine specialties like blueberry pancakes.

Hostess: Ann M. Dubay
Rooms: 2 (SB) $65
Full Breakfast
Credit Cards: none
Notes: 2, 8, 9, 10

The Inn on South Street

5 South Street; PO Box 478A, 04046
(207) 967-5151; (800) 963-5151;
FAX (207) 967-4385
E-mail: edowns@innonsouthst
Web site: http://www.innonsouthst.com

Now approaching its 200th year, this stately Greek Revival house is found in Kennebunkport's historic district. Located on a quiet street, the inn is within walking distance of restaurants, shops, and the water. There are three beautifully decorated guest rooms and one luxury apartment/suite. Private baths, queen-size beds, fireplaces, a common room, afternoon refreshments, and early morning coffee are offered. Breakfast is always special and is served in the large country kitchen with views of the river and ocean or, weather permitting, in the garden. Rated A+ and excellent by ABBA.

Hosts: Eva and Jaques Downs
Rooms: 4 (PB) $99-225
Full Breakfast
Credit Cards: A, B
Notes: 2, 8, 9, 10, 12

Kennebunkport Inn

1 Dock Square; PO Box 111, 04046
(207) 967-2621; (800) 248-2621;
FAX (207) 967-3705
Web site: http://www.thekennebunkportinn.com

Classic country inn located in the heart of Kennebunkport near shops and the historic district, beaches, boating, and golf. Originally a sea captain's home, the inn maintains its charm with antique furnishings in each of the thirty-four rooms, which all include private baths, phones, TVs, and AC. Serving breakfast and dinner, May–October, in two elegant dining rooms with fireplaces. The inn also features a Victorian pub with piano bar. The rooms are open year-round.

Hosts: Rick and Martha Griffin
Rooms: 35 (PB) $69.50-229
Full Breakfast
Credit Cards: A, B, C
Notes: 2, 4, 5, 7, 8, 9, 10, 12

King's Port Inn

PO Box 1070, 04046
(207) 987-4340; (800) 286-5767;
FAX (207) 967-4810
E-mail: info@kingsport.com
Web site: http://www.kingsport.com

King's Port Inn combines affordable rates with unique amenities and convenience to famous Dock Square, Kennebunkport's shops, restaurants, and beaches. Most rooms offer color cable TV, telephone, refrigerator, full private bath, and AC. Choose one of the luxurious deluxe rooms with king bed, dual shower, and private two-person Jacuzzi. Other features include surround-sound theater entertainment and a pantry sideboard breakfast buffet.

Hosts: Bill and Rosita Greer
Rooms: 32 (PB) $49-135 (seasonal)
Continental Breakfast
Credit Cards: A, B, D
Notes: 2, 5, 7, 8, 9, 10, 11, 12

Maine Stay Inn

PO Box 500-A, 04046
(207) 967-2117; (800) 950-2117;
FAX (207) 967-8757
E-mail: innkeeper@mainestayinn.com
Web site: http://www.mainestayinn.com

A grand Victorian inn that exudes charm from its wraparound porch to its perennial flower garden and spacious lawn. The

Maine Stay Inn

white clapboard house, built in 1860 and listed on the National Historic Register, and the adjoining cottages sit grandly in Kennebunkport's historic district. The Maine Stay features a variety of delightful accommodations, all with private baths, color cable TV, and air-conditioning. Many rooms have fireplaces. A sumptuous full breakfast and afternoon tea are included. The inn is an easy walk from the harbor, shops, galleries, and restaurants. AAA three-diamond- and Mobil three-star-rated.

Hosts: Lindsay and Carol Copeland
Rooms: 17 (PB) $95-225
Full Breakfast
Credit Cards: A, B, C
Notes: 5, 7, 8, 9, 10, 12

KITTERY

Enchanted Nights Bed and Breakfast

29 Wentworth Street, 03904
(207) 439-1489
E-mail: info@enchanted-nights-bandb.com
Web site: http://www.enchanted-nights-bandb.com

Enchanted Nights Bed and Breakfast offers affordable luxury 75 minutes north of

Boston in coastal Maine. The home is fanciful and whimsical for the romantic at heart. French and Victorian furnishings with CATVs. Just 3 minutes from historic Portsmouth dining, dancing, concerts in the park, historic homes, the theater, harbor cruises, cliff walks, scenic ocean drives, beaches, charming neighboring resorts, a water park, and outlet malls. Enjoy the whirlpool tub for two. A full breakfast is served (or pay $12 less), and you may enjoy a Portsmouth cafe. Pets welcome. No smoking indoors.

Hosts: Nancy Bogenberger and Peter Lamandid
Rooms: 8 (6PB; 2SB) $52-182
Full Breakfast
Credit Cards: A, B, C, D
Notes: 2, 5, 6, 8, 9, 10, 12

LONG ISLAND

Cushing Homestead Bed and Breakfast

Box 266, 04050
(207) 766-2846; (207) 774-4754

Located on Long Island, a 45-minute ferry ride from Portland, the bed and breakfast is a small island getaway. After a day at the beach or exploring the island, relax on the porch and watch the sunset. In the morning, enjoy a continental breakfast of homemade muffins or coffee cake. We also have a three-bedroom cottage and a two-bedroom unit next door, for rent by the week or night. No smoking.

Hosts: Sue and Sam Longanecker
Rooms: 8 (1PB; 7SB) $49-86
Continental Breakfast
Credit Cards: none
Notes: 2, 8, 9

LUBEC

Breakers by the Bay

37 Washington, 04652
(207) 733-2487

Breathtaking views of the Bay, Campobello Island, Grand Mansion Island, and lighthouses from private decks. Antique beds, handmade quilts, and crocheted tablecloths. Gas log fireplaces. Rooms have private entrances and decks, TVs, refrigerators. Close to International Bridge to Campobello and FDR house, Quaddy Head State Park, four lighthouses.

Host: E.M. Elg
Rooms: 5 (3PB; 2SB) $50-75
Full Breakfast
Credit Cards: none
Notes: 2, 8, 10

NAPLES

The Augustus Bove House

RR1, Box 501, 04055
(207) 693-6365

Historic Hotel Naples, visited in the '20s by Enrico Caruso and Joseph P. Kennedy. In horse-and-buggy days, it was one of the area's first "summer hotels." Within easy walking distance of the causeway, restaurants, recreation, and shops. Naples, a four-season area of activity, has something of interest for everyone. Our guest rooms have elegant yet homey furnishings and feature queen, twin, and king beds. Hot tub. Most feature modern, private baths. Robes furnished. AC, TV, phones.

Hosts: Dave and Arlene Stetson
Rooms: 10 (8PB; 2SB) $59-139 (seasonal)
Full Breakfast
Credit Cards: A, B, C, D
Notes: 2, 5, 6, 7, 8, 9, 10, 11

Inn at Long Lake

PO Box 806; Lakehouse Road, 04055
(207) 693-6226; (800) 437-0328

Enjoy romantic elegance and turn-of-the-century charm at the Inn at Long Lake, nestled amid the pines and waterways of the lake region of western Maine. The inn has sixteen restored rooms with TV, air-conditioning, and private baths. Situated near the causeway, the inn is close to four-season activities and fine dining.

Hosts: Maynard and Irene Hincks
Rooms: 16 (PB) $59-150
Continental Breakfast
Credit Cards: A, B, D
Notes: 2, 7, 9, 10, 11, 12

OGUNQUIT

The Pine Hill Inn

PO Box 2336, 03907
(207) 361-1004
Web site: http://www.chronbooks.com

One-hundred-year-old renovated Victorian, quiet and secluded, just a 5-minute walk from Perkins Cove, which abounds with lobster boats, shops, restaurants, and the rocky coast of Maine. Spacious rooms, private bath, ceiling fan, individually controlled heat. The inn is nestled among pines, off the beaten path—a bird-watcher's paradise. Enjoy a book and sip tea on the 50-foot screened-in porch.

Hosts: Frank and Lou-Ann Agnelli
Rooms: 5 (PB) + 2-bedroom cottage (minimum stay three nights, cottage); $85-120 suites, $300 and up, cottage
Continental Breakfast
Credit Cards: A, B, F
Notes: 2, 5, 9, 10

The Terrace by the Sea

PO Box 831, 03907
(207) 646-3232
E-mail: innkeeper@terracebythesea.com
Web site: http://www.terracebythesea.com

The Terrace by the Sea blends the elegance of our Colonial inn and our deluxe motel accommodations. Both offer spectacular ocean views in a peaceful, secluded setting across from the beach. All rooms have private baths, air-conditioning, telephones, color cable televisions, heat, refrigerators, and some efficiency kitchens. The Terrace by the Sea is within easy walking distance of the beautiful sandy beach, Marginal Way, shops, restaurants, and a link to the trolleys. Come share the charm and hospitality of New England!

Hosts: John and Daryl Bullard
Rooms: 36 (PB) $46-160
Continental Breakfast
Credit Cards: none
Notes: 2, 4, 8, 9, 10

PORTLAND

Inn on Carleton

46 Carleton Street, 04102
(207) 775-1910; (800) 639-1779;
FAX (207) 761-0956
Web site: http://www.innoncarleton.com

The innkeepers graciously welcome you to their restored 1869 Victorian home located in Portland's historic Western Promenade neighborhood. Situated on a quiet, tree-lined street in a unique residential neighborhood of Victorian architecture, the Inn on Carleton is close to the center of downtown Portland. A short walk to the Portland Museum of Art, Maine Medical

Center, the Performing Arts Center, and the city's business district. Close at hand are Casco Bay's Calendar Islands; the international ferry to Nova Scotia; and the Old Port area with its cobbled streets, colorful shops, and many fine restaurants.

Hosts: Phil and Sue Cox
Rooms: 7 (6PB;1SB) $65-160
Full Breakfast
Credit Cards: A, B, D
Notes: 2, 5, 7 (9+), 8, 9, 10, 11, 12

West End Inn

146 Pine Street, 04102
(207) 772-1377 (voice and FAX);
(800) 338-1377

Built in 1871, this historic town house blends the architecture and beauty of yesteryear with all the comforts and conveniences of today. Each of our guest rooms is unique in design and has a private bath for your privacy and convenience. A full, hot breakfast starts your day of enjoyment in this beautiful seaport city.

Host: John Leonard
Rooms: 6 (PB) $109-179
Full Breakfast
Credit Cards: A, B, C
Notes: 2, 5, 10, 11, 12

SACO

The Crown 'n' Anchor Inn

121 North Street; PO Box 228, 04072
(207) 282-3829; (800) 561-8865;
FAX (207) 282-7495

Our North Street location places the Crown 'n' Anchor Inn at the hub of local attractions. Delight in this Greek Revival two-story house with ornate Victorian furnishings, period antiques, and many collectibles. Guests desiring to take time out from their busy schedules are invited to socialize in our parlor, curl up with a good book in our library, or just relax and enjoy the garden views from the comfort of our front porch. Just minutes from Kennebunkport, Wells, Ogunquit, Kittery, and more.

Hosts: John Barclay and Martha Forester
Rooms: 6 (PB) $60-110
Full Breakfast
Credit Cards: A, B, C
Notes: 2, 5, 6, 7 (by arrangement), 8, 9, 10, 11, 12

SEARSPORT

Brass Lantern Inn

81 W. Main Street, 04974
(207) 548-0150; (800) 691-0150
E-mail: brasslan@agate.net
Web site: http://www.agate.net/~brasslan/brasslantern.html

Nestled at the edge of the woods, this gracious Victorian inn, built in 1850 by a sea captain, overlooks Penobscot Bay. Features include an ornate tin ceiling in the dining room, where full breakfasts are served by candlelight. A ground floor room is available. Two of our rooms can sleep three. The Brass Lantern Inn is within walking distance of the ocean. Leave stress behind; relax and unwind with us. This is a smoke-free inn.

Hosts: Dick and Maggie Zieg
Rooms: 5 (PB) $65-90
Full Breakfast
Credit Cards: A, B, D
Notes: 2, 5, 7, 8, 9, 10, 11, 12

Captain Green Pendleton Bed and Breakfast

428 E. Main Street, 04974
(800) 949-4403

The Captain Green Pendleton is a fine sea captain's home near the Penobscot Bay. Enjoy bright, airy bedrooms with charming and simple furnishings of the late 1800s, with parlour and bedroom fireplaces. The main house, attached farmhouse, and barn are set on sweeping lawns, overlooking a large, spring-fed pond, backed by nearly 80 wooded acres. A walking path circles the meadow, and a cross-country ski trail goes through the woods. We serve a full, cooked breakfast.

Hosts: Richard and Kathleen Greiner
Rooms: 3 (1PB; 2SB) $55-65
Full Breakfast
Credit Cards: A, B
Notes: 2, 5, 10, 11

Thurston House Bed and Breakfast Inn

8 Elm Street; PO Box 686, 04974
(207) 548-2213; (800) 240-2213; call about FAX
E-mail: thurston@acadia.net
Web site: http://www.obs-us.com/chesler/thurstonhousebnbinn

This beautiful Colonial home, circa 1830, with ell and carriage house was built as a parsonage house for Stephen Thurston, uncle of Winslow Homer, who visited often. Now you can visit in a casual environment. The quiet village setting is steps from Penobscot Marine Museum, beach park on Penobscot Bay, restaurants, churches, galleries, antiques, more. Relax in one of our four guest rooms—one with a bay view, two that are great for kids. Enjoy the "forget about lunch" breakfasts.

Hosts: Carl and Beverly Eppig
Rooms: 4 (2PB; 2SB) $50-65
Full Breakfast
Credit Cards: A, B, C
Notes: 2, 5, 7, 8, 9, 10, 11, 12

SOUTHWEST HARBOR

Inn at Southwest

PO Box 593, 04679
(207) 244-3835; FAX (207) 244-9879
E-mail: innatsw@acadia.net
Web site: http://acadia.net/innatsw

This Second Empire Victorian B&B has welcomed guests since 1884. The wicker-filled wraparound porch is the perfect spot to enjoy our Victorian garden and the harbor view. Enjoy spacious rooms, private baths, and gourmet breakfasts. Beautiful Acadia National Park is 5 minutes from our doorstep; it offers spectacular coastlines and 150 miles of hiking trails. Southwest Harbor is on the "quiet side" of Mt. Desert Island, near Bar Harbor.

Hostess: Jill Lewis
Rooms: 9 (PB) $60-135 (seasonal)
Full Breakfast
Credit Cards: A, B, D
Notes: 2, 7 (8 and older), 9, 10

The Island House

Clark Point Road; PO Box 1006, 04679
(207) 244-5180
E-mail: islandab@acadia.net
Web site: http://www.acadia.net/island_house

Relax in a gracious, restful seacoast home on the quiet side of Mt. Desert Island. We serve such Island House favorites as blueberry scones and fresh fruit crepes. A charming, private loft apartment is available. Acadia National Park is only a 5-minute drive away. Located across the street from the harbor, near swimming, sailing, biking, and hiking.

Hosts: Ann and Charles Bradford
Rooms: 4 + efficiency apartment (3PB; 2SB) $50-95
Full Breakfast
Credit Cards: A, B (for overseas guests & room guarantee)
Notes: 5, 7 (over 5 and well-supervised), 8, 9, 10, 11, 12

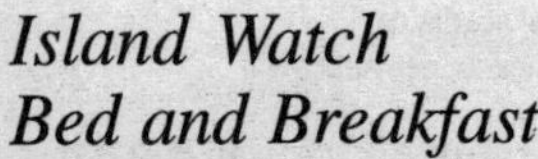

Island Watch Bed and Breakfast

73 Freeman Ridge Road; PO Box 1359, 04679
(207) 244-7229

Wake to the rising sun over Cadillac Mountain and the majestic sea, high atop Freeman Ridge in the heart of Mt. Desert Island. A 15-minute walk to Acadia National Park, 5 minutes to the village and harbor. A bird-watcher's paradise where wildlife abounds. Smoke-free. Private baths and hearty breakfasts.

Hostess: Maxine Clark
Rooms: 6 (PB) $75-85
Full Breakfast
Credit Cards: none
Notes: 2, 8, 9, 10

The Lambs Ear Inn

60 Clark Point Road, 04679
(207) 244-9828; FAX (207) 244-9924

Our old Maine house was built in 1857. It is comfortable and scenic, away from the hustle and bustle. Private baths, comfortable beds with crisp, fresh linens. Enjoy the sparkling harbor views. Breakfast to

The Lambs Ear Inn

remember. Come and be a part of this special village and of Mt. Desert Island, surrounded by Acadia National Park.

Hostess: Elizabeth Hoke
Rooms: 6 (PB) $85-165
Full Breakfast
Credit Cards: A, B, C, D
Notes: 2, 8, 9, 10, 12

THOMASTON

Cap'n Frost Bed and Breakfast

241 Main Street; U.S. Route 1, 04861
(207) 354-8217

Our 1840 Cape home is furnished with country antiques, some of which are for sale. If you are visiting our midcoastal area, we offer you a comfortable overnight stay, situated close to Monhegan Island and a 2-hour drive from Acadia National Park. Reservations are helpful. Personal checks are accepted. All the guest rooms have private baths.

Hosts: Arlene and Harold Frost
Rooms: 3 (PB) $50
Full Breakfast
Credit Cards: none
Notes: 2

WATERFORD

Kedarburn Inn

Route 35, Box 61, 04088
(207) 583-6182; FAX (207) 583-6424
E-mail: kedar01@aol.com
Web site: http://members.aol.com/kedar01/index.html

Located in historic Waterford Village, a place to step back in time while you enjoy the comforts of today. Charming bedrooms decorated with warm country touches, including quilts handmade by Margaret, will add pleasure to your visit. Each day will start with a hearty breakfast. In the evening, relax and enjoy the elegant dinner (served daily). Whether you come for outdoor activities or simply to enjoy the countryside, let us pamper you in our relaxed and friendly atmosphere.

Hosts: Margaret and Derek Gibson
Rooms: 7 (5PB; 2SB) $71-88
Full Breakfast
Credit Cards: A, B, C, D
Notes: 2, 4, 5, 6, 7, 9, 10, 11, 12

WELLS (WELLS BEACH)

The Purple Sandpiper

1058 Post Road, 04090
(207) 646-7990; (800) 484-5040, 7990
E-mail: sb@cybertours.com
Web site: http://purplesandpiper.apexhosting.com

Enjoy your summer vacation in a relaxed, comfortable atmosphere. All rooms have private bath, private entrance, CCTV, and refrigerator. We are just 1 mile from Wells Beach, or choose to lounge by our inground pool. Breakfast includes fresh-baked muffins, pastry, breads, cereal, juice, and coffee. During your stay, pamper yourself at Amy's Beauty Shoppe, our on-site salon. Beaches, antique shops, and fine seafood restaurants nearby. Conveniently located between Kennebunkport and Ogunquit.

Hosts: Stephen and Amy Beauregard
Rooms: 5 (PB) $59-99 (seasonal)
Continental Breakfast
Credit Cards: A, B
Notes: 5, 7, 9

Homestead Inn Bed and Breakfast

YORK BEACH

Homestead Inn Bed and Breakfast

8 S. Main Street, Route 1A, 03910
(207) 363-8952 (voice and FAX)
E-mail: HomstedBB@aol.com
Web site: http://members.aol.com/HomstedBB

Friendly, quiet, homey—four rooms in a 1905 boardinghouse converted to our home in 1969. Panoramic view of ocean and shore hills. Walk to two beaches, shops, and Nubble Lighthouse. Great for small, adult groups. Living room fireplace. Breakfast served in barn-board dining room and outside on private sun deck.

Hosts: Dan and Danielle Duffy
Rooms: 4 (SB) $55-65
Continental Plus Breakfast
Credit Cards: none
Notes: 2, 8, 9, 10, 12

YORK HARBOR

Bell Buoy B&B

PO Box 445, 03911
(207) 363-7264

At the Bell Buoy Bed and Breakfast, there are no strangers, only friends who have never met. The home is located only minutes from I–95 and U.S. 1, minutes from the Kittery outlet malls, and a short walk from sandy beaches—or you may want to stroll the Marginal Way along the ocean shore a short distance away. Enjoy the fireplace and cable television. Homemade bread or muffins are served with breakfast in the dining room each morning, or on the front porch.

Hosts: Wes and Kathie Cook
Rooms: 5 (3PB; 2SB) $60-90
Full Breakfast
Credit Cards: none
Notes: 2, 5, 7 (over 6), 9, 10

York Harbor Inn

Route 1A; PO Box 573, 03911
(207) 363-5119; (800) 343-3869;
FAX (207) 363-7151
E-mail: garyinkeep@aol.com
Web site: http://www.yorkharborinn.com

In the heart of York Harbor, our historic inn enjoys a spectacular setting. Rooms offer antiques, period accessories, fireplaces, ocean-view decks, Jacuzzi spas. Our romantic ocean-view dining room offers top-rated cuisine and fine wines; our Celler Pub features fireplaces and entertainment. Banquet and meeting facilities. Walk to Harbor Beach across the street. Boating, fishing, sea kayaking, golf, and tennis are nearby. Ask about packages.

Hosts: Garry and Nancy Dominguez
Rooms: 33 (PB) $89-239
Continental Breakfast
Credit Cards: A, B, C, E
Notes: 2, 3, 4, 5, 7, 8, 9, 10, 12

Maryland

ALSO SEE LISTINGS UNDER DISTRICT OF COLUMBIA.

ANNAPOLIS

The Barn on Howard's Cove

500 Wilson Road, 21401
(410) 266-6840; FAX (410) 266-7293
E-mail: gdgutsche5@aol.com
Web site: http://www.bnbweb.com/Howard's-Cove.html

The Barn on Howard's Cove welcomes you with warm hospitality to a converted 1850s horse barn overlooking a beautiful cove of the Severn River. You will be located just outside the hubbub of Annapolis and convenient to both Baltimore and Washington, DC. Begin the day with a choice of full breakfasts served in the dining area, on a sunny deck, or in a solarium—all overlooking the river. Our guests enjoy the beautiful gardens, rural setting, antiques, quilts, Oriental rugs, and the charming Noah's ark collection. Two guest bedrooms, each with a private bathroom, await you. One room has a sleeping loft and private deck on the river. Both guest rooms overlook the river. Docking in deep water is provided. Canoes and a kayak are available for guests to use.

Hosts: Graham and Libbie Gutsche
Rooms: 2 (PB) $90
Full Breakfast
Credit Cards: none
Notes: 2, 5, 7, 8, 10, 12

Chez Amis B&B

85 East Street, 21401
(410) 263-6631; (888) 224-6455
Web site: http://www.chezamis.com

Around 1900, Chez Amis "House of Friends" was a grocery store. Still evident are the original oak display cabinet, tin ceiling, and pine floors. One-half block from the capital, 1 block from the harbor, and minutes by foot from the naval academy. "European country" decor with antiques and quilts. Four guest rooms with private baths. King and queen brass beds, TVs, central AC, robes, coffee service, and down comforters in every room. Don is a retired army lawyer, Mickie a former tour guide. They welcome you with true "southern" Christian hospitality!

Hosts: Don and Mickie Deline
Rooms: 4 (PB) $95-120
Full Breakfast
Credit Cards: A, B
Notes: 2, 5, 12

---

welcome; 7 Children welcome; 8 Tennis nearby; 9 Swimming nearby; 10 Golf nearby; 11 Skiing nearby; 12 May be booked through travel agent.

MARYLAND

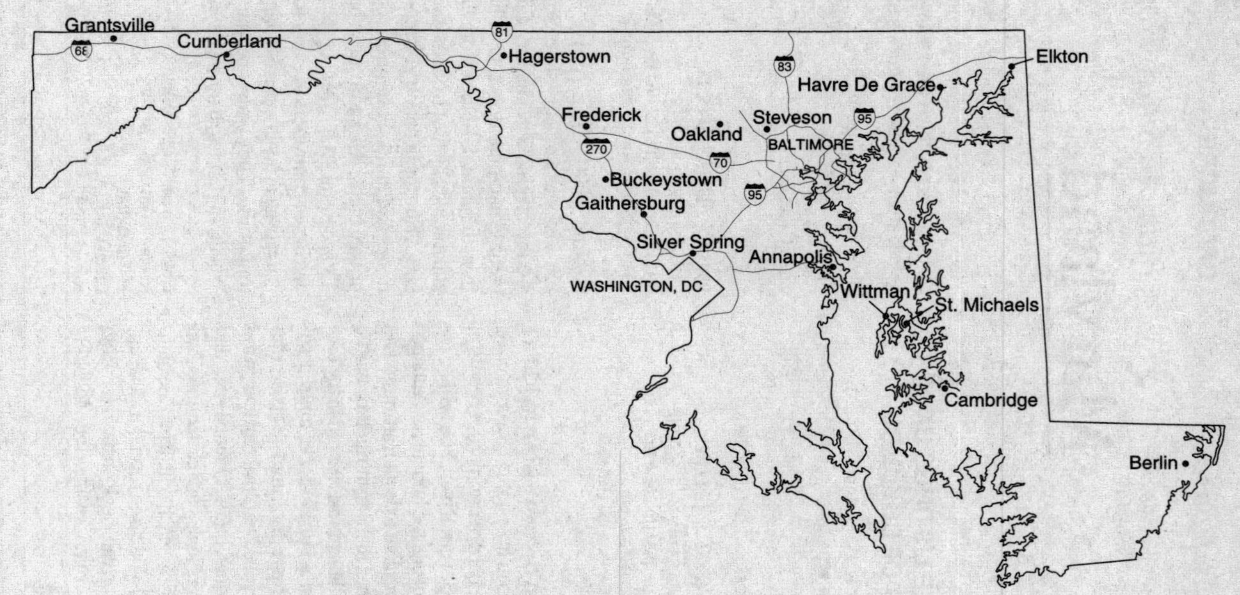

Grantsville
68
Cumberland
81
Hagerstown
83
Elkton
Havre De Grace
Frederick
Steveson
95
Oakland
BALTIMORE
270
70
Buckeystown
95
Gaithersburg
Silver Spring
Annapolis
WASHINGTON, DC
Wittman
St. Michaels
Cambridge
Berlin

Eastport House

101 Severn Avenue, 21403
(410) 295-9710; FAX (410) 295-9711
E-mail: eastporths@toad.net

Less than a block from water's edge, this circa-1870 home touts a colorful history as a grocery store, school, church meeting place, and now a bed and breakfast. Five theme rooms capture the essence of the Chesapeake Bay and create a casual, relaxing environment. A full breakfast is served in the dining room or (seasonally) on the porch. Each guest room has cable television and a private phone line with answering machine. Bicycles are available for guests' use. Fireplace in the parlor. Air-conditioning. Parking is plentiful.

Hosts: Barry and Susan Norfolk
Rooms: 5 (3PB; 2SB) $105-140
Full Breakfast
Credit Cards: none
Notes: 2, 5, 7

The Gloucester House

151 Duke of Gloucester Street, 21401
(410) 268-6323; (410) 216-9189

Come enjoy our cozy elegance and modern comfort. Beautifully renovated 1850 home located in the historic district. Just a short walk from the USNA, city dock, and other attractions. We serve a full breakfast each morning in our formal dining room. Our garden is delightful and the fireplace is cheerful! All private baths.

Hosts: Jim and Phyllis Ward
Rooms: 1 room, 1 suite (PB) $110-135
Full Breakfast
Credit Cards: A, B, D

BALTIMORE

Biltmore Suites Hotel

205 W. Madison Street, 21201
(410) 728-6550; (800) 868-5064;
FAX (410) 728-5829
Web site: http://www.inn-guide.com/Biltmoresuites

A Victorian B&B just a few blocks from the central business district, within the historic Mt. Vernon area, adjacent to "antique row" and within walking distance of the Inner Harbor, convention center, Baltimore arena, museums, art gallery, and Oriole and Ravens Park.

Host: Gul Baz
Rooms: 26 (PB) $99-139 (directory discount)
Continental Breakfast
Credit Cards: A, B, C, D, E
Notes: 5, 6 (fee), 7, 8, 9, 12

BERLIN

Merry Sherwood Plantation B&B

8909 Worcester Highway, 21811
(410) 641-2112; (800) 660-0358;
FAX (410) 641-9528

Guests at this elegant Victorian (circa 1859) can truly relax amid the beautiful formal and parklike gardens, a setting conducive to weddings and special events, located near Ocean City and Assateague. It's in the heart of a growing golf community; recreational activities are available.

Host: W. Kirk Burbage
Rooms: 8 (6PB; 2SB) $95-175
Full Breakfast
Credit Cards: A, B
Notes: 5, 7 (over 8), 8, 9, 10

NOTES: Credit cards accepted: A Master Card; B Visa; C American Express; D Discover; E Diners Club; F Other; 2 Personal checks accepted; 3 Lunch available; 4 Dinner available; 5 Open all year; 6 Pets welcome; 7 Children welcome; 8 Tennis nearby; 9 Swimming nearby; 10 Golf nearby; 11 Skiing nearby; 12 May be booked through travel agent.

CAMBRIDGE

Glasgow Inn, Circa 1760

1500 Hambrooks Boulevard, 21613
(410) 228-0575; FAX (410) 221-0297
E-mail: glasgow@shorenet.net

Experience life in a classic Colonial, riverside plantation in a 7-acre park, circa 1760. National Register historic places nearby. Ideal for biking, sailing, hunting. Bird walks through Blackwater National Refuge. Corporate meetings, writers' retreats, reunions, weddings, receptions, parties, cycling tours. AC, fireplaces.

Hostesses: Louiselee Roche and Martha Ann Rayne
Rooms: 6 (2PB; 4SB) $100-150
Full Breakfast
Credit Cards: none
Notes: 2, 5, 8, 10, 12

CUMBERLAND

The Inn at Walnut Bottom

120 Greene Street, 21502-2934
(301) 777-0003; (800) 286-9718;
FAX (301) 777-8288

Classic country inn on historic Cumberland's oldest street. Twelve guest rooms and family suites. Two cozy sitting rooms for reading and relaxing. Color cable TV and telephone in each room. A small shop offers beautiful and unique items by local artisans. Afternoon refreshments and a full breakfast included with lodging. Excellent restaurant on premises. The inn is within walking distance of the Western Maryland Scenic Railroad, the historic district, and several antique shops. Extraordinary hiking, biking, and sight-seeing close by. AAA-rated, three diamonds.

Hosts: Grant M. Irvin and Kirsten O. Hansen
Rooms: 10 + 2 suites (8PB; 4SB) $75-115
Full Breakfast
Credit Cards: A, B, C, D
Notes: 2, 3, 4, 5, 7, 9, 10, 11, 12

ELKTON

Garden Cottage at Sinking Springs

234 Blair Shore Road, 21921-8025
(410) 398-5566; FAX (410) 392-2389

With an early plantation house, including a 400-year-old sycamore, the cottage nestles at the edge of a meadow flanked by herb gardens and a historic barn with a gift shop. Sitting room with fireplace, bedroom, bath, air-conditioning, electric heat. Freshly ground coffee and herbal teas are offered with breakfast. Longwood Gardens and Winterthur Museum are 50 minutes away. Chesapeake City is nearby (excellent restaurants!). Sleeps three in two rooms; third person pays only $25. Enter at Elk Forest Road.

Hosts: Bill and Ann Stubbs
Rooms: 1 cottage (PB) $93
Full Country Breakfast
Credit Cards: A, B
Notes: 2, 5, 6, 7, 8, 10, 12

FREDERICK

Catoctin Inn

PO Box 243, **Buckeystown,** 21717
(301) 874-5555

The Catoctin Inn is a memorable getaway and a business traveler's home away from home, located in the historic village of Buckeystown, south of Frederick. We offer sixteen antique-filled guest rooms, king beds, two-person whirlpool baths, fireplaces, color TV/VCRs (with free movies), phones with computer access, and an outdoor hot tub! Available for meetings and weddings. Ask about our two-night specials. Horseback riding, Civil War history nearby.

Hosts: Terry and Sarah MacGillivray
Rooms: 16 (PB) $85-150
Full Breakfast
Credit Cards: A, B, C, D, E
Notes: 2, 4 (limited days), 5, 7, 8, 9, 10, 11, 12

Middle Plantation Inn

9549 Liberty Road, 21701-3246
(301) 898-7128
E-mail: BandB@MPInn.com
Web site: http://www.MPInn.com

From this charming inn built of stone and log, you can drive through horse country to the village of Mt. Pleasant. The inn is located several miles east of Frederick on 26 acres. Each guest room is furnished with antiques and has a private bath, television, and air-conditioning. The keeping room, a common room, features stained glass and a stone fireplace. Nearby you can find antique shops, museums, and a number of historic attractions. Middle Plantation Inn is located within 40 minutes of such Civil War-era sites as Gettysburg, Antietam Battlefield, and Harper's Ferry.

Hosts: Shirley and Dwight Mullican
Rooms: 4 (PB) $95-110
Continental Breakfast
Credit Cards: A, B, C
Notes: 2, 5, 8, 9, 10, 12

GAITHERSBURG

Gaithersburg Hospitality Bed and Breakfast

18908 Chimney Place, 20886
(301) 977-7377
E-mail: pjdanil@bellatlantic.net

This luxury host home just off I–270 with all the amenities, including private parking, is located in the beautifully planned community of Montgomery Village, near churches, restaurants, and shops. It is 10 minutes from a DC Metro station, and a convenient drive south to Washington, DC, and north to historic Gettysburg, Pennsylvania, and Harper's Ferry. This spacious bed and breakfast has two rooms with private baths; one has a queen bed. Also offered are a large, sunny third room with twin beds and a fourth room with a single bed. Hosts delight in serving full, home-cooked breakfasts with your pleasure and comfort in mind.

Hosts: Suzanne and Joe Danilowicz
Rooms: 4 (2PB; 2SB) $62-72
Full Breakfast
Credit Cards: none
Notes: 2, 7, 8, 9, 10, 12

GRANTSVILLE

Walnut Ridge B&B

92 Main Street; PO Box 368, 21536
(301) 895-4248 (voice and FAX);
(800) 419-2568
E-mail: walnutridge@usa.net
Web site: http://www.gcnet.net/ggba/walnut

Experience country hospitality in our quiet, quaint, peaceful inn. Located in western Maryland's Appalachian Mountains with Amish countryside, historical sites, local artisans, and year-round recreation. Walnut Ridge is a restored farmhouse dating to 1864 with antiques, handmade quilts, and country collectibles. Fireplaces, wood-fired hot tub, garden gazebo, antique player piano, video library, and country suite add to the charm. Hiking, fishing, boating, cross-country skiing, alpine, and white-water rafting available. Antique and craft shops within walking distance, as well as our own gift shoppe. We have one fully remodeled log cabin. Easy to find, right off I–68 Exit 19 into Grantsville. "We love to cater to our guests, helping them create wonderful, warm memories."

Hosts: Tim and Candy Fetterly
Rooms: 3 + suite + log cabin (PB) $75-125
Full Breakfast (Continental Breakfast for cabin)
Credit Cards: A, B
Notes: 2, 5, 7, 8, 9, 10, 11, 12

HAGERSTOWN

Lewrene Farm B&B

9738 Downsville Pike, 21740
(301) 582-1735
E-mail: lewrenebedandbreakfast@juno.com

Enjoy our quiet, Colonial country home on 125 acres near I–70 and I–81, a home away from home for tourists, businesspeople, and families. We have ample room for family celebrations. Sit by the fireplace or enjoy the great outdoors. Antietam Battlefield and Harper's Ferry are nearby; Washington and Baltimore are 1½ hours away. Quilts for sale.

Lewrene Farm Bed and Breakfast

Hosts: Irene and Lewis Lehman
Rooms: 6 (3PB; 3SB) $50-105
Full Breakfast
Credit Cards: A, B
Notes: 2, 5, 8, 9, 10, 11

Sunday's Bed and Breakfast

39 Broadway, 21740
(301) 797-4331; (800) 221-4828
E-mail: info@sundaysbnb.com
Web site: http://www.sundaysbnb.com

This elegant 1890 Queen Anne Victorian home is situated in the historic north end of Hagerstown. You may relax in any of the many public rooms and porches or explore the numerous historic attractions, antique shops, golf courses, museums, ski areas, and shopping outlets nearby. You'll experience special hospitality and many personal touches at Sunday's Bed and Breakfast. A full breakfast, afternoon tea and desserts, evening refreshments, fruit basket, fresh flowers, special toiletries, and late-night cordial and chocolate are just some of the offerings at Sunday's Bed and Breakfast. Less than 90 minutes from Baltimore and Washington.

Host: Bob Ferrino
Rooms: 4 (PB) $75-115
Full Breakfast
Credit Cards: A, B, E
Notes: 2, 4, 5, 7 (12 and older), 8, 9, 10, 11, 12

Currier House

HAVRE DE GRACE

Currier House

800 S. Market Street, 21078
(410) 939-7886; (800) 827-2889
E-mail: janec@currier-bb.com
Web site: http://www.currier-bb.com

Casual comfort in the historic residential district overlooking the Chesapeake Bay. One block from the lighthouse, museums, and park. Fully renovated house dating from 1800. Four guest rooms, each with a queen bed and private bath. Central AC. Full "waterman's" breakfast might include sautéed oysters and Maryland stewed tomatoes (in season, of course).

Hosts: Jane and Paul Belbot
Rooms: 4 (PB) $85-95
Full Breakfast
Credit Cards: A, B, C, D
Notes: 2, 5, 10, 12

OAKLAND

The Oak and Apple B&B

208 N. Second Street, 21550
(301) 334-9265
E-mail: Laam66B@Prodigy.com

Circa 1915, this restored Colonial Revival sits on a beautiful large lawn with mature trees. It includes a large, columned front porch, enclosed sunporch, parlor with fireplace, and cozy gathering room with television. Awaken to a fresh continental breakfast served at fireside in the dining room or on the sunporch. The quaint town of Oakland offers a wonderful small-town atmosphere. Deep Creek Lake, Wisp Ski Resort, and state parks with hiking, fishing, swimming, bicycling, boating, and skiing are nearby.

Hostess: Jana Brown
Rooms: 5 (3PB; 2SB) $65-90
Continental Breakfast
Credit Cards: A, B
Notes: 2, 5, 8, 9, 10, 11, 12

ST. MICHAELS

Kemp House Inn Bed and Breakfast

412 Talbot Street; PO Box 638, 21663
(410) 745-2243

Built in 1807 by Col. Joseph Kemp, this superbly crafted home is one of a small collection of Federal-period brick structures in St. Michaels. Elegant Federal details are evident throughout the house. Each of the rooms is tastefully furnished with period decor. Cozy antique four-poster beds with patchwork quilts, down pillows, wing-back sitting chairs, and Queen Anne tables grace each room. Old-fashioned nightshirts, low-light sconces, and working fireplaces create an ambience of the early 19th century.

Hosts: Stephen and Diane Cooper
Rooms: 8 (6PB; 2SB) $80-120
Continental Breakfast
Credit Cards: A, B, D
Notes: 2, 5, 8, 9, 10, 12

Parsonage Inn

210 N. Talbot Street, 21663
(410) 745-5519; (800) 394-5519
E-mail: wworkman@ix.netcom.com
Web site: http://www.bestinns.net

This circa-1883 Victorian was lavishly restored in 1985 with guest rooms, private baths, and brass beds with Laura Ashley linens. Fireplaces in three rooms. The parlor and dining room are in the European tradition. Striking architecture! Two blocks from the maritime museum, shops, and restaurants. Mobil, AAA three-star ratings.

Host: Gayle Lutz
Rooms: 8 (PB) $100-160
Full Breakfast
Credit Cards: A, B
Notes: 2, 5, 7, 8, 9, 10, 12

Wades Point Inn

PO Box 7, 21663
(410) 745-2500; (888) 923-3466;
FAX (410) 745-3443
E-mail: wadesinn@wadespoint.com
Web site: http://www.wadespoint.com

For those seeking the serenity of the country and the splendor of the bay, we invite you to charming Wades Point Inn, just a few miles from St. Michaels. Complemented by the ever-changing view of boats, birds, and water lapping the shoreline, our 120 acres of fields and woodlands, with a mile of walking or jogging trail, provide a peaceful setting for relaxation and recreation on Maryland's eastern shore. Closed January–March.

Hosts: Betsy and John Feiler
Rooms: 14 winter, 23 summer (16PB; 7SB) $95-230
Continental Breakfast
Credit Cards: A, B
Notes: 2, 8, 9, 10

SILVER SPRING

Varborg Bed and Breakfast

2620 Briggs Chaney Road, 20905
(301) 384-2842; FAX (301) 384-4379

This suburban, Colonial home in the countryside is convenient to Washington, DC, and Baltimore, just off Route 29 and close to Route 95. Three guest rooms with a shared bath are available. Your hosts will be happy to share their knowledge of excellent nearby restaurants. The specialty of Varborg Bed and Breakfast is our homemade bread.

Hosts: Bob and Pat Johnson
Rooms: 3 (SB) $50
Full Breakfast
Credit Cards: none
Notes: 2, 5, 7, 8, 9, 10

STEVENSON

Gramercy Mansion Bed and Breakfast

1400 Greenspring Valley Road, 21153-0119
(410) 486-2405; (800) 553-3404;
FAX (410) 486-1765
Web site: http://www.angelfire.com/md/Gramercy

Gramercy Mansion Bed and Breakfast is a 1902 English Tudor-style mansion on a 45-acre estate in historic Greenspring Valley. The bed and breakfast rooms are beautifully decorated, some having fireplaces and Jacuzzi tubs. Only 10 miles from downtown Baltimore. Our gourmet breakfasts are delicious; guests get to choose what they want from a menu. In summer, guests enjoy the Olympic-size pool, the tennis court, our nature trails, and our 7-acre organic herb farm.

Hosts: Anne Pomykala, Cristin Kline, Maria Webb
Rooms: 10 (5PB; 5SB) $90-260
Full Breakfast (gourmet and vegetarian available)
Credit Cards: A, B, C, D
Notes: 2, 5, 7, 8 and 9 (onsite), 10, 12

WITTMAN (ST. MICHAELS)

The Inn at Christmas Farm

8873 Tilghman Island Road, 21676
(410) 745-5312; (800) 987-8436
Web site: http://www.virtualcities.com

Located just 7 miles west of St. Michaels, our waterfront inn and farm (circa 1830) contain a unique collection of historic buildings, including St. James Chapel (1893)—saved from destruction, moved to the farm, and restored as the Gabriel and Bell Tower suites. The inn is set back from Route 33 just past the general store in the small village of Wittman. The beauty of the Chesapeake and its wildlife bring visitors from afar. Enjoy the peaceful tranquillity; sit by our spring-fed pond (or swim, in warm weather!); walk along the shore. Bike into St. Michaels, where the Chesapeake Bay Maritime Museum, antiques, seafood delicacies, and sights in the charming colonial town await. You may visit nearby Tilghman Island, where the last sailing oyster fleet is harbored. The full gourmet breakfast features our signature Christmas Farm quiche; it's served on our enclosed farmhouse porch overlooking field, farm, and woods. You can observe our "toy" farm animals—peacocks, sheep, chickens, and miniature horses. Waterfowl are also part of our special world.

Hosts: Paul Curtis and Susan Rockwell
Rooms: 4 (PB) $110-165
Full Breakfast
Credit Cards: A, B
Notes: 2, 5, 7, 8, 10

welcome; 7 Children welcome; 8 Tennis nearby; 9 Swimming nearby; 10 Golf nearby; 11 Skiing nearby; 12 May be booked through travel agent.

MASSACHUSETTS

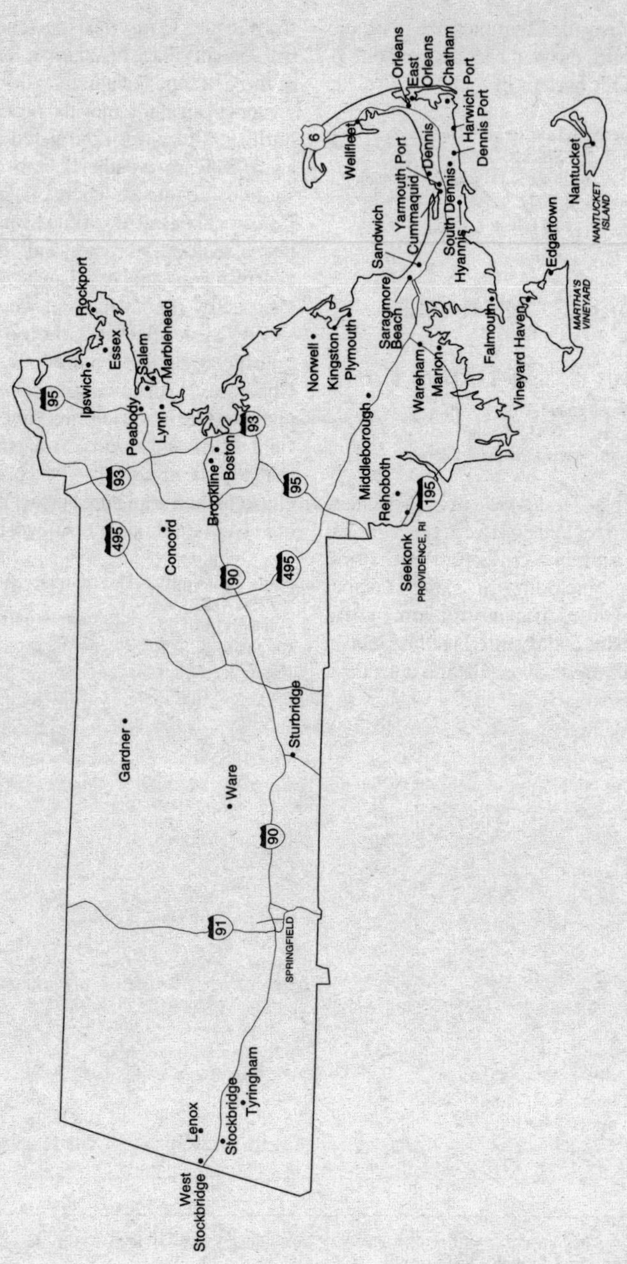

Massachusetts

BOSTON

A B&B Agency of Boston (and Boston Harbor Bed and Breakfast)

47 Commercial Wharf, 02110-3804
(617) 720-3540; (800) 248-9262;
FAX (617) 523-5761

Downtown Boston's largest selection of guest rooms in historic bed and breakfast homes, including Federal and Victorian town houses and beautifully restored 1840s waterfront lofts. Available nightly, weekly, monthly. Or choose from the lovely selection of fully furnished, private studios, one- and two-bedroom condos, corporate suites, and lofts with all amenities, including fully furnished kitchens, private baths (some with Jacuzzis), TVs, and phones. Exclusive locations include waterfront, Faneuil Hall/Quincy Market, North End, Back Bay, Beacon Hill, Copley Square, and Cambridge.

Hostess: Ferne Mintz
Rooms: 140 (100PB; 40SB) $65-120
Continental Breakfast
Credit Cards: A, B, C
Notes: 2, 5, 7, 12

Greater Boston Hospitality

PO Box 1142, **Brookline,** 02446
(617) 277-5430
E-mail: bdfd@channell.com
Web site: http://www.channell.com/BnB

Greater Boston Hospitality offers hundreds of Georgian, Federal, Victorian, and Brownstone private homes and condos throughout the greater Boston area. All include breakfast; many include parking. Most are in historic areas. We provide on-call service to both business and pleasure travelers. Discounts available for longer stays. Wide range of accommodations, $75-260. MC, Visa accepted. Lauren Simonelli and Kelly Simpson, proprietors.

CAPE COD

Liberty Hill Inn on Cape Cod

77 Main; Route 6-A, **Yarmouth Port,** 02675
(508) 362-3976; (800) 821-3977;
FAX (508) 362-6485
E-mail: libertyh@capecod.net
Web site: http://www.capecod.net/libertyhillinn

An elegant Cape Cod B&B, the Liberty Hill Inn welcomes travelers to historic

NOTES: Credit cards accepted: A Master Card; B Visa; C American Express; D Discover; E Diners Club; F Other; 2 Personal checks accepted; 3 Lunch available; 4 Dinner available; 5 Open all year; 6 Pets welcome; 7 Children welcome; 8 Tennis nearby; 9 Swimming nearby; 10 Golf nearby; 11 Skiing nearby; 12 May be booked through travel agent.

Liberty Hill Inn on Cape Cod

Main Street in a seaside village. Meander country lanes to Cape Cod Bay and nature trails. Take a run on the beach. Stroll to village shops and first-class restaurants. Mobile three-star-rated. Honeymoon packages. Cable TV, AC, canopy beds, luxurious double whirlpool, romantic fireplaces, gourmet breakfast. The central location is ideal for exploring Cape Cod.

Hosts: Jack and Beth Flanagan
Rooms: 9 (PB) $95-185
Full Breakfast
Credit Cards: A, B, C
Notes: 2, 5, 7, 8, 9, 10, 12

CHATHAM (CAPE COD)

The Old Harbor Inn

22 Old Harbor Road, 02633
(508) 945-4434; (800) 942-4434;
FAX (508) 945-7665
E-mail: brazohi@capecod.net
Web site: http://www.virtualcapecod.com/oldharborinn

We feel our guests can speak better than ourselves. Excerpts from the guest book: "What a lovely, great retreat," "spectacular place," "very special," "wonderful hosts," "it feels as though we are leaving good friends," "heavenly place," "all this and whales too!" "warm and cozy atmosphere," "relaxing nights," "good company," "excellent service," "delicious food," "absolutely charming," "lovely, quiet," "made us feel at home," "we'll be back."

Hosts: Judy and Ray Braz
Rooms: 8 (PB) $109-229
Deluxe (Healthy) Continental Breakfast
Credit Cards: A, B, C, D, E
Notes: 2, 5, 8, 9, 10, 12

CONCORD

Hawthorne Inn

462 Lexington Road, 01742
(978) 369-5610; FAX (978) 287-4949
E-mail: res@concordmass.com
Web site: http://www.concordmass.com

Beside the Battle Road the minutemen marched along in 1775, the inn was constructed c. 1870 on land owned by Emerson, Hawthorne, and the Alcott family (*Little Women*) and surveyed by Thoreau. Amidst aged trees, bountiful gardens, tree house, and frog pond, it is filled with original art, antiques, games, and books. Our town is alive with history, beauty, and peace. We hope we have captured a small part of what is Concord.

Hosts: G. Burch and M. Mudry
Rooms: 7 (PB) $150-220
Continental Breakfast
Credit Cards: A, B, C, D
Notes: 2, 5, 7, 8, 9, 11, 12

DENNIS (CAPE COD)

Isaiah Hall B&B Inn

152 Whig Street; PO Box 1007, 02638
(508) 385-9928; (800) 736-0160;
FAX (508) 385-5879
E-mail: isaiah@capecod.net
Web site: http://www.virtualcapecod.com/isaiahhall

Enjoy country ambience and hospitality in the heart of Cape Cod. Tucked away on

NOTES: Credit cards accepted: A Master Card; B Visa; C American Express; D Discover; E Diners Club; F Other; 2 Personal checks accepted; 3 Lunch available; 4 Dinner available; 5 Open all year; 6 Pets

a quiet, historic side street, this lovely 1857 farmhouse is within walking distance of the beach, restaurants, shops, and playhouse. Delightful gardens surround the inn; country antiques, Oriental rugs, and quilts are within. Rooms have private baths and air-conditioning, and most have queen beds. Some have balconies or fireplaces. Near biking, golf, and tennis. Rated AAA three diamonds and ABBA three crowns.

Hostess: Marie Brophy
Rooms: 9 + 1 suite (PB) $89-156
Continental Breakfast
Credit Cards: A, B, C
Notes: 2, 7 (over 7), 12

DENNISPORT (CAPE COD)

The Rose Petal Bed and Breakfast

152 Sea Street, 02639
(508) 398-8470
E-mail: rosepetl@capecode.net
Web site: http://www.virtualcapecod.com/market/rosepetal

A picturesque 1872 New England home, complete with picket fence, invites guests to share this historic, delightful seaside resort neighborhood. Stroll past century-old homes to a sandy beach. Home-baked pastries highlight a full breakfast. A comfortable parlor offers TV, piano, and reading. Enjoy queen-size beds, antiques, hand-stitched quilts, and spacious, bright baths. Convenient to all Cape Cod attractions. Open all year. AAA three diamonds.

Hosts: Gayle Kelly
Rooms: 3 (2PB; 1SB) $59-98
Full Breakfast
Credit Cards: A, B, C
Notes: 2, 5, 7, 8, 9, 10, 12

EAST ORLEANS (CAPE COD)

The Farmhouse at Nauset Beach

163 Beach Road, 02653
(508) 255-6654

Be our guest at an 1870 Greek Revival–style home with old-fashioned hospitality. A short walk to the beautiful sand dunes and surf of Nauset Beach (Atlantic Ocean). This historic farmhouse is situated on 1.6 acres, 90 feet from the road in a lovely, quiet residential area. Some oceanview rooms. Open year-round. Close to many activities and fine restaurants. Begin the day with a lovely sunrise.

Hostess: Dot Standish
Rooms: 8 (PB) $52-105
Continental Plus Breakfast
Credit Cards: A, B
Notes: 2, 5, 7 (over 5), 8, 9, 10, 12

Nauset House Inn

143 Beach Road; PO Box 774, 02643
(508) 255-2195
E-mail: jvessell@capecod.net
Web site: http://www.nausethouseinn.com

A real, old-fashioned, country inn farmhouse, circa 1810, is located on 3 acres with an apple orchard, ½ mile from Nauset Beach. A quiet, romantic getaway. Large common room with fireplace; brick-floored dining room where breakfast is served. Cozily furnished with antiques, eclectic—a true fantasy.

Hosts: Diane and Al Johnson, Cindy and John Vessella
Rooms: 14 (8PB; 6SB) $75-135
Full Breakfast
Credit Cards: A, B, D
Notes: 2, 8, 9, 10

Ship's Knees Inn

186 Beach Road; PO Box 756, 02643
(508) 255-1312; FAX (508) 240-1351
Web site: http://www.capecod.com/shipskneesinn

This 170-year-old restored sea captain's home is a 3-minute walk from beautiful, sand-duned Nauset Beach. Inside the warm, lantern-lit doorways are nineteen rooms individually appointed with special colonial color schemes and authentic antiques. Some rooms feature authentic ship's knees, hand-painted trunks, old clipper ship models, braided rugs, and four-poster beds. Tennis and swimming are available on the premises. Three miles away, overlooking Orleans Cove, the Cove House offers three rooms, a one-bedroom efficiency, and two cottages.

Hosts: Jean and Ken Pitchford
Rooms: 22 + 1 efficiency + 2 cottages (PB) $50-110
Continental Breakfast
Credit Cards: A, B
Notes: 2, 5, 7 (Cove House), 8 and 9 (on premises), 10, 12

EDGARTOWN —MARTHA'S VINEYARD

The Arbor Inn

222 Upper Main Street; PO Box 1228, 02539
(508) 627-8137

This charming Victorian home originally was built on the island of Chappaquiddick and moved by barge to its present location. A short stroll to the village shops, fine restaurants, and bustling activity of the Edgartown harbor. The rooms are typically New England, furnished with antiques, and filled with the fragrance of fresh flowers. Central air-conditioning. Peggy gladly will direct you to unspoiled beaches, walking trails, fishing, and all the delights of Martha's Vineyard. A small, one-bedroom house is available on a weekly basis.

Hostess: Peggy Hall
Rooms: 10 (8PB; 2SB) $80-120
Continental Breakfast
Credit Cards: A, B
Notes: 2, 7 (over 12), 8, 9, 10, 12

Captain Dexter House of Edgartown

Captain Dexter House of Edgartown

35 Pease's Point Way; PO Box 2798, 02539
(508) 627-7289; FAX (508) 627-3328
E-mail: mvcc@vineyard.net
Web site: http://www.mvy.com/captdexter

Built in 1840 by a seafaring merchant, this country Colonial inn is traditionally New England, from its white clapboard siding and black shutters to its double-width floorboards. Most of the inn's eleven rooms have canopied four-poster beds, period antiques, and working fireplaces. All have their own baths. Start your day with a home-baked continental breakfast. Relax at the end of the day in our landscaped garden, sipping lemonade or an evening aperitif. The inn is a short stroll from town and the harbor. The hospitality

NOTES: Credit cards accepted: A Master Card; B Visa; C American Express; D Discover; E Diners Club; F Other; 2 Personal checks accepted; 3 Lunch available; 4 Dinner available; 5 Open all year; 6 Pets

of the live-in innkeepers is nationally known. Open April 15–October 31.

Hostess: Roberta Pieczenik
Rooms: 11 (PB) $95-195
Continental Breakfast
Credit Cards: A, B, C
Notes: 2, 8, 9, 10, 12

ESSEX

George Fuller House

148 Main Street, 01929
(978) 768-7766; (800) 477-0148;
FAX (978) 768-6178
E-mail: rcameron@shore.net
Web site: http://www.cape-ann.com/fullerhouse

Built in 1830, this handsome Federalist home retains its 19th-century charm, including Indian shutters and captain's staircase. Three working fireplaces. There are handmade quilts, braided rugs, and caned Boston rockers. Breakfast might include such items as French toast drizzled with brandy lemon butter. Close to Gordon College and Gordon Conwall Seminary.

Hosts: Cindy and Bob Cameron
Rooms: 7 (PB) $100-125
Full Breakfast
Credit Cards: A, B, C, D
Notes: 2, 5, 7, 8, 9, 10, 12

FALMOUTH (CAPE COD)

Captain Tom Lawrence House

75 Locust Street, 02540
(508) 540-1445; (800) 266-8139;
FAX (508) 457-1790
E-mail: capttom@capecod.net
Web site: http://www.sunsol.com/captaintom/

An 1861 whaling captain's residence in a historic village close to beach, bikeway, ferries, bus station, ships, and restaurants. Explore the entire cape, vineyard, and Plymouth by day trips. Six beautiful guest rooms have private baths and firm beds, some with canopies. Fully furnished, air-conditioned apartment with kitchenette sleeps two to four people. Color TVs in all rooms. Children welcome in apartment. Antiques, Steinway piano, fireplace in sitting room. Homemade, delicious breakfasts include specialties from organic grain. German is spoken here. On National Register of Historic Homes. All rooms have central AC. No smoking! AAA- and Mobil-rated. Closed in January.

Captain Tom Lawrence House

Hostess: Barbara Sabo-Feller
Rooms: 6 plus efficiency apartment (PB) $85-140
Full Breakfast
Credit Cards: A, B
Notes: 2, 7, 8, 9, 10

The Inn at One Main St.

One Main Street, 02540
(508) 540-7469
E-mail: innat1main@aol.com
Web site: http://www.bbonline.com/ma/onemain

The inn is a decorative, shingled 1892 Victorian with Queen Anne accents, an open front porch, and a two-story turret, surrounded by a white picket fence and tastefully landscaped grounds. Wake to a hot

welcome; 7 Children welcome; 8 Tennis nearby; 9 Swimming nearby; 10 Golf nearby; 11 Skiing nearby; 12 May be booked through travel agent.

gourmet breakfast with fresh fruit and various sweetbreads. The inn is ideally situated in the midst of the historic district and within walking distance of the ferry shuttle to Nantucket and Martha's Vineyard.

Hosts: Jeanne Dahl and Ilona Cleveland
Rooms: 6 (PB) $95-125
Full Breakfast
Credit Cards: A, B, C, D
Notes: 5, 8, 9, 10

The Palmer House Inn

81 Palmer Avenue, 02540
(508) 548-1230; (800) 472-2632;
FAX (508) 540-1878
E-mail: innkeepers@palmerhouseinn.com
Web site: http://www.palmerhouseinn.com

Enjoy the warmth and charm of a Victorian home. Built in 1901, the inn with its adjacent guest house and romantic Cottage Suite is listed on the National Register of Historic Places. The stained-glass windows; rich, hand-rubbed woodwork; gleaming hardwood floors; and antique furnishings let the weary traveler step back in time to a more genteel era. Breakfast is a gourmet delight. Some guest rooms have whirlpool tubs and fireplaces.

Hosts: Ken and Joanne Baker
Rooms: 12 + cottage (PB) $78-199
Full Gourmet Breakfast
Credit Cards: A, B, C, D, E
Notes: 2 (deposit only), 5, 7 (10 and over), 8, 9, 10, 12

Village Green Inn

40 Main Street, 02540
(800) 237-1119; FAX (508) 457-5051
E-mail: Village.Green@cape.com; VGI40@aol.com
Web site: http://www.vsc.cape.com/~villageg

Village Green Inn

This gracious old 1804 Colonial-Victorian is ideally located on Falmouth's historic village green. Walk to fine shops and restaurants, or bike to beaches and picturesque Woods Hole along the Shining Sea Bike Path. Enjoy 19th-century charm and warm hospitality amidst elegant surroundings. Four lovely guest rooms and one romantic suite all have private baths and unique fireplaces (two are working). A full gourmet breakfast features delicious house specialties. Many thoughtful amenities are included. Air-conditioned, CCTV.

Hosts: Diane and Don Crosby
Rooms: 5 (PB) $85-150
Full Gourmet Breakfast
Credit Cards: A, B
Notes: 2 (deposit only), 5, 8, 9, 10, 12

FALMOUTH HEIGHTS (CAPE COD)

Grafton Inn

261 Grand Avenue S., 02540
(508) 540-8688; (800) 642-4069;
FAX (508) 540-1861
Web site: http://www.sunsol.com/graftoninn

Oceanfront Victorian. Thirty steps to a sandy beach. Breathtaking views of Martha's Vineyard. Comfortable queen and king beds. Period antiques. A sumptuous, full breakfast is served at individual tables overlooking Nantucket Sound. AC/heat,

NOTES: Credit cards accepted: A Master Card; B Visa; C American Express; D Discover; E Diners Club; F Other; 2 Personal checks accepted; 3 Lunch available; 4 Dinner available; 5 Open all year; 6 Pets

CCTV. Thoughtful amenities. Fresh flowers, homemade chocolates, evening wine and cheese. Beach chairs and towels. Eight-minute walk to island ferry. Dining 1 block away. AAA/Mobil, three stars.

Hosts: Liz and Rudy Cvitan
Rooms: 11 (PB) $85-169
Full Breakfast
Credit Cards: A, B, C
Notes: 2 (deposit only), 8, 9, 10, 12

Inn on the Sound

313 Grand Avenue, 02540
(508) 457-9666; (800) 564-9668;
FAX (508) 457-9631
Web site: http://www.falmouth-capecod.com/fww/inn.on.the.sound

This oceanfront bed and breakfast offers ten spacious guest rooms; nine with water views; all with serene, casual, and comfortable beachhouse-style atmosphere. Enjoy the magnificent view from the 40-foot deck, sample the full gourmet breakfast, relax with a favorite book in front of the fireplace, or visit the many year-round attractions from our ideally located inn. Walk to the Martha's Vineyard ferry. Bicycle rentals, great restaurants, and, of course, the beach. Reservations recommended, especially in the summer.

Hosts: Renee Ross and David Ross
Rooms: 10 (PB) $60-160 (seasonal)
Full Breakfast
Credit Cards: A, B, C, D
Notes: 2, 5, 8, 9, 10, 12

The Moorings Lodge

207 Grand Avenue, 02540
(508) 540-2370; (800) 398-4007
Web site: http://www.bbonline.com/ma/moorings

Capt. Frank Spencer built this large, lovely Victorian home in 1905. It is directly across from a sandy beach with lifeguard safety, and it is within walking distance of good restaurants and the island ferry. Your homemade, buffet breakfast is served on a glassed-in porch overlooking the island, Martha's Vineyard. Airy rooms with private baths add to your comfort. Call us home while you tour the cape!

The Moorings Lodge

Hosts: Ernie and Shirley Benard
Rooms: 8 (PB) $75-110
Full Breakfast
Credit Cards: A, B, C
Notes: 2, 7, 8, 9, 10, 12

GARDNER

The Hawke Bed and Breakfast

162 Pearl Street, 01440
(978) 632-5909

A Colonial farmhouse on 1 acre of lawn and gardens. Enjoy the ambience of a quieter, gentler time. Relax on the screened porch or the backyard swing. Fresh berries and flowers, in season, from our gardens. Wake to a full homemade breakfast featuring Nancy's delicious muffins or scones. Area amenities include hiking, biking, skiing, mountain climbing, golf, crafts, antiques, art galleries, museums, flea market, furniture outlets, and specialty shops.

Hosts: Robert and Nancy Hawke
Rooms: 3 (SB) $50-60
Full Breakfast
Credit Cards: none
Notes: 2, 5, 7, 8, 9, 10, 11

HARWICH PORT (CAPE COD)

Augustus Snow House

528 Main Street, 02646
(508) 430-0528; (800) 320-0528;
FAX (508) 432-7995 (x 15)
E-mail: snowhouse1@aol.com
Web site: http://www.augustussnow.com

This romantic 1901 Victorian inn offers luxurious accommodations. Each of the five exquisitely decorated bedrooms offers queen- or king-size beds, fireplaces, TVs, AC, telephones, and elegant private baths (some with Jacuzzis). A wonderful gourmet breakfast and afternoon refreshment are served each day. The private beach is just a 3-minute stroll from the inn. Wonderful restaurants, shops, and the ferry are all within walking distance. "With Victorian ambience and contemporary amenities, each guest is promised a memorable and pampered visit."

Hosts: Joyce and Steve Roth
Rooms: 5 (PB) $100-160
Full Breakfast
Credit Cards: A, B, C, D
Notes: 2, 5, 8, 9, 10, 12

Harbor Walk

6 Freeman Street, 02646
(508) 432-1675

This Victorian summer guest house was built in 1880 and is furnished with eclectic charm. A few steps from the house will bring you into view of Wychmere Harbor and, further along, to one of the fine beaches of Nantucket Sound. The village of Harwich Port is only ½ mile from the inn and contains interesting shops and some of the finest restaurants on Cape Cod. Harbor Walk offers six comfortable rooms with twin or queen beds. An attractive garden and porch are available to guests for sitting, lounging, and reading. Open May–October.

Hosts: Marilyn and Preston Barry
Rooms: 6 (4PB; 2SB) $50-75
Full Breakfast
Credit Cards: none
Notes: 2, 7, 8, 9, 10, 12

The Inn on Sea Street

HYANNIS (CAPE COD)

The Inn on Sea Street

358-363 Sea Street, 02601
(508) 775-8030; FAX (508) 771-0878
E-mail: innonsea@capecod.net
Web site: http://www.capecod.net/innonsea

An elegant ten-room Victorian inn just steps from the beach and ferries. Antiques, canopy beds, Persian rugs, and *objets d'art* abound in this friendly, unpretentious, hospitable atmosphere. A full gourmet breakfast of fresh fruit and home-baked delights is served at individual tables set with the hosts' finest sterling silver, china, and crystal. One-night stays are welcomed. Reservations suggested.

Hosts: Lois Nelson and J.B. Whitehead
Rooms: 9 rooms + cottage (8PB; 2SB) $78-125
Full Breakfast
Credit Cards: A, B, D
Notes: 2, 8, 9, 10, 12

Sea Breeze Inn

397 Sea Street, 02601
(508) 771-7213; FAX (508) 862-0663
E-mail: seabreeze@capecod.net
Web site: http://www.capecod.net/seabreeze

Sea Breeze Inn is a beautiful B&B by the sea. Five-minute drive to the ferries, downtown, and the Kennedy Compound. Rooms are very comfortably furnished with private baths, AC, telephones, TVs. An expanded continental breakfast of cereals, homemade muffins, scones, and fresh fruit is served every morning.

Hostess: Patricia Gibney
Rooms: 14 (PB) $50-130
Continental Breakfast
Credit Cards: A, B, C, D
Notes: 2, 5, 7, 8, 9, 10, 12

IPSWICH

Town Hill Bed and Breakfast

16 N. Main Street, 01938
(978) 356-8000 (voice and FAX);
(800) 457-7799
Web site: http://www.ipswichma.com

Historic Greek Revival home built in 1845. Features eleven individually decorated rooms close to beautiful Crane Beach. Walk to shops, restaurants, train to Boston. Golf nearby, whale-watching, antique hunting, canoeing, bird-watching, polo, and much more.

Hosts: Chere and Bob Statho
Rooms: 11 (9PB; 2SB) $75-150
Full Breakfast
Credit Cards: A, B, C

KINGSTON

1760 Peabody Bradford Homestead

6 River Street, 02364
(781) 585-2646

Elegant historic home in rural setting. Overlooks Jones River, which was named after the *Mayflower* captain. Abuts conservation lands with wildlife and walking trails. Sitting room for reading, TV, conversation. Minutes from Plymouth's historic sites, shops, restaurants. Nearby are Duxbury Art Complex, King Caesar and John Alden homes.

Hosts: Gertrude and Jerry Powell
Rooms: 3 (PB) $70+
Continental Breakfast
Credit Cards: none
Notes: 2, 5

LENOX

Garden Gables Inn

141 Main Street; PO Box 52, 01240
(413) 637-0193; FAX (413) 637-4554
E-mail: gardeninn@aol.com
Web site: http://www.lenoxinn.com

A 250-year-old Colonial inn in the center of historic Lenox village, a mile from

Tanglewood. The inn features eighteen lodging rooms and an outdoor pool on 5 acres of secluded grounds. A full buffet breakfast is featured.

Hosts: Mario and Lynn Mekinda
Rooms: 18 (PB) $110-225
Full Breakfast
Credit Cards: A, B, C, D
Notes: 2, 5, 8, 10, 11

Diamond District Breakfast Inn

LYNN

Diamond District Breakfast Inn

142 Ocean Street, 01902-2007
(781) 599-4470; (800) 666-3076;
FAX (781) 599-5122
E-mail: diamonddistrict@msn.com
Web site: http://www.BBHost.com/diamonddistrict

Architect-designed Georgian mansion in the historic "Diamond District," built in 1911. Gracious foyer and grand staircase, fireplace, living and dining room with ocean view, French doors to veranda overlooking the gardens, ocean. Guest rooms offer antiques, air-conditioning, TVs, phones, down comforters, some fireplaces, whirlpool, deck, ocean views, and private baths. Three hundred feet off 3-mile sandy beach for swimming, walking, jogging. Walk to restaurants. Home-cooked breakfast; vegetarian, lowfat available. Eight miles northeast of Boston.

Hosts: Sandra and Jerry Caron
Rooms: 11 (7PB; 4SB) $90-235
Full Breakfast
Credit Cards: A, B, C, D, E
Notes: 2, 5, 7 (not childproof), 9, 10, 12

MARBLEHEAD

Harbor Light Inn

58 Washington Street, 01945
(781) 631-2186; FAX (781) 631-2216
E-mail: hli@shore.net
Web site: http://www.innbook.com/harborl.html

Winner of many national awards, including *Vacation Magazine*, "America's Best Romantic Inns." Elegant furnishings grace the two connected Federalist mansions. Formal fireplaced parlors, dining room, and bedchambers; double Jacuzzis, sundecks, patio, outlet garden, and outdoor heated pool combine to ensure the finest in New England hospitality. Located in the heart of the historic Harbor District of fine shops, art galleries, and restaurants.

Hosts: Peter and Suzanne Conway
Rooms: 21 (PB) $95-245
Continental Breakfast
Credit Cards: A, B, C
Notes: 2, 5, 7 (inquire), 8, 9, 10, 12

Harbor Light Inn

Harborside House

23 Gregory Street, 01945-3241
(781) 631-1032
E-mail: swliving@shore.net
Web site: http://www.shore.net/~swliving

This 1850 home overlooks Marblehead Harbor. Guests enjoy water views from fireplaced living room, period dining room, sunny breakfast porch, and third-story deck. A generous breakfast includes fresh fruit, home-baked goods, and cereals. Antique shops, gourmet restaurants, historic sites, and beaches are a pleasant stroll away. The owner is a professional dressmaker and nationally ranked competitive swimmer. Harborside House is a smoke-free bed and breakfast.

Hostess: Susan Livingston
Rooms: 2 (SB) $70-85
Expanded Continental Breakfast
Credit Cards: none
Notes: 2, 5, 7 (over 10), 8, 9

MARION

Pineywood Farm Bed and Breakfast

599 Front Street, 02738
(508) 748-3925; (800) 858-8084
E-mail: gmcturk@capecod.net
Web site: http://www.virtualcities.com

Pineywood Farm is a charming, 1815 farmhouse with a carriage house. It has been completely restored, yet retains the warmth and ambience of a bygone era, complete with wide-plank, white pine floors; four working fireplaces; a large screened porch; and a "good morning" staircase. We offer spacious rooms with air-conditioning, cable TV, paddle fans, and private baths, overlooking a lovely perennial garden and private swimming pool. Pineywood Farm Bed and Breakfast is located on a 3-acre estate, 1½ miles from the Tabor Academy. The town beach is at the end of our street. The bed and breakfast is open year-round.

Pineywood Farm Bed and Breakfast

Hosts: Beverly and George McTurk
Rooms: 5 (3PB; 2SB) $85-100
Continental Breakfast
Credit Cards: A, B, C
Notes: 2, 5, 8, 9, 10

MIDDLEBORO

1831 Zachariah Eddy House Bed and Breakfast

51 S. Main Street, 02346
(508) 946-0016; FAX (508) 947-2603
E-mail: zacheddy@aol.com
Web site: http://www.bbhost.com/zacheddyhouse

Quiet, comfortable elegance in this lovely 19th-century home with unique "chapel bath." Within 35 miles of Boston, Plymouth, Cape Cod, Providence, Newport. Whale-watching, fishing, beaches, museums, theater at your fingertips. Weather and tide permitting, there may even be an invitation to join the innkeepers as they haul the day's catch of lobsters from the ocean floor. House specialties: clam chowder and lobster omelet. Ask about the free lobster dinner offer!

Hosts: Brad and Cheryl Leonard
Rooms: 3 (1-2PB; 2SB) $85-125
Full Breakfast
Credit Cards: A, B, C, D
Notes: 2, 4, 5, 8, 9, 10, 12

On Cranberry Pond B&B

43 Fuller Street, 02346
(508) 946-0768
FAX (508) 947-8221

Enjoy a restful night's sleep in the comfort and quiet of the country. Wake up to the heavenly aroma of coffee and a gourmet breakfast. Nestled between Cranberry Pond and picturesque New England cranberry bogs in the heart of the "Cranberry Capital of the World." Walking trails and mountain bikes available. Centrally located, 40 minutes from Boston, Cape Cod, and Providence, Rhode Island; 20 minutes from Plymouth Rock.

Hosts: Jeannine LaBossiere and Son Tim
Rooms: 5 (3PB; 2SB) $85-160
Full Breakfast
Credit Cards: A, B, C, D, E
Notes: 2, 5, 8, 9, 10, 11, 12

NANTUCKET

Inn at Captain's Corner

89 Easton Street; PO Box 628, 02554
(508) 228-1692; (800) 319-9990;
FAX (978) 740-0036
E-mail: captainscorners@nii.net
Web site: http://www.our2inns.homesite.net

The peace and quietude of Nantucket in elegant comfort. This 1890s captain's home boasts leaded windows, fireplaces, and hardwood floors. Enjoy an afternoon of reading in our yard or refreshment on our shaded front porch. A short walk from Main Street and its wonderful shops and galleries, a quick bus ride from many beautiful beaches. Let The Inn at Captain's Corner be your home away from home.

Host: B. Bowman
Rooms: 15 (11PB; 4SB) $79-160
Continental Breakfast
Credit Cards: A, B, C
Notes: 2, 7, 8, 9, 10, 12

Martin House Inn

61 Centre Street, 02554
(508) 228-0678; (508) 325-4798;
E-mail: martinn@nantucket.net
Web site: http://www.nantucket.net/lodging/martinn

In a stately 1803 mariner's home in Nantucket's historic district, a romantic sojourn awaits you. A glowing fire in a spacious, charming living/dining room; large, airy guest rooms—four with fireplaces—with authentic period pieces, including four-poster and canopy beds; lovely yard and veranda for peaceful summer afternoons. Our deluxe continental breakfast includes inn-baked breads and muffins, fruit, yogurt, and homemade granola.

Hosts: Debbie Wasil
Rooms: 13 (9PB; 4SB) $50-185
Continental Breakfast
Credit Cards: F
Notes: 2 (business check)

The Woodbox Inn

29 Fair Street, 02554
(508) 228-0587
Web site: http://www.woodboxinn.com

The Woodbox is Nantucket's oldest inn, built in 1709. Located 1½ blocks from the center of Nantucket, the inn serves "the best breakfast on the island" and offers gourmet dinners by candlelight. Queen-size beds, private baths. One- and two-bedroom suites have working fireplaces.

Host: Dexter Tutein
Rooms: 9 (PB) $140-240
Full Breakfast Available
Credit Cards: none
Notes: 2, 4, 7, 8, 9, 10

NORWELL

1810 House B&B

147 Old Oaken Bucket Road, 02061
(781) 659-1810
E-mail: tuttle1810@aol.com

A comfortable B&B lovingly restored and enlarged. The antique half Cape features original beamed ceilings, wide-pine floors, and stenciled walls. Three bright, cheery rooms share two full baths. Breakfast is served next to the fireplace in the country kitchen or, weather permitting, on the screened porch. The large, fireplaced family room with piano, TV, and VCR welcomes you to relax after a busy day. Oceanfront dining, interesting antique shops, major highways just minutes away.

Hosts: Susanne and Harold Tuttle
Rooms: 3 (2PB; 2SB for families or 2 couples together) $75-95
Full Breakfast
Credit Cards: none
Notes: 2, 5, 8, 9, 10, 12

PEABODY

Joan's Bed and Breakfast

210 R. Lynn Street, 01960
(978) 532-0191

Joan's Bed and Breakfast is in a prime New England location, only 10 minutes from historic Salem, 25 minutes from Boston, and 1 hour from the many shopping outlets. Numerous great restaurants, theaters, and shopping malls are in the area. The 16-by-32-foot in-ground pool is available for use by guests. Make my home your home!

Hostess: Joan Hetherington
Rooms: 3 (SB; PB can be arranged) $55-75
Full Breakfast
Credit Cards: none
Notes: 2, 5, 7, 9, 10

PLYMOUTH

Foxglove Cottage Bed and Breakfast

101 Sandwich Road, 02360
(508) 747-6576; (800) 479-4746;
FAX (508) 747-7622
E-mail: tranquility@foxglove-cottage.com
Web site: http://www.foxglove-cottage.com

Elegant and romantic lodging for the discerning traveler. Lovingly restored 1820 Cape in a pastoral setting, away from the bustle of tourist traffic but close to Plantation and beaches. All our antique-furnished rooms have en-suite private baths, AC/heat, sitting area, and working fireplaces. Enjoy a full breakfast on our deck off the large common room. Foxglove Cottage is the perfect "hub" for day trips to Boston, the Islands, Newport, and Cape Cod. Listed in Fodor's *Best Bed and Breakfast in America.*

Hosts: Mr. and Mrs. Charles K. Cowan
Rooms: 3 (PB) $85-90
Full Breakfast
Credit Cards: none

REHOBOTH (NEAR PROVIDENCE, RI)

Gilbert's Tree Farm B&B

30 Spring Street, 02769
(508) 252-6416
E-mail: jeanneg47@aol.com

Our 15-acre tree farm provides a quiet place to enjoy the beauty of nature and God's bountiful gifts. The body is nourished with hearty breakfasts and refreshed with hikes through the woods and exercise in the in-ground swimming pool.

Hostess: Jeanne D. Gilbert
Rooms: 4 (1PB; 3SB) $60-80
Full Breakfast
Credit Cards: $20 credit card charge
Notes: 2, 5, 6 (horses only), 7, 8, 9, 10, 12

Perryville Inn B&B

157 Perryville Road, 02769
(508) 252-9239; (800) 439-9239;
FAX (508) 252-9054

This 19th-century restored Victorian (listed on the National Register of Historic Places) is located on 4½ wooded acres featuring a quiet brook, millpond, stone walls, and shaded paths. Bicycles are available (including a tandem) for exploring the unspoiled countryside. The inn overlooks an eighteen-hole public golf course. All rooms are furnished with antiques and accented with colorful handmade quilts. Nearby you will find antique shops, museums, Great Woods Performing Arts Center, fine seafood restaurants, and even an old-fashioned New England clambake—or arrange for a horse-drawn hayride or a hot-air balloon ride. Within 1 hour's drive of Boston, Plymouth, Newport, and Mystic; 7 miles from Providence, Rhode Island. Central air-conditioning.

Perryville Inn B&B

Hosts: Tom and Betsy Charnecki
Rooms: 4 (PB) $65-95
Continental Breakfast
Credit Cards: A, B, C, D
Notes: 2, 5, 7, 8, 10, 12

ROCKPORT

The Inn on Cove Hill

37 Mt. Pleasant Street, 01966
(978) 546-2701; (888) 546-2701
Web site: http://www.cape-ann/covehill

A friendly atmosphere with the option of privacy is available in this painstakingly restored, 200-year-old Federal home in a perfect setting only 2 blocks from the harbor and shops. The cozy bedrooms are meticulously appointed with antiques; some have canopy beds. Wake up to the aroma of hot muffins and enjoy breakfast at the umbrella tables in the pump garden. Your comfort is enhanced in our individually air-conditioned rooms and nonsmoking environment.

Hosts: John and Marjorie Pratt
Rooms: 11 (9PB; 2SB) $48-115
Continental Breakfast
Credit Cards: A, B
Notes: 2, 8, 9, 10

Linden Tree Inn

Linden Tree Inn

26 King Street, 01966
(978) 546-2494; (800) 865-2122;
FAX (978) 546-3297
E-mail: ltree@shore.net
Web site: http://www.shore.net/~ltree

Located on one of Rockport's many picturesque streets, the inn is a haven for a restful, relaxing vacation. We are a leisurely, 800-foot walk from the sandy beach, restaurants, art galleries, unique shops, and the train station. Inside our Victorian-style home are fourteen individually decorated guest rooms, all with private baths. Guests enjoy the inn's formal living room, sunporch, bay and pond views from the cupola, spacious yard, and Dawn's made-from-scratch breakfasts, served buffet-style in the dining room.

Hosts: Jon and Dawn Cunningham
Rooms: 18 (PB) $72-109
Hearty Homemade Continental Breakfast
Credit Cards: A, B
Notes: 2, 5, 7, 8, 9, 10, 12

The Seafarer Inn

50 Marmion Way, 01966
(978) 546-6248; (800) 394-9394
Web site: http://www.rockportusa.com/seafarer

The seafarer is a quiet, intimate inn serving persons since 1890. Ocean views are spectacular from every room. Three rooms have kitchens or kitchenettes. Our living room is informal, warm in winter with a working fireplace, perfect for a group gathering. Our inn is only 1 hour from Boston area attractions.

Host: David Cantrell
Rooms: 8 (7PB; 1SB) $85-110
Continental Breakfast
Credit Cards: A, B
Notes: 2, 5, 7, 8, 9, 10, 12

The Tuck Inn Bed and Breakfast

The Tuck Inn Bed and Breakfast

17 High Street, 01966
(978) 546-7260; (800) 789-7260
E-mail: tuckinn@shore.net
Web site: http://www.rockportusa.com/tuckinn

This welcoming 1790 Colonial home is located on a quiet secondary street just 1 block from the village center. The nearby train station offers convenient access to Boston, as well. Featuring antiques, colorful quilts, and local artwork throughout, the inn offers all private baths, CCTVs, air-conditioning, and an in-ground pool.

Nonsmoking, pet-free environment. Breakfast each morning is a hearty, home-baked buffet. The Woods graciously invite you to "*come stay with us*!"

Hosts: Liz and Scott Wood
Rooms: 11 (PB) $55-95
Continental Plus Breakfast
Credit Cards: A, B
Notes: 2, 5, 7, 8, 9, 10, 11, 12

SAGAMORE BEACH (CAPE COD)

Widow's Walk Bed and Breakfast

152 Clark Road, Box 605, 02562
(508) 888-0762

Located 200 feet from beautiful Sagamore Beach on Cape Cod Bay, the Widow's Walk B&B provides a soothing atmosphere that encourages you to relax and enjoy the magnificence of old Cape Cod. Bask in the sunshine by day, walk for miles on a quiet, sandy beach, or marvel over the romantic sunset on the bay in the evening. Our Cape-style country home gives you that "homecoming feeling," with wide plank floors, three fireplaces, and an authentic widow's walk. Start your day with a delicious breakfast in our country kitchen or on the deck. Two beautiful bedrooms on the second floor share a bath and are separated by a "gathering room" with a fireplace. We also offer a fully equipped apartment with its own entrance on the ground level. No smoking.

Hosts: Bill and Meredith Chase
Rooms: 2 (2SB) $60-85
Full Breakfast
Credit Cards: none
Notes: 2, 5, 7, 8, 9, 10

Amelia Payson House

SALEM

Amelia Payson House

16 Winter Street, 01970
(978) 744-8304
E-mail: bbamelia@aol.com
Web site: http://www.salemweb.com/biz/ameliapayson

Built in 1845, 16 Winter Street is one of Salem's finest examples of Greek Revival architecture. Elegantly restored and beautifully decorated, each room is furnished with period antiques and warmed by a personal touch. Private baths, AC, cable TV. Located in the heart of Salem's historic district; a 5-minute stroll finds downtown shopping, historic houses, museums, and Pickering Wharf's waterfront dining. The seaside towns of Rockport and Gloucester are a short drive up the coast; downtown Boston is only 30 minutes by car, or easily can be reached by train or bus. Color brochure available. No smoking. Celebrating 15 years as a B&B. Closed January–February.

Hosts: Ada and Donald Roberts
Rooms: 4 (PB) $65-125
Continental Breakfast
Credit Cards: A, B, C
Notes: 8, 9, 10

The Salem Inn

7 Summer Street, 01970
(978) 741-0680; (800) 446-2995;
FAX (978) 744-8924
E-mail: saleminn@earthlink.net
Web site: http://www.salemweb.com/biz/saleminn

Salem, one of America's oldest cities, has an enduring maritime past. The Salem Inn, comprising The West House (c. 1834), The Curwen House (c. 1854), and The Peabody House (c. 1874) testifies to those days of glory. These historic homes are a short walk from an impressive array of activities. The inn's individually decorated rooms provide an ensemble of amenities: private bath, color TV, telephone, and queen or king bed, as well as kitchenettes, fireplaces, and Jacuzzis. Antiques and tasteful furnishings grace all the buildings.

Hosts: Richard and Diane Pabich
Rooms: 39 (PB) $99-200
Continental Breakfast
Credit Cards: A, B, C, D, E, F
Notes: 2, 4, 5, 6, 7, 9, 10, 12

SANDWICH (CAPE COD)

Captain Ezra Nye House

152 Main Street, 02563
(508) 888-6142; (800) 388-2278;
FAX (508) 833-2897
E-mail: captnye@aol.com
Web site: http://www.captainezranyehouse.com

Whether you come to enjoy summer on Cape Cod, a fall foliage trip, or a quiet winter vacation, the Captain Ezra Nye House is a great place to start. It is located only 60 miles from Boston, 20 miles from Hyannis, and within walking distance of many noteworthy attractions, including the Heritage Plantation, Sandwich Glass Museum, and the Cape Cod Canal. Award-winning "Readers Choice," named "Best Bed and Breakfast, Upper Cape," by *Cape Cod Life* magazine for four years; named one of the top fifty inns in America by *Inn Times*.

Hosts: Elaine and Harry Dickson
Rooms: 6 (PB) $75-110
Full Breakfast
Credit Cards: A, B, C, D, F
Notes: 2, 5, 7 (over 10), 8, 9, 10, 12

Cranberry House Bed and Breakfast

50 Main Street, 02563
(508) 888-1281

The Cranberry House is a friendly place to stay on Cape Cod. A full breakfast is served in the dining room or on the deck. Relax in the den overlooking the beautifully landscaped yard. Hosts offer cable TV and complimentary soft drinks. Sandwich, the cape's oldest town, has many shops, restaurants, museums, gardens, and beaches. The Cape Cod Canal has walking and biking trails. No smoking inside.

Hosts: John and Sara Connolly
Rooms: 4 (PB) $75
Full Breakfast
Credit Cards: none
Notes: 2 (and traveler's checks), 5, 7 (over 10), 8, 9, 10

The Summer House

158 Main Street, 02563
(508) 888-4991; (800) 241-3609
E-mail: sumhouse@capecod.net
Web site: http://www.capecod.net/summerhouse

This exquisite 1835 Greek Revival home, featured in *Country Living* magazine, is

The Summer House

located in the heart of historic Sandwich village. It features antiques; working fireplaces; hand-stitched quilts; flowers; large, sunny rooms; and English-style gardens. The Summer House is within strolling distance of dining, museums, shops, a pond, and the boardwalk to the beach. Guests are served bountiful breakfasts and afternoon tea in the garden. The home is open year-round.

Hosts: Erik Suby and Phyllis Burg
Rooms: 5 (PB) $65-105
Full Breakfast
Credit Cards: A, B, C, D
Notes: 2, 5, 7, 8, 9, 10, 12

SOUTH DARTMOUTH

The Little Red House

631 Elm Street, 02748
(508) 996-4554

The Little Red House is a charming gambrel Colonial home located in the lovely coastal village of Padanaram. This home is beautifully furnished with country accents, antiques, lovely living room with fireplace, and luxuriously comfortable four-poster or brass-and-iron beds. A full homemade breakfast in the romantic, candlelit dining room is a delectable treat. Close to the harbor, beaches, and historic sites; a short distance to New Bedford, Newport, Plymouth, Boston, and Cape Cod. The Martha's Vineyard ferry is just 10 minutes away.

Hostess: Meryl Zwirblis
Rooms: 3 (1PB; 2SB) $55-75
Full Breakfast
Credit Cards: none
Notes: 2, 5, 9, 10, 12

SOUTH DENNIS (CAPE COD)

Captain Nickerson Inn

333 Main Street, 02660
(508) 398-5966 (voice and FAX);
(800) 282-1619
Web site: http://www.bbonline.com/ma/captnick

Delightful Victorian sea captain's home located on a bike path in the historic section of Dennis. This is the midcape area, close to all points of interest. Comfortable front porch is lined with white wicker rockers. Guest rooms are decorated in period four-poster or white iron queen beds and Oriental or hand-woven rugs. Cozy terry robes and AC available in all rooms. The fireplaced living room is comfortable yet lovely and has cable TV, VCR, and stained-glass windows. The dining room is also fireplaced and has parqueted floors

Captain Nickerson Inn

and a stained-glass window. Popular board games available. Walk to Indian lands trail and the Bass River. Bike to Cape Cod (20-plus-mile bike trail is only ½ mile from the inn); complimentary bicycles. Championship golf courses, world-class beaches, paddleboats, horseback riding, ferry service, museums, Cape Playhouse, fishing, craft and antique shops, etc. Children welcome! Smoking outside only.

Hosts: Pat and Dave York
Rooms: 5 (3PB; 2SB) $65-95
Full Breakfast
Credit Cards: A, B, D
Notes: 2, 4 (weekends only), 5, 7, 9, 10, 12

STOCKBRIDGE

Arbor Rose B&B

8 Yale Hill Road, 01262
(413) 298-4744
Web site: http://www.arborrose.com

A charming 1810 mill and farmhouse with flowing pond, gardens, antiques, home baking, tranquillity, and smiles. Close to Stockbridge center, museums, restaurants, and Berkshire Theatre. Four-poster beds, fireplaces, gallery shop, and ski packages. No smoking. Families welcome.

Hostess: Christina Alsop
Rooms: 5 (PB) $85-175
Full Breakfast
Credit Cards: A, B, C
Notes: 2, 5, 7, 8, 9, 10, 11, 12

Four Seasons on Main

47 Main Street; PO Box 634, 01262
(413) 298-5419

Lovingly restored and refurbished 1860 Greek Revival home in the heart of Stockbridge, "Norman Rockwell's Main Street." Beautiful gardens and large front porch. We have private baths, AC, and fine heirloom antiques. Fireplace and television in front parlor. An easy walk from fine restaurants, Berkshire Theater, and several churches, as well as the National Shrine of Divine Mercy. Afternoon refreshments. Minimum stay July, August, and holiday weekends.

Hosts: Greg and Pat O' Neill
Rooms: 3 (PB) $125-165
Full Breakfast
Credit Cards: A, B, C
Notes: 2, 5, 8, 9, 10, 11

STURBRIDGE

Sturbridge Country Inn

530 Main Street, 01566
(508) 347-5503; FAX (508) 347-5319

At this historic 1840s inn, each room has a fireplace and private whirlpool tub. It is located close to Old Sturbridge Village and within walking distance of restaurants, shops, and antiques. Breakfast is available in your room.

Host: Mr. MacConnell
Rooms: 9 (PB) $59-159
Continental Breakfast
Credit Cards: A, B, C, D
Notes: 2, 4, 5, 7, 8, 9, 10, 11, 12

TYRINGHAM

The Golden Goose

123 Main Road; Box 336, 01264
(413) 243-3008

Two private country getaways in peaceful valley, ½ mile off the Appalachian Trail. Minutes from Stockbridge, Tanglewood, and fine restaurants. Small studio with kitchen, shower bath, queen-size bed, plus full double sofa bed. Large barn loft with king and double bed, cooking facilities, tub and shower bath, double sink. Each furnished with antiques. Breakfast provided in room. Rates vary with length of stay. Ask for our brochure.

Hosts: Lilja and Joe Rizzo
Rooms: 2 (PB) $100-180
Continental Plus Breakfast
Credit Cards: A, B, C
Notes: 2, 5, 7, 8, 9, 10, 11, 12

VINEYARD HAVEN (MARTHA'S VINEYARD)

Captain Dexter House of Vineyard Haven

92 Main Street; Box 2457, 02568
(508) 693-6564; FAX (508) 693-8448
E-mail: mvcc@vineyard.net
Web site: http://www.mvy.com/captdexter

Built in 1843 for a sea captain, the house has been meticulously restored and exquisitely furnished to reflect the charm and elegance of that period of New England's history. You are surrounded by flowers from our garden and pampered by innkeepers who believe in old-fashioned hospitality. The inn's romantic guest rooms are distinctively decorated to create the warmth and ambience of an elegant private home. Several rooms have working fireplaces (as does the parlor) and four-poster canopy beds. The town and ferry are only a short stroll away.

Hosts: Roberta Pieczenik
Rooms: 8 (PB) $75-185
Continental Breakfast
Credit Cards: A, B, C
Notes: 2, 5, 8, 9, 10, 12

WARE (STURBRIDGE)

Antique 1880 Inn

14 Pleasant Street, 01082
(413) 967-7847

Built in 1876, this Colonial-style inn has pumpkin and maple hardwood floors, beamed ceilings, six fireplaces, and antique furnishings. Afternoon tea is served by the fireplace, breakfast in the dining room or on the porch, weather permitting. It is a short, pretty country ride to historic Old Sturbridge Village and Old Deerfield Village. Hiking, fishing nearby. Midway between Boston and the Berkshires.

Hosts: Margaret and Stan Skutnik
Rooms: 5 (2PB; 3SB) $40-65
Full Breakfast
Credit Cards: none
Notes: 2, 5, 8, 9, 10, 11, 12

WAREHAM

Mulberry B&B

257 High Street, 02571-1407
(508) 295-0684; FAX (508) 291-2909

Mulberry Bed and Breakfast sits on a ½-acre lot shaded by a majestic, seven-trunk mulberry tree. This Cape Cod–style home, built in 1847 by a blacksmith, offers three cozy guest rooms with two shared baths

Mulberry Bed and Breakfast

and a hearty, homemade breakfast. Mulberry is 1 mile from I–195 and I–495. The historic, picturesque cities of Boston, Newport, New Bedford, and Plymouth are within an hour's drive.

Hostess: Frances A. Murphy
Rooms: 3 (SB) $55-75
Full Breakfast
Credit Cards: A, B, C, D
Notes: 2, 5, 7, 8, 9, 10, 11 (cross-country), 12

WELLFLEET (CAPE COD)

The Inn at Duck Creeke

70 Main Street; Box 364, 02667
(508) 349-9333; FAX (508) 349-0234 or 9333
E-mail: duckinn@capecod.net
Web site: http://www.capecod.net/duckinn

Just ½ mile from the center of town is this wonderful, rambling, old-fashioned inn. The 1800s inn sits on five acres, on a knoll between a duck pond and a tidal salt marsh leading to the bay. The feeling is cozy and comfortable. The hospitality is warm and welcoming. Many rooms have views. Larger rooms on the third floor are suited for groups or families.

Hosts: Bob Morrill and Judy Pihl
Rooms: 25 (17PB; 8SB) $40-95 (seasonal)
Continental Breakfast
Credit Cards: A, B, C
Notes: 4, 7, 8, 9, 10, 12

WEST STOCKBRIDGE

Card Lake Inn

PO Box 38, 01266
(413) 232-0272; FAX (413) 232-0294
E-mail: cardlakeinn@bcn.net
Web site: http://www.cardlakeinn.com

Card Lake Inn is located only minutes from Tanglewood, the Norman Rockwell museum, and the Butternut Ski Area. We offer our guests fine dining and lodging at reasonable prices. The guest rooms are colonially furnished, many of them with brass beds. The home is air-conditioned for your comfort. Our restaurant and rooms are smoke-free.

Hosts: Ed and Lisa Robbins
Rooms: 8 (PB) $65-150
Full Breakfast
Credit Cards: A, B, D
Notes: 2, 3, 4, 5, 7, 8, 9, 10, 11, 12

WEST YARMOUTH (CAPE COD)

The Manor House Bed and Breakfast

57 Maine Avenue, 02673
(508) 771-3433; (800) 962-6679;
FAX (508) 790-1186
E-mail: manorhse@capecod.net
Web site: http://www.capecod.net/manorhouse

The Manor House is a lovely, 1920s Dutch Colonial located in a quiet residential neighborhood just a block from the beach. All rooms have private baths and are comfortably decorated with a mixture of antiques and country. We are ideally located mid-Cape on the southern side, with easy access to virtually everything Cape Cod has to offer. We offer a bountiful breakfast, afternoon refreshments, and friendly hospitality. Beach chairs and towels are available for our guests.

Hosts: Rick and Liz Latshaw
Rooms: 6 (PB) $78-128
Full Breakfast
Credit Cards: A, B, C
Notes: 2, 5, 8, 9, 10, 12

MICHIGAN (UPPER PENINSULA)

Houghton
Chassell
75
Mackinac Island

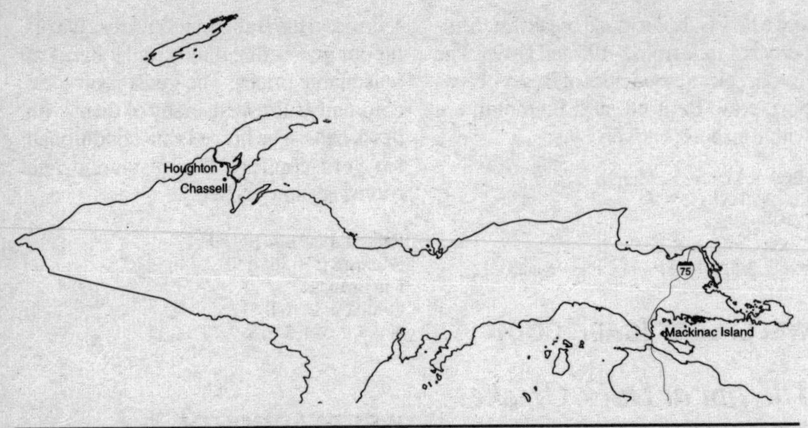

MICHIGAN

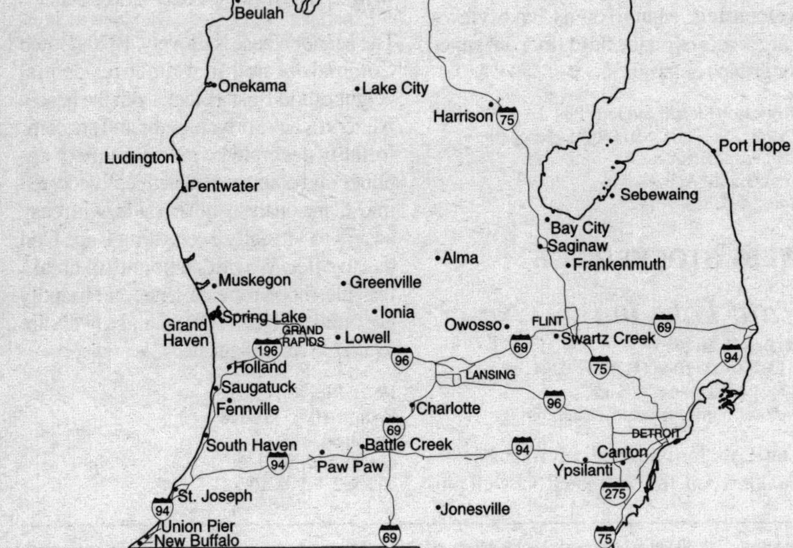

Ellsworth
Boyne City
Beulah
Onekama
Lake City
Harrison
75
Port Hope
Ludington
Pentwater
Sebewaing
Bay City
Saginaw
Frankenmuth
Alma
Muskegon
Greenville
Ionia
Spring Lake
Grand Haven
GRAND RAPIDS
Lowell
Owosso
FLINT
69
Swartz Creek
196
96
69
LANSING
75
94
Holland
Saugatuck
Fennville
Charlotte
96
69
DETROIT
South Haven
Battle Creek
94
94
Canton
Paw Paw
Ypsilanti
St. Joseph
275
94
Jonesville
Union Pier
New Buffalo
69
75

Michigan

ALMA

Saravilla Bed and Breakfast

633 N. State Street, 48801-1640
(517) 463-4078; FAX (517) 463-8624
E-mail: ljdarrow@saravilla.com
Web site: http://www.saravilla.com

Enjoy the charm and original features of this 11,000-square-foot Dutch Colonial home dating to 1894. You may enjoy the pool table, the fireplace in the library, and the hot tub in the sunroom. Guest rooms are spacious and quiet; several have fireplaces, and one has a whirlpool tub. A full breakfast is served each morning in the elegant turret dining room. The casino is 20 minutes away.

Hosts: Linda and Jon Darrow
Rooms: 7 (PB) $70-110
Full Breakfast
Credit Cards: A, B, D
Notes: 2, 5, 7, 8, 10, 12

BATTLE CREEK

Greencrest Manor

6174 Halbert Road E., 49017
(616) 962-8633; FAX (616) 962-7254

To experience Greencrest Manor is to step back in time to a way of life that is rare

Saravilla Bed and Breakfast

NOTES: Credit cards accepted: A Master Card; B Visa; C American Express; D Discover; E Diners Club; F Other; 2 Personal checks accepted; 3 Lunch available; 4 Dinner available; 5 Open all year; 6 Pets welcome; 7 Children welcome; 8 Tennis nearby; 9 Swimming nearby; 10 Golf nearby; 11 Skiing nearby; 12 May be booked through travel agent.

today. From the moment you enter the iron gates, you will be mesmerized. This French Normandy mansion, situated on the highest elevation of St. Mary's Lake, is constructed of sandstone, slate, and copper. The three levels of formal gardens include fountains, stone walls, iron rails, and cut sandstone urns. The home offers AC. Greencrest Manor was the featured "Inn of the Month" in *Country Inns* magazine, August 1992, and was chosen as one of the magazine's top twelve inns in the nation for that year.

Hosts: Kathy and Tom VanDaff
Rooms: 8 (6PB; 2SB) $75-200
Continental Breakfast
Credit Cards: A, B, C, E
Notes: 2, 5, 8, 10

BAY CITY

Clements Inn

1712 Center Avenue, 48708-6122
(517) 894-4600; (800) 442-4605;
FAX (517) 895-8535
Web site: http://www.laketolake.com/clements

This 1886 Queen Anne Victorian home features six fireplaces, magnificent woodwork, oak staircase, amber-colored glass windows, working gas lamps, organ pipes, and two claw-foot tubs. Each of the six bedrooms includes cable television, VCR, telephone, private bath, and AC. Special features include in-room gas fireplaces, in-room whirlpool tubs, and the 1,200-square foot Ballroom Suite with fireplace, whirlpool, and furnished kitchen.

Hosts: Brian and Karen Hepp
Rooms: 6 (PB) $70-175
Continental Breakfast
Credit Cards: A, B, C, D, E
Notes: 2, 5, 7, 8, 10, 11, 12

BEULAH

Brookside Inn —Hotel Frankfort

115 U.S. 31, 49617
(616) 882-9688; FAX (616) 882-4600
E-mail: brookside@brooksideinn
Web site: http://www.brooksideinn.com

Rekindle the wonderous feeling of love and togetherness. Rooms for intimate seclusion with Polynesian spa, plush carpets, soft music, and little log stove. A king-size canopy waterbed will create the mood of serenity. Full breakfast and dinner for two are included; tax and tips included for two.

Hosts: Pam and Kirk Corenz, Scott Powell
Rooms: 30 (PB) $220-285
Full Breakfast
Credit Cards: A, B, C, D, E, F
Notes: 2, 3, 4, 5, 8, 9, 10, 11, 12

BOYNE CITY

Deer Lake Bed and Breakfast

00631 E. Deer Lake Road, 49712
(616) 582-9039; FAX (616) 582-5385
E-mail: info@deerlakebb.com
Web site: http://www.deerlakebb.com

Deer Lake is a contemporary waterfront bed and breakfast in a quiet country setting. Breakfast is served in the parlor at tables set with fine china and crystal, by candlelight. Guest rooms each have air-conditioning and individual heat. Between the home and the lake is a small pond that's perfect for a quick swim or provides a place to sit in the morning with a cup of

Deer Lake Bed and Breakfast

coffee and watch the countryside wake up. A jewelry class is available.

Hosts: Shirley and Glenn Piepenburg
Rooms: 5 (PB) $80-105
Full Breakfast
Credit Cards: A, B, D
Notes: 2, 5, 7, 8, 9, 10, 11, 12

CANTON

Willow Break Inn B&B

44255 Warren Road, 48187
(734) 454-0019; (888) 454-1919;
FAX (734) 451-1126

Childhood memories. . .pampering pleasures. Between Ann Arbor and Detroit. Seclusion, wandering brook, flower gardens, hammock, deck, and hot tub on a wooded acre. Comfortable antiques, feather beds, quilts, fluffy robes, gourmet candlelight breakfast. In-room television/VCR, CD system. Nearby are the Henry Ford Museum and Greenfield Village.

Hosts: Bernadette and Michael Van Lenten
Rooms: 3 (PB) $95-125
Full Breakfast
Credit Cards: A, B, C
Notes: 2, 3, 4, 5, 6, 7, 8, 9, 10,
11 (cross-country), 12

CHARLOTTE

Schatze Manor Bed and Breakfast

1281 W. Kinsel Highway, 48813
(517) 543-4170; (800) 425-2244

Come and enjoy quiet elegance in our Victorian Oak Suite with red Oriental soaking tub, or enjoy sleeping in the 1948 Chevy Woody Room, or feel like a celebrity and relax in our Movie Star Room. All with private baths, distinctive hand-carved woodwork, unique decoration, full breakfast, evening dessert, and a nonsmoking atmosphere. Golf and dinner/theater packages. Lansing is 20 miles away.

Hosts: Donna and Paul Dunning
Rooms: 3 (PB) $60-105
Full Breakfast
Credit Cards: A, B, C
Notes: 2, 5, 8, 9, 10

ELLSWORTH

Historic Ellsworth House Bed and Breakfast

9510 Lake Street, 49729
(616) 588-7001; (888) 388-1876
E-mail: historicellsworthhouse@juno.com

This historic inn was the first house built in the village of Ellsworth. Situated at the head of the "oxbow" on Lake St. Claire and Lake Ellsworth, in 1876 the Historic Ellsworth House served as an inn to many lumbermen. It later housed area teachers. Renovated in 1998, the house was restored on the inside to reflect the colors and decor of the time period in which it was constructed. Beautiful acre of grounds.

Hosts: Marcella and Eric Nuffer
Rooms: 3 (PB) $95
Full Breakfast
Credit Cards: A, B
Notes: 2, 3, 5, 6, 7, 8, 9, 10, 11

The Kingsley House

FENNVILLE

The Kingsley House

626 W. Main Street, 49408
(616) 561-6425; FAX (616) 561-2593
E-mail: GaryKing@occn.org
Web site: http://www.bbonline.com/mi/kingsley

This elegant Queen Anne Victorian was built by the prominent Kingsley family in 1886 and selected by *Inn Times* as one of the fifty best bed and breakfasts in America. Also featured in *Insider* magazine. Near Holland, Saugatuck, Allegan State Forest, sandy beaches, and cross-country skiing. Bicycles available. We have three rooms with whirlpool baths and fireplaces and a getaway honeymoon suite. Enjoy beautiful surroundings and family antiques. Breakfast is served in the formal dining room.

Hosts: Gary and Kari King
Rooms: 8 (PB) $80-165
Full Breakfast
Credit Cards: A, B, C, D
Notes: 2, 4, 5, 8, 9, 10, 11, 12

Ridgeland

6875 126th Avenue, 49408
(616) 857-1633

Take a walk back in time to the turn of the century and experience a stay in one of the original guest homes of the Lakeshore area. We are a family-oriented bed and breakfast with antique furnishings. Located near the Saugatuck-Douglas area in a rural setting by Lake Michigan. See wildlife in its natural setting. Private bath and Jacuzzi. Nonsmoking.

Hosts: Carl and Michelle Nicholson
Rooms: 3 (PB) $85-90
Full Breakfast
Credit Cards: A, B
Notes: 2, 5, 7, 9, 10, 11

FRANKENMUTH

Bavarian Town Bed and Breakfast

206 Beyerlein Street, 48734
(517) 652-8057
E-mail: btbedb@juno.com

Beautifully decorated Cape Cod dwelling with central air-conditioning and private half baths in a peaceful, residential district of Michigan's most popular tourist town, just 3 blocks from Main Street. Bilingual hosts are descendants of original German settlers. Will serve as tour guides of the area, including historic St. Lorenz Lutheran Church. Color television with comfortable sitting area in each room. Shared kitchenette. Enjoy leisurely served full breakfasts with homemade, baked food. We share recipes and provide superb hospitality.

Hosts: Kathy and Louie Weiss
Rooms: 2 (private half baths, shared shower) $65-70
Full Breakfast
Credit Cards: none
Notes: 2, 5, 7, 8, 9, 10

Bed and Breakfast at the Pines

Bed and Breakfast at the Pines

327 Ardussi Street, 48734
(517) 652-9019

Welcome to our clean, casual, comfortable, ranch-style home located in a quiet neighborhood within walking distance of main tourist attractions and famous restaurants. Relax and enjoy reading or visiting with other guests in our "great room" overlooking our perennial garden and bird feeders. Guest rooms are individually furnished with double/twin beds, cotton sheets, terry robes, and ceiling fans. Modified full breakfast of homemade breads, fresh seasonal fruits, and specialty beverages. This smoke-free home was established in 1986.

Hosts: Richard and Donna Hodge
Rooms: 2 (1PB; 1SB) $50
Modified Full Breakfast
Credit Cards: none
Notes: 2, 5, 6, 7

GRAND HAVEN

Boyden House Inn B&B

301 S. 5th, 49417
(616) 846-3538

Built in 1874, our charming Victorian inn is decorated with treasures from faraway places, antiques, and original art. Enjoy the comfort of air-conditioned rooms with private baths and two whirlpool baths. Some rooms feature fireplaces or balconies. Relax in our common room and veranda surrounded by a beautiful perennial garden. Full, homemade breakfast served in our lovely dining room. Within walking distance of boardwalk beaches, shopping, and restaurants.

Hosts: Corrie and Bernend Snoeyer
Rooms: 7 (PB) $75-120
Full Breakfast
Credit Cards: A, B, C, D
Notes: 2, 5, 7, 8, 9, 10, 11, 12

Seascape Bed and Breakfast

20009 Breton, **Spring Lake,** 49456
(616) 842-8409 (voice and FAX)
Web site: http://www.bbonline.com/mi/seascape

Located on private, sandy Lake Michigan Beach. Scenic, relaxing lakefront rooms. Enjoy the warm hospitality and "country feeling" ambience of our nautical lakeshore home. A full homemade breakfast is served in the gathering room with fieldstone fireplace or on the large sundeck. Either offers a panoramic view of Grand Haven Harbor. Stroll or cross-country ski on dune land nature trails. Open all year, offering a kaleidoscope of scenes with the changing of the seasons.

Hostess: Susan Meyer
Rooms: 4 (PB) $75-150
Full Breakfast
Credit Cards: A, B
Notes: 2, 5, 8, 9, 10, 11

Gibson House Bed and Breakfast

GREENVILLE

Gibson House Bed and Breakfast

311 W. Washington Street, 48838
(616) 754-6691; FAX (616) 754-3904

Enjoy the warmth and hospitality of this state historic landmark. This Colonial Revival mansion was home to the Gibson refrigeration and appliance family for three generations. Restored to its original grace and beauty, the home features beautiful woodwork, stained glass, and Victorian antiques that compliment our elegant but comfortable rooms. Enjoy tea at fireside, take a stroll around our 200-year-old Mulberry tree, or hop on our bicycle built for two and take a spin around Baldwin Lake. Gift certificates available.

Hosts: Herb and Kathryn Heie
Rooms: 5 (PB) $65-98
Full Breakfast weekends, Continental Breakfast weekdays
Credit Cards: A, B, C
Notes: 5, 8, 9, 10, 11

HARRISON

The Carriage House Inn

1515 Grant Avenue; PO Box 757, 48625
(517) 539-1300; FAX (517) 539-5661
E-mail: carhsinn@glccomputers.com
Web site: http://www.carriagehouseinn.com

The Carriage House Inn is nestled in a pine plantation overlooking beautiful Budd Lake, offering its guests intimate accommodations on 127 acres. The seven guest rooms have private baths; most also have whirlpool tubs, color TV/VCR, cable, telephone, coffeemaker, wet bar refrigerator, and air-conditioning. Executive retreat accommodations and private retreat reception and training facilities are available. Breakfast features a variety of samplings each morning.

Hosts: John and Connie Mlinarcik
Rooms: 7 (PB) $95-135
Continental Breakfast
Credit Cards: A, B
Notes: 2, 5, 7, 8, 9, 10, 11, 12

HOLLAND

Dutch Colonial Inn

560 Central Avenue, 49423
(616) 396-3664; FAX (616) 396-0461
E-mail: dutchcolonialinn@juno.com
Web site: http://www.bbonline.com/mi/dutch

Relax and enjoy a gracious 1928 Dutch Colonial. Your hosts have elegantly decorated their home with family heirloom antiques and furnishings from the 1930s. Guests enjoy the cheery sunporch, honeymoon suites with fireplaces, and rooms with televisions and double whirlpool tubs. Festive touches abound during the Christmas season. Nearby are Dutch attractions, charming downtown shopping, Hope College, Michigan's finest beaches, bike paths, and cross-country ski trails, plus the Tulip Festival. Corporate rates are available for business travelers.

Hosts: Bob and Pat Elenbaas
Rooms: 4 (PB) $90-150
Full Breakfast
Credit Cards: A, B, C, D
Notes: 2, 5, 8, 9, 10, 11

HOUGHTON

Charleston House Historic Inn

918 College Avenue, 49931
(906) 482-7790; (800) 482-7404;
FAX (906) 482-7068

Turn-of-the-century Georgian house with double veranda, ceiling fans, and wicker furniture. The inn features ornate woodwork, leaded- and beveled-glass windows, a library with fireplace, and grand interior staircase. Comfortable period reproduction and antique furnishings with king canopy and twin beds. All private baths, air-conditioning, cable color TV, and telephones. Full breakfast. Walk to university and downtown. Smoking limited to the garden.

Charleston House Historic Inn

Hosts: John and Helen Sullivan
Rooms: 5 (PB) $90-165
Full Breakfast
Credit Cards: A, B, C
Notes: 5, 7 (12+), 8, 9, 10, 11, 12

IONIA

Union Hill Inn B&B

306 Union Street, 48846
(616) 527-0955

This elegant 1868 Italianate-style home served as a station for the underground

Union Hill Inn B&B

welcome; 7 Children welcome; 8 Tennis nearby; 9 Swimming nearby; 10 Golf nearby; 11 Skiing nearby; 12 May be booked through travel agent.

railroad. The home is beautifully furnished with antiques. Enjoy the living area with its fireplace, piano, porcelain village, and dolls. The home is air-conditioned. Flower beds surround the home, noted for its expansive veranda and panoramic view overlooking the historic city. With all the beauty at Union Hill Inn, the greatest thing you will experience is God's love and peace that abide here.

Hosts: Tom and Mary Kay Moular
Rooms: 6 (1PB; 5SB) $50-95
Full Breakfast
Credit Cards: none
Notes: 2, 5, 7, 8, 9, 10, 12

JONESVILLE

The Munro House

202 Maumee, 49250
(517) 849-9292; (800) 320-3792
Web site: http://www.getaway2smi.com/munro

This 1840 Greek Revival structure was built by George C. Munro, a brigadier general during the Civil War. Visitors can see the secret room used to hide runaway slaves as part of the underground railway. The seven cozy guest rooms, all with private baths, are furnished with period antiques, many with working fireplaces and Jacuzzis. We have five common area rooms, including a library and breakfast room with an open-hearth fireplace. An evening snack is offered.

Hostess: Joyce Yarde
Rooms: 7 (PB) $75-150
Full Breakfast
Credit Cards: A, B, D
Notes: 2, 5, 7, 8, 9, 10, 11, 12

LAKE CITY

Bed and Breakfast in the Pines

1940 Schneider Park Road, 49651
(616) 839-4876
Web site: http://www.laketolake.com

A quaint chalet nestled among the pines on shimmering Sapphire Lake. Each bedroom has its own outside door leading to its own deck facing the lake. Enjoy our large fireplace and warm hospitality. Handicap ramp. Thirteen miles east of Cadillac. No alcohol, smoking, or pets. Enjoy downhill/cross-country skiing, fishing, swimming, hiking, biking, and boating. Two-week advance reservation only.

Hostess: Reggie Ray
Rooms: 2 (1PB; 1SB) $100; extra beds $25 each
Full Breakfast
Credit Cards: none
Notes: 2, 5, 8, 9, 10, 11

LOLAND

Manitou Manor

PO Box 864, 49654
(616) 256-7712
Web site: http://www.laketolake.com

A spacious country estate makes staying in Leelanau County a peaceful experience. Open year-round, the home features private baths and family-style breakfasts. Unique guest rooms have inviting themes. A perfect place to celebrate the seasons.

Hosts: Mike and Sandy Lambdin
Rooms: 5 (PB) $85-159
Full Breakfast
Credit Cards: A, B, D
Notes: 2, 5, 7, 8, 9, 10, 11

NOTES: Credit cards accepted: A Master Card; B Visa; C American Express; D Discover; E Diners Club; F Other; 2 Personal checks accepted; 3 Lunch available; 4 Dinner available; 5 Open all year; 6 Pets

McGee Homestead Bed and Breakfast

LOWELL

McGee Homestead Bed and Breakfast

2534 Alden Nash NE, 49331
(616) 897-8142

Join us in the country! An 1880 farmhouse with a barn full of petting animals. Five acres surrounded by orchards, next to a golf course. Guests can use the separate entrance to a living room with fireplace, parlor, and small kitchen, furnished with antiques. Big country breakfast.

Hosts: Bill and Ardie Barber
Rooms: 4 (4PB) $38-58
Full Breakfast
Credit Cards: A, B, C, D
Notes: 2, 7, 8, 9, 10, 11

LUDINGTON

Doll House Inn

709 E. Ludington Avenue, 49431
(616) 843-2286; (800) 275-4616
Web site: http://www.bbonline.com/mi/dollhouse

The Doll House Inn is a gracious 1900 American Foursquare with seven rooms, including a bridal suite with whirlpool tub for two. Enclosed porch. We offer smoke- and pet-free adult accommodations. A full, heart-smart breakfast is served each morning. The home is air-conditioned. Corporate rates, bicycles, cross-country skiing, walk to beach and town, and special weekend and murder mystery packages in fall and winter. Transportation available to and from car ferry/airport. Closed November–March.

Hosts: Barb and Joe Gerovac
Rooms: 7 (PB) $60-110
Full Breakfast
Credit Cards: A, B
Notes: 2, 8, 9, 10

Doll House Inn

The Inn at Ludington

701 E. Ludington Avenue, 49431
(616) 845-7055; (800) 845-9170
Web site: http://www.bbonline.com/mi/ludington

Enjoy the charm of the past with the comfort of today. No stuffy, hands-off museum atmosphere here—our vintage furnishings invite you to relax and feel at home. The bountiful breakfast will sustain you for a day of beachcombing, biking, or antiquing. In winter, cross-country skiing awaits at Ludington State Park. Looking for something different? Murder mysteries are a specialty. Make this your headquarters for a Ludington/Lake Michigan adventure. Just look for the "painted lady" with the

---

welcome; 7 Children welcome; 8 Tennis nearby; 9 Swimming nearby; 10 Golf nearby; 11 Skiing nearby; 12 May be booked through travel agent.

three-story turret. The Inn at Ludington is a nonsmoking home.

Hosts: Diane Shields and David Nemitz
Rooms: 6 (PB) $70-90
Full Buffet Breakfast
Credit Cards: A, B, C
Notes: 2, 3 (picnic), 5, 7, 8, 9, 10, 11, 12

Snyder's Shoreline Inn

903 W. Ludington Avenue; PO Box 667, 49431
(616) 845-1261; FAX (616) 843-4441
E-mail: sharon@snydersshoreinn.com
Web site: http://www.snydersshoreinn.com

Snyder's Shoreline Inn offers a beautiful location on the edge of town and tremendous views of Lake Michigan. Guests enjoy watching freighters, fishing boats, and spectacular Lake Michigan sunsets from private covered balconies. Sleep comfortably in our pleasant guest rooms, each one immaculate and individually decorated with a charm that reflects the owners' personal touch. Explore local antique shops and miles of nearby sandy beaches. The inn features in-room spas, quilts, and stenciled walls. Continental breakfast. Outdoor pool/spa. Smoke-free. No pets.

Hosts: Angie Snyder and Kate Whitaker
Rooms: 44 (PB) $65-229
Continental Breakfast
Credit Cards: A, B, C, D
Notes: 2, 8, 9, 10

MACKINAC ISLAND

Haan's 1830 Inn

PO Box 123, 49757
(906) 847-6244

The earliest Greek Revival home in the Northwest Territory, the completely restored inn is on the Michigan Historic Registry. It is located in a quiet neighborhood 3 blocks around Haldiman Bay from the bustling 1800s downtown and Old Fort Mackinac. Adjacent to St. Anne's Church and gardens. Rooms are furnished with antiques. Experience the 19th-century ambience of horse-drawn buggies and wagons. Closed late October–mid-May.

Hosts: Nancy and Nicholas Haan
Rooms: 8 (6PB; 2SB) $85-160
Continental Breakfast
Credit Cards: none
Notes: 2, 7, 8, 9, 10

MUSKEGON

Port City Victorian Inn

1259 Lakeshore Drive, 49441
(616) 759-0205 (voice and FAX); (800) 274-3574
E-mail: pcvicinn@gte.net
Web site: http://www.bbonline.com/mi/portcity

An 1877 romantic Victorian getaway on the bluffs of Muskegon Lake. Minutes from

Snyder's Shoreline Inn

NOTES: Credit cards accepted: A Master Card; B Visa; C American Express; D Discover; E Diners Club; F Other; 2 Personal checks accepted; 3 Lunch available; 4 Dinner available; 5 Open all year; 6 Pets

Lake Michigan beaches, state parks, theaters, sports arena, and restaurants. Five bedrooms with private baths, two featuring suites with lake views and private double whirlpools. Rooftop balcony, TV/VCR room with a view of the lake. The main floor is all common area for our guests' enjoyment. Includes two parlors—one with a fireplace—large dining room, sunroom, and music room with piano. All rooms have air-conditioning, cable TV, and phones. FAX and bicycles available.

Hosts: Barbara and Fred Schossau
Rooms: 5 (PB) $95-125
Full Breakfast
Credit Cards: A, B, C, D, E, F
Notes: 2, 5, 7, 8, 9, 10, 11, 12

Sans Souci Euro Inn

NEW BUFFALO

Sans Souci Euro Inn

19265 S. Lakeside Road, 49117
(616) 756-3141; FAX (616) 756-5511
E-mail: sans-souci@worldnet.att.net
Web site: http://www.sans-souci.com

Sans Souci ("without a care") is far removed from the hustle of everyday life. Inside our gates, you will find silence and serenity. Lakeside cottages, honeymoon suites, vacation homes with whirlpools and fireplaces. Enjoy a 50-acre nature retreat with private lake (fishing, swimming, skating) and wondrous wildlife. Birder's paradise—spring and fall migration stopover. Fine dining, antiques, art galleries, golf courses nearby. Family reunions, small seminars welcome. AAA-approved. Chicago only 70 miles.

Hostess: Angelika Siewert
Rooms: 9 (PB) $98-185
Full Breakfast
Credit Cards: A, B, C, D
Notes: 2, 5, 6, 7, 8, 9, 10, 11 (cross-country), 12

ONEKAMA

Lake Breeze House

5089 Main Street, 49675-0301
(616) 889-4969
Web site: http://www.manistee.com/lakebreeze.html

Our two-story frame house on Portage Lake is yours with a shared bath, living room, and breakfast room. Each room has its own special charm with family antiques. Come, relax, and enjoy our back porch and the sounds of the babbling creek. By reservation only. Boating and charter service available.

Hosts: Bill and Donna Erickson
Rooms: 3 (1P half B; 2SB) $55-65
Full Breakfast
Credit Cards: none
Notes: 2, 7, 8, 9, 10, 11

OWOSSO

Rossman's R&R Ranch

308 E. Hibbard Road, 48867
(517) 723-2553; FAX (517) 725-5392

A newly remodeled farmhouse from the 1900s, the ranch sits on 130 acres overlooking the Maple River Valley. A large concrete, circular drive with white board fences leads to stables of horses and cattle. Area wildlife includes deer, fox, rabbits, pheasant, quail, and songbirds. Observe and explore from the farm lane, river walk, or outside deck. Countrylike accents adorn the farmhouse interior, and guests are welcome to use the family parlor, garden, game room, and fireplace. Newly installed central air-conditioning.

Hosts: Jeanne and Carl Rossman
Rooms: 3 (SB) $45
Continental Breakfast
Credit Cards: none
Notes: 2, 5, 6, 7, 10

Sylverlynd

3452 McBride Road, 48867
(517) 723-1267

Sylverlynd is located on 18 acres in the countryside west of Owosso. It was designed and built by the owners, Rev. and Mrs. Schweikert, with the counsel of an architect friend. A small woods and a pond stocked with fish are part of the landscaping. The design elements include touches of English tudor, Swiss chalet, and contemporary. Balconies and decks with a view across open countryside open off each room. A circular fireplace, barn beams, fieldstone walls, and fireplace are part of the inside design. The home is furnished with antiques, French Provincial, country pieces, and owner-designed and -built pieces, plus interesting souvenirs and artifacts from the owners' residence in Australia and their world travels.

Hosts: Rev. Ed and Leona Schweikert
Rooms: 2 (SB) $60-70 (by reservation only)
Continental Breakfast
Credit Cards: none
Notes: 2, 5, 6, 7, 8, 10, 12

PAW PAW

Carrington Country House

43799 60th Avenue, 49079
(616) 657-5321
E-mail: r.m.carrington@aol.com

Carrington's Country House is a 150-year-old farmhouse built in the center of fruit and grape vineyards near I–94. Just down the street is public access to spring-fed Lake Cora, a short walking distance from the house. The picturesque country road leading to the house is lined with large old sugar maples that form a canopy of gold and green throughout the year.

Host: Wm. Carrington
Rooms: 3 (SB)
Continental Breakfast
Credit Cards: none
Notes: 2, 5, 6, 7, 9, 10

PENTWATER

The Historic Nickerson Inn

262 Lowell; PO Box 986, 49449
(616) 869-6731; FAX (616) 869-6151

The Historic Nickerson Inn has been serving guests with "special hospitality" since 1914. Our inn was totally renovated in 1991. All our rooms have private baths and AC. We have two Jacuzzi suites with fireplaces and balconies overlooking Lake Michigan. Two short blocks to Lake Michigan beach, and 3 blocks to shopping district. New ownership. Open all year. Casual, fine dining in our eighty-seat

NOTES: Credit cards accepted: A Master Card; B Visa; C American Express; D Discover; E Diners Club; F Other; 2 Personal checks accepted; 3 Lunch available; 4 Dinner available; 5 Open all year; 6 Pets

restaurant. Excellent for retreats, workshops, and year-round recreation.

Hosts: Gretchen and Harry Shiparski
Rooms: 11 (PB) $90-225
Full Breakfast
Credit Cards: A, B, D
Notes: 2, 4, 5, 7 (12 and older), 9, 10, 11 (cross-country), 12

The Pentwater "Victorian" Inn

180 E. Lowell Street, 49449
(616) 869-5909; FAX (616) 869-7002
Web site: http://www.bbonline.com/mi/pentwater/special.html

This beautiful Victorian inn, built in the 1800s, has an attractive gingerbread exterior and stained-glass windows that have been lovingly preserved. Located a short walk from the village shops, fine dining, and Lake Michigan Beach with its spectacular sunsets. This popular inn provides comfort and hospitality, from the personal greeting by your hosts to the evening snack to the elegant, three-course breakfast made from scratch and served in the dining room. Each of the bedrooms is tastefully decorated with British and American antiques the hosts collected while living in England. A heart-shaped Jacuzzi for two is in the Garden Suite. Three porches grace the inn; the back porch has an enclosed hot tub room. No smoking.

The Pentwater "Victorian" Inn

Hosts: Quintus and Donna Renshaw
Rooms: 5 (PB) $85-125
Full Breakfast
Credit Cards: A, B
Notes: 2, 5, 7, 8, 9, 10, 11 (cross-country), 12

The Stafford House

PORT HOPE

The Stafford House

4489 Main Street; PO Box 204, 48468
(517) 428-4554

From a delicious full buffet-style breakfast, afternoon refreshments, or special dinner packages, enjoy staying in our 1886 country Victorian home with all its original woodwork. You can delight in viewing the spring, summer, and fall flowers in bloom. There are many amenities to leave you with lasting memories. From spectacular sunrises to moonlit nights, enjoy golf, charter fishing, scenic lighthouses, antiquing, lakeshore parks, beaches, and more.

Hosts: Greg and Kathy Gephart
Rooms: 4 (PB) $60-85
Full Breakfast
Credit Cards: A, B, D
Notes: 2, 4, 5, 7 (over 10), 9, 10, 11, 12

welcome; 7 Children welcome; 8 Tennis nearby; 9 Swimming nearby; 10 Golf nearby; 11 Skiing nearby; 12 May be booked through travel agent.

SAGINAW

Cousins B&B

4694 Brockway Road, 48603
(517) 790-1728

Enjoy second-floor privacy, queen-size bed, private bath with dressing room, sitting area with television and VCR, desk with phone (a FAX is available), refrigerator, and coffeemaker. There is a wicker-and-glass summer porch, living room with fireplace, central AC, and large, parklike setting. The home is furnished with fine artwork and antiques. Airport transportation is provided to and from Cousins. No smoking, please. Office space available. The B&B is in a central location, within walking distance of three to six churches (how far do you want to walk?). Pets welcome, with prior approval; space for pets not always available.

Hosts: Pat and Jim Hess
Rooms: 2 (PB) $125 per night, $200 weekend package
Full Breakfast
Credit Cards: A, B
Notes: 2, 5, 6, 8, 9, 10, 11, 12

ST. JOSEPH

South Cliff Inn B&B

1900 Lakeshore Drive, 49085
(616) 983-4881; FAX (616) 983-7391

An English country-style B&B. The exterior of the inn is English cottage–style, with decks overlooking Lake Michigan, a beautiful formal garden, and sunsets beyond compare. The interior is English country–style, with many antiques, imported fabrics, and custom furnishings.

South Cliff Inn Bed and Breakfast

Several rooms have balconies that overlook the lake. Each guest room is individually decorated. The atmosphere is warm and friendly. Homemade breakfasts, created by the retired chef and owner, are something you will not want to miss.

Host: Bill Swisher
Rooms: 7 (PB) $75-165
Full or Continental Breakfast
Credit Cards: A, B, C, D
Notes: 5, 8, 9, 10, 11, 12

SAUGATUCK

"The Porches" Bed and Breakfast

2297 Lakeshore Drive, **Fennville,** 49408
(616) 543-4162; FAX (616) 543-4264
E-mail: rjohnson@accn.org
Web site: http://www.saugatuck.com

Built in 1897, "The Porches" offers five guest rooms, each with private bath. Located 3 miles south of Saugatuck, we have a private beach and hiking trails. The large common room has a TV. We overlook Lake Michigan, where you can view beautiful sunsets from the front porch.

Hosts: Bob and Ellen Johnson
Rooms: 5 (PB) $75-85
Full Breakfast Sunday, Continental Plus midweek
Credit Cards: A, B
Notes: 2, 7 (ask), 8, 9, 10, 12

NOTES: Credit cards accepted: A Master Card; B Visa; C American Express; D Discover; E Diners Club; F Other; 2 Personal checks accepted; 3 Lunch available; 4 Dinner available; 5 Open all year; 6 Pets

Sherwood Forest Bed and Breakfast

Sherwood Forest B&B

938 Center Street; PO Box 315, 49453
(616) 857-1246; (800) 838-1246;
FAX (616) 857-1996
E-mail: sherwoodforest@hayburn.com
Web site: http://travelassist.com/reg/m10021.html

Surrounded by woods, this Victorian-style home offers antique-furnished guest rooms with private baths, cozy wing chairs, and Persian rugs. Two suites available with Jacuzzi/fireplace. Another room sports a hand-painted mural that transforms the room into a canopied tree loft, complemented by a gas fireplace. Heated pool, bicycles, ½ block from Lake Michigan public beach and spectacular sunsets. In winter, cross-country ski or hike wooded paths. Cottage also available.

Hosts: Keith and Susan Charak
Rooms: 5 (PB) $85-165
Continental Breakfast
Credit Cards: A, B, D, E, F
Notes: 2, 7, 8, 9, 10, 12

Twin Gables Country Inn

900 Lake Street; PO Box 881, 49453
(616) 857-4346; (800) 231-2185;
FAX (616) 857-1092
Web site: http://www.bbonline.com/mi/twingables

Overlooking Kalamazoo Lake, the state historic inn has central air-conditioning throughout. Twin Gables features fourteen charming guest rooms with private baths, some with fireplaces, furnished in antiques and country decor. Cross-country skiers may relax in the large indoor hot tub and cozy up to a warm, crackling fireplace, while summer guests may take a refreshing dip in the heated outdoor pool and enjoy glorious sunsets from the front veranda. Three separate one- and two-bedroom cottages, one with fireplace, also available.

Hosts: Michael and Denise Simcik
Rooms: 14 (PB) $68-119
Full Breakfast
Credit Cards: A, B, C, D, E
Notes: 2, 5, 7, 8, 9, 10, 11, 12

SEBEWAING

Rummel's Tree Haven

41 N. Beck (M-25), 48759
(517) 883-2450
E-mail: erummel@avcl.net

We're open year-round to accommodate you whenever you're in the area. This is fishing and hunting country on Saginaw Bay—plenty of perch, walleye, geese, ducks, and deer. A quiet, pleasant area—fresh, clean atmosphere.

Hosts: Carl and Erma Rummel
Rooms: 2 (PB) $50
Full Breakfast
Credit Cards: none
Notes: 2, 5, 7

SOUTH HAVEN

Carriage House B&B

233 Dyckman Avenue, 49090
(616) 639-1776, 639-2161; FAX (616) 639-2308
Web site: http://www.theinnplace.com

"The Inn Place" is a luxurious, romantic retreat in two unique locations. One home overlooks the harbor; the other overlooks the park. Beautiful Victorian homes, newly renovated. Twenty guest rooms—nineteen with fireplaces, fourteen with whirlpools, eight with decks overlooking the harbor. Old-fashioned country breakfast. Outstanding hors d'oeuvres. Walk to beach, town, restaurants, and marina.

Hosts: Jay and Joyce Yelton
Rooms: 20 (PB) $95-180
Full Breakfast
Credit Cards: A, B, C
Notes: 2, 5, 9, 10, 11

The Seymour House

The Seymour House

1248 Blue Star Highway, 49090
(616) 227-3918; FAX (616) 227-3010
E-mail: seymour@cybersol.com
Web site: http://www.bbonline.com/mi/seymour

Spectacular grounds surround this 1862 Italianate mansion and guest log cabin. The 11-acre estate offers a 1-acre pond for fishing and swimming, trails through the woods, and unequalled privacy. Only minutes from the resort towns of Saugatuck/ South Haven and ½ mile from Lake Michigan. The area offers biking trails, golf, antiquing, sandy beaches, lighthouse, and awesome Lake Michigan sunsets. Superior accommodations include five guest rooms with private baths, some with Jacuzzis and fireplaces. Air-conditioning, gourmet breakfast.

Hosts: Tom and Gwen Paton
Rooms: 5 + log cabin (PB) $80-135
Full Breakfast
Credit Cards: A, B
Notes: 2, 5, 9, 10, 11, 12

SWARTZ CREEK

Pink Palace Farms Bed and Breakfast

6095 Baldwin Road, 48473-9118
(810) 655-4076; FAX (810) 655-8308

Enjoy old-fashioned charm and gracious hospitality in the countryside 10 miles southwest of Flint. The house was built in 1888 and is on the National Register of Historic Places. TV/VCR room. Smoking restricted. Spacious lawn and gardens. Full breakfast served in country dining room (or in bed, if you prefer). Fruit in season, homemade breads with jams, and home-churned butter.

Hosts: Blaine and Jeannette Pinkston
Rooms: 3 (1PB; 2SB) $39.95-59.95
Full Breakfast
Credit Cards: none
Notes: 2, 7, 8, 9, 10, 11

UNION PIER

The Inn At Union Pier

9708 Berrien; PO Box 222, 49129
(616) 469-4700; FAX (616) 469-4720
Web site: http://www.innatunionpier.com

Located just 75 minutes from Chicago and 200 steps from the beach, the Inn at Union

Pier blends casual elegance with barefoot informality. Choose from our sixteen charming, spacious rooms. Most feature antique Swedish wood-burning fireplaces and porches overlooking landscaped grounds. Take one of the inn's bicycles out for a spin on a quiet country road, unwind in the outdoor hot tub and sauna, or enjoy Michigan wines and popcorn, which are served every evening in the inn's Great Room. A bountiful breakfast and afternoon refreshments are included every day. The Inn at Union Pier also hosts corporate retreats in a productive environment.

Hosts: Joyce Erickson Pitts and Mark Pitts
Rooms: 16 (PB) $135-205
Full Gourmet Breakfast
Credit Cards: A, B, D
Notes: 2, 5, 8, 9, 10, 11

YPSILANTI

Parish House Inn B&B

103 S. Huron Street, 48197
(734) 480-4800; (800) 480-4866;
FAX (734) 480-7472
E-mail: ParishInn@aol.com
Web site: http://www.laketolake.com

This former parsonage of the First Congregational Church is a totally restored Queen Anne–style house. The guest rooms have antique furniture, Victorian colors and wallpaper—yet, they offer guests all the modern conveniences. Awake to the aroma of freshly brewed coffee, baking breads, and sizzling bacon. The location is ideal for travelers on I–94 and U.S. 23 going to the University of Michigan, EMU, an area event, or a local business.

Hostess: Mrs. Chris Mason
Rooms: 9 (PB) $75-125
Full Breakfast
Credit Cards: A, B, C, D
Notes: 2, 5, 8, 9, 10, 11, 12

MINNESOTA

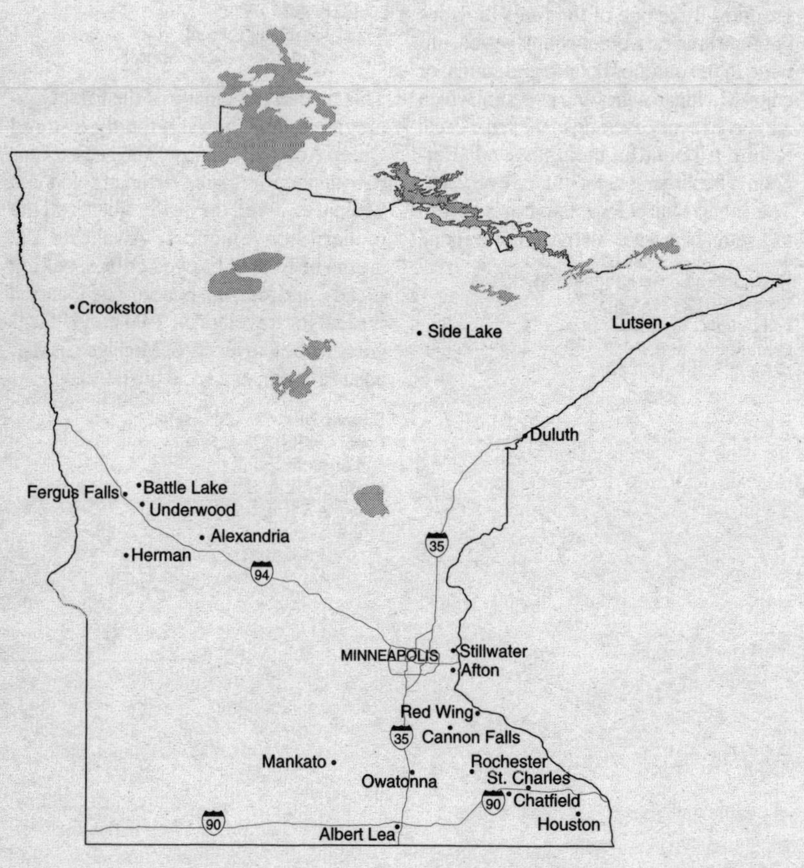

Crookston
Side Lake
Lutsen
Duluth
Fergus Falls
Battle Lake
Underwood
Alexandria
Herman
35
94
MINNEAPOLIS
Stillwater
Afton
Red Wing
35
Cannon Falls
Mankato
Rochester
Owatonna
St. Charles
90
Chatfield
90
Houston
Albert Lea

Minnesota

AFTON

Afton House Inn

3291 S. St. Croix Trail; PO Box 326, 55001
(651) 436-8883; FAX (651) 436-6859

The historic Afton House Inn is located on the scenic St. Croix River. Our inn has fifteen rooms, each individually decorated with a country antique decor. The inn offers fine dining in our main dining room and casual dining in the Catfish Saloon. Public Sunday champagne brunch cruises, May–October. Come visit Afton—a great getaway with small-town charm.

Hosts: Gordy and Kathy Jarvis
Rooms: 15 (PB) $60-140
Continental Breakfast
Credit Cards: A, B, C, D
Notes: 2, 3, 4, 5, 7, 8, 9, 10, 11

ALBERT LEA

The Victorian Rose Inn

609 W. Fountain Street, 56007
(507) 373-7602; (800) 252-6558
E-mail: vicrose@deskmedia.com

Queen Anne Victorian home (1898) in virtually original condition, with fine woodwork, stained glass, gingerbread, antique light fixtures. Antique furnishings, down comforters. Spacious rooms, one with fireplace. AC. A full breakfast is served each day. Business/extended-stay rates and gift certificates offered. Children by arrangement; no pets; no smoking.

Hosts: Darrel and Linda Roemmich
Rooms: 4 (PB) $40-80
Full Breakfast
Credit Cards: A, B
Notes: 2, 5, 7, 8, 10, 12

ALEXANDRIA

Cedar Rose Inn

422 7th Avenue W., 56308
(320) 762-8430; (888) 203-5333;
FAX (320) 762-8044
E-mail: cedarose@getel.com
Web site: http://www.echopress.com/cedarose

From the wild blooming roses in the summer to the warm crackling fire in the winter, the Cedar Rose Inn offers year-round comfort for anyone away from home. Conveniently located within walking distance of downtown Alexandria, with its quiet shops and friendly people. The inn

Cedar Rose Inn

is located in the spectacular Minnesota lake country.

Hosts: Aggie and Florian Ledermann
Rooms: 4 (PB) $75-125
Full Breakfast
Credit Cards: A, B
Notes: 2, 5, 8, 9, 10, 11, 12

BATTLE LAKE

Xanadu Island B&B

Route 2, Box 51, 56515
(218) 864-8096; (800) 369-9043
E-mail: xanadu@prtel.com
Web site: http://www.xanadu.cc

This 1920s large lodge-style home is located on a private 7-acre island. Jacuzzis and fireplaces in some of the rooms. Full breakfast served on four-season porch overlooking the lake. Use of fishing boats and canoe included. Sandy swimming beach. Located 3 miles outside a small, charming lake town with unique shops. Golfing, hiking, cross-country skiing, fine dining, and antiquing nearby.

Hosts: Janet and Bryan Lonski
Rooms: 5 (PB) $75-140
Full Breakfast
Credit Cards: A, B, D
Notes: 2, 5, 9, 10, 11 (cross-country), 12

CANNON FALLS

Quill & Quilt

615 W. Hoffman Street, 55009
(507) 263-5507; (800) 488-3849;
FAX (507) 263-4066
E-mail: gataway@cannon.net

Circa-1897 home boasts oak woodwork and spacious, airy common areas. It is decorated with Victorian wallpapers, antiques, and handmade quilts. Large suite with double whirlpool is a favorite. Near the Cannon Valley bike trail, 35 miles from the Mall of America. Midweek rates and gift certificates available.

Hosts: Staci and Jim Smith
Rooms: 4 (PB) $55-145
Full Breakfast
Credit Cards: A, B
Notes: 2, 5, 8, 9, 10, 11

CHATFIELD

Liund's Guest House

218 SE Winona Street, 55923
(507) 867-4003

Two old-fashioned guest houses redone to provide the charm of the old and the amenities of the new. Each house has a large screened-in front porch, small screened-in back porch, old-fashioned furniture in kitchen, dining rooms, parlor, four bedrooms with private baths, central air-conditioning, soft water. Very homey and comfortable. One hundred miles from Minneapolis, 20 miles from Rochester, 17 miles from Lanesboro.

Hosts: Shelby and Marion Lund
Rooms: 8 (PB) $65 w/breakfast; $60 without
Continental Plus Breakfast
Credit Cards: none
Notes: 2, 5, 6 and 7 (check with owner), 9, 10, 11

NOTES: Credit cards accepted: A Master Card; B Visa; C American Express; D Discover; E Diners Club; F Other; 2 Personal checks accepted; 3 Lunch available; 4 Dinner available; 5 Open all year; 6 Pets

Elm Street Inn Bed and Breakfast

CROOKSTON

Elm Street Inn B&B

422 Elm Street, 56716
(218) 281-2343; FAX (218) 281-1756
E-mail: legal@beltrami.means.net

The Elm Street Inn is a Georgian Revival (1910) home with antiques, hardwood floors, and stained and beveled glass. Guests enjoy the wicker-filled sunporch, old-fashioned beds, quilts, and fresh flowers—and the memorable full breakfast by candlelight. A community pool is next-door. Children are permitted by prior arrangement. No pets. No smoking.

Hosts: John and Sheryl Winters
Rooms: 4 (PB) $65
Full Breakfast
Credit Cards: A, B
Notes: 2, 5, 8, 9, 10, 12

DULUTH

The Mansion B&B

3600 London Road, 55804
(218) 724-0739
Web site: www.eskimo.com/~my3sons/mansion

This magnificent home was built in 1928. The 7-acre estate is nestled on 525 feet of Lake Superior beach with manicured lawns, woods, and gardens. Guests are encouraged to make themselves at home on the grounds and inside the mansion. Common rooms for guests include the library, living room, three-season porch, gallery, dining room, and trophy room. Come to the lake and let us share our home with you!

Hosts: Warren, Sue, and Andrea Monson
Rooms: 10-13 (6 PB; 4SB) $115-235
Full Breakfast
Credit Cards: A, B
Notes: 2, 5

FERGUS FALLS

Bakketopp Hus Bed and Breakfast

RR 2, Box 187-A, 56537
(218) 739-2915; (800) 739-2915
E-mail: DDN@PRTel.com
Web site: http://www.bbonline.com/mn/bakketopp

Quiet, spacious lake home with vaulted ceilings, fireplaces, private spa, flower garden patio, and lakeside decks. Antique furnishings from family homestead; four-poster, draped, French canopy bed; and private baths. Here you can listen as loons call to each other across the lake in the still of dusk, witness the falling foliage splendor, relax by the crackling fire, or sink into the warmth of the spa after a day of hiking or skiing. Near antique shops and Maplewood State Park. Ten minutes off I–94. Gift certificates available. Reservation with deposit.

Hosts: Dennis and Judy Nims
Rooms: 3 (PB) $70-105
Full Breakfast
Credit Cards: A, B, D
Notes: 2, 5, 8, 9, 10, 11

HERMAN

Lawndale Farm Bed and Breakfast

Route 2, Box 50, 56248
(320) 677-2687

This historic inn features a two-bedroom suite, deck, Belgian Waffles, adjacent lily pond, wild flower garden, waterfowl area, wildlife art gift shop. Hiking and biking trails. Many flowers and herbs. You can view ducks, geese, swans, deer—and puppies raised on the farm/pond!

Hosts: Gordon and Gay Ekberg
Rooms: 1 suite (2PB) $65
Full Breakfast
Credit Cards: none
Notes: 2, 6, 7, 11

Addie's Attic Bed and Breakfast

HOUSTON

Addie's Attic Bed and Breakfast

117 S. Jackson Street; PO Box 677, 55943
(507) 896-3010; FAX (507) 896-4010

Beautiful home, circa 1903. Cozy front parlor with curved-glass window. Games, TV, player piano. Rooms are decorated and furnished with "attic finds." Hearty breakfast served in dining room. Near hiking, biking, cross-country ski trails, canoeing, antique shops. Weekday rates.

Hosts: Fred and Marilyn Huhn
Rooms: 3 (SB) $45-50
Full Breakfast
Credit Cards: none
Notes: 5, 8, 9, 10, 11

Lindgren's Bed and Breakfast

LUTSEN

Lindgren's B&B

5552 County Road 35; PO Box 56, 55612-0056
(218) 663-7450

This is a 1920s log lodge home in Superior National Forest on a walkable shoreline of Lake Superior. The knotty cedar interior is decorated with wildlife trophies. Massive stone fireplaces, Finnish sauna, whirlpool, baby grand piano, and TVs/VCRs/CD. In center of area known for skiing, golf, stream and lake fishing, mountain biking, snowmobiling, horseback riding, the skyride, alpine slide, kayaking, snowshoeing, fall colors, and Superior Hiking Trail. Near the Boundary Waters Canoe Area entry point. You'll enjoy the

NOTES: Credit cards accepted: A Master Card; B Visa; C American Express; D Discover; E Diners Club; F Other; 2 Personal checks accepted; 3 Lunch available; 4 Dinner available; 5 Open all year; 6 Pets

secluded, spacious, manicured grounds. Located ½ mile off Highway 61 on the Lake Superior Circle Tour.

Hostess: Shirley Lindgren
Rooms: 4 (PB) $85-125
Full Northwoods Country Breakfast
Credit Cards: A, B
Notes: 2, 5, 7 (over 12), 8, 9, 10, 11, 12

MANKATO

Butler House

704 S. Broad Street, 56001
(507) 387-5055; FAX (507) 388-5462
E-mail: Butter@mnic.net

This English-style (1905) mansion is elegantly furnished and includes a palatial porch, beautiful suites, canopy beds, whirlpool, fireplace, and private baths. Features include hand-painted murals, Steinway grand piano, window seats, and a conference room. No smoking. Near state trail, civic center, biking, skiing, golfing, and antiquing. Come join us for an escape into a world of comfort and relaxation.

Hosts: Ron and Sharry Tschida
Rooms: 5 (PB) $55-115 (deposit required)
Full Breakfast, weekends; Continental, weekdays
Credit Cards: A, B, C
Notes: 2, 5, 9, 10, 11, 12

Butler House

OWATONNA

The Northrop-Oftedahl House Bed and Breakfast

358 E. Main Street, 55060
(507) 451-4040; FAX (507) 451-2755

This 1898 Victorian with stained glass is 3 blocks from downtown. It has pleasant porches, a grand piano, a 6-foot footed bathtub, and souvenirs (antiques and collectibles). The house is family-owned and -operated; it is one of twelve historic homes in the area, rich in local history, with an extensive library, backgammon, croquet, badminton, bocce, and more. Near hiking and biking trails, parks, tennis, and snowmobiling. Thirty-five miles from Mayo Clinic, 50 miles from Mall of America. Special group retreat rates. Bikers' bunks.

Hosts: Jean and Darrell Stewart
Rooms: 6 (2PB; 4SB) $54.95-84.95
Full Breakfast
Credit Cards: none
Notes: 2, 3 and 4 (by reservation), 5, 6 (by arrangement), 7, 8, 9, 10, 11

RED WING

The Red Wing Blackbird

722 W. 5th Street, 55066
(612) 388-2292
E-mail: blackbird@pressenter.com

The Red Wing Blackbird bed and breakfast is a fine example of Queen Anne architecture, built in 1880. A charming, three-season porch was added recently. The inn is located in the historic district, within walking distance of the Sheldon Theatre for the performing arts, downtown shopping, and antique alley. The hosts look forward to sharing their Norwegian culture and musical talents.

Hosts: Lois and Paul Christenson
Rooms: 2 (PB) $90-135
Full Breakfast
Credit Cards: A, B
Notes: 2, 5, 8, 9, 10, 11

ROCHESTER

Inn at Rocky Creek

2115 Rocky Creek Drive NE, 55906
(507) 288-1019; (800) 388-1019
Web site: http://www.innsandouts.com

A beautiful new inn created with the ambience and character of a bygone era. Only minutes from the Mayo Clinic.

Hosts: Robert and Jane Hanson
Rooms: 3 (PB) $69-125
Full or Continental Breakfast
Credit Cards: A, B
Notes: 2, 5, 7, 8, 9, 10, 12

ST. CHARLES

Thoreson's Carriage House Bed and Breakfast

606 Wabasha Avenue, 55972
(507) 932-3479

Located near beautiful Whitewater State Park with its swimming, trails, and demonstrations by the park naturalist. Horseback riding available nearby. We are in Amish territory and minutes from the world-famous Mayo Clinic. Piano and videos available. Write for brochure.

Hostess: Moneta Thoreson
Rooms: 2 (SB) $40-45
Full Breakfast
Credit Cards: none
Notes: 2, 5, 7, 8, 9, 10

SIDE LAKE

McNair's B&B

7694 Highway 5; PO Box 155, 55781
(218) 254-5878

Located in the Hibbing/Chisholm area in a beautiful forest setting. The French Colonial inn features romantic apartment-size, honeymoon-style suites complete with fireplaces, Jacuzzis, kitchens, elegant furnishings, decorator fabrics. Full gourmet breakfast served in suite; homemade dessert, complimentary beverages.

Hosts: Don and Louise McNair
Rooms: 3 (PB) $90-130
Full Breakfast
Credit Cards: none
Notes: 2, 5, 8, 9, 11, 12

STILLWATER

James A. Mulvey Residence Inn

622 W. Churchill Street, 55082
(612) 430-8008; (800) 820-8008;
FAX (612) 430-2801
Web site: http://www.cotn.com/bb

This is an enchanting place. Built in 1878 by lumberman James A. Mulvey, the

James A. Mulvey Residence Inn

NOTES: Credit cards accepted: A Master Card; B Visa; C American Express; D Discover; E Diners Club; F Other; 2 Personal checks accepted; 3 Lunch available; 4 Dinner available; 5 Open all year; 6 Pets

Italianate residence and stone carriage house grace the most visited historic river town in the upper Midwest. Exclusively for you are the grand parlor, formal dining room, Victorian sunporch, and five fabulously decorated guest rooms filled with exquisite art and antiques. Four-course breakfast, double whirlpools, mountain bikes, fireplaces, and air-conditioning. Welcome refreshments. Grace-filled service from innkeepers who care.

Hosts: Truett and Jill Lawson
Rooms: 7 (PB) $99-179
Full Breakfast
Credit Cards: A, B, D
Notes: 2, 5, 8, 9, 10, 11, 12

UNDERWOOD

Aloft in the Pines

Route 2, Box 294, 56586
(218) 495-2862; (888) 457-6301
Web site: http://tecn.com/mn.tourism/accom/ac12114.html

In a rustic log home, lounge in your own living room with a sunken hot tub overlooking crystal clear Pickerel Lake, and relax in one of the sun-filled guest rooms. Enjoy breakfast by the wood cookstove, on one of the many decks, or on the sunporch. Minutes from historic Phelps Mill, Fergus Falls, antique/gift shops, state parks, hiking trails, cross-country skiing, and golf. Boat mooring. Weekly, weekday special rates. No pets or smoking.

Hosts: Mary and John Peterson
Rooms: 3 (2PB; 1SB) $50-70
Full Breakfast
Credit Cards: none
Notes: 2, 5, 7, 8, 9, 10, 11, 12

welcome; 7 Children welcome; 8 Tennis nearby; 9 Swimming nearby; 10 Golf nearby; 11 Skiing nearby; 12 May be booked through travel agent.

MISSISSIPPI

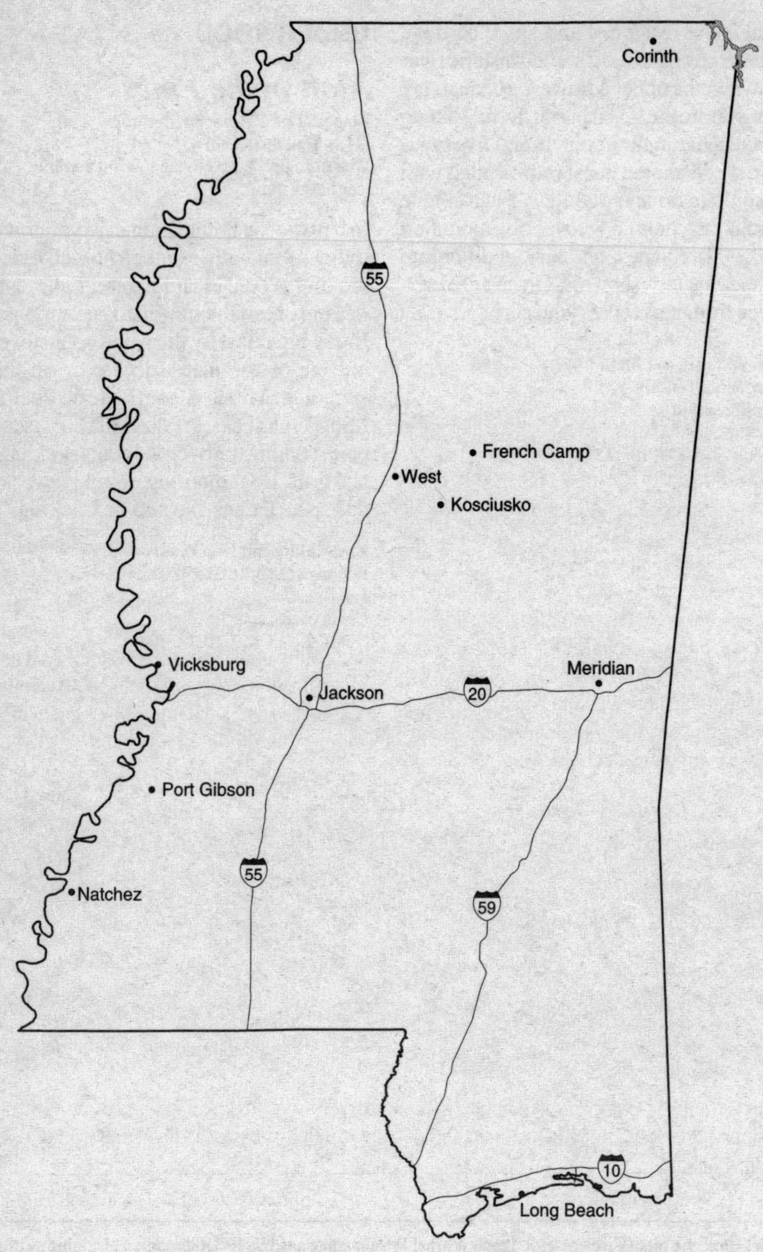

Mississippi

Natchez Trace B&B Reservation Service

PO Box 193, **Hampshire, TN,** 38461
(913) 285-2777; (800) 377-2770
E-mail: natcheztrace@worldnet.att.net
Web site: http://www.bbonline.com/natcheztrace

This reservation service is unusual in that all the homes listed are close to the Natchez Trace, the delightful National Parkway running from Nashville, Tennessee, to Natchez, Mississippi. Kay Jones can help you plan your trip along the Trace, with homestays in interesting and historic homes along the way. Locations of homes include Ashland City, Columbia, FairView, Franklin, Hohenwald, and Nashville, **Tennessee;** Florence and Cherokee, **Alabama;** and Church Hill, Corinth, French Camp, Kosciusko, Lorman, Natchez, New Albany, Tupelo, and Vicksburg, **Mississippi**. Rates $60-125.

CORINTH

The Generals' Quarters

924 Fillmore Street, 38834
(601) 286-3325; FAX (601) 287-8188
E-mail: genqtrs@tsixroads.com
Web site: http://www.tsixroads.com/~genqtrs

The Generals' Quarters is a beautifully restored Victorian home in the historic district of the old Civil War town. The rooms are decorated with period antiques and contemporary pieces. All rooms have private baths, cable TVs, and phones. The suite boasts a 140-year-old, four-poster canopy bed. There is a second-floor lounge with veranda, beautiful parlor, and porch on the first floor, and lovely gardens to relax in after a day of sight-seeing, antiquing, playing golf, or touring the Civil War sights in Corinth and outlying areas. Our resident chef prepares a delicious full breakfast and evening snack. Situated close to Shiloh National Military Park and the Tennessee-Tombigbee Waterway. The home provides some of the best hospitality the South has to offer. The Generals' Quarters is rated AAA three diamonds, ABBA three crowns.

Hosts: Charlotte and Luke Doehner
Rooms: 5 (PB) $70-100
Full Breakfast
Credit Cards: A, B, D
Notes: 2, 4, 5, 8, 9, 10, 12

Ravenswood Bed and Breakfast

1002 Douglas Street (at Linden), 38834-4227
(601) 665-0044

Ravenswood is a 1929 Arts & Crafts home in a historic north Mississippi Civil

---

NOTES: Credit cards accepted: A Master Card; B Visa; C American Express; D Discover; E Diners Club; F Other; 2 Personal checks accepted; 3 Lunch available; 4 Dinner available; 5 Open all year; 6 Pets welcome; 7 Children welcome; 8 Tennis nearby; 9 Swimming nearby; 10 Golf nearby; 11 Skiing nearby; 12 May be booked through travel agent.

Ravenswood Bed and Breakfast

War town. Casual home-stay atmosphere; many public areas. On 1½ parklike acres with wildlife and Civil War earthworks. Walk to information center, museum, historic homes. Located near Pickwick Dam watersports, Natchez Trace Parkway, Shiloh National Battlefield, and Tupelo. Eighty-five miles east of Memphis. You can walk to local churches in historic downtown—sixty-four churches are in the county, most denominations.

Hosts: Ron Wayne Smith and Timothy Hodges
Rooms: 3 (PB) $75-90
Continental Breakfast
Credit Cards: A, B
Notes: 2, 6, 7, 8, 9, 10

Samuel D. Bramlitt House

1125 Cruise Street, 38834
(601) 286-5370; (800) 484-1107, 7645
E-mail: thom112@avsia.com
Web site: http://www.tsixroads.com/corinth/bramlitt.html

Starry skies. Soft breezes. Sweet fragrance of magnolia and roses. The aroma of freshly baked bread. A good book. A few pleasures offered at the Bramlitt House, circa 1892. Filled with antiques, this gracious Victorian mansion promises a return to days when life was not so hectic. Walk to Mississippi's oldest drugstore and soda fountain. Explore streets lined with historic homes, steeped in Civil War history.

Hosts: Cindy and Kevin Thomas
Rooms: 3 (PB) $75-85
Full Breakfast
Credit Cards: A, B, C, D, F
Notes: 2, 4 (except Sunday), 5, 7 (well-behaved), 8, 9, 10, 11 (water)

FRENCH CAMP

French Camp Bed and Breakfast Inn

PO Box 120, 39745
(601) 547-6835

The inn is located on the historic Natchez Trace National Parkway, halfway between Jackson and Tupelo. It has been constructed from two restored, authentic, hand-hewn log cabins, each of them more than 100 years old. Indulge in southern cooking at its finest: fresh orange juice, "scratch" muffins, creamy grits, skillet-fried apples, fresh cheese, scrambled eggs, crisp slab bacon, and lean sausage, with two kinds of homemade bread and three kinds of homemade jellies.

Hosts: Ed and Sallie Williford
Rooms: 5 (PB) $60
Full Breakfast
Credit Cards: B
Notes: 2, 3, 4, 5, 6, 7, 8, 9, 12

French Camp Bed and Breakfast Inn

NOTES: Credit cards accepted: A Master Card; B Visa; C American Express; D Discover; E Diners Club; F Other; 2 Personal checks accepted; 3 Lunch available; 4 Dinner available; 5 Open all year; 6 Pets

Fairview Inn

JACKSON

Fairview Inn

734 Fairview Street, 39202
(601) 948-3429; (888) 948-1908;
FAX (601) 948-1203
E-mail: fairview@fairviewinn.com
Web site: http://www.fairviewinn.com

The Fairview Inn is a Colonial Revival mansion listed on the National Historic Register. Its elegant and comfortable ambience is accented by fine fabrics and antiques in a historic neighborhood. Near churches, shopping, two colleges, and major medical complexes. AAA award, four diamonds; "Top Inn of 1994" award by *Country Inns* magazine.

Hosts: Carol and William Simmons
Rooms: 8 (PB) $115-165
Full Breakfast
Credit Cards: A, B, C, D
Notes: 2, 4 (by reservation), 5, 8, 9, 10, 12

KOSCIUSKO

Redbud Inn

121 N. Wells Street, 39090
(601) 289-5086 (voice and FAX); (800) 379-5086

Christened The Redbud Inn, the house defies its classification as commercial property. With an emphasis on preservation—a practice of all former owners—the house stands as a visual example of a lifestyle and culture to be found only in history books. The stately, two-storied structure is characterized by the traditional wide center hall; heart-pine wainscoting, doors, and woodwork; and ornate mantles accented with tiles. Featured in *Colonial Homes*, *Southern Living*, *The New York Times,* and many other periodicals.

Hostesses: Maggie Garrett and Ruth Aldridge
Rooms: 5 (4PB; 1SB) $85-100
Full Breakfast
Credit Cards: A, B, C, D
Notes: 2, 3, 4, 5, 7, 8, 10, 12

LONG BEACH

Red Creek Inn, Vineyard, and Racing Stable

7416 Red Creek Road, 39560
(228) 452-3080; (800) 729-9670;
FAX (228) 452-4450

Raised French cottage built in 1899 by a retired Italian sea captain to entice his young bride away from her parents' home in New Orleans. Red Creek Inn, Vineyard, and Racing Stable is situated on 11 acres with ancient live oaks and fragrant magnolias, and delights itself in its peaceful comforts. With a 64-foot-long porch, including porch swings, our inn is furnished in antiques for guests' enjoyment. A new marble Jacuzzi awaits in the Victorian Room. A ministerial discount of 10 percent is offered.

Hosts: Karl and "Toni" Mertz
Rooms: 7 (5PB; 2SB) $49-124
Continental Plus Breakfast
Credit Cards: none
Notes: 2, 3 and 4 (advance request), 5, 7, 9, 10, 12

MERIDIAN

Lincoln Ltd. Bed and Breakfast

2303 23rd Avenue; PO Box 3479, 39303-3479
(601) 482-5483; (800) 633-6477;
FAX (601) 693-6477
Web site: http://www.tnn4bnb.com

This reservation service offers bed and breakfast accommodations in historic homes and inns in the whole state of **Mississippi,** as well as southeastern **Louisiana** and **Alabama**. Take advantage of one-phone-call convenience for your bed and breakfast reservations and trip planning through Mississippi. Experience history—antebellum mansions, historic log houses, and contemporary homes. There is a B&B suite on the premises. Call for details and brochure. Barbara Lincoln Hall, coordinator.

NATCHEZ

The Bed and Breakfast Mansions of Natchez

200 State Street; PO Box 347, 39121
(601) 446-6631; (800) 647-6742;
FAX (601) 446-8687
E-mail: tours@natchezpilgrimage.com
Web site: http://www.natchezpilgrimage.com

More than thirty magnificent B&B inns offer exquisite accommodations in pre-Civil War mansions, country plantations, and charming Victorian elegance. Historic Natchez, situated on high buffs that overlook the Mississippi River, offers visitors year-round tours of historic homes, horse-drawn carriage tours, plus the famous spring and fall pilgrimages featuring some of America's most splendid historic homes.

Host: Natchez Pilgrimage Tours
Rooms: more than 100 (PB) starting at $85
Full Southern Breakfast (at most inns)
Credit Cards: A, B, C, D
Notes: 2, 12

Dunleith

Dunleith

84 Homochitto, 39120
(601) 446-8500; (800) 433-2445

Dunleith Bed and Breakfast, circa 1856, is a national historic landmark. No children under 18. Full southern breakfast. Private baths, fireplaces. Three rooms in the main house, eight in the courtyard wing. Close to downtown Natchez on 40 acres. Open for tours daily. No smoking.

Host: W.F. Heins, III
Rooms: 11 (PB) $95-140
Full Breakfast
Credit Cards: A, B, D
Notes: 8, 10

PORT GIBSON

Oak Square Plantation

1207 Church Street, 39150
(601) 437-4350; (800) 729-0240;
FAX (601) 437-5768
E-mail: kajunmade@aol.com

This restored antebellum mansion of the Old South is in the town Gen. U. S. Grant

NOTES: Credit cards accepted: A Master Card; B Visa; C American Express; D Discover; E Diners Club; F Other; 2 Personal checks accepted; 3 Lunch available; 4 Dinner available; 5 Open all year; 6 Pets

said was "too beautiful to burn." On the National Register of Historic Places, it has family heirloom antiques and canopied beds and is air-conditioned. Your hostess' families have been in Mississippi 200 years. Christ is the Lord of this house. "But as for me and my house, we will serve the Lord" (Joshua 24:15). Located on U.S. Highway 61, adjacent to the Natchez Trace Parkway.

Hostess: Mrs. W.D. Lum
Rooms: 12 (PB) $85-105
Full Breakfast
Credit Cards: A, B, C, D
Notes: 2, 5, 7 (limited), 12

Annabelle Bed and Breakfast

VICKSBURG

Annabelle Bed and Breakfast

501 Speed Street, 39180
(601) 638-2000; (800) 791-2000;
FAX (601) 636-5054
E-mail: annabelle@vicksburg.com
Web site: http://www.missbab.com/annabelle

Let George and Carolyn Mayer welcome you and personally extend you the true grace and hospitality of the deep South. At Annabelle, you can relax in luxurious comfort in king- or queen-size beds, enjoy fine art and antiques, refresh in the sparkling swimming pool, and unwind in a whirlpool tub. Awarded AAA three diamonds; Mobil Travel Guide three stars. Featured in *Southern Living*; Fodor's *The South's Best B&Bs*; *Country Inns*; etc.

Hosts: George and Carolyn Mayer
Rooms: 6 + 1 suite (PB)
Full Breakfast
Credit Cards: A, B, C, D, E
Notes: 2, 5, 8, 9, 10, 12

WEST

The Alexander House Bed and Breakfast

11 Green Street; PO Box 187, 39192
(601) 967-2266; (800) 350-8034

Step inside the front door of the Alexander House Bed and Breakfast and go back in time to a more leisurely and gracious way of life. Victorian decor at its prettiest and country hospitality at its best are guaranteed to please your senses. Capt. Alexander, Dr. Joe, Ulrich, Annie, and Miss Bealle are all rooms waiting to cast their spells over those who visit. Day trips to historic or recreational areas may be charted or chartered. Located just 3 miles off I–55.

Hosts: Ruth Ray and Woody Dinstel
Rooms: 5 (3PB; 2SB) $65
Full Breakfast
Credit Cards: A, B, C, D
Notes: 2, 4, 5, 12

MISSOURI

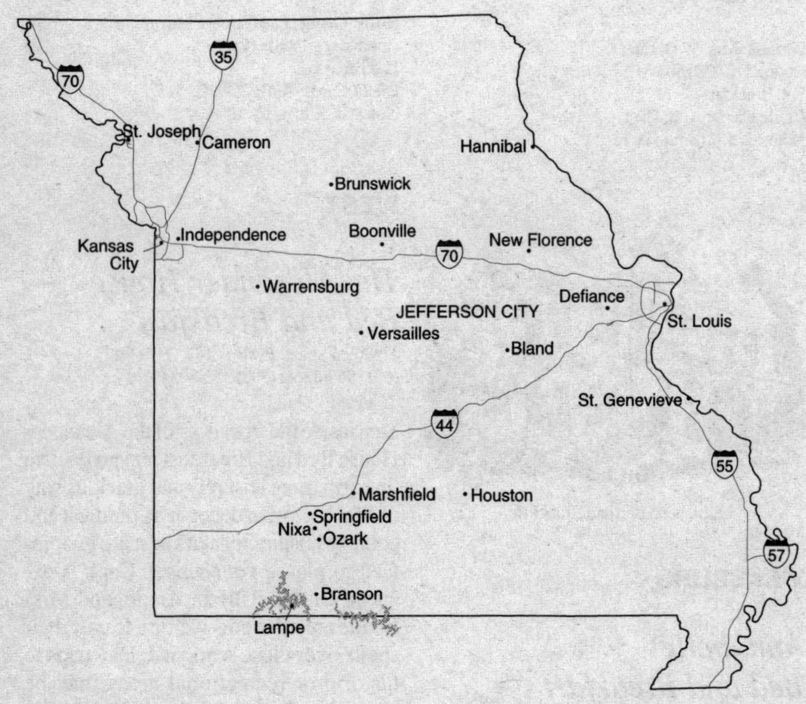

70
35
St. Joseph
Cameron
Hannibal
Brunswick
Independence
Boonville
70
New Florence
Kansas City
Warrensburg
Defiance
JEFFERSON CITY
St. Louis
Versailles
Bland
St. Genevieve
44
55
Marshfield
Houston
Springfield
Nixa
Ozark
57
Branson
Lampe

Missouri

Ozark Mountain Country Bed and Breakfast Service

PO Box 295, 65615
(417) 334-4720 (voice and FAX); (800) 695-1546
E-mail: MGCameron@aol.com

Ozark Mountain Country has been arranging accommodations for guests in southwestern Missouri and northwestern Arkansas since 1982. Our services are free. In the current list of more than 100 homes and small inns, some locations offer private entrances, fantastic views, guest sitting areas, swimming pools, Jacuzzis, and/or fireplaces. Most locations are available all year. Personal checks accepted. Some homes welcome children; a few welcome pets (even horses). Write for complimentary host brochure describing the B&Bs available, listing, and discount coupons. Coordinator: Kay Cameron. $35–145. Major credit cards welcomed.

BLAND

Caverly Farm & Orchard

100 Cedar Ridge Road, 65014
(573) 646-3732

Our remodeled 1860 farmhouse on 57 acres of Ozark Hill country features three bedrooms with private baths, a parlor for visiting, and a dining room and screened porch for meals. A three-bedroom guest house is available for family gatherings. The farm has a stocked pond for fishing, a fresh-water creek, and space to walk and play. Antique shopping, winery tours, country auctions, and county fairs are nearby. Our home is accessible.

Hosts: David and Nancy Caverly
Rooms: 3 (PB) $50
Full Breakfast
Credit Cards: none
Notes: 2, 4, 5, 7

BOONVILLE

Morgan Street Repose

611 E. Morgan Street, 65233
(660) 882-7195; (800) 248-5063

An 1869 National Historic Registered home delightfully restored for a romantic, gracious, hospitable stay. Enjoy heirlooms,

Morgan Street Repose

NOTES: Credit cards accepted: A Master Card; B Visa; C American Express; D Discover; E Diners Club; F Other; 2 Personal checks accepted; 3 Lunch available; 4 Dinner available; 5 Open all year; 6 Pets welcome; 7 Children welcome; 8 Tennis nearby; 9 Swimming nearby; 10 Golf nearby; 11 Skiing nearby; 12 May be booked through travel agent.

antiques, books, games, and curiosities. Our extravagant breakfasts are formally served in one of three dining rooms or the Secret Garden. One block from antique/specialty shops, restaurants, and the Katy biking/hiking trail. Rental bikes available. Afternoon tea served.

Hostess: Doris Shenk
Rooms: 3 (PB) $65-95
Full Breakfast
Credit Cards: none
Notes: 2, 5, 7 (older), 12

BRANSON

Cameron's Crag

PO Box 295, 65726
(417) 335-8134 (voice and FAX); (800) 933-8529
E-mail: mgcameron@aol.com

High on a bluff overlooking Lake Taneycomo and the valley, just 3 miles south of Branson. Guests enjoy a spectacular view from a new, spacious, detached, private suite with whirlpool tub, kitchen, living-and-bedroom area. Two-room suite with indoor hot tub and private bath. A third room has a great view of the lake and a private hot tub on the deck. All rooms have king-size beds, hot tubs, private entrances, TV/VCRs, and a video library.

Hosts: Kay and Glen Cameron
Rooms: 3 (PB) $75-95
Full Breakfast
Credit Cards: A, B, C, D
Notes: 2, 5, 7, 8, 9, 10, 11, 12

Josie's Peaceful Getaway

HCR 1 Box 1104, 65616
(417) 338-2978; (800) 289-4125
Web site: http://www.bbonline.com/mo/josies

Pristine, gorgeous lakefront scenery on Table Rock Lake where sunsets and moonlit nights lace the sky. Contemporary design featuring cathedral ceilings and stone fireplaces mingled with a Victorian flair. Cozy wood-burning fireplaces, lavish Jacuzzi spas, candlelight, and fresh flowers abound. Dine in luxury as you enjoy breakfast served on china and crystal. Celebrate your honeymoon or anniversary in style. Eight miles from Branson and music shows; 5 minutes from Silver Dollar City/Marina. Smoke-free environment.

Hosts: Bill and Jo Anne Coats
Rooms: 3 (PB) $60-110
Full and Continental Breakfast
Credit Cards: A, B, C, D
Notes: 2, 5, 7 (with restrictions), 9, 10, 12

Lakeshore Bed and Breakfast

HC#1 Box 935, 65616
(417) 338-2698 (voice and FAX); (800) 285-9739

A peaceful place on beautiful Table Rock Lake, 2 miles from Silver Dollar City. Great for family or church groups up to twelve people—also honeymoons and anniversaries. A contemporary home with boat dock and swim deck, covered patio with picnic table and grill, glider swing. Two units have private entrances, queen-size beds, hide-a-beds, coffee bars, refrigerators, microwaves, televisions, VCRs, AC,

Lakeshore Bed and Breakfast

NOTES: Credit cards accepted: A Master Card; B Visa; C American Express; D Discover; E Diners Club; F Other; 2 Personal checks accepted; 3 Lunch available; 4 Dinner available; 5 Open all year; 6 Pets

and private baths with showers; one has a whirlpool tub. One unit has a double bed and private bath. A nutritious, hearty breakfast is served.

Hostess: Gladys Lemley
Rooms: 3 (PB) $50-75
Full Breakfast
Credit Cards: none
Notes: 2, 5, 7, 8, 9, 10, 11, 12

Patchwork Quilt Bed and Breakfast

PO Box 126, 65615
(417) 334-7999

A comfy, rustic, cedar home on 4 wooded acres in Branson, just 5 minutes from the Grand Palace and many other top music shows, attractions, and lakes. Private hot tub on the large porch, king-size bed, refrigerator, microwave, coffee pot, television, VCR and tapes, telephone in your room. A big country breakfast is served each morning.

Hostess: Jewell Schroll
Rooms: 2-bedroom suite (PB) $45-75
Full Breakfast
Credit Cards: none
Notes: 2, 5, 6, 7, 8, 9, 10, 11 (water), 12

BRANSON WEST

Martindale Bed and Breakfast

HCR 4, Box 3570, 65737
(417) 338-2588; (888) 338-2588
E-mail: ELMardale@aol.com
Web site: http://www.bbim.org/martindale

Table Rock lakefront home built to pamper you. Balcony separates two elegantly decorated bedrooms with lake view, private baths and entrance. Enjoy luxurious cherry scroll beds, mirrored armoires, VCR, and cable TV. Relish seclusion from hot tub, screened-in porch, or deck. Ozarkians' breakfast is "sumpt'n" special. Picturesque drive to area attractions.

Hosts: Ellis and Luci Martin
Rooms: 2 (PB) $65
Full Breakfast
Credit Cards: none
Notes: 2, 7 (ask)

Sycamore Valley Farm Bed and Breakfast

BRUNSWICK

Sycamore Valley Farm Bed and Breakfast

RR 2, Box 159, 65236
(660) 548-3283

An abundance of photos, keepsakes, memorabilia, and antiques invite you to share in the rich heritage of the Reichert family during your stay. Matt, Tina, and their four children extend an invitation to "be our guest." You can take in the tranquillity of the wide-open spaces of this rural farmstead; unwind and relax while swinging on the porch swing overlooking the lush, rolling farmland; or take a peaceful stroll down the lane. "We strive to make all our guests feel at home, whether your stay be for business or pleasure."

Hosts: Matt and Tina Reichert
Rooms: 2 (1PB; 1SB) $45
Full Breakfast
Credit Cards: A, B
Notes: 2, 5, 7

CAMERON

Cook's Country Cottage Bed and Breakfast

7880 NE Bacon Road, 64429
(816) 632-1776

A perfect country hideaway to escape the fast pace of today's society. Relax in luxury and have your every whim catered to. Water gardens, lake to fish, trails to walk, birds and wildlife to watch, and porches to rock on are a few options to enjoy. "Coming home" never gets better!

Hosts: Don and Loura Cook
Rooms: 2 (PB) $50-65
Full Country Breakfast
Credit Cards: none
Notes: 2, 3, 4, 5, 8, 9, 10, 11

DEFIANCE

The Parsons House Bed and Breakfast

211 Lee Street; PO Box 38, 63341
(314) 798-2222; (800) 355-6878;
FAX (314) 798-2220
E-mail: makeyes@compuserve.com

Stately 1842 Federalist home overlooks the Missouri River Valley. Listed in the Historic Survey, it features fireplaces, a large gathering room, and many antiques. For your enjoyment: a piano, organ, large library, porches, gardens, and hot tub. Close by are the Katy Bicycle Trail, Daniel Boone Home, and Missouri wineries—yet downtown St. Louis is only 35 miles away. A generous country breakfast is served in the gathering room by the fireplace in cool weather, on the porch or in the gardens during the summer.

The Parsons House Bed and Breakfast

Hosts: Al and Carol Keyes
Rooms: 3 (PB) $80-95
Full Breakfast
Credit Cards: A, B
Notes: 2, 5, 7 (limited), 10

HANNIBAL

Fifth Street Mansion Bed and Breakfast Inn

213 S. Fifth Street, 63401
(573) 221-0445; (800) 874-5661

Built in 1858 in Italianate style by friends of Mark Twain. Antique furnishings complement the stained glass, ceramic fireplaces, and original gaslight fixtures of the house. Two parlors, dining room, and library with hand-grained walnut paneling, plus wraparound porches, provide space for conversation, reading, TV, and games. Walk to the Mark Twain historic district, shops, restaurants, and riverfront. The Fifth Street Mansion blends Victorian charm with plenty of old-fashioned hospitality. The whole house is available for reunions and weddings.

Hosts: Mike and Donalene Andreotti
Rooms: 7 (PB) $65-90
Full Breakfast
Credit Cards: A, B, C, D
Notes: 2, 5, 7, 8, 9, 10, 12

Fifth Street Mansion Bed and Breakfast Inn

HERMANN

"A Little Log Cabin in the Woods" B&B

142 Whiteside School Road, **New Florence,** 63363
(573) 252-4301

Enjoy a secluded, modern log house in the woods (owners live nearby) on 275 acres near Hermann. Central air, fireplace, full kitchen, dining room, living room with TV (satellite dish, VCR, videos). Two bedrooms with king-size beds (one with full-size bed), two bathrooms. Porch, trails, restored 1900 one-room schoolhouse to tour. Fantastic bird-watching opportunities, large creek bed for fossil hunting, dark country nights for star-gazing and complete privacy.

Hosts: Clyde and Ellen Waldo
Rooms: 1 log cabin (3 bedrooms, 2 baths) $60-89
Full Breakfast
Credit Cards: none
Notes: 2, 5, 7 (by arrangement), 10

HOUSTON

Windstone House

539 Cleveland Road, 65483
(417) 967-2008

Windstone House is a large, two-story home with a spacious wraparound porch and balcony, sitting in the middle of more than 80 acres that provide a breathtaking view of the Ozarks countryside. The home has been tastefully furnished with a collection of antiques. In warm weather, breakfast is served on the balcony overlooking a spectacular panorama of meadows and woodland. If you are bent on unwinding, then this is the place for you.

Hostess: Barbara Kimes
Rooms: 3 (1PB; 2SB) $60
Full Breakfast
Credit Cards: none
Notes: 2, 5, 7 (over 12), 9, 10

Windstone House

INDEPENDENCE

Woodstock Inn Bed and Breakfast

1212 W. Lexington, 64050
(816) 833-2233
Web site: http://www.independence-missouri.com

Nestled within Independence's famous historical district, the Woodstock Inn is just a short stroll from all the sites you came to Independence to see! We have eleven warm and inviting rooms, each with a distinct personality and private bath. After a restful night's sleep, wake up to a piping hot cup of coffee and take a seat at our long oak dining table. Tempt your palate with our house specialty, gourmet Belgian waffles topped off with powdered sugar and smothered with specialty syrups or fresh fruit sauce. Our full breakfast is exactly what you need to start off a wonderful day of sight-seeing!

Hosts: Todd and Patricia Justice
Rooms: 11 (PB) $59-99
Full Breakfast
Credit Cards: A, B, C, D
Notes: 2, 5, 7, 12

KANSAS CITY

The Doanleigh Inn

217 E. 37th Street, 64111
(816) 753-2667; FAX (816) 531-5185
E-mail: doanleigh@aol.com
Web site: http://www.doanleigh.com

In the heart of the city, the Doanleigh Inn is ideally located between the famed Country Club Plaza and Hallmark Crown Center. Lovely European and American antiques enhance the Georgian architecture of the inn. Wine and hors d'oeuvres await you each evening and a full gourmet breakfast is served each morning. Fireplaces and Jacuzzis provide the ultimate in relaxation. Other amenities include afternoon cookies, daily newspapers, free local calls and FAXES, and in-room computer modem access.

The Doanleigh Inn

Hosts: Cynthia Brogdon and Terry Maturo
Rooms: 5 (PB) $95-150
Full Breakfast
Credit Cards: A, B, C, D
Notes: 2, 5, 8, 12

Reservation Service: Bed and Breakfast Kansas City

PO Box 14781, **Lenexa, KS,** 66285
(913) 888-3636

Accommodations are available in Kansas City, Weston, Liberty, Independence, and St. Joseph. Thirty-five inns and homestays range from circa 1845 to a contemporary geodesic dome in the woods. Amenities include hot tubs, Jacuzzis, queen and king beds, private baths, and full gourmet

NOTES: Credit cards accepted: A Master Card; B Visa; C American Express; D Discover; E Diners Club; F Other; 2 Personal checks accepted; 3 Lunch available; 4 Dinner available; 5 Open all year; 6 Pets

breakfasts. Prices from $50 to $150. Major credit cards welcome at the individual inns. Edwina Monroe, coordinator.

Southmoreland on the Plaza

116 E. 46th Street, 64112
(816) 531-7979 (voice and FAX)

Award-winning Southmoreland's 1913 Colonial Revival style brings New England to the heart of Kansas City's historic arts, entertainment, and shopping district—the country club plaza. Business and leisure guests enjoy individually decorated rooms offering decks, fireplaces, or Jacuzzi baths. Business travelers find respite at Southmoreland with its rare mix of business support services. In-room phones, FAX, copier, message center, modem hookups, 24-hour access, switchboard. Six-time winner of Mobil four-star award. New deluxe carriage house with fireplace and double Jacuzzi!

Hostesses: Penni Johnson and Susan Moehl
Rooms: 12 + carriage house (PB) $125-225
Full Breakfast
Credit Cards: A, B, C
Notes: 2, 5, 8

Southmoreland on the Plaza

LAMPE

Grandpa's Farm B&B

HC3, Box 476, 65681
(417) 779-5106; (800) 280-5106;
FAX (417) 779-2050
E-mail: keithpat@inter-line.net
Web site: http://www.iaswww.com/grandpa

A real old-time, 116-acre Ozark Mountain farm with plenty of friendly animal life. Luxurious Honeymoon Suite with spa, Red Bud Suite with large whirlpool tub, Dogwood Suite with kitchenette, and Mother Hen Room. Near Branson, Missouri, and Eureka Springs, Arkansas. Big country breakfast served on screened-in porch. Secret hideout lofts for children.

Hosts: Keith and Pat Lamb
Rooms: 4 (PB) $65-90
Full Breakfast
Credit Cards: A, B, D
Notes: 2, 5, 7, 9, 12

MARSHFIELD

The Dickey House Bed and Breakfast Inn

331 S. Clay Street, 65706
(417) 468-3000; (800) 450-7444
Web site: http://www.bbonline.com/mo/dickeyhouse

This mansion situated on 1 acre of parklike grounds is one of Missouri's finest bed and breakfast inns. The Dickey House offers three antique-filled guest rooms with private baths, plus three spectacular suites with luxuriously appointed decor, double Jacuzzi, fireplace, and cable TV. The inn and dining room are enhanced by a display of fine American and European art and antiques. A gourmet breakfast is served in Victorian style amid fine china, silver, and crystal. The bed and breakfast has a four-diamond AAA rating.

Hosts: Larry and Michalene Stevens
Rooms: 6 (PB) $60-105
Full Breakfast
Credit Cards: A, B, D
Notes: 2, 5, 8, 9, 10, 12

NIXA

Wooden Horse B&B

1007 W. Sterling Court, 65714
(417) 724-8756; (800) 724-8756
Web site: http://www.nixa.com/chamber/WoodenHorse

At this quiet country setting, you'll experience the warm, homey atmosphere of the Rocking Horse Room or the shimmering floral decor of the Carousel Room. Enjoy the sprinkling of antiques, various collections, and wood-burning stone in the living room with TV/VCR. Relaxing outside includes trees to meander through, a deck, the spa, gardens, and a swing in the big oak tree. Near Springfield, Branson, and Silver Dollar City.

Hosts: Larry and Valeta Hammar
Rooms: 2 (PB) $60-70
Full Breakfast
Credit Cards: none
Notes: 2, 5, 6, 8, 9, 10

OZARK

Dear's Rest B&B

1408 Capp Hill Ranch Road, 65721
(417) 581-3839; (800) 588-2262
E-mail: info@dearsrest.com
Web site: http://www.dearsrest.com

Dear's Rest Bed and Breakfast

Slip away from stress and relax surrounded by nature "with a view." Our Amish-built cedar home waits for "only you" (up to six), where hiking through the forest or stream snorkeling in clear, spring-fed Bull Creek are just part of the fun. The fireplace and homey antiques give Dear's Rest a peaceful feeling of bygone days. If antique shopping and Branson shows get too strenuous, try our hot tub "under the stars." Inspected and approved by Bed & Breakfast Inns of Missouri and Christian County Health Department.

Hosts: Linda and Allan Schilter
Rooms: 2-bedroom suite (PB) $85-130
Full Breakfast
Credit Cards: A, B, D
Notes: 2, 5, 7, 9, 12

ST. GENEVIEVE

Inn St. Gemme Beauvais

78 N. Main Street, 63670
(573) 883-5744; (800) 818-5744;
FAX (573) 883-3899

Jacuzzis, hors d'oeuvres, and private suites filled with antiques only serve to begin your pampering stay in Missouri's oldest continually operating bed and breakfast. The romantic dining room with working fireplace is the perfect setting for an intimate breakfast. The inn has been redecorated and is within walking distance of many shops and historical sites. Packages available for that special occasion, as well as picnics to take on hiking trails.

Hostess: Janet Joggerst
Rooms: 7 (PB) $69-149
Full Breakfast
Credit Cards: A, B, D
Notes: 2, 3, 5, 7, 8, 9, 10

ST. JOSEPH

Harding House B&B

219 N. 20th Street, 64501
(816) 232-7020; FAX (816) 232-5467
Web site: http://www.stjomo.com/harding_house.html

Gracious turn-of-the-century home. Elegant, oak woodwork, and pocket doors. Antiques and beveled-, leaded-glass windows. Historic area near museums, churches, and antique shops. Four unique guest rooms. Eastlake has a romantic wood-burning fireplace and queen-size bed; the Blue Room has an antique water lily quilt on the wall. Children welcome. Full breakfast with homemade pastry.

Hosts: Glen and Mary Harding
Rooms: 4 (2PB; 2SB) $45-65
Full Breakfast
Credit Cards: A, B, C, D
Notes: 2, 5, 7, 8, 10, 12

ST. LOUIS

Geandaugh House

3835 S. Broadway, 63118
(314) 771-5447; FAX (314) 773-1576
E-mail: popp-inn@juno.com

Experience midwestern hospitality at its finest. Downtown St. Louis, the gateway to the West, is just 5 minutes by car from this 16th-century home. Geandaugh House, the oldest house in the city, was lovingly rescued from demolition in 1985. The Popps have furnished it with period antiques and many collectibles. They offer a Christian atmosphere for travelers who are looking for a peaceful spot in the city. The breakfasts are profuse, the hospitality profound.

Hosts: Gea and Wayne Popp
Rooms: 4 (PB) $60-70
Full Breakfast
Credit Cards: none
Notes: 2, 5, 7

Lafayette House Bed and Breakfast

2156 Lafayette Avenue, 63104
(314) 772-4429

This 1876 Queen Anne mansion is in historic Lafayette Square, only minutes from downtown St. Louis. Attend a baseball or football game; shop at historic Union Station; visit the St. Louis Arch, science center, and zoo; or simply stroll through lovely Lafayette Square Park. From the moment you arrive, you'll be surrounded by this bed and breakfast's unique personality! Annalise will treat you to a full gourmet breakfast, which may include homemade breads, muffins, crab-stuffed quiche, or Belgian waffles with warm blueberry compote. The house is furnished comfortably with antiques and traditional furniture. The suite on the third floor, accommodating six, has a private bath and kitchen. Maybe you'll prefer our Victorian Room with its fireplace and Jacuzzi for that romantic getaway. For business guests we offer FAX service, in-room phones, flexible breakfast hours. ABBA-inspected and -approved. Resident cats!

Hosts: Annalise Millet and Nancy Hammersmith
Rooms: 6 (3PB; 3SB) $60-150
Full Breakfast
Credit Cards: A, B, C, D, E, F
Notes: 2, 5, 7, 8, 9, 10, 11, 12

SPRINGFIELD

Virginia Rose B&B

317 E. Glenwood, 65807-3543
(417) 883-0693; (800) 345-1412
E-mail: VROSEBB@MOCOM.net

This two-story farmhouse, built in 1906, offers country hospitality right in town. Situated on a tree-covered acre, our home is furnished with early-1900s antiques, quilts on queen-size beds, and rockers on the porch. Relax in the parlor with a book, puzzle, or game, or watch a movie on the TV/VCR. We are located only minutes from BASS Pro Outdoor World, restaurants, shopping, antique shops, and miniature golf, and only 40 miles from Branson. Inspected and approved by the B&B Inns of Missouri.

Hosts: Jackie and Virginia Buck
Rooms: 5 (PB) $50-100
Full Breakfast
Credit Cards: A, B, C, D
Notes: 2, 5, 7, 9, 10, 12

VERSAILLES

The Hilty Inn

206 E. Jasper, 65084
(573) 378-2020; (800) 667-8093
Web site: http://www.bbim.org/hilty/rates.html

A Victorian setting near the historic Morgan County Courthouse. We have a court-

The Hilty Inn

yard with outdoor dining, when weather permits. A place to get away from it all, relax, and enjoy being catered to. It is a fun place for reunions or for friends to meet and have good visits together.

Hostess: Doris Hilty
Rooms: 4 (PB) $55-95
Full or Continental Breakfast
Credit Cards: A, B, C
Notes: 2, 4, 5, 7 (inquire first), 10

WARRENSBURG

The Camel Crossing Bed and Breakfast

210 E. Gay Street, 64093
(660) 429-2973; FAX (660) 429-2722
E-mail: camelx@iland.net

Ride a magic carpet to this bed and breakfast that is homey in atmosphere but museumlike in its decor. Brass, copper, hand-tied carpets, and furnishings from the Far East will captivate your imaginations. An oasis for mind and body. If you come a stranger, you'll leave as a friend.

Hosts: Joyce and Ed Barnes
Rooms: 4 (2PB; 2SB) $55-75
Full Breakfast
Credit Cards: A, B
Notes: 2, 5, 8, 9, 10

Montana

BOZEMAN

Cottonwood Inn

13515 Cottonwood Canyon Road, 59718
(406) 763-5452; (888) TRY-INNS (879-4667);
FAX (406) 763-5638
E-mail: info@cottonwood-inn.com
Web site: http://www.cottonwood-inn.com

On the forested edge of the Gallatin Mountains is our inn of pine, redwood, cedar, and stained glass. The area is home to moose, elk, deer, and other wildlife. We are less than 1 hour from Yellowstone and Big Sky Resort. Enjoy moonlit evenings in our outdoor hot tub and sumptuous gourmet breakfasts. All five deluxe guest rooms have private baths. We are a smoke-free inn.

Hosts: Joe and Debbie Velli
Rooms: 5 (PB) $65-120
Full Breakfast
Credit Cards: A, B
Notes: 2, 5, 7 (over 12), 8, 9, 10, 11, 12

The Lehrkind Mansion

719 N. Wallace Avenue, 59715
(406) 585-6932 (voice and FAX; call first);
(800) 992-6932
E-mail: lehrkindmansion@imt.net
Web site: http://www.imt.net/~lehrkindmansion

The Lehrkind Mansion

Listed in the National Register and built in 1897, The Lehrkind Mansion offers one of Montana's finest examples of Victorian Queen Anne architecture. A spacious yard and gardens, porches, and the large corner tower are among this three-story mansion's spectacular features. Period antiques throughout. The music parlor features Victrolas and a rare 1897 Regina music box—7 feet tall! Queen beds, comforters, and overstuffed chairs. A large hot tub will soak away the aches of an active day. Seven blocks off the historic Main Street shopping district.

Hosts: Jon Gerster and Christopher Nixon
Rooms: 5 (4PB; 1SB) $75-155
Full Breakfast
Credit Cards: A, B, C
Notes: 2, 5, 7, 8, 9, 10, 11, 12

---

welcome; 7 Children welcome; 8 Tennis nearby; 9 Swimming nearby; 10 Golf nearby; 11 Skiing nearby; 12 May be booked through travel agent.

MONTANA

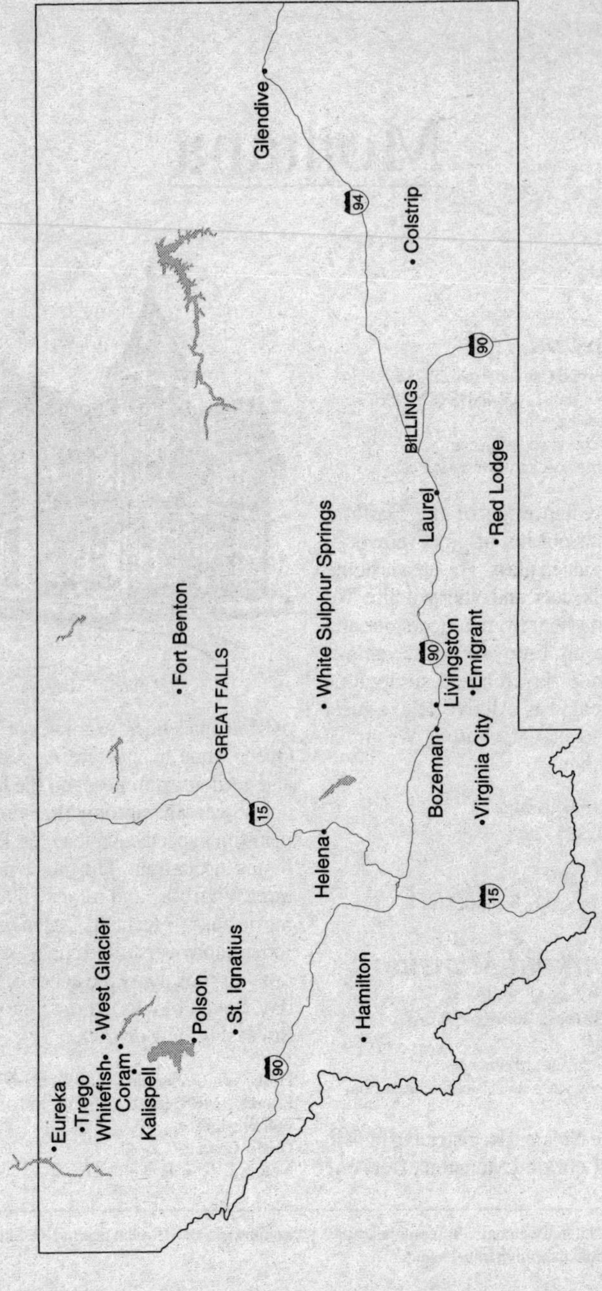

Glendive
94
Colstrip
90
BILLINGS
Laurel
Red Lodge
Fort Benton
GREAT FALLS
White Sulphur Springs
90
Livingston
Emigrant
Bozeman
Virginia City
15
Helena
15
West Glacier
St. Ignatius
Polson
Hamilton
Eureka
Trego
Whitefish
Coram
Kalispell
90

Lindley House Bed and Breakfast

202 Lindley Place, 59715
(406) 587-8403; (800) 787-8404;
FAX (406) 582-8112
E-mail: lindley@avicom.net
Web site: http://www.avicom.net/lindley

A charming and distinctive Victorian manor house listed on the National Historic Register and located close to the downtown area, within walking distance of the university, theaters, fine restaurants, quaint shops, and galleries. The Lindley House has undergone a complete restoration, with dramatic French wall coverings, antique beds, fireplaces, stained-glass windows, and an enclosed English garden.

Hostess: Stephanie Volz
Rooms: 8 (6PB; 2SB) $90-250
Full Breakfast
Credit Cards: A, B, D
Notes: 2, 5, 8, 9, 10, 11, 12

COLSTRIP

Lakeview Bed and Breakfast and Specialty Dining

7437 Castle Rock Lake Drive; PO Box 483, 59323
(406) 748-3653; (888) LAKE BNB (525-3262)

In the heart of southeastern Montana, weary travelers can enjoy the peaceful beauty of Castle Rock Lake. Boating, fishing, swimming, bird-watching, lovely walking path. Nearby golf course. Thirty miles from Lewis and Clark Trail. An hour's drive to Custer Battlefield. Garden, Woodland, Castle Rooms have gorgeous queen

Lakeview Bed and Breakfast

beds, phones, TVs. Delicious full breakfast. Evening refreshments. Other meals offered. Relax in beautiful, comfortable surroundings while we take care of the little details and make you feel right at home.

Hostess: Debby Vetsch
Room: 3 (1PB; 2SB) $57.20-69.68
Full Breakfast
Credit Cards: A, B, C
Notes: 2, 3, 4, 5, 7, 8, 9, 10, 12

EMIGRANT (NEAR NORTH ENTRANCE, YELLOWSTONE)

Paradise Gateway B&B and Guest Log Cabin

PO Box 84, 59027
(406) 333-4063; (800) 541-4113;
FAX (406) 333-4626
E-mail: paradise@gomontana.com

Paradise Gateway B&B, just minutes from Yellowstone National Park, offers quiet, charming, comfortable guest rooms in the shadow of the majestic Rocky Mountains. As day breaks, enjoy a country, gourmet breakfast by the banks of the Yellowstone River, a noted blue-ribbon trout stream. A "cowboy treat tray" is served in the afternoon. Enjoy summer and winter sports. Only entrance open to Yellowstone year-round. Call for reservations. Also, the

Emigrant Peak Log Cabin is located on 28 acres of Yellowstone River frontage next to the bed and breakfast. Modern, two-bedroom cabin with laundry services and complete kitchen. Decorated in country charm. Extremely private. $150 a night. Member of the Montana Bed and Breakfast Association.

Hosts: Pete and Carol Reed
Rooms: 4 (PB) $85-110; cabin $150
Full Breakfast in B&B, Continental in cabin
Credit Cards: A, B
Notes: 2, 5, 8, 9, 10, 11, 12

EUREKA

Huckleberry Hannah's Bed and Breakfast

3100 Sophie Lake Road, 59917
(888) 889-3381 (for reservations, free brochure)
E-mail: huckhana@libby.org
Web site: http://www.libby.org/huckleberryhannah

Welcome to nearly 5,000 square feet of old-fashioned charm. Fifty wooded acres, fabulous trout-filled lake with glorious views of the Rockies. Depicts a quieter time in history when the pleasures of life represented a walk in the woods or moonlight swim. Or maybe a little early morning relaxation in a porch swing, sipping a fresh cup of coffee and watching the sun rise. The surrounding area is mostly public lands—perfect for hiking, biking, hunting, fishing, and swimming. Skier's dream. Comfortable, sunny rooms and home-cooked food. Owned and operated by the author of one of the Northwest's best-selling cookbooks, *Huckleberry Hannah's Country Cooking Sampler*. Questions cheerfully answered. Inquire about accommodations for pets. Smoking outside only. Senior discounts.

Hosts: Jack and Deanna Doying
Rooms: 5 + cottage (PB) $55-90
Full Breakfast
Credit Cards: A, B
Notes: 2, 3, 4, 5, 6 (some), 7, 8, 9, 11, 12

FORT BENTON

Long's Landing Bed and Breakfast

1011 17th Street; Box 935, 59442
(406) 622-3461
E-mail: longsbnb@juno.com
Web site: http://www.innsandouts.com

Forty minutes north of Great Falls, just off Highway 87, near the Missouri River in the birthplace of Montana. Three charming guest rooms await. Enjoy two museums, a golf course, Old Fort Park, river trips, and other points of interest. Open May 1–November 1. No smoking.

Hostess: Amy Long
Rooms: 3 (1PB; 2SB) $45
Continental Breakfast
Credit Cards: none
Notes: 2, 7 (over 10), 8, 9, 10, 12

GLACIER NATIONAL PARK

A Wild Rose Bed and Breakfast

10280 Highway 2 E.; PO Box 130369, **Coram,** 59913-0396
(406) 387-4900 (voice and FAX)
E-mail: wildrose@cyberport.net
Web site: http://www.cyberport.net/wildrose

Set in the mountains, A Wild Rose offers the finest luxury accommodations, 6 miles

NOTES: Credit cards accepted: A Master Card; B Visa; C American Express; D Discover; E Diners Club; F Other; 2 Personal checks accepted; 3 Lunch available; 4 Dinner available; 5 Open all year; 6 Pets

from spectacular Glacier National Park. Our immaculate and richly detailed rooms are beautifully decorated with a Victorian flair and have exquisite mattresses, natural linens, hair dryers, Neutrogena amenities, and plush robes for guests to use while enjoying our inn. Our romantic whirlpool suites are perfect for honeymoons and special occasions. We offer onsite massages, a therapeutic spa, and packages for special occasions.

Hosts: Joseph and Brenda Mihalko
Rooms: 6 (PB) $100-150
Full Breakfast
Credit Cards: A, B, D, F
Notes: 2, 4, 5, 7 (over 12), 9, 10, 11, 12

GLENDIVE

The Hostetler House Bed and Breakfast

113 N. Douglas Street, 59330
(406) 365-4505; (800) 965-8456;
FAX (406) 365-8456

Two blocks from downtown shopping and restaurants, The Hostetler House Bed and Breakfast is a charming, 1912 historic home with two comfortable guest rooms, sitting room, sunporch, tandem bicycle, and hot tub. Full gourmet breakfast is served on Grandma's china. On I–94 and the Yellowstone River, close to parks, swimming pool, tennis courts, golf course, antique shops, and churches. Craig and Dea invite you to "arrive as a guest and leave as a friend."

Hosts: Craig and Dea Hostetler
Rooms: 2 (SB) $50
Full Gourmet Breakfast
Credit Cards: A, B, D
Notes: 2, 5, 8, 9, 10, 11 (cross-country), 12

HAMILTON

Trout Springs Bed and Breakfast

721 Desta Street, 59840
(406) 375-0911; (888) 67-TROUT (678-7688);
FAX (406) 375-0988
E-mail: Tsprings@bitterroot.net
Web site: http://www.wtp.net/go/troutsprings

Catching trout and breakfast are the specialties here. Guests are encouraged to catch trout from our ponds. We serve a four-course breakfast. All bedrooms have king-size beds. There are fireplaces, TV, laundry, and spacious decks overlooking the trout ponds and beautiful gardens. Also an evening campfire. Honeymoon suite and Jacuzzi room available. The home features original western art designed and built by the proprietors in their own gallery on the premises.

Hosts: Maynard and Brenda Gueklenhaar
Rooms: 6 (PB) $70-90
Full Breakfast
Credit Cards: A, B, C, D
Notes: 2, 5, 8, 9, 10, 11

HELENA

The St. James Bed and Breakfast

114 N. Hoback Street, 59601
(406) 449-2623

The St. James B&B was built in 1889 as the St. James African Methodist Episcopal Church. Renovation was completed in 1994 and includes two comfortable bedrooms. Enjoy the sauna, salon (hair styling), and host Loren Kovich's art studio and gallery.

Hosts: Loren and Jan Kovich
Rooms: 2 (PB) $65
Full Breakfast
Credit Cards: A, B
Notes: 2, 5, 7, 8, 10, 11

KALISPELL

Bonnie's Bed and Breakfast

265 Lake Blaine Road, 59901
(406) 755-3776; (800) 755-3778
Web site: http://www.wtp.net/go/montana/sites/bonnie.html

At Bonnie's Bed and Breakfast, we feature three very special rooms with distinctive personalities to suite you. A deposit for the first night is required to guarantee a reservation and is fully refundable with a 7-day cancellation notice. While staying at Bonnie's Bed and Breakfast, you'll enjoy a smoke-free environment. Sorry, we are unable to accommodate pets.

Hosts: Leonard and Bonnie Boles
Rooms: 4 (2PB; 2SB) $75-115
Full Breakfast
Credit Cards: A, B
Notes: 2, 5, 10, 11, 12

LAUREL

Riverside Bed and Breakfast

2231 Thiel Road, 59044
(406) 628-7890; (800) 768-1580
E-mail: RiversideBB@cwz.com

Just off I–90, 15 minutes from Billings, on a main route to skiing and Yellowstone National Park. Fly-fish the Yellowstone from our backyard; soak away stress in the hot tub; llinger and llook at the llovable llamas; take a spin on our bicycle built for two; enjoy a peaceful sleep, a friendly visit, and a fantastic breakfast.

Hosts: Lynn and Nancy Perey
Rooms: 2 (PB) $65
Full Breakfast
Credit Cards: A, B, C
Notes: 2, 5, 7 (age restriction), 10, 11, 12

LIVINGSTON

Greystone Inn Bed and Breakfast

122 S. Yellowstone Street, 59047
(406) 222-8319

We invite you to "step back in time." Built at the turn of the century from hand-cut sandstone, the Greystone is one of the most historic homes in this small railroad town. Your hosts have lovingly restored this classic home over the years. They offer you a peaceful, relaxed pace for your get-away-from-it-all vacation. Ask us about our cabin in the mountains, if you're looking for a real escape.

Hosts: Lin and Gary Lee
Rooms: 2 (1PB; 1SB) $70-90
Full Breakfast
Credit Cards: none
Notes: 2, 5, 7, 8, 9, 10, 11, 12

POLSON

Hawthorne House

304 3rd Avenue E., 59860
(406) 883-2723; (800) 290-1345

In the small western Montana town of Polson, at the foot of Flathead Lake, you'll

NOTES: Credit cards accepted: A Master Card; B Visa; C American Express; D Discover; E Diners Club; F Other; 2 Personal checks accepted; 3 Lunch available; 4 Dinner available; 5 Open all year; 6 Pets

find Hawthorne House, an English Tudor home on a quiet, shady street. In summer, cheerful window boxes welcome the weary traveler. The house is furnished with antiques from Karen's grandparents. There are plate collections, Indian artifacts, and glassware. The kitchen also has interesting collections. Breakfast is always special, with something baked fresh each morning. Nearby attractions include Glacier National Park, the National Bison Range, Kerr Dam, and great scenic beauty. Golf abounds. There are always activities on the lake and river.

Hosts: Gerry (pronounced *Gary*) and Karen Lenz
Rooms: 4 (SB) $40 (breakfast $5 per person)
Full Breakfast
Credit Cards: none
Notes: 2, 5, 7 (over 12), 8, 9, 10

Swan Hill Bed and Breakfast

460 Kings Point Road, 59860
(406) 883-5292; (800) 537-9489;
FAX (406) 883-5314

Ours is a blessed, spacious redwood home, modern in amenities, that has the warmth of the Christian family. Awaken to our gourmet breakfasts, which change daily. You may choose to breakfast in our formal dining room or under an umbrella table on the deck overlooking the lake and trees. Our home is in a secluded area with queen bedrooms and private baths. There is an indoor pool surrounded by outdoor decks overlooking Flathead Lake. All a refreshing experience.

Hosts: Sharon and Larry Whitten
Rooms: 5 (PB) $85-150
Full Breakfast
Credit Cards: A, B
Notes: 2, 5, 6, 10

RED LODGE

Willows Inn Bed and Breakfast

224 S. Platt Avenue; PO Box 886, 59068
(406) 446-3913
Web site: http://www.bbhost.com/willowsinn

Nestled beneath the majestic Beartooth Mountains in a quaint historic town, this delightful turn-of-the-century Victorian, complete with picket fence and porch swing, awaits you. A light and airy atmosphere with warm, cheerful decor greets the happy wanderer. Five charming guest rooms, each unique, are in the main inn. Two delightfully nostalgic cottages with kitchen and laundry are also available. Home-baked pastries are a specialty. Videos, books, games, afternoon refreshments, and sundeck.

Hosts: Kerry, Carolyn, and Elven Boggio
Rooms: 5 + 2 cottages (3PB; 2SB) $55-80
Continental Plus Breakfast
Credit Cards: A, B, D
Notes: 2, 5, 7 (restricted), 8, 9, 10, 11, 12

ST. IGNATIUS

Mission Falls Ranch Bed and Breakfast

15338 Hillside, 59865
(406) 745-3375

Experience a working cattle ranch in scenic Montana. The ranch is located on the Hothead Indian Reservation at the foot of the Mission Mountains, where we raise and train working border collies along with the cattle. Within a few miles, you can backpack into the Mission Mountains

Tribal Wilderness or visit the National Bison Range and Ninepipes National Wildlife Refuge. To the north is Flathead Lake and Glacier National Park. Horseback riding and a trout stream are nearby. Rodeos and pow-wows are held locally in the summer.

Hosts: Lynn and Joan Mason
Rooms: 3 (1PB; 2SB) $70
Full Breakfast
Credit Cards: none
Notes: 2, 4, 6, 7, 9

Stonehouse Inn Bed and Breakfast

VIRGINIA CITY

Stonehouse Inn Bed and Breakfast

Box 205; 306 E. Idaho, 59755
(406) 843-5504

Located on a quiet street only blocks from the historic section of Virginia City, this Victorian stone home is listed on the National Register of Historic Places. Brass beds and antiques in every room give the inn a romantic touch. Five bedrooms share two baths. Full breakfasts are served each morning, and smoking is allowed on our porches. Skiing, snowmobiling, golfing, hunting, and fly-fishing nearby.

Hosts: John and Linda Hamilton
Rooms: 5 (SB) $55
Full Breakfast
Credit Cards: A, B
Notes: 2, 5, 7, 8, 9, 10, 12

WEST GLACIER

Mountain Timbers Wilderness Lodge

PO Box 127, 59936
(406) 387-5830; (800) 841-3835;
FAX (406) 387-5835

Tucked in the heart of northwestern Montana stands Mountain Timbers, a magnificent, hand-hewn hideaway that provides wilderness, wildlife, and spectacular vistas into Glacier National Park. Inside the spacious lodge you'll find massive rock and stone fireplaces, comfortable sitting areas, a fully stocked library, and outstanding views from almost every window. Beyond the calm of our lodge stretch miles of high-country adventures—white-water rafting, fishing in clear mountain streams, horseback riding and hiking in Glacier, big-game hunting, or golfing on one of the Flathead Valley's many championship courses. In the winter, try our 15 kilometers of groomed, private, cross-country ski trails, with downhill skiing at the Big Mountain, located only 25 miles away.

Hosts: Dave and Betty Rudisill
Rooms: 6 (4PB; 2SB) $75-125
Full Breakfast
Credit Cards: A, B, C
Notes: 2, 5, 7, 9, 10, 11, 12

WHITE SULFUR SPRINGS

Sky Lodge Bed and Breakfast

4260 Highway 12 E; PO Box 428, 59645
(406) 547-3999; (800) 965-4305

Find affordable luxury in a spacious log lodge, situated in the heart of one of Montana's prime outdoor recreation areas. Sky Lodge Bed and Breakfast is located in the beautiful Smith River Valley of central Montana, surrounded by three mountain ranges and acres of National Forests. It's midway between Yellowstone and Glacier national parks. Our guests enjoy outdoor hot tubs with great views of the mountains.

Hosts: Marc and Debbie Steinberg
Rooms: 4 (PB) $62-72
Full Breakfast
Credit Cards: A, B
Notes: 4, 5, 7, 9, 11

WHITEFISH

The Crenshaw House

5465 Highway 93 S., 59937
(406) 862-3496; (800) 453-2863;
FAX (406) 862-4742
E-mail: bedandbook@in-tch.com
Web site: http://www.whitefishmt.com

If you are looking for a place to unwind, this is the place to stay. Located just outside Whitefish in a quiet, relaxing country setting. This B&B features private baths, hot tub, fireplaces, and great food—including the house specialty, huckleberry popovers, served at your door to wake you in the morning. Children are welcome. No smoking or pets inside. A kennel is available for your pet.

Hostess: Anni Crenshaw-Rieker
Rooms: 3 (PB) $75-105
Full Breakfast
Credit Cards: A, B, C, D
Notes: 2, 3 and 4 (on request), 5, 6 (outside kennel), 7, 8, 9, 10, 11, 12

NEBRASKA

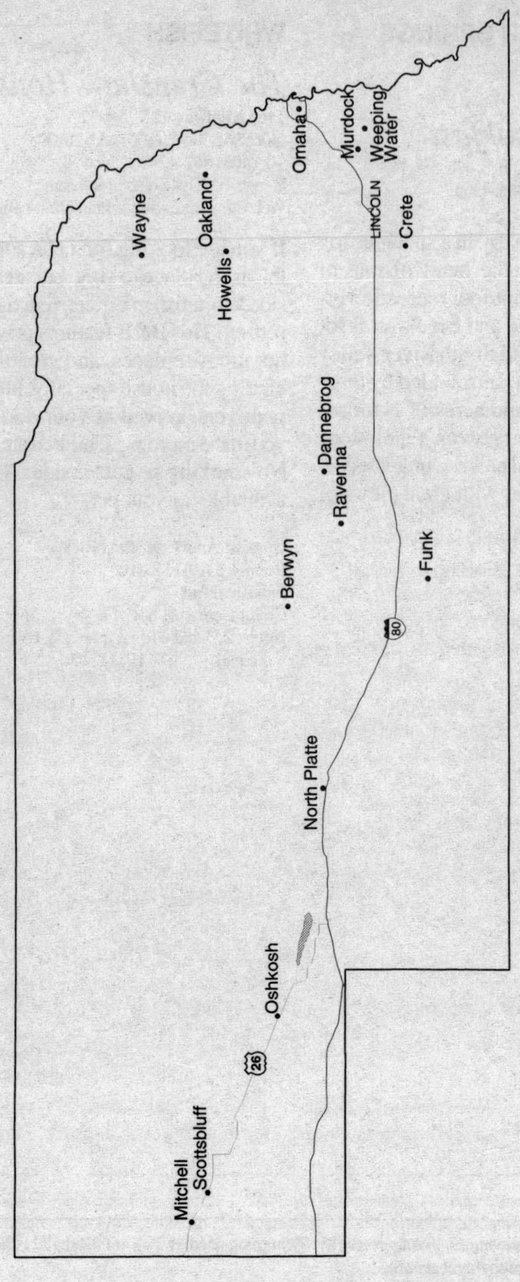

Wayne
Oakland
Howells
Omaha
Murdock
Weeping Water
LINCOLN
Crete
Dannebrog
Ravenna
Berwyn
Funk
80
North Platte
Oshkosh
26
Mitchell
Scottsbluff

Nebraska

BERWYN

1909 Heritage House B&B at Berwyn

101 Curran Avenue, 68819
(308) 935-1136

A warm welcome awaits you in this lovely, three-story Victorian country home with air-conditioned rooms. Heritage House is located in central Nebraska on Highway 2, one of America's most scenic highways. Enjoy a country breakfast in an elegant dining room, country kitchen, sunroom, or the Garden Room. Relax in the therapy spa and sauna. Visit the country chapel and gift shop in Heritage House Park. Refreshments served in the Garden Room.

Hosts: Meriam and Dale Thomas
Rooms: 5 (1PB; 4SB) $55-90
Full Breakfast
Credit Cards: none
Notes: 2, 3, 4, 5, 8, 9, 10

CRETE

The Parson's House

638 Forest Avenue, 68333
(402) 826-2634

The Parson's House

Enjoy warm hospitality in a restored four-square home that was built at the turn of the century, furnished with antiques and a modern whirlpool tub. Located near Doane College's beautiful campus. Breakfast is served in the formal dining room.

Hostess: Sandy and Harold Richardson
Rooms: 2 (SB) $45
Full Breakfast
Credit Cards: none
Notes: 2, 5, 8, 9

DANNEBROG

Nestle Inn-Dannebrog

209 E. Roger Welsch Avenue; PO Box 91, 68831
(308) 226-8252

Lovingly restored 1908 bungalow in the Danish capital of Nebraska with oak floors, library, and covered porch with swing for your pleasure. Have your first

---

NOTES: Credit cards accepted: A Master Card; B Visa; C American Express; D Discover; E Diners Club; F Other; 2 Personal checks accepted; 3 Lunch available; 4 Dinner available; 5 Open all year; 6 Pets welcome; 7 Children welcome; 8 Tennis nearby; 9 Swimming nearby; 10 Golf nearby; 11 Skiing nearby; 12 May be booked through travel agent.

cup of coffee in the sunny breakfast nook or lovely gazebo before you walk the short block to "Harriett's Danish" for a full breakfast. Nearby hike and bike trail and sand-green golf course. Enjoy the Danish Independence Day Festival in June and Danish Christmas Festival in December. Candlelight dinners by reservation.

Hosts: Gaylord and Judy Mickelsen
Rooms: 3 (SB) $50
Full Breakfast
Credit Cards: none
Notes: 4 (by reservation)

FUNK

Uncle Sam's Hilltop Lodge

Box 110, RR 1, 68940
(308) 995-2204; (308) 995-5568 evenings

Uncle Sam says, "We want you for our guest." Five minutes from I–80 and a suburb of Kearney. Sandhill cranes are nearby in spring. Our 1979 solar home is built into Nebraska's sandhills with four levels. An indoor sand pile and game room are available. Enjoy the view or relax in the tub for two. Free full breakfast and farm tours.

Hosts: Sam and Sharon Schrock
Rooms: 2 (1PB; 1SB) $48-55
Full Breakfast
Credit Cards: none
Notes: 2, 5, 6, 7, 8, 9

HOWELLS

Beran Bed and Breakfast

1604 Road 16, 68641-3043
(402) 986-1358

Enjoy the peace of the country in our grand, gabled farmhouse, among century-old cottonwoods and rock gardens. You'll feel like you're staying at grandma's in our 1905 home. Breakfast includes Czech pastries. Gift shop features our homemade jellies and crafts.

Hosts: Emil and Nadine Beran
Rooms: 3 (SB) $45
Full Breakfast
Credit Cards: none
Notes: 2, 5, 6, 7

Barn Again Bed and Breakfast

MITCHELL

Barn Again Bed and Breakfast

170549 County Road L, 69357
(308) 632-8647; FAX (308) 632-5518
E-mail: barnagin@ricochet.net
Web site: http://www.prairieweb.com/barnagain

Enjoy a country formal setting in this "reborn" 100-year-old barn located just minutes west of Scottsbluff in the shadow of Scotts Bluff National Monument and Museum. Very close to the historic Oregon Trail. Guest rooms furnished in Victorian antique furniture and appointments. Leisure room and sunroom. The formal dining room is surrounded by a mural of the farm in 1910. Breakfast by candlelight. Mini-museum and antique shop. Peace and

NOTES: Credit cards accepted: A Master Card; B Visa; C American Express; D Discover; E Diners Club; F Other; 2 Personal checks accepted; 3 Lunch available; 4 Dinner available; 5 Open all year; 6 Pets

quiet guaranteed. Double occupancy—husband/wife.

Hosts: Dick and Jane Snell
Rooms: 4 (PB) $75-80
Full Breakfast
Credit Cards: A, B, C, D, E
Notes: 2, 5, 8, 9, 10

MURDOCK

The Farm House

32617 Church Road, 68407
(402) 867-2062

Built in 1896, The Farm House provides a glimpse back to country life of the past. The home is complete with expansive, 10-foot ceilings, wood floors, an oak spindle staircase, antiques, and even a front porch swing. Room decor and furnishings throughout provide a feeling of comfortable, country elegance with many quilts and Pat's collection of angels. AC. Half hour from Lincoln and Omaha.

Hosts: Mike and Pat Meierhenry
Rooms: 3 (1PB; 2SB) $35-45
Full Breakfast
Credit Cards: none
Notes: 2, 5, 6, 7, 8, 9, 10

The Farm House

NORTH PLATTE

Derryberry Inn

302 S. Jeffers, 69101
(308) 534-5550

An antique-filled Romantic Revival home built in 1912. Bedroom decor in different time periods. Master bedroom has whirlpool tub. Only minutes from Scout's Rest Ranch, Union Pacific Bailey Yards, Lincoln County Historical Museum, and Lake Maloney. Less than an hour's drive from Lake McConahay. Exit 177; north on Highway 83 to C Street; west 1 block.

Hosts: Dan and Allison Fanning-Huebner, Donna Fanning
Rooms: 5 (2PB; 3SB) $50-80
Full Breakfast
Credit Cards: A, B
Notes: 5, 7, 8, 9, 10

Knoll's Country Inn Bed and Breakfast

Route 2, Box 458, 69101
(308) 368-5634; (800) 337-4526
Web site: http://www.bbonline.com/ne/knolls

Knoll's Country Inn is a modern home in the country where it is peaceful and quiet. Take a walk and enjoy a beautiful sunset across the prairie. Relax in a whirlpool bathtub or under the stars in our outdoor spa. After a refreshing night's sleep, you will wake to the aroma of a delicious home-cooked breakfast. Weather permitting, you can take breakfast on the deck and enjoy the flower gardens and birds.

Hosts: Arlene and Robert Knoll
Rooms: 5 (1PB; 4SB) $60-75
Full Breakfast
Credit Cards: none
Notes: 2, 5, 7 (inquire first), 8, 9, 10, 11 (water)

OAKLAND

Benson Bed and Breakfast

402 N. Oakland Avenue, 68045
(402) 685-6051
E-mail: sanderson@genesisnet.net

Located in the center of a small town. Benson Bed and Breakfast is beautifully decorated and offers a breakfast you won't soon forget, served in the dining room with all its finery. Features include a large collection of soft-drink collectibles, a library full of books, a beautiful garden room to relax in, and a large whirlpool tub with color TV on the wall. All rooms are on the second level. Craft and gift shops are on the main floor. Three blocks west of Highway 77. No smoking.

Hosts: Stan and Norma Anderson
Rooms: 3 (SB) $50-60
Full Breakfast
Credit Cards: none
Notes: 2, 5, 8, 9, 10, 12

OMAHA

The Jones'

1617 S. 90th Street, 68124
(402) 397-0721

Large, private residence with large deck and gazebo in the back. Fresh cinnamon rolls are served for breakfast. Your hosts' interests include golf, travel, needlework, and meeting other people. Located 5 minutes from I-80.

Hosts: Theo and Don Jones
Rooms: 3 (1PB; 2SB) $25
Continental Breakfast
Credit Cards: none
Notes: 2, 5, 6, 7, 8

OSHKOSH

The Locust Tree B&B

400 W. 5th Street, 69154
(308) 772-3530

Enjoy small-town hospitality in a contemporary family home. The large brick home is graced with majestic spruce and locust trees. Gracious guest rooms with baths. Continental breakfast. Access to free summer swimming, Pony Express route, Ash Hollow State Park and Museum.

Hosts: Pete and Ardena Regier
Rooms: 2 (1PB; 1SB) $45-75
Continental Breakfast
Credit Cards: none
Notes: 2, 5, 7, 9, 10

RAVENNA

Aunt Betty's B&B

804 Grand Avenue, 68869
(308) 452-3739; (800) 632-9114

Enjoy the peace of a small, central Nebraska town while staying at Aunt Betty's three-story Victorian bed and breakfast. Four bedrooms are furnished in antiques and decorated with attention to detail. Relax in the sitting room while awaiting a delicious, full breakfast that includes Aunt Betty's "Sticky Buns" and homemade goodies. Flower garden with fishpond for relaxation. Accommodations for hunters in the hunter's loft. An antique shop is part of the bed and breakfast. Golf and tennis nearby. Only ½ hour from I–80.

Hosts: Harvey and Betty Shrader
Rooms: 4 (SB) $45-55
Full Breakfast
Credit Cards: A, B
Notes: 2, 3, 4 (by appointment), 5, 7, 8, 9, 10

NOTES: Credit cards accepted: A Master Card; B Visa; C American Express; D Discover; E Diners Club; F Other; 2 Personal checks accepted; 3 Lunch available; 4 Dinner available; 5 Open all year; 6 Pets

SCOTTSBLUFF

Fontenelle Inn Bed and Breakfast

1424 Fourth Avenue, 69361
(308) 632-6257
E-mail: ptdlady@prairieweb.com

Welcome to the historic Fontenelle Inn Bed and Breakfast! This 1917 "castlelated" inn provides a uniquely regal setting on the Oregon Trail. The Fontenelle Inn is the perfect place for receptions, tea parties, banquets, luncheons, reunions, or simply enjoying an evening in one of our luxurious guest rooms, followed by a gourmet breakfast. We hope you enjoy your stay with us.

Hosts: Bill and Brenda Dean
Rooms: 12 (PB) $65-85
Full Breakfast
Credit Cards: A, B, D
Notes: 2, 3, 4, 5, 7, 8, 9, 10, 12

WAYNE

Grandma Butch's Bed and Breakfast

502 Logan Street, 68787
(402) 375-2759

Ardyce Kniesche and Ken Murphy will make you feel at home in this restored 1907 two-story "Victorian" with wraparound front porch. The homey quality of rich wood and beautiful windows is characteristic of the period. Kennel for pets.

Hosts: Ardyce Kniesche and Ken Murphy
Rooms: 4 (1PB; 3SB) $40-50
Full Breakfast
Credit Cards: A, B
Notes: 2, 5, 7, 8, 9, 10

WEEPING WATER

Lauritzen's Blue Heron Bed and Breakfast

5102 Highway 50; PO Box 292, 68463
(402) 267-3295; (888) 915-5559

Country pleasures will be yours at Ken and Alice's comfortable farm. Roam around the working farm and experience the country life of raising crops and cattle. Wander through the gardens or enjoy the acres of woods filled with wildlife. Enjoy a star-filled sky while relaxing in the spa. The Larkspur or Hollyhock Rooms (each with private bath) will assure you a restful night's sleep. Homemade Danish and American specialties and gourmet coffee fill the house with delightful aromas to waken you. Hot tub. Located 25 minutes from Omaha or Lincoln.

Hosts: Ken and Alice Lauritzen
Rooms: 2 (PB)
Full Breakfast
Credit Cards: A, B
Notes: 2, 4, 5, 9, 10, 11, 12

---

welcome; 7 Children welcome; 8 Tennis nearby; 9 Swimming nearby; 10 Golf nearby; 11 Skiing nearby; 12 May be booked through travel agent.

NEVADA

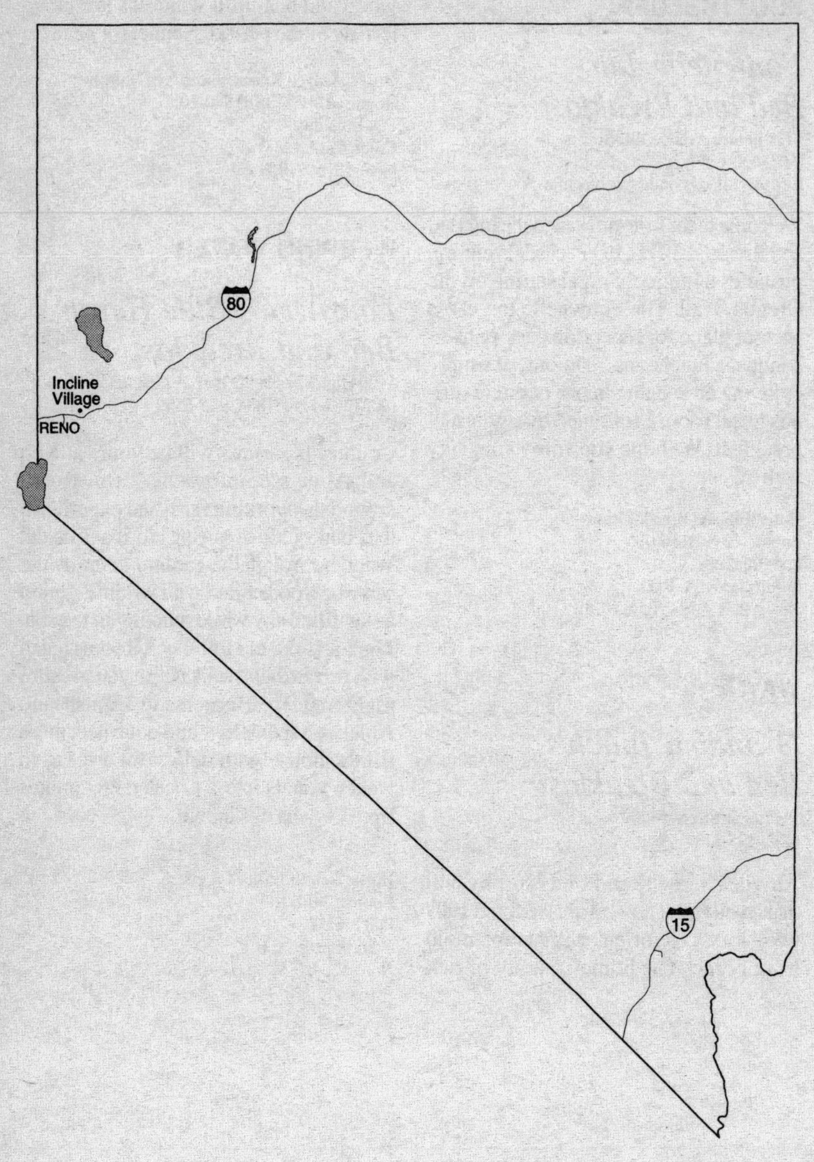

Nevada

Advance Reservations Inn Arizona/Mi Casa Su Casa/Old Pueblo Homestays B&B RSO

PO Box 950, **Tempe, AZ,** 85280-0950
(602) 990-0682; (800) 456-0682 (reservations);
FAX (602) 990-3390
E-mail: micasa@primenet.com
Web site: http://www.micasa.com

Since 1981, we proudly have listed inspected, clean, comfortable B&B inns, homestays, cottages, and ranches in Arizona and the Southwest. We list about 200 B&Bs that are modest to luxurious, historic to contemporary. In **Nevada,** we list Henderson and Las Vegas. (See also our entries in Arizona, New Mexico, and Utah.) We also represent two luxury villas, one in Puerto Vallarto, **Mexico,** and the second in the Costa Brava area of **Spain.** Most rooms have private baths and range from $50 to $275, based on double occupancy. Continental to gourmet breakfasts. A book with individual descriptions and pictures is available for $9.50. Ruth Young, coordinator.

INCLINE VILLAGE

Haus Bavaria Bed and Breakfast

593 N. Dyer Circle; PO Box 9079, 89452
(702) 831-6122; (800) 731-6222;
FAX (702) 831-1238
E-mail: chewitt440@aol.com
Web site: www.hausbavaria.com

This European-style residence in the heart of the Sierra Nevada Mountains is within walking distance of Lake Tahoe. Each of the five guest rooms opens onto a balcony, offering lovely views of the mountains. Breakfast, prepared by your host, includes a selection of home-baked goodies, fruit, juices, freshly ground coffee, and teas. A private beach and swimming pool are available to guests. You may enjoy skiing at Diamond Peak, Mt. Rose, Heavenly Valley, and other nearby areas.

Host: Bick Hewitt
Rooms: 5 (PB) $85-155
Full Breakfast
Credit Cards: A, B, C, D
Notes: 2, 5, 7, 8, 9, 10, 11, 12

NOTES: Credit cards accepted: A Master Card; B Visa; C American Express; D Discover; E Diners Club; F Other; 2 Personal checks accepted; 3 Lunch available; 4 Dinner available; 5 Open all year; 6 Pets welcome; 7 Children welcome; 8 Tennis nearby; 9 Swimming nearby; 10 Golf nearby; 11 Skiing nearby; 12 May be booked through travel agent.

NEW HAMPSHIRE

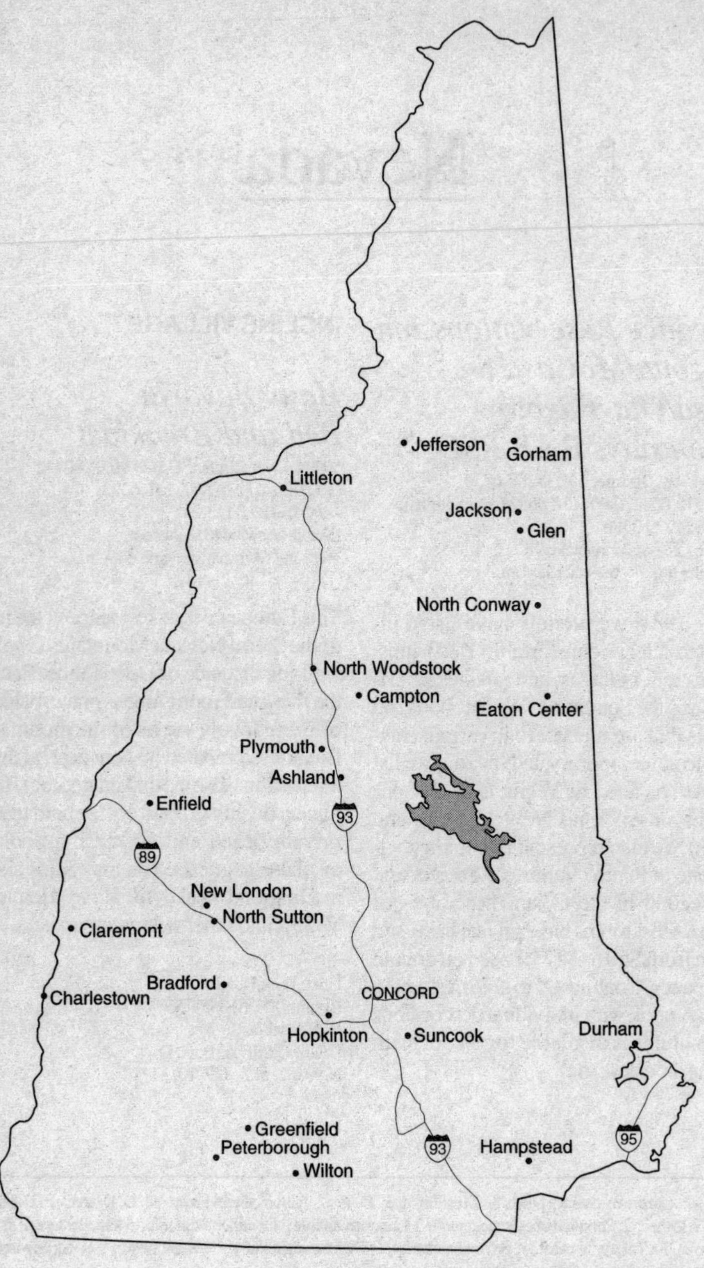

New Hampshire

ALLENTOWN—SUNCOOK

White Rabbit Inn B&B

62 Main Street, **Suncook Village,** 03275
(603) 485-9494 (voice and FAX)
Web site: http://www.whtrabbit.com

The stately, circa-1760 White Rabbit Inn provides true privacy, complemented by attentive hospitality. Delicious aromas wafting from the huge, modern and immaculate kitchen remind you that your host, executive chef Gregory Martin, has an exclusive, first-class international culinary background. The solid brick, marble, and hardwood construction; tall ceilings and spacious hallways; beautiful, ornate wood paneling; extravagant fireplaces; and lavish moldings contribute to the serene and secluded atmosphere. The White Rabbit Inn is a splendid choice.

Host: Gregory Martin
Rooms: 5 (2PB; 3SB)
Full or Continental Breakfast
Credit Cards: A, B, C, D, F
Notes: 2, 5, 7 (by exception), 8, 9, 10, 11, 12

ASHLAND

Glynn House Inn Bed and Breakfast

43 Highland Street, 03217
(603) 968-3775; (800) 637-9599;
FAX (603) 968-3129
E-mail: glynnhse@lr.net
Web site: http://nettx.com/glynnhouse

The Glynn House Inn is nestled among the lakes and mountains of New Hampshire in the heart of the state. The inn is a fully restored Queen Anne Victorian featuring nine rooms, all offering private baths. Some have fireplaces and whirlpool tubs. A full breakfast is served. The inn is located within easy access of I–93, Exit 24, only 2 hours from Boston. A quiet, romantic escape where attention to detail is our hallmark.

Hosts: Karol and Betsy Paterman
Rooms: 9 (PB) $85-145
Full Breakfast
Credit Cards: A, B, C, D, E, F
Notes: 2, 5, 7 (over 10), 8, 9, 10, 11, 12

NOTES: Credit cards accepted: A Master Card; B Visa; C American Express; D Discover; E Diners Club; F Other; 2 Personal checks accepted; 3 Lunch available; 4 Dinner available; 5 Open all year; 6 Pets welcome; 7 Children welcome; 8 Tennis nearby; 9 Swimming nearby; 10 Golf nearby; 11 Skiing nearby; 12 May be booked through travel agent.

Candlelite Inn Bed and Breakfast

BRADFORD

Candlelite Inn B&B

5 Greenhouse Lane, 03221
(603) 938-5571; (888) 812-5571;
FAX (603) 938-2564
Web site: http://www.virtualcities.com/ons/nh/y/nhyb601.htm

An 1897 country Victorian inn nestled on 3 acres in the Lake Sunapee Region. We serve a full breakfast—down to dessert—in our sunroom, which overlooks the pond. Relax on the gazebo porch while sipping lemonade on a lazy summer day, or curl up in the living room in front of the corner fireplace. Skiing, hiking, antiquing, restaurants minutes away. No smoking.

Hosts: Les and Marilyn Gordon
Rooms: 6 (PB) $65-95
Full Breakfast
Credit Cards: A, B, C, D
Notes: 2, 5, 8, 9, 10, 11, 12

CAMPTON

Mountain Fare Inn

Mad River Road; PO Box 553, 03223
(607) 726-4283
E-mail: mtnfareinn@cyberportal.net

Lovely 1840s village home with the antiques, fabric, and feel of country cottage living. Gardens in summer, foliage in fall, a true skier's lodge in winter. Accessible, peaceful, warm, friendly, affordable. Unspoiled beauty from Franconia Notch to Squam Lake. Four-season sports, soccer field, music, theatre. Featuring hiking vacations, tennis, championship golf course, family reunions.

Hosts: Susan and Nick Preston
Rooms: 10 (9 PB; 1 SB) $60-105
Full Breakfast
Credit Cards: none
Notes: 2, 3, 4, 5, 6, 7, 8, 9, 10, 11, 12

CHARLESTOWN

MapleHedge

355 Main Street; PO Box 638, 03603
(603) 826-5237 (voice and FAX);
(800) 9-MAPLE-9 (962-7539)
E-mail: debrine@fmis.net

Rather than just touring homes 2½ centuries old, make one your "home away from home" while visiting western New Hampshire or eastern Vermont. MapleHedge offers distinctly different bedrooms, with antiques that complement the individual decor. It has very tastefully added all modern-day amenities such as central AC, fire sprinkler system, and queen beds. Enjoy a gourmet breakfast in the grand dining room of this magnificent home that is on the National Register and situated among 200-year-old maples and lovely gardens. Day trips show local attractions. Brochure sent on request. Highly rated by Mobil and ABBA. Closed January–March.

Hosts: Joan and Dick DeBrine
Rooms: 5 (PB) $85-100
Full Three-Course Breakfast
Credit Cards: A, B
Notes: 2, 7 (over 12), 8, 9, 10, 11, 12

NOTES: Credit cards accepted: A Master Card; B Visa; C American Express; D Discover; E Diners Club; F Other; 2 Personal checks accepted; 3 Lunch available; 4 Dinner available; 5 Open all year; 6 Pets

Goddard Mansion Bed and Breakfast

CLAREMONT

Goddard Mansion Bed and Breakfast

25 Hillstead Road, 03743
(603) 543-0603; (800) 736-0603;
FAX (603) 543-0001
E-mail: goddardmansion@usa.net

Circa 1905, this mansion with adjacent garden tea house is set amid acres of lawns and gardens with panoramic mountain views. The beautifully restored, English manor–style, eighteen-room mansion has expansive porches and ten uniquely decorated guest rooms. The living room has a fireplace and window seats for cuddling up with a good book and enjoying a vintage baby grand piano. A 1939 Wurlitzer jukebox lights up a corner of the walnut-paneled dining room where a full, natural breakfast awaits guests each morning. Four-season activities, historic sites, cultural events, fun, and "fine" dining are nearby. The area is an antique buff's adventureland! Brochure available. Families welcome.

Hostess: Debbie Albee
Rooms: 10 (3PB; 7SB) $65-125
Full Breakfast
Credit Cards: A, B, C, D
Notes: 2, 5, 7, 8, 9, 10, 11

CONWAY

The Darby Field Country Inn & Restaurant

PO Box D, 03818
(603) 447-2181; (800) 426-4147;
FAX (603) 447-5726
E-mail: marc@darbyfield.com
Web site: http://www.darbyfield.com

The Darby Field Country Inn & Restaurant, situated near New Hampshire's scenic Kancamagus Highway, is a perfect setting for weekend getaways, extended vacations, reunions, weddings, honeymoons, and receptions. Nearby North Conway offers great shopping and antiquing. The White Mountain National Forest abutting our property affords opportunities for nordic and alpine skiing, snowshoeing, hiking, mountain biking, canoeing, and fishing. Return to the inn for a swim in our sparkling pool, quiet relaxation, fine dining, and friendly hospitality.

Hosts: Marc and Maria Donaldson
Rooms: 16 (14PB; 2SB) $80-220
Full Breakfast
Credit Cards: A, B
Notes: 2, 4, 5 (except April), 7, 9, 10, 11, 12

DURHAM

Three Chimneys Inn, Ffrost Sawyer Tavern

17 Newmarket Road, 03824
(603) 868-7800; FAX (603) 868-5011
E-mail: chimney3@nh.ultranet.com
Web site: http://www.threechimneysinn.com

A newly restored 1649 homestead and carriage house overlooking formal gardens and the old Mill Falls. Guest rooms have fireplaces, four-poster canopy beds with Edwardian bed drapes, phones with data ports, full private baths, and Jacuzzis. "Maples" with its four fireplaces and Georgian furnishings offers fine dining in a candlelit atmosphere. Dine in the shade of an Old English grape arbor in "The Conservatory." Portsmouth, Strawberry Banke living museum, and the seacoast are only minutes away.

Hostess: Jane Peterson
Rooms: 24 (PB) $149-189
Full Breakfast
Credit Cards: A, B, C, D
Notes: 2, 3, 4, 5, 8, 9, 10

The Inn at Crystal Lake

EATON CENTER (CONWAY)

The Inn at Crystal Lake

Route 153; PO Box 12, 03832
(603) 447-2120; (800) 343-7336;
FAX (603) 447-3599

Unwind in the comforts of our 1884 Victorian inn, nestled in peaceful Eaton village, just 6 miles south of Conway. The tastefully decorated guest rooms are furnished with antiques. Begin each day with a full country breakfast in old-fashioned elegance at your own private table. A short drive down a country road will bring you to all the activities of the Mt. Washington Valley. Shopping, dining, and five major ski areas will keep you happily entertained—or just relax here and enjoy our historic village, beautiful Crystal Lake, and the hospitality of your hosts. Experience New England in a country inn.

Hosts: Richard and Janice Octeau
Rooms: 11 (PB) $70-100
Full Breakfast
Credit Cards: A, B, C, D, E
Notes: 2, 5, 7 (over 6), 8, 9, 10, 11, 12

ENFIELD

Boulder Cottage on Crystal Lake

RR 1 Box 257, 03748
(603) 632-7355

A turn-of-the-century Victorian cottage owned by our family for 73 years. Our home faces beautiful Crystal Lake, a small, private lake centrally located in the Dartmouth-Sunapee Region. We promise guests an unspoiled environment with classic views of the lake and mountains. Enjoy swimming, canoeing, boating, fishing, hiking, or just relaxing on our comfortable screened porch or sunny decks. Weekly rates can be arranged. Children over 10 welcome. No pets, no smoking. Advance reservations required.

Hosts: Barbara and Harry Reed
Rooms: 4 (2PB; 2SB) $45-70
Full Breakfast
Credit Cards: none
Notes: 2, 7 (over 10), 9, 10, 12

NOTES: Credit cards accepted: A Master Card; B Visa; C American Express; D Discover; E Diners Club; F Other; 2 Personal checks accepted; 3 Lunch available; 4 Dinner available; 5 Open all year; 6 Pets

GLEN

Covered Bridge House

Route 302; PO Box 989, 03838
(603) 383-9109; (800) 232-9109;
FAX (603) 383-8089
E-mail: cbhouse@landmarknet.net
Website: http://www.netlx.com/coveredbridge.html

Feel at home in our cozy bed and breakfast on the Saco River next to a restored 1850s covered bridge. With just six guest rooms and a cozy living room, our inn offers a comfortable, informal atmosphere. Awaken to a hearty country breakfast. In warm weather, enjoy the beauty of the Saco River in our backyard—swim, tube, fish, or sunbathe on the rocks. Just minutes from Attitash, where in winter you can enjoy some of the best skiing in the East. AAA three diamonds.

Hosts: Dan and Nancy Wanek
Rooms: 6 (4PB; 2SB) $49-89
Full Breakfast
Credit Cards: A, B, C, D
Notes: 2, 5, 7, 9, 10, 11, 12

GORHAM

Libby House Bed and Breakfast

55 Main Street; Box 267, 03581
(603) 466-2271; (800) 453-0023
E-mail: libbyhouse@worldnet.att.net

The Libby House Bed and Breakfast is a turn-of-the-century Victorian home located on the town common in Gorham. We offer three guest rooms, each with a private bath, queen-size bed, and mountain view. The Northern White Mountains National Forest is only minutes away, with numerous outdoor activities that are available year-round. Gorham's many wonderful shops and restaurants are within easy walking distance of the B&B.

Libby House Bed and Breakfast

Hosts: Paul, Margaret, and Lila Kuliga
Rooms: 3 (PB) $55-95
Full Breakfast
Credit Cards: A, B, C, D
Notes: 2, 5, 7, 8, 9, 10, 11, 12

GREENFIELD

The Greenfield Bed and Breakfast Inn

PO Box 400, 03047
(603) 547-6327; (800) 678-4144;
FAX (603) 547-2418
E-mail: innkeeper@greenfieldinn.com
Web site: http://www.greenfieldinn.com

Renovations in 1998 include whirlpool tubs, Jacuzzis, and fireplaces. We can sleep six in the hayloft suite, hideaway suite, or carriage house. Canopied beds, Victorian comforters, AC, TV/VCR, phone system, hot tubs. Children welcome. Multiday discounts, low weekly and monthly rates.

Hosts: Barbara and Vic Mangini
Rooms: 13 including cottage (10PB; 3SB) $49-169
Full Breakfast
Credit Cards: A, B, C
Notes: 2, 5, 7 (restrictions), 8, 9, 10, 11, 12

Stillmeadow Bed and Breakfast at Hampstead

HAMPSTEAD

Stillmeadow B&B at Hampstead

545 Main Street; PO Box 565, 03841
(603) 329-8381; FAX (603) 329-4075
E-mail: rover@tiac.net

Historic 1850 home with five chimneys, three staircases, hardwood floors, Oriental rugs, and woodstoves. Set on rolling meadows adjacent to conservation trails. Single, doubles, and suites, all with private baths. Families are welcome, with amenities such as a fenced-in play yard and children's playroom. Easy commute to Manchester and Boston. Complimentary refreshments—and the cookie jar is always full! Formal dining/living rooms.

Hosts: Lori Offord
Rooms: 4½ (4PB) $60-90
Expanded Continental Breakfast
Credit Cards: A, B, C, D
Notes: 2, 5, 7, 8, 9, 10, 11, 12

HOPKINTON

The Country Porch B&B

281 Moran Road, 03229
(603) 746-6391

Situated on 15 peaceful acres of lawn, pasture, and forest, this B&B is a reproduction of an 18th-century Colonial. Sit on the wraparound porch and gaze over the meadow, bask in the sun, and then cool off in the pool. The comfortably appointed rooms have a Colonial, Amish, or Shaker theme and have king or twin beds. Summer and winter activities are plentiful, and fine country dining is a short drive away. "Come and sit a spell." No smoking.

Hosts: Tom and Wendy Solomon
Rooms: 3 (PB) $60-75
Full Breakfast
Credit Cards: A, B
Notes: 2, 5, 9, 10, 11

JACKSON

Ellis River House

PO Box 656, 03846
(603) 383-9339; (800) 233-8309;
FAX (603) 383-4142
E-mail: innkeeper@erhinn.com
Web site: http://www.erhinn.com

Sample true New England hospitality at this enchanting, small hotel/country inn within a short stroll of the village. The house has comfortable king and queen guest rooms decorated with Laura Ashley prints, some with fireplaces and two-person Jacuzzis, cable TV, scenic balconies, and period antiques; all with individually controlled heat and AC. Two-room and family suites, riverfront cottage, hot tub, sauna, and heated pool, sitting and game rooms, sundeck overlooking the pristine Ellis River. Enjoy a breakfast with homemade breads or a delicious trout dinner. Relax with libations and billiards in the pub.

Hosts: Barry and Barbara Lubao
Rooms: 19 (PB) $79-259
Full Country Breakfast
Credit Cards: A, B, C, D, E
Notes: 2, 4, 5, 6 and 7 (limited), 8, 9, 10, 11, 12

JEFFERSON

Applebrook Bed and Breakfast

Route 115A, 03583
(603) 586-7713; (800) 565-6504
E-mail: applebrook@aol.com
Web site: http://www.applebrook.com

Taste our midsummer raspberries while enjoying spectacular mountain views. Applebrook is a comfortable, casual bed and breakfast in a large Victorian farmhouse with a peaceful, rural setting. After a restful night's sleep, you will enjoy a hearty breakfast before venturing out for a day of hiking, fishing, antique hunting, golfing, swimming, or skiing. Near Santa's Village and Six-Gun City. Dormitory available for groups. Brochures available. Hot tub under the stars.

Hosts: Martin Kelly and Sandra Conley
Rooms: 14 (7PB; 7SB) $55
Full Breakfast
Credit Cards: A, B
Notes: 2, 6, 7, 8, 9, 10, 11, 12

LITTLETON

Continental 93 Travelers Inn

516 Meadow Street, Exit 42, I–93; 03561
(603) 444-5366 (voice and FAX); (800) 544-9366
E-mail: info@continental93.com
Web site: http://www.continental93.com

The newest sparkle in New Hampshire's White Mountains. This newly renovated resort offers year-round recreation, a location central to White Mountain attractions, and quality accommodations. Queen and double beds. Fully air-conditioned. Free breakfast. Fifty-six units on 117 acres. Two trout ponds with free fishing (no license required). Heated pool, sauna, hot tub. Canadian cash at par all year. Conference and banquet facilities. AAA and senior discounts.

Hostess: Lynn T. McArdle
Rooms: 56 (PB) $49-79
Continental Breakfast
Credit Cards: A, B, C, D, E
Notes: 4, 5, 6, 7, 8, 9, 10, 11, 12

The Inn at Pleasant Lake

NEW LONDON

The Inn at Pleasant Lake

125 Pleasant Street; PO Box 1030, 03257
(603) 526-6271; (800) 626-4907;
FAX (603) 526-4111
E-mail: bmackenz@kear.tds.net
Web site: http://www.innatpleasantlake.com

Descending 500 feet from Main Street, visitors will find the inn situated on the shore of Pleasant Lake with Mt. Kearsarge as its backdrop. All twelve well-appointed guest rooms have private baths and are furnished with antiques. Mornings start with a bountiful continental and hot breakfast. Upon checking in, guests are invited to afternoon tea. A five-course dinner is served. Reservations required. Hiking, boating, swimming, skiing, biking, and cozy accommodations make this inn a destination, not just a place to stay.

Hosts: Brian and Linda MacKenzie
Rooms: 12 (PB) $95-145
Full Breakfast
Credit Cards: A, B, D
Notes: 2, 4, 5, 7, 8, 9, 10, 11, 12

NORTH CONWAY

The 1785 Inn

3582 White Mountain Highway; PO Box 1785, 03860-1785
(603) 356-9025; (800) 421-1785; FAX (603) 356-6081
E-mail: the1785inn@aol.com
Web site: http://www.the1785inn.com

A relaxing place to vacation any time of year. The inn is famous for its views and food. Located at the Scenic Vista, popularized by the White Mountain School of Art, its famous scene of Mt. Washington is virtually unchanged from when the inn was built more than two centuries ago. The homey atmosphere will make you feel right at home, and the food and service will make you eagerly await your return.

Hosts: Becky and Charlie Mallar
Rooms: 17 (12PB; 5SB) $59-169
Full Breakfast
Credit Cards: A, B, C, D, E
Notes: 2, 4, 5, 7, 8, 9, 10, 11, 12

Buttonwood Inn on Mt. Surprise

Mt. Surprise Road; PO Box 1817, 03860
(603) 356-2625; (800) 258-2625 (U.S.); FAX (603) 356-3140
E-mail: button_w@moose.ncia.net
Web site: http://www.buttonwoodinn.com

The Buttonwood Inn is nationally recognized for superior innkeeping. Visit our 1820s farmhouse on 17 secluded acres, 2 miles from the village of North Conway. Our guests enjoy a peaceful, rural setting, with the convenience of being close to everything. Decorated with Shaker furniture, stenciling, and antiques. Breakfasts are second to none. Award-winning perennial gardens surround the inn. You can hike or cross-country ski from the back door. Individually prepared daily itineraries are available. A memorable blend of hospitality, laughter, and kindness.

Hosts: Peter and Claudia Needham
Rooms: 10 (PB) $85-200
Full Breakfast
Credit Cards: A, B, C, D
Notes: 2, 7, 8, 9, 10, 11, 12

Eastman Inn

Eastman Inn

2331 White Mountain Highway, Route 16; PO Box 882, 03860
(603) 356-6707; (800) 626-5855 (reservations only, please); FAX (606) 356-7708
E-mail: eastman@eastmaninn.com
Web site: http://www.eastmaninn.com

A 1777 Victorian with panoramic mountain views. Furnished with antiques. Spacious rooms with queen- or king-size beds; some with fireplaces and balconies facing the mountains. Within minutes of all attractions, shopping, dining, golfing, hiking, skiing, and canoeing. Nonsmoking inn. AAA

NOTES: Credit cards accepted: A Master Card; B Visa; C American Express; D Discover; E Diners Club; F Other; 2 Personal checks accepted; 3 Lunch available; 4 Dinner available; 5 Open all year; 6 Pets

three-diamond rating. A warm, Christian environment of hospitality.

Hosts: Peter and Carol M. Watson
Rooms: 15 (14PB; 2SB) $65-165
Full Breakfast
Credit Cards: A, B, D
Notes: 5, 8, 9, 10, 11, 12

Merrill Farm Resort

428 White Mountain Highway, 03860
(603) 447-3866; (800) 445-1017;
FAX (603) 447-3867
E-mail: info@merrillfarm.com
Web site: http://www.merrillfarm.com

Once a working farm, Merrill Farm has been an accommodation for more than 100 years. Modern amenities in a rustic country atmosphere. Family lofts, fireplace/kitchenettes, or whirlpool units are available. Fully air-conditioned, year-round recreation. Free breakfast. On crystal clear Saco River—free canoeing. Handy to ten major ski areas. Handy to all White Mountain attractions. AAA and senior discounts. Canadian cash at par 90% of the year.

Hostess: Emily Harper
Rooms: 60 (PB) $49-119
Continental Breakfast
Credit Cards: A, B, C, D, E
Notes: 5, 7, 8, 9, 10, 11, 12

NORTH SUTTON

Follansbee Inn on Kezar Lake

(603) 927-4221; (800) 626-4221;
FAX (603) 927-4107
E-mail: follansbeeinn@conknet.com
Web site: http://www.follansbeeinn.com

Take a "step into the past" at our lakeside country inn. Our 1840s B&B is nestled in a tiny village surrounded by wooded hills. Relax on our old-fashioned wraparound porch. Use our canoe or rowboat. Guest rooms are furnished with antiques and comfortable beds. A full, family-style breakfast is included. Termed an "affordable luxury" by *CI* magazine. AAA three diamonds, Mobile three stars.

Hosts: Sandy and Dick Reilein
Rooms: 23 (11PB; 12SB) + lakefront cottage $80-110; cottage weekly, $675 (breakfast extra)
Full Breakfast
Credit Cards: A, B
Notes: 2, 8, 9, 10, 11

NORTH WOODSTOCK

Wilderness Inn

RFD 1, Box 69, 03262
(603) 745-3890; (800) 200-9453;
FAX (603) 745-6367
E-mail: Wildernessinn@juno.com
Web site: http://www.musar.com/wildernessinn

A 1912 Craftsman house with seven bedrooms and cottage, the Wilderness Inn is the quintessential country inn. Snuggled within the White Mountain National Forest, 5 miles south of Franconia Notch. The Old Man Profile, Flume, Lost River, Cannon and Loon Mountain ski areas, and Mount Washington are all nearby. Your delicious gourmet breakfast includes homemade muffins, fresh fruit salad, juice, tea or freshly ground coffee, pancakes, French toast, crepes, or omelets. Enjoy a relaxed country house ambience.

Hosts: Rosanna and Michael Yarnell
Rooms: 7 (5PB; 2SB) + cottage $40-115
Full Breakfast
Credit Cards: A, B, C
Notes: 2, 5, 7, 8, 9, 10, 11, 12

PETERBOROUGH

Apple Gate Bed and Breakfast

199 Upland Farm Road, 03458
(603) 924-6543

The Apple Gate Bed and Breakfast is a charming 1832 Colonial home nestled among gardens, trees, and apple orchards. It is conveniently located just 2 miles from downtown Peterborough, Thornton Wilder's "Our Town," and the center for cultural and outdoor activities in the Monadnock region. There are four guest bedrooms (the Cortland, the Granny Smith, the Crispin, and the McIntosh), all with Laura Ashley bed linens, stencil-decorated walls, and private baths. Here guests can relax in a house filled with country elegance and enjoy a full candlelight breakfast served by a crackling fire.

Hosts: Ken and Dianne Legenhausen
Rooms: 4 (PB) $65-80
Full Breakfast
Credit Cards: A, B
Notes: 2, 5, 9, 10, 11

PLYMOUTH

Col. Spencer Inn

RR 1, Box 206, 03264
(603) 536-3438

Col. Spencer Inn

A 1764 center-chimney Colonial with antique furnishings, wide pine floorboards, hand-hewn beams, and Indian shutters. Seven antique-appointed bedrooms with private baths welcome guests. A full country breakfast is served in a fireplaced dining room. The inn is convenient to both lake and mountain attractions, at Exit 27 off I–93, ½ mile south on Route 3.

Hosts: Carolyn and Alan Hill
Rooms: 7 (PB) $45-65
Full Breakfast
Credit Cards: none
Notes: 2, 5, 7, 8, 9, 10, 11, 12

WILTON CENTER

Stepping Stones B&B

6 Bennington Battle Trail, 03086
(603) 654-9048; (800) 654-9048;
FAX (603) 654-6821

A fine, small B&B at the edge of one of southern New Hampshire's most charming villages. In friendly European tradition, the hostess invites guests to share an unusually interesting 19th-century house and garden. Stepping Stones is in the Monadnock region of south-central New Hampshire, just off Route 101, in the countryside beyond the picturebook hamlet of Wilton Center (sometimes confused with the town of Wilton, 4 miles east).

Hostess: D. Ann Carlsmith
Rooms: 3 (PB) $55-60
Full Breakfast
Credit Cards: none
Notes: 2, 5, 6 (under control), 7 (supervised), 10, 11, 12

NOTES: Credit cards accepted: A Master Card; B Visa; C American Express; D Discover; E Diners Club; F Other; 2 Personal checks accepted; 3 Lunch available; 4 Dinner available; 5 Open all year; 6 Pets

New Jersey

BAY HEAD

The Bentley Inn

694 Main Avenue, 08742
(732) 892-9589; FAX (732) 701-0030
Web site: http://www.bentleyinn.com

A charming century-old-plus inn filled with original handcrafts and decorations. The atmosphere is friendly and relaxed, with teal carpeting throughout each unique guest room. Fireplace and candlelit tea during the off season. Cooled by AC or ocean breezes, relax on our second-floor wraparound porch. Hearty, full breakfasts, beach passes, reserved parking, outdoor shower and changing area, soda machine, daily maid service, spectacular sunrises and sunsets eagerly await you.

Hosts: brother/sister Tony and Alessandra Matteo
Rooms: 20 (8PB; 12SB) $50-195 (private baths available off-season only)
Full Breakfast
Credit Cards: A, B, C, D, E
Notes: 2, 4, 5, 7, 8, 9, 10, 12

BELMAR

The Inn at the Shore

301 4th Avenue, 07719
(732) 681-3762; FAX (732) 280-1914
E-mail: tomvolker@aol.com
Web site: http://www.bbianj.com/innattheshore

The inn is located within sight of the Atlantic Ocean and Belmar's wide, beautiful beaches and boardwalk, and just steps from serene Silver Lake, home to the first flock of swans bred in America. Enjoy casual Victorian ambience on our expansive, wraparound porch, where relaxing in a rocker takes you to the seashore of days gone by. Spacious common areas include a cafe-style brick patio ready for barbecues or refreshing beverages, our large living room with its lovely stone fireplace and state-of-the-art entertainment center, and the grand dining room and library—perfect for quiet moments of reading, writing, or unwinding by our tranquil aquarium. Bikes, beach badges, AC available. The guest pantry has a refrigerator, microwave, dishes, etc. Available for family reunions, retreats, and weddings. The inn is child-friendly.

Hosts: Tom and Rosemary Volker
Rooms: 12 (3PB; 9SB) $55-125
Extended Continental Breakfast
Credit Cards: A, B, C
Notes: 2, 5, 7, 8, 9, 10, 11, 12

The Inn at the Shore

welcome; 7 Children welcome; 8 Tennis nearby; 9 Swimming nearby; 10 Golf nearby; 11 Skiing nearby; 12 May be booked through travel agent.

NEW JERSEY

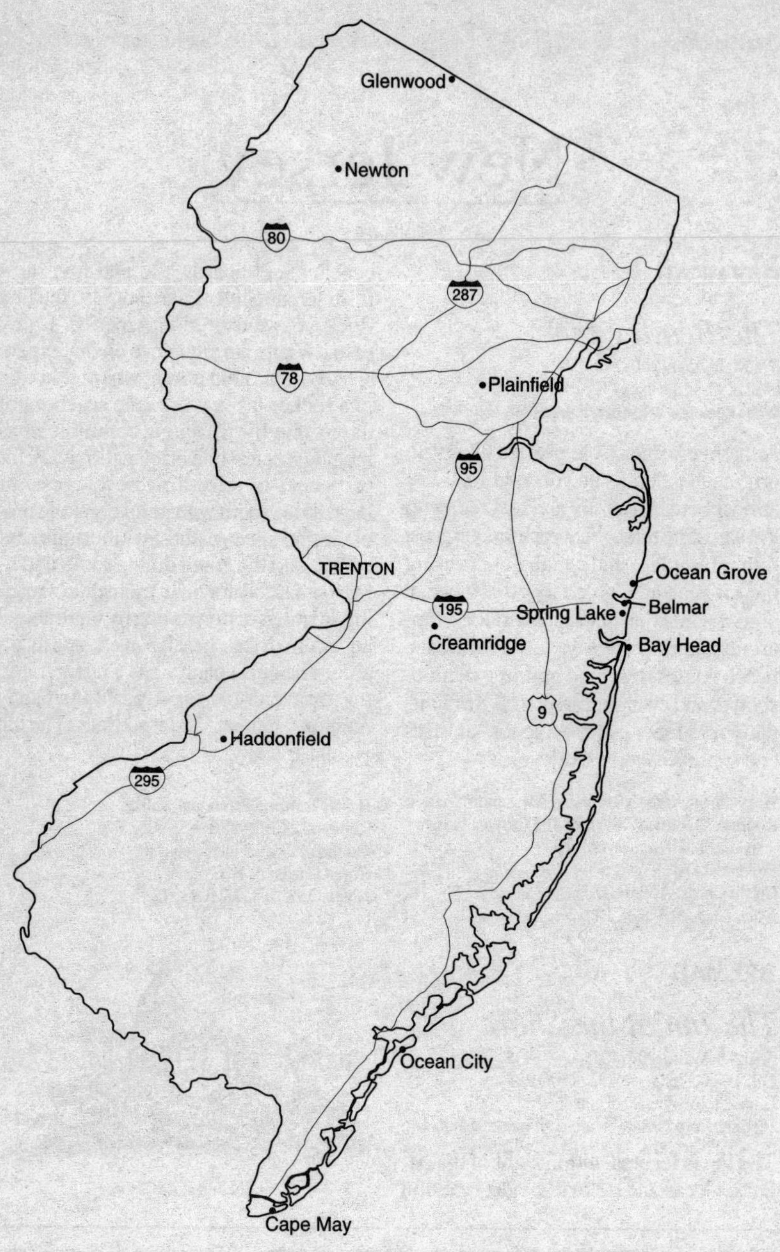

Glenwood
Newton
80
287
78
Plainfield
95
TRENTON
195
Creamridge
Ocean Grove
Belmar
Spring Lake
Bay Head
9
Haddonfield
295
Ocean City
Cape May

CAPE MAY

Angel of the Sea B&B

5-7 Trenton Avenue, 08204
(609) 884-3369; (800) 848-3369;
FAX (609) 884-3331
Web site: http://www.angelofthesea.com

Angel of the Sea is a romantic Victorian mansion with ocean views, twenty-seven rooms with private baths, gourmet breakfasts, afternoon tea, wine and cheese, bikes. Rated in Reed Travel Group's 1996 *Official Hotel Guide* as one of the top two bed and breakfasts in North America. A stay at the Angel will be an unforgettable experience filled with good friends, good food, and cherished memories.

Hosts: Gregg and Lorie Whissell
Rooms: 27 (PB) $95-285
Full Breakfast
Credit Cards: A, B, C
Notes: 2, 5, 8, 9, 10

The Henry Sawyer Inn

722 Columbia Avenue, 08204-2332
(609) 884-5667; (800) 449-5667;
FAX (609) 884-9406
Web site: http://www.beachcomber.com/Bbs/sawyer.html

An elegant 1877 Victorian bed and breakfast inn. All our spacious, airy rooms and suites have private baths, refrigerators, air-conditioners, TVs, and hair dryers. Some accommodations have other amenities, including a private veranda, fireplaces, a whirlpool tub, and VCRs. All accommodations include a full breakfast and afternoon refreshments; the use of beach tags, towels, and chairs; private hot and cold beach showers; and off-street parking. A short walk to the Washington Street Mall, Washington Square stores, major antique shops, tennis courts, ocean promenade and beach, and fine restaurants.

Hostesses: Mary and Barbara Morris
Rooms: 5 (PB) $85-175
Full Breakfast
Credit Cards: A, B, C, D
Notes: 2, 5, 7

The Inn on Ocean

25 Ocean Street, 08204
(609) 884-7070; (800) 304-4477;
FAX (609) 884-1384
E-mail: innocean@bellatlantic.net
Web site: http://www.capenet.com/capemay/innocean

An intimate, elegant Victorian inn. Fanciful Second Empire style with an exuberant personality. Beautifully restored. King and queen beds. Private baths. Fireplaces. Fully air-conditioned. Full breakfasts. Wicker-filled ocean-view porches. Billiard room. Open all seasons. Free onsite parking available. Guests say: "A slice of Heaven for a few days." "Great time—God bless!"

Hosts: Jack and Katha Davis
Rooms: 5 (PB) $99-229
Full Breakfast
Credit Cards: A, B, C, D, E
Notes: 2, 5, 8, 9, 10, 12

John Wesley Inn

30 Gurney Street, 08204
(609) 884-1012

This is a Carpenter Gothic 1869 Victorian, exquisitely and romantically restored. Lace curtains and American antiques decorate each room. Guests are refreshed

---

NOTES: Credit cards accepted: A Master Card; B Visa; C American Express; D Discover; E Diners Club; F Other; 2 Personal checks accepted; 3 Lunch available; 4 Dinner available; 5 Open all year; 6 Pets welcome; 7 Children welcome; 8 Tennis nearby; 9 Swimming nearby; 10 Golf nearby; 11 Skiing nearby; 12 May be booked through travel agent.

by the breeze-filled verandas and the air-conditioned rooms and apartments. The inn is centrally located in Cape May's primary historic district. Only ½ block from the beach, with onsite parking.

Hosts: John and Rita Tice
Rooms: 8 (6PB; 2SB) $95-165
Continental Breakfast
Credit Cards: none
Notes: 2, 5, 7, 8, 9, 10

The Kings Cottage

The Kings Cottage

9 Perry Street, 08204
(609) 884-0415
Web site: http://www.beachcomber.com

This three-story "Stick Style" Victorian cottage is an exquisite example of the work done by noted architect Frank Furness. Taking full advantage of its location, the guest rooms—all with private baths—and the two wicker-filled verandas optimize the ocean views. The interior has been lovingly restored and furnished in true Victorian fashion to reflect the grandeur of that period. Antiques abound, especially in the parlor and formal dining room, where a full breakfast is served, utilizing fine china, crystal, and silver—all the trappings that make life that much more enjoyable. You may enjoy afternoon tea on the veranda or in the formal garden.

Hosts: Patricia and Tony Marino
Rooms: 9 (PB) $95-275
Full Breakfast
Credit Cards: A, B
Notes: 5, 8, 9, 10

The Mason Cottage

625 Columbia Avenue, 08204
(609) 884-3358; (800) 716-2766

Built in 1871 for a wealthy Philadelphia businessman, the inn is in the French Empire style. The Mason family purchased the house in 1945 and started welcoming guests in 1946. The curved, wood-shingle mansard roof was built by local shipyard carpenters. Restored original furniture remains in the house. The house has endured the 1878 Cape May fire and several hurricanes. Honeymoon packages and gift certificates available. One block from the ocean. AC in all rooms and suites.

Hosts: Dave and Joan Mason
Rooms: 5 + 4 suites (PB) $95-265
Full Breakfast
Credit Cards: A, B, C
Notes: 2, 7 (over 12), 8, 9, 10, 12

The Mooring

801 Stockton Avenue, 08204
(609) 884-5425; FAX (609) 884-1357
Web site: http://www.themooring.com

Built in 1882, the Mooring is one of Cape May's original guest houses. Enjoy the comfortable elegance of this classic Second Empire inn, with its grand entrance hall and wide, spiral staircase leading to the spacious guest rooms—each of which has period furnishings, private bath, and ceiling fan; most have air-conditioning. A full breakfast and afternoon tea are served in the dining room at tables for two. The Mooring is a block from the beach, within easy walking distance of shops and restaurants. Free onsite parking; low weekday rates off-season.

Hostess: Leslie Valenza
Rooms: 12 (PB) $75-165
Full Breakfast
Credit Cards: A, B
Notes: 2, 7 (over 5), 8, 9, 10, 12

The Queen Victoria®

102 Ocean Street, 08204
(609) 884-8702
E-mail: qvinn@bellatlantic.net
Web site: http://www.queenvictoria.com

The Queen Victoria includes three 19th-century homes that have been restored and furnished with antiques. There are two parlors, one with a fireplace and one with TV and games. Two dining rooms serve a hearty, country breakfast and afternoon tea. Special services include free bicycles, beach showers and towels, and turned-down beds with a special chocolate on your pillow. All rooms have AC and private baths—many with whirlpool tubs.

Hosts: Joan and Dane Wells
Rooms: 21 (PB) $105-290
Full Breakfast
Credit Cards: A, B
Notes: 2, 5, 7, 8, 9, 10, 12

Sea Holly B&B

815 Stockton Avenue, 08204
(609) 884-6294; FAX (609) 884-5157

Located in the Victorian area of historic Cape May, the Sea Holly is an elegant, three-story Gothic cottage with Italianate detailing. Rooms are furnished with authentic Renaissance Revival and Eastlake antiques. All rooms have private baths; some have ocean views. Guest rooms are airy and comfortable, each having AC for summer and central heating for a cozy winter stay. The Sea Holly is 1 block from the ocean, within walking distance of the Victorian Mall and restaurants.

Hostess: Christy Lacey-Igoe
Rooms: 8 (PB) $50-200
Full Breakfast
Credit Cards: A, B, C
Notes: 2 (deposit only), 5, 8, 9, 10, 12

White Dove Cottage

White Dove Cottage

619 Hughes Street, 08204
(609) 884-0613; (800) 321-3683

Elegant 1886 bed and breakfast situated in the center of the historical district on a quiet, gaslit, residential street. Two blocks from the beach, 1 block from the shopping area. Room AC in the summer. Suites with fireplace and Jacuzzi, all rooms with private bath. A full breakfast is served; afternoon tea or snacks. Weekend murder mysteries, January–March.

Hosts: Frank and Sue Smith
Rooms: 6 (PB) $80-215
Full Breakfast
Credit Cards: none
Notes: 2, 5, 8, 9, 10, 12

welcome; 7 Children welcome; 8 Tennis nearby; 9 Swimming nearby; 10 Golf nearby; 11 Skiing nearby; 12 May be booked through travel agent.

Windward House

24 Jackson Street, 08204
(609) 884-3368; FAX (609) 884-1575
Web site: http://www.beachcomber.com/capemay/bbs/windward.html

The elegant Edwardian, seaside inn has an entryway and staircase that are perhaps the prettiest in town. Spacious guest rooms filled with antiques have king and queen beds, AC, and TVs. Three sun and shade porches, cozy parlor fireplace, Christmas finery. The inn is located in the historic district, a half block from the beach and shopping mall. Rates include homemade breakfast, afternoon refreshments, beach passes, and parking. Midweek discounts; off-season weekend packages.

Hosts: Sandy and Owen Miller
Rooms: 8 (PB) $85-179
Full Breakfast
Credit Cards: A, B
Notes: 2, 5, 7 (over 8), 8, 9, 10, 12

The Wooden Rabbit Inn

The Wooden Rabbit Inn

609 Hughes Street, 08204
(609) 884-7293; FAX (609) 898-6081

Charming country inn in the heart of Cape May, surrounded by Victorian cottages. Cool, shady street—the prettiest in Cape May. Two blocks to beaches, 1 block to shops and fine restaurants. Guest rooms have air-conditioning, private baths, and TVs, and comfortably sleep two to four. Country decor with a relaxed family atmosphere. Delicious breakfasts, afternoon tea. Three pet cats to fill your laps. Open year-round. Families welcome.

Hosts: Nancy and Dave McGonigle
Rooms: 4 (PB) $90-200
Full Breakfast
Credit Cards: A, B
Notes: 2, 5, 7, 8, 9, 10, 12

CREAM RIDGE

Earthfriendly B&B

17 Olde Noah Hunt Road, 08514
(609) 259-9744; FAX (732) 308-9796

Located 2 miles from Six Flags Great Adventure and 30 miles from Jersey Shore. Small B&B on an 8-acre organic farm. Bright, modern home catering to children. The partially solar-heated home was designed by your host, a retired airline captain and world traveler.

Host: Jim Schmitt
Rooms: 3 (1PB; 2SB) $65-80
Full Breakfast
Credit Cards: none
Notes: 2 (in advance), 5, 7, 12

GLENWOOD

Apple Valley Inn

927 Route 517; PO Box 302, 07418
(973) 764-3735; FAX (973) 764-1050

Elegant B&B in the Early American tradition. An 1831 Colonial mansion. Pool, trout stream, apple orchard, antique shop,

Old Grist Mill, skiing, water park, Appalachian Trail, West Point, Botanical Gardens, two state parks, and Hudson Valley attractions are within a short drive. Holidays. Two-night minimum. Reduced rates for 6+ days. Special events weekends.

Hostess: Mitzi Durham
Rooms: 7 (2PB; 5SB) $70-120
Full Breakfast
Credit Cards: A, B, D
Notes: 2, 3 (picnic), 5, 7 (over 13), 8, 9, 10, 11, 12

HADDONFIELD

Queen Anne Inn

44 West End Avenue, 08033
(609) 428-2195; (800) 269-0014;
FAX (609) 354-1273
E-mail: QAInn@aol.com

This Victorian jewel in historic Haddonfield is proud of its theatrical productions, symphony orchestra, museums, art center, idyllic parks, dinosaur discovery, unique shops, and restaurants. Take a carriage ride or walking tour of period homes and churches. Short train ride to Philadelphia. Elegant surroundings with small hotel amenities. "Hospitality, history, and home."

Hosts: Fred and Nancy Lynn Chorpita
Rooms: 9 (PB) $99-159
Full Breakfast
Credit Cards: A, B, C, D
Notes: 2, 5, 7 (10+), 8, 9, 10, 12

NEWTON

The Wooden Duck B&B

140 Goodale Road, 07860
(973) 300-0395 (voice and FAX)
Web site: http://www.bbianj.com/woodenduck

The Wooden Duck is a secluded, 17-acre mini-estate about 1 hour's drive from New York City. Located on a country road in rural Sussex County, it is close to antiques, golf, the Delaware Water Gap, Waterloo Village, and winter sports. The rooms are spacious with private bath, television, VCR, phone, and desk. Features include central air-conditioning, an inground pool, game room, and living room with see-through fireplaces. The home features antique furnishings and reproductions. Biking and hiking are at the doorstep, with a 1,000-acre state park across the street and a "Rails to Trails" (abandoned railway maintained for hiking and biking) running behind the property. Wildlife abounds in the area.

Hosts: Bob and Barbara (B&B) Hadden
Rooms: 7 (PB) $100-150
Full Breakfast
Credit Cards: A, B, C, D
Notes: 2, 5, 8, 9, 10, 11

OCEAN CITY

BarnaGate Bed and Breakfast

637 Wesley Avenue, 08226
(609) 391-9366; FAX (609) 399-5048

We are an old-fashioned bed and breakfast promoting hospitality as our specialty. Located on a barrier island 8 miles long and approximately 1 mile wide, where the sea air and ocean sounds prevail. Designated by the Historic Commission as an Ocean City seashore cottage, our B&B has five Victorian rooms with the modern conveniences of queen-size beds (one with twin beds), and air-conditioners in all guest rooms. A large front porch is furnished with wicker rockers and chairs. Guests may relax under burgundy awnings after a day on the beach, walking our 2½-mile boardwalk, investigating our quaint Asbury Avenue stores, or researching the antiques along Route 9.

Hosts: Frank and Lois Barna
Rooms: 5 (1PB; 4SB) $80-160
Continental Breakfast
Credit Cards: A, B, C
Notes: 2, 5, 8, 9, 10

Delancey Manor

869 Delancey Place, 08226
(609) 398-6147

Delancey Manor is a turn-of-the-century summer house situated just 100 yards from a great beach and our 2.45-mile boardwalk. Summer fun is available for families and friends at "America's greatest family resort." We have two breezy porches with ocean views. Guests can walk to nearby restaurants, boardwalk fun, and the Tabernacle with its renowned speakers. The inn is located in a residential neighborhood in a dry town. Larger family rooms are available on request. Advance reservations are recommended.

Hosts: Stewart and Pam Heisler
Rooms: 4 (PB) $65-85
Morning Coffee (no breakfast)
Credit Cards: none
Notes: 2, 7, 8, 9, 10

New Brighton Inn Bed and Breakfast

519 5th Street, 08226
(609) 399-2829; FAX (609) 398-7786
E-mail: ddhand@aol.com
Web site: http://www.newbrighton.com

This charming 1880 Queen Anne Victorian has been magnificently restored to its original beauty. All guest rooms and common areas (living room, library, and sunporch) are furnished elegantly and comfortably with antiques. The front veranda is furnished with rockers and a large swing. Rates include beach tags and the use of bicycles.

Hosts: Daniel and Donna Hand
Rooms: 6 (PB) $95-125
Full Breakfast
Credit Cards: A, B, C, D
Notes: 2, 5, 8, 9, 10

OCEAN GROVE

Bellevue Stratford Inn

7 Main Avenue, 07756
(732) 775-2424; (877) 775-2424;
FAX (732) 774-0007
E-mail: bbergen335@aol.com
Web site: http://www.oceangrovenj.com/bsinn

Built in 1875 as a Victorian seaside inn, the Bellevue Stratford is charming and furnished in a uniquely comfortable, romantic style. All our rooms are equipped with ceiling fans and sinks and have private or shared baths. We offer oceanside accommodations and a warm, friendly atmosphere just steps from our commerce-free boardwalk and beach. Come enjoy our breezy porches, warm welcome, and renewal of the mind and body. An "expanded" continental breakfast is served at the Stratford on weekend and holiday mornings. Beach badges, sand chairs, towels available. Open May–October.

Hosts: James Bovasso and Barbara Bergen
Rooms: 20 (2PB; 18SB) $60-85
Expanded Continental Breakfast
Credit Cards: A, B, C
Notes: 2, 7, 8, 10

NOTES: Credit cards accepted: A Master Card; B Visa; C American Express; D Discover; E Diners Club; F Other; 2 Personal checks accepted; 3 Lunch available; 4 Dinner available; 5 Open all year; 6 Pets

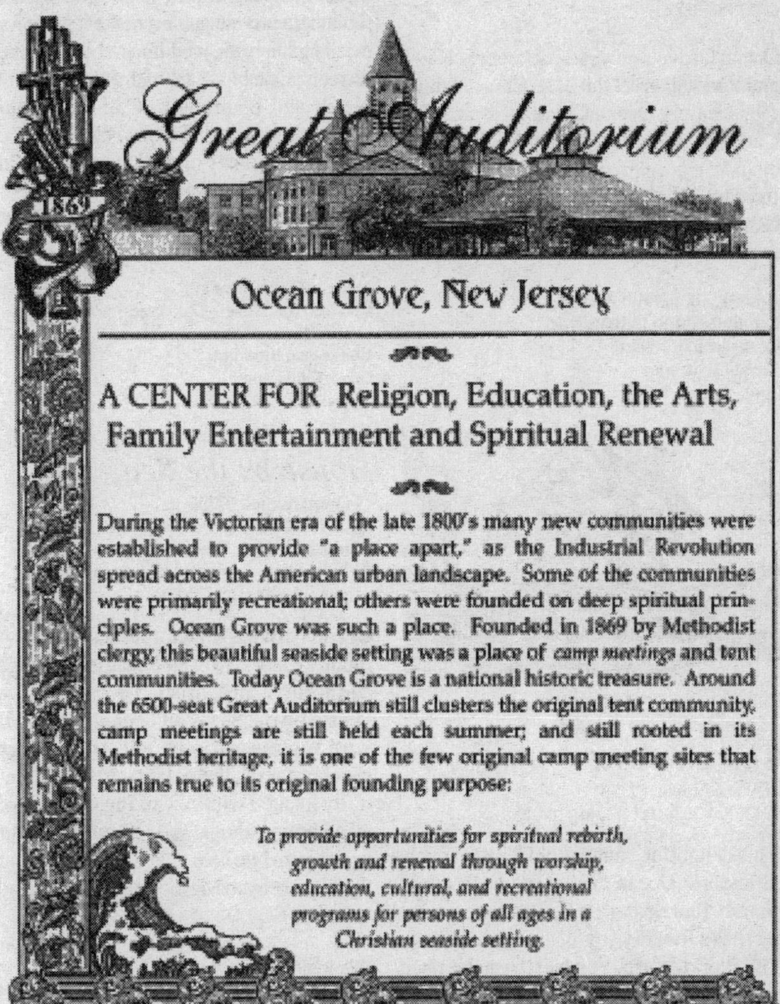

welcome; 7 Children welcome; 8 Tennis nearby; 9 Swimming nearby; 10 Golf nearby; 11 Skiing nearby; 12 May be booked through travel agent.

The Carriage House Bed and Breakfast

18 Heck Avenue, 07756
(732) 988-3232

Ocean Grove's newest! Innkeepers Kathi and Phil will greet the 21st century with a 19th-century Ocean Grove treasure. The Carriage House is a gem of Victorian elegance, a block from the ocean, a block from town, in the heart of Ocean Grove's charming historic section. We are open all seasons to pamper you.

Hosts: Kathi and Phil Franco
Rooms: 18 (5PB; 13SB) $60-95
Continental Breakfast
Credit Cards: none

The Cordova

The Cordova

26 Webb Avenue, 07756
(732) 774-3084; fax (732) 897-1666

This delightful, century-old Victorian inn at historic Ocean Grove (a beach community founded as a religious retreat center) has a friendly, joyful atmosphere with Old World charm. You feel like a member of an extended family as you chat over breakfast. Surrounded by antiques, quiet and family-oriented, the Cordova was selected by *New Jersey* magazine as "one of the seven best on the Jersey shore." Also featured in *O' New Jersey*. Guest kitchen, living room, BBQ and picnic tables in a private garden make it great for family gatherings, weddings, showers, and retreats. One block from the magnificent beach and boardwalk. Call about our murder mysteries, Tai Chi weekends, food fests, and comedy nights. Saturday night refreshments. Midweek specials. Religious programs and concerts in the 6,700-seat Great Auditorium.

Hostess: Doris Chernik
Rooms: 16 + 2 suites + 2 cottages (5PB; 15SB) $48-99
Continental Breakfast
Credit Cards: none
Notes: 2, 5, 7, 8, 9, 10, 12

House by the Sea

14 Ocean Avenue, 07756
(732) 775-2847; FAX (732) 502-0403
E-mail: housebysea@monmouth.com
Web site: http://www.travelguides.com/bb/house_by_the_sea

Ocean Grove is a Victorian seaside community founded in 1869, featuring a large auditorium for Christian worship. The House by the Sea is an oceanfront B&B with eighteen rooms and three large porches facing the Atlantic Ocean. Centrally located within walking distance of all activities, shops, and restaurants. Your innkeepers live here year-round and share their home from Memorial Day weekend to Labor Day.

Hosts: Sally and Alyn Heim
Rooms: 18 (10PB; 8SB) $55-99
Continental Breakfast
Credit Cards: none
Notes: 2, 8, 9 (beach), 10

The Lillagaard Inn

5 Abbott Avenue, 07756
(732) 988-1216
Web site: http://www.lillagaard.com

Dick and Jane Wehr look forward to welcoming guests to their charming inn. The Lillagaard is a twenty-four-room Victorian adhering to the charm of an earlier time, offering a quiet interlude for visitors to the Jersey shore with its warm, friendly atmosphere. We are steps from the beach, providing ocean-view rooms.

Hosts: Dick and Jane Wehr
Rooms: 24 (14PB; 10SB) $60-95
Continental Breakfast
Credit Cards: none

Ocean Plaza Inn

Ocean Plaza Inn

18 Ocean Pathway, 07756
(732) 774-6552; (888) 891-9442;
FAX (732) 869-1180

Guests have regarded the award-winning Ocean Plaza Inn as their "home away from home." Warm hospitality; bright, sunny, newly renovated rooms; and the beach 1 block away make the Ocean Plaza the ultimate bed and breakfast experience. All of the guest rooms have brand-new bathrooms, TV, VCR combinations, and central air-conditioning. The foyer is always welcoming for guests to relax and listen to classical music or read a book. The salty smell of ocean breezes and a fine view can be enjoyed on any of the wraparound porches. After a visit, one feels like part of the Ocean Plaza family.

Hosts: Valerie and Jack Green
Rooms: 18 (PB)
Continental Breakfast
Credit Cards: A, B
Notes: 2, 5, 8, 9 (summer), 10

Ocean Vista

13 Ocean Avenue, 07756
(732) 776-2500

Located on the oceanfront, Ocean Vista offers three gracious porches filled with rocking chairs and morning sun. With rooms reminiscent of turn-of-the-century beachfront rooming houses, we offer both private and shared baths. Coffee/tea and muffins are served each morning while you take in the beautiful ocean view. Children are welcome but must be chaperoned. Ocean Vista is a smoke-free building.

Hosts: Peter and Diane Herr
Rooms: 27 (14PB; 13SB) $60-150
Continental Breakfast
Credit Cards: A, B, C

Pine Tree Inn

10 Main Avenue, 07756
(732) 775-3264; FAX (732) 775-2939

A small Victorian inn offering a quiet interlude for visitors to the Jersey shore—truly a bed and breakfast adhering to the charm of an earlier time. Enjoy breakfast each morning amidst midsummer ocean breezes on our front porch or sideyard. A popular seaside resort since 1869, our village is a historic landmark. Commercial-free boardwalk, uncrowded beaches.

Hostess: Karen Mason
Rooms: 12 (4PB; 7SB) $45-110
Continental Plus Breakfast
Credit Cards: A, B
Notes: 2, 5, 7 (12 and older), 8, 9, 10, 11

PLAINFIELD

The Pillars of Plainfield

922 Central Avenue, 07060
(908) 753-0922; (800) 888-PILLARS (745-5277)
E-mail: pillars2@juno.com
Web site: http://www.bestinns.net/usa/nj/pillars.html

A restored mansion in the Van Wyck Brooks Historic District. Close to I–95, GS Parkway, and the Newark airport. Take the train to NYC. Full Swedish breakfast. Rooms have phone, TV, AC. Relax in front of our wood-burning fireplaces, use our library, or play the organ. We want you to feel at home.

Hosts: Chuck and Tom Hale
Rooms: 6 (PB) $79-109
Full Breakfast
Credit Cards: A, B, C
Notes: 2, 5, 6 (dogs), 7 (over 12), 8, 9, 10, 11, 12

The Pillars of Plainfield

SPRING LAKE

Hamilton House Inn

15 Mercer Avenue, 07762
(732) 449-8282; FAX (732) 449-0206
E-mail: relax@hamiltonhouseinn.com
Web site: http://www.hamiltonhouseinn.com

The aroma of fresh-baked bread beckons you to our cheery dining room for breakfast served at intimate tables. Sip iced tea by our backyard pool, enjoy the ocean view from our front porch, stroll the boardwalk, or spend the day on the white, sandy Atlantic beaches a few steps away. Relax in our spacious parlor with central air in summer and cozy fireplaces during the cool seasons. Old-world hospitality.

Hosts: Anne and Bud Benz
Rooms: 8 (PB) $115-225
Full Breakfast
Credit Cards: A, B, C, D, E
Notes: 2, 5, 8, 9 (on premises), 10

White Lilac Inn

414 Central Avenue, 07762
(732) 449-0211; FAX (732) 295-3976

We are in the shore region! The White Lilac Inn, circa 1888, with its triple-tiered porches, reflects the graciousness of a southern style that allows guests to relax and enjoy the simple life of an earlier time. Sit by the fire and enjoy friendly hospitality. Breakfast is full, leisurely, homemade, and served at tables for two in our Garden Room and enclosed porch. Discover the romance at the end of each day. Closed January 1–February 10.

Host: Mari and Chuck Slocum
Rooms: 10 (8PB; 2SB) $89-159
Full Breakfast
Credit Cards: A, B, C, D
Notes: 2, 7 (14 and older), 8, 9, 10, 12

NOTES: Credit cards accepted: A Master Card; B Visa; C American Express; D Discover; E Diners Club; F Other; 2 Personal checks accepted; 3 Lunch available; 4 Dinner available; 5 Open all year; 6 Pets

New Mexico

Advance Reservations Inn Arizona/Mi Casa Su Casa/Old Pueblo Homestays B&B RSO

PO Box 950, **Tempe, AZ,** 85280-0950
(602) 990-0682; (800) 456-0682 (reservations);
FAX (602) 990-3390
E-mail: micasa@primenet.com
Web site: http://www.micasa.com

Since 1981, we have listed inspected, clean, comfortable homestays, inns, cottages, and ranches in Arizona and the Southwest. We list about 200 modest-to-luxurious, historic-to-contemporary B&Bs. In **New Mexico,** we list Albuquerque, Algodones, Bernalillo, Chama, Chimayo, Corrales, Espanola, Lincoln, Las Cruces, Santa Fe, and Taos. (See also our entries in Arizona, Nevada, and Utah.) We also represent two luxury villas, one in Puerto Vallarto, **Mexico,** and the second in the Costa Brava area of **Spain.** Most rooms have private baths and range from $50 to $275, based on double occupancy. Continental to gourmet breakfasts. A book with individual descriptions and pictures of the venues is available for $9.50. Ruth Young, coordinator.

ALBUQUERQUE

Böttger-Koch Mansion Bed & Breakfast Inn

110 San Felipe NW, 87104
(505) 243-3639; (800) 758-3639;
FAX (505) 243-4378
E-mail: bottgerk@aol.com
Web site: http://www.bottger.com

The Böttger-Koch Mansion is an elegant, romantic, and historic Victorian inn. It was the first bed and breakfast in New Mexico to receive the prestigious Inn of the Year award from the New Mexico Hotel and Motel Association. The inn is the only lodging in Old Town Proper, Albuquerque's largest and most historic visitors' attraction. Guests can walk to everything: restaurants, galleries, and shops. The inn is convenient to downtown and the airport. This is a AAA three-diamond award-winning bed and breakfast. Truly enchanted. For more information, visit our World Wide Web page (listed above).

Hosts: Yvonne and Ron Koch
Rooms: 7 (PB) $99-179
Full Breakfast
Credit Cards: A, B, C
Notes: 2, 5, 7, 8, 9, 10, 11, 12

NEW MEXICO

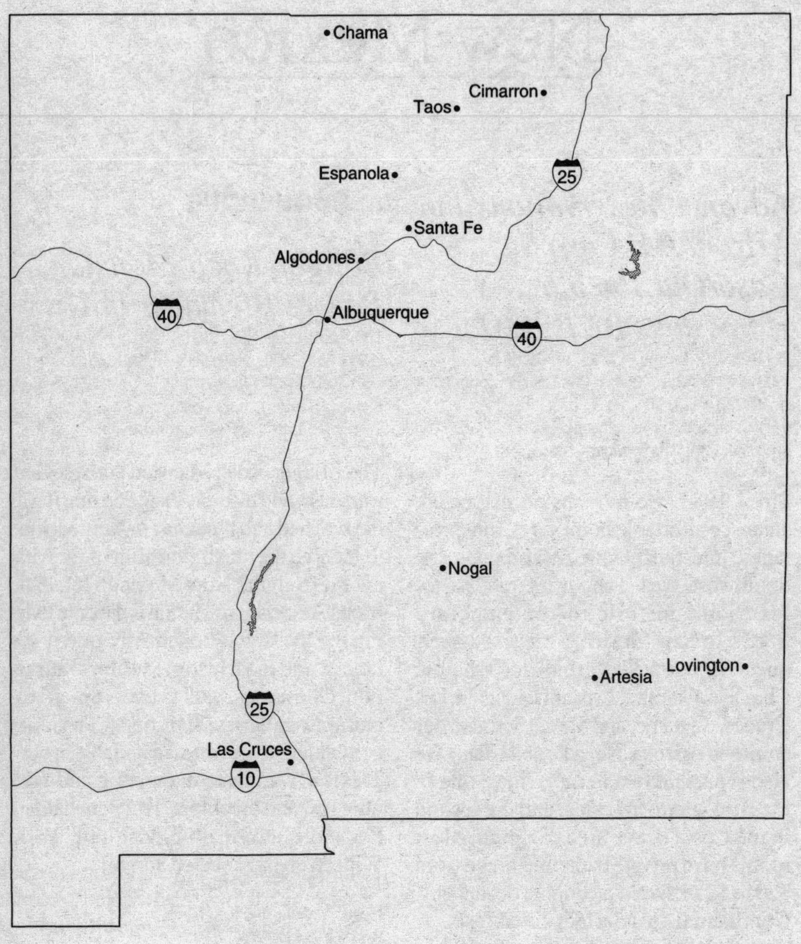
Chama
Cimarron
Taos
Espanola
25
Santa Fe
Algodones
40
Albuquerque
40
Nogal
Lovington
Artesia
25
Las Cruces
10

Canyon Crest B&B

5804 Canyon Crest NE, 87111
(505) 821-4898
Web site: http://www.rt66.com/~cmansure/ccb&b.htm

A comfortable, cozy hideaway awaits you in this contemporary southwestern home. Enjoy the splash of color with the hosts' prize-winning batik pictures. Angels, antiques, and collectibles from traveling and teaching in Africa are sprinkled throughout. After a great day of skiing, museums, and art galleries, come home to a cup of tea or coffee. Indulge in a quiet night's sleep. Start the day refreshed with a delicious continental breakfast.

Hosts: Jan and Chip Mansure
Rooms: 2 (SB) $75
Continental Breakfast
Credit Cards: A, B, C, D
Notes: 2, 5, 7, 8, 9, 10, 11

Enchanted Vista B&B

10700 Del Rey NE, 87122
(505) 823-1301

Excellent location in Albuquerque. Large suites near mountains, overlooking city lights. Forty minutes from Santa Fe and close to the airport and the old town; 10 minutes from the Balloon Fiesta and "The Tram." Beautiful gardens. Perfect for a longer stay. Pets welcome. All suites have private entrances and private baths!

Hosts: Tillie and Al Gonzales
Rooms: 2 (PB) $62-74
Continental Breakfast
Credit Cards: none
Notes: 2, 5, 6, 7, 8, 9, 10, 11, 12

ARTESIA

Adobe Rose Bed and Breakfast

1614 N. 13th Street, 88210
(505) 748-3082 (voice and FAX);
(888) 909-ROSE
E-mail: adobe@pvtnetworks.net

Enjoy a southwestern atmosphere with beautiful sunsets and quiet evenings. Our adobe getaway is complete with lovely gardens and a courtyard that boasts a quaint goldfish pond. All rooms offer a private entrance, bathroom, television, phone, and refrigerator. Each room has its own charm, with custom lodgepole pine furniture. Handicap-accessible room with roll-in shower. Smoke-free. Free laundry facilities available. Located only 1 hour from Carlsbad Caverns and the UFO Museum in Roswell.

Hosts: Sunny and Lacy Dilts
Rooms: 4 (PB) $50-75
Continental Breakfast
Credit Cards: A, B, C, E
Notes: 2, 5, 7, 12

CHAMA

Refuge Bed and Breakfast

804 7th Street; PO Box 819, 87520
(505) 756-2136; (800) 566-4799

Impeccably adorned yet comfortable guest rooms, more than 1,000 feet of screened and covered porches, and magnificent views of the 20,400-acre wildlife refuge directly across the river from this country inn. Relaxed atmosphere with horseshoe pits, an outdoor fire pit, hiking, outdoor sports, and watchable wildlife. You'll enjoy sumptuous breakfasts and personal service and hospitality. Located only 0.6 mile from the train.

Hosts: Jeff and Jackie Nettleton
Rooms: 5 (PB) $90-120
Full Gourmet Breakfast
Credit Cards: A, B
Notes: 2, 4, 5, 7, 11, 12

CIMARRON

Casa del Gavilan

Highway 21 S.; PO Box 518, 87714
(505) 376-2246; (800) GAVILAN (428-4526);
FAX (505) 376-2247

Nestled in the majestic foothills of the Sangre de Christo Mountains, the Casa del Gavilan is a place of spirit, where hawk and eagle soar. It is a secluded turn-of-the-century adobe villa. Enjoy elegant hospitality and breathtaking views in a historic setting. Four guest rooms plus a two-room suite. Join us and experience the uncommon tranquillity of Casa del Gavilan.

Hosts: Bob and Helen Hittle
Rooms: 5 (PB) $70-100
Full Breakfast
Credit Cards: A, B, C, D
Notes: 2, 5, 7, 12

ESPANOLA

Casa del Rio

PO Box 92, 87532
(505) 753-2035
E-mail: casadelr@roadrunner.com
Web site: http://www.fourcorners.com/nm/inns/casadelrio

Casa del Rio is a micro-mini southwestern ranch with Arabian horses and fine-wool sheep. It is of authentic adobe construction, set against a magnificent cliff, known locally as Los Palacios, at the base of which runs the Chama River. The home is furnished with hand-carved, traditional, Spanish Colonial furniture and crafts. A coffee or tea tray is delivered to each room as a wake-up. Gold Medallion–certified, three-diamond rating.

Hostess: Eileen Sopanen
Rooms: 2 (PB) $90-125
Full Breakfast
Credit Cards: A, B (for reservations only)
Notes: 2, 5, 6 (horses only), 9, 11

The Inn of La Mesilla

Route 1, Box 368A, 87532
(505) 753-5368 (voice and FAX; call first);
(888) 276-7703
Web site: http://www.bestinns.net/usa/nm/lames.html

A beautiful Pueblo-style home, The Inn of La Mesilla is rural elegance in the heart of the Eight Northern Indian Pueblos. It is high on a hill with fabulous views. Quiet. Full breakfast and afternoon tea are served. Guests enjoy a Jacuzzi on a large redwood deck with views. Two rooms both have private, full baths, color televisions, and ceiling fans. Two English springer spaniels, Pork Chop and Te-Bon! Baby grand piano in great room near fireplace. Equidistant to Santa Fe and Taos. Hiking, fishing, golf courses nearby; 18 miles to the famed Santa Fe Opera.

Hostess: Yolanda F. Hoemann
Rooms: 2 (PB) $90
Continental Plus Breakfast
Credit Cards: none
Notes: 2, 5, 10, 11

LAS CRUCES

Hilltop Hacienda Bed and Breakfast

2600 Westmoreland, 88012
(505) 382-3556 (voice and FAX)
E-mail: hilltop@zianet.com
Web site: http://www.travelassist.com/reg

A secluded, romantic retreat with breathtaking sunrises, sunsets, and star-filled nights atop 18 acres. Spectacular views of Las Cruces, the Rio Grande Valley, and the Organ Mountains. Unique, two-story arched adobe brick dwelling of Moorish architecture with spacious verandas and patios. Guest rooms are beautifully decorated. Spacious baths. Enjoy romantic walks through lovely rose and desert gardens. Gourmet full breakfast is served. Lots of wonderful amenities. Loved pets welcome. Only minutes from downtown Las Cruces and Old Mesilla.

Hosts: Bob and Teddi Peters
Rooms: 3 (PB) $65-85
Full Breakfast
Credit Cards: A, B
Notes: 2, 5, 6, 8, 9, 10, 12

LOVINGTON

Pyburn House Bed and Breakfast

203 N. Fourth Street, 88260
(505) 396-3460; FAX (505) 396-7315

This folklore two-story house, built in 1935 by John Pyburn, is listed on the state and national registers of historic places. A very comfortable and romantic atmosphere, where each guest room has a special ambience and is furnished with lovely antiques, luxury linens, thick towels, and plush baths. Amenities include cable TV/VCRs; full, queen, and king beds; Jacuzzi; fireplace; and bicycle built for two. Smoking permitted outside.

Hosts: Don and Sharon Ritchey
Rooms: 4 (PB) $55-125
Continental Breakfast
Credit Cards: A, B, D
Notes: 2, 5, 8, 9, 10

NOGAL

Monjeau Shadows Bed and Breakfast

HC 67, Box 87, 88341
(505) 336-4191
E-mail: reidland@Lookingglass.net

Four-level Victorian farmhouse on ten acres of beautiful, landscaped grounds. Picnic area, nature trails. King and queen beds, honeymoon suite. Antiques. Just minutes from Lincoln National Park and White Mountain Wilderness. Fishing, cross-country skiing, fishing, horseback riding. Enjoy Monjeau Shadows' year-round comfort.

Hosts: Billie and Gil Reidland
Rooms: 4 (PB) $75-100
Full Breakfast
Credit Cards: A, B
Notes: 2, 5, 10, 11

SANTA FE

El Paradero

220 W. Manhattan, 87501
(505) 988-1177; FAX (505) 988-3577
E-mail: elpara@trail.com
Web site: http://www.elparadero.com

El Paradero is located on a quiet downtown side street, ideal for exploring the heart of historic Santa Fe. The inn's owners have turned the old, adobe Spanish farmhouse into a warm and relaxing experience of true southwestern camaraderie and hospitality. The inn is furnished in the southwestern tradition with folk art and has an eccentric, rambling character typical of old adobe homes. Breakfasts are huge and special.

Hosts: Ouida MacGregor and Thom Allen
Rooms: 14 (10PB; 4SB) $65-150
Full Breakfast
Credit Cards: A, B
Notes: 2, 5, 6, 7, 8, 9, 10, 11, 12

Hacienda Vargas Bed and Breakfast

PO Box 307, 87001
(505) 867-9115; (800) 261-0006;
FAX (505) 867-1902
E-mail: hacvar@swcp.com
Web site: http://www.swcp.com/hacvar

Hacienda Vargas Bed and Breakfast offers elegance, romance, and privacy. Conveniently located between Albuquerque and Santa Fe on the historic El Camino Real, the site has been both a stagecoach stop and an Indian trading post. Complete with an adobe chapel. Care has been taken to preserve the spirit of the Old West, the influence of original Spanish settlers, and the presence of the Pueblo Indian culture. Guests appreciate the variety of activities to be found within minutes of Hacienda Vargas: golfing, snow skiing, horseback riding, and casino gambling. All rooms and suites have private baths and entrances, and fireplaces. A picturesque setting for private parties and garden weddings.

Hosts: Paul and Jule De Vargas
Rooms: 8 (PB) $69-139
Full Breakfast
Credit Cards: A, B
Notes: 5, 7, 10, 11, 12

TAOS

Orinda Bed and Breakfast

Box 4451, 87571
(505) 758-8581; (800) 847-1837;
FAX (505) 751-4895
E-mail: orinda@newmex.com
Web site: http://www.taosnet.com/orinda

A 50-year-old adobe home. Dramatic pastoral setting on 2 acres. View of Taos Mountains, surrounded by elms and cottonwood. Decorated in a southwestern design. Original art in rooms and common areas. *Kiva* fireplaces in suites. Quiet, on a private road, but only a 15-minute walk to galleries, plaza, and restaurants. Passes to local spa are provided at no charge.

Hosts: Cary and George Pratt
Rooms: 4 (3PB; 1SB) $70-90
Full Breakfast
Credit Cards: A, B, C, D
Notes: 2, 5, 7, 8, 9, 10, 11, 12

Orinda Bed and Breakfast

NOTES: Credit cards accepted: A Master Card; B Visa; C American Express; D Discover; E Diners Club; F Other; 2 Personal checks accepted; 3 Lunch available; 4 Dinner available; 5 Open all year; 6 Pets

New York

ALBION

Friendship Manor

349 S. Main Street, 14411
(716) 589-2983
E-mail: baker@iinc.com

This circa-1880 home is tastefully landscaped with roses, herb gardens, and shade trees. A swimming pool and tennis court are provided. Our intimate interior is an artful blend of Victorian-style furnishings and complementing antiques throughout. Enjoy a breakfast of homemade breads and preserves in our formal dining room. Centrally located between Niagara Falls/Buffalo and Rochester, it is the perfect stop when traveling through or planning an intimate getaway.

Hosts: Jack and Marylin Baker
Rooms: 3 (1PB; 2SB) $55-65
Continental Plus Breakfast
Credit Cards: A, B, D
Notes: 2, 3, 4, 5, 7, 8, 9, 10

AVERILL PARK

Ananas Hus B&B

148 South Road, 12018
(518) 766-5035

The Tomlinsons invite you to share the beautiful, tranquil, smoke-free, and pet-free environment of their hillside home on 30 acres with a panoramic view of the Hudson River Valley. Ananas Hus serves breakfast by the fire in winter and, in fair weather, under the roofed patio. AC is available. Ananas Hus is located 0.8 mile off Route 43 on County Road 23 in West Stephenton, convenient to western Massachusetts and the Capitol District of New York State; this area abounds with cultural, natural, historical, and sports attractions. Great downhill and cross-country skiing is nearby.

Hosts: Clyde H. Tomlinson, Jr., and Thelma Olsen Tomlinson
Rooms: 3 (2PB; 1SB) $65-80
Full Breakfast
Credit Cards: C
Notes: 2, 7 (over 12), 9, 10, 11, 12

BAINBRIDGE

Berry Hill Gardens Bed and Breakfast

242 Ward Loomis Road, 13733
(607) 967-8745; (800) 497-8745;
FAX (607) 967-2227
E-mail: fowlerj@ibm.net
Web site: http://www.bbhost.com/berryhillgardens

This restored 1820s farmhouse on a hilltop is surrounded by extensive herb and

---

welcome; 7 Children welcome; 8 Tennis nearby; 9 Swimming nearby; 10 Golf nearby; 11 Skiing nearby; 12 May be booked through travel agent.

NEW YORK

Canton
South Colton
Wellesley Island
Crown Point
Bolton Landing
Warrensburg
Queensbury
Saratoga Springs
Valley Falls
ALBANY
Rensselaer
Averill Park
Fair Haven
Albion
Lewiston
Niagara Falls
Mumford
Palmyra
Baldwinsville
Oneida
Dolgeville
Elbridge
Syracuse
Utica
Jamesville
Clarence
Le Roy
Gorham
Hamburg
Penn Yan
Cooperstown
Branchport
Portageville
Dundee
Fillmore
Watkins Glen
Ithaca
Oneonta
Hobart
Gowanda
Hunt
Hammondsport
Burdett
Madrid
Meridale
Windham
Round Top
Bainbridge
Bovina Center
Palenville
Mayville
Chautauqua
Cuba
Corning
Spencer
Candor
Windsor
Oliverea
Pine Bush
Mahopac
Tomkins Cove
Long Island City
New York City
Hampton Bays
Westhampton Beach
87
81
90
390
88
84
684
495

perennial gardens and 180 acres where you can hike, swim, bird-watch, skate, cross-country ski, or sit on the wrap-around porch and watch nature parade. Our rooms are furnished with comfortable antiques. A 10-minute drive takes you to restaurants, golf, tennis, auctions, and antique centers. You can buy plants, dried flowers, and wreaths grown and hand-crafted on the farm to take home with you. Cooperstown and most local colleges are only 45 minutes away. Three hours from New York City.

Hosts: Jean Fowler and Cecilio Rios
Rooms: 5 (1PB; 4SB) $60-80
Full Breakfast
Credit Cards: A, B, C
Notes: 2, 5, 7, 8, 9, 10, 11, 12

BALDWINSVILLE

Pandora's Getaway

83 Oswego Street, 13027
(315) 635-9571; (888) 638-8668
E-mail: PGetaway@worldnet.att.net

Pandora's Getaway is a 150-year-old Greek Revival in a quiet village setting, minutes from all locations in Syracuse. Lots of antiques, collectibles, and country charm. Cozy fireplace in one bedroom and living room. Enjoy the front porch. Easy access to thruway, fairgrounds, SU, and SUNY Oswego. Near all central New York locations.

Hostess: Sandy Wheeler
Rooms: 4 (3PB; 1SB) $60-85
Full Breakfast
Credit Cards: A, B, D
Notes: 2, 5, 7, 8, 9, 10, 11, 12

BOLTON LANDING

Hilltop Cottage Bed and Breakfast

4825 Lakeshore Drive, 12814–0186
(518) 644-2492

Hilltop Cottage is a clean, comfortable, renovated farmhouse near Lake George in the beautiful eastern Adirondack Mountains. Walk to restaurants, marinas, and beach. Enjoy a helpful, homey atmosphere with hearty breakfasts on the screen porch. In the summer, this is a busy resort area. Autumn foliage is beautiful.

Hostess: Anita Richards
Rooms: 3 (PB) $65-85
Full Breakfast
Credit Cards: A, B
Notes: 2

BOVINA CENTER

The Swallow's Nest Bed and Breakfast

Bramley Mt. Road; Box 112, 13740
(607) 832-4547
Web site: http://www.delawarecounty.org/dcbba

We are an 1850 farmhouse with four bedrooms and a large dining room where you are served a special breakfast. We have a large room available for seminars, workshops, or just to relax in. There is hiking on our property and swimming in our pond. Nearby you will find horseback riding, fishing, hunting, golf, antiquing, and auctions. Or you may just sit under a tree or by the brook and unwind. We are located only 9 miles from Delhi College and 19 miles from Oneonta. Reservations are appreciated one week in advance, with a 50% deposit. Three days' cancellation notice required. Check-in after 1 PM; check-out by 11 AM.

Hosts: Walter and Gunhilde Kuhnle
Rooms: 4 (1PB; 3SB) $65-70
Full Breakfast
Credit Cards: A, B
Notes: 2, 3, 4, 5, 7, 9, 10, 11

BRANCHPORT

Gone With the Wind Bed and Breakfast on Keuka Lake

453 W. Lake Road, 14418
(607) 868-4603; FAX (607) 868-0388

The name paints the picture—an 1887 stone Victorian on 14 acres overlooking our quiet lake cove adorned by an inviting picnic gazebo. Feel the magic of total relaxation and peace of mind in the solarium hot tub; gather your gifts of imagination on our pleasant nature trails; unlock your unique, God-given gifts to see the purpose for your life accomplished. Fireplaces, delectable breakfasts, private beach and dock. Reserve "The Sequel," a log lodge, for small retreats, business, and friendly gatherings. One hour south of Rochester in the New York Finger Lakes.

Hosts: Linda and Robert Lewis
Rooms: 6+; $70-130
Full Breakfast
Credit Cards: none
Notes: 2, 5, 8, 9, 10, 11

BURDETT

The Red House Country Inn

4586 Picnic Area Road, 14818–9716
(607) 546-8566; FAX (607) 546-4105 (call first)
E-mail: redhsinn@aol.com
Web site: http://www.fingerlakes.net/redhouse

Located in the 13,000-acre Finger Lakes National Forest. Twenty-eight miles of maintained hiking and cross-country ski trails. Six award-winning wineries are within 10 minutes of the completely restored 1840s farmstead on 5 acres of groomed lawns and flower gardens. Enjoy beautifully appointed rooms, country breakfasts, in-ground pool, and fully equipped kitchen. Twelve minutes from Ithaca, 30 from Corning.

Hostesses: Joan Martin and Sandy Schmanke
Rooms: 5 (SB) $49-89
Full Breakfast
Credit Cards: A, B, C, D
Notes: 2, 4 (November–April), 5, 7 (over 12), 8, 9 (on premises), 10, 11, 12

CANDOR

The Edge of Thyme Inn Bed and Breakfast

6 Main Street; PO Box 48, 13743
(607) 659-5155 (voice and FAX); (800) 722-7365
Web site: http://www.edgeofthyme.baka.com

Featured in *Historic Inns of the Northeast.* Located in this quiet rural village is a large, gracious Georgian home. Leaded glass, windowed porch, marble fireplaces, period sitting rooms, gardens, and pergola. Epicurean breakfast served in a genteel manner. The location is central to Cornell,

NOTES: Credit cards accepted: A Master Card; B Visa; C American Express; D Discover; E Diners Club; F Other; 2 Personal checks accepted; 3 Lunch available; 4 Dinner available; 5 Open all year; 6 Pets

The Edge of Thyme Inn Bed and Breakfast

Ithaca College, Corning, Elmira, Watkins Glen, and wineries. Gift shoppe. High tea is served by appointment.

Hostess: Eva Mae Musgrave
Rooms: 5 (3PB; 2SB) $65-125
Full Breakfast
Credit Cards: A, B
Notes: 2, 5, 7 (well-behaved), 8, 9, 10, 11 (cross-country), 12

CANTON

Misty Meadows Bed and Breakfast

1609 State Highway 68, 13617
(315) 379-1563 (call about FAXING)
E-mail: syrettp@northweb.com
Web site: http://www.northweb.com/~syrettp

Modern center hall Colonial built in 1991. Rooms are equipped with color TV, cable, telephone, and clock radio. Office area available with computer, printer, scanner, and FAX. Conveniently located to Potsdam and Canton and their colleges. Two rooms—one with queen and one with full and twin beds—both are air-conditioned.

Hosts: Marcia and Peter Syrett
Rooms: 2 (SB) $50-60
Full Breakfast
Credit Cards: none
Notes: 2, 5, 7, 8, 10, 11

Ostrander's Bed and Breakfast

1675 State Highway 68, 13617
(315) 386-2126; FAX (315) 386-3843
E-mail: ostbbinn@northnet.org

A 22-acre country estate surrounded by board and stone fences and farm pastures. Two spacious guest rooms in our 1996 Cape Cod home are decorated with antiques. A guest cottage with kitchen overlooks an acre pond. Cable TV, ceiling fans, private baths. Awaken to the aroma of baked-apple French toast and muffins to be served in the large country kitchen, or on the front porch or rear deck. Within 10 minutes of St. Lawrence and Clarkson universities, SUNY Canton and Potsdam, three eighteen-hole golf courses, ultramodern and family farms, antique shopping, cycling, canoeing, and hiking trails. We are a working sheep farm; we raise border collie dogs and have a sheepskin shop.

Hosts: Rita and Alan Ostrander
Rooms: 3 (PB) $65-85
Full Breakfast
Credit Cards: A, B
Notes: 2, 5, 8, 9, 10, 11

White Pillars Bed and Breakfast

395 Old State Road, 13617
(315) 386-2353; (800) 261-6292

Experience classic antiquity and modern luxury in this beautifully renovated 1850s homestead. Whirlpool tub, marble and oak floors, air-conditioning, cable TV, down feather beds, and expansive windows. The home overlooks 100 acres of meadows. This quiet, rural setting is located 6 miles from Canton, the county seat

White Pillars Bed and Breakfast

and home of several colleges. Summer guests are invited to use the facilities of their hosts' cottage on Trout Lake, 20 minutes away, for swimming, canoeing, sailing, fishing, and tennis.

Hosts: John and Donna Clark
Rooms: 4 (2PB; 2SB) $50-75
Full Breakfast
Credit Cards: A, B, C
Notes: 2, 5, 7, 8, 9, 10, 11, 12

CHAUTAUQUA

Plumbush B&B

Chautauqua-Stedman Road; PO Box 864, 14722
(716) 789-5309; FAX (716) 357-9727
Web site: http://www.chautauquainfo.com

A gracious, circa-1865 Victorian Italianate hilltop villa. Antique furnishing, cordial parlor, library and garden room, five bedrooms with private baths. Country view from every window. Enjoy hiking, biking, or skiing our 15 rolling acres. One mile from the Chautauqua Institution and a twenty-seven-hole golf course.

Hosts: Gary and Mary Doebler
Rooms: 5 (PB) $90-140
Full or Continental Breakfast (seasonal)
Credit Cards: none
Notes: 2, 5, 8, 9, 10, 11

CLARENCE

Asa Ransom House

10529 Main Street, 14031
(716) 759-2315; FAX (716) 759-2791
E-mail: asaransom@aol.com
Web site: http://www.asaransom.com

The Asa Ransom House, an intimate village inn located in historic Clarence Hollow, is minutes from downtown Buffalo and only 28 miles from Niagara Falls. The inn features nine beautifully appointed guest rooms, all with private baths and most with fireplaces, porch, or balcony. Voted "#1 Bed and Breakfast" by a recent *Buffalo News* reader survey. The Asa Ransom House was awarded grand prize for the "Waverly Room of the Year," and our country gourmet cuisine has been featured in *Bon Appetit* and *Gourmet*. Clarence Hollow is known throughout the East for its treasured antique shops.

Host: Robert
Rooms: 9 (PB) $95-145
Full Breakfast
Credit Cards: A, B, D
Notes: 2, 3, 4, 7, 10, 12

COOPERSTOWN

Berrywick II

2836 Middlefield Center Road, 13326
(607) 547-2052

Located 6 miles from Cooperstown, home of the Baseball Hall of Fame, the Farmer's Museum, and the New York State Historical Association—Fenimore House and the Glimmerglass Opera House. All beautifully situated around 9-mile-long Otsego Lake. Berrywick II is a renovated 19th-century farmhouse with separate entrance for guests to a converted, two-bedroom apartment. Queen, double, and twin rooms with kitchen/sitting room and bath are perfectly suited for a couple of couples or for families with well-behaved children. Sorry, no pets and no smoking.

Hosts: Helen and Jack Weber
Rooms: 3 (SB—converted apartment) $75-85
Continental or Full Breakfast
Credit Cards: none
Notes: 2, 5, 7, 9, 10

1865 White Birch Bed and Breakfast

CORNING

1865 White Birch Bed and Breakfast

69 E. First Street, 14830
(607) 962-6355

The White Birch, Victorian in structure but decorated in country, has been refurbished to show off its winding staircase, hardwood floors, and wall window in the dining room that overlooks the backyard. We are located in a residential area, 2 blocks from restored historic Market Street and 6 blocks from the Corning Museum of Glass. A warm fire during the colder months welcomes guests in the common room, where TV and great conversation are available. A full gourmet breakfast is served each morning.

Hosts: Kathy and Joe Donahue
Rooms: 4 (2PB; 2SB) $71.50-80
Full Breakfast
Credit Cards: A, B, C
Notes: 2, 5, 7, 8, 9, 10

Delevan House

188 Delevan Avenue, 14830
(607) 962-2347

This Southern Colonial house sits on a hill overlooking Corning. It is charming, graceful, and warm, in quiet surroundings. Delicious breakfast served from 8 to 9 AM. Check-in time 3 PM; check-out time 10:30 AM. Free transportation from airport. We are 2 minutes from Market Street and Glass Center by car. TV in all rooms. Very private. Enjoy a cool refreshment on the lovely screened-in porch.

Hostess: Mary M. DePumpo
Rooms: 3 (1PB; 1½SB) $65-85
Full Breakfast
Credit Cards: none
Notes: 2, 5, 7 (over 10), 10, 11, 12

CROWN POINT

Crown Point B&B (The Wyman House)

Route 9N, Main Street; PO Box 490, 12928
(518) 597-3651
E-mail: cpbb@cptelco.net
Web site: http://www.cptelco.net/~crwnptbb

An elegant "painted lady" Victorian manor house on 5½ acres. The gracious interior is filled with period antiques. Each of five bed chambers is distinctively decorated and has its own ambience and private bath. The house boasts woodwork panels of six types of wood. Outside are three porches and a fountain amidst blooming gardens. Homemade breakfast. Located near Lake Champlain, the area has museums, historical sites, and antiques.

Hosts: Hugh and Sandy Johnson
Rooms: 5 (PB) $60-120
Continental Plus Breakfast
Credit Cards: A, B, C, D
Notes: 2, 5, 7, 8, 9, 10, 12

CUBA

Helen's Tourist Home

7 Maple Street, 14727
(716) 968-2200

Your hostess has been welcoming tourists to her comfortable, turn-of-the-century home for 43 years. Located on a quiet residential street. Guests have the run of the house, including the large living room with TV. Coffee, a toaster, and a refrigerator always are available. Visit the Cuba Lake, Cuba Cheese Shop, and Seneca Oil Springs—first oil discovered in America. A restaurant is just around the corner, a small shopping center nearby.

Hostess: Dora W. Wittmann
Rooms: 5 (1PB; 4SB) $35-40
Credit Cards: none (traveler's check okay)
Notes: 2, 5, 7, 9, 10, 11

DOLGEVILLE

Adrianna B&B

44 Stewart Street, 13329
(315) 429-3249; (800) 335-4233
Web site: http://www.virtualcities.com/~virtual

Adrianna Bed and Breakfast is located in a rural Little Falls area near I–90, Exit 29A. The cozy residence blends antique and contemporary furnishings. It is convenient to Saratoga, Cooperstown, and historic sites, and to snowmobiling, cross-country skiing, and hiking trails. Four guest rooms are offered, two with private baths. A full breakfast is served. Smoking is restricted. The home is air-conditioned.

Hostess: Adrianna Naizby
Rooms: 4 (2PB; 2SB) $55-65
Full Breakfast
Credit Cards: A, B
Notes: 2, 5, 6 (well-behaved), 7 (over 5), 9, 10, 11, 12

South Glenora Tree Farm Bed and Breakfast

DUNDEE

South Glenora Tree Farm Bed and Breakfast

546 S. Glenora Road, 14837
(607) 243-7414
Web site: http://www.fingerlakes.net/treefarm

Just 7 miles above Watkins Glen, situated on a 60-acre tree farm, this 1850 converted barn has five queen-size bedrooms with private baths. The barn has central air-conditioning, an extra furnished great room, and a guest kitchen. Enjoy the wraparound front porch, picnic pavilion, or hiking trails.

Host: Steve Ebert
Rooms: 4 + 1 suite (PB) $75-120
Continental Plus Breakfast
Credit Cards: A, B, D
Notes: 5, 7, 9, 10

NOTES: Credit cards accepted: A Master Card; B Visa; C American Express; D Discover; E Diners Club; F Other; 2 Personal checks accepted; 3 Lunch available; 4 Dinner available; 5 Open all year; 6 Pets

FAIR HAVEN

Black Creek Farm B&B

PO Box 390, 13064
(315) 947-5282 (voice and FAX)
E-mail: ksarber@redcreek.com
Web site: http://www.fairhavenny.com/bcf

Black Creek Farm is a 20-acre slice of serenity waiting to help you unwind from city life. Stroll the gardens, nap on the hammock, borrow our bicycle built for two, or read a book on the wicker-filled porch. We provide clean rooms, some with private baths and queen beds, and a hearty country-style breakfast featuring our fruit in season. Two miles from Fair Haven Beach State Park, Lake Ontario, and the Sterling Renaissance Festival, so there is always something to see and do. Check out our antique shop in the barn. If total privacy is what you are looking for, we have a guest house hidden away overlooking our 2-acre pond. Built in 1996 just for our guests to enjoy the quiet solitude of the country. There are ducks and geese on the pond, turkey and deer in the woods, and bass in the pond. Spend a week or weekend in total serenity.

Hosts: Bob and Kathy Sarber
Rooms: 4 (2PB; 2SB) $50-75 (guest house $100)
Full Breakfast
Credit Cards: A, B
Notes: 2, 3, 5, 8, 9, 10, 12

FILLMORE

Just a "Plane" B&B

11152 Route 19-A, 14735
(716) 567-8338

Enjoy a relaxing, peaceful stay at Just a "Plane." Situated on the banks of the historic Genesee Valley Canal, the three-story Dutch Colonial home was constructed in 1926. Renovated in 1995, it has four guest rooms, each with a private bath. The "Plane" in the name refers to the scenic airplane rides, offered for an additional fee. Your host Craig, a licensed commercial pilot, flies a Piper PA-22, which is hangared on the farm. In the morning, enjoy a full country breakfast in the dining room or sunroom.

Hosts: Craig and Audrey Smith
Rooms: 4 (PB) $57
Full Breakfast
Credit Cards: A, B, C
Notes: 2, 5, 7, 8, 10, 11

Hart House Bed and Breakfast

FINEVIEW

Hart House Bed and Breakfast

PO Box 70, 13640
(315) 482-5683 (voice and FAX); (888) 481-5683
Web site: http://www.1000islands.com/host

In the heart of the 1,000 Islands, our grand gentleman's cottage is a true destination for your special occasion. Adjacent to a golf course, with a fine St. Lawrence River view, we're just minutes from major boat cruises. Accessible by car, located just 5 minutes from I–81 and 10 minutes from the Canadian border, 1,000 Islands is an all-season getaway—with a difference! We offer luxury accommodations: canopied beds with decorator sheeting, cozy fireplaces, and private whirlpool baths featuring Italian ceramic tile.

Hosts: Rev. Dudly and Kathy Danielson
Rooms: 5 (PB) $125-195
Full Breakfast
Credit Cards: A, B
Notes: 2, 4 (special occasions only), 5, 7, 8, 9, 10, 11, 12

GORHAM

Gorham House Bed and Breakfast

4752 E. Swamp Road; PO Box 43, 14461-0043
(716) 526-4402 (voice and FAX)
E-mail: GORHAM.HOUSE@juno.com
Web site: http://www.angelfire.com/biz/GorhamHouse

A circa-1887, fourteen-room country Colonial-style farmhouse decorated with family antiques is yours to enjoy in the heart of the Finger Lakes. The Gorham House features spacious, beautifully appointed guest rooms. In the kitchen you will find a large collection of advertising tins, while the eat-in pantry features framed cream of wheat advertisements from the early 1900s. Guests may walk our 5 acres; explore the many different wildflowers, berry bushes, fruit trees, and herbs; relax on one of our three porches.

Hosts: Nancy and Al Rebmann
Rooms: 3 (1PB; 2SB) $70-110
Full Breakfast
Credit Cards: none
Notes: 2, 5, 7 (well-behaved, over 12), 8, 9, 10, 11

GOWANDA

The Teepee

14396 Four Mile Level Road, 14070
(716) 532-2168

The Teepee is operated by full-blooded Seneca Indians on the Cattaraugus Indian Reservation. Max is of the Turtle Clan and Phyllis of the Wolf Clan. Tours of the reservation are available, as are tours of the nearby Amish community. Good base when visiting Niagara Falls.

Hosts: Max and Phyllis Lay
Rooms: 4 (SB) $50
Full Breakfast
Credit Cards: none
Notes: 2, 5, 7, 8, 9, 10, 11

HAMBURG

Sharon's Lake House

4862 Lakeshore Road, 14075-5542
(716) 627-7561

Built on the shore of Lake Erie. Rooms offer a magnificent view of the Buffalo city skyline and the Canadian border, only 15 minutes west of the city. Rooms are new and beautifully decorated, with waterfront views. Food is prepared gourmet-style. New hot tub room and widow's watch overlooking Lake Erie available. Reservations and a two-night minimum stay are required. We offer discounts every month—for example, one free night with a two-night stay.

Hosts: Sharon and Vince DiMaria
Rooms: 2 (1PB; 1SB) $100-110
Full Gourmet Breakfast
Credit Cards: none
Notes: 2, 3, 4, 5, 7 (by reservation), 9, 10, 11

HAMMONDSPORT

The Amity Rose B&B

8264 Main Street, 14840
(607) 569-3408; (800) 982-8818;
FAX (607) 569-2504
E-mail: amtyrose@ptd.net
Web site: http://www.amityroseinn.com

A 1900 home decorated like country. Just as you enter the Village, Keabemaid Dinner Boat and the lake are nearby. Located in the Finger Lakes wine country of New York State. Four lovely rooms, all with private baths and air, two with whirlpool soaking tubs. Balcony, downstairs porch, large living room fireplace. Full breakfast, all queen beds.

Hosts: Frank and Ellen Laufersweiler
Rooms: 4 (PB) $85-115
Full Breakfast
Credit Cards: F
Notes: 2

The Blushing Rose Bed and Breakfast

The Blushing Rose B&B

11 William Street, 14840
(607) 569-3402; (800) 982-8818;
FAX (607) 569-2504
E-mail: blusrose@ptd.net
Web site: http://www.blushingroseinn.com

An 1843 Italianate inn in the historic village of Hammondsport. Lake nearby. Shopping, restaurants, museum. We have four lovely, large rooms, queen beds, air, private baths, in-room coffee, sitting areas. Wicker front porch parlor and breakfast room with full breakfast.

Hosts: Ellen and Frank Laufersweiler
Rooms: 4 (PB) $85-105
Full Breakfast
Credit Cards: F
Notes: 2, 8, 9, 10

HAMPTON BAYS

House on the Water

Box 106, 11946
(516) 728-3560

Quiet waterfront residence in Hampton Bays surrounded by 2 acres of gardens on Shinnecock Bay. A pleasant neighborhood on a peninsula, good for jogging and walking. Two miles to ocean beaches, 7 miles to Southampton. Kitchen facilities, bicycles, boats, lounges, and umbrellas. A full breakfast from 8 AM to noon is served on the terrace overlooking the water. Watch the boats and swans go by. Adults only. No pets. Rooms have water views and private baths and entrances. German, French, and Spanish are spoken.

Hostess: Mrs. Ute
Rooms: 3 (2PB; 1SB) $95-115
Full Breakfast
Credit Cards: none
Notes: 2, 7 (over 12), 8, 9, 10, 12 (10 percent)

HOBART

Breezy Acres Farm

RD 1, Box 191, 13788
(607) 538-9338

For a respite from busy, stressful lives, visit us. We offer cozy accommodations with private baths in our circa-1830s farmhouse. You'll awaken refreshed to wonderful aromas from the kitchen. A full, homemade breakfast will be served to you while you plan your day. You could spend a week here leisurely exploring the museums, Howe Caverns, and the Baseball Hall of Fame—but leave some time every day to roam our 300 acres, or to sit in a wicker swing on our old-fashioned, pillared porches, soaking in the views of meadows, pastures, and rolling hills. Or make use of the golfing, tennis, fishing, and skiing facilities nearby.

Hosts: Joyce and David Barber
Rooms: 3 (PB) $60-75
Full Homemade Breakfast
Credit Cards: A, B, C
Notes: 2, 5, 7 (some restrictions), 8, 9, 10, 11

HUNT

Edgerley Bed and Breakfast

9303 Creek Road, 14846–9740
(716) 468-2149
E-mail: snuggs2@juno.com

Edgerley Bed and Breakfast is located on 14 quiet acres in the beautiful Genesee Valley of western New York, 5 minutes from Letchworth State Park and 10 minutes from Swain Ski Resort. We have a cottage that sleeps ten. Swimming, golf, and horseback riding are available. Hot tub solarium room, fireplaces, library. Two guest rooms have Jacuzzis. We welcome Christian retreats.

Hosts: Jane and Ed Peterson
Rooms: 5 (PB) $95-150
Full Breakfast
Credit Cards: none
Notes: 2, 5, 9, 10, 11

ITHACA

Log Country Inn B&B of Ithaca

PO Box 581, 14851
(607) 589-4771; (800) 274-4771;
FAX (607) 589-6151
E-mail: wanda@logtv.com
Web site: http://www.logtv.com/inn

Escape to the rustic charm of a log house at the edge of 7,000 acres of state forest in the Finger Lakes region. Modern accommodations provided in the spirit of international hospitality. Awaken to the sound of birds and explore the peaceful surroundings. Enjoy full European breakfasts with blintzes or Russian pancakes. Sauna and afternoon tea available. Access to hiking and cross-country trails. Cornell University, Ithaca College, Corning Glass Center, wineries close by. Your hostess is a biologist.

Hostess: Wanda Grunberg
Rooms: 5 (3PB; 2SB) $55-85
Full Breakfast
Credit Cards: A, B, C
Notes: 2, 5, 6, 7, 8, 9, 10, 11, 12

A Slice of Home

178 N. Main Street, **Spencer,** 14883
(607) 589-6073; FAX (607) 589-4698
E-mail: slice@lightlink.com
Web site: http://www.fingerlakes.net/sliceof home

A Slice of Home is a newly remodeled,150-year-old farmhouse with four bedrooms. Enjoy our country cooking with hearty breakfasts each morning. The home is located in the Finger Lakes winery area, just 20 minutes from Ithaca and Watkins Glen. Hiking, tenting, bicycle tours, and cross-country skiing are available. Hospitality is our specialty.

Hostess: Bea Brownell
Rooms: 5 (PB) $45-150
Full Breakfast
Credit Cards: none
Notes: 2, 5, 6 (outside), 7, 8, 9, 10, 11, 12

Heart's Desire Bed and Breakfast

LE ROY

Heart's Desire Bed and Breakfast

147 E. Main Street, 14482
(716) 768-4486

You will receive genuine hospitality in this 1913 Colonial home located in the quaint village of Le Roy in western New York. The master suite features a wood-burning fireplace and Jacuzzi. Enjoy an evening snack in our sitting room next to the fire, or stroll the lovely tree-lined streets of our historical village. It's the perfect spot to enjoy many nearby attractions such as Niagara Falls, Wyoming Gaslight Village, Letchworth Falls, and the Genesee Country Museum.

Hosts: Fred and Susan Holmes,
Dale and Mariann Conner
Rooms: 4 (2PB; 2SB) $65-95
Full Breakfast
Credit Cards: none
Notes: 2, 5, 7, 8, 10

Oatka Creek Bed and Breakfast

71 E. Main Street, 14482
(716) 768-6990

Enjoy warm hospitality and comfortable accommodations at Oatka Creek Bed and Breakfast located in the quaint village of Le Roy—the birthplace of Jello. The air-conditioned guest rooms feature antique and reproduction furnishings. A full breakfast awakens your tastebuds each morning. Walk to picturesque Oatka Creek, shops, and fine dining. The perfect overnight hub for exploring Rochester, Buffalo/ Niagara Falls, Finger Lakes, museums, colleges, antiquing, and Letchworth State Park—"The Grand Canyon of the East." Getaway packages start at $140.

Hosts: Craig and Lynn Bateman
Rooms: 4 (PB) $65-85; packages from $140
Full Breakfast
Credit Cards: A, B
Notes: 2, 5, 7, 8, 10

MADRID

Brandy-View Bed and Breakfsat

24 Walker Road, 13660
(315) 322-4429; (315) 322-4678
E-mail: hargrave@northnet.org
Web site: http://www.unidial.com/~llskinsci

Country brick home built in 1849 by Jim's great-grandfather. Located in St. Lawrence County, bordering the U.S.–Canada border. The home is furnished with family heirlooms. Snuggle under homemade quilts, relax in claw-foot tubs. This is a chance to see a modern dairy farm in action; guests are encouraged to tour the milking facility, help feed the many baby calves, or meander through thc meadows and woods. Nearby are the Adirondack Mountains, the St. Lawrence Seaway, the 1,000 Islands, and many Canadian landmarks and attractions.

Hosts: Grace and James Hargrave
Rooms: 4 (SB) $60
Full Breakfast
Credit Cards: none
Notes: 2, 5, 7, 9, 10, 11, 12

Chipman Acres Guest House

207 Brandy Brook Road, 13660
(315) 322-5588
E-mail: kpacres@northnet.org

A charming and spacious new home adjacent to the family farm communicates warmth and distinctive character with a solarium and five guest rooms. Convenient to area colleges and the majestic St. Lawrence River. Depending on the seasonal whims of the weather, there may be good cross-country skiing, fishing, skating, sailing, and swimming.

Hostess: Marion Acres
Rooms: 5 (3-4PB; 2SB) $60-70
Full Breakfast
Credit Cards: none
Notes: 2, 5, 7, 9, 10, 11

MAHOPAC

Mallard Manor

345 Lakeview Street, 10541
(914) 628-3595; FAX (914) 225-1664

Encounter the country—just 50 miles north of New York City in the lower Hudson Valley. Surrounded by informal gardens, this 25-year-old Dutch Colonial offers city dwellers a warm, relaxing country experience. Hand-painted mural and stenciling add old-world charm to the guest rooms. A homemade breakfast completes guests' restful getaway.

Hosts: Jean and Joe Costello
Rooms: 2 (SB) $70
Full Breakfast
Credit Cards: none
Notes: 2, 5, 10

The Village Inn Bed and Breakfast

MAYVILLE (CHAUTAUQUA)

The Village Inn Bed and Breakfast

111 S. Erie Street, 14757
(716) 753-3583
Web site: http://www.busdir.com/thevilinn/index.html

The Village Inn is a turn-of-the-century Victorian home located near the shores of Lakes Chautauqua and Erie, 3 miles from Chautauqua Institution and less than a 30-minute drive from Peek'n Peak and

Cockaigne ski centers. We offer comfort in both single and double rooms in a home furnished with many antiques and trimmed in woodwork crafted by European artisans. In the morning, enjoy a breakfast of homemade waffles, nut kuchen, in-season fruit, coffee, and juice in our sunny breakfast room.

Host: Dean Hanby
Rooms: 3 (SB) $55-60
Full Breakfast
Credit Cards: C
Notes: 2, 5, 6, 7, 8, 9, 10, 11, 12

MERIDALE

The Old Stageline Stop Bed and Breakfast

PO Box 125; Catskill Turnpike Road, 13806
(607) 746-6856
Web site: http://www.delawarecounty.org/dcbba/toss.htm

This early-1900s farmhouse, once part of a dairy farm, is high on a hill overlooking the peaceful countryside. Comfortable rooms are decorated tastefully with country furnishings. Guests enjoy a variety of attractions, relaxing on the porch, and taking walks to absorb the beautiful views. A full breakfast and afternoon treats are served with pleasure. Delhi, Oneonta, and Hartwick Colleges are nearby. The house is within a short drive of Cooperstown and many other attractions—antiques, fairs, auctions, and historical sites such as Hanford Mills.

Hostess: Rose Rosino
Rooms: 4 (1PB; 3SB) $60-70
Full Breakfast
Credit Cards: A, B
Notes: 2, 5, 8, 10

MUMFORD

The Genesee Country Inn, c. 1833

948 George Street, 14511–0340
(716) 538-2500; (800) NYSTAYS (697-8297); FAX (716) 538-4565
E-mail: gbarcklow@aol.com
Web site: http://www.geneseecountryinn.com

Near Rochester, at the edge of Finger Lakes, 1 hour from Buffalo, this old stone mill on 8 private acres of Spring Creek offers you history, hospitality, nature, and quiet country elegance. Tea, gift shop, private baths, TV, air-conditioning, gourmet breakfast by candlelight. Ask about Friday–Saturday dining—Italian Trattoria cuisine. Some fireplaces, canopy bed, near millpond. Walk to Genesee Country Museum near Letchworth State Park. No smoking. Resident pets. History and romance packages. AAA three diamonds.

Hosts: Glenda Barcklow and Kim Rasmussen
Rooms: 9 (PB) $85-140
Full Breakfast
Credit Cards: A, B, C, D, E
Notes: 2, 5, 8, 9, 10, 11

NEW YORK CITY

Alma Mathews House Bed and Breakfast

275 W. 11th Street, 10014
(212) 691-5931/32; FAX (212) 727-9746

A pleasant but inexpensive guest house/conference center for persons in New York for nonprofit business. In a quiet corner of Greenwich Village, the splendid facility is offered as an act of stewardship by the Women's Division of the General Board of Global Ministries of the Methodist Church. It accommodates up to thirty-five persons overnight in nineteen rooms—twelve doubles, six singles, and one sofa-couch room. Ideal for meetings—two conference rooms, a common TV lounge, two formal parlors, plus laundry and kitchenette facilities. No meals are served; delicatessen arrangements can be made for groups. Handicap-accessible. Convenient to public transportation and neighborhood restaurants and shops.

Hosts: Alison A. Proft and Victor M. Fontanez
Rooms: 19 (3PB; 16SB) $45-95
Credit Cards: A, B
Notes: 2 (with ID)

Holy Family Bed and Breakfast

10-11 49th Avenue, **L.I.C.,** 11101
(718) 392-7597; FAX (718) 786-3640

Close to the core of the Big Apple, the B&B is just a 3- to 5-minute subway ride to midtown Manhattan. The daily rate includes breakfast provisions, use of fully equipped kitchen and dining room, and a host of amenities like telephone, a small library, organ/piano, and TV/VCR. Within walking distance are family restaurants, diners, coffee shops, and a beautiful state park offering a panoramic view of the Manhattan skyline and East River. Across from the B&B is St. Mary's Catholic Church. Traveler's checks accepted.

Hosts: Tom and Sonia Salerni
Rooms: 3 (SB) $40-75 single, depending on number of nights
Continental Breakfast
Credit Cards: A, B, C
Notes: 5, 7, 8

Urban Ventures

38 W. 32nd Street, 10001
(212) 594-5650; FAX (212) 947-9320
E-mail: urbanven@ziplink.net
Web site: http://www.nyurbanventures.com

Urban Ventures, a reservation service, was started in 1979 and has been growing ever since. We're now up to about 900 accommodations in NYC. These are divided among unhosted apartments (ranging from studios to three-bedroom, three-bath extravaganzas) and B&B homes. Whatever amenities you choose, with breakfast, advice, and the loan of an umbrella. Each accommodation is inspected by UV staff.

Rooms: Approximately 900 (P&SB) $75+ for B&B, $105-600 for apartment or home
Continental Breakfast
Credit Cards: A, B, C, D, E
Notes: 2, 5, 12

NIAGARA FALLS

The Cameo Inn

4710 Lower River Road, Route 18-F, **Lewiston,** 14092
(716) 745-3034
E-mail: cameoinn@juno.com
Web site: http://www.cameoinn.com

Imagine the ambience of our gracious Queen Anne Victorian authentically furnished with family heirlooms and period antiques, all with a breathtaking view of the Niagara River. Situated on an 80-foot bluff, the inn offers the tranquillity of days past with the comforts of today. Three lovely guest rooms with shared or private baths are available, as well as our romantic "Riverview Suite." Breakfast is served at Cameo Manor (our other location) each morning. Smoke-free. No pets, please. Come and enjoy.

Hosts: Greg and Carolyn Fisher
Rooms: 4 (2PB; 2SB) $65-115
Full Breakfast
Credit Cards: A, B, D
Notes: 5, 7, 8, 9, 10, 11, 12

Cameo Manor North

3881 Lower River Road (Route 18-F), **Youngstown,** 14174
(716) 745-3034
E-mail: cameoinn@juno.com
Web site: http://www.cameoinn.com

Located just 7 miles north of Niagara Falls, our English manor house is the perfect spot for that quiet getaway you have been dreaming about. Situated on 3 secluded acres, Cameo Manor North offers a great room with fireplaces, solarium, library, and an outdoor terrace for your enjoyment. Our beautifully appointed guest rooms include suites with private sunrooms and cable television. A breakfast buffet is served daily.

Hosts: Greg and Carolyn Fisher
Rooms: 5 (3PB, 2SB) $65-130
Full Breakfast
Credit Cards: A, B, D
Notes: 5, 7, 8, 9, 10, 11, 12

The Country Club Inn

5170 Lewiston Road, **Lewiston,** 14092
(716) 285-4869; (716) 285-5614
E-mail: ctyclubinn@ccnn.net
Web site: http://www.CountryClubInn.com

Located just minutes from Niagara Falls, The Country Club Inn is a nonsmoking bed and breakfast. Three large and beautifully decorated guest rooms with private bath,

The Country Club Inn

queen-size bed, and cable TV. A great room with a wood-burning fireplace and pool table leads to a covered patio overlooking the golf course. A full breakfast is served at guests' convenience in our elegant dining room. Convenient to the NYS thruway and bridges to Canada.

Hosts: Barbara Ann and Norman Oliver
Rooms: 3 (PB) $75-90
Full Breakfast
Credit Cards: none
Notes: 2, 5, 7, 9, 10

Manchester House Bed and Breakfast

653 Main Street, 14301
(716) 285-5717; (800) 489-3009;
FAX (716) 282-2144
E-mail: slenkc@compuserve.com
Web site: http://www.manchesterhouse.com

This brick-and-shingle residence was built in 1903 and used as a doctor's residence and office for many years. After extensive renovation, Manchester House opened as a bed and breakfast in 1991. Carl and Lis received a Niagara Falls beautification award for their work. Manchester House is within easy walking distance of the falls, aquarium, and geological museum. Off-street parking.

Hosts: Lis and Carl Slenk
Rooms: 3 (PB) $75-95
Full Breakfast
Credit Cards: A, B
Notes: 5, 7, 12

OLIVEREA

Slide Mt. Forest House

805 Oliverea Road, 12410
(914) 254-4269
Web site: http://www.slidemountain-inn.com

Nestled in the Catskill Mountain State Park, our inn offers the flavor and charm of the old country. Come and enjoy our beautiful country setting, superb lodging, fine dining, and chalet rentals. Family-run for more than 60 years, we strive to give you a pleasant and enjoyable stay. German and continental cuisine, lounge, pool, tennis, hiking, fishing, antiquing, and more are available for your pleasure.

Hosts: Ralph and Ursula Combe
Rooms: 21 (17PB; 4SB) $50-75
Full Breakfast
Credit Cards: A, B, D
Notes: 2, 3, 4, 5 (chalets only), 7, 8, 9, 10, 11

ONEONTA

The Murphy House Bed and Breakfast

33 Walnut Street, 13820
(607) 432-1367
E-mail: mmurphy@digital-marketplace.net

Comfortable accommodations in the historic district of Oneonta, a small, rural city nestled among the hills of upstate New York. This 1920 bed and breakfast home is within walking distance of shops and restaurants. Tastefully prepared breakfasts and hospitality abound. Nearby attractions include college-based activities, national soccer and baseball halls of fame, the beauty of God's four seasons, and cultural events ranging from opera to dancing under the stars. Located only 30 minutes from Cooperstown, 3.5 hours from New York City.

Hosts: Mike and Nancy Murphy
Rooms: 2 (PB) $75-85
Full Breakfast
Credit Cards: none
Notes: 2, 5, 7, 8, 9, 10, 11

PALMYRA

Canaltown B&B

119 Canandaigua Street, 14522
(315) 597-5553

This 1850s historic village home of Greek Revival architecture is situated near antique stores, Eric Coverlet Museum, country store museum, Eric Canal hiking trail, and canoe rentals. Rooms are furnished with iron and brass beds and antiques. Living room fireplace.

Hosts: Robert and Barbara Leisten
Rooms: 2 (SB)
Full Breakfast
Credit Cards: C
Notes: 2, 3, 5, 7, 10, 11, 12

PENN YAN

Wagener Estate B&B

351 Elm Street, 14527
(315) 536-4591; FAX (315) 536-6985

The Wagener Estate Bed and Breakfast is a fifteen-room 1790s home, furnished with antiques and country charm. It's located at the edge of the village on 4 scenic acres with shaded lawns, apple trees, and gentle breezes. The pillared, wicker-furnished veranda is a perfect spot for quiet reflection, conversation, and refreshments. Penn Yan is in the heart of Finger Lakes wine country, close to Corning Glass and Watkins Glen.

Hosts: Joanne and Scott Murray
Rooms: 6 (4PB; 2SB) $75-95
Elegant Breakfast
Credit Cards: A, B, C, D
Notes: 2, 5, 8, 9, 10, 12 (no commission)

PINE BUSH

The Milton Bull House

1065 Route 302, 12566
(914) 361-4770

A traditional bed and breakfast, this historic house has nine rooms furnished with antiques. The house is Greek Revival in style. There are two large, airy guest rooms. Located in the beautiful Hudson Valley, near the Shawangank Ridge, it offers wonderful opportunities for hiking, rock climbing, shopping, and visits to nearby antique marts and wineries. Several churches are nearby. Old-fashioned farm breakfast with home baking.

Hosts: Graham and Ellen Jamison
Rooms: 2 (1PB; 2SB) $75
Full Breakfast
Credit Cards: none
Notes: 2, 5, 7, 9, 10

PORTAGEVILLE

Broman's Genesee Falls Inn

Main and Hamilton Streets, Route 436;
PO Box 238, 14536
(716) 493-2484; FAX (716) 468-5654

An 1870 inn with beautiful Victorian dining room and guest rooms. Chef-owned, family-operated. Fine food and wine selections, large appetizer list. Varied menu: steaks, seafood, chicken, prime rib. Delicious dinners for two. Homemade soups, dressing, breads, desserts. One-half mile from south entrance to Letchworth State Park. The history and old-world charm will bring you here; the friendly atmosphere and fine food will bring you back.

Hosts: JB and Carol Broman
Rooms: 12 (10PB; 2SB) $57-92
Full Breakfast
Credit Cards: A, B
Notes: 3, 4, 5, 7, 9, 10, 11

QUEENSBURY (ADIRONDACK AREA)

Crislip's Bed and Breakfast

693 Ridge Road, 12804
(518) 793-6869

Located in the Adirondack area just minutes from Saratoga Springs and Lake George, this landmark Federal home provides spacious accommodations with period antiques, four-poster beds, and down comforters. The country breakfast menu features such items as buttermilk pancakes, scrambled eggs, and sausages. Your hosts invitc you to rclax on thcir porchcs and enjoy the beautiful mountains of Vermont.

Hosts: Ned and Joyce Crislip
Rooms: 3 (PB) $65-75
Full Breakfast
Credit Cards: A, B
Notes: 2, 5, 7, 8, 9, 10, 11

RENSSELAER

Tibbitts House Inn

100 Columbia Turnpike, Routes 9 and 20, 12144
(518) 472-1348

Our inn is a 140-year-old restored farmhouse that has accepted guests for the past

welcome; 7 Children welcome; 8 Tennis nearby; 9 Swimming nearby; 10 Golf nearby; 11 Skiing nearby; 12 May be booked through travel agent.

Tibbitts House Inn

70 years. My grandparents, the Tibbitts, became hosts to travelers then, and we have continued introducing countless patrons to the pleasures of country living. Our grounds are spacious, tree-filled, and serene. Cheery wallpapers, handcrafted quilts, and braided and rag rugs complement the guest accommodations. Antiques are prevalent and become conversation pieces. Comfortable, cozy, and tranquil—that's Tibbitts House Inn. We are located just 1.5 miles from Albany, the New York state capital.

Hosts: Herb and Claire Rufleth
Rooms: 4 + 1 suite (1PB; 4SB) $54-80
Full and Continental Breakfast
Credit Cards: none
Notes: 2, 5, 7, 8, 9, 10

ROUND TOP (PURLING)

Tumblin' Falls House Bed and Breakfast

PO Box 281, 12473
(518) 622-3981 (voice and FAX)
E-mail: tfallsbb@francomm.com
Web site: http://www.tumblinfalls.com

Nestled in the hamlet of Purling, where the clear, cool waters of the Shinglekill have drawn visitors since the early 1800s. Hidden among the trees, perched high atop a cliff, sits Tumblin' Falls House Bed and Breakfast. Fall asleep to the soothing sounds of gentle waters. Wake up to a wonderful country breakfast served on the front porch overlooking the falls. Situated in an area rich in history, Greene County offers an abundance of vacation activities for people of all ages. Antiquing, bird-watching, hiking, fishing, skiing, and much, much more are nearby.

Hosts: Linda and Hugh Curry
Rooms: 4 (1PB; 3SB) $55-125; weekly rates available
Full Breakfast
Credit Cards: A, B, C
Notes: 2, 3, 4, 5, 6, 7, 9, 10, 11, 12

SARATOGA SPRINGS

The Lombardi Farm Bed and Breakfast

41 Locust Grove Road, 12866
(518) 587-2074 (voice and FAX)

Restored Victorian farmhouse just 2 miles from the center of Saratoga Springs. Newly decorated, private baths, AC, four-course gourmet breakfast, hot tub, and Jacuzzi. Near performing arts center, Skidmore College, National Museum of Racing, National Museum of Dance, mineral baths with massage, pools, lakes, golf, skiing, antiquing, track. Bottle-feed a baby goat on the 10-acre farm in springtime. A recreational center at the B&B has exercise machines and bicycles for the guests.

Hosts: Dr. Vincent and Kathleen Lombardi
Rooms: 4 (PB) $100-130
Gourmet Breakfast
Credit Cards: none
Notes: 2, 5, 7, 8, 9, 10, 11, 12

SOUTH COLTON

Braeside Bed and Breakfast

20A Cold Brook Drive, 13687
(315) 262-2553

Braeside, a modified Cape Cod riverfront home with a large deck and two docks, is situated on a hill on the Raquet River, nestled in the northern foothills of the Adirondacks. Great day hikes and walks very nearby. Antique furnishings and collections. Four cozy, comfortable country guest rooms. Nature beckons you to hike, bike, canoe, bird-watch, fish, kayak, cross-country ski, or just relax on the premises. Rowboat and canoe available. Golf, museums, antiquing. Colleges nearby. Freshly prepared, full breakfast at riverside. Package deals.

Hostess: Joann E. Ferris
Rooms: 4 (SB) $60; extended-stay discounts
Full Breakfast
Credit Cards: none
Notes: 2, 3 (bag), 4 (sometimes with package), 5, 7, 8, 9, 10, 11 (cross-country), 12

SYRACUSE

Bed and Breakfast Wellington

707 Danforth Street, 13208
(315) 474-3641; (800) 724-5006;
FAX (315) 474-2557
E-mail: BBW@ix.netcom.com
Web site: http://www.flbba.com/wellington

"Salt City's finest." Nationally recognized, historic 1914 brick-and-stucco, Tudor-style home designed by the prolific architect Ward Wellington Ward. Contains rich wood interiors, ample interior glass, tiled fireplaces, and cozy porches. Antiques abound. Central to downtown, medical centers, the Carousel Center, Armory Square, and universities. Short drive to Finger Lakes Outlet Center. Spacious suites, rooms with private baths. Gift certificates available. Professional B&B consulting services/classes available. Children over 6 welcome.

Hosts: Wendy Wilber and Ray Borg
Rooms: 5 (4PB; 1SB) $65-125
Full Gourmet Breakfast, weekends;
Continental Breakfast, weekdays
Credit Cards: A, B, C, D, E
Notes: 2 (and traveler's checks), 5, 7 (special arrangement), 8, 9, 10, 11, 12

Giddings Garden Bed and Breakfast

Giddings Garden Bed and Breakfast

290 W. Seneca Turnpike, 13207
(315) 492-6389; (800) 377-3452
E-mail: giddingsb-b@webtv.net
Web site: http://www.flash.net/~vault/giddings.htm

An early morning stroll through the luscious gardens, with the sounds of birds and waterfalls, enhances your appetite for breakfast. We are an upscale, historic B&B, circa 1810. Three rooms, all with

welcome; 7 Children welcome; 8 Tennis nearby; 9 Swimming nearby; 10 Golf nearby; 11 Skiing nearby; 12 May be booked through travel agent.

exquisite baths with marble and mirrored walls. Queen poster beds, fireplaces, color cable TV, and air-conditioning. Choose your favorite mood: The Honey Room—romantic; The Executive—masculine; The Country Garden—flowery.

Hosts: Pat and Nancie Roberts
Rooms: 3 (PB) $75-125
Full Gourmet Breakfast
Credit Cards: A, B, C, D
Notes: 2, 5, 7, 8, 9, 10, 11, 12

SYRACUSE AREA

Elaine's Bed and Breakfast Selections

Mailing address: 4987 Kingston Road, **Elbridge,** 13060–9773
(315) 689-2082

Elaine's Bed and Breakfast Selections is a reservation service that lists bed and breakfasts in **New York State** in the following towns: Auburn, Baldwinsville, Canastota, Cincinnatus, Cleveland on Oneida Lake, Clinton, DeWitt, Durhamville, Elbridge, Fair Haven, Fayetteville, Geneva, Glen Haven, Gorham, Groton, Homer, Jamesville, Lafayette, Liverpool, Lyons, Marathon, Marcellus, Minoa, Oneida Castle, Oneida, Ovid, Owasco Lake, Port Ontario, Preble, Rome, Seneca Falls, Sheldrake-on-Cayuga, Skaneateles, Sodus Bay on Lake Ontario, South Otselic, Spencer, Sherrill, Syracuse, Tully, Vernon, Vesper, Wampsville, and New Lebanon in the Berkshires; also, Kennebunkport, **Maine.** A descriptive catalog is available for $3 *cash* along with a self-addressed, stamped (64 cents) #10 envelope. Elaine N. Samuels, director.

High Meadows Bed and Breakfast

3740 Eager Road, **Jamesville,** 13078
(315) 492-3517; (800) 519-7533
E-mail: nmentz1@aol.com

Enjoy country hospitality at High Meadows, high in the hills 10 miles south of Syracuse. We have two guest rooms with a shared bath, a private suite, and a furnished bedroom apartment. Enjoy a plant-filled solarium and wraparound deck with a magnificent 50-mile view. A continental breakfast featuring fresh fruit, muffins, and homemade jams can be served on the deck, weather permitting. Explore scenic, lush central New York with its many lakes, nature centers, and vineyards.

Hosts: Al and Nancy Mentz
Rooms: 3 + furnished apartment (2PB; 2SB) $60-110
Continental Breakfast
Credit Cards: none
Notes: 2, 5, 7, 8, 9, 10, 11, 12

TOMKINS COVE

Cove House Bed and Breakfast

PO Box 81, 10986
(914) 429-9695
E-mail: dpscis@aol.com
Web site: http://www.pojonews.com/covehouse

The Cove House B&B is a modern but rustic home with a majestic view of the Hudson River. Enjoy coffee and pastries in the sunny, intimate solarium on the large, airy deck. History buffs can tour Stony Point Battlefield and the U.S. Military Academy at West Point. Nature lovers can hike for miles through the scenic woods

NOTES: Credit cards accepted: A Master Card; B Visa; C American Express; D Discover; E Diners Club; F Other; 2 Personal checks accepted; 3 Lunch available; 4 Dinner available; 5 Open all year; 6 Pets

of Bear Mountain and Harriman state parks. Weekend foragers will find the village of Nyack perfect for antiquing and lunch. All just minutes away.

Hosts: Pat and Dan Sciscente
Rooms: 3 (1PB; 2SB) $70-90
Full Breakfast
Credit Cards: none
Notes: 2, 9, 10, 11

UTICA

The Iris Stonehouse B&B

16 Derbyshire Place, 13501–4706
(315) 732-6720; (800) 446-1456;
FAX (315) 732-6854

Enjoy city charm close to everything, 3 miles south of I–90, Exit 31. This stone Tudor house has leaded-glass windows that add charm to the eclectic decor of the four guest rooms. A sitting room for guests offers a comfortable area for relaxing, reading, watching television, or just socializing in a smoke-free atmosphere. The Iris Stonehouse Bed and Breakfast has central air-conditioning.

Hosts: Shirley and Roy Kilgore
Rooms: 4 (2PB; 2SB) $50-80
Full Breakfast
Credit Cards: A, B, C, D
Notes: 2, 5, 8, 10, 12

VALLEY FALLS

Maggie Towne's B&B

351 Phillips Road, 12185
(518) 663-8369; (518) 686-7331

This lovely old Colonial home is located amid beautiful lawns and trees. Guests may enjoy a cup of tea or glass of wine before the huge fireplace in the family room. Use the music room or curl up with a book on the screened porch. Mornings, your host serves home-baked goodies. She gladly will prepare a lunch for you to take on tour or enjoy at the house. It's 20 miles to historic Bennington, 30 to Saratoga.

Hostess: Margaret D. Towne
Rooms: 3 (SB) $45
Full Breakfast
Credit Cards: none
Notes: 2, 3, 5, 6 (sometimes), 7, 8, 9, 10, 11

WARRENSBURG

White House Lodge

3760 Main Street, 12885
(518) 623-3640

An 1847 Victorian home in the heart of the queen village of the Adirondacks—an antiquer's paradise. The lodge is furnished with many Victorian antiques that send you back in time. Five minutes to Lake George, Fort William Henry, and Great Escape. Walk to restaurants and shopping. Enjoy the air-conditioned television lounge for guests only. Wicker rockers and chairs on front porch. Window and Casablanca fans.

Hosts: Jim and Ruth Gibson
Rooms: 3 (SB) $85 (double)
Continental Breakfast
Credit Cards: A, B
Notes: 5, 7 (over 7), 9, 10, 11

WATKINS GLEN

Clarke House B&B

102 Durland Avenue, 14891
(607) 535-7965

Clarke House is a charming Tudor-style home, circa 1920, completely remodeled and furnished with new queen-size and twin mattresses. Charming antique decor is found throughout the house. We feature a hearty breakfast, central AC, and private baths. Walk to area restaurants, attractions, and churches.

Hosts: Jack and Carolyn Clarke
Rooms: 4 (3PB; 1SB) $75-85
Full Breakfast
Credit Cards: A, B, C, D
Notes: 2, 8, 9, 10

WESTHAMPTON BEACH

1880 House Bed and Breakfast

2 Seafield Lane; PO Box 648, 11978
(516) 288-1559; (800) 346-3290
Web site: http://getawaysmag.com

The Seafield House is a hidden, 100-year-old country retreat perfect for a romantic hideaway, a weekend of privacy, or just a change of pace from city life. Located only 90 minutes from Manhattan, Seafield House is ideally situated on Westhampton Beach's exclusive Seafield Lane. The estate includes a swimming pool and tennis court and is a short, brisk walk from the ocean beach. The area offers outstanding restaurants, shops, and opportunities for antique hunting. Indoor tennis, Guerney's International Health Spa, and Montauk Point are nearby.

Hostess: Elsie Collins
Rooms: 3 suites (PB) $100-195
Full Breakfast
Credit Cards: A, B, C
Notes: 5, 8, 9, 10, 12

Albergo Allegria Bed and Breakfast

WINDHAM

Albergo Allegria Bed and Breakfast

Route 296, 12496
(518) 734-5560; (800) 625-2374;
FAX (518) 734-5570
E-mail: albergo@aol.com
Web site: http://www.AlbergoUSA.com

Italian for the "Inn of Happiness," Albergo Allegria seeks to pamper all who walk through its doors. This sprawling Queen Anne mansion (circa 1876) is a registered historic site and New York State's four-diamond bed and breakfast. It provides twenty-one gracious guest rooms with 20th-century amenities. Two acres of manicured grounds are home to the country gardens, creek with waterfall, mountain views, open fields, and quiet places. Albergo Allegria is an enchanting inn nestled in the Catskill Mountain Forest Preserve. Recreation year-round.

Hosts: Vito and Lenore Radelich
Rooms: 21 (PB) $65-225
Full Breakfast
Credit Cards: A, B, D, E
Notes: 5, 7, 8, 9, 10, 11, 12

Country Suite B&B

PO Box 700, 12496
(518) 734-4079 (voice and FAX); (888) 883-0444
E-mail: ctrysuite@aol.com
Web site: http://www.virtualcities.com/ons/ny/c/nyc6701.htm

Spacious 150-year-old farmhouse in the northern Catskills. Heirlooms and antiques provide country elegance with urban flair. Gourmet breakfasts, après-ski, afternoon treats. Restored by current owners to accommodate guests seeking comfortable yet affordable elegance. Living room with fireplace. On 10½ beautiful acres complemented by gardens and gazebo. Antique shop onsite. "A treasure to be discovered over and over again"—*Inn Review*.

Hostesses: Sondra Clark and Lorraine Seidel
Rooms: 5 (PB) $99-149
Full Breakfast
Credit Cards: C
Notes: 2, 5, 7 (well-behaved), 8, 9, 10, 11

WINDSOR

Country Haven Bed and Breakfast

66 Garrett Road, 13865
(607) 655-1204 (voice and FAX)
E-mail: CntryHaven@aol.com

Country Haven is a restored 1800s farmhouse in a quiet country setting on 350 acres. It is a haven for today's weary traveler as well as a weekend hideaway where warm hospitality awaits you. Browse through our gift shop. Additional rooms are available in a new log home. The house is located 1 mile from Route 17-E, Exit 78; 12 miles east of Binghamton; 7 miles from Route 81.

Hostess: Rita Saunders
Rooms: 6 (4PB; 2SB) $45-65
Full Breakfast
Credit Cards: A, B, D
Notes: 2, 5, 7, 9, 10

welcome; 7 Children welcome; 8 Tennis nearby; 9 Swimming nearby; 10 Golf nearby; 11 Skiing nearby; 12 May be booked through travel agent.

NORTH CAROLINA

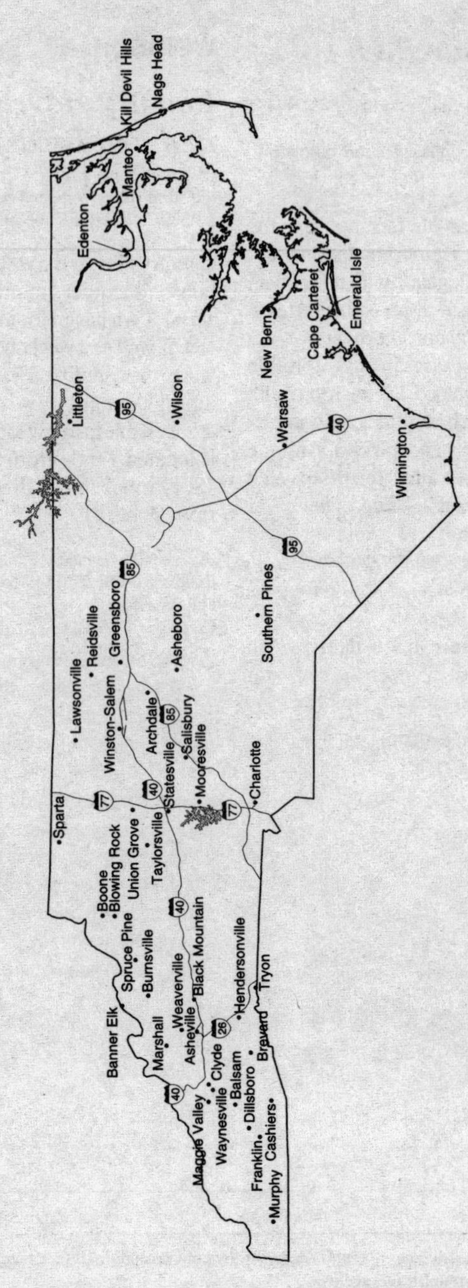

North Carolina

ASHEBORO

The Doctor's Inn

716 S. Park Street, 27203
(336) 625-4916, 625-4822

The Doctor's Inn is a home filled with antiques. It offers its guests the utmost in personal accommodations. Amenities include a gourmet breakfast served on fine china and silver, fresh flowers, terry cloth robes and slippers, and ice cream parfaits. Nearby are more than sixty potteries and the North Carolina Zoo (5 miles).

Hosts: Marion and Beth Griffin
Rooms: 2 (1PB; 1SB) $95
Full Breakfast
Credit Cards: none
Notes: 2, 5, 8, 9, 10

The Doctor's Inn

ASHEVILLE

Albemarle Inn Bed and Breakfast

86 Edgemont Road, 28801
(828) 255-0027; (800) 621-7435;
FAX (828) 236-3397
E-mail: info@albemarleinn.com
Web site: http://www.albemarleinn.com

Albemarle Inn is a distinguished Greek Revival mansion with an exquisitely carved oak staircase, balcony, paneling, and high ceilings. Located in a beautiful residential area, it is included in the National Register of Historic Places. Spacious, tastefully decorated, comfortable guest rooms have TVs, telephones, air-conditioning, and private baths with claw-foot tubs and showers. Delicious full breakfast served in our dining room and on the sunporch. Swimming pool. Unmatched hospitality. AAA three-diamond-rated.

Hosts: Diana and Tony Morris
Rooms: 11 (PB) $95-160
Full Breakfast
Credit Cards: A, B, D
Notes: 2, 5, 7 (over 13), 8, 9, 10, 12

NOTES: Credit cards accepted: A Master Card; B Visa; C American Express; D Discover; E Diners Club; F Other; 2 Personal checks accepted; 3 Lunch available; 4 Dinner available; 5 Open all year; 6 Pets welcome; 7 Children welcome; 8 Tennis nearby; 9 Swimming nearby; 10 Golf nearby; 11 Skiing nearby; 12 May be booked through travel agent.

Cairn Brae

217 Patton Mountain Road, 28804
(828) 252-9219
E-mail: cairnebrae@compuserve.com
Web site: http://ourworld.compuserve.com/homepages/mrichardson

Cairne Brae is a mountain retreat located just above Asheville on 3 wooded acres. Secluded, quiet—but only minutes from downtown. Enjoy beautiful views and walking trails. A full breakfast is served. Air-conditioned. Approved by Mobil and AAA (three diamonds).

Hosts: Millie and Ed Adams
Rooms: 4 (PB) $95-120
Full Breakfast
Credit Cards: A, B, D
Notes: 2, 8, 9, 10, 12

Cedar Crest Victorian Inn

674 Biltmore Avenue, 28803
(828) 252-1389; (800) 252-0310;
FAX (828) 253-7667
E-mail: stay@cedarcrestvictorianinn.com
Web site: http://www.cedarcrestvictorianinn.com

This 1890 Queen Anne mansion is listed on the National Register of Historic Places. One of the largest and most opulent residences surviving Asheville's 1890s boom period. A captain's walk, projecting turrets, and expansive verandas welcome guests to lavish interior woodwork and stained glass. All rooms are furnished with antiques, with satin and lace trim.

Hosts: Jack and Barbara McEwan
Rooms: 11 (PB) $135-225
Full Breakfast
Credit Cards: A, B, C, D, E
Notes: 2, 5, 7 (over 10), 8, 10, 12

Dry Ridge Inn Bed and Breakfast

26 Brown Street, **Weaverville,** 28787
(828) 658-3899; (800) 839-3899;
FAX (828) 658-8022
E-mail: dryridgeinn@msn.com
Web site: http://www.bbonline.com/nc/dryridge

This casually elegant bed and breakfast is quietly removed, 10 minutes north of Asheville's many attractions. Country-style antiques and contemporary art enhance the unique 1800s village farmhouse. A full breakfast is served, with individual seating. Relax in our outdoor spa or with quality, spiritual reading after enjoying a day of mountain adventure.

Hosts: Paul and Mary Lou Gibson
Rooms: 7 (PB) $90-120
Full Breakfast
Credit Cards: A, B, C, D
Notes: 2, 5, 7, 8, 9, 10, 11, 12

The Old Reynolds Mansion

100 Reynolds Heights, 28804
(828) 254-0496

An antebellum mansion in a country setting. This elegant, restored inn has mountain views from all rooms, huge verandas, wood-burning fireplaces, swimming pool, and AC. A continental breakfast and evening beverage are served. Listed on the National Register of Historic Places. Come see history brought back to life!

Hosts: Fred and Helen Faber
Rooms: 11 (9PB; 2SB) $60-130
Continental Breakfast
Credit Cards: none
Notes: 2, 8, 9, 10, 11

BALSAM

Balsam Mountain Inn

PO Box 40, 28707
(828) 456-9498; (800) 224-9498;
FAX (828) 456-9298
E-mail: merrily@dnet.net
Web site: http://www1.aksi.net/~cmark/balsam.htm

Nestled among lofty peaks in the Great Smoky Mountains just off the Blue Ridge Parkway, this historic inn was built in 1908, restored in 1991, and now offers fifty cheerful rooms, two 100-foot porches with rockers and a view, a 2,000-volume library, and gracious dining. Plump pillows and soft comforters will inspire pleasant dreams, while the friendly staff attend to your every need.

Hostess: Merrily Teasley
Rooms: 50 (PB) $90-150
Full Breakfast
Credit Cards: A, B, D
Notes: 2, 3 (Sunday only), 4, 5, 7, 8, 9, 10, 12

BANNER ELK

The Banner Elk Inn Bed and Breakfast

407 Main Street E., 28604
(828) 898-6223
Web site: http://www.boonechamber.com/bannerelkinn

A charming, cozy inn built in 1912, renovated and furnished with antiques collected from around the world. Five guest rooms, private baths, elegant breakfasts served on fine china, great room with stone fireplace, lovely perennial gardens with stone fountain. Ask about our honeymoon loft.

The Banner Elk Inn Bed and Breakfast

The inn is located in town, close to fine shops and restaurants.

Hostess: Beverly Lait
Rooms: 5 (4PB; 1SB) $90-115
Full Breakfast, weekends; Continental Breakfast, weekdays
Credit Cards: A, B
Notes: 2, 5 (reservations), 6, 7, 8, 9, 10, 11, 12

BLACK MOUNTAIN

Friendship Lodge Bed and Breakfast

PO Box 877, 28711
(828) 669-9294 (summer);
(813) 895-4964 (November 25–May10)

A cozy, ten-bedroom bed and breakfast in Ridgecrest, 2 miles east of Black Mountain. We're dedicated to the task of helping our guests enjoy the natural beauty and abundant attractions of our area. Start each day with a sumptuous breakfast. Most of our cozy bedrooms have two double beds and private baths; each room is delightfully different. Close to Montreat, Blue Ridge Assembly, and Christmount.

Hosts: Bob and Sarah LaBrant
Rooms: 10 (8PB; 2SB) $50-55
Full Breakfast
Credit Cards: none
Notes: 2, 7, 8, 9, 10

welcome; 7 Children welcome; 8 Tennis nearby; 9 Swimming nearby; 10 Golf nearby; 11 Skiing nearby; 12 May be booked through travel agent.

BLOWING ROCK

Inn at Ragged Gardens

PO Box 1927, 28605
(828) 295-9703
E-mail: Ragged-Gardens.INN@BlowingRock.com
Web site: http://Ragged-Gardens.com

Surrounded by an acre of formal and "ragged" gardens, our 1900s manor-style house offers an enchanting hideaway in the heart of the village of Blowing Rock. Each of our eight guest rooms is complete with a ceiling fan, goose-down comforters and pillows, and a whirlpool bath, complemented by a beautiful breakfast. We look forward to welcoming everyone into our 100-year-old home that's filled with God's presence.

Hosts: Lee and Jama Hyett
Rooms: 8 (PB) $105-150
Full Breakfast
Credit Cards: A, B
Notes: 2, 5, 7 (over 12), 8, 9, 10, 11, 12

BOONE

The Gragg House Bed and Breakfast

210 Ridge Point Drive, 28607
(828) 264-7289

Located 10 minutes from the beautiful Blue Ridge Parkway and blessed with mountain views, The Gragg House opens to a lush landscape of native wildflowers and rhododendron. Bird songs are nearly the only sound to break the silence of this secluded getaway. Hospitality at the Gragg House is an important supplement to the home's glorious setting. Your hosts like to offer friendly small touches without imposing too much activity or attention on guests who would rather be alone. A sumptuous breakfast can truly be the unexpected.

Hosts: Judy and Robert Gragg
Rooms: 3 (1PB; 2SB) $75-95
Full Gourmet Breakfast
Credit Cards: none
Notes: 2, 5, 7 (by arrangement), 8, 9, 10, 11, 12

Prospect Hill Bed and Breakfast

(See description under Mountain City, Tennessee.)

The Red House Bed and Breakfast

BREVARD

The Red House Bed and Breakfast

412 W. Probart Street, 28712
(828) 884-9349

The Red House was built in 1851 and has served as a trading post, a railroad station, the county's first courthouse, and the first post office. It has been lovingly restored and is now open to the public. Charmingly furnished with turn-of-the-century antiques. Convenient to the Blue

---

NOTES: Credit cards accepted: A Master Card; B Visa; C American Express; D Discover; E Diners Club; F Other; 2 Personal checks accepted; 3 Lunch available; 4 Dinner available; 5 Open all year; 6 Pets

Ridge Parkway, Brevard Music Center, and Asheville's Biltmore Estate. Closed January–March.

Hostess: M.O. Ong
Rooms: 7 (5PB; 2SB) $45-79
Full Breakfast
Credit Cards: A, B
Notes: 2, 8, 9, 10

Womble Inn

301 W. Main Street, 28712
(828) 884-4770

Relax in a welcoming, comfortable atmosphere. Each guest room is especially furnished in antiques and decorated to make you feel cared for. All guest rooms have private baths and air-conditioning. Your breakfast will be served to you on a silver tray, or you may prefer to be seated in the dining room. The inn is ½ mile from the exciting Brevard Music Center.

Hosts: Beth and Steve Womble
Rooms: 6 (PB) $58-68
Continental Breakfast
Credit Cards: A, B, D
Notes: 2, 3, 4 (Thursday/Friday), 5, 7, 8, 9, 10

BURNSVILLE

A Little Bit of Heaven

937 Bear Wallow Road, 28714
(828) 675-5379; FAX (828) 675-0364
Web site: http://www.inngetaways.com/nc/features/alittle.html

Get away from the day-to-day routine for a while and enjoy "A Little Bit of Heaven." This charming home offers spectacular mountain views all around. Guest rooms are beautifully decorated and furnished with queen or twin beds and private baths. While guests visit, they can enjoy an abundance of activities in the area or just relax around the house and be pampered by the warm hospitality of their hosts.

Hosts: John and Shelley Johnson
Rooms: 4 (PB) $65-85
Full Breakfast
Credit Cards: A, B
Notes: 2, 5, 7, 8, 9, 10, 11

CAPE CARTERET

Harborlight Guest House

332 Live Oak Drive, 28584
(919) 393-6868 (voice and FAX);
(800) 624-VIEW (8439)
Web site: http://www.nando.net/nao/ads/harborlight

The Harborlight, located on the central North Carolina coast, is situated on a peninsula; all suites offer panoramic water views. All suites also offer private entrances and private baths; luxury suites feature two-person Jacuzzis, fireplaces, and in-room breakfast. The guest house is minutes from area beaches, secluded island excursions, and the outdoor drama "Worthy is the Lamb"—a passion play that depicts the life of Christ.

Hosts: Bobby and Anita Gill
Rooms: 9 (PB) $75-200
Full Breakfast
Credit Cards: A, B, C
Notes: 5, 8, 9, 10

CASHIERS

Millstone Inn

PO Box 949, 28717
(828) 743-2737; (888) 645-5786;
FAX (828) 743-0208

Selected by *Country Inns* magazine as one of the best twelve inns, Millstone Inn has breathtaking views of the Nantahala forest. The exposed beams are complemented by carefully selected antiques and artwork. Enjoy a gourmet breakfast in our glass-enclosed dining room overlooking Whiteside Mountain. At 3,500 feet, it's always cool for a hike to the nearby Silver Slip Falls—or enjoy the nearby golf, tennis, restaurants, and antique shops.

Hosts: Paul and Patricia Collins
Rooms: 11 (PB) $84-154
Full Breakfast
Credit Cards: A, B, C, D
Notes: 2, 8, 9, 10, 11, 12

CHARLOTTE

The Carmel B&B

4633 Carmel Road, 28226
(704) 542-9450; FAX (704) 544-8278
E-mail: lindamoag@worldnet.att.net

Classic elegance and charm. Four guest rooms, all with private baths. Located in southeast Charlotte, minutes from the premier Phillips Place complex, with gourmet restaurants, elegant shops, and ten theatre/movie houses. Golf nearby. Easy access to I–485, 85, and 77. Nonsmoking house. Children over 12 welcome.

Hosts: Tom and Linda Moag
Rooms: 4 (PB) $79-109
Full Breakfast
Credit Cards: A, B, C
Notes: 2, 5, 7 (over 12), 10, 12

The Elizabeth B&B

2145 E. 5th Street, 28204
(704) 358-1368
Web site: http://www.bbonline.com/nc/ncbbi

This 1923 lavender "lady" is located in historic Elizabeth, second-oldest neighbor-

The Elizabeth Bed and Breakfast

hood in Charlotte. European country-style rooms are beautifully appointed with antiques, ceiling fans, decorator linens, and unique collections. All rooms have central air and private baths; some have TV and phones. Enjoy a generous breakfast, then relax in our garden courtyard, complete with a charming gazebo—or stroll beneath giant oak trees to convenient restaurants and shopping. Nearby attractions include the Mint Museum of Art, Blumenthal Performing Arts Center, Discovery Place, and professional sporting events.

Hostess: Joan Mastny
Rooms: 4 (PB) $79-109
Full Breakfast
Credit Cards: A, B, D
Notes: 2, 5, 9, 12

The Homeplace B&B

5901 Sardis Road, 28270
(704) 365-1936; FAX (704) 366-2729

This restored 1902 country Victorian home with its wraparound porch and tin roof is nestled among 2½ wooded acres. Secluded "cottage-style" gardens with a gazebo, brick walkways, and a 1930s log barn further enhance this nostalgic oasis in southeast Charlotte. Experienced innkeepers offer a full breakfast. Opened in

1984, The Homeplace is a "reflection of the true bed and breakfast."

Hosts: Frank and Peggy Dearien
Rooms: 2 + 1 suite (PB) $108-150
Full Breakfast
Credit Cards: A, B, C
Notes: 2, 5, 12

CLYDE

Windsong: A Mountain Inn

459 Rockcliffe Lane, 28721
(828) 627-6111; FAX (828) 627-8080
E-mail: themancinis@compuserve.com
Web site: http://www.bbonline.com/nc/windsong

A secluded, romantic log inn high in the Smoky Mountains offering fabulous views, hearty gourmet breakfasts, deluxe rooms with fireplaces, tubs for two, and deck or patio. Also, two-bedroom cottage suites with living room, dining room, full kitchen, fireplace, tub for two, deck, BBQ. Extensive continental breakfast provided in cottage suites. Outdoor hot tub, heated pool, tennis, hiking, llamas.

Hosts: Russ and Barbara Mancini
Rooms: 5 (PB) $130-175
Full Breakfast
Credit Cards: A, B, D
Notes: 2, 5, 8, 9, 10, 11, 12

Windsong: A Mountain Inn

DILLSBORO

Applegate Inn

163 Hemlock Street; PO Box 1051, 28725
(828) 586-2397 (voice and FAX)
E-mail: applegate@wcu.campus.mci.net
Web site: http://www.inngetaways.com/nc/features/applegat.html

Newly decorated, on one level. Footbridge to railroad and shops. Relax in the screened-in gazebo or on the deck out by Scott's Creek. All rooms have private baths and central air, and include a huge breakfast. Minisuites have kitchenettes and cable TV. All credit cards, traveler's checks accepted. AAA-rated.

Hosts: John and Andree Faulk
Rooms: 9 (PB) $65-100
Full Breakfast
Credit Cards: A, B, C, D, E, F
Notes: 2, 5, 10, 11, 12

Albemarle House Bed and Breakfast

EDENTON

Albemarle House Bed and Breakfast

204 W. Queen Street, 27932
(252) 482-8204
E-mail: reuelmari@ecsu.campus.mci.net
Web site: http://www.bbonline.com/nc/albemarle

Enjoy welcoming refreshments on the porch or in the parlor of our circa-1900 country Victorian home. Located in Edenton's historic district, we are just 2 blocks from Albemarle Sound. Our air-conditioned home is furnished with antiques and reproductions, stenciling, art, quilts, and collections. The three spacious guest rooms are complete with queen beds, TVs, and private baths. A family suite is available. Coffee awaits outside your door each morning. An elegant full breakfast is served by candlelight. Bicycles and sailing cruises are offered to guests.

Hosts: Marijane and Reuel Schappel
Rooms: 3 (PB) $80
Full Breakfast
Credit Cards: A, B
Notes: 2, 5, 7 (over 10), 8, 9, 10

Captain's Quarters Inn

202 W. Queen Street, 27932
(252) 482-8945; (800) 482-8945
Web site: http://www.captainsquartersinn.com

This Colonial Revival, circa-1907 inn is an elegant bed and breakfast with each guest room (queen/king/twin beds) offering private, modern bath (one Jacuzzi), TV, and phone. Located in the heart of the Edenton historic district. A 65-foot front porch overlooks gardens and is 2 blocks from Albemarle Sound. Each room is designed in sailing captain theme. Welcome refreshments (afternoon tea, wine, beer, cheese, etc.), a continental breakfast brought to your door (homemade muffins, breads), and as a three-course breakfast served in the "Harbor Room" Monday–Saturday and our Sunday breakfast buffet. Four- and five-course gourmet dining is offered with the mystery weekends October–March and the sailing or golf weekends April–October ($296–299 per couple). Guided trolley tours, walking tours, biking, antiquing, plantations, and art galleries are additional attractions.

Captain's Quarters Inn

Hosts: Bill and Phyllis Pepper
Rooms: 8 (PB) $80-95
Full and Continental Breakfast
Credit Cards: A, B
Notes: 2, 4, 5, 7 (8 and older), 8, 9, 10, 12

Trestle House Inn at Willow Tree Farm

632 Soundside Road, 27932
(252) 482-2282; (800) 645-8466;
FAX (252) 482-7003
E-mail: thinn@coastalnet.com
Web site: http://www.edenton.com/trestlehouse

On a wildlife refuge surrounded on three sides by water in historic Edenton. Birding, canoeing, fishing, biking, sight-seeing, and relaxing are our guests' favorite activities. The inn's interior has massive California redwood beams that came from a railroad trestle from the Southern Railroad. These beams come from trees estimated to be more than 450 years old.

Host: Peter L. Bogus
Rooms: 5 (PB) $80-95
Full Breakfast
Credit Cards: A, B, C
Notes: 2, 5, 7, 8, 9, 10, 12

EMERALD ISLE

Emerald Isle Inn and B&B by the Sea

502 Ocean Drive, 28594
(252) 354-3222
E-mail: adetwiller@coastalnet.com

Located at the ocean, this jewel of a Crystal Coast inn is truly a treasure to be discovered. A peaceful haven to all who seek a quiet, restful, sun-filled getaway. Your stay includes a full gourmet breakfast with freshly ground coffee and other tempting samplings. Suites include Victorian, French country, tropical, and our new luxury suite. New king suite, ocean views, porch swing. All suites have private entrances and bathrooms. With direct beach access, you are only steps away from discovering the gentle shoreline treasures. We are minutes from antiquing, fine restaurants, historic sites, and the outdoor drama passion play "Worthy is the Lamb." Come to your home away from home for a visit you'll always remember! AAA-rated.

Host: Marilyn Detwiller
Rooms: 4 suites (PB) $75-150
Full Breakfast
Credit Cards: A, B
Notes: 2, 5, 7, 8, 9, 10

FRANKLIN

The Franklin Terrace

159 Harrison Avenue, 28734
(282) 524-7907; (800) 633-2431
E-mail: terrace@dnet.net
Web site: http://www.intertekweb.com/terrace

The Franklin Terrace, built as a school in 1887, is listed on The National Register of Historic Places. The Terrace is a lovely two-story bed and breakfast that offers nostalgic charm and comfortable accommodations. Its wide porches and large guest rooms filled with period antiques will carry you to a time gone by when southern hospitality was at its best. The Terrace offers a casual shopping experience where you can browse through the antiques, crafts, and gifts for sale on the main floor. You also will be within walking distance of Franklin's famous gem shops, clothing boutiques, and fine restaurants.

Hosts: Ed and Helen Henson
Rooms: 9 (PB) $52-69
Full Breakfast
Credit Cards: A, B, C, D
Notes: 7 (over 3 years), 8, 9, 10, 12

GREENSBORO

Greenwood Bed and Breakfast

205 N. Park Drive, 27401
(336) 274-6350 (voice and FAX); (800) 535-9363
Web site: http://www.zip2.com/mainstreet/greenwoodb&b

"A culinary escape where great conversation is standard fare." In a turn-of-the-century, twenty-two-room chalet in the park. All five guest rooms have private baths. We offer a swimming pool and a New Orleans chef who prepares high-end, restaurant-quality breakfasts, cooked to order, served when you want (and you may have guests in for breakfast).

Hosts: Bob and Dolly Guertin
Rooms: 5 (PB) $95-160
Full Breakfast
Credit Cards: A, B, C, D, E
Notes: 2, 3, 4 (if all 5 rooms are booked by one group or family), 5, 7 (over 16), 8, 9, 10, 12

Apple Inn

HENDERSONVILLE

Apple Inn

1005 White Pine Drive, 28739
(828) 693-0107; (800) 615-6611;
FAX (828) 693-0173
Web site: http://www.wncguide.com/hend_co/appleinn/Welcome.html

There's no place like home—unless it's the Apple Inn! Only 2 miles from downtown Hendersonville, the inn is situated on 3 acres featuring charmingly comfortable rooms, each with modern private baths that await your arrival. Delicious home-cooked breakfasts, fresh flowers, and antiques complement the ambience of this turn-of-the-century home. Enjoy billiards, tennis, swimming, hiking, antiquing, bird-watching, or just relaxing.

Hosts: Bob and Pam Hedstrom
Rooms: 5 + cottage (PB) $79-89
Full Breakfast
Credit Cards: A, B
Notes: 2, 5, 7, 8, 9, 10, 11, 12

Claddagh Inn

755 N. Main Street, 28792
(828) 697-7778; (800) 225-4700;
FAX (828) 697-8664
E-mail: InnKeepers@Claddaghinn.com
Web site: http://www.Claddaghinn.com

The Claddagh Inn, Hendersonville's first bed and breakfast, is located just 2 blocks from the beautiful Main Street Promenade. All guest rooms have private baths, telephones, air-conditioning, and TVs. Guests awaken to a full country Irish breakfast, relax in the library and parlor with an evening sherry, or just enjoy the charm of rocking on the veranda. Listed on the National Register of Historic Places. AAA-approved. Group catering available for parties and meetings.

Hosts: Augie and Gerrie Emanuele
Rooms: 14 + 2-bedroom suite (PB) $89-135
Full Breakfast
Credit Cards: A, B, C, D
Notes: 2, 5, 7, 8, 9, 10, 12

Waverly Inn

783 N. Main Street, 28792
(828) 693-9193; (800) 537-8195;
FAX (828) 692-1010
E-mail: waverlyinn@ioa.com
Web site: http://www.waverly.com

Listed on the National Register, this is the oldest inn in Hendersonville. Recently renovated, there is something for everyone, including claw-foot tubs, king and queen canopy beds, a suite, telephones, rocking chairs, and sitting rooms. All rooms have private baths. Enjoy our complimentary soft drinks and fresh-baked goods. Walk to exceptional restaurants, antique stores, and shopping. Biltmore Estate, the Blue Ridge Parkway, and Connemara are nearby. Full country breakfast included in rates. The inn was rated as one of 1993's top ten bed and breakfasts in the United States by *INNovations*.

Hosts: John and Diane Sheiry, Darla Olmstead
Rooms: 14 (PB) $79-185
Full Breakfast
Credit Cards: A, B, C, D
Notes: 2, 5, 7, 8, 9, 10, 12

HIGH POINT

The Bouldin House Bed and Breakfast

4332 Archdale Road, 27263
(336) 431-4909; (800) 739-1816;
FAX (336) 431-4914
E-mail: lmiller582@aol.com
Web site: http://www.bbonline.com/nc/bouldin

Fine lodging and hospitality amidst America's finest home furnishings showrooms! Our finely crafted, historic bed and breakfast sits on 3 acres of a former tobacco farm. Quiet, country atmosphere; casual and relaxed, yet elegant. Warmly decorated rooms combined old and new, each with spacious, modern, private baths. Awaken to an early morning coffee/tea service. Follow the aroma of our chef's choice, gourmet breakfast to the dining room, paneled in oak. Come; indulge.

Hosts: Ann and Larry Miller
Rooms: 4 (PB) $85-115
Full Gourmet Breakfast
Credit Cards: A, B, C, D
Notes: 2, 5, 8, 10, 12

KILL DEVIL HILLS

Cherokee Inn

500 N. Virginia Dare Trail, 27948
(252) 441-6127; (800) 554-2764;
FAX (252) 441-1072
Web site: http://chaela.com/cherokeeinn

Our beach house, located on the Outer Banks of North Carolina, is 600 feet from the Atlantic Ocean beach. Fine food, history, sports, and adventure galore. We welcome you for a restful, active, or romantic getaway. Enjoy the cypress interior, wraparound porch, bicycles, or beach chairs at our friendly, smoke-free inn.

Hosts: Bob and Kaye Combs
Rooms: 6 (PB) $65-105
Continental Breakfast
Credit Cards: A, B, C
Notes: 2, 8, 9, 10, 12

LAWSONVILLE

Southwyck Farm B&B

1070 Southwyck Farm Road, 27022–9768
(336) 593-8006 (voice and FAX)
E-mail: SowyckFarm@aol.com
Web site: http://www.sowyckfarm@aol.com

Visit our New England–style, custom-built home with 18th-century elegance on a 38-acre estate with a magnificent view of the Blue Ridge Mountains. Antiques, waterfowl paintings and carvings, and other treasures from around the world enhance our home. Have your choice of a gourmet or traditional country breakfast before you venture off to Hanging Rock State Park, the Blue Ridge Parkway, or an adventure on the Dan River. One hour from Greensboro or Winston-Salem.

Hosts: Diana Carl and David Hoskins
Rooms: 3 (1PB; 2SB) $90
Full Breakfast
Credit Cards: A, B
Notes: 2, 3, 4, 5, 9, 10, 12

LITTLETON (LAKE GASTON)

Littleton's Maplewood Manor Bed and Breakfast

120 College Street; PO Box 1165, 27850
(919) 586-4638 (voice and FAX); (800) 420-0638

A small hometown B&B offering you a nice, clean, spacious room with king, queen, or twin beds, shared bath, and full breakfast. There are books, games, videos, CDs, and tapes. There will be tea in the afternoon, wine and crackers in the evening. The grounds are parklike; benches and chairs are placed around for guests to use. The screened porch is a great place to relax. Multinight and multiroom discounts. Traveler's checks accepted.

Hosts: Helen and Alan Burtchell
Rooms: 2 (SB) $60
Full Breakfast
Credit Cards: A, B
Notes: 5, 9, 10

MAGGIE VALLEY

Wynne's Creekside Lodge Bed and Breakfast

152 Bunny Run Lane, **Waynesville,** 28786
(828) 926-8300; (800) 849-4387;
FAX (828) 926-0888
E-mail: righton@primeline.com
Web site: http://www.innsandouts.com/p150311.html

Situated on trout-stocked Jonathan Creek in the scenic western North Carolina mountains, Wynne's Creekside Lodge lies on 2½ country acres, 5 minutes outside Maggie Valley. The 1926 two-story farmhouse recently was raised and set upon a wood-and-stone contemporary addition. Six-person outdoor Jacuzzi, mountain bike rentals, and fishing. Breakfast includes homemade bread, jams, pastry. Complimentary cappuccino or refreshments. Christian atmosphere. Church staff retreats welcome.

Hosts: Les and Gail Wynne
Rooms: 4 (PB) $55-65
Full Breakfast
Credit Cards: A, B
Notes: 2, 5, 7 (over 6), 8, 9, 10, 11

MANTEO

Tranquil House Inn

405 Queen Elizabeth Avenue; PO Box 2045, 27954
(252) 473-1404; (800) 458-7069;
FAX (252) 473-1526
E-mail: djust1587@aol.com
Web site: http://www.tranquilinn.com

The Tranquil House Inn is a beautiful 19th-century style inn with 20th-century convenience. Relax on our second-floor deck and enjoy the cool coastal breezes. Listen to the soothing sounds of the marina as you enjoy the deluxe continental breakfast, lemonade, and wine and cheese reception. Use our bikes as you sight-see, shop, and discover the history of Roanoke Island. You will be minutes from the beaches but a world apart.

Hosts: Don and Lauri Just
Rooms: 25 (PB) $79-169
Continental Breakfast
Credit Cards: A, B, C, D
Notes: 2, 4, 5, 7, 8, 9, 10, 12

MARSHALL

Marshall House B&B

100 Hill Street; PO Box 865, 28753
(828) 649-9205; FAX (828) 649-2999

Built in 1903, the inn overlooks the peaceful town of Marshall and the French Broad River. This country inn, listed on the National Historic Register, is decorated with fancy chandeliers, antiques, and pictures. Four fireplaces, formal dining room, parlor, and upstairs TV/reading room. Enjoy storytelling about the house, the town, the people, and the history. Our loving house pets gladly will welcome your pets, also.

The toot of a train and good service make your visit a unique experience.

Hosts: Ruth and Jim Boylan
Rooms: 9 (2PB; 7SB) $39.50-75
Continental Plus Breakfast
Credit Cards: A, B, C, D, E
Notes: 3, 4, 5, 6, 7, 9, 10, 11, 12

MOORESVILLE (LAKE NORMAN)

Spring Run B&B

172 Spring Run Drive, **Lake Norman,** 28115
(704) 664-6686; FAX (704) 664-9282

Enjoy an award-winning, three-course, gourmet breakfast at this home on Lake Norman, where you'll find many great lakeside eateries. Each room has private bath, cable TV, and free movie channel. Amenities include an exercise room with game table, paddleboat, lake swimming, boat hook-up at the pier, and fishing. Enjoy a round of golf at the course across the street. We are 25 minutes north of Charlotte and 20 minutes south of I–40. Spring Run Bed and Breakfast has been awarded three diamonds from the AAA, and for 8 years in a row has earned a perfect score from the BOH.

Hostess: Mary Farley
Rooms: 2 (PB) $95-120
Full Gourmet Breakfast
Credit Cards: A, B
Notes: 2, 5, 8, 9, 10, 12

MURPHY

Park Place B&B

100 Hill Street, 28906
(828) 837-8842

Welcome to your home away from home! For your comfort, Park Place—a two-story clapboard/brick house, circa 1900—offers three well-appointed guest rooms and serves a full gourmet breakfast. The hosts greatly enjoy sharing with guests the home's congenial atmosphere and its eclectic decor of family treasures, antiques, collectibles, and hand-knotted Oriental rugs. While relaxing on the screened, tree-top-level porch, guests love shooting the breeze or just rocking the time away. *Willkommen—Wir sprechen Deutsch!*

Hosts: Rikki and Neil Wocell
Rooms: 3 (PB) $65-90
Full Breakfast
Credit Cards: none
Notes: 2, 5, 8, 9, 10

NAGS HEAD

First Colony Inn®

6720 S. Virginia Dare Trail, 27959
(252) 441-2343; (800) 368-9390;
FAX (252) 441-9234
E-mail: innkeeper@firstcolonyinn.com
Web site: http://www.firstcolonyinn.com

At this AAA four-diamond inn, the Lawrence family welcome guests with real southern hospitality. English antiques grace public areas and bedrooms. Buffet breakfast and afternoon tea are included. All bedrooms have private baths, phones, refrigerators, and microwaves. Luxury rooms boast wet bars or kitchenettes; some have Jacuzzis, sitting areas, or screened porches. Amenities include a large, secluded outdoor pool; wraparound porches; gazebo overlooking the ocean; and direct ocean access. Smoke-free.

Hosts: The Lawrences
Rooms: 26 (PB) $80-275 (seasonal)
Full Breakfast
Credit Cards: A, B, C, D
Notes: 5, 7, 8, 9, 10, 12

welcome; 7 Children welcome; 8 Tennis nearby; 9 Swimming nearby; 10 Golf nearby; 11 Skiing nearby; 12 May be booked through travel agent.

NEW BERN

The Aerie Inn

509 Pollock Street, 28562
(252) 636-5553 (voice and FAX); (800) 849-5553
E-mail: Aerie@cconnect.net

Relax and enjoy the warmth and charm of this 1880 inn, reminiscent of period homes along the coast. One block from Tryon Place in the heart of the historic district, The Aerie is within an easy walk of all of New Bern's treasures. Furnished with antiques and period reproductions. Each guest room has private bath, AC, TV, and telephone. The sitting room with its player piano and library provides a comfortable gathering place for guests. A full gourmet, candlelit breakfast; afternoon tea; and evening refreshments are included.

Hosts: Howard and Dee Smith
Rooms: 7 (PB) $89-99
Full Breakfast
Credit Cards: A, B, C, D
Notes: 2, 5, 7, 8, 9, 10, 12

Howard House Victorian Bed and Breakfast

207 Pollock Street, 28560
(252) 514-6709; (800) 705-5261;
FAX (252) 514-6710
E-mail: howardhouse@coastalnet.com

Step back in time to a gracious, elegant era by staying in this 1890 Victorian-style bed and breakfast. Located in the downtown historic district of New Bern, the Howard House is within walking distance of the riverfront, a variety of restaurants, historic homes, and sites like Tryon Place and specialty shops. The Wynns offer desserts, refreshments, and good conversation on the front porch or in the parlor as you return from a busy day around town. A bountiful breakfast is served each morning in the formal dining room. We await your arrival. . . .

Howard House Victorian Bed and Breakfast

Hosts: Steven and Kimberly Wynn
Rooms: 4 (PB) $85-95
Full Breakfast
Credit Cards: A, B, C, D
Notes: 2, 5, 9, 10

Magnolia House

315 George Street, 28562
(252) 633-9488 (voice and FAX); (800) 601-9488

We invite you to romance yourselves with a stay at New Bern's Magnolia House. You may choose from three uniquely decorated guest rooms, each with private bath. Located two doors from Tryon Place, once home to the royal governor of North Carolina, Magnolia House is centrally located in the heart of the historic district. Fine restaurants, quaint shops, museums, and antiquing are within walking distance.

Magnolia House is furnished with local estate antiques and family pieces. A full breakfast is served at your convenience; you may choose to have it served under the magnolia tree for which the inn is named. Honeymoon and anniversary packages are our specialties. Gift certificates are available.

Hosts: Kim and John Trudo
Rooms: 3 (PB) $90-100
Full Breakfast
Credit Cards: A, B, C, D
Notes: 2, 5, 7 (over 8), 10, 12

REIDSVILLE

Fairview Farm Bed and Breakfast

1891 Harrison Crossroads Road, 27320
(336) 349-6910 (voice and FAX)
E-mail: pburton@juno.com
Web sites: http://www.bbonline.com/nc/ncbb1
http://www.bestinns.net/usa/nc/fairview.html

Fairview Farm, a southern farmhouse with wrap-around porch, sits on 135 acres of a former tobacco farm belonging to the owner's family for five generations. The house, with its beaded-board ceilings and heart-pine floors, is furnished with family pieces and other antiques, including mechanical musical instruments, clocks, china, hats, and quilts. Onsite are an ESSO country store, antique automobiles, and antique horse-drawn and farm equipment. China-Penn Plantation, antique shops, and outlets are nearby.

Hosts: John and Peggy Burton
Rooms: 2 (PB) $70
Full Breakfast
Credit Cards: none
Notes: 2, 5, 7 (12+ years), 10

SALISBURY

Rowan Oak House

208 S. Fulton Street, 28144-4845
(704) 633-2086; (800) 786-0437;
FAX (704) 633-2084
Web site: http://www.bbonline.com/nc/rowanoak

An elegant high Victorian located in the historic district. Stained and leaded glass, seven fireplaces, wraparound porch, and gardens adorn this 100-year-old mansion. Each of the four guest rooms is lavishly furnished with antiques, sitting area, desk, phone, duvet with down comforter, reading lights, fruit, and flowers. Private baths (one room has a double Jacuzzi). Central air-conditioning and heat. Color TV, books, magazines, and board games are in the upstairs parlor. Smoking limited. Full gourmet breakfast served. Close to furniture shopping and Charlotte Motor Speedway. Walking distance to downtown churches, antique shopping, historic buildings, and fine restaurants.

Hosts: Barbara and Les Coombs
Rooms: 4 (PB) $85-125
Full Breakfast
Credit Cards: A, B, C, D
Notes: 2, 5, 7 (over 12), 8, 9, 10, 12

SOUTHERN PINES

Knollwood House Bed and Breakfast

1495 W. Connecticut Avenue, 28387
(910) 692-9390; FAX (910) 692-0609

The English manor house stands among 5 acres of longleaf pines, dogwoods, azaleas, towering holly trees, and 40-foot

Knollwood House Bed and Breakfast

magnolias. From a terrace where Glenn Miller's orchestra once gave a concert, Knollwood's lawns roll down to the fifteenth fairway of a famous golf course. Furnished with late-18th-century/early-19th-century antiques, both suites and guest rooms are available. Special golf package rates are available on request.

Hosts: Dick and Mimi Beatty
Rooms: 6 (PB) $100-150
Full Breakfast
Credit Cards: A, B
Notes: 2, 5, 7, 8, 9, 10, 12

SPARTA

Turby-Villa Bed and Breakfast

2072 NC Highway 18 N., 28675
(336) 372-8490

At 3,000 feet, this contemporary two-story home is the centerpiece of a 20-acre farm located 2 miles from Sparta. The house is surrounded by an acre of trees and manicured lawn with a lovely view of the Blue Ridge Mountains. Breakfast is served either on the enclosed porch with its white wicker furnishings or in the formal dining room with its Early American furnishings. Mrs. Mimi Turbiville takes justifiable pride in her attractive, well-maintained bed and breakfast.

Hostess: Maybelline R. Turbiville
Rooms: 3 (PB) $35 single, $50 couple
Full Breakfast
Credit Cards: none
Notes: 2, 5, 7, 8, 10

SPRUCE PINE

Richmond Inn B&B

101 Pine Avenue, 28777
(828) 765-6993
E-mail: billxlee@m-y.net

A rambling country estate, the Richmond Inn is Spruce Pine's premier bed and breakfast. Located in a scenic mountain setting, the half-century-old inn is shaded by towering white pines and landscaped with native dogwood trees, mountain laurel, and rhododendron. The tranquil surroundings belie the fact that the quaint little town of Spruce Pine is within 3 blocks of the inn. The terrace of the Richmond Inn overlooks the valley of the North Toe River. Four miles beyond the river valley is the crest of the Blue Ridge Mountains, crowned by the Blue Ridge Parkway.

Hosts: Bill Ansley and Lendre (Lee) Boucher
Rooms: 7 (PB) $55-75
Full Breakfast
Credit Cards: A, B, D
Notes: 2, 5, 7, 8, 9, 10, 11, 12

Richmond Inn Bed and Breakfast

NOTES: Credit cards accepted: A Master Card; B Visa; C American Express; D Discover; E Diners Club; F Other; 2 Personal checks accepted; 3 Lunch available; 4 Dinner available; 5 Open all year; 6 Pets

STATESVILLE

Aunt Mae's B&B

532 E. Broad Street, 28677
(704) 873-9525

Enjoy a nostalgic journey with a Victorian flair. Aunt Mae kept much of the history of her dishes, linens, knick-knacks, and books. . .and these are for your browsing pleasure while enjoying your stay in her 1891 home. Our location within walking distance of historic downtown and at the crossroads of I–40/I–77 in the beautiful North Carolina piedmont makes us a good vacation spot, special getaway, or stop-over when traveling.

Hosts: Sue and Richard Rowland
Rooms: 2 (PB) $60
Full Breakfast
Credit Cards: A, B
Notes: 2, 5, 8, 10, 12

Cedar Hill Farm

778 Elmwood Road, 28625
(704) 873-4332; (800) 948-4423

An 1840 farmhouse and private cottages on a 32-acre sheep farm in rolling hills. Antique furnishings, air-conditioning, cable television, and phones in rooms. After your full country breakfast, swim, play badminton, or relax in a porch rocker or hammock. For a busier day, visit two lovely towns with historic districts, Old Salem, or two larger cities within a 45-mile radius. Convenient to restaurants, shopping, and three interstate highways.

Hosts: Brenda and Jim Vernon
Rooms: 3 (PB) $70-95
Full Breakfast
Credit Cards: A, B, C
Notes: 2, 5, 6 (limited), 7, 9, 10, 12

Madelyn's in the Grove —A Bed & Breakfast

1836 West Memorial Highway; PO Box 249, **Union Grove,** 28689
(704) 539-4151; (800) 948-4473;
FAX (704) 539-4080
E-mail: madelyns@yadtel.com
Web site: http://www.madelyns.com

Listen to the birds and unwind. We have moved our B&B to Union Grove, only 15 minutes north of Statesville and I–40 and only 2 minutes from I–77, Exit 65. There are many things to see and do. After a fun-filled day, come back and have cheese and crackers and a glass of lemonade. Sit on one of the porches or the gazebo, watch the stars, and be glad you are at Madelyn's in the Grove. Personal checks preferred.

Hosts: Madelyn and John Hill
Rooms: 5 (PB) $75-135
Full Breakfast
Credit Cards: A, B, C
Notes: 2, 5, 7, 10, 12

TAYLORSVILLE

The Mountain of Grace "Cottage on the Peak"

251 Harrelson Ridge Road, 28681
(828) 635-7300

Unique, breathtaking, and beautiful. Amazing grace is what you will find in this fully equipped Victorian cottage atop a 2,800-foot mountain. Secluded and private—a perfect getaway. Enjoy sunrises over the Catawba Valley and mountain range. Stroll the wooded lane or hike the mountain. Choice of breakfast served to the cottage or poolside. Private covered porch and swing, plus BBQ and patio.

Enjoy sunsets or gaze at the stars. Close to eighty-room Hickory Furniture Mart and fine or casual dining. Plan a day trip (Asheville, Blowing Rock, etc.). Television, VCR, AC, heat. Warmth and hospitality await you. Great place for a game of croquet on the ridge of the mountain! Inquire about additional activities and attractions. Deposit required. Cash or check.

Hosts: Allen and Debbie Jones
Rooms: 1 cottage $85-125
Full and Continental Breakfast
Credit Cards: F
Notes: 2, 5, 9, 10, 11, 12

The Fox Trot Inn

TRYON

The Fox Trot Inn

PO Box 1561, 28782
(828) 859-9706

This lovingly restored residence, circa 1915, is situated on 6 wooded acres within the city limits of Tryon. It is convenient to everything, yet secluded with a quietly elegant atmosphere. Guests are treated to a full gourmet breakfast; heated swimming pool; and fully furnished guest house with two bedrooms, kitchen, living room, fireplace, deck, and outstanding mountain views. Two of the guest rooms have sitting rooms. Both the inn and guest house are fully air-conditioned.

Host: Wim Woody
Rooms: 4 (PB) $80-125; guest house $550 weekly
Full Breakfast
Credit Cards: none
Notes: 2, 5, 6 (in guest house), 7, 8, 9, 10, 12

WARSAW

The Vintage Inn

748 NC Highways 24 and 50, 28398
(910) 296-1727; FAX (910) 296-1431

"Your inn for something special." Our rural setting adds to the privacy and relaxed atmosphere for a feeling of "getting away from it all." After a restful night, walk on brick sidewalks and rustic paths flanked by tall pines and towering oaks. The "Squire's" guest house nearby has four rooms with private baths and antique furnishings. Adjacent is the famous Country Squire Restaurant. Weekend package available. Take Exit 364 from I–40. Rated by AAA and Mobil Travel Guide.

Hostess: Iris Lennon
Rooms: 16 (PB) $65-79
Continental Breakfast
Credit Cards: A, B, C, E
Notes: 2, 3, 4, 5, 7, 10, 12

WAYNESVILLE

Wynne's Creekside Lodge

152 Bunny Run Lane, 28786
(828) 926-8300; (800) 849-4387;
FAX (828) 926-0888
E-mail: righton@primeline.com
Web site: http://www.innsandouts.com/p150311.html

Situated on trout-stocked Jonathan Creek in the scenic western North Carolina

NOTES: Credit cards accepted: A Master Card; B Visa; C American Express; D Discover; E Diners Club; F Other; 2 Personal checks accepted; 3 Lunch available; 4 Dinner available; 5 Open all year; 6 Pets

mountains, Wynne's Creekside Lodge lies on 2½ country acres, 5 minutes outside Maggie Valley. The 1926 two-story farmhouse recently was raised and set upon a wood-and-stone contemporary addition. Six-person outdoor Jacuzzi, mountain bike rentals, and fishing. Breakfast includes homemade bread, jams, pastry. Complimentary cappuccino or refreshments. Christian atmosphere. Church staff retreats welcome.

Hosts: Les and Gail Wynne
Rooms: 4 (PB) $55-65
Full Breakfast
Credit Cards: A, B
Notes: 2, 5, 7 (over 6), 8, 9, 10, 11

Live Oaks Bed and Breakfast

WILMINGTON

Live Oaks B&B

318 S. 3rd Street, 28401
(910) 762-6733; (800) 762-6732
E-mail: liveoak318@aol.com
Web site: http://www.liveoaks.com

Located in the historic downtown area, this circa-1883 home has been restored to its original grandeur and decorated in Victorian style with antiques and reproductions. Within walking distance are wonderful shops and restaurants, antiquing, museums, and galleries. Take a horse-drawn carriage ride, a walking tour, or a house tour and relive a bit of the past. Golf and beaches are just 20 minutes away.

Hosts: Margi and Doug Erickson
Rooms: 3 (PB) $95-125
Full Breakfast
Credit Cards: A, B, D, E
Notes: 2, 5, 6 (under 25 pounds), 7 (12 and older), 9, 10, 12

Rosehill Inn B&B

114 S. Third Street, 28401
(910) 815-0250; (800) 815-0250;
FAX (910) 815-0350
E-mail: rosehill@rosehill.com
Web site: http://www.rosehill.com

Rosehill Inn offers travelers the warmth and security of returning home after a long day's journey. Fully renovating the B&B in 1995, the owners have endeavored to maintain the comfort and charm of this beautiful home. Located just a block from the Cape Fear River, it is only a few minutes from fine dining and fun shopping. Included in your stay is a generous breakfast of homemade delights.

Hosts: Laurel Jones and Dennis Fietsch
Rooms: 6 (PB)
Full or Continental Breakfast
Credit Cards: A, B, C, D
Notes: 2, 5, 7 (12 and older), 8, 9, 10, 12

Taylor House Inn

14 N. Seventh Street, 28401
(910) 763-7581; (800) 382-9982

Located in the downtown historic district, just blocks from the Cape Fear River. A haven of warm southern hospitality and

welcome; 7 Children welcome; 8 Tennis nearby; 9 Swimming nearby; 10 Golf nearby; 11 Skiing nearby; 12 May be booked through travel agent.

thoughtfulness. The five bedrooms are filled with period antiques, fresh flowers, and beautiful linens. A full gourmet breakfast is served in the formal dining room by candlelight. A slice of heaven—be pampered and enjoy the Cape Fear area.

Hosts: Scott and Karen Clark
Rooms: 5 (PB) $95-110
Full Gourmet Breakfast
Credit Cards: A, B, C
Notes: 2, 5, 8, 9, 10

Miss Betty's Bed and Breakfast Inn

WILSON

Miss Betty's Bed and Breakfast Inn and Executive Suite

600 W. Nash Street, 27893-3045
(919) 243-4447 (voice and FAX); (800) 258-2058

Selected as one of the "best places to stay in the South," Miss Betty's is ideally located midway between Maine and Florida along the main north-south route, I–95. Comprised of four beautifully restored structures in the downtown historic section, the National Registered Davis-Whitehead-Harriss House (circa 1858), the Riley House (circa 1900), Rosebud (circa 1942), and the Queen Anne (circa 1911) have recaptured the elegance and style of quiet Victorian charm, but with modern conveniences. Guests can browse for antiques in the inn or visit numerous shops that give Wilson the title "Antique Capital of North Carolina." A quiet town famous for its barbecue, Wilson has four beautiful golf courses and many tennis courts. Rooms include three king suites.

Hosts: Betty and Fred Spitz
Rooms: 10 + 4 executive suites (PB) $60-80
Full Breakfast
Credit Cards: A, B, C, D, E
Notes: 2, 5, 8, 9, 10

WINSTON-SALEM

Lady Anne's Victorian Bed and Breakfast

612 Summit Street, 27101
(336) 724-1074
Web site: http://www.bbonline.com/nc/ladyannes

Warm, southern hospitality surrounds you in this 1890 Victorian home, listed on the National Register of Historic Places. An aura of romance touches each suite or room. All are individually decorated with period antiques, treasures, and modern luxuries. Some rooms have two-person whirlpools, cable TVs, HBO, stereos, telephones, coffee, refrigerators, private entrances, and balconies. An evening dessert and full breakfast are served. Lady Anne's is ideally located near downtown attractions, performances, restaurants, shops, and Old Salem Historic Village. Smoking only on the porch!

Hostess: Shelley Kirby
Rooms: 4 (PB) $55-170
Full Breakfast
Credit Cards: A, B, C, D
Notes: 5, 8, 9, 10

North Dakota

McCLUSKY

Midstate Bed and Breakfast

980 Highway 200 NE, 58463
(701) 363-2520 (voice and FAX); (888) 434-2520

In central North Dakota, this country home is very easy to locate: Mile Marker 232 on ND 200. Built in 1980. The guest entrance takes you to a complete and private lower level containing your bedroom and bath, plus a large TV lounge with fireplace and kitchenette. Additional bedrooms are on the upper level. Breakfast is served in the formal dining room or the plant-filled atrium. In an area of great hunting; guests are allowed hunting privileges on more than 4,000 acres. Good fishing nearby. Air-conditioned.

Hostess: Grace Faul
Rooms: 4 (1PB; 3SB) $35-40
Full Breakfast
Credit Cards: none
Notes: 2, 3, 4, 5, 6 (conditional), 7, 8, 9

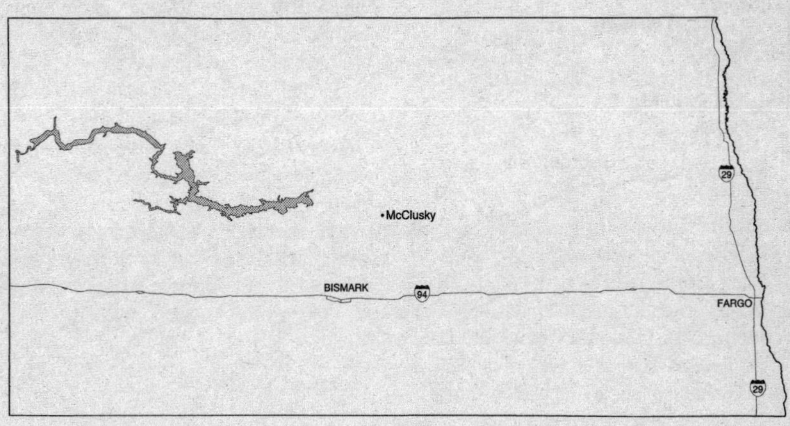

welcome; 7 Children welcome; 8 Tennis nearby; 9 Swimming nearby; 10 Golf nearby; 11 Skiing nearby; 12 May be booked through travel agent.

OHIO

Fayette
Wauseon
TOLEDO
80
Lakeside
Marblehead
Sandusky
90
Mesopotamia
Defiance
Milan
Wakeman
80
Tiffin
AKRON/CANTON
76
Poland
75
77
71
Wooster
Crestline
Fredericksburg
Wilmot
Millersburg
Berlin
Strasburg
Sugarcreek
Dover
Dellroy
Fresno
Sidney
Greenville
Plain City
Delaware
70
Tipp City
70
Columbus
70
Dayton
Blue Rock
Caldwell
Somerset
Camden
71
Germantown
Sugar Grove
Oxford
77
75
Lebanon
Hamilton
CINNCINNATI
Georgetown
Ripley

Ohio

Donna's Premier Lodging

BERLIN

Donna's Premier Lodging

PO Box 307, 44610
(330) 893-3068; (800) 320-3338;
FAX (330) 893-0037
E-mail: info@donnasb-b.com
Web site: http://www.donnasb-b.com

Prepare yourself for the ultimate romantic experience in the heart of Ohio's Amish country. Couples in love can relax in a heart-shaped waterfall Jacuzzi while the fireplace warms a luxurious bridal suite or snuggle under warm covers and await the delivery of a scrumptious breakfast to the cottage. Romantics can indulge in a spacious, classy chalet complete with pool table, while nature lovers may like to recline in hickory rockers on the front porch of a log cabin.

Hosts: Johannes and Donna Marie Schlabach
Rooms: 2 chalets, 5 cottages, 1 log cabin, 2 suites, 3 B&B rooms (PB) $45-225
Full or Continental Breakfast (inquire)
Credit Cards: A, B, D
Notes: 2, 5, 7, 8, 9, 10, 12

The Oaks Bed and Breakfast

4752 State Route 62; PO Box 421, 44610
(330) 893-3061; (800) 893-3061

Charming, three-story red brick home nestled in the heart of Berlin in picturesque Holmes County. The Oaks Bed and Breakfast is "your home away from home." Four rooms, including two suites; one is a master lofted suite with its own sitting room, skylights, and whirlpool. All rooms have private baths, TV/VCR units, and AC, and are smoke-free. Relax on our porches surrounded by oak trees, or stroll uptown to more than twenty-five craft or gift shops. Ideal for couples or families.

NOTES: Credit cards accepted: A Master Card; B Visa; C American Express; D Discover; E Diners Club; F Other; 2 Personal checks accepted; 3 Lunch available; 4 Dinner available; 5 Open all year; 6 Pets welcome; 7 Children welcome; 8 Tennis nearby; 9 Swimming nearby; 10 Golf nearby; 11 Skiing nearby; 12 May be booked through travel agent.

Rent for one night or a whole week. Call for more information.

Hosts: Steve and Ruth Schlabach
Rooms: 4 (PB) $65-125 (seasonal)
Continental Breakfast
Credit Cards: A, B, D
Notes: 2, 5, 7, 8, 9, 10, 12

BLUE ROCK

McNutt Farm II/ Outdoorsman Lodge

6120 Cutler Lake Road, 43720-9740
(740) 674-4555

Country bed and breakfast in rustic quarters on a working farm in the quiet of the Blue Rock hill country. Only 11 miles from I–70, 35 miles from I–77, and 60 miles from I–71. Guests enjoy their own private kitchen, living room with fireplace or wood-burner, private bath, porch with swing, and beautiful view with forests and pastured livestock. Choose the log cabin or the carriage house. For those who want more than an overnight stay, please ask about our log cabin by the week or weekend. A cellar house cabin (somewhat primitive) is also available. Sleep to the sounds of whippoorwills and tree frogs. Awaken to the crowing rooster and the wild turkey calling; sometimes the bleating of a newborn fawn can be heard. We welcome you by reservation and deposit.

Hosts: Don R. and Patty L. McNutt
Rooms: 2 suites (PB) $40-100
Continental Breakfast
Credit Cards: none
Notes: 2 (deposit, cash for balance), 5, 6 and 7 (prearranged), 9, 10

CALDWELL

The Harkins House Inn

715 West Street, 43724
(740) 732-7347
E-mail: icocca@nobleconet.com

Come spend an enchanted evening in this immaculately restored home. Built in 1905 by an influential family of the Caldwell area (ancestors of the proprietors), the inn features bountiful original woodwork with oak and heart pine flooring and a stately library with fireplace and French doors. Enjoy your stay in one of our rooms with air-conditioning and cable television. Then savor breakfast in the formal dining room. Caldwell is only 25 minutes between Cambridge and Marietta.

Hosts: Jeff and Stacey Lucas
Rooms: 2 (PB) $53-65
Full Breakfast
Credit Cards: A, B, C
Notes: 2, 5, 7, 8, 9, 10

CAMDEN

Pleasant Valley Bed and Breakfast

7343 Pleasant Valley Road, 45311
(937) 787-3800

Welcome to our very country bed and breakfast home. This huge Victorian brick is a centerhall design. The home is garnished with lovely woodwork, fireplaces, and screened porches for your enjoyment. We have a billiard room, white-sand volleyball court, and a big bark barn with deck that overlooks a pond. Pleasant Valley will host your private party or dinner. We also can do luncheons, retirement gatherings,

NOTES: Credit cards accepted: A Master Card; B Visa; C American Express; D Discover; E Diners Club; F Other; 2 Personal checks accepted; 3 Lunch available; 4 Dinner available; 5 Open all year; 6 Pets

Pleasant Valley Bed and Breakfast

family reunions, home weddings, and barn weddings for our guests.

Hosts: Tim and Peggy Lowman
Rooms: 4 (2PB; 2SB) $55-65
Full Breakfast
Credit Cards: none
Notes: 2, 3, 4, 6, 7, 8, 9, 10, 11 (water)

COLUMBUS

Shamrock Bed and Breakfast

5657 Sunbury Road, 43230
(614) 337-9849

Half mile from I–270, close to the airport, 15 minutes from downtown and major attractions. All guest rooms are on the first floor. More than an acre of landscaped gardens, patio, arbor, and pond. Queen-size bedrooms, quiet ambience of antiques and art. Very restful. Guests have complete use of the first floor (living room, TV and music, large solarium). Close to Polaris, New Easton Shoppes, gardens, movies, galleries. Air-conditioned.

Host: Tom L. McLaughlin
Rooms: 2 (PB) $50-75
Full Breakfast
Credit Cards: none
Notes: 2, 5, 7, 10

DAYTON

Candlewick Bed and Breakfast

4991 Bath Road, 45424
(937) 233-9297

This tranquil Dutch Colonial home sits atop a hill on 5 rolling acres. George, a retired engineer, and Nancy, a retired schoolteacher, invite you to spend a peaceful night in comfortable rooms containing a blend of antiques and colonial and country furnishings. Full breakfast includes fresh fruit and juice, choice homemade pastries, and freshly brewed coffee. Weather permitting, enjoy breakfast on the screened porch overlooking a large pond often visited by wild ducks and geese. Convenient to the Air Force Museum and major universities, Candlewick is a perfect retreat for either business or pleasure.

Hosts: George and Nancy Thompson
Rooms: 2 (SB) $55-60
Full Breakfast
Credit Cards: none
Notes: 2, 5

DEFIANCE

Sanctuary Ministries

20277 Schick Road, 43512
(419) 658-2069

Sanctuary Ministries is a quiet getaway in a Christian atmosphere. A cedar-sided, two-story home with air-conditioning; a 6-acre lake; a pond; and 5 acres of woods make for a peaceful getaway. This is a favorite fishing hole for many, with rowboat and canoe. Picnicking and bird-watching from our porch swings add to the tranquil atmosphere for relaxation.

Hosts: Emil and Barbara Schoch
Rooms: 2 (SB) $35-50
Full Breakfast
Credit Cards: none
Notes: 2, 5, 7, 9, 10

DELAWARE

Welcome Home Inn

6640 Home Road, 43015
(740) 881-6588; (800) 484-4693, 6716
Web site: http://www.bbonline.com/oh/welcomehome

Located on 6 wooded acres, Welcome Home Inn is a southern farmhouse-style house filled with oak antiques. A grand piano sits beneath stained-glass windows in a spacious dining room, where guests are served breakfast. Or they can dine on the screened porch. Enjoy sitting on the large, wraparound porch filled with wicker furniture. Only minutes away are restaurants, the Columbus Zoo, Powell with its quaint antique shops, and golf courses.

Hosts: Forrest and Brenda Williams
Rooms: 4 (2PB; 2SB) $60-95
Full Breakfast
Credit Cards: none
Notes: 2, 5, 10

DELLROY

Candleglow Bed and Breakfast

4247 Roswell Road SW, 44620
(330) 735-2407
Web site: http://www.raex.com/~carroll/candleglow

Today's comfort in yesterday's Victorian atmosphere. Romantic, casual elegance. Three spacious guest rooms with king or queen beds. Private baths with claw-foot or whirlpool tubs. Full breakfast, afternoon tea, and snack in room. Atwood Lake Resort Area. Swimming, boating, hiking, horseback riding, tennis, golf, and antique shops are all close by.

Hostess: Audrey Genova
Rooms: 3 (PB) $90 (summer; call for winter rates)
Full Breakfast
Credit Cards: none
Notes: 2, 5, 8, 9, 10

Mowrey's Welcome Home Bed and Breakfast

DOVER

Mowrey's Welcome Home Bed and Breakfast

4489 Dover-Zoar Road NE, 44622
(330) 343-4690

A serene, homey atmosphere and old-fashioned hospitality set the scene in this contemporary but traditional country home. Congenial hosts are retired teachers who welcome you to visit or to enjoy the privacy of your large, comfortable suite. Books, fireplaces, grand piano, old clocks, and other antiques provide interest throughout the house. Explore the woods and creek, or enjoy the hillside view from the porches. Wildlife abounds. Second bedroom available for larger parties. Central air. Many interesting sites nearby.

Hosts: Paul and Lola Mowrey
Rooms: 2 (1PB; 1SB) $45-70
Full Breakfast
Credit Cards: none
Notes: 2, 5, 7 (over 9), 8, 9, 10, 12

Olde World Bed and Breakfast

2982 State Route 516 NW, 44622
(330) 343-1333; (800) 447-1273;
FAX (330) 364-8022
E-mail: owbb@tusco.net
Web site: http://www.oldeworldbb.com

My childhood dream of restoring this Victorian home is truly a fairytale I would love to share with you. Old-world tradition is reflected in our uniquely appointed suite, including Victorian, Oriental, Parisian, Mediterranean, and Alpine influences. An antiquer's delight, our entire home is open to our guests, including parlor, veranda, and dining room. Your stay is complete with a soak in our private, two-person hot tub. Centrally located near Amish Country and other historical sites.

Hostess: Jonna Sigrist
Rooms: 5 (PB) $55-100
Full Breakfast
Credit Cards: A, B, D
Notes: 2, 3, 5, 9, 10, 12

FAYETTE

Red Brick Inn

206 W. Main Street, 43521
(419) 237-2276

Guests will enjoy a visit to our 125-year-old Victorian home filled with antique furnishings—many of them family heirlooms. Three bedrooms are available, each with private bath. Two rooms have a private porch and are handicap-accessible. We are located in northwestern Ohio near Harrison Lake State Park and Fayette's historic opera house, at the corner of routes 66 and 20.

Hosts: Don and Jane Stiriz
Rooms: 3 (PB) $55
Full Breakfast
Credit Cards: none
Notes: 2, 5, 8, 9, 10

FREDERICKSBURG

Gilead's Balm Manor Bed and Breakfast

8690 CR 201, 44627
(330) 695-3881

Nestled among the Amish farms of Holmes County, 14 minutes north of Berlin, you will find 5 landscaped acres of Amish country elegance. We have added four luxurious and spacious suites with 12-foot ceilings to our manor house. Each suite includes a two-person Jacuzzi, fireplace/gas logs, kitchen, private bath, satellite TV, air-conditioner, and double French doors with round-top windows overlooking our 2½-acre lake. Just minutes from shops and restaurants. Our guests say it's like experiencing the luxurious accommodations of a European estate. The hosts are of Amish and Mennonite backgrounds.

Hosts: David A. and Sara Mae Stutzman
Rooms: 4 (PB) $125-175
Continental Breakfast
Credit Cards: A, B, C, D
Notes: 2, 5, 7, 8, 9, 10, 12

GEORGETOWN

Bailey House B&B

112 N. Water Street, 45121
(937) 378-3087

The Bailey House is on the National Register of Historic Places. The three-story Greek Revival home is furnished in antiques and features three bedrooms with washstands and antique beds. The Bailey House is ½ block from Ulysses S. Grant's boyhood home; private tours are available.

Hostesses: Nancy Purdy and Jane Sininger
Rooms: 4 (SB) $55
Full Breakfast
Credit Cards: none
Notes: 2, 5, 6, 7, 8, 9, 10

GERMANTOWN

Gunckel Heritage Bed and Breakfast

33 W. Market Street, 45327–1353
(937) 855-3508

Located in the heart of the Gunckel Town Plat historic district, our bed and breakfast is a Federal-style brick home with Victorian influences. It features a front-to-back foyer with a grand staircase. The six fireplaces, beautiful woodwork, and original interior shutters add to the ambience. Enjoy a full breakfast by candlelight in our elegant dining room, on the covered balcony, or on the porch furnished in wicker, weather permitting. We like to spoil guests with complimentary refreshments and access to our ice cream sundae bar. Rooms are decorated in period antiques, with romantically furnished bedchambers. Antiquing, museums, parks, covered bridges, bike trails, and a nature center are all nearby. Ten-percent dinner coupon at the famous Florentine Hotel, two doors east.

Hosts: Lynn and Bonnie (Gunckel) Koogle
Rooms: 4 (PB) $70-95
Full Breakfast
Credit Cards: A, B, D
Notes: 2, 5, 7, 8, 9, 10, 11 (water)

GREENVILLE

The Waring House

304 W. Third Street, 45331
(937) 548-2682

The Waring House is an 1869 Victorian home restored to reflect the elegance of this romantic era. The ten-room Italianate home includes a double parlor, library, four bedrooms and guest bath, formal dining room, and kitchen, along with a lovely garden and in-ground pool. Your hosts individualize the accommodations to ensure a memorable stay for every guest. A highlight of your visit will be a home-cooked breakfast, which will be served in the formal dining room.

Hosts: Mike and Judy Miller
Rooms: 3 (SB) $60-75
Full Breakfast
Credit Cards: D
Notes: 2, 5, 7, 8, 9, 10

HAMILTON

Eaton Hill Bed and Breakfast

1951 Eaton Road, 45013
(513) 856-9552

Eaton Hill Bed and Breakfast has a country feel, although it is incorporated into the city of Hamilton, Ohio. The white Colonial home is surrounded by fields, trees, and flowers. It is 10 miles from the Miami University campus, conveniently located for parents, guests, and friends of the university and Butler County residents. A portable crib and highchair are available.

Hostess: Mrs. Pauline Zink
Rooms: 3 (1PB; 2SB) $50-60
Full Breakfast
Credit Cards: none
Notes: 2, 5, 6 (caged), 7, 8, 9, 10

LAKESIDE

Idlewyld Bed and Breakfast

350 Walnut, 43440
Mail: 17600 Detroit, #908, Lakewood, 44107
(419) 798-4198

Idlewyld has a homey ambience in which guests can relax and enjoy the tranquil beauty, friendly atmosphere, and timeless charm of 19th-century Lakeside. The home has a large, wraparound porch where guests can relax in comfort on Amish rockers. Rooms are clean, comfortable, and tastefully decorated; many amenities and pleasant surprises await guests. Nowhere is it possible to find a breakfast equal to that served at Idlewyld—we are fussy about what we serve, and it shows. Lakeside is a special place; lively activity coexists with spiritual calm. Spiritual, cultural, intellectual, and physical programs foster traditional Christian and family values.

Hosts: Dan and Joan Barris
Rooms: 15 (5PB; 10SB) $40-60
English Sideboard Breakfast
Credit Cards: A, B, D
Notes: 2, 7, 8, 9, 10

LEBANON

Burl Manor Bed and Breakfast

230 S. Mechanic Street, 45036
(513) 934-0400; FAX (513) 934-0402
Web site: http://www.lebanon-ohio.com/burlmanor.html

Located in historic Lebanon, Burl Manor was built in the mid-1800s by the editor and publisher of Ohio's oldest weekly newspaper, William H.P. Denney. This Italianate home reflects the past with spacious parlor, formal dining room, grandiose chandeliers, hand-crafted woodwork, and a unique fireplace. Outdoor activities include a swimming pool, lawn croquet, and pool volleyball. Harmon Golf and Tennis Center with a public park are just a block away.

Hosts: Jay and Liz Jorling
Rooms: 4 (PB) $80
Full Breakfast
Credit Cards: A, B
Notes: 2, 5, 7, 8, 9 (onsite), 10, 12

MARBLEHEAD

The Ivy House Bed and Breakfast

504 Ottawa Drive, 43440
(419) 798-4944
E-mail: lawyer@comp-res.com

Located on a rise above Lake Erie's western basin, The Ivy House offers a quiet wooded setting for your relaxation. Rent one room or the entire house (sleeps thirteen; nine beds) for a family or social gathering. Kitchen use possible; private beach pass; full breakfast served family-style. Walk to ferry dock, park, shops, and restaurant. We offer off-season and second-night discounts to help you save $ for play.

Hosts: Ray and Susan Lawyer
Rooms: 4 (SB) $55-65
Full Breakfast
Credit Cards: A, B, C, D
Notes: 2, 3 and 4 (pre-order), 6 (considered), 7, 9, 10, 12

MESOPOTAMIA

Old Stone House Bed and Breakfast

8505 Route 534; Box 177, 44439
(440) 693-4186

Wake your fondest memories in this setting from the past, built circa 1830 from sandstone used in northeastern Ohio's landmark buildings. Guests are intrigued by the oversize windowsills and immense walls of this architectural curiosity. Immerse yourself in the quaint life of the Amish and village commons built by Connecticut settlers as part of Ohio's Western Reserve. Retreat to our country room with fireplace and indulge in natural beauty. Private dining in Amish home, buggy ride, historic tours available. Three suites (two hydrotherapy whirlpools), sitting areas overlooking rolling countryside. Children welcome; no smoking. Evening snack and beverage. Forty-one miles east of Cleveland; approximately 30 minutes from Sea World.

Hosts: Sam and Darcy Miller
Rooms: 3 (PB) $85
Full Breakfast
Credit Cards: none
Notes: 6, 7

MILLERSBURG

Indiantree Farm Bed and Breakfast

5488 State Route 515, 44654
(330) 893-2497; (888) 267-5607

Peaceful lodging in a guest house on a picturesque hilltop farm in the heart of Amish country, a mile from Walnut Creek. Large front porch, farming with horses, hiking trails. Apartments with kitchen and bath for the price of a room. An oasis where time slows and the mood is conversation, not television.

Host: Larry D. Miller
Rooms: 3 (PB) $60-75
Continental Breakfast
Credit Cards: none
Notes: 2, 5, 11

NEW BEDFORD

Valley View Inn of New Bedford

32327 State Route 643, 43824
(330) 897-3232; (800) 331-VIEW (8439);
FAX (330) 897-0636
E-mail: valleyvu@bright.net
Web site: http://www.ez-page.com/valleyview

This Christian-owned and -operated inn is located in the midst of Ohio's Amish country. Relax by the cozy fireplace in the sitting room or enjoy the casual atmosphere of the family room. While there are no TVs to interrupt the serenity of the inn, a player piano, Ping-Pong table, checkers, or dart games await our guests. Shop in the nearby towns of Berlin, Walnut

Creek, or Charm, then stay at our inn for total stress relief.

Hosts: Dan and Nancy Lembke
Rooms: 10 (PB) $75-105
Full Breakfast (Continental on Sunday)
Credit Cards: A, B
Notes: 2, 5, 7 (13 and older), 10

OXFORD

The Duck Pond

6391 Morning Sun Road; PO Box 504, 44056
(513) 523-8914

An 1863 farmhouse situated 3 miles north of Miami University and uptown Oxford, 2 miles south of Hueston Woods State Park—which has an eighteen-hole golf course, nature trails, boating, swimming, and fishing. Antiquing awaits 15 miles away. Come and enjoy the quaintness that only a bed and breakfast can offer. Be our guest and enjoy our famous Hawaiian French toast. Reservations are required, so please call in advance. The Duck Pond is a member of the Ohio Bed and Breakfast Association and has met OBBA inspection standards.

Hosts: Don and Toni Kohlstedt
Rooms: 4 (1PB; 3SB) $55-75
Full Breakfast
Credit Cards: none
Notes: 2, 5, 8, 9, 10

PLAIN CITY

Yoder's Bed and Breakfast

8144 Cemetery Pike, 43064
(614) 873-4489

Located on a 107-acre farm northwest of Columbus. Big Darby Creek runs along the front yard. Excellent bird-watching. Within minutes of Amish restaurants, gift shops, cheese house, Amish furniture store, bookstores, and antique shops. King and queen beds, air-conditioning. No smoking or pets.

Hostess: Claribel Yoder
Rooms: 4 (1PB; 3SB) $55-68
Full Breakfast
Credit Cards: none
Notes: 2, 5, 9, 10

Inn at the Green

POLAND

Inn at the Green

500 S. Main Street, 44514
(330) 757-4688

An 1876 classic Victorian town house sharing the village green with a Presbyterian church founded in 1802. The inn retains 12-foot ceilings, large moldings, five working Italian marble fireplaces, interior window shutters, and poplar floors. The inn is decorated with antiques, American art, and Oriental rugs. Poland is a preserved Western Reserve village in which President William McKinley grew up.

Hosts: Ginny and Steve MeLoy
Rooms: 4 (PB) $60
Continental Breakfast
Credit Cards: A, B, D
Notes: 2, 5, 7, 8, 9, 10, 12

RIPLEY

The Baird House Bed and Breakfast

201 N. Second Street, 45167
(513) 392-4918

On the Historic Register, built in 1825 just 500 feet from the Ohio River on scenic State Route 52, 50 miles east of Cincinnati. Three porches, swings, rockers, beautiful sunsets, large historical area, museums, parks, and battle site areas nearby. Nine churches (several within walking distance), offstreet parking. Large parlor and library. Books, games, music, good food, snacks, and warm hospitality. His and her bicycles. Central air. Tea served at 4. Check-in at 3, check-out at 10. Full "gourmet" breakfast. Celebrating tenth anniversary in business; buy two nights and receive third night free.

Hosts: Glenn and Patricia Kittles
Rooms: 3 (2PB; 1SB) $95-150
Full Breakfast
Credit Cards: none
Notes: 2, 8, 10

Misty River Bed and Breakfast

206 N. Front Street, 45167
(937) 392-1556 (voice and FAX)

"A charming riverfront home" in Ripley's historic district. The decor is country and antique—both comfortable and welcoming—with private baths. Wood-burning fireplace in living room and spacious front porch for river-watching. Sunsets are spectacular. Ulysses S. Grant boarded here at age 16. Ripley was important in the "underground railroad." Full breakfast and wonderful homemade cinnamon rolls.

Hostess: Dotty Prevost
Rooms: 2 (PB) $75
Full Breakfast
Credit Cards: none
Notes: 2, 5, 12

The Signal House

The Signal House

234 N. Front Street, 45167
(937) 392-1640; FAX (937) 392-1240

This stately 1830 historic home overlooks the scenic Ohio River, offering relaxing porches and beautiful sunsets for romantic getaways or rural business trips. Guests enjoy central air, gardens, yard, and fireside parlor games. FAX and copier on premises. Five Civil War officers lived here. Legends tell of the "underground railroad." Ripley has 55 acres on the National Register of Historic Places. Named "Best Night Out" by *Cincinnati Magazine.*

Hosts: Vic and Betty Billingsley
Rooms: 2 (PB) $75
Full Breakfast
Credit Cards: A, B, D
Notes: 2, 5, 8, 10, 11 (water), 12

SANDUSKY

The 1890 Queen Anne Bed and Breakfast

714 Wayne Street, 44870
(419) 626-0391; FAX (419) 626-3064

Spacious accommodations with charm and elegance await at the 1890 Queen Anne B&B in downtown Sandusky. Built of native limestone, this 108-year-old Victorian home lends ambience and romance for its guests. Three large, air-conditioned rooms offer tranquil luxury for relaxation. Beauty abounds in the regal outdoors as viewed from a screened porch, where continental plus breakfasts are enjoyed. Easy access to beaches, Lake Erie island boat trips, Cedar Point, shopping, and other recreational opportunities. Brochure on request.

Host: Dr. Robert Kromer
Rooms: 3 (PB) $105-130
Continental Breakfast
Credit Cards: A, B, D
Notes: 2, 5, 8, 9, 10

Wagner's 1844 Inn

230 E. Washington Street, 44870
(419) 626-1726; FAX (419) 626-8465
E-mail: wagnersinn@sanduskyohio.com
Web site: http://www.lrbcg.com/wagnersinn

Located in the historic district in an 1844 Victorian home. All rooms have private baths, queen beds, and AC. Within walking distance of the bay, parks, museums, tennis courts, swimming pool, and ferries to Cedar Point and the Lake Erie Islands.

Hosts: Walt and Barb Wagner
Rooms: 3 (PB) $70-100
Continental Breakfast
Credit Cards: A, B, D
Notes: 5, 6, 8, 9, 10

SHELBY

Bethel Bed and Breakfast

4885 State Route 39, **Crestline,** 44827
(419) 347-3054
E-mail: spry641365@aol.com

A Christian atmosphere on 6 acres in farm country. We have a half-acre stocked pond, sand volleyball pit, horseshoe pits, herb and vegetable gardens, flowerbeds, fruit trees, sitting porches, and a Watchman Nee book room. Common living room with piano, board games, magazines, and door to the deck outside. Located between Shelby and Tiro on State Route 39. Call for brochure.

Hostess: Sue Pry
Rooms: 4 (1PB; 3SB)
Full Breakfast
Credit Cards: None
Notes: 2, 3, 4, 5, 7 (call first), 8, 9, 10, 11, 12

SIDNEY

GreatStone Castle

429 N. Ohio Avenue, 45365
(937) 498-4728; FAX (937) 498-9950
E-mail: greatstone@wesnet.com
Web site: http://www.bbhost.com/greatstonecastle_oh

GreatStone Castle, registered with the National Historical Society, is a 100-year-old mansion on 2 beautiful acres. The castle is constructed of 18-inch limestone with three turrets and is finished with rare, imported hardwood. Antique furniture, fireplaces, and fine furnishings help complete the elegant setting. A deluxe continental breakfast is served each morning in the mansion's conservatory.

Hosts: Frederick and Victoria Keller
Rooms: 5 (3PB; 2SB) $80-110
Continental Breakfast
Credit Cards: A, B, C
Notes: 2, 5, 8, 9, 10, 11, 12

SOMERSET

Somer Tea Bed and Breakfast

200 S. Columbus Street; Box 308, Route 13, 43783
(740) 743-2909

"Somer Tea" is named for the collection of more than 400 teapots and the friendly village of Somerset. An 1850s brick, two-story home on the National Register of Historic Places. Two bedrooms furnished with old, new, and cherished family pieces. Comfortable porch and deck. Tea always available. Somerset was settled in 1804 and was the boyhood hometown of Civil War Gen. Phil Sheridan. Air-conditioning throughout the house.

Hosts: Richard and Mary Lou Murray
Rooms: 2 (SB) $45-55
Full Breakfast
Credit Cards: none
Notes: 2, 5, 6, 7

Somer Tea Bed and Breakfast

STRASBURG

Ellis's Bed and Breakfast

104 Fourth Street SW, 44680
(330) 878-7863

Our turn-of-the-century home is comfortably furnished for your "home away from home." A big-screen TV in the sunken living room and a secluded patio are for your relaxation. A tasty, complete breakfast, different each morning, is served in the dining room using our best china, silver, etc. We are conveniently located for Zoar, Amish country, Dover/New Philadelphia, and Canton. Antiques, flea markets, gift shops, and restaurants abound. No smoking, please.

Hosts: Tom and Grace Ellis
Rooms: 3 (SB) $55
Full Breakfast
Credit Cards: none
Notes: 2, 5, 7

SUGAR GROVE

Hickory Bend Bed and Breakfast

7541 Dupler Road SE, 43155
(740) 746-8381
E-mail: ppeery@ohiohills.com

Nestled in the Hocking Hills of southeastern Ohio on 10 wooded acres. "So peaceful, we go out to watch *the car* go by on Sunday afternoon," says Pat. Patty is a spinner and weaver. The cozy, private room is outside the home in the midst of dogwood, poplar, and oak trees. Guests come for breakfast and conversation.

Hickory Bend Bed and Breakfast

Heated in the winter and cooled in the summer. Write for brochure.

Hosts: Pat and Patty Peery
Rooms: 1 (PB) $50
Full Breakfast
Credit Cards: none
Notes: 2, 8, 9, 10

SUGARCREEK

Breitenbach Bed and Breakfast

307 Dover Road, 44681
(330) 343-3603; (800) THE WINE;
FAX (330) 343-8290

Splendid accommodations in a quaint Swiss village in the heart of Amish country. This home is artistically furnished with a mixture of antiques, ethnic treasures, and local arts and crafts. Nearby Amish restaurants, cheese houses, flea markets, antique malls, and quilt and craft shops.

Breitenbach Bed and Breakfast

Evening refreshments and a full gourmet breakfast are served.

Hostess: Deanna Bear
Rooms: 4 (PB) $65-85
Full Breakfast
Credit Cards: A, B, C
Notes: 2, 5, 8, 10

Marbeyo Bed and Breakfast

2370 County Road 144, 44681
(330) 852-4533; FAX (330) 852-3605

Hosted by an Amish/Mennonite family, nestled in the heart of the Amish country in eastern Holmes County. Three bedrooms, private baths, AC. Relax in the quiet country; take leisurely walks on the farm; see the animals. Enjoy a delicious breakfast at your convenience.

Hosts: Mark and Betty Yoder
Rooms: 3 (PB) $55-75
Full Breakfast
Credit Cards: A, B
Notes: 2, 5, 7, 10

TIFFIN

Fort Ball Bed and Breakfast

25 Adams Street, 44883
(419) 447-0776; (888) 447-0776;
FAX (419) 447-3499

Our restored Queen Anne Revival house was built in 1894 by John King for his family. King was the master builder who constructed the Tiffin Court House and College Hall at Heidelberg College. The whole house is arranged for guests' enjoyment. Relax in the family room with TV/VCR or

Fort Ball Bed and Breakfast

the formal parlor with a book or an old issue of *National Geographic*.

Hosts: Charles and Lenora Livingston
Rooms: 4 (2PB; 2SB) $55-85
Full Breakfast
Credit Cards: A, B, D
Notes: 2, 5, 7, 10

TIPP CITY

Willow Tree Inn

1900 W. State Route 571, 45371
(937) 667-2957

Nestled on 5 country acres and surrounded by broad, rolling fields, the Willow Tree Inn is the perfect getaway for weary travelers. An ancient willow tree drowses by a spring-fed pond while ducks lazily paddle past. It's a wonderful place to relax, kick your shoes off, and enjoy good, old-fashioned hospitality. Built in 1830, our 6,000-square-foot historic estate has been fully restored. The original wide plank, ash floors and built-in bookshelves add special elegance to the front parlor, where our guests enjoy gathering in the evening for complimentary refreshments.

Hosts: Jolene and Chuck Sell
Rooms: 4 (3PB; 1SB) $65-85
Full Breakfast
Credit Cards: A, B
Notes: 2, 5, 6, 7, 9, 10, 12

TOLEDO

Cummings House Bed and Breakfast

1022 N. Superior Street, 43604–1961
(419) 244-3219 (voice and FAX); (888) 708-6998
E-mail: BnBToledo@aol.com

Nestled in Toledo's oldest neighborhood, the Vistula Historic District, the Cummings House B&B offers Victorian elegance to

Cummings House Bed and Breakfast

NOTES: Credit cards accepted: A Master Card; B Visa; C American Express; D Discover; E Diners Club; F Other; 2 Personal checks accepted; 3 Lunch available; 4 Dinner available; 5 Open all year; 6 Pets

travelers looking for a home away from home. Our home is a walk from downtown attractions and business centers. Our accommodations allow you to surround yourself with the grandeur of the 1890s while enjoying the comfortable amenities of the 1990s, including a secluded chapel in our third-floor tower.

Hosts: Lowell Greer and Lorelei Crawford
Rooms: 4 (2PB; 2SB) $60-90
Full or Continental Breakfast
Credit Cards: none
Notes: 2, 5, 9, 10

WAKEMAN

Melrose Farm Bed and Breakfast

727 Vesta Road, 44889
(419) 929-1867
E-mail: melrose@accnorwalk.com

Halfway between Ashland and Oberlin, Melrose Farm is a peaceful country retreat. Each of the three lovely guest rooms in the 125-year-old brick house has a private bath. Guests enjoy the tennis court, stocked pond, perennial gardens, and quiet, rural setting. Thirty miles from Cedar Point, an hour's drive from Cleveland or Toledo, 2 hours from Columbus. Air-conditioned comfort with old-fashioned, relaxed hospitality. Special Monday–Thursday rates for a multinight stay.

Hosts: Abe and Eleanor Klassen
Rooms: 3 (PB) $75
Full Breakfast
Credit Cards: none
Notes: 2, 3, 5, 7, 8 (onsite), 9, 10

WAUSEON

1910 House Bed and Breakfast

147 N. Franklin Street, 43567
(419) 335-7742; (888) 822-4566

Just a block from the Wauseon downtown area, our 1910 House is one of the oldest in the county. Built in the Georgian Revival style, it is tastefully decorated. The large guest rooms have a king bed and two twins in a separate room with private bath. A sumptuous breakfast of fresh fruit, home-baked bread/pastries, and hot entrée will ready you for a day's activities.

Hosts: Luz and Jose Tabilon
Rooms: 4 (2PB; 2SB) $65-85
Full Breakfast
Credit Cards: A, B
Notes: 2, 5, 8, 10

Hasseman House

WILMOT

Hasseman House

925 U.S. 62; PO Box 215, 44689
(330) 359-7904; FAX (330) 359-7159
Web site: http://www.amishdoor.com

Situated at the door to Ohio's Amish country is the Hasseman House. This charming and warm, early-1900s Victorian bed and breakfast invites you to unpack your bags and relax. Furnished with antiques, the Hasseman House is indeed a step back into a bygone era. Four cozy rooms complete with private baths and air-conditioning. Full breakfast. You will fall in love with the intricate woodwork and original stained glass. Amish restaurant and many shops nearby. Walk-ins welcome!

Hosts: Milo and Kathryn Miller
Rooms: 4 (PB) $69-110
Full Breakfast
Credit Cards: A, B, D
Notes: 2, 5, 9, 10

Raber's Tri-County View Bed and Breakfast

PO Box 155, 44689
(330) 359-5189

Raber's Tri-County View is located in the world's largest Amish settlement, with lots of rolling hills and fields all around. Each room has a unique, peaceful atmosphere and decor, with private bath, queen-size bed, central heating and air-conditioning, microwave, refrigerator, and coffeepot. From a garden swing, you can relax and enjoy the view of three different counties. No smoking inside. One mile from Wilmot, 10 miles from Berlin, Walnut Creek, and Kidron in Amish country. Lots of quilts, antiques, and craft shops, cheese houses, furniture stores, and the best restaurants in the state.

Hosts: Ed and Esther Raber
Rooms: 3 (PB) $55-85
Full Breakfast
Credit Cards: A, B
Notes: 2, 5, 7, 8, 9, 10

WOOSTER

Historic Overholt House

1473 Beall Avenue, 44691
(330) 263-6300; (800) 992-0643;
FAX (330) 263-9378
E-mail: overholtBB@aol.com
Web site: http://www.bbonline.com/oh/overholt

This "stick-style Victorian" home with a rare, solid walnut "flying staircase" is located at the gateway to Amish country. Adjacent to the College of Wooster, within walking distance of the Ohio Light Opera. Executive candlelight breakfast, hot tub, Christmas parlor, two fireplaces, parklike setting. Special rates for small groups who stay two days and occupy all four rooms. Full money-back guarantee.

Hostesses: Sandy Pohalski and Bobbie Walton
Rooms: 4 (PB) $63-70
Executive Continental Breakfast
Credit Cards: A, B, C, D
Notes: 2, 5, 7, 8, 9, 10

Millennium Classic B&B

1626 Beall Avenue, 44691
(330) 264-6005; (800) 937-4199;
FAX (330) 264-5008
Web site: http://www.bbonline.com/oh/millennium

Millennium Classic is located in the heart of Wooster. Close to the College of Wooster, hospital, shopping mall, restaurants, and grocery store. Post-Victorian exterior, with a traditional, classic theme inside. Lots of decks, porches, quiet sitting areas, and shade trees. You'll enjoy the friendly, homelike atmosphere.

Host: John Byler
Rooms: 4 (PB) $55-95
Extended Continental Breakfast
Credit Cards: A, B, C, D
Notes: 2, 5, 7, 8, 9, 10, 12

Oklahoma

ALINE

Heritage Manor Bed and Breakfast

RR 3, Box 33, 73716
(580) 463-2563; (800) 295-2563

Heritage Manor is a country getaway on 80 acres that was settled in the 1893 Land Run in northwestern Oklahoma. Two prestatehood homes have been joined and restored by the innkeepers, using a Victorian theme. Enjoy beautiful sunrises, sunsets, stargazing from the rooftop deck, relaxing in the hot tub, and reading a book from the 5,000-volume library. Ostriches, donkeys, and Scottish Highland cattle roam a fenced area. Located close to Selenite Crystal digging area and several other attractions.

Hosts: A.J. and Carolyn Rexroat
Rooms: 4 (2 PB; 2SB) $75-150
Full Breakfast
Credit Cards: none
Notes: 2, 3 and 4 (by reservation), 5, 6 and 7 (by arrangement), 9, 10 (30 miles)

CHICKASHA

Campbell-Richison House Bed and Breakfast

1428 Kansas Avenue, 73018
(405) 222-1754; FAX (405) 224-1190
E-mail: davidratcliff@worldnet.att.net

The Campbell-Richison House, built in 1909, recaptures the charm and hospitality of a past era. The house shares the histories of three families: C. M. George Hollingsworth, C. B. and Margaret Campbell, and Cori and Beth Richison, all Grady County pioneers in their own way. At present, the Campbell-Richison House is a family-run bed and breakfast guest house. David and Kami purchased the home in 1993 and are restoring it to its original grandeur. The guest rooms are uniquely and warmly decorated.

Hosts: David and Kami Ratcliff
Rooms: 3 (1PB; 2SB) $45-65
Full Breakfast
Credit Cards: A, B, C
Notes: 2, 5, 7, 8, 10

---

welcome; 7 Children welcome; 8 Tennis nearby; 9 Swimming nearby; 10 Golf nearby; 11 Skiing nearby; 12 May be booked through travel agent.

OKLAHOMA

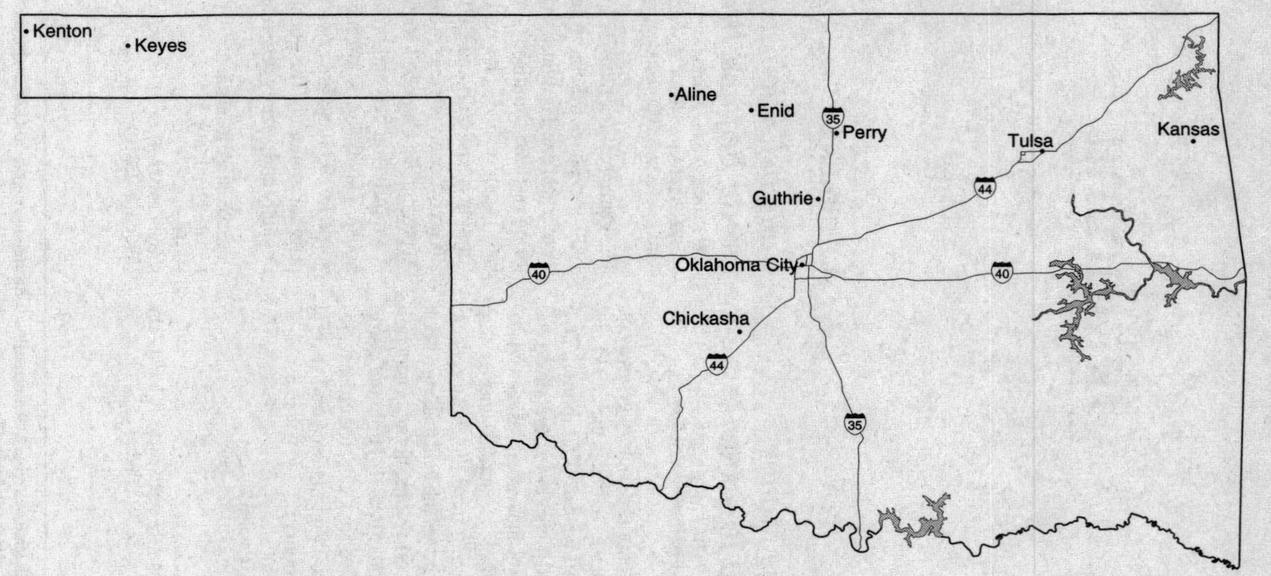

Kenton
Keyes
Aline
Enid
35
Perry
Tulsa
Kansas
44
Guthrie
40
Oklahoma City
40
Chickasha
44
35

ENID

Worthington House —the Bed and Breakfast of Enid

1224 W. Main Street, 73703
(580) 237-9202; (888) 242-5009;
FAX (580) 233-6193
E-mail: worthing@enid.com

This 90-year-old Colonial Revival home wraps you in a relaxed, casual atmosphere, surrounded by warm hominess. Leave behind the stress and struggles of everyday life. Relax and visit in our country library, or enjoy the goldfish pond in the garden area. Three lovely bedrooms with private baths await you with unexpected amenities. TV/VCRs in rooms. Gourmet breakfast. Corporate rates Sunday–Thursday. Share our gift of hospitality.

Hosts: Gary and Cindy Worthington
Rooms: 3 (PB) $65-75
Full Breakfast
Credit Cards: A, B
Notes: 2

GUTHRIE

Victorian Rose Bed and Breakfast

415 E. Cleveland, 73044
(405) 282-3928

The 100-year-old Queen Anne home, built in 1894, mixes the charm of the past with the comforts of the present. Located on a brick street, it features a wraparound porch with gingerbread accents, with a porch swing and garden area. Lovely restoration with quality workmanship: beautiful oak floors; exquisite, original beveled windows; gleaming brass light fixtures; and antiques. Three blocks from historic downtown (the largest urban historical district in the U.S.). Three beautiful Victorian guest rooms offer queen beds and private baths. Full, complimentary gourmet breakfast. Family rates and gift certificates available.

Victorian Rose Bed and Breakfast

Hosts: Linda and Foy Shahan
Rooms: 3 (PB) $69-89
Full Gourmet Breakfast
Credit Cards: A, B, D
Notes: 2, 5, 8, 9, 10, 12

KANSAS

Hanner House Hideaway

650 Highland Road, 74347
(918) 597-2121
E-mail: hanhouse@sstelco.com
Web site: http://telstar1.com/hanhouse.htm

Hanner House Hideaway is nestled among pines and oaks near the Illinois River. It is a restful, secluded home that overlooks a small lake. Come listen to the whippoorwills and gaze at the stars. The property has a large pool, two hot tubs, sauna, some whirlpool tubs, dessert in the evening, and a large breakfast.

Host: Damon Waggoner
Rooms: 6 + loft (for groups) (PB) $65-110
Full Breakfast
Credit Cards: A, B
Notes: 2, 4 (some days), 5, 7, 8, 10

KENTON

Black Mesa Bed and Breakfast

PO Box 81, 73946
(580) 261-7443; (800) 866-3009
E-mail: BMBB1@juno.com
Web site: http://www.ccccok.org/bmbb.html

Located 2 miles north of Kenton at the foot of the Black Mesa, this 1910 rock ranch house boasts the best in country hospitality. Whether hiking, rock hounding, fishing, hunting, birding, or escaping the routine, rest in a double-occupancy or family suite (sleeps eight) at Black Mesa Bed and Breakfast.

Hosts: Monty Joe and Vicki Roberts
Rooms: 2 (PB)
Full Breakfast
Credit Cards: A, B, D
Notes: 2, 3, 4, 5, 6, 7, 10

KEYES

Cattle Country Inn Bed and Breakfast

HC 1, Box 34, 73947
(580) 543-6458; (800) 406-6458

We are truly country-located. If you like wide-open spaces where you can see for miles and not be in hearing distance of any highway traffic, come stay with us. Located in the panhandle between Guymon and Boise City, the inn is a nice stopping place on the way to or from the Rockies. Come experience the hospitality and hearty cookin' served up by your host in the beautiful, spacious, very modern ranch-style home. Located 38 miles west of Guymon on Highway 64, then 8½ miles south on dirt roads. Cimarron County, the last county west, has many points of interest, as well as plenty of good prairie dog and pheasant hunting.

Hosts: Lane and Karen Sparkman
Rooms: 6 (1PB; 5SB) $55
Full Breakfast
Credit Cards: A, B, C
Notes: 2, 5, 7

OKLAHOMA CITY

The Grandison at Maney Park

1200 N. Shartel, 73103
(405) 232-8778; (800) 240-4667;
FAX (405) 232-5039
E-mail: grandison@juno.com
Web site: http://www.bbonline.com/ok/grandison/history.html

Nine bedrooms feature antique furnishings, queen and king beds, private baths with double Jacuzzi and shower, and gas fireplaces. Built in 1904 and moved to its present location in 1909, the home features carved mahogany woodwork, a massive entry with curved staircase, original stained-glass and brass fixtures—charming details at every turn. We offer romantic getaways and executive services.

NOTES: Credit cards accepted: A Master Card; B Visa; C American Express; D Discover; E Diners Club; F Other; 2 Personal checks accepted; 3 Lunch available; 4 Dinner available; 5 Open all year; 6 Pets

Television and phone are available in rooms on request. Refreshment bar, workout room, and gift shop.

Hosts: Bob and Claudia Wright
Rooms: 9 (PB) $75-135
Full Breakfast weekends, Continental weekdays
Credit Cards: A, B, C, D
Notes: 2, 3 and 4 (10+ people), 5, 6 and 7 (limited), 12

PERRY

Oklahoma Territory 1893

Route 3, Box 50, 73077
(580) 336-9452 (voice and FAX);
(888) OKT-1893 (658-1893)
Web site: http://www.bbonline.com/ok/territory

Located just 9 miles east of the ranching community of Perry, Oklahoma Territory 1893 sits on 15 acres of romantic Oklahoma prairie land. Centrally located within an hour of 400 antique dealers, historical sights and museums, rodeos and Native American powwows, quail and pheasant hunting, Oklahoma State University, and The Lazy E. Arena. It is within a 90-minute drive of Oklahoma City and Tulsa. A pasture and roping arena are available to guests by prior arrangement.

Hosts: Jo and Mary McGuire
Rooms: 5 (2PB; 3SB) $59-85
Full or Continental Breakfast
Credit Cards: A, B

TULSA

Hideaway Bed and Breakfast

6130 W. 39th Street S., 74107–4818
(918) 445-2838

The perfect place for that much-needed getaway. Relax with morning coffee or have a quiet evening under the stars on your private deck. Bring along your favorite movie and spend a cozy romantic night in the privacy of your guest room. Come and let us pamper you. We'd love to have you as our guests.

Hosts: Mark and Pam Hollie
Rooms: 1 (PB) $80-135
Full Breakfast (optional)
Credit Cards: none
Notes: 2, 5

OREGON

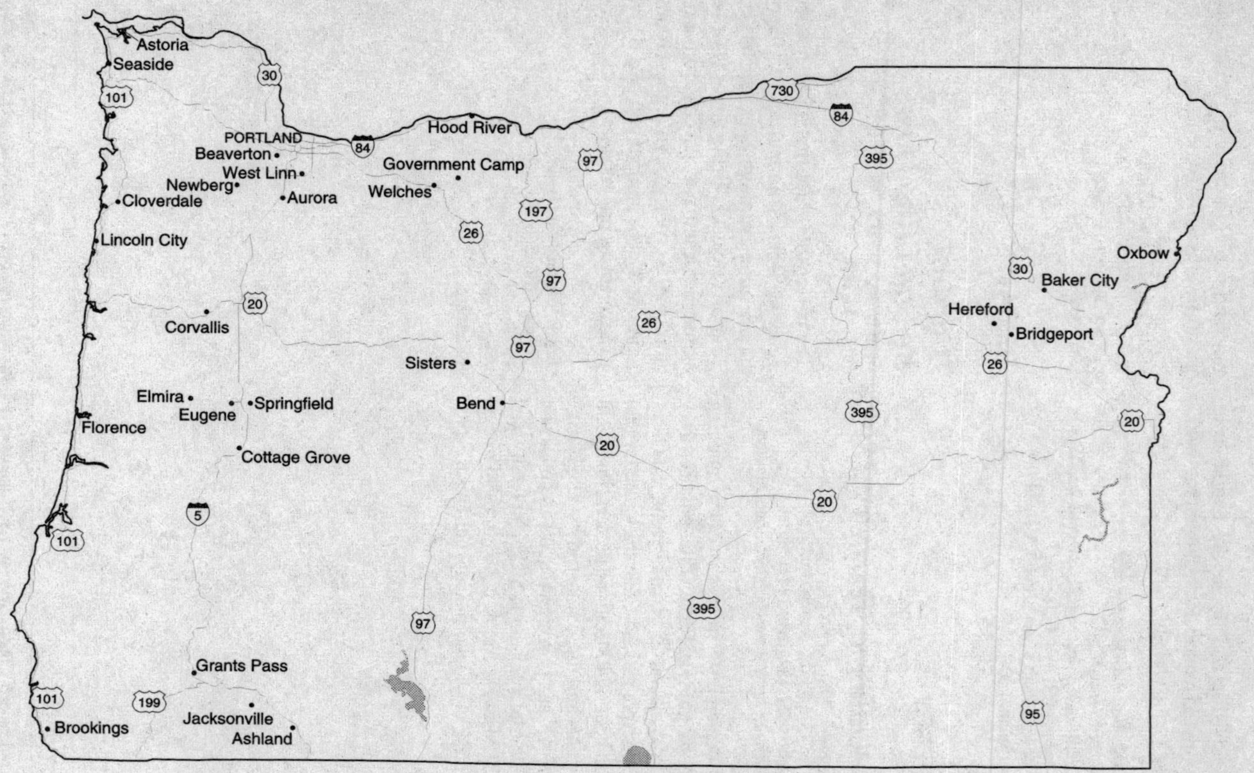

Astoria
Seaside
PORTLAND
Beaverton
West Linn
Newberg
Cloverdale
Aurora
Hood River
Government Camp
Welches
Lincoln City
Corvallis
Sisters
Bend
Elmira
Eugene
Springfield
Florence
Cottage Grove
Oxbow
Baker City
Hereford
Bridgeport
Grants Pass
Jacksonville
Ashland
Brookings
30
101
84
730
395
97
197
26
20
5
199
95

Oregon

ASHLAND

Cowslip's Belle Bed and Breakfast

159 N. Main Street, 97520
(541) 488-2901; (800) 888-6819;
FAX (541) 482-6138
E-mail: stay@cowslip.com
Web site: http://www.cowslip.com/cowslip

Teddy bears, chocolate truffles, cozy down comforters, and scrumptious breakfasts. Cowslip's Belle Bed and Breakfast is a delightful 1913 Craftsman bungalow and carriage house in the heart of the historic district. The B&B, a nationally recognized award winner, has been featured in 1) *McCall's* (one of the "Most Charming Inns in America"), 2) *Country Accents,* 3) *Northwest Best Places,* 4) *The Best Places to Kiss in the Northwest,* and 5) *Weekends for Two in the Pacific Northwest—50 Romantic Getaways.*

Hosts: Jon and Carmen Reinhardt
Rooms: 4 (PB) $95-140
Full Breakfast
Credit Cards: A, B
Notes: 2, 5, 8, 9, 10, 11, 12

Mt. Ashland Inn

Mt. Ashland Inn

550 Mt. Ashland Ski Road, 97520
(541) 482-8707 (voice and FAX); (800) 830-8707
Web site: http://www.mtashlandinn.com

Beautifully handcrafted log lodge and sauna/spa terrace command spectacular views from a mountain ridge just south of Ashland. Rock fireplace, Oriental rugs, and antique furnishings create a warm, luxurious atmosphere. Hike or ski the Pacific Crest Trail from the front door. Quality snowshoes and mountain bikes available

---

NOTES: Credit cards accepted: A Master Card; B Visa; C American Express; D Discover; E Diners Club; F Other; 2 Personal checks accepted; 3 Lunch available; 4 Dinner available; 5 Open all year; 6 Pets welcome; 7 Children welcome; 8 Tennis nearby; 9 Swimming nearby; 10 Golf nearby; 11 Skiing nearby; 12 May be booked through travel agent.

at no charge. "A magical mountain retreat," says *Country Home*. Three stars, *Northwest Best Places*. AAA, Mobil. "A retreat for all seasons. . .promises renewal, relaxation, and adventure!" says *Country Living* magazine.

Hosts: Chuck and Laurel Biegert
Rooms: 5 (PB) $79-190
Full Breakfast
Credit Cards: A, B, C, D
Notes: 2, 5, 8, 9, 10, 11, 12

Benjamin Young Inn

ASTORIA

Benjamin Young Inn

3652 Duane Street, 97103
(503) 325-6172; (800) 201-1286
E-mail: benyoung@willapabay.org
Web sites: http://www.ohwy.com/or/b/benyoung.htm
http://www.morian.com/inns

This Queen Anne Victorian built in 1888 is ideal for romantic getaways. Relax in the Jacuzzi tub of our Fireplace Suite with king bed, fireplace, and television/VCR, or enjoy the Honeymoon Suite. Ken often performs weddings. Five rooms, views, private baths, gourmet breakfasts. Catering for groups of 8–100+. National Register of Historic Places.

Hosts: Carolyn and Rev. Ken Hammer
Rooms: 5 (PB) $75-135
Full Breakfast
Credit Cards: A, B, C, D, E
Notes: 2, 5, 7 (well-behaved), 8, 9, 10, 12

Columbia River Inn

1681 Franklin Avenue, 97103
(503) 325-5044; (800) 953-5044

Columbia River Inn is charming in every way. Built in 1870, this beautiful "painted lady" Victorian has a gazebo for weddings and parties in the beautifully landscaped garden. Come see the "stairway to the stars," a unique terraced garden view of the celebrated Columbia River. Aquatic center and seafood lab nearby. An eight-screen theater 2 blocks away is coming in 1999. The inn offers four elegantly furnished rooms, one with a working fireplace and Jacuzzi. Beautiful side garden added, with cobblestone sidewalk. My specialty is hospitality—"Home is where the heart is. . . ." Guests may use offstreet parking. Gift certificates available.

Hostess: Karen N. Nelson
Rooms: 4 (PB) $75-125
Full Breakfast
Credit Cards: A, B
Notes: 2, 5, 7 (6 and older), 9, 10

Grandview Bed and Breakfast

1574 Grand Avenue, 97103
(503) 325-5555; (800) 488-3250
Web site: www.bbonline.com/or/grandview

Antiques and white wicker furnishings grace this Victorian home, born in 1896.

Ivy and alders grow profusely on the west side, sheltering birds and birdhouses. Most rooms have birdcages for decoration. Some rooms overlook the Columbia River. Breakfast, served in the tower of the bullet turret, may include smoked salmon, cream cheese, and bagels. Astoria was established in 1811. Fur trading, then salmon and logging gave this town its start.

Hostess: Charlene Maxwell
Rooms: 9 (7PB; 2SB) $55-105
Full Breakfast
Credit Cards: A, B, D
Notes: 5, 7 (over 8), 8, 9, 10

The Inn at Aurora

AURORA

The Inn at Aurora

15109 2nd Street NE, 97002
(503) 678-1932; (888) 799-1374
E-mail: weaver@hevanet.com
Web site: http://www.ohwy.com/or/i/innataur.htm

Designed to reflect the Old Aurora Colony, this new inn is located in the National Historic District near the Old Aurora Colony Museum and numerous antique shops. Champoeg State Park by the Willamette River and Silver Falls State Park are nearby for hiking and biking. All rooms have king beds, AC, cable TV, and phones. The suite is hearthside with a spa tub. Upper rooms offer pleasant views of Aurora and the natural landscape.

Hostess: Fay and Dave Weaver
Rooms: 4 (PB) $89-119
Full Breakfast
Credit Cards: A, B, C
Notes: 2, 5, 10, 12

BAKER CITY

Baer House B&B

2333 Main Street, 97814
(541) 524-1812
E-mail: baerhouse@triax.com
Web site: http://www.triax.com/baerhouse

Rendezvous with history. Experience luxury on the Oregon Trail. Enjoy an 1882 Victorian Italianate listed on the National Register, with Christian hosts. Two rooms share a new bath, and the large, two-room suite has a private bath with claw-foot tub and pedestal sink. Laundry and kitchenette are provided. Convenient Main Street location. Year-round recreational opportunities, including skiing and the National Oregon Trail Interpretive Center.

Hosts: Judy and Nick Greear
Rooms: 3 (1PB; 2SB)
Full Breakfast
Credit Cards: A, B, C, D
Notes: 5, 9, 10, 11

BEAVERTON

The Yankee Tinker

5480 SW 183rd Avenue, 97007
(503) 649-0932 (voice and FAX); (800) 846-5372
E-mail: yankeet676@aol.com
Web site: http://www.yankeetinker.com

Easy access to Beaverton, Hillsboro business; 10 miles west of Portland in Washington County wine country. Comfortable

welcome; 7 Children welcome; 8 Tennis nearby; 9 Swimming nearby; 10 Golf nearby; 11 Skiing nearby; 12 May be booked through travel agent.

home operating as a B&B since 1988, filled with heirlooms, antiques, quilts, and flowers. Private yard/gardens. Spacious deck. Quiet retreat, perfect for a day or week. Fireplace in guest sitting room. AC. Acclaimed breakfasts, timed and scaled to meet your needs, utilize the abundant variety of locally grown fruits and berries. Featured in *Hidden Oregon*.

Hosts: Jan and Ralph Wadleigh
Rooms: 3 (2PB; 1SB) $65-75
Full Breakfast
Credit Cards: A, B, C, D, E
Notes: 2, 5, 9, 10, 12

BEND

Gazebo B&B

21679 Obsidian Avenue, 97702
(541) 389-7202

Come visit our country home with a panoramic view of the Cascades from Mt. Hood to Mt. Bachelor. Relax among our antique furnishings or in the rock garden and gazebo. Enjoy nearby skiing, hiking, fishing, rafting, and the best golfing in Oregon. Minutes from town. Family-style breakfast. Smoking outdoors only.

Hosts: Gale and Helen Estergreen
Rooms: 2 (1PB; 1SB) $50-60
Full Breakfast
Credit Cards: none
Notes: 2, 5, 7, 8, 9, 10, 11

BRIDGEPORT

Bruno Ranch

PO Box 51, 97819
(561) 446-3468

Bruno Ranch is a ranch cottage in the country, 25 miles from Baker City. Come stay with us to rest and recharge. It's like going to a real "grandma's house!" Open all year. Bird-watching, hunting, and fishing are nearby.

Bruno Ranch

Hostess: Maria Bruno
Rooms: 2 (SB) $30
Full Breakfast
Credit Cards: none
Notes: 3 and 4 (can be arranged), 5, 7

BROOKINGS

Chetco River Inn

21202 High Prairie Road, 97415
(541) 670-1645; (800) 327-2688
Web site: http://www.chetcoriverinn.com

Chetco River Inn is a back-country inn situated right on a wild and scenic river. Areas of forest provide you with privacy and an opportunity to stop the time. You will be pampered with big country breakfasts, down beds, private baths, and all the cookies and coffee you want. Hiking, fishing, swimming, star-gazing, and nature-watching are waiting. Brookings is a

NOTES: Credit cards accepted: A Master Card; B Visa; C American Express; D Discover; E Diners Club; F Other; 2 Personal checks accepted; 3 Lunch available; 4 Dinner available; 5 Open all year; 6 Pets

coastal town. The Kalmiopsis Wilderness Area is close by.

Hostess: Sandra Brugger
Rooms: 5 (PB) $115-135
Full Breakfast
Credit Cards: A, B
Notes: 2, 4, 5, 7 (if old enough to take their own rooms), 9 (river)

CLOVERDALE

Sandlake Country Inn

8505 Galloway Road, 97112
(503) 965-6745

Sshhh. . . .We're a secret hideaway on the awesome Oregon coast—a private, peaceful place for making memories. This 1894 shipwreck-timbered farmhouse on the Oregon Historic Registry is tucked into a bower of old roses. You will find hummingbirds, Mozart, cookies at midnight, marble fireplaces, whirlpool baths for two, a honeymoon cottage, vintage movies, and breakfast en suite. This is a nonsmoking, wheelchair-accessible inn.

Hosts: Femke and David Durham
Rooms: 4 (PB) $90-135
Full Breakfast
Credit Cards: A, B, C, D
Notes: 2, 12

CORVALLIS

A B&B on the Green

(Formerly Abed & Breakfast at Sparks' Hearth)
2515 SW 45th Street, 97333
(541) 757-7321; (888) 757-7321;
FAX (541) 753-4332
E-mail: sparks@bandbonthegreen.com
Web site: http://www.bandbonthegreen.com

Critique passing golfers from our back deck or spoil yourself in the outdoor spa—we furnish plush body towels and robes; you bring a suit. Visit on red velvet Victorian furnishings and Oriental carpets in the living room, or crash in comfort in the TV/reading room. Sleep in country quiet on a king bed in a king bedroom. Awaken to a breakfast of fresh fruit compote, a hot entrée, and homemade pie, served on china and crystal. Life is good!

Hosts: Neoma and Herb Sparks
Rooms: 4 (2PB; 2SB) $70-85
Full Breakfast
Credit Cards: A, B, C, D, E
Notes: 2, 5, 7 (over 8), 8, 9, 10, 12

COTTAGE GROVE

Apple Inn Bed and Breakfast

30697 Kenady Lane, 97424
(541) 942-2393; (800) 942-2393;
FAX (541) 767-0402
E-mail: appleinn@pond.net
Web site: http://www.pond.net/~bnbassoc/appleinn.html

Lovely country home snuggled in our 190-acre forest and tree farm. Close to I–5 and Cottage Grove with covered bridges, antiques, golf, and lakes. Two rooms with private baths charmingly decorated in country and antiques, comfortable beds, view, TV/VCR, phone, luxury hot tub. Featured in the Sunday *Oregonian* travel section. Homemade breakfast plus snacks. Smoking outside, children by arrangement. Cookbook available. Privacy and pampering. Be our guests!

Hosts: Harry and Kathe McIntire
Rooms: 2 (PB) $75-95
Full Breakfast
Credit Cards: D
Notes: 2, 5, 7, 8, 9, 10

McGillivray's Log Home Bed and Breakfast

ELMIRA

McGillivray's Log Home Bed and Breakfast

88680 Evers Road, 97437
(541) 935-3564

Fourteen miles west of Eugene, on the way to the coast, you will find the best of yesterday and the comforts of today. King beds, air-conditioning, and quiet. Old-fashioned breakfasts usually are prepared on an antique, wood-burning cookstove. This built-from-scratch 1982 log home is near Fern Ridge Lake.

Hostess: Evelyn R. McGillivray
Rooms: 2 (PB) $70-80
Continental Breakfast
Credit Cards: A, B
Notes: 2, 5

EUGENE

Camille's Bed and Breakfast

3277 Onyx Place, 97405
(541) 344-9576; FAX (541) 345-9970
E-mail: wkievith@aol.com

A 1963 contemporary home in a woodsy older neighborhood furnished in American country antiques. Rooms offer wonderfully comfortable queen beds, artistic touches. Cozy guest sitting room has a phone and cable TV. Two rooms, one with private bath (you and your party are the only guests). Close to the University of Oregon, minutes from downtown. Near one of Eugene's most popular restaurants. Full, healthy breakfast (guests have menu options). Smoke-free environment. Dutch spoken by host.

Hosts: Bill and Camille Kievith
Rooms: 2 (1PB; 1SB) $50-60
Full Breakfast
Credit Cards: none
Notes: 2, 5, 8, 9, 10

The Campbell House, A City Inn

252 Pearl Street, 97401
(541) 343-1119; (800) 264-2519;
FAX (541) 343-2258
E-mail: campbellhouse@campbellhouse.com
Web site: http://www.campbellhouse.com

Splendor and romance in the tradition of a fine European hotel. Each of the elegant rooms features private bath, TV/VCR, telephone, and robes. Selected rooms feature a four-poster bed, fireplace, and jetted or claw-foot tub. Take pleasure from the Old World ambience of the parlor and library with a fine selection of books and videos. Within walking distance of restaurants, theaters, museums, and shops. Two blocks from 9 miles of riverside bike paths and jogging trails.

Hostess: Myra and Roger Plant
Rooms: 12 + 6 luxury suites (PB) $80-275
Full Breakfast
Credit Cards: A, B, C, D
Notes: 5, 7, 8, 9, 10, 12

NOTES: Credit cards accepted: A Master Card; B Visa; C American Express; D Discover; E Diners Club; F Other; 2 Personal checks accepted; 3 Lunch available; 4 Dinner available; 5 Open all year; 6 Pets

FLORENCE

Betty's Barn Home Bed and Breakfast

05659 Canary Road, 97439
(541) 997-2764

"Country on the Coast." Back to the real thing in the bed and breakfast experience. Quiet, peaceful surroundings. Tall trees, green lawns, beautiful landscaping amid Oregon's National Recreation Area, ¼ mile from the famous Jessie M. Honeyman State Park. Boating, swimming.

Host: Betty (Marion E.) Westfall
Rooms: 2 (SB) $55-65
Full Breakfast
Credit Cards: none
Notes: 2, 5, 7, 8, 9, 10, 11 (water)

Flery Manor Bed and Breakfast

GRANTS PASS

Flery Manor Bed and Breakfast

2000 Jumpoff Joe Creek Road, 97526
(541) 476-3591; FAX (541) 471-2303
E-mail: flery@flerymanor.com
Web site: http://www.flerymanor.com

Elegant, romantic, secluded. Nestled on 7 mountain view acres near the Rogue River. Four elegantly decorated rooms. Full private baths. Central air. The suite has a king bed, fireplace, Jacuzzi tub, and private balcony. The living room is two stories high with 20-foot high windows to expose the magnificent view, including numerous varieties of birds and wildlife. Ponds, paths, and flowers grace the lower yard. Our new gazebo, with its waterfall and koi pond, is the perfect place to relax or enjoy a BBQ. We also offer a library, parlor with piano, huge balcony, and formal dining room where we serve a three-course gourmet breakfast on fine china. Our guests can enjoy a luxurious, private health club.

Hosts: John and Marla Vidrinskas
Rooms: 4 (PB) $75-125
Full Gourmet Breakfast
Credit Cards: A, B
Notes: 2, 4, 5, 7 (over 10 years), 8, 9, 10, 11, 12

The Ivy House

139 SW "T" Street, 97526
(541) 474-7363

Enjoy fine English tradition in downtown Grants Pass. Within easy walking distance of historic district, shops, and restaurants. This 1908 brick home offers beautifully appointed rooms, friendly and cheery. Tea and biscuits in bed are offered. Followed by a full English breakfast. Jacuzzi bathtub for your pleasure. King, queen, full,

The Ivy House

welcome; 7 Children welcome; 8 Tennis nearby; 9 Swimming nearby; 10 Golf nearby; 11 Skiing nearby; 12 May be booked through travel agent.

and twin beds. We have air-conditioning and a pure-water alpine air cleaner.

Hostess: Doreen Pontius
Rooms: 5 (1PB; 4SB) $65-90
Full Breakfast
Credit Cards: A, B
Notes: 2, 5, 6, 7, 8, 9, 10, 11, 12

Fort Reading Bed and Breakfast

HEREFORD

Fort Reading Bed and Breakfast

20588 Highway 245, 97837
(541) 446-3478 (voice and FAX); (800) 573-4285

We are a working cattle ranch 40 miles southwest of Baker City in the Burnt River Valley. While you're with us, enjoy a stroll around the ranch, the country charm of your own two-bedroom cottage, and a ranch-style breakfast in the ranch house breakfast room. Squirrel, deer, and elk hunts can be arranged. There are streams and a lake nearby for fishing. No smoking. Open April–September.

Hosts: Daryl and Barbara Hawes
Rooms: 2 (SB) $45-75
Full Ranch-Style Breakfast
Credit Cards: none
Notes: 2, 3, 4, 6, 7

HOOD RIVER

Columbia Gorge Hotel

4000 Westcliff Drive, 97031
(541) 386-5566; (800) 345-1921;
FAX (541) 387-5414
E-mail: cghotel@gorge.net
Web site: http://www.gorge.net/lodging/cghotel

The Columbus Gorge Hotel, 60 miles east of Portland, was built in 1921 as a gracious oasis for travelers along the Columbia River Gorge Scenic Highway. At the top of a 208-foot waterfall, above the majestic Columbia River, the hotel has a national reputation for fine cuisine and elegant surroundings. The hotel boasts forty unique nonsmoking guest rooms, award-winning dining, and exquisite wedding facilities on 11 beautiful acres. All rooms have private baths and include "The World Famous Farm Breakfast."®

Hosts: Boyd and Halla Graves, Chavalla Lopez
Rooms: 40 (PB)
Special Breakfast
Credit Cards: none

JACKSONVILLE

The Touvelle House Bed and Breakfast

455 N. Oregon Street; PO Box 1891, 97530
(541) 899-8938; (800) 846-8422
E-mail: touvelle@wave.net
Web site: http://www.wave.net/upg/touvelle

A 1916 Craftsman-style mansion on two acres, 2 blocks from the village. Six charming, individually decorated bedrooms, all with private baths and air-conditioning. Watch the "world go by" from our covered verandas. You will enjoy the pool, spa, library, and fireplace in the great room. Come be pampered like hotel guests of a time gone by.

Hosts: Dennis and Carolee Casey
Rooms: 6 (PB) $90-115
Full Breakfast
Credit Cards: A, B, C, D, E
Notes: 2, 5, 8, 9 (onsite), 10, 11, 12

LINCOLN CITY

Brey House "Ocean View" B&B Inn

3725 NW Keel Avenue, 97367
(541) 994-7123
Web site: http://www.moriah.com/breyhouse

The ocean awaits you just across the street. Enjoy whale-watching, storm-watching, or just beachcombing. We are conveniently located a short walking distance from local restaurants and retail shops. Guests have four beautiful rooms to choose from, all with private baths and queen beds. Flannel sheets and electric blankets are in all the guest rooms. Enjoy Milt and Shirley's talked-about breakfast. Brey House is a three-story, Cape Cod–style home.

Hosts: Milt and Shirley Brey
Rooms: 4 (PB) $70-135
Full Breakfast
Credit Cards: A, B, D
Notes: 2, 5, 9, 10, 12

Pacific Rest Bed and Breakfast

1611 NE 11th Street, 97367
(541) 994-2337; (888) 405-7378
E-mail: jwaetjen@wcn.net

Newer home on a hillside within walking distance of shops, restaurants, lake, and

Pacific Rest Bed and Breakfast

beach. Two spacious suites with private baths and decks. Also available: a two-bedroom, two-bath, fully furnished, ocean-view cottage with hot tub, TV, VCR. Can accommodate small retreats and family reunions. Timeless Treasures suite sleeps three; My Favorite Things sleeps five. Family-operated with gracious hospitality and personal service. Well-behaved children welcome. Christian counseling available. We serve a full candlelight breakfast and gourmet coffee, teas, and snacks.

Hosts: Ray and Judy Waetjen
Rooms: 4 (PB) $80-150
Full Breakfast
Credit Cards: none
Notes: 2, 5, 6, 7, 9, 10, 12

MT. HOOD AREA

Falcon's Crest Inn

87287 Government Camp Loop Highway;
PO Box 185, **Government Camp,** 97028–0185
(503) 272-3403; (800) 624-7384 (reservations);
FAX (503) 272-3454
E-mail: falconscrest@earthlink.net
Web site: http://www.virtualcities.com/or/falconcrestinn.htm

Falcon's Crest Inn is a beautiful mountain lodge/chalet-style house, architecturally designed to fit into the quiet natural forest

welcome; 7 Children welcome; 8 Tennis nearby; 9 Swimming nearby; 10 Golf nearby; 11 Skiing nearby; 12 May be booked through travel agent.

and majestic setting of Oregon's Cascade Mountains. Conveniently located at the intersection of Highway 26 and the Government Camp Loop Highway, the inn is within walking distance of Ski Bowl, a year-round playground featuring downhill skiing in the winter and the Alpine Slide in the summer! Five suites, all with private baths. Each guest room is individually decorated with interesting and unique collectibles and beautiful views of mountains and forests. Phones are available in each suite. Smoking restricted. A fine-dining restaurant is on the premises. Ski packages available! Multiple-night discounts.

Hosts: BJ and Melady Johnson
Rooms: 5 (PB) $95-179
Full Mountain Breakfast
Credit Cards: A, B, C, D
Notes: 2, 4, 5, 8, 9, 10, 11, 12

Old Welches Inn

26401 E. Welches Road, **Welches,** 97067
(503) 622-3754; FAX (503) 622-5370
Web site: http://www.innsandouts.com/property/old_welches_inn.html

Enjoy casual elegance in a riverside retreat. The inn is the oldest building on the west/southwest side of Mt. Hood. Lots of private places to sit and enjoy the scenery of the surrounding mountains.

Old Welches Inn

Hosts: Judith and Ted Mondun
Rooms: 3 + cottage (P&SB) $85-130
Full Breakfast
Credit Cards: A, B, C, D
Notes: 2, 5, 6 (check first), 7 (12+), 8, 9, 10, 11, 12

Smith House Bed and Breakfast

NEWBERG

Smith House B&B

415 N. College Street, 97132–2650
(503) 538-1995; (503) 537-0508

Built in 1904, this Queen Anne Victorian, furnished with comfortable antiques, is located in the heart of Oregon's wine country, near downtown Newberg and George Fox University. Treat yourself to an evening reminiscing on the porch swing or relaxing on the patio. Enjoy coffee and cookies fresh from the oven, fruit and flowers, evening bed turn-down, and a full homemade breakfast. One-hour drive from the coast, 30 minutes from Portland.

Hosts: Glen and Mary Post
Rooms: 2 (SB) $65-70
Full Breakfast
Credit Cards: none
Notes: 2, 5, 8, 9, 10

NOTES: Credit cards accepted: A Master Card; B Visa; C American Express; D Discover; E Diners Club; F Other; 2 Personal checks accepted; 3 Lunch available; 4 Dinner available; 5 Open all year; 6 Pets

OXBOW

Hells Canyon Adventures/ S. Hells Canyon Lodge

PO Box 159, 97840
(541) 785-3352; (800) 422-3568;
FAX (541) 785-3353
E-mail: jeatboat@pdx.oneworld.com
Web site: http://www.hellscanyonadventures.com

Located along a private road into the southern part of the Hells Canyon Recreation area, overlooking the Hells Canyon Reservoir. Accessible through eastern Oregon on Highway 86 and southwestern Idaho by Highway 71. Minutes from White Water Jetboat Tours and Rafting, fishing, hiking, snowmobiling, and cross-country skiing. The lodge has three very spacious guest rooms, two with private bath. All rooms offer comfort to stretch out and relax. The lodge also works well for small corporate meetings. We surprise you each morning with our full country breakfast, fresh-baked goodies, juice, and all the trimmings. We speak German.

Hosts: Doris and Bret Armacost
Rooms: 3 (2PB; 1SB) $150+
Full Breakfast
Credit Cards: A, B, D
Notes: 2, 3, 4, 5, 9 (river), 11 (cross-country)

SEASIDE

10th Avenue Inn

125 10th Avenue, 97138
(503) 738-0643; (800) 569-1114;
FAX (503) 717-1688
E-mail: 10thaveinn@seasurf.net
Web site: http://www.obbg.org

Four guest rooms with private baths, one room with two beds. Enjoy this ocean-view home just steps from the beach and a short walk on the promenade from restaurants and shopping. The "right balance of personal and private." Light, airy guest rooms, decorated in soft colors, sprinkled with antiques, include TVs. Full breakfast. No smoking or pets. A separate cottage sleeps seven.

Hosts: Francie and Vern Starkey
Rooms: 4 (PB) $55-75
Full Breakfast
Credit Cards: A, B, C, D
Notes: 2, 5, 8, 9, 10, 12

Sand Dollar Bed and Breakfast

Sand Dollar B&B

606 N. Holladay Drive, 97138
(503) 738-3491; (800) 738-3491

Historic Craftsman bungalow includes two upstairs bedrooms with private baths and comfy beds—or you may prefer our cottage with its spectacular view and full kitchen. Children are always welcome. Only a short walk to the beach, shops, or restaurants. Your hosts are a retired minister and his wife. The Sand Dollar is a no-smoking bed and breakfast.

Hosts: Bob and Nita Hempfling
Rooms: 3 (PB) $65-125
Full Breakfast
Credit Cards: A, B, D
Notes: 2 ,5, 7, 8, 9, 10

SISTERS

Conklin's Guest House

69013 Camp Polk Road, 97759
(541) 549-0123; (800) 549-4262;
FAX (541) 549-4481
Web site: http://www.informat.com/bz/conklins

Conklin's Guest House is surrounded by a sprawling meadow with a panoramic backdrop of snowcapped peaks. Rich in history, the near-century-old homesite gives evidence that early settlers chose the most beautiful sites first! Modern conveniences and attention to detail ensure a comfortable and restful stay. A truly peaceful environment within walking distance of Sisters' bustling shops and restaurants. Guests may use the barbecue, swimming pool, and laundry facilities, and otherwise to *be at home!* The ponds are stocked with trout for catch-and-release fishing. The Sisters area has something for everyone, from rafting and rock climbing to dining and shopping and much more.

Hosts: Frank and Marie Conklin
Rooms: 5 (PB) $90-120
Full Breakfast
Credit Cards: none
Notes: 2, 5, 7 (12+), 8, 9 (heated pool), 10, 11

SPRINGFIELD/EUGENE

McKenzie View, A Riverside B&B

34922 McKenzie View Drive, 97478
(541) 726-3887; (888) McKVIEW (625-8439);
FAX (541) 726-6968
E-mail: mckenzieview@worldnet.att.net
Web site: http://design-web.com/mckenzieview

Spacious country getaway on a quiet bend of the McKenzie River, but only 15 minutes from Eugene and the university. Douglas firs and perennial gardens fill 6 acres. Picture-window views of the river can be enjoyed throughout the house. Guest rooms are elegantly decorated, with antique furnishings and comfortable seating areas. Let the river lull you to sleep, rest in a hammock, or relax in front of a fire. McKenzie View refreshes body and spirit.

Hosts: Roberta and Scott Bolling
Rooms: 4 (PB) $85-215
Full Breakfast
Credit Cards: A, B
Notes: 2, 5, 8, 9

WEST LINN

Swift Shore Chalet Bed and Breakfast

1190 Swift Shore Circle, 97068
(503) 650-3853; FAX (503) 656-2105
E-mail: swiftshore@aol.com

The perfect getaway. . .a place to relax in the quiet surroundings of a beautiful home, surrounded by a panoramic view of green hillsides, a garden filled with fragrant flowers, and the songs of birds. A full breakfast is beautifully served on the deck or in the dining room. Specialties include Mandarin orange scones, raspberry cream cheese coffee cake, Belgian waffles, Dutch oven pancakes, and Pacific crab quiche. Be pampered and served with quiet attention to detail. Minutes from downtown Portland and scenic beauties. A wonderful setting for families.

Hosts: Nancy and Horace Duke
Rooms: 2 (1PB; 1SB) $80
Full Breakfast
Credit Cards: none
Notes: 5, 7, 10

NOTES: Credit cards accepted: A Master Card; B Visa; C American Express; D Discover; E Diners Club; F Other; 2 Personal checks accepted; 3 Lunch available; 4 Dinner available; 5 Open all year; 6 Pets

Pennsylvania

A Bed and Breakfast Connection/Bed and Breakfast of Philadelphia

PO Box 21, **Devon,** 19333
(610) 687-3565; (800) 448-3619;
FAX (610) 995-9524
E-mail: bnb@bnbphiladelphia.com
Web site: http://www.bnbphiladelphia.com

From elegant town houses in historic **Center City Philadelphia** to a manor house in scenic **Bucks County;** from an elegant home-within-a-barn in the **suburbs** to charming Victorian inns in **York,** A Bed and Breakfast Connection/Bed and Breakfast of Philadelphia offers a wide variety of styles and locations in its scores of inspected homes, guest houses, and inns. For example, choose from accommodations just 3 blocks from "America's most historic square mile," **Independence National Historical Park;** or within easy distance of **Valley Forge Park;** or in the heart of the **Brandywine Valley** area with its magnificent historic estates and museums. Stay in the Amish country of Lancaster County. Accommodations from $30 to $200 per night. We offer houses with one guest room and inns with many rooms. We cover seven counties in the southeastern corner of Pennsylvania. Major credit cards accepted. Mary Alice Hamilton and Peggy Gregg, co-owners.

Rest and Repast Bed and Breakfast Reservations

PO Box 126, **Pine Grove Mills,** 16868
(814) 238-1484; FAX (814) 234-9890
Web site: http://iul.com/bnbinpa

Come to central Pennsylvania to see the Nittany Lions play Big Ten football and basketball. Stay to visit the plethora of historic sites, hike the mountainsides at our many state parks, or tour charming 19th-century villages and shops. Since 1982, Rest and Repast has represented inspected bed and breakfasts in central Pennsylvania. Our fifty-plus properties include scenic farms near famous fly-fishing streams, estates on the National Register, comtemporary homes within walking distance of campus, and several private apartments and cottages. The 140 guest rooms vary widely, with private or shared baths. Rates: $60-125, double-occupancy. Corporate rates available, as well as long-term rates. Deposit required; cash or check only. Brochure available on request.

PENNSYLVANIA

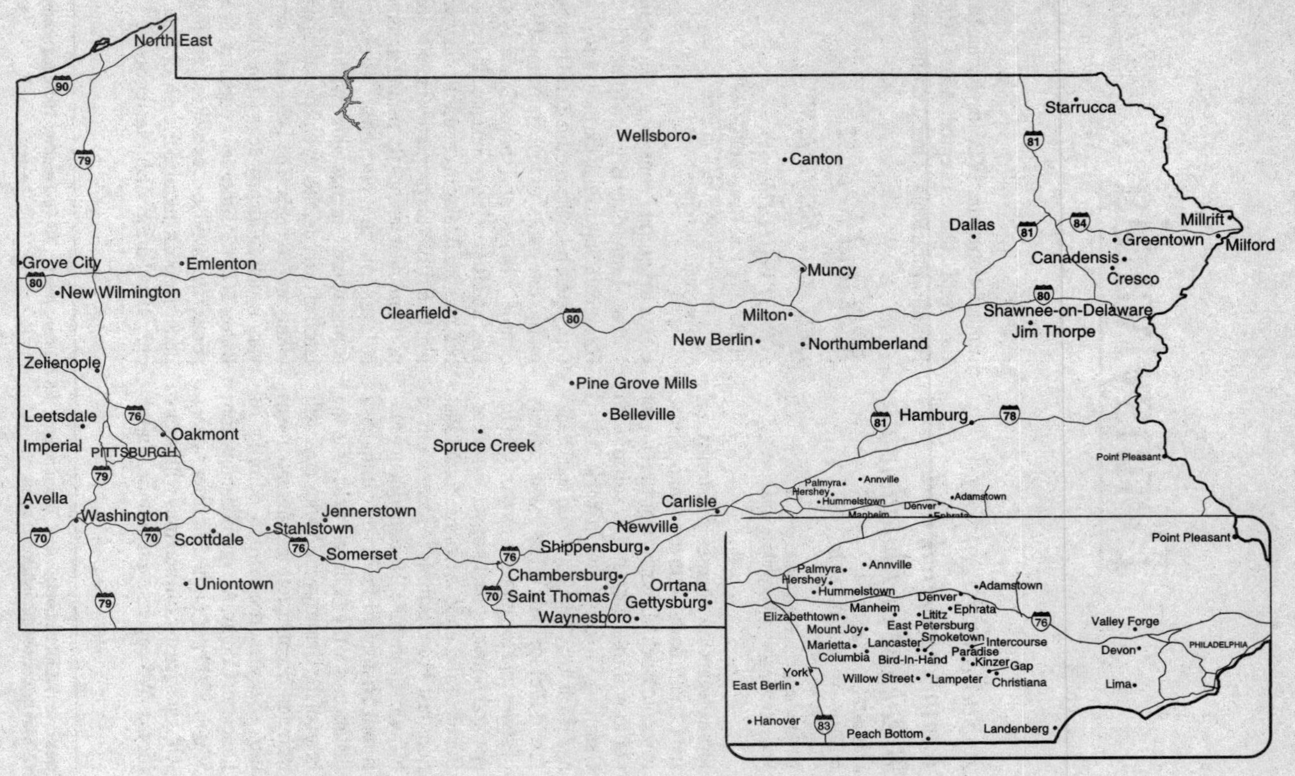

ADAMSTOWN

Adamstown Inn Bed and Breakfast

62 W. Main Street, 19501–0938
(717) 484-0800; (800) 594-4808;
FAX (717) 484-1384
E-mail: adaminn@ptd.net
Web site: http://www.Adamstown.com

Experience simple elegance in two Victorian homes resplendent with leaded-glass windows and door, magnificent chestnut woodwork, and Oriental rugs. All seven guest rooms are decorated with family heirlooms, handmade quilts, lace curtains, and many distinctive touches. Accommodations range from antique to king beds. Five of the rooms have Jacuzzi tubs for two, and three rooms feature gas fireplaces. The inns are located in a small town brimming with antiques dealerships. The homes are located only minutes from Reading and Lancaster.

Hosts: Tom and Wanda Berman
Rooms: 7 (PB) $70-135
Continental Breakfast
Credit Cards: A, B
Notes: 2, 5, 8, 9, 10, 12

ANNVILLE

Swatara Creek Inn

RD 2, Box 692, 17003
(717) 865-3259

An 1860s Victorian mansion situated on four acres in the peaceful country. All rooms have private baths, canopied queen beds, and air-conditioning, and include a full breakfast. Sitting room, dining room, and gift shop on the first floor. Wheelchair-accessible. Close to Hershey, Mt. Hope Winery, Mt. Gretna, Reading outlets, and the Lancaster Amish area. Near historical sites: Cornwall Mines, Ephrata Cloisters, Gettysburg, etc. No smoking inside.

Host: Dick Hess
Rooms: 10 (PB) $55-80
Full Breakfast
Credit Cards: A, B, C, D, E
Notes: 2, 5, 7, 8, 9, 10, 12

BELLEVILLE

Twin Oaks B&B

73 S. Dryhouse Road, 17004
(717) 935-2026

In the heart of the Kishacoquillas Valley, only 30 minutes from Penn State. Norman and Sarah welcome their guests to a new facility with clean, spacious rooms. In a quiet country setting with a panoramic view of Stone and Jacks Mountains. A full breakfast is served. Children are welcome. Open all year.

Hosts: J. Norman and Sarah Glick
Rooms: 4 (1PB; 3SB) $45-60
Full Breakfast
Credit Cards: none
Notes: 2, 5, 7, 12

BIRD-IN-HAND

The Village Inn of Bird-in-Hand

2695 Old Philadelphia Pike; PO Box 253, 17505
(717) 293-8369; (800) 914-2473;
FAX (717) 768-1117
E-mail: smucker@bird-in-hand.com
Web site: http://www.bird-in-hand.com/villageinn

Listed on the National Historic Register, our inn is located on Route 340, 5 miles east of Lancaster in the heart of the Pennsylvania Dutch country. Each room features its own private bath and includes a continental plus breakfast, free use of indoor and outdoor pools and tennis courts (within walking distance), and a complimentary 2-hour tour of the surrounding Amish farmlands. Reservations suggested. Package available.

Hosts: Nancy Kauffman
Rooms: 11 (PB) $69-139
Continental Plus Breakfast
Credit Cards: A, B, C, D
Notes: 2, 5, 8, 9, 10, 12

CANADENSIS

Brookview Manor Bed and Breakfast Inn

RR 1, Box 365, 18325
(717) 595-2451; (800) 585-7974;
FAX (717) 595-5065

Situated on 4 picturesque acres, the inn offers the traveler an ideal retreat from the workaday world. Enjoy the simple pleasures of hiking trails or a cozy glider on a spacious wraparound porch. Each room offers a panoramic view of the forest, mountains, and stream; all have private baths. Breakfast is served in our cheery dining room and includes fruits, juices, fresh muffins, and a hearty entrée.

Hosts: Mary Anne Buckley, George and Donna Marie Mason
Rooms: 10 (PB) $100-150
Full Breakfast
Credit Cards: A, B, C, D, E
Notes: 2, 5, 7 (over 12), 8, 9, 10, 11, 12

Dreamy Acres

Route 447 and Seese Hill Road, 18325–0007
(717) 595-7115

Esther and Bill Pickett started Dreamy Acres as a bed and breakfast inn in 1959—doing bed and breakfast before it was in style. Situated on 3 acres with a stream and pond, Dreamy Acres is in the heart of the Pocono vacationland, close to stores, churches, gift shops, and recreational facilities. Guest rooms have AC and color cable TV; some have VCRs.

Hosts: Esther and Bill Pickett
Rooms: 6 (4PB; 2SB) $38-55
Expanded Continental Breakfast
Credit Cards: none
Notes: 2, 5, 8, 9, 10, 11

CANTON

M-mm Good B&B

RD 1, Box 71, 17724
(717) 673-8153

Located along Route 414, 3 miles east of Canton in the quiet country in the center of the Endless Mountains. Clean, comfortable rooms and a breakfast including homemade muffins or sticky buns. Picnic tables under maple trees. Hiking, fishing.

Hosts: Melvin and Irene Good
Rooms: 3 (SB)
Full Breakfast
Credit Cards: None
Notes: 2, 5, 7

CARLISLE

Line Limousin Farmhouse Bed and Breakfast

2070 Ritner Highway, 17013
(717) 243-1281; FAX (717) 249-5537
E-mail: bline@planetcable.net
Web site: http://www.pafarmstay.com/line/index.html

Step back in time and stay with us in our 1864 brick and stone farmhouse, which has always been owned by the Line family. French Limousin cattle are raised on our 100-acre farm. Cross over our stone fences to spot wildlife and a large variety of birds. After a large breakfast, join us for worship at our historic First Presbyterian Church. Two rooms have comfortable king beds, private baths, AC, and TV. Nonsmoking. Open April–October.

Hosts: Bob and Joan Line
Rooms: 4 (2PB; 2SB) $68.90-79.50
Full Breakfast
Credit Cards: none
Notes: 2, 5, 7 (over 8), 10

Pheasant Field B&B

150 Hickorytown Road, 17013
(717) 258-0717 (voice and FAX)
E-mail: pheasant@pa.net
Web site: http://www.pa.net/pheasant

Pheasant Field Bed and Breakfast

Stay in this lovely old brick farmhouse set in quiet country surroundings. Wake up to a full country breakfast including fresh bread or muffins, fresh fruit, a hot entrée, and plenty of hot coffee. After a game of tennis or a hike on the Appalachian Trail, relax in the family room or living room and help yourself to a homemade cookie (or two). Feel free to bring your horse—we offer overnight boarding, when space is available. Collector car shows, antiquing, and fly-fishing are nearby. Smoking is permitted outside. We can arrange for your pets at local kennels. AAA three-diamond rating. "Come home to the country."

Hostess: Denise (Dee) Fegan
Rooms: 4 (2PB; 2SB) $65-105
Full Breakfast
Credit Cards: A, B, C
Notes: 2, 5, 7, 8 (onsite), 9, 10, 11, 12

CHAMBERSBURG

Falling Spring Inn

1838 Falling Spring Road, 17201
(717) 267-3654; FAX (717) 267-2584

Enjoy country living only 2 miles off I–81, Exit 6, and Route 30, on a working farm with animals and Falling Spring, a nationally renowned, freshwater trout stream. A large pond, lawns, meadows, ducks, and birds all make a pleasant stay. Historic Gettysburg is only 25 miles away. Relax in our air-conditioned rooms with queen beds. One room with spa. One room wheelchair-accessible.

Hosts: Adin and Janet Frey
Rooms: 5 (PB) $49-89
Full Breakfast
Credit Cards: A, B
Notes: 2, 5, 7, 8, 9, 10, 11, 12

CHRISTIANA

Georgetown B&B

1222 Georgetown Road, 17509
(717) 786-4570

Once a miller's home, the original structure was converted to a B&B for the enjoyment of guests in a relaxing home away from home. Entrance to the house is by a brick walkway. A herb garden lets guests smell thc lavender and mint—just two of the herbs used to garnish morning breakfasts. There is a choice of three bedrooms decorated with antiques and collectibles. Lancaster County Amish, a unique group of people who travel in horse-drawn carriages, pass in front of the Georgetown. Visit the local Strasburg Train Museum.

Hostess: Doris W. Woerth
Rooms: 3 (1PB; 2SB) $40-50
Full Breakfast
Credit Cards: none
Notes: 2, 5, 9, 10

Spruce Edge Guest House

1586 Georgetown Road, 17509
(717) 529-2712, 529-3979

Relax and enjoy this charming, rustic 19th-century bed and breakfast cottage situated on a working dairy farm. Originally a summer kitchen, Spruce Edge Guest House has been meticulously restored. Minutes from many local attractions, the guest house is nestled among beautiful Lancaster County farms.

Hosts: Ed and Arlene Harnish
Rooms: 1 cottage (PB) $40-60
Full Breakfast
Credit Cards: none
Notes: 2, 7, 10

Victorian Loft Bed and Breakfast

CLEARFIELD

Victorian Loft Bed and Breakfast

216 S. Front Street, 16830
(814) 765-4805; (800) 798-0456;
FAX (814) 765-9596
E-mail: pdurant@csrlink.net
Web site: http://www.virtualcities.com/ons/pa/z/paza601.htm

An elegant 1894 Victorian riverfront home in the Clearfield historic district. Memorable breakfast, air-conditioning, skylights, balcony, private kitchen and dining, guest entertainment center, family movies, and whirlpool bath. Weaving/sewing studio; spinning demonstrations by request. Hosts are Bible college graduates. Perfect stop on I–80—3 miles off Exit 19 in rural west-central Pennsylvania. Also, a completely equipped three-bedroom cabin on 8 forested acres, located just 2 miles from Parker Dam and Elliot State Parks with swimming, fishing, boating, and numerous outdoor activities.

Hosts: Tim and Peggy Durant
Rooms: 4 + cabin (2PB; 2SB) $50-100
Full Breakfast
Credit Cards: A, B, C, D
Notes: 2, 5, 6 (call ahead), 7, 8, 9, 10, 11, 12

NOTES: Credit cards accepted: A Master Card; B Visa; C American Express; D Discover; E Diners Club; F Other; 2 Personal checks accepted; 3 Lunch available; 4 Dinner available; 5 Open all year; 6 Pets

CLINTON (PITTSBURGH)

Country Road B&B

199 Moody Road, **Imperial,** 15126
(412) 899-2528; FAX (412) 899-2579
E-mail: croadbb.com
Web site: http://www.bnb.lm.com

A peaceful, quiet farm setting just 5 miles from the Greater Pittsburgh Airport, with pick-up service available, and 20 minutes from downtown. A restored 100-year-old farmhouse with trout pond, in-ground swimming pool, and screened-in front porch. Recently a cottage (once a springhouse) and 200-year-old log cabin were restored and made available to guests. Golf course within walking distance, and air tours available in vintage Piper restored aircraft. New poolside one-bedroom apartment, fireplace, Jacuzzi. Great corporate rental.

Hosts: David and Janice Cornell
Rooms: 5 (4PB; 1SB) $95-110
Full Breakfast
Credit Cards: A, B, D
Notes: 2, 5, 7, 10

COLUMBIA

Clocktower Bed and Breakfast

441 Chestnut Street, 17512
(717) 684-5869; (800) 422-5869
E-mail: bedandb@aol.com
Web site: http://user.aol.com/bedandb/clock.html

This turn-of-the-century brick Victorian home has dark woodwork throughout and an ornate stained-glass window over the staircase. Located in the small historic town of Columbia, along the Susquehanna River, it is the perfect spot to relax and unwind. Convenient to Lancaster, York, Hershey, and Gettysburg, the Clocktower B&B is also only a brief stroll from museums, antiques, shops, and restaurants. Microwave/refrigerator available. Exercise room on premises. Offstreet parking and AC. Packages, gift certificates available.

Hosts: Chris and Becky Will
Rooms: 3 (PB) $60-70
Continental Breakfast
Credit Cards: A, B
Notes: 2, 5, 8, 9, 10, 11

The Columbian, A Bed and Breakfast

360 Chestnut Street, 17512
(717) 684-5869; (800) 422-5869
E-mail: bedandb@aol.com
Web site: http://user.aol.com/bedandb

Circa 1897. Centrally located in the small historic river town of Columbia, the Columbian, a brick Colonial Revival mansion, features an ornate stained-glass window and magnificent tiered staircase. Large, air-conditioned rooms offer queen-size beds, private baths, and CATV. Suite with balcony and/or fireplaces available. Come relax and unwind in our lovely home

The Columbian

and browse through the antique shops, art galleries, outlets, and museums only a brief stroll away. Getaway packages, gift certificates available.

Hosts: Chris and Becky Will
Rooms: 8 (PB) $70-115
Full Breakfast
Credit Cards: A, B
Notes: 2, 5, 7, 8, 9, 10, 11

CRESCO

LaAnna Guest House

RR 2, Box 1051, 18326
(717) 676-4225 (voice and FAX)

The 111-year-old Victorian home is furnished with Victorian and Empire antiques. It has spacious guest rooms, quiet surroundings, and a trout pond. You can walk to waterfalls and mountain views; deer and other wildlife are seen nearby.

Hostess: Kay Swingle
Rooms: 4 (SB) $40
Continental Breakfast
Credit Cards: none
Notes: 2, 5, 7, 8, 9, 10, 11

DALLAS (WILKES-BARRE)

Ponda-Rowland Bed and Breakfast Inn

RR 1, Box 349, 18612–9604
(717) 639-3245; (800) 854-3286;
FAX (717) 639-5531

Ponda-Rowland Bed and Breakfast Inn is a circa-1850 inn on a large, scenic farm in the Endless Mountains of Pennsylvania. King beds, private baths, AC, beamed ceilings, ceiling fans. Completely furnished with museum-quality country antiques. Mountain views, thirty-four-acre private wildlife sanctuary with trails, and ponds. Fishing, canoeing, ice-skating, tobogganing, hay rides, horses, sheep, goats, turkeys, pot-bellied pig, donkeys, and more to see, do, and touch. Refreshments afternoon and evening. Large stone fireplace. Breakfast by candlelight. Nearby are air tours, swimming, horseback riding, downhill skiing, and fine restaurants. Approved by AAA, ABBA, and Mobil.

Hosts: Jeanette and Cliff Rowland
Rooms: 6 (PB) $75-125
Full Breakfast
Credit Cards: A, B, C, D
Notes: 2, 5, 7, 10, 11, 12

DENVER

Cocalico Creek B&B

224 S. 4th Street, 17517
(717) 336-0271; (888) 208-7334
Web site: http://www2.epix.net/~bblanco/cocalico.html

Situated in northern Lancaster County, the 1927 classic stone Colonial offers casual elegance in a country setting. Four tastefully decorated bedrooms with queen beds and private baths; one room has a private balcony. AC for summer comfort; heated beds with down comforters for winter chills. Minutes from antiquing, outlet shopping, golf, and farmers markets. Explore the history, culture, and rural scenic beauty.

Hostess: Charlene Sweeney
Rooms: 4 (PB) $72-87
Full Breakfast
Credit Cards: A, B
Notes: 2, 5, 7, 9, 10

EAST BERLIN

Copper Lantern Inn Bed and Breakfast

213 W. King Street, 17316
(717) 244-6280

Our Copper Lantern Inn is located minutes from popular tourism attractions in Pennsylvania: antique shops, Pennsylvania Dutch country, Hershey Park, Gettysburg Battlefield, farmers markets, outlet malls, and outstanding restaurants. The Inner Harbor in Baltimore is only 1 hour away. Some of the finer golf courses are just minutes away, including "The Bridges" in Abbottstown, a new eighteen-hole course.

Hosts: Yvonne and John Myers, Barb and Charles Bubb
Rooms: 3 (1PB; 2SB) $49-69
Full Breakfast
Credit Cards: none
Notes: 2, 5, 10

EAST PETERSBURG

George Zahm House Bed and Breakfast

6070 Main Street, 17520
(717) 569-6026

The George Zahm House, built in 1854, is a restored Federal period home in beautiful Lancaster County. The inn features three bedrooms with private baths and a first-floor suite that offers a sitting room, bedroom, and private bath. The inn has 10-foot ceilings throughout and is furnished with an eclectic collection of antiques. Breakfast is served in the dining room and features homemade muffins, breads, Belgian waffles, granolas, and seasonal fresh fruit.

Hosts: Robyn and Jeff Keeports, Daneen Kemple
Rooms: 4 (PB) $65-85
Expanded Continental Breakfast
Credit Cards: A, B
Notes: 2, 5, 7 (over 12), 8, 9, 10, 12

ELIZABETHTOWN

West Ridge Guest House

1285 W. Ridge Road, 17022
(717) 367-7783; FAX (717) 367-8468
E-mail: wridgeroad@aol.com
Web site: http://www2.epix.net/~bblanco/westridge.html

Country estate setting midway between Harrisburg and Lancaster. Nine guest rooms, four in the main house, five in a guest house that offers complete privacy. Some have fireplaces, Jacuzzis, decks; all rooms have phones, TVs, VCRs (movie library available), private baths. Full breakfast is served. Local attractions: Hershey Park, Lancaster County Amish

West Ridge Guest House

community, outlet shopping, Gettysburg. Four-star-rated by the American Bed & Breakfast Association.

Hostess: Alice P. Heisey
Rooms: 9 (PB) $60-110
Full Breakfast
Credit Cards: A, B, C
Notes: 2, 5, 7, 8, 10, 12

EPHRATA

Historic Smithton Inn

900 W. Main Street, 17522
(717) 733-6094
Web site: http://www.smithtoninn.com

Smithton, an American pre-Revolutionary inn opened 235 years, has been fully restored. It is in Lancaster County, perhaps the most spiritually focused county in America and home of the Amish, Mennonite, and Brethren people. A romantic and picturesque place. Its big, square rooms are bright and sunny. Each room has its own working fireplace and can be candlelit during evening hours. There is a sitting area in each guest room with comfortable leather upholstered chairs, reading lamps, soft goose down pillows, and handmade Pennsylvania Dutch quilts. Smithton's Dahlia Gardens feature a striking display of blossoms grown from tubers that were all winners in American Dahlia Society competitions. Mannerly children and pets welcome; please make prior arrangements. Smoking prohibited.

Hostess: Dorothy R. Graybill
Rooms: 8 (PB) $75-175
Full Breakfast
Credit Cards: A, B, C
Notes: 2, 5, 6 and 7 (by arrangement), 8, 9, 10, 12

The Inns at Doneckers

318-324 N. State Street, 17522
(717) 738-9502; FAX (717) 738-9554
E-mail: donecker@doneckers.com
Web site: http://www.doneckers.com

Relax in country elegance in historic Lancaster County. Four inns of forty distinctive rooms, decorated in fine antiques, some fireplace/Jacuzzi suites. Steps from the Doneckers community. A 38-year-old family-owned business of exceptional fashion stores for the family and home, an award-winning gourmet restaurant, art/craft/quilt galleries, art studios. Minutes from antique/collectible markets, Amish farmlands. "An oasis of sophistication in PA Dutch Country"—*Country Inns.*

Host: H. William Donecker
Rooms: 40 (38PB; 2SB) $65-210
Continental Breakfast
Credit Cards: A, B, C, D, E, F
Notes: 2, 3, 4, 5, 7, 8, 9, 10

Martin House

Martin House

265 Ridge Avenue, 17522
(717) 733-6804; (888) 651-8418
E-mail: vmartin@ptd.net
Web site: http://www.innformation.com/pa/martin

Located in Pennsylvania Dutch country, our contemporary home is set against a wooded area. There are antique markets, outlet malls, Hershey Park, historical places, and golf courses within a few miles. For your comfort: spacious rooms with

NOTES: Credit cards accepted: A Master Card; B Visa; C American Express; D Discover; E Diners Club; F Other; 2 Personal checks accepted; 3 Lunch available; 4 Dinner available; 5 Open all year; 6 Pets

king or queen beds and a private hot tub! A living room and large, sunny deck are available for guests to use. Discount for three nights or more.

Hosts: Moses and Vera Martin
Rooms: 3 (PB) $75-115
Full Breakfast
Credit Cards: A, B
Notes: 2, 5, 7, 9, 10

Meadow Valley Farm

Meadow Valley Farm

221 Meadow Valley Road, 17522
(717) 733-8390

Stay a while on the farm overlooking the pond with swans. Watch our sons milk sixty cows. Watch or help our daughter pack approximately 30,000 eggs daily. Pet cats and calves, and see Shep bring in the cows. The original summer house from the 1800s has three cozy bedrooms, fully equipped kitchen, and antique furnishings. Located in the Lancaster County farming countryside, with covered bridges, local fresh produce, markets, and auctions. Explore the back roads. Nice restaurants. Amish dinners arranged. No smoking.

Hosts: Walter and Marlene Hurst
Rooms: 3 (1PB; 2SB) $30-35
No Breakfast (coffee and juice provided)
Credit Cards: none
Notes: 4 (can be arranged), 7

GETTYSBURG

Appleford Inn

218 Carlisle Street, 17325
(717) 337-1711; (800) 275-3373;
FAX (717) 334-6228
E-mail: jwiley@cvn.net
Web site: http://www.bbonline.com/pa/appleford

History, elegance, hospitality, and comfort greet you at this stately 1867 Victorian in-town mansion. Located 2 blocks north of Gettysburg's town circle (Lincoln Square). Walk to restaurants, antique shops, historic attractions, and battlefield. The inn offers ten charming, antique-furnished guest rooms with private baths, AC, numerous amenities, and spacious common areas with fireplaces, grand piano, and collections. You are served a sumptuous breakfast each morning surrounded by candlelight and classical music.

Hosts: John and Jane Wiley
Rooms: 10 (PB) $85-125
Full Breakfast
Credit Cards: A, B, C, D
Notes: 2, 5, 7 (8 years +), 8, 9, 10, 11, 12

The Brafferton Inn

44 York Street, 17325
(717) 337-3423
Web site: http://www.bbhost.com/braffertoninn

The Brafferton Inn is one of historic Gettysburg's gracious landmarks. The elegant 1786 fieldstone home, listed on the National Register of Historic Places, has been fully restored to include a private bath for each of the ten guest rooms. Featured in *Country Living,* the inn has exquisite antiques and original artistry throughout. The inn combines elegance and ease. Warm-colored Orientals, comfortable wing-backs, and a tall 1800 grandfather clock grace the living room. The dining room boasts a stunning folk art mural. Other surprising nooks and crannies, a deck, and an in-town garden provide guests with getaway spots. The spirit of an earlier time pervades.

Hosts: Jane and Sam Back
Rooms: 10 (PB) $90-135
Full Breakfast
Credit Cards: A, B, C, D
Notes: 2, 5, 7 (over 7), 8, 9, 10, 11, 12

The Doubleday Inn

104 Doubleday Avenue, 17325
(717) 334-9119
Web site: http://www.bbonline.com/pa/doubleday

Located directly on the Gettysburg battlefield, this beautifully restored Colonial country inn enjoys splendid views of historic Gettysburg and the battlefield. Guests enjoy candlelit country breakfasts, afternoon refreshments, and the cozy comfort of a centrally air-conditioned inn surrounded by lovely antiques and Civil War memorabilia. Free presentations by battlefield historians on selected evenings.

Hosts: Charles and Ruth Anne Wilcox
Rooms: 9 (5PB; 4SB) $84-104
Full Breakfast
Credit Cards: A, B, D
Notes: 2, 5, 7 (8 and older), 8, 9, 10, 11, 12

Keystone Inn

231 Hanover Street, 17325
(717) 337-3888
Web site: http://www.virtualcities.com/ons/pa/pag6601.htm

The Keystone Inn is a large, brick Victorian home built in 1913. The high-ceilinged rooms are decorated with lace and flowers, and a handsome chestnut staircase rises to the third floor. The guest rooms are bright, cheerful, and air-conditioned. Each has a reading nook and writing desk. Choose your own breakfast from our full breakfast menu. One suite available.

Hosts: Wilmer and Doris Martin
Rooms: 5 (PB) $69-109
Full Breakfast
Credit Cards: A, B, D
Notes: 2, 5, 7, 8, 9, 10, 11

GREENTOWN

Hall's Inn Bed and Breakfast

RR 1, Box 137, 18426
(717) 676-3429

Located on Route 390 in Promised Land State Park, Hall's Inn offers you clean and comfortable rooms with a serene atmosphere. Guests may relax on the wraparound porch and enjoy the tranquillity and fresh mountain air while watching the deer. A beautiful lake with beach and picnicking are enjoyed. In winter, cross-country skiing and snowmobiling are popular, with hiking all year. An outside grill and picnic tables are available to our guests.

Hosts: John and Lois Hall
Rooms: 9 (2PB; 7SB) $55-65
Continental Breakfast
Credit Cards: A, B
Notes: 2, 5, 7, 9, 11

GROVE CITY

Snow Goose Inn

112 E. Main Street, 16127
(724) 458-4644; (800) 317-4644
Web site: http://www.bbonline.com/pa/snowgoose

The Snow Goose Inn is a large house, circa 1895, formerly a doctor's home. It has a large, wraparound front porch with an old-fashioned porch swing. Comfortable, air-conditioned guest rooms have private baths. Each is decorated with antiques and touches of country. A full breakfast is served, along with homemade muffins, home-baked breakfast rolls, etc.

Hosts: Orvil and Dorothy McMillen
Rooms: 4 (PB) $65
Full Breakfast
Credit Cards: A, B
Notes: 2, 5, 7, 8, 9, 10, 11, 12

HAMBURG

Come Aside Inn

800 Schappell Road, 19526
(610) 562-9293

Located conveniently off Interstate 78, close to the Reading outlets and Hawk Mountain, is our country home—a tranquil respite. The wicker porch furniture invites you to "come aside and rest awhile." Winter brings the relaxing glow of the fireplace. A candlelight, expanded continental breakfast is served in the open-beamed dining room with a southern hospitality touch. Loretta's apple quiche and homemade breads are a favorite.

Hosts: Bob and Loretta Miller
Rooms: 3 (1PB; 2SB) $50-65
Continental Plus Breakfast
Credit Cards: F
Notes: 2, 5, 8, 9, 10, 11

HANOVER

Beechmont Inn

315 Broadway, 17331
(717) 632-3013; (800) 553-7009

Elegant, 1834 Federal inn with seven guest rooms, all with private baths. Fireplaces, AC, afternoon refreshments, and gourmet breakfasts. One large suite has a private whirlpool tub and canopy beds. Gettysburg battlefield, Lake Marburg, golf, and great antiquing are nearby. Convenient location for visits to Hershey, York, or Lancaster. Weekend and golf packages and romantic honeymoon or anniversary packages are offered. Picnic baskets are available. Great area for biking and hiking. AAA- and Mobil-approved.

Hosts: Bill and Susan Day
Rooms: 7 (PB) $80-135
Full Breakfast
Credit Cards: A, B, C, D
Notes: 2, 3, 5, 8, 9, 10, 11, 12

HERSHEY

Nancy's Guest House

235 Hershey Road, 17036
(717) 566-9844
E-mail: marnan@paonline.com

Comfort, hominess, and privacy are what you find at our guest house. You are our only guests. Located 2 miles from Hershey Park, our second-floor, one-unit, non-smoking apartment has a private entrance and a large deck. There are two bedrooms, a living room, a kitchen, and a bath with laundry. Color television and AC add to the comfort. Eat in or go out, choosing from fast food or fine dining. Traveler's checks or cash are accepted; checks limited. A ten-percent discount for five nights or more. Located 3½ miles from I–81 on Route 39.

Hosts: Marlin and Nancy Geesaman
Rooms: 2-bedroom apartment (PB) $65-85
Credit Cards: none
Notes: 7, 8, 9, 10, 11

Pinehurst Inn

50 Northeast Drive, 17033
(717) 533-2603; (800) 743-9140;
FAX (717) 534-2639

Spacious brick home surrounded by lawns and countryside. There is a warm, welcoming, many-windowed living room and old-fashioned porch swing. The inn is within walking distance of all Hershey attractions: Hershey Museums, Rose Gardens, Hershey Park, and Chocolate World. Less than 1 hour's drive from Gettysburg and Lancaster County. Each room welcomes you with a queen-size bed and a Hershey Kiss on each pillow.

Hosts: Roger and Phyllis Ingold
Rooms: 15 (2PB; 13SB) $47-67
Full Breakfast
Credit Cards: A, B
Notes: 2, 5, 7, 8, 9, 10, 12

Shepherd's Acres B&B

RD 3, Box 370, Bell Road, **Palmyra,** 17078
(717) 838-3899

Welcome to the Hershey-Lancaster area! You'll enjoy it more if you stay on our 20-acre farmette overlooking the scenic Lebanon Valley. Our new, spacious Cape Cod home is filled with Margy's hand-sewn quilts and wall hangings, with some antique furniture accenting the "country theme," as well. The eat-in enclosed porch area is a great place to enjoy both beauty and tranquillity as you watch the sheep in the pasture or the deer in the fields.

Hosts: Jerry and Margy Allebach
Rooms: 3 (1PB; 2SB) $45-60
Full Breakfast
Credit Cards: none
Notes: 2, 5, 8, 9, 10, 11

JENNERSTOWN

The Olde Stagecoach Bed and Breakfast

1760 Lincoln Highway; PO Box 337, 15547
(814) 629-7440; FAX (814) 629-9244

The Olde Stagecoach Bed and Breakfast is a renovated, 200-year-old farmhouse that, during the 1700s and 1800s, was a stagecoach rest stop. It now has four lovely bedrooms decorated with antiques, adding country charm, each with its own private bath. Guests relax in the Victorian-style common room. It is a place to stay in all four seasons, located on the historical Lincoln Highway. Nearby are the oldest professional summer theater, antique shops, golfing, outlet shopping, skiing, and cross-country skiing.

Hosts: Carol and George Neuhof
Rooms: 4 (PB) $65
Full Breakfast
Credit Cards: A, B
Notes: 2, 5, 10, 11

JIM THORPE

The Inn at Jim Thorpe

24 Broadway, 18229
(717) 325-2599; (800) 329-2599;
FAX (717) 325-9145
E-mail: innjt@ptd.net
Web site: http://www.innjt.com

The inn rests in a unique and picturesque setting in the heart of historic Jim Thorpe. Elegant rooms are complete with private baths and color TVs/HBO, and are furnished with Victorian reproductions. Suites have fireplaces and whirlpools. Enjoy shopping, historic mansion and museum

NOTES: Credit cards accepted: A Master Card; B Visa; C American Express; D Discover; E Diners Club; F Other; 2 Personal checks accepted; 3 Lunch available; 4 Dinner available; 5 Open all year; 6 Pets

tours, mountain biking, and white-water rafting—all right outside our doors!

Host: David Drury
Rooms: 33 (PB) $65-250
Continental Breakfast
Credit Cards: A, B, C, D, E
Notes: 3, 4, 5, 7, 9, 11, 12

KINZERS

Sycamore Haven Farm

35 S. Kinzer Road, 17535
(717) 442-4901

We have approximately forty milking cows and many young cattle and cats for children to enjoy. Our farmhouse has three guest rooms, all with double beds and one single. Cots and playpen. Shared bath. Fifteen miles east of Lancaster city. Route 30 to Kinzer Road; turn right at the first farm on the left.

Hosts: Charles and Janet Groff
Rooms: 3 (SB) $30-40
Continental Breakfast
Credit Cards: none
Notes: 2, 5, 6, 7, 8, 9, 10

LANCASTER

1725 Historic Witmer's Tavern, Inn, and Museum

2014 Old Philadelphia Pike, 17602
(717) 299-5305

Witmer's Tavern is Lancaster's oldest and only pre-Revolutionary War inn still lodging travelers in the original building. Reflects rural and historic flavor of the area. Restored to the simple, authentic, pioneer style that was familiar to European immigrants who joined the Conestoga wagon trains being provisioned at the inn for the western and southern treks into the wilderness areas. Fresh flowers, working fireplaces, antique quilts, and antiques in all the romantic rooms. Pandora's Antique Shop is on the premises. Bird-in-Hand and Intercourse villages, other antique shops, and auctions just beyond. Valley Forge, Hershey, Gettysburg, Winterthur, Chadds Ford, and New Hope all within a 90-minute drive. On the National Register of Historic Places, and a national landmark. Beautiful park across the street; Amish cow pasture in the rear.

Host: Brant Hartung
Rooms: 7 (2PB; 5SB) $60-90
Continental Plus Breakfast
Credit Cards: none
Notes: 2, 5, 8, 9, 10, 11, 12

Australian Walkabout Inn

Australian Walkabout Inn

837 Village Road; PO Box 294, **Lampeter,** 17537
(717) 464-0707; FAX (717) 464-2501
Web site: http://www.bbonline.com/pa/walkabout/index.html

This 1925 restored Mennonite farmhouse is in a village setting convenient to major attractions. There are large, wraparound porches, English and wildflower gardens,

welcome; 7 Children welcome; 8 Tennis nearby; 9 Swimming nearby; 10 Golf nearby; 11 Skiing nearby; 12 May be booked through travel agent.

a lily pond, and period antiques. A full candlelight breakfast is served. Guest rooms have fireplaces, canopies, Jacuzzis, or hot tubs. A fantasy cottage is available.

Hosts: Richard and Margaret Mason
Rooms: 5 (PB) $99-199
Full Breakfast
Credit Cards: A, B, C
Notes: 2, 3, 4, 5, 7, 8, 9, 10, 12

Bed and Breakfast —The Manor

830 Village Road, 17602–1627
(717) 464-9564

A cozy farmhouse in scenic Amish country, 3 miles west of Strasburg Railroad, 5 minutes from all attractions. Full gourmet buffet breakfast, deluxe in-ground pool. Children welcome. Amish dinners arranged. Reserve a room for two nights and receive a free Amish dinner for two.

Hostesses: Jackie Curtis and Mary Lou Paolini
Rooms: 6 (4PB; 2SB) $79-99
Full Buffet Breakfast
Credit Cards: A, B
Notes: 2, 5, 7, 8, 9

Country Living Inn

2406 Old Philadelphia Pike, 17602
(717) 295-7295
Web site: http://padutchwelcome.com/ctryliv.html

Just like "home!" Warm, inviting hospitality. Country decor with quilts on the full, queen, or king beds. New Shaker furniture, glider rockers, or sofas in the deluxe suite or queen rooms. Romantic suite with a whirlpool for two. Amish farms on the north and west sides. Coffee, tea, and hot chocolate served daily. Pastries served weekends (May–October) on the porch. The front porches have rockers and benches for visiting, relaxing, or watching Amish buggies go by.

Country Living Inn

Hosts: Bill and Judy Harnish
Rooms: 34 (PB) $43-130
Continental Breakfast
Credit Cards: A, B
Notes: 5, 10, 12

Flowers and Thyme Bed and Breakfast

238 Strasburg Pike, 17602
(717) 393-1460; FAX (717) 399-1986
E-mail: padutchbnb@aol.com
Web site: http://members.aol.com/padutchbnb

Enjoy lodging and breakfast in a serene country setting. Our B&B overlooks a picturesque working farm and is surrounded by English cottage gardens. Tastefully created interiors. Genuine hospitality. Minutes from outlets and music theatres. Clean, comfortable rooms with queen beds. Baths are private; one has a Jacuzzi. Beautiful country breakfasts are served in the spacious gathering room. Dinner with an Amish family can be arranged.

Hosts: Don and Ruth Harnish
Rooms: 3 (PB) $80-100
Full Breakfast
Credit Cards: A, B, C
Notes: 2, 5, 7 (over 12), 8, 9, 10

Gardens of Eden Bed and Breakfast

1894 Eden Road, 17601
(717) 393-5179; FAX (717) 393-7722
Web site: http://www.padutchinns.com

Victorian ironmaster's home built circa 1860 on the banks of the Conestoga River, 3 miles northeast of Lancaster. Antiques and family collections of quilts and coverlets fill the three guest rooms, all with private baths. The adjoining guest cottage (restored summer kitchen) features a walk-in fireplace, dining room, bedroom, and bath on the second floor. Marilyn's floral designs are featured and are for sale. Three acres of gardens feature herbs, perennials, and wildflowers among the woodsy trails. Local attractions are personalized by a tour guide service and dinner in an Amish couple's home. A canoe and rowboat are available. Two bike trails pass the house.

Hosts: Marilyn and Bill Ebel
Rooms: 4 (PB) $95-130
Full Breakfast
Credit Cards: A, B
Notes: 2, 5, 7 (in guest house), 8, 9, 10, 12

Lincoln Haus Inn Bed and Breakfast

1687 Lincoln Highway E., 17602
(717) 392-9412
Web site: http://www.800padutch.com/linchaus.html

Lincoln Haus Inn is the only inn in Lancaster County with a distinctive hip roof. It is furnished with antiques and rugs on gleaming hardwood floors, with natural oak woodwork. I am a member of the Old Amish Church, serving family-style breakfast in a homey atmosphere. Convenient location, close to Amish farmlands, malls, historic Lancaster (including farmers market), Gettysburg, and Hershey; 5 minutes from Route 30 and the Pennsylvania Dutch Visitors' Bureau. Amish dinners can be arranged.

Hostess: Mary K. Zook
Rooms: 6 + 2 apartments (PB) $55-80
Full Breakfast
Credit Cards: none
Notes: 2, 4 (at Amish homes), 5, 7, 8, 9, 10, 12

Meadowview Guest House

2169 New Holland Pike, 17601
(717) 299-4017

This Dutch Colonial home is located in the heart of the Pennsylvania Dutch Amish area. Three guest rooms and kitchen on the second floor. There is a stove, refrigerator, sink, and dishes. A breakfast tray is put in the kitchen in the morning for each guest room. Close to many historic sites and to farmers and antique markets. Excellent restaurants and many attractions help guests enjoy the beautiful country. Personalized maps are provided.

Hosts: Edward and Sheila
Rooms: 3 (1PB; 2SB) $35-50
Continental Breakfast
Credit Cards: none
Notes: 2 (deposit only), 5, 7 (over 6) , 8, 9, 10, 12

New Life Homestead Bed and Breakfast

1400 E. King Street, 17602–3246
(717) 396-8928; FAX (717) 396-0461
E-mail: wgiersch@redrose.net
Web site: http://www.bbonline.com/pa/newlife

Located in the heart of Amish country, close to all attractions. If you ever wanted

New Life Homestead Bed and Breakfast

to know about the Amish and Mennonite people, this is where to learn. The home features antiques and heirlooms. Full breakfasts and evening refreshments are served. Your hosts are a Mennonite family with traditional family values. Private baths, air-conditioning.

Hosts: Carol and Bill Giersch
Rooms: 3 (2PB; 1SB) $65-85
Full Family-Style Breakfast
Credit Cards: none
Notes: 2, 5, 7, 8, 9, 10, 12

O'Flaherty's Dingeldein House Bed and Breakfast

1105 E. King Street, 17602
(717) 293-1723; (800) 779-7765;
FAX (717) 293-1947
E-mail: oflahbb@lancnews.infi.net
Web site: http://800padutch.com/ofhouse.html

Come visit one of Lancaster County's most unique bed and breakfasts. Gracious accommodations in our beautiful Dutch Colonial home (former residence of the Armstrong family, of floor tile fortune). Minutes from scenic Amish country. Convenient to farmers markets, downtown Lancaster, outlets, Hershey, and Gettysburg. O'Flaherty's offers elegant breakfasts, beautiful gardens, itineraries, maps, and abundant hospitality. Queen beds, private baths. AAA three-star-rated. "Try us; you'll like us."

Hosts: Jack and Sue Flatley
Rooms: 5 (PB) $80-100
Full Breakfast
Credit Cards: A, B, D
Notes: 2, 5, 7, 8, 9, 10

LANCASTER COUNTY (PENNSYLVANIA DUTCH COUNTRY) (SEE ALSO—BIRD-IN-HAND, CHRISTIANA, COLUMBIA, DENVER, EAST PETERSBURG, ELIZABETHTOWN, EPHRATA, KINZERS, LANCASTER, MANHEIM, MARIETTA, MOUNT JOY, PARADISE, PEACH BOTTOM, AND SMOKETOWN)

The Apple Bin Inn Bed and Breakfast

2835 Willow Street Pike, **Willow Street,** 17584
(717) 464-5881; (800) 338-4296;
FAX (717) 464-1818
E-mail: bininn@aol.com
Web site: http://www.applebininn.com

Experience the hospitality and charm at one of the area's finest B&Bs. This 1865 home is nestled in the county's oldest village, 3 miles south of Lancaster. We offer distinctive country decor in a comfortable, relaxed setting. Enjoy the two-room suites,

The Apple Bin Inn Bed and Breakfast

NOTES: Credit cards accepted: A Master Card; B Visa; C American Express; D Discover; E Diners Club; F Other; 2 Personal checks accepted; 3 Lunch available; 4 Dinner available; 5 Open all year; 6 Pets

balcony, and patios. Try our restored carriage house (two-story, with fireplace) for a unique getaway. Awaken to the aroma of a homemade breakfast. AC, TV, phone in room. FAX available.

Hosts: Barry and Debbie Hershey
Rooms: 4 + carriage house (PB) $95-135
Full Breakfast
Credit Cards: A, B, C
Notes: 2, 5, 8, 9, 10

Ben Mar Farm B&B

5721 Old Philadelphia Pike, **Gap,** 17527
(717) 768-3309

Come stay on our working dairy farm. We are located in the heart of the famous Amish country. Experience quiet country life while staying in the large, beautifully decorated rooms of our 200-year-old farmhouse. Our efficiency apartment is a favorite; it includes a full kitchen and queen and double beds with private bath. Enjoy a fresh continental breakfast brought to your room. The home is air-conditioned.

Hosts: Herb and Melanie Benner
Rooms: 3 (PB) $45-65
Continental Breakfast
Credit Cards: none
Notes: 2, 5, 7, 8, 9

Carriage Corner B&B

3705 E. Newport Road; PO Box 371, **Intercourse,** 17534–0371
(717) 768-3059; (800) 209-3059;
FAX (717) 768-0691

"A comfortable bed, a hearty breakfast, a charming village, and friendly hosts" has been used to describe our B&B. We have comfortable rooms with country decor, Amish quilt hangings, and private baths. Our home offers a relaxing country atmosphere with hand-crafted touches of folk art and country. Rooms have AC. We are centered in the heart of beautiful farms and a culture that draws many to the nearby villages of Intercourse, Bird-in-Hand, and Strasburg. Amish dinners sometimes can be arranged. There is much to learn from these calm and gentle people.

Hosts: Mr. and Mrs. Gordon Schuit
Rooms: 5 (PB) $65-85
Full Breakfast
Credit Cards: A, B
Notes: 2, 5, 7, 12

Homestead Lodging

184 E. Brook Road (Route 896), 17576
(717) 393-6927; FAX (717) 393-1424

Come to our beautiful Lancaster County setting where you can hear the clippety-clop of horse-drawn Amish buggies and experience the sights and sounds of their unique culture. . .while you enjoy the freshness of well-kept farmlands. Enjoy a walk down the lane to the Amish farm adjacent to us, or enjoy a quiet evening on the porch. Clean country rooms with cable TV, refrigerator, queen and double beds, individually controlled heat and AC. Microwave available.

Hosts: Robert and Lori Kepiro
Rooms: 5 (PB) $39-64
Continental Breakfast
Credit Cards: A, B, C, D
Notes: 2 (deposit only), 5, 7, 8, 9, 10, 12

The Inn at Hayward Heath

2048 Silver Lane, **Willow Street,** 17584
(717) 464-0994; (800) 482-6432
Web site: http://www.ristenbatt.com/hayward

Located in the gently rolling Lancaster County hills, our 1887 farmhouse has been

The Inn at Hayward Heath

beautifully restored to replicate colonial living. Reflect on America's past in our Shaker-style room with queen canopy bed, or enjoy the romantic touch of our spacious country garden room with queen bed, sitting area, and attached private bath with two-person whirlpool. Our first-floor rose bedroom features a queen bed and a large private bath. A two-bedroom suite is available. Large living room for visiting, reading, or viewing TV. A sumptuous breakfast is served in the formal dining room. Close to historic areas; tourist attractions; outlet shopping malls; Amish farms; and craft, antique, and quilt shops.

Hosts: Joan and David Smith
Rooms: 4 (PB) $85-120
Full Breakfast
Credit Cards: A, B, D
Notes: 2, 5, 8, 10

LANDENBERG

Cornerstone Inn

300 Buttonwood Road, 19350
(610) 274-2143; FAX (610) 274-0734
E-mail: corner3000@aol.com
Web site: http://www.belmar.com/cornerstone

A fine 18th-century country inn just minutes from Longwood Gardens, Winterthur, Wyeth Museum, and Amish country. Fireplaces, Jacuzzis, air-conditioning, canopy beds galore!

Hostess: Linda Chamberlin
Rooms: 8 (PB) $75-150
Full Breakfast
Credit Cards: A, B, D
Notes: 2, 5, 8, 9, 10

Hamanassett Bed and Breakfast

LIMA (BRANDYWINE VALLEY)

Hamanassett Bed and Breakfast

PO Box 129, 19037
(610) 459-3000 (voice and FAX)
E-mail: hamanasset@aol.com
Web site: http://www.bbonline.com/pa/hamanassett

Enjoy an early-19th-century mansion on 48 secluded, peaceful acres of woodlands, gardens, and trails in the Brandywine Valley near Winterthur, Hagley, Nemours, Brandywine (Wyeth) museums, and Longwood Gardens. Well-appointed guest quarters have queen, double, twin, and canopied king beds; private baths; TV; and amenities. Beautiful Federalist living room and extensive library. Full country breakfast—sophisticated cuisine. Near tennis, golf, and excellent dining. An elegant, quiet weekend escape along the

U.S. Route 1 corridor and a world away. Two-night minimum. No smoking. Closed July 15–August 30.

Hostess: Evelene H. Dohan
Rooms: 9 (7PB; 2SB) $90-125
Full Breakfast
Credit Cards: none
Notes: 2, 8, 10

LITITZ

Alden House B&B

62 E. Main Street, 17543
(717) 627-3363
E-mail: inn@aldenhouse.com
Web site: http://www.aldenhouse.com

Fully restored 1850 Victorian/Colonial located in the heart of the town's historic district. All local attractions and shops are within a short walk. Home of the nation's oldest pretzel bakery. Spacious suites, central air-conditioning, offstreet parking, and bicycle storage available. Antiques abound in this area, as well as handmade quilts. Enjoy old-fashioned hospitality.

Hosts: Fletcher and Joy Coleman
Rooms: 5 (PB) $85-120
Full Breakfast
Credit Cards: A, B
Notes: 2, 5, 8, 9, 10, 12

MANHEIM (LANCASTER AREA)

Country Comforts of Jonde Lane Farm

1103 Auction Road, 17545
(717) 665-4231

The Nissleys invite you to share life on their 140-year-old working family farm. Relax on the back porch and enjoy the serenity, or participate in daily chores. Feed a calf, milk a goat, gather eggs! Children are welcome—and there is plenty for them to do! Rooms feature comfortable country decor and are air-conditioned. You are welcome to join us at the Mennonite church on Sunday morning. The farm is located only 30 minutes from Hershey and Amish country.

Hosts: Elaine and John Nissley
Rooms: 6 (3PB; 3SB) $45-70
Full Breakfast
Credit Cards: A, B
Notes: 2, 5, 7

Dutch Pride Guest House, Bed and Breakfast

1383 Lancaster Road, 17545
(717) 665-5083

Relax in the heart of Lancaster County tucked between Lancaster and Lebanon. Our stone ranch house is restful, with screened gazebo, flower gardens, and sunroom. Efficiency suite, full kitchen, air-conditioning, television, telephone, office, private bath, queen and regular beds, plus guest rooms. The guest house is smoke-free. Located close to Hershey Chocolate town and the Gettysburg battlefield. Harrisburg, the renaissance fair, farmers markets, Amish farms, outlet shopping, antiques, covered bridges, restaurants, airports, and auctions are nearby. Country setting. Easy to find.

Hosts: Roy and Mary Jane Sauder
Rooms: 3 (2PB; 1SB) $75-90
Full or Continental Breakfast
Credit Cards: A, B
Notes: 2, 5, 7, 8, 9, 10, 12

Penn's Valley Farm

6182 Metzler Road, 17545
(717) 898-7386

Quiet farm setting on 64 acres. One Victorian room in farmhouse and private guest house separate from farmhouse. Easy access to Amish rural areas and Hershey Park. Continental or full breakfast, as you prefer. Guest house can sleep seven.

Hosts: Mel and Gladys Metzler
Rooms: 2 (1PB; 1SB) $50-65
Full Breakfast
Credit Cards: A, B, C
Notes: 2, 5, 7

Wenger's B&B

571 Hossler Road, 17545
(717) 665-3862

Relax and enjoy your stay in the quiet countryside of Lancaster County. Our ranch-style house is within walking distance of our son's 100-acre dairy farm. The spacious rooms will accommodate families. Take a guided tour through the Amish farmland. Hershey, Pennsylvania's state capital at Harrisburg, and the Gettysburg battlefield are within an hour's drive.

Hosts: Arthur and Mary K. Wenger
Rooms: 2 (PB) $60-65
Full Breakfast
Credit Cards: none
Notes: 2, 5, 7

MARIETTA

Historic Linden House

606 E. Market Street, 17547–1808
(717) 426-4697; (800) 416-4697;
FAX (717) 426-4138
E-mail: lindenhous@aol.com

The Historic Linden House is a Federal-style home built in 1806 and listed on the National Historic Register. When built, it was considered one of the finest mansions in south-central Pennsylvania, costing $16,000–17,000 to build. Marietta is a charming town along the Susquehanna River which time has forgotten; 48% of its buildings are in the historic district. The home historically is known for its staircase—the longest original, preserved, continuous handrail staircase in Lancaster County. Guests enjoy queen beds, private baths, and fresh flowers in season. Spend a relaxing evening in the parlor by two crackling fireplaces (the house has sixteen fireplaces). Special packages and discounts are available.

Hosts: Henry, Jeanene, and David Hill
Rooms: 4 (PB) $55
Full Breakfast
Credit Cards: A, B
Notes: 2, 5, 7

The River Inn Bed and Breakfast

The River Inn Bed and Breakfast

258 W. Front Street, 17547–1405
(717) 426-2290; (888) 824-6622;
FAX (717) 426-2966

Bordering the Susquehanna River in western Lancaster County, the town of Marietta offers quiet streets with hundreds of restored homes and architectural treasures.

NOTES: Credit cards accepted: A Master Card; B Visa; C American Express; D Discover; E Diners Club; F Other; 2 Personal checks accepted; 3 Lunch available; 4 Dinner available; 5 Open all year; 6 Pets

Located in the historic district, the 200-year-old River Inn welcomes guests with its meticulous 18th-century restoration and special attention to detail. The six working fireplaces, a wide open stairway, crown molding, and tin lighting add to the inn's charming colonial atmosphere. Our guests can relax on the enclosed porch, stroll through the gardens, or bike the streets of Marietta.

Hosts: Bob and Joyce Heiserman
Rooms: 3 (PB) $60-80
Full Breakfast
Credit Cards: A, B, D, E, F
Notes: 2, 5, 7 (10+), 10, 12

MILFORD

Cliff Park Inn and Golf Course

155 Cliff Park Road, 18337
(717) 296-6491; (800) 225-6535;
FAX (717) 296-3982

Historic country inn on a secluded 600-acre estate. Spacious rooms with private baths, phone, and climate control. Furnishings are Victorian-style. Fireplaces. Golf at the door on one of America's oldest golf courses (1913). Cross-country ski or hike on 7 miles of marked trails. Golf and ski equipment rentals. Golf school. Full-service restaurant rated three stars by Mobil. MAP or B&B plans available. Specialists in business conferences and country weddings.

Host: Harry W. Buchanan, III
Rooms: 18 (PB) $90-155
Full Breakfast
Credit Cards: A, B, C, D, E
Notes: 2, 3, 4, 5, 7, 8, 9 (onsite), 10, 11, 12

MILL RIFT

Bonny Bank Bungalow

PO Box 481, 18340
(717) 491-2250

Let the rush of the rapids lull you to sleep in this cozy bungalow perched on the banks of the Upper Delaware National Scenic and Recreational River. Located on a dead-end road in a small town. Private entrance and private bath. TV available, if you can take your eyes off the view. River access for swimming and tubing (tubes available at no charge). Canoe/raft rentals and hiking on public lands nearby.

Hosts: Doug and Linda Hay
Rooms: 1 (PB) $50
Full Breakfast
Credit Cards: none
Notes: 2, 8, 9, 10

MILTON

Pau-Lyn's Country B&B

RD 3, Box 676, 17847
(717) 742-4110

The beautiful Susquehanna Valley of central Pennsylvania is unique. Varied, pleasant experiences await those who want to be in touch with God's handiwork and observe agriculture, scenic mountains, rivers, and valleys. Recreation abounds—underground railroad stops and much more. The innkeepers provide nostalgic memories throughout the antique-furnished, 1850 Victorian brick house, 2 miles from I–80. Air-conditioned. "A restful haven."

Hosts: Paul and Evelyn Landis
Rooms: 7 (4PB; 3SB) $45-55
Full Breakfast
Credit Cards: none
Notes: 2, 5, 7, 8, 9, 10, 11, 12

MOUNT JOY

Cedar Hill Farm

305 Longenecker Road, 17552
(717) 653-4655 (voice and FAX)
Web site: http://www.800padutch.com/cedarhill.html

This 1817 stone farmhouse overlooks a peaceful stream and was the birthplace of the host. Stroll the acreage or relax on wicker rockers on the large front porch. Enjoy the singing of the birds and serene countryside. A winding staircase leads to the comfortable rooms, each with a private bath. Central AC. A room for honeymooners offers a private balcony. Breakfast is served beside a walk-in fireplace. Midway between the Lancaster and Hershey areas, where farmers markets, antique shops, and good restaurants abound. Gift certificates for anniversary or holiday giving. Open all seasons.

Hosts: Russel and Gladys Swarr
Rooms: 5 (PB) $75-80
Continental Plus Breakfast
Credit Cards: A, B, C, D
Notes: 2, 5, 7, 8, 10

Hillside Farm Bed and Breakfast

607 Eby Chiques Road, 17552
(717) 653-6697; (888) 249-3406;
FAX (717) 653-5233 (call first)
E-mail: hillside3@juno.com
Web site: http://www2.epix.net/~bblanco/hillside.html

Quiet, secluded 1863 brick farm homestead overlooking Chiques Creek, dam, and waterfall. Located 10 miles west of downtown Lancaster and entirely surrounded by farmland. Comfortable, cozy, country furnishings include dairy antiques and milk bottles. Hot tub for six on porch. Family reunions welcome. Seasonal packages. Close to Amish country, Hershey, antique shops, flea markets, auctions, wineries, and trails for hiking and biking. Bike trail maps available. Dinner arranged in advance with Amish. Strictly nonsmoking. Air-conditioned.

Hillside Farm Bed and Breakfast

Hosts: Gary and Deb Lintner
Rooms: 5 (3PB; 2SB) $60-75
Full Breakfast
Credit Cards: A, B, D
Notes: 2, 5, 7 (10 and older), 8, 9, 10, 11, 12

MUNCY

The Bodine House Bed and Breakfast

307 S. Main Street, 17756
(570) 546-8949; FAX (570) 546-0607
E-mail: BODINE@PSCPOWER.NET

The Bodine House, featured in the December 1991 issue of *Colonial Homes* magazine, is located on tree-lined Main Street in Muncy's historic district. Constructed in 1805, the house has been authentically restored and now is listed on the National Register of Historic Places.

NOTES: Credit cards accepted: A Master Card; B Visa; C American Express; D Discover; E Diners Club; F Other; 2 Personal checks accepted; 3 Lunch available; 4 Dinner available; 5 Open all year; 6 Pets

Most of the furnishings are antiques. The center of Muncy, with its shops, restaurants, library, and churches, is just a short walk down the street. No smoking.

Hosts: David and Marie Louise Smith
Rooms: 4 (PB) $65-70; Carriage House (up to six guests) $125
Full Breakfast
Credit Cards: A, B, C, D
Notes: 2, 5, 7 (over 6), 8, 9, 10, 11, 12

NEW BERLIN

The Inn at Olde New Berlin

321 Market Street, 17855
(717) 966-0321; FAX (717) 966-9557
E-mail: john@newberlin-inn.com
Web site: http://www.newberlin-inn.com

"A luxurious base for indulging in a clutch of quiet pleasures" is *The Philadelphia Inquirer*'s apt description of this elegantly appointed Victorian inn. The superb dining opportunities at Gabriel's Restaurant (onsite) coupled with the antique-filled lodging accommodations provide romance and ambience. An upscale experience in a rural setting, located 1 hour north of Harrisburg. Guests relay that they depart feeling nurtured, relaxed, yet—most of all—inspired. Gifts, herb garden, air-conditioning. AAA- and Mobil-approved. Full line of Radko Christmas ornaments available at Gabriel's Gifts.

Hosts: John and Nancy Showers
Rooms: 9 + 2 suites (5PB; 4SB) $90-180
Full Breakfast
Credit Cards: A, B, D
Notes: 2, 3, 4, 5, 7, 8, 9, 10, 12

Behm's Bed and Breakfast

NEW WILMINGTON

Behm's Bed and Breakfast

166 Waugh Avenue, 16142
(412) 946-8641; (800) 932-3315

Located but 1 block from Westminster College campus, Behm's 100-year-old bed and breakfast is comfortably furnished with family, primitive, and collected antiques. Located within walking distance of shops and restaurants, Behm's is surrounded by rural, Old Order Amish. Nationally recognized watercolorist Nancy Behm's gallery is onsite. Lighted, offstreet parking is available for guests. The homemade breakfast varies daily and is served in our dining room.

Hosts: Nancy and Bob Behm
Rooms: 4 (2PB; 2SB) $50-65
Full Breakfast
Credit Cards: A, B
Notes: 2, 5, 7, 8, 9, 10, 11

welcome; 7 Children welcome; 8 Tennis nearby; 9 Swimming nearby; 10 Golf nearby; 11 Skiing nearby; 12 May be booked through travel agent.

NEWVILLE

Nature's Nook Farm B&B

740 Shed Road, 17241
(717) 776-5619 (voice and FAX)

Located in a quiet, peaceful setting along the Blue Mountains. Warm Mennonite hospitality and clean, comfortable lodging await you. Enjoy freshly brewed garden tea and fresh fruit, in season. Homemade cinnamon rolls, muffins, and coffee cakes. Perennial flower garden. Close to Colonel Denning State Park with hiking trails, fishing, and swimming. Two hours to Lancaster, 1 hour to Harrisburg, and 1½ hours to Gettysburg and Hershey. The home is wheelchair-accessible.

Hosts: Don and Lois Leatherman
Rooms: 1 (PB) $50-58
Continental Breakfast
Credit Cards: none
Notes: 2, 5, 7 (8 and older), 8, 9, 10

NORTH EAST

Vineyard Bed and Breakfast

10757 Sidehill Road, 16428
(814) 725-8998; (888) 725-8998

Your hosts welcome you to the "Heart of Grape Country" on Lake Erie, surrounded by vineyards and orchards. Our turn-of-the-century farmhouse is quiet and peaceful, with rooms furnished with queen or king beds and tastefully decorated to complement our home.

Hosts: Clyde and Judy Burnham
Rooms: 4 (PB) $65-75
Full Breakfast
Credit Cards: A, B, C, D
Notes: 2, 5, 7, 9, 10, 11

NORTHUMBERLAND

Campbell's Bed and Breakfast

707 Duke Street, 17857–1709
(717) 473-3276

Campbell's Bed and Breakfast is a country inn built in 1859. Three large bedrooms with queen-size beds await your occupancy. Enjoy a refreshing swim in the large, heated, in-ground pool surrounded by the rose garden, or relax beside the fireplace in the home's spacious living room during the cool months.

Hosts: Bob and Millie Campbell
Rooms: 3 (2PB; 1SB) $50-65
Full Breakfast
Credit Cards: A, B
Notes: 2, 5, 7 (call first), 8, 9 (onsite), 10, 12

ORRTANNA

Hickory Bridge Farm Bed and Breakfast

96 Hickory Bridge Road, 17353
(717) 642-5261
E-mail: hickory@mail.cvn.net
Web site: http://www.gettysburg.com/gcvb/hbf.htm

Only 8 miles west of historic Gettysburg. Unique country dining and B&B. Cozy cottages with woodstoves and private baths are located in secluded, wooded settings along a stream. Lovely rooms are available in the farmhouse with antiques, private baths, and whirlpool tubs. Full, farm breakfast served at the farmhouse, which was built in the late 1700s. Country dining offered on Fridays, Saturdays, and Sundays in a 130-year-old barn with many

---

NOTES: Credit cards accepted: A Master Card; B Visa; C American Express; D Discover; E Diners Club; F Other; 2 Personal checks accepted; 3 Lunch available; 4 Dinner available; 5 Open all year; 6 Pets

antiques. Family-owned/-operated for more than 20 years.

Hosts: Robert and Mary Lynn Martin
Rooms: 9 (PB) $79-89
Full Breakfast
Credit Cards: A, B, D
Notes: 2, 4 (weekends), 5, 8, 9, 10, 11

PALMYRA

The "Hen-Apple" B&B

409 S. Lingle Avenue, 17078
(717) 838-8282
Web site: http://www.visithhc.com/henapple.html

Our lovingly restored 19th-century farmhouse is surrounded by more than an acre of lawn and gardens for guests to enjoy. Quaint and "country." Inside and out you'll find antiques, folk art, and an abundance of old-fashioned charm. Breakfast is a delight in our cozy dining room or on our screened veranda in warm weather. With several porches and common areas to enjoy, guests always find time to relax.

Hosts: Harold and Flo Eckert
Rooms: 6 (PB) $65-75
Full or Continental Breakfast
Credit Cards: A, B, C, D, F (all Novas)
Notes: 2, 5, 8, 9, 10, 12

PARADISE

The Parson's Place

37 Leacock Road, 17562
(717) 687-8529
Web site: http://www2.epix.net/~allseaso/parsons.html

Mid-1700s stone house with stone patio overlooking flower gardens and a picturesque road that is traveled by horse-drawn buggies to the Amish village-mecca of Intercourse (tourist center of Lancaster County), 3 miles to the east. Share this charming home, furnished with country decor, with a former pastor and wife.

The Parson's Place

Hosts: Robert and Margaret Bell
Rooms: 3 (2PB; 1SB) $50-80
Full Breakfast
Credit Cards: A
Notes: 2, 5

PEACH BOTTOM

Pleasant Grove Farm

368 Pilottown Road, 17563
(717) 548-3100

Located in beautiful, historic Lancaster County, this 160-acre dairy farm has been a family-run operation for 110 years, earning the title of Century Farm by the Pennsylvania Department of Agriculture. As a working farm, it lets guests experience daily life in a rural setting. Built in 1814, 1818, and 1820, the house once served as a country store and post office. A full country breakfast is served by candlelight.

Hosts: Charles and Labertha Tindall
Rooms: 4 (1PB; 3SB) $45-60
Full Breakfast
Credit Cards: none
Notes: 2, 5, 7, 9, 10

PITTSBURGH

The Inn at Oakmont

PO Box 103, **Oakmont**, 15139
(412) 828-0410; FAX (412) 828-1358
Web site: http://www.bnb.lm.com

Nestled in the historic village of Oakmont, we are next to Oakmont Country Club and 20 minutes from Pittsburgh. Built in 1994, this meticulously designed B&B has become a mecca for the traveler seeking the service and charm of a more gracious era. All rooms include television, radio, telephone, and sleep machines. Some rooms have whirlpool tubs and fireplaces.

Hostess: Shelley Smith
Rooms: 8 (PB) $130-140
Full Breakfast
Credit Cards: A, B, C, D
Notes: 2, 5, 10, 12

POCONO MOUNTAINS (SEE ALSO—CANADENSIS AND CRESCO)

Eagle Rock Lodge

Eagle Rock Lodge

River Road; PO Box 265, **Shawnee-on-the-Delaware,** 18356
(717) 421-2139

This century-old inn sits on 10½ Delaware River acres adjacent to the scenic Delaware Water Gap National Recreation Area and the Pocono Mountains. Breakfast is served on an 80-foot screened porch overlooking the river. Step back in time to a relaxed, bygone era. Group rentals.

Hosts: Jim and Jane Cox
Rooms: 8 (1PB; 6SB) $70-100
Full Breakfast
Credit Cards: C
Notes: 2, 5, 7, 8, 9, 10, 11, 12

POINT PLEASANT (NEW HOPE)

Tattersall Inn

Cafferty and River Roads; PO Box 569, 18950
(215) 297-8233; (800) 297-4988;
FAX (215) 297-5093
E-mail: NRHG17A@Prodigy.com

This 18th-century, plastered, fieldstone home with broad porches and manicured lawns recalls an unhurried bygone era. Enjoy the richly wainscoted entry hall, formal dining room with marble fireplace, and vintage phonographs. Step back in time when you enter the colonial common room with its beamed ceiling and walk-in fireplace. Spacious guest rooms with antiques, some with fireplaces. AC.

Hosts: Gerry and Herb Moss
Rooms: 6 (PB) $70-130
Full Breakfast
Credit Cards: A, B, C, D
Notes: 2, 5, 7, 8, 9, 12

SAINT THOMAS

Heavenly Sent B&B

7886 Lincoln Way West, 17252
(717) 369-5882
E-mail: gbrady@epix.net

Gregg and Karen have lovingly and completely restored this 1800-era house. The

NOTES: Credit cards accepted: A Master Card; B Visa; C American Express; D Discover; E Diners Club; F Other; 2 Personal checks accepted; 3 Lunch available; 4 Dinner available; 5 Open all year; 6 Pets

inn offers generous-size rooms with original hardwood floors. Guests may enjoy the warmth of their private bubbling whirlpool, or a fireplace in the sitting room with its own scenic view. You will be awakened from your slumber by the tantalizing, divine aroma of freshly ground and brewed gourmet coffee. A culinary feast has been prepared and awaits in the romantic, candlelit dining room where soft music is being played. Guests have an abundance of options for ultimate relaxation.

Hosts: Gregg and Karen Brady
Rooms: 5 (3PB; 2SB) $80-150
Full Breakfast
Credit Cards: A, B
Notes: 2, 3 and 4 (extra), 5, 7 (well-behaved), 8, 9, 10, 11, 12

SCOTTDALE

Pine Wood Acres Bed and Breakfast

Route 1, Box 634, 15683
(724) 887-5404; FAX (724) 887-3111
E-mail: horsch@mph.org
Web site: http://www.laurelhighlands.org/pinewoodacres

Experience gracious hospitality in our circa-1880 farmhouse. Enjoy the seasonal changes to the landscape of our tranquil country setting. Antiques, quilts, herb and perennial gardens, bountiful breakfasts, and afternoon tea. Close to Wright's Fallingwater and Kentuck Knob. Ten miles south of the I–70/I–76 junction at New Stanton.

Hosts: Ruth and James Horsch
Rooms: 3 (2PB; 1SB) $68.90-79.50
Full Breakfast
Credit Cards: some
Notes: 2, 5, 6, 7, 8, 9, 10, 11, 12

Zephyr Glen Bed and Breakfast

Zephyr Glen B&B

205 Dexter Road, 15683
(724) 887-6577; FAX (724) 887-6177 (call first)
E-mail: zephyr@hhs.net

Our 1822 Federal-style Mennonite farmhouse is nestled on 3 wooded acres. The house is filled with antiques, old quilts, and seasonal decorations. We feature caring Christian hospitality, warm country decor, afternoon tea, bed turn-down, and a hearty breakfast. Sit by the fireplace, rock on the wide porch, or stroll through herb, flower, and fruit gardens. Antiques, Fallingwater, hiking, biking, white water, and historic sites are nearby. We'll help you find your favorite. Come and enjoy!

Hosts: Noreen and Gil McGurl
Rooms: 3 (PB) $75-80
Full Breakfast
Credit Cards: A, B, D
Notes: 2, 5, 7 (over 12), 8, 10, 11, 12

SEWICKLEY

The Whistlestop B&B

195 Broad Street, **Leetsdale,** 15056
(724) 251-0852
Web site: http://www.mountainsky.com

A quaint brick Victorian home built in 1888 by the Harmonist Society, a Christian communal group similar to the Shakers. It features the "Upper Berth," a third-floor suite with a small kitchen and dining area, and the "Lower Berth" with a sofa bed and private entrance. Kids stay free with parents. Your hostess is well-known for her country cooking, specializing in breads, muffins, pastries, and jams. Leetsdale is located on the Ohio River, 12 miles west of Pittsburgh (the airport is 20 minutes away) and close to the classic American village of Sewickley, where fine examples of historic architecture are well-maintained. The home is smoke-free.

Hosts: Steve and Joyce Smith
Rooms: 2 (PB) $60-70
Full Country Breakfast
Credit Cards: A, B, C, D
Notes: 2, 5, 7

Field and Pine Bed and Breakfast

SHIPPENSBURG

Field and Pine Bed and Breakfast

2155 Ritner Highway, 17257
(717) 776-7179; (717) 776-0076
E-mail: fieldpine@aol.com
Web site: http://www.virtualcities.com

Surrounded by stately pine trees, Field and Pine is a family-owned B&B with the charm of an Early American stone house on an 80-acre gentleman's farm. Built in 1790, the house has seven working fireplaces, original wide-pine floors, and stenciled walls. Bedrooms are furnished with antiques, quilts, and comforters. A gourmet breakfast is served in the formal dining room. Three miles from I–81, between Carlisle and Shippensburg.

Hosts: Mary Ellen and Allan Williams
Rooms: 3 (1PB; 2SB) $65-75
Full Breakfast
Credit Cards: A, B
Notes: 2, 5, 7 (over 12), 8, 9, 10, 11

SOMERSET

Quill Haven Country Inn

1519 N. Center Avenue, 15501
(814) 443-4514; FAX (814) 445-1376
E-mail: quill@quillhaven.com
Web site: http://www.quillhaven.com

A 1918 "gentleman's farmhouse" furnished with antiques and reproductions. Four uniquely decorated guest rooms with private baths, AC, and cable TV. Common room with fireplace, sunroom where breakfast is served, private deck with hot tub. AAA-rated, three diamonds. Pennsylvania Travel Council-rated. Near Hidden Valley and Seven Springs ski resorts; Frank Lloyd Wright's Fallingwater; Youghiogheny Reservoir; Ohiopyle for hiking, biking, and white-water sports; outlet mall; golf courses; and antique shops. Located 1.2 miles from the Pennsylvania Turnpike, Exit 10.

Hosts: Carol and Rowland Miller
Rooms: 4 (PB) $75-95
Full Breakfast
Credit Cards: A, B, D
Notes: 2, 5, 7 (well-behaved), 8, 9, 10, 11

NOTES: Credit cards accepted: A Master Card; B Visa; C American Express; D Discover; E Diners Club; F Other; 2 Personal checks accepted; 3 Lunch available; 4 Dinner available; 5 Open all year; 6 Pets

SPRUCE CREEK

Cedar Hill at Spruce Creek

HC-01, Box 26, 16683
(814) 632-3804; (800) 764-9790
E-mail: llv1@epsu.edu
Web site: http://www.cedarhill-sprucecreek.com

A naturally graceful 1820 stone house. Original fireplaces, floors, and modern baths. Relaxing farm atmosphere near Penn State, Lake Raystown, fishing streams, caves, antiques, mountain paths, Amish farms, bicycle trails, and vacation opportunities. Bicycle trips, murder mystery weekends, fall foliage, farm activities. Wedding receptions, small retreats, and family reunions can be arranged. We are three generations of Vances committed to providing a quality, memorable experience.

Hosts: Barry and Linda, Aaron and Jennifer Vance
Rooms: 4 (PB) $65-117
Full Breakfast
Credit Cards: A, B, D

The Marshall House

HC 01, Box 10; Route 45, 16683
(814) 632-8319

Our country home is located near the village of Spruce Creek. Spend time on the front porch listening to the creek, reading, or just resting. Family activities available at Old Bedford Village, Raystown Lake, Horse Shoe Curve, Bland's Park, Lincoln and Indian caverns, and Penn State University. Fishers and hunters welcome.

Hosts: Sharon and Jim Dell
Rooms: 2 (SB) $35-50
Full Breakfast
Credit Cards: A, B
Notes: 2, 5, 7, 10, 11

STAHLSTOWN

Thorn's Cottage

RD 1, Box 254, 15687
(724) 593-6429

Located in the historic Ligonier Valley area of the Laurel Mountains, 7 miles from the Pennsylvania Turnpike, 50 miles east of Pittsburgh, the cottage offers homey, woodland privacy. Relax on the sunporch or in the herb garden with its swing. Near Fallingwater, white-water rafting, biking and hiking trails, and the quaint town of Ligonier with shops, dining, amusement park. Breakfast includes home-baked muffins and scones. Full kitchen.

Hosts: Larry and Beth Thorn
Rooms: 3-room cottage (PB) $55
Full Breakfast
Credit Cards: none
Notes: 2, 5, 7, 9, 10, 11

STARRUCCA

Nethercott Inn

6 Starrucca Creek Road; PO Box 26, 18462
(717) 727-2211; FAX (717) 727-3811
E-mail: netneinn@nep.net

This lovely, 1893 Victorian home is nestled in a small village in the Endless Mountains and furnished in country and antiques. All rooms have queen beds and private baths. Three and one-half hours from New York City and Philadelphia, 8 from Toronto. "The Loft" sleeps eight and has a kitchen and two baths. Available for ski rentals, family reunions, etc.

Hosts: Charlotte and John Keyser
Rooms: 7 (PB) $75-110
Full Breakfast
Credit Cards: A, B, C, D
Notes: 2, 5, 7, 11, 12

UNIONTOWN

Inne at Watson's Choice

RD 3, Box 363, 15401
(724) 437-4999
E-mail: bross@watsonschoice.com
Web site: http://www.watsonschoice.com

The Inne at Watson's Choice is a carefully restored, circa-1820 western Pennsylvania farmhouse. Here your family, friends, and business acquaintances can lodge in the warmth and hospitality of a B&B. For a night or for a week, a special anniversary or a weekend getaway, your visit to the Inne at Watson's Choice can become your quiet retreat from the bustle of everyday life. Located in the village of Balsinger. Mobil three stars, AAA three diamonds, and PA Travel Council.

Hosts: Bill and Nancy Ross
Rooms: 7 (PB) $89-125
Full Breakfast
Credit Cards: A, B, C, D
Notes: 5, 8, 9, 10, 11

VALLEY FORGE

Association of Bed and Breakfasts

PO Box 562, 19481–0562
(610) 783-7838; (800) 344-0123 (reservations);
FAX (610) 783-7783
E-mail: pa@bnbassociation.com

There is a B&B for you!—whether business, vacation, getaways, or relocating. Also serving **Bucks** and **Lancaster Counties.** More than 500 rooms are available in historic city/country inns, town houses, unhosted estate cottages, and suites. Family plan, Jacuzzi, fireplace, pool. Free brochure or descriptive directory ($3). Services include gift certificates, dinner reservations, weddings/special occasions/photography at unique bed and breakfasts, personal attention, gracious hospitality. No reservation fee. Featured in *Philadelphia Magazine*. Rate range: $35-135. Major credit cards accepted. Carolyn J. Williams, coordinator.

WASHINGTON

Rush House Bed and Breakfast

810 E. Maiden Street, 15301
(724) 223-1890
E-mail: jwheeler@cobweb.net

Rush House is a 100-year-old Victorian house built to accommodate Catfish Creek, which flows through a tunnel under the house. The bedrooms are decorated with antique pieces, and antique clocks abound throughout the house. A buffet breakfast is served each morning in the spacious dining room.

Hosts: Jim and Judy Wheeler
Rooms: 4 (PB) $75-110
Full Breakfast
Credit Cards: A, B
Notes: 2, 5, 8, 9

WAYNESBORO

The Shepherd and Ewe Bed and Breakfast

11205 Country Club Road, 17268
(717) 762-8525; (888) 937-4393;
FAX (717) 762-5880
Web site: http://www.bbonline.com/pa/shepherd

Renowned for its rich shepherding heritage, The Shepherd and Ewe extends that

The Shepherd and Ewe Bed and Breakfast

same nurturing tradition to its guests, who are invited to unwind in one of four guest rooms or the spacious master suite. Three rooms have private, full baths. Filled with Victoriana and lovingly restored antiques, each room is clean and inviting. Hot country breakfast includes homemade breads, muffins, and other delights to garnish the main course. Located high atop lush acres of rolling farmland, the B&B is a short drive from Gettysburg and Mercersburg. Lancaster's Dutch Country and Washington are a bit farther—they can be for your second day. Fine restaurants, state parks, hiking trails, art galleries, antique shops.

Hosts: Robert and Twila Risser
Rooms: 5 (3PB; 2SB) $75-85
Full Breakfast
Credit Cards: A, B, C, D
Notes: 2, 5, 7, 8, 9, 10, 11

WELLSBORO

Kaltenbach's Bed and Breakfast

RD 6, Box 106A, Stony Fork Road (Kelsey Street), 16901
(717) 724-4954; (800) 722-4954
Web site: http://www.pafarmstay.com

This sprawling, country home with room for thirty-two guests offers comfortable lodging, home-style breakfasts, and warm hospitality. Set on a 72-acre farm, Kaltenbach's provides opportunities for walks through meadows, pastures, and forests; picnicking; and watching the sheep, pigs, rabbits, and wildlife. All-you-can-eat country breakfasts. Honeymoon suites have tub or Jacuzzi for two. Hunting and golf packages are available. Pennsylvania Grand Canyon. Hiking and biking on Pine Creek's all-new "Rail Trails," built on the old Conrail bed. Kaltenbach's was awarded a two-star rating in the Mobil Travel Guide for its accommodations and hospitality. Professional Association of Innkeepers international inn member.

Host: Lee Kaltenbach
Rooms: 12 (9PB) $60-125
Full Breakfast
Credit Cards: A, B
Notes: 2, 3, 4, 5, 7, 8, 9, 10, 11

YORK

Friendship House Bed and Breakfast

728 E. Philadelphia Street, 17403
(717) 843-8299

An 1890s vintage town house located close to markets, shopping, and recreation. Spacious bedrooms with queen beds. Property has a beautiful private yard with quaint gardens. Also has a three-car garage. A country breakfast is served most mornings. Free hostess gift.

Hostesses: Karen Maust and Becky Detwiler
Rooms: 3 (2PB; 1SB) $55-65
Full Breakfast
Credit Cards: none
Notes: 2, 5, 7, 8, 9, 10, 11

ZELIENOPLE

Benvenue Manor

160 Manor Drive, 16063
(724) 452-1710
Web site: http://www.innkeepersonly.com

"Benvenue," the original name of our 1816 stone manor home, means a "Good Welcome." Guests enjoy a spectacular view, relax by the open fire, and feast on a gourmet breakfast. Four Victorian bedrooms are available, two with private baths, and a guest living room. Gracious hospitality. High tea is served at 3 PM Tuesday and Thursday, and Saturday by special arrangement. We can host birthday parties and showers. Children welcome. Located 35 minutes from downtown Pittsburgh.

Hostess: Margo Hogan
Rooms: 4 (3PB) $55-100
Full Breakfast
Credit Cards: B
Notes: 2, 3, 4, 5, 7, 8, 9, 10

The Inn on Grandview

310 E. Grandview Avenue, 16063
(724) 452-0469; FAX (724) 452-0200
E-mail: GrandInn@aol.com
Web site: http://www.bnb.lm.com

Nestled in the historic town of Zelienople, the Inn on Grandview was built in the early 19th century. Within ½ hour, you can drive to Pittsburgh to the south or to Amish farm country to the north. Your hosts will be happy to direct you to the many antique, craft, and gift shops that grace the surrounding countryside. The inn is beautifully restored and very comfortable, and will make your stay in Zelienople a memorable experience.

Hosts: Rich and Juanita Eppinger
Rooms: 4 (PB) $85-105
Full Breakfast
Credit Cards: A, B, C, D
Notes: 2, 5, 7, 8, 9, 10, 12

Rhode Island

BLOCK ISLAND

The Barrington Inn

Corner of Beach and Ocean Avenues; PO Box 397, 02807
(401) 466-5510; FAX (401) 466-5880
E-mail: barrington@ids.net
Web site: http://www.blockisland.com/barrington

Known for its warmth and hospitality, The Barrington Inn is an 1886 farmhouse on a knoll overlooking the New Harbor area of Block Island. Six individually decorated guest rooms and two housekeeping apartments. A light breakfast is served. Amenities include two guest sitting rooms (one with TV), refrigerator, ceiling fans, comfortable beds, front porch, back deck, and afternoon beverages. No smoking.

Hosts: Joan and Howard Ballard
Rooms: 6 + 2 apartments (PB)
Continental Plus Breakfast
Credit Cards: A, B, D
Notes: 2, 7, 8, 9

The Rose Farm Inn

Roslyn Road, Box E, 02807
(401) 466-2034; FAX (401) 466-2053
E-mail: rosefarm@blockisland.com
Web site: http://www.blockisland.com/rosefarm

Experience the romance of the Victorian era. Treat yourself to a romantic room beautifully furnished with antiques and king- or queen-size canopy bed. Enjoy the peaceful tranquillity of the farm from shaded decks cooled by gentle ocean breezes. Gaze at the ocean from your window, or share a whirlpool bath for two. Awaken to a light buffet breakfast in a charming porch dining room with an ocean view. Bicycle rentals available.

Hostess: Judith B. Rose
Rooms: 19 (17PB; 2SB) $89-195
Continental Plus Breakfast
Credit Cards: A, B, C, D
Notes: 2, 7 (over 12), 8, 9

The Sheffield House Bed and Breakfast

High Street; PO Box 1557, 02807
(401) 466-2494; (800) 466-8329;
FAX (401) 466-8890
E-mail: info@sheffieldhouse.com
Web site: http://www.shefieldhouse.com

Beautiful 1888 Victorian B&B located in the historic district. Comfortable rooms, each individually decorated with family pieces, antiques, and island finds. Private back garden and wraparound front porch. Five-minute walk to beach, ferry, or downtown shopping. Beach towels provided. Family-owned and -operated. For the visitor who wants a place to stay that

---

welcome; 7 Children welcome; 8 Tennis nearby; 9 Swimming nearby; 10 Golf nearby; 11 Skiing nearby; 12 May be booked through travel agent.

RHODE ISLAND

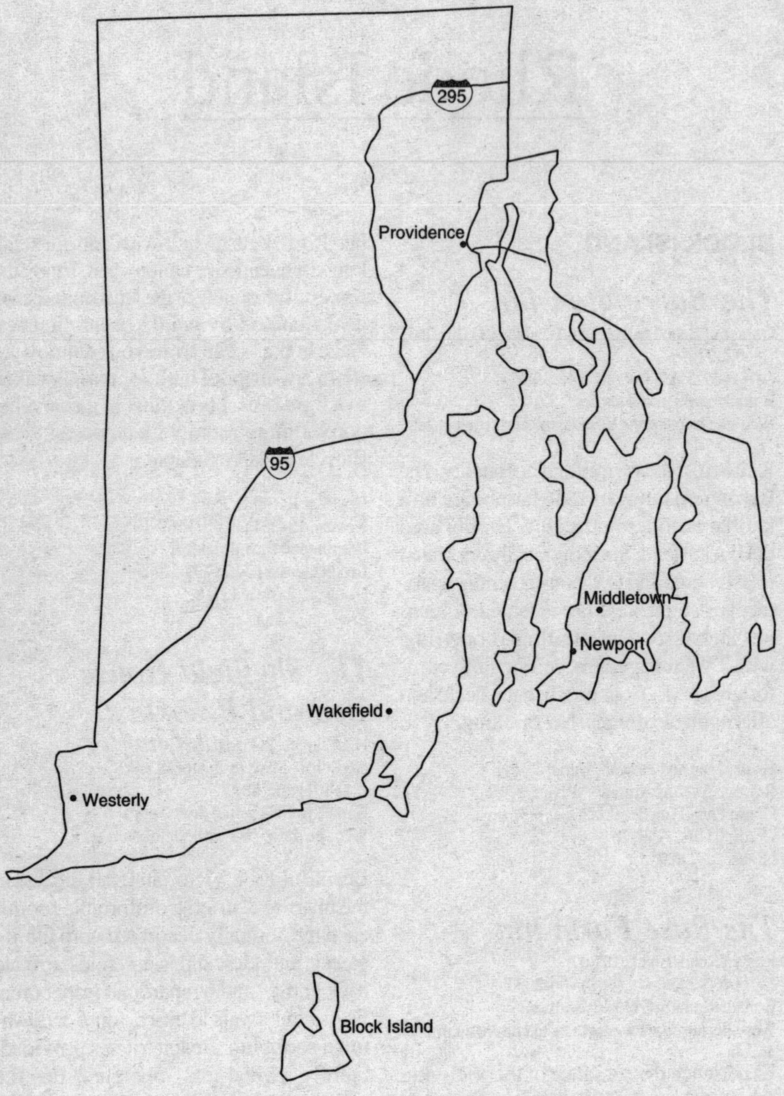

295
Providence
95
Middletown
Newport
Wakefield
Westerly
Block Island

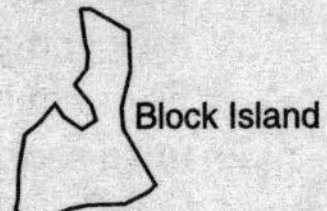

The Sheffield House Bed and Breakfast

matches the island in quiet ambience, grace, and friendly informality.

Hosts: Molly and Chris O'Neill
Rooms: 7 (5PB; 2SB) $50-165 (seasonal)
Continental Breakfast
Credit Cards: A, B, C, D
Notes: 2, 5, 8, 12

MIDDLETOWN (NEWPORT)

The Inn at Shadow Lawn

120 Miantonomi Avenue, 02842
(401) 847-0902; (800) 352-3750;
FAX (401) 848-6529
E-mail: randy@shadowlawn.com
Web site: http://www.shadowlawn.com

Shadow Lawn is a 142-year-old Victorian mansion. Eight rooms, private baths, TV with cable and VCR, telephones, air-conditioning, fireplaces, refrigerator, and complimentary wine. Also available for weddings, meetings, retreats, etc.

Hosts: Selma and Randy Fabricant
Rooms: 8 (PB) $54-175
Full Breakfast
Credit Cards: A, B, C, D, E
Notes: 5, 7, 8, 9, 10, 12

Lindsey's Guest House

6 James Street, 02842
(401) 846-9386
E-mail: 103611.2760@compuserve.com
Web site: http://www.goodnet.com/~eb66090/RI01.html

Walk to beaches and restaurants. Five minutes from Newport's famous mansions, Ocean Drive, Cliff Walk, boat and bus tours, and bird sanctuary. Quiet residential neighborhood with offstreet parking. Large yard and deck. Ask about events and discounts. Split-level, owner-occupied home. One room is accessible to 28-inch wheelchairs.

Hostess: Anne Lindsey
Rooms: 4 (2PB; 2SB) $55-85
Expanded Continental Breakfast
Credit Cards: A, B
Notes: 2, 5, 7, 8, 9, 10, 12

Lindsey's Guest House

NOTES: Credit cards accepted: A Master Card; B Visa; C American Express; D Discover; E Diners Club; F Other; 2 Personal checks accepted; 3 Lunch available; 4 Dinner available; 5 Open all year; 6 Pets welcome; 7 Children welcome; 8 Tennis nearby; 9 Swimming nearby; 10 Golf nearby; 11 Skiing nearby; 12 May be booked through travel agent.

NEWPORT

Brinley Victorian Inn

23 Brinley Street, 02842–3238
(401) 849-7645; (800) 999-8523;
FAX (401) 845-9634

Romantic year round, the inn becomes a Victorian Christmas dream come true. Comfortable antiques and fresh flowers fill every room. Walking to most attractions. Offroad parking. Friendly, unpretentious service. AAA-rated.

Hosts: John and Jennifer Sweetman
Rooms: 16 (14PB; 2SB) $89-199
Continental Breakfast
Credit Cards: A, B, C
Notes: 5, 7 (over 8), 8, 9, 10, 12

The Burbank Rose

111 Memorial Boulevard W., 02840
(401) 849-9457; (888) 297-5800

The Burbank Rose, built in 1850, is located in the historic downtown harborfront area. Walk to everything in town. Close to all attractions. Special off-season and midweek rates. Clean, comfortable rooms with private baths and AC. Free parking for our guests.

Hosts: John and Bonnie McNeely
Rooms: 4 (PB) $69-149
Full Breakfast
Credit Cards: C, D
Notes: 2, 5, 8, 9, 10, 11, 12

Cliffside Inn

2 Seaview Avenue, 02840
(401) 847-1811; (800) 845-1811;
FAX (401) 848-5850
E-mail: cliff@wsii.com
Web site: http://www.cliffsideinn.com

Perfectly located on a quiet, tree-lined street, Cliffside is just 1 block from the Cliffwalk, a 5-minute walk from the beach, and a short stroll from the famed Gilded Age Mansions. Accommodations offer a relaxed but elegant blend of fine period antiques, luxury fabrics, and thoughtful designer detailing. Most rooms and suites contain fireplaces and whirlpool baths.

Hosts: Stephen Nicolas
Rooms: 15 (PB) $185-450
Full Breakfast
Credit Cards: A, B, C, D, E
Notes: 5, 8, 9, 10, 12

Stella Maris Inn

91 Washington Street, 02840
(401) 849-2862

The newly renovated Stella Maris Inn is located in the historic "Point" section of Newport, just a few blocks from downtown. Guests will enjoy tastefully furnished rooms, all with private baths, and several with ocean views and fireplaces.

Hosts: Dorothy and Ed Madden
Rooms: 10 (PB) $75-175
Continental Upscale Breakfast
Credit Cards: none
Notes: 2, 5, 7 (over 10), 8, 9, 10

PROVIDENCE

Historic Jacob Hill Farm Bed and Breakfast Inn

120 Jacob Street, **Seekonk, Massachusetts,** 02771
(508) 336-9165; (888) 336-9165;
FAX (508) 336-0951
E-mail: jacob-hill-farm@juno.com
Web site: http://inn-providence-ri.com

Built in 1722, the inn has a long history of hosting some of America's most affluent families, including the Vanderbilts. Recently

NOTES: Credit cards accepted: A Master Card; B Visa; C American Express; D Discover; E Diners Club; F Other; 2 Personal checks accepted; 3 Lunch available; 4 Dinner available; 5 Open all year; 6 Pets

updated rooms are spacious, with queen and king canopied beds and private baths. Individually appointed with antiques and traditional wall coverings, some have fireplaces and Jacuzzi tubs. On the premises is an in-ground pool, tennis court, and gazebo where you can relax and watch the sunset after a busy day of sight-seeing or local antique shopping. Centrally located 1 hour from Boston or Cape Cod. Newport is 45 minutes, Fall River (for factory shopping) 20 minutes, and Providence just 10 minutes (Brown University and Rhode Island School of Design).

Hosts: Bill and Eleonora Rezek
Rooms: 5 suites (PB)
Full Breakfast
Credit Cards: A, B, C, D
Notes: 5, 8, 9, 10, 11, 12

The Old Court Bed and Breakfast

144 Benefit Street, 02903
(401) 751-2002; FAX (401) 272-4830
E-mail: reserve@oldcourt.com
Web site: http://www.oldcourt.com

The Old Court Bed and Breakfast is filled with antique furniture, chandeliers, and memorabilia from the 19th century, with each room designed to reflect period tastes. All rooms have private baths. The antique, Victorian beds are comfortable and spacious. Just a 3-minute walk from the center of downtown Providence, near Brown University and Rhode Island School of Design.

Host: David Dolbashian
Rooms: 11 (PB) $85-250
Full Breakfast
Credit Cards: A, B, D
Notes: 2, 5, 8, 9, 12

The State House Inn Bed and Breakfast

43 Jewett Street, 02908
(401) 351-6111; FAX (401) 351-4261

Conveniently located minutes from downtown in a quiet and quaint neighborhood, The State House Inn offers business and vacation travelers privacy and personal service. Each guest room has a private bath and is decorated in Shaker or colonial furnishings. A hearty and healthy breakfast is served in our dining room.

Hosts: Monica Hopton
Rooms: 10 (PB) $89-119
Full Breakfast
Credit Cards: A, B, C, D
Notes: 5, 7, 8, 9, 10, 12

WAKEFIELD

Larchwood Inn Bed and Breakfast

521 Main Street, 02879
(401) 783-5454; (800) 275-5450;
FAX (401) 783-1800

Watching over the main street of the quaint New England town for more than 160 years, this grand old house, surrounded by lawns and shaded by stately trees, dispenses hospitality and good food and spirits from early morning to late at night. Historic Newport, picturesque Mystic Seaport, salty Block Island, and Foxwoods Casino are a short ride away.

Hosts: Francis and Diann Browning
Rooms: 18 (12PB; 6SB) $65-130
Full Breakfast
Credit Cards: A, B, C, D, E
Notes: 2, 3, 4, 5, 6, 7, 8, 9, 10, 11, 12

WESTERLY

Woody Hill Bed and Breakfast

149 S. Woody Hill Road, 02891
(401) 322-0452
E-mail: woodyhill@ri.connect.com
Web site: http://www.visitri.com/south/bospages/woodyhill

Woody Hill Bed and Breakfast

This Colonial reproduction is set on a hill overlooking 20 acres of informal gardens, woods, and fields. Antiques, wide-board floors, handmade quilts, and fireplaces create an Early American atmosphere. Guests enjoy a full breakfast and the use of a secluded, 40-foot in-ground pool. Close to Newport, Block Island, Mystic, and casino.

Hostess: Ellen L. Madison
Rooms: 4/5 (4PB; 2SB) $75-125
Full Breakfast
Credit Cards: none
Notes: 2, 5, 7, 8, 9, 10

NOTES: Credit cards accepted: A Master Card; B Visa; C American Express; D Discover; E Diners Club; F Other; 2 Personal checks accepted; 3 Lunch available; 4 Dinner available; 5 Open all year; 6 Pets

South Carolina

BEAUFORT

TwoSuns Inn Bed and Breakfast

1705 Bay Street, 29902
(843) 522-1122 (voice and FAX); (800) 532-4244
E-mail: twosuns@islc.net
Web site: http://www.twosunsinn.com

Enjoy the charm of a small, resident-host bed and breakfast in a remarkably beautiful, nationally landmarked historic district about midway between Charleston and Savannah—complete with a panoramic bay-view veranda, individually appointed king or queen guest rooms, an informal afternoon "tea and toddy hour," and sumptuous breakfasts. The setting is idyllic; the atmosphere is casually elegant: a restored 1917 grand home with modern baths and amenities, accented throughout with collectibles and antiques.

Hosts: Carrol and Ron Kay
Rooms: 6 (PB) $105-151
Full Breakfast
Credit Cards: A, B, C, D, E
Notes: 2, 5, 8, 9, 10, 12

The Breeden Inn and Carriage House

BENNETTSVILLE

The Breeden Inn and Carriage House

404 E. Main Street, 29512
(843) 479-3665; FAX (843) 479-7998
Web site: http://www.bbonline.com/sc/breeden

This 1886 southern mansion offers a relaxing stay in elegant, comfortable surroundings. Uniquely decorated guest rooms offer a multitude of tasteful period pieces, collectibles, cable TV, and seasoned oak and heart of pine throughout both houses. The inn is located in Bennettsville's historic district and is 20 minutes off I–95 (a great halfway point

---

welcome; 7 Children welcome; 8 Tennis nearby; 9 Swimming nearby; 10 Golf nearby; 11 Skiing nearby; 12 May be booked through travel agent.

SOUTH CAROLINA

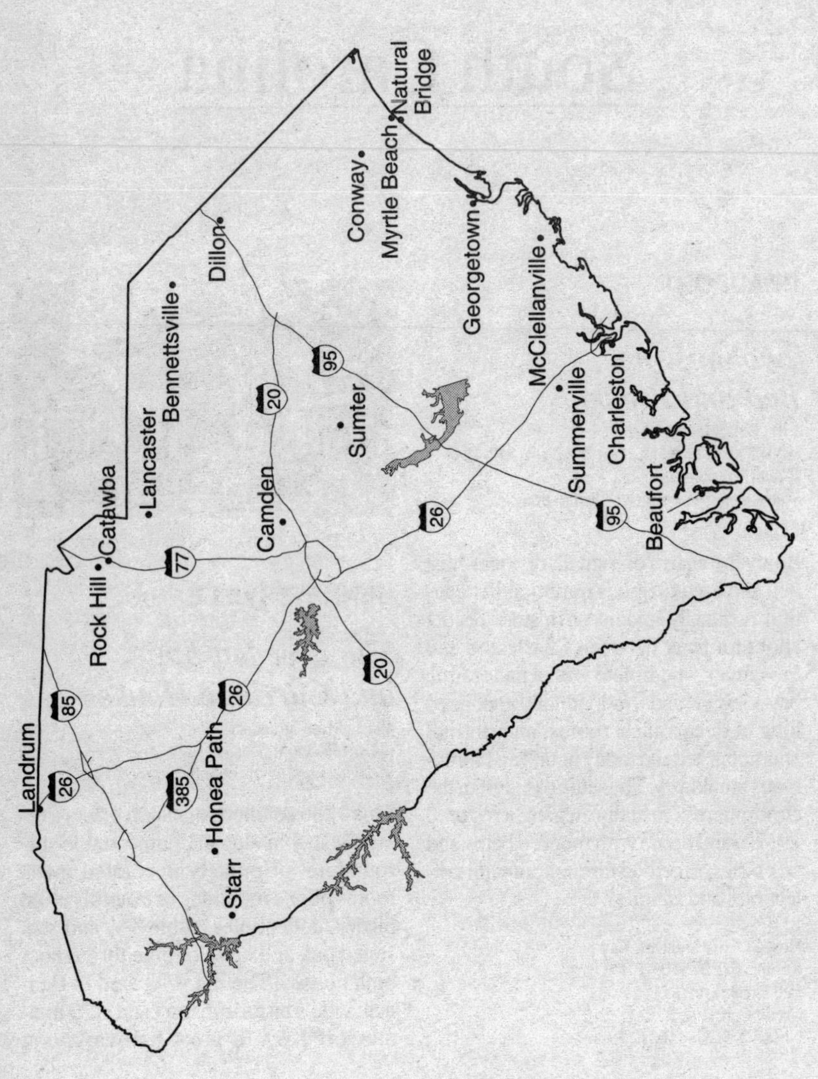

between Florida and New York). Quiet and secluded grounds provide many huge shade trees—perfect for birding (binoculars and field guides provided)—in-ground pool; twenty-nine-column, wraparound veranda; and portico with rockers, swings, and ceiling fans. Visit our inn's antique shop. Enjoy a self-guided historic walking, driving, or local antique shop tour (guides provided). Begin your day with a delicious, elegant breakfast. Allow us to impart gracious southern hospitality to your memory making. National Register and designated Backyard Wildlife Habitat property. Owned by a Christian family.

Hosts: Wesley and Bonnie Park
Rooms: 6 (PB) $75-95
Full Breakfast
Credit Cards: A, B
Notes: 2 (personal & traveler's), 5, 7, 9, 10, 12

CAMDEN

Candlelight Inn

1904 Broad Street, 29020
(803) 424-1057

Two acres of gardens with native southern plantings surround this candlelit Cape Cod–style inn. The decor is a delightful, tasteful mix of country, with quilts, handcrafted samplers, poster beds, family antiques, and traditional furnishings. Enjoy a unique, hearty breakfast on the sunporch; the menu and place setting change daily. Or how about breakfast in the garden?

Hosts: Jo Ann and George Celani
Rooms: 3 (PB) $75-125
Full Breakfast
Credit Cards: A, B, C, D
Notes: 2, 5, 8, 10, 12

1837 Bed and Breakfast/Tearoom

CHARLESTON

1837 Bed and Breakfast/Tearoom

126 Wentworth Street, 29401
(843) 723-7166

Enjoy accommodations in a wealthy cotton planter's home and brick carriage house centrally located in Charleston's historic district. Canopied, poster, rice beds. Walk to boat tours, the old market, antique shops, restaurants, and main attractions. Near Charleston Place (convention center) and College of Charleston. Gourmet breakfast is served in the formal dining room and includes sausage-and-grits casserole, raspberry French toast, ham frittata with Mornay sauce, and home-baked breads. The 1837 Tea Room serves afternoon tea to guests and public. Offstreet parking. Special winter rates.

Hosts: Sherri Weaver and Richard Dunn
Rooms: 8 (PB) $69-135
Full Gourmet Breakfast
Credit Cards: A, B, C
Notes: 2, 5, 7 (7 and older), 8, 9, 10, 12

Ashley Inn

201 Ashley Avenue, 29403
(843) 723-1848; (800) 581-6658;
FAX (843) 579-9080

Stay in a stately, historic, circa-1835 home. So warm and hospitable, the Ashley Inn offers seven intimate bedrooms featuring canopy beds, private baths, fireplaces, and air-conditioning. Delicious breakfasts are served on a grand columned piazza overlooking a beautiful Charleston garden or in the formal dining room. Relax with tea and cookies after touring nearby historic sites or enjoying the complimentary touring bicycles. The Ashley Inn offers simple elegance in a warm, friendly home noted for true southern hospitality.

Hosts: Bud and Sally Allen
Rooms: 8 (PB) $79-180
Full Breakfast
Credit Cards: A, B, C, D
Notes: 2, 5

Belvedere B&B

40 Rutledge Avenue, 29401
(843) 722-0973

A Colonial Revival mansion built in 1900 with an exquisite Adamesque interior taken from the circa-1800 Belvedere Plantation house. In the downtown historic district on Colonial Lake, within walking distance of historical points of interest, restaurants, and shopping. Guests may use the public areas and piazzas in this romantic, beautifully restored mansion. Closed December 1–February 10.

Hosts: David S. Spell and Rick Zender
Rooms: 3 (PB) $125-150
Continental Breakfast
Credit Cards: none
Notes: 2, 7 (over 8), 8, 9, 10

Cannonboro Inn

184 Ashley Avenue, 29403
(843) 723-8572; (800) 235-8039;
FAX (843) 723-8007
E-mail: cannon@cchat.com
Web site: http://www.cchat.com/cannon

This 1853 home offers beautifully decorated bedrooms with antique four-poster and canopied beds. Cannonboro Inn is a place to be pampered. You may sleep in until the aroma of sizzling sausage and home-baked biscuits lures you to a full breakfast on the columned piazza overlooking a Low Country garden and fountain. After breakfast, tour nearby historic sites on complimentary bicycles, and return to more pampering with afternoon sherry, tea, and sumptuous home-baked goods. Our private baths, offstreet parking, color TV, and AC, along with that very special southern hospitality, demonstrate this is what Charleston is all about!

Hosts: Bud and Sally Allen, Lynn Bartosh
Rooms: 6 (PB) $79-180
Full Breakfast
Credit Cards: A, B, C, D
Notes: 2, 5, 7 (10+), 8, 9 (beach), 10, 12

Country Victorian B&B

105 Tradd Street, 29401–2422
(843) 577-0682

Come relive the charm of the past. Relax in a rocker on the piazza of this historic home and watch the carriages go by. Walk to antique shops, churches, restaurants, art galleries, museums, and all historic points of interest. The house, built in 1820, is located in the historic district south of Broad. Rooms have private entrances and contain antique iron and brass beds, old quilts, antique oak and wicker furniture, and braided rugs over heart-of-pine floors.

Homemade cookies will be waiting. Many extras! Featured in *Country Quilts Magazine*, fall 1997.

Hostess: Diane Deardurff
Rooms: 2 (PB) $85-130
Continental Breakfast
Credit Cards: none
Notes: 2, 5, 7 (over 10), 8, 9, 10, 11 (water)

East Bay Bed and Breakfast

301 E. Bay Street, 29401
(843) 722-4186; FAX (843) 720-8528

Elegant 200-year-old Federal single house and birthplace of Civil War heroine Phoebe Pember. Easy walk to the old city market, King Street shops, College of Charleston, Medical University, restaurants, and day spa. Exquisitely decorated. Silver tray service. Private carriage house also available. Meeting and reception space. Desks, FAX, telephone, cable TV, and offstreet parking. Smoking permitted on piazzas only. Inquire about accommodations for children.

Hostesses: Carolyn Rivers and Zibby Teague
Rooms: 2 + 2 suites (PB) $125-185
Continental Breakfast
Credit Cards: A, B, C
Notes: 2, 5

John Rutledge House Inn

116 Broad Street, 29401
(843) 723-7999; (800) 476-9741;
FAX (843) 720-2615
E-mail: jrh@charminginns.com
Web site: http://www.charminginns.com

Built in 1763 by a signer of the U.S. Constitution. Antiques and reproductions give each room its own warmth and distinctions. Choose among rooms and suites in the main house or the privacy of one of the inn's two carriage houses.

Hostess: Linda Bishop
Rooms: 19 (PB) $170-265
Continental Breakfast
Credit Cards: A, B, C, D, E
Notes: 2, 5, 7, 9, 10, 12

King George IV Inn

32 George Street, 29401
(843) 723-9339; (888) 723-1667;
FAX (843) 723-7749
Web site: http://www.bbonline.com/sc/kinggeorge

A 200-year-old house in the heart of the historic district. The inn is Federal-style, with three levels of Charleston side porches. The house has 10 x 12-foot ceilings with decorative plaster moldings, wide-planked hardwood floors, old furnishings, and antiques. Private baths, offstreet parking, air-conditioning, TVs. One-minute walk to King Street, 5 minutes to the market.

Hosts: Debra, Terry, and Debbie
Rooms: 10 (8PB; 2SB) $75-149
Continental Plus Breakfast
Credit Cards: A, B
Notes: 2, 5, 7, 8, 9, 10, 12

The Kitchen House (Circa 1732)

126 Tradd Street, 29401
(843) 577-6362; FAX (843) 965-5615

Nestled in the heart of the historic district, The Kitchen House is a totally restored 18th-century dwelling. You'll enjoy the southern hospitality, absolute privacy, fireplaces, and antiques. Private patio, colonial herb garden, fish pond, and fountain. Concierge service. The home has been featured in *Colonial Homes*, *The New York Times*, and *Best Places to Stay in the South.*

Hostess: Lois Evans
Rooms: 3 (PB) $150-250
Full Breakfast
Credit Cards: A, B
Notes: 2, 5, 7, 12

Rutledge Victorian Inn

Rutledge Victorian Inn

114 Rutledge Avenue, 29401
(843) 722-7551; (888) 722-7553;
FAX (843) 727-0065
Web sites: http://www.bbonline.com/sc/rutledge
http://www.virtualcities.com
http://www.webpost.com/hia/listings/rutledge.htm

Elegant Charleston home in downtown historic district. Century-old house with rare, decorative, Italianate architecture with beautiful ceiling moldings. Rooms have mahogany and oak fireplaces, 12-foot ceilings, hardwood floors, 10-foot doors and windows, and antiques. Lovely, 120-foot porch with rocking chairs and joggling board overlooking the park and Roman Columns, remains of the Confederate soldiers' reunion hall. Relaxed atmosphere, AC, parking, and TVs. Lovely formal dining rooms where complimentary continental plus breakfast is served. Short walk to historic sites. Our Kitchen House (#6 Ambrose Alley) also is available.

Hosts: Lyn, Dave, and Norm
Rooms: 11 (7PB; 4SB) $150-280
Continental Plus Breakfast
Credit Cards: A, B
Notes: 2, 5, 7 (12 and older), 8, 9, 10, 12

The Thomas Lamboll House

19 King Street, 29401
(843) 723-3212; (888) 874-0793;
FAX (843) 723-5222
E-mail: lamboll@aol.com
Web site: http://www.lambollhouse.com

This 1735 single house is located on the corner of Lamboll and King Streets, just north of The Battery. It offers two large, handsome bedrooms with private baths and French doors leading to the balcony. The bedrooms, furnished with antiques, have AC, fireplaces, cable TV, and phones. Offstreet parking.

Hosts: Marie and Emerson Read
Rooms: 2 (PB) $100-145
Continental Breakfast
Credit Cards: A, B
Notes: 2, 5, 7, 8, 9, 10

Villa de La Fontaine

138 Wentworth Street, 29401
(843) 577-7709
Web site: http://charleston.cityinformation.com/villa

Villa de La Fontaine is a columned Greek Revival mansion in the heart of the historic district. It was built in 1838 and boasts a ¾-acre garden with fountain and terraces.

Restored to impeccable condition, the mansion is furnished with museum-quality furniture and accessories. The hosts are retired ASID interior designers and have decorated the rooms with 18th-century American antiques. Several of the rooms feature canopy beds. Breakfast is prepared by a master chef who prides himself on serving a different menu every day. Parking on the property, with 7-foot brick walls and iron gates! It is in the safest part of Charleston, near the College of Charleston. Minimum-stay requirements for weekends and holidays.

Hosts: William Fontaine and Aubrey Hancock
Rooms: 4 (PB) $100-150
Full Breakfast
Credit Cards: none
Notes: 2, 5, 7 (12 and older), 8, 9, 10

The Cypress Inn

CONWAY

The Cypress Inn

16 Elm Street; PO Box 495, 29528
(843) 248-8199; (800) 575-5307;
FAX (843) 248-0329
Web site: http://www.bbonline.com/sc/cypress

Coastal South Carolina is the location of this divine bed and breakfast where you'll find excellence in the little details. This is where your memories are created. On the edge of the Waccamaw River, overlooking a private marina. Guests enjoy Jacuzzis, TVs, and phones with dataports for the business traveler. Morning breakfast is alive with delicious aromas and enthusiastic voices. Days are spent bird-watching, taking ocean walks, exploring sculpture gardens, and much more.

Hosts: Jim and Carol Ruddick
Rooms: 12 (PB) $95-140
Full Breakfast
Credit Cards: A, B, C, E
Notes: 2, 5, 8, 9, 10, 12

DILLON

Magnolia Inn

601 E. Main Street, 29536
(843) 774-0679 (voice and FAX)
E-mail: http://innmagnolia@aol.com

Warm hospitality and beautiful decor with antiques grace this century-old Greek Revival home located just 2 miles from Exit 190 on I–95. It's only 60 minutes from Myrtle Beach and 40 minutes from Darlington Speedway.

Hosts: Eileen and Alan Kemp
Rooms: 4 (PB) $65
Continental Breakfast
Credit Cards: A, B, C, D
Notes: 2, 5

GEORGETOWN

Ashfield Manor

3030 S. Island Road, 29440
(843) 546-0464; (800) 483-5002

This Christian home offers southern hospitality in the style of a real southern plantation. Ashfield Manor has an elegant but comfortable setting. All rooms are oversize and decorated with period furnishings. They have private entrances and color remote TVs. Expanded continental breakfast is served in your room, in the parlor, or on our 57-foot screen porch overlooking our lake (home to much waterfowl and an alligator!). Georgetown is quaint and historic, with many attractions close by.

Hosts: Dave and Carol Ashenfelder
Rooms: 4 (2PB; 2SB) $55-65
Continental Breakfast
Credit Cards: A, B, D
Notes: 2, 5, 7, 8, 10, 12

The Shaw House

The Shaw House

613 Cypress Court, 29440
(843) 546-9663

The Shaw House is a spacious, two-story Colonial home in a natural setting with a beautiful view overlooking miles of marshland—perfect for bird-watchers. Within walking distance of downtown and great restaurants on the waterfront. Rooms are large, with many antiques and private baths. Breakfast is served at our guests' convenience. Also included are nighttime chocolates on each pillow, turnbacks, and some loving extras. Guests leave with a little gift—prayers, recipes, and/or jellies. Approved by AAA, Mobil, and ABBA.

Hosts: Mary and Joe Shaw
Rooms: 3 (PB) $50-65
Full Breakfast
Credit Cards: none
Notes: 2, 5, 7, 8, 9, 10

"Ship Wrights" Bed and Breakfast

609 Cypress Court, 29440
(843) 527-4475

Three-thousand-plus square feet of beautiful, quiet, clean home is yours to use when you stay. It's nautically attired and tastefully laced with family heirlooms. Guests say they feel like they just stayed at their best friend's home. The bedrooms and baths are beautiful and very comfortable. You'll never get "Grandma Eicker's Pancakes" anywhere else (the inn is famous for them; there's a great story behind the pancakes!). The view from the large porch is breathtaking, perfect for bird-watching. Five minutes from Ocean Beach. AAA-approved.

Hostess: Leatrice M. Wright
Rooms: 2 (PB) $60
Full Breakfast
Credit Cards: none
Notes: 2, 5, 7, 8, 9, 10

HONEA PATH

"Sugarfoot Castle"

211 S. Main Street, 29654
(864) 369-6565

Enormous trees umbrella this lovely brick Victorian home. Fresh flowers grace the

14-inch-thick-walled rooms furnished with family heirlooms. You can enjoy the living room's interesting collections or the library's comfy chairs, TV, VCR, books, fireplace, desk, and game table. Upon arising, guests find coffee and juice outside their doors, followed by a breakfast of hot breads, cereal, fresh fruit, and beverages served by candlelight in the dining room. Rock away the world's cares on a screened porch overlooking peaceful grounds. AAA-approved.

Hosts: Gale and Cecil Evans
Rooms: 3 (SB) $64
Continental Breakfast
Credit Cards: A, B (prefer cash or personal check)
Notes: 2, 5, 8, 9, 10

LANCASTER

Wade-Beckham House Bed and Breakfast

3385 Great Falls Highway, 29720
(803) 285-1105

A pastoral setting for this 1800s plantation home offers serenity, spacious porches, heirloom family antiques, and interesting historical artifacts. Guests may choose the Rose Room, Summer House Room, or Wade Hampton Room, all located upstairs. Horses, cows, chickens, an old barn, and an antique store are on the property. The home is listed on the National Register.

Hostess: Jan Duke
Rooms: 3 (PB) $75
Full Breakfast
Credit Cards: none
Notes: 2, 8, 10

LANDRUM

The Red Horse Inn

310 N. Campbell Road, 29356
(864) 895-4968 (voice and FAX); (864) 909-1575
Web site: http://www.bbhost.com/redhorseinn

The Red Horse Inn is located on 190 acres in the foothills of the Blue Ridge Mountains. Five Victorian cottages are luxuriously appointed. Each offers a kitchen, bathroom, bedroom, living room with fireplace, deck or patio, color television, and air-conditioning. Three have Jacuzzis and a sleeping loft. The sweeping mountain views, hiking trails, and peaceful countryside offer spiritual renewal.

Hosts: Mary and Roger Wolters
Rooms: 5 cottages (PB) $95
Continental Breakfast
Credit Cards: A, B
Notes: 2, 5, 6 (ask), 7, 8, 9, 10, 12

Laurel Hill Plantation

McCLELLANVILLE

Laurel Hill Plantation

8913 N. Highway 17; PO Box 190, 29458
(843) 887-3708; (888) 887-3708
Web site: http://www.bbonline.com/sc/laurelhill

A nature lover's delight! Laurel Hill faces the Atlantic Ocean. Wraparound porches provide spectacular views of creeks and marshes. The reconstructed house is furnished with antiques that reflect the Low Country lifestyle. A perfect blend of yesterday's nostalgia and today's comfort in a setting of unparalleled coastal vistas. Located on Highway 17, 30 miles north of Charleston, 25 miles south of Georgetown, and 60 miles south of Myrtle Beach.

Hosts: Jackie and Lee Morrison
Rooms: 4 (PB) $95-115
Full Breakfast
Credit Cards: A, B, C, D, E
Notes: 2, 5, 7 (restricted), 9, 10, 12

MYRTLE BEACH

Serendipity Inn

407 - 71st Avenue N., 29572–3634
(843) 449-5268; (800) 762-3229

An award-winning, Spanish-style inn—unique, elegant, and secluded—is situated just 300 yards from the Atlantic beach. Guests may enjoy the heated pool and hot tub. Rooms are air-conditioned and have TVs, private baths, and refrigerators. More than seventy golf courses are nearby, as well as fishing, tennis, restaurants, theaters, and shopping. Serendipity Inn is located near all the famous Myrtle Beach country music theaters. Myrtle Beach is 90 miles from historic Charleston.

Serendipity Inn

Hosts: Terry and Sheila Johnson
Rooms: 14 (PB) $59-149
Continental Breakfast
Credit Cards: A, B
Notes: 7, 8, 9, 10, 12

ROCK HILL

East Main Guest House

600 E. Main Street, 29730
(803) 366-1161 (voice and FAX)

Located in the historic district and just 20 minutes from downtown Charlotte, this bed and breakfast offers guest rooms with queen-size beds, fireplaces, televisions, and phones. The honeymoon suite has stained-glass windows, canopy bed, and a whirlpool bath. A sitting/game room is provided, and a FAX is available. A continental breakfast is served each morning in the gracious dining room or, weather permitting, under the garden pergola. AAA three diamonds.

Hosts: Melba and Jerry Peterson
Rooms: 3 (PB) $59-79
Expanded Continental Breakfast
Credit Cards: A, B
Notes: 2, 5, 8, 9, 10, 12

Harmony House Bed and Breakfast

3485 Harmony Road, 29704
(803) 329-5886; (888) 737-0016
Web site: http://www.bbonline.com/sc/harmony

Victorian-style farmhouse built in 1991, nestled on a 36-acre countryside tract just 4 miles off I–77 on the outskirts of Rock Hill. Beautifully decorated with antiques

Harmony House Bed and Breakfast

and family treasures. Two common sitting areas, one with drinks, snacks, etc. Peace and tranquillity are definite assets, with city life just minutes away. Ample attractions nearby. Wraparound porch with swings, goldfish pond, and garden.

Hosts: Winky and Cecil Staton
Rooms: 3 (PB) $65-75
Continental Plus Breakfast
Credit Cards: none

STARR

The Gray House

111 Stone's Throw Avenue, 29684
(864) 352-6778; FAX (864) 352-6777

This turn-of-the-century home is the perfect romantic getaway, with beautiful gardens, tranquil pond, quiet walking trail, and horse-drawn carriage rides (by appointment). Two suites offer private baths with whirlpools and private dining alcoves. Enjoy breakfast in your suite. Two-bedroom farmhouse also available. Restaurant serves southern fare.

Hostess: Kathy Stone
Rooms: 2 + 2-bedroom farmhouse (PB) $65-125
Full Breakfast
Credit Cards: A, B, C
Notes: 2, 3, 4, 5, 10, 12

SUMMERVILLE

Linwood Historic Home and Gardens

200 S. Palmetto Street, 29483
(843) 871-2620 (voice and FAX)
Web site: http://www.bbonline.com/sc/linwood/index.html

Once the home of a 19th-century plantation owner. Gracious hospitality abounds at Linwood, a beautifully restored Victorian home featuring high ceilings, chandeliers, period antiques, and wide porches. Nestled on 2 acres of lush gardens, Linwood is in the center of the charming village of Summerville, near shops and restaurants. Linwood has a lovely, large inground pool. Famous plantations, golf courses, beaches, and historic Charleston are nearby. Recreation or retreat—we are here to serve you.

Hosts: Peter and Linda Shelbourne
Rooms: 3 (PB) $75-90
Continental Breakfast and Afternoon English Tea
Credit Cards: none
Notes: 2, 5, 7, 8, 9, 10, 12

SUMTER

The Bed and Breakfast of Sumter

6 Park Avenue, 29150
(803) 773-2903; (888) 786-8372;
FAX (803) 775-6943

Charming, 1896 home facing a lush park in the historic district. Large front porch with swing and rocking chairs. Gracious guest rooms with antiques, fireplaces, and all private baths. Formal Victorian parlor and TV sitting area. FAX machine available. Gourmet breakfast includes fruit, entrée, and home-baked breads. Antiques, Swan Lake, and fifteen golf courses are close by.

Hosts: Suzanne and Jess Begley
Rooms: 5 (PB) $65-75
Full Gourmet Breakfast
Credit Cards: A, B, D
Notes: 2, 5, 8, 10, 12

Magnolia House Bed and Breakfast

Magnolia House Bed and Breakfast

230 Church Street, 29150
(803) 775-6694; (888) 666-0296
E-mail: http://magnoliahouse@sumter.net

Our Greek Revival home with its five fireplaces, stained-glass windows, and inlaid oak floors has been home to only four families. It was built by C.A. Lemmon in what is now Sumter's Historic District. This warm, inviting home with its five guest rooms, each decorated in antiques from a different era, comes with domestic pets and is within walking distance of the downtown area of Sumter and Hampton Park. You may enjoy an afternoon refreshment in the formal backyard garden.

Hosts: Buck and Carol Ann Rogers
Rooms: 4 + 2-room suite (4PB; 1SB) $75-125
Full Breakfast
Credit Cards: A, B, C
Notes: 2, 5, 6, 7, 10, 12 (10-percent commission)

NOTES: Credit cards accepted: A Master Card; B Visa; C American Express; D Discover; E Diners Club; F Other; 2 Personal checks accepted; 3 Lunch available; 4 Dinner available; 5 Open all year; 6 Pets

South Dakota

CANOVA

Skoglund Farm Bed and Breakfast

Route 1, Box 45, 57321
(605) 247-3445

Skoglund Farm brings back memories of Grandpa and Grandma's home. It is furnished with antiques and collectibles. A full, home-cooked evening meal and breakfast are served each day. Guests may sightsee in the surrounding area, visit Little House on the Prairie Village, hike, or just relax. Several country churches are located nearby.

Skoglund Farm Bed and Breakfast

Hosts: Alden and Delores Skoglund
Rooms: 5 (SB) $30/adult; $20/teen; $15/child; children 5 and under free
Full Breakfast
Credit Cards: none
Notes: 2, 3, 4 (included), 5, 6, 7, 8, 9, 10, 12

CHAMBERLAIN

Riverview Ridge

HC 69, Box 82A, 57325
(605) 734-6084
Web site: http://www.bbonline.com/sd/riverviewridge

Contemporary home on a bluff overlooking a Missouri River bend. Located on the Lewis and Clark Trail. King and queen beds, full breakfast, and secluded country peace. Three and one-half miles from downtown Chamberlain on Highway 50. Enjoy outdoor recreation; visit museums, Indian reservations, and casinos; or relax and make our home your home.

Hosts: Frank and Alta Cable
Rooms: 3 (1PB; 2SB) $55-70
Full Breakfast
Credit Cards: A, B
Notes: 2, 5, 7, 9, 10

---

welcome; 7 Children welcome; 8 Tennis nearby; 9 Swimming nearby; 10 Golf nearby; 11 Skiing nearby; 12 May be booked through travel agent.

SOUTH DAKOTA

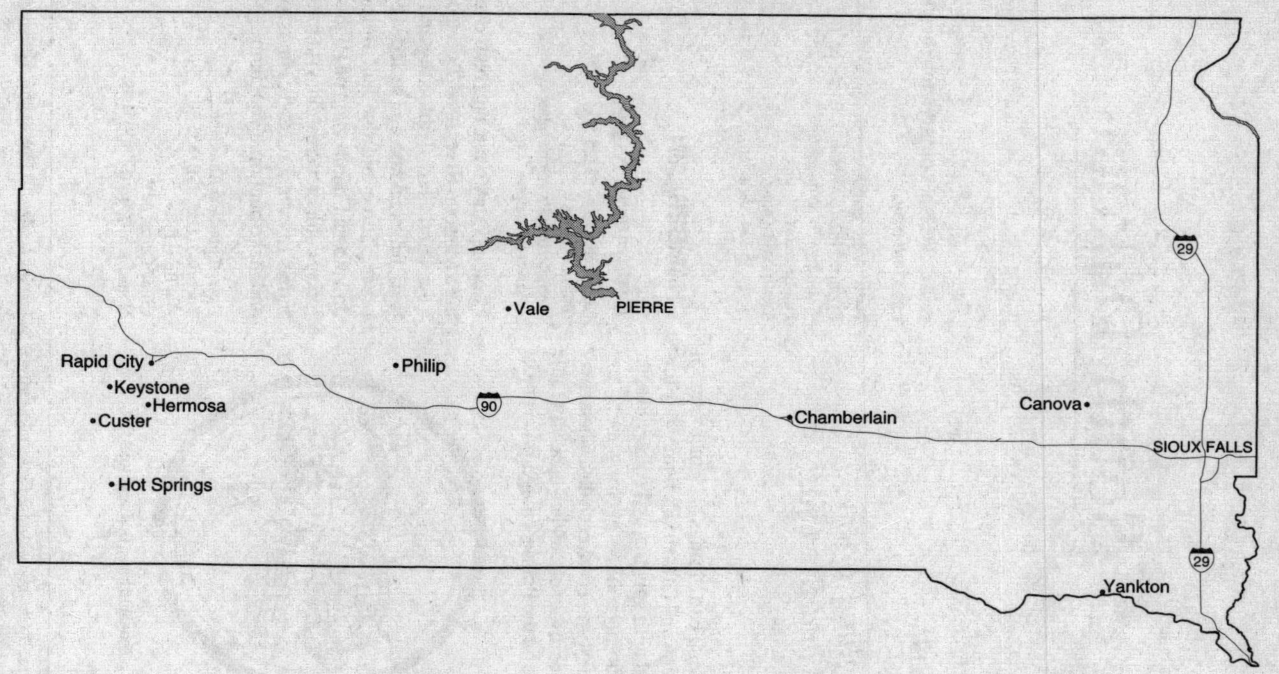

Custer Mansion Bed and Breakfast

CUSTER

Custer Mansion Bed and Breakfast

35 Centennial Drive, 57730
(605) 673-3333; FAX (605) 673-3033
E-mail: carmilse@gwtc.net

Enjoy the nostalgia of an authentic 1891 Victorian Gothic home listed on the National Register of Historic Places. Transoms, stained glass, and antiques feature Victorian elegance and country charm with western hospitality. Lovely, individually decorated rooms are named for songs. All-you-can-eat, home-cooked breakfast. Two honeymoon suites, one with Jacuzzi tub. Central to all Black Hills attractions: Mt. Rushmore, Crazy Horse Memorial, Custer State Park, and many more. Minimum stay of two nights, holidays and peak season; reduced rates, off-season. Recommended by *Bon Appetit,* AAA, and Mobil Travel Guide; member of BBISD.

Hosts: Mill and Carole Seaman
Rooms: 4 + 1 family suite (PB) $68-115
Full Breakfast
Credit Cards: none
Notes: 2, 5, 7, 8, 9, 10, 11

HERMOSA

Bunkhouse Bed and Breakfast

14630 Lower Spring Creek Road, 57744
(605) 342-5462; (888) 756-5462
Web site: http://www.bbonline.com/sd/bunkhouse

A small working ranch in the foothills of the Black Hills of South Dakota, our special feature is a facility for guests to bring their own horses to ride. Our decor is western/antique, and our guests enjoy a peaceful night's sleep with only the sounds of the creek, the coyotes, and crickets. They awaken to the sounds of birds singing and the smell of our sumptuous all-you-can-eat ranch breakfast. Spend the day exploring God's country.

Hosts: Chuck and Carol Hendrickson
Rooms: 3 (1PB; 2SB) $80-100
Full Breakfast
Credit Cards: A, B
Notes: 2, 7, 9, 10, 12

HOT SPRINGS

The "B and J" Bed and Breakfast

HCR 52, Box 101-B, 57747
(605) 745-4243

Nestled in the southern Black Hills, this charming 1890 log cabin, decorated in antiques, provides guests with a unique pioneer setting. Enjoy peaceful mountain scenery while listening to the Fall River that never freezes. Early mornings, deer and wild turkey may be seen. True western hospitality and a home-cooked breakfast are waiting in Bill and Jeananne's kitchen.

Down the entrance road, enjoy horseback riding. One mile south of Hot Springs on U.S. 385/18. In Hot Springs, swim at the historic Evans Plunge, where the water is always 87 degrees. Visit the world's largest find of Columbian Mammoth bones. Golf at one of the Midwest's most challenging, beautiful courses. Minutes from Angostura Lake, Wind Cave National Park, and Custer State Park, where buffalo, antelope, elk, and prairie dogs roam.

Hosts: William and Jeananne Wintz
Rooms: 1 + log cabin (PB) $100-125
Full Breakfast
Credit Cards: none
Notes: 2, 7, 8, 9, 10, 11

KEYSTONE

The Anchorage Bed and Breakfast

24110 Leaky Valley Road, 57751
(605) 574-4740; (800) 318-7018
E-mail: anchragebb@aol.com
Web site: http://www.bbonline.com/sd/theanchorage

Drop your anchor in a peaceful harbor. The Anchorage offers a guest house (sleeps two–eight) within hiking distance of Mt. Rushmore. Hot tub under the stars after a day of hiking, sight-seeing, or snow-mobiling. Breakfast with your hosts may include pumpkin waffles, hot apple butter, smoked turkey sausage, fresh-baked breakfast breads, fruit, gourmet coffee, assorted teas, and juice. Your needs are our priority.

Hosts: Jim and Lin Gogolin
Rooms: 1 guest house (PB) $95
Full Breakfast
Credit Cards: A, B, D
Notes: 2, 5, 7, 12

PHILIP

Triangle Ranch Bed and Breakfast

HCR 1, Box 62, 57567
(605) 859-2122; (888) 219-1774
Web site: http://www.bbonline.com/sd/triangleranch

Welcome to our historic, five-generation, working cattle ranch located on the prairie, 20 minutes northeast of Badlands National Park. You'll be greeted on the front porch of the "Alhambra," our ornate, mission-style Sears home. Built in 1923, restored and listed on National Register of Historic Places. Enjoy vintage rooms. Hike, picnic, stargaze, and relax. Real peace and quiet. Bring *your* horse and ride our rolling pastureland or the majestic Badlands nearby.

Hosts: Lyndy and Kenny Ireland
Rooms: 5 (3PB; 2SB) $60-80
Full Breakfast
Credit Cards: A, B
Notes: 2, 3, 4, 5, 7, 9

RAPID CITY

Abend Haus Cottages and Audrie's Bed and Breakfast

23029 Thunderhead Falls Road, 57702–8524
(605) 342-7788
Web site: http://www.pahasapa.com/wp/audries

The ultimate in charm and old-world hospitality. We have been family-owned and -operated since 1985 and are the area's first B&B establishment. Our spacious suites and cottages are furnished in comfortable European antiques. All feature a private entrance, private bath, patio, hot tub, and full Black Hills–style breakfast. Each suite provides a setting that quiets your heart. Our country home, the Cranbury House, has two suites. If the past intrigues you, the Old Powerhouse is for you. Das Abend Haus Cottage (the Evening House) is a restful, creekside hideaway, tucked into a mountainside; its two suites are designed after a German cottage in the Black Forest. The individual log cottages are also reminiscent of Germany. Soak in your private hot tub and watch Rapid Creek flow along. These accommodations are unsurpassed anywhere.

Hosts: Hank and Audry Kuhnhauser
Rooms: 9 (PB) $95-145
Full Breakfast
Credit Cards: none
Notes: 2, 5, 8, 9, 10, 11

Alex Johnson Hotel

Alex Johnson Hotel

523 6th Street, 57701
(605) 342-1210; (800) 888-2539;
FAX (605) 342-7436
E-mail: info@alexjohnson.com
Web site: http://www.alexjohnson.com

Visit the Alex Johnson Hotel and stay at a historic landmark. Since 1928, "the Alex" has provided a long line of celebrities and other guests with service excellence. It offers 143 newly restored guest rooms. Old-world charm is combined with award-winning hospitality. This legendary hotel offers guests a piece of old-west history in the heart of downtown Rapid City. It is listed on the National Register of Historic Places.

Hosts: The Didiers
Rooms: 143 (PB) $73.50-104.50
Full Breakfast
Credit Cards: A, B, C, D, E
Notes: 2, 3, 4, 5, 6, 7, 8, 9, 10, 11, 12

STURGIS

Dakota Shepherd Bed and Breakfast

RR 3, Box 25C, **Vale,** 57788
(605) 456-2836
Web site: http://www.bbonline.com/sd/dakotashepherd

Enjoy luxury in the prairie and headquarter at our authentic sheep farm/ranch while exploring nearby Black Hills attractions, Bear Butte State Park, or Devil's Tower. Our modern ranch home offers spacious, romantic guest rooms beautifully decorated with vintage 1940s furniture and family heirlooms. Savor delicious homemade breakfasts, then relax and enjoy the panoramic landscape. Shop in "Gift Closet" or help with farm chores. Dinner available.

Hosts: Sheryl and Robert Trohkimoinen
Rooms: 4 (2PB; 2SB) $60-70
Full Breakfast
Credit Cards: A, B
Notes: 2, 3, 4, 5, 10, 11, 12

YANKTON

Mulberry Inn

512 Mulberry Street, 57078
(605) 665-7116
E-mail: cameron@hdc.net

The beautiful Mulberry Inn offers the ultimate in comfort and charm in a traditional setting. Built in 1873, the inn features parquet floors, six guest rooms furnished with antiques, two parlors with marble fireplaces, and a large porch. Minutes from the Lewis and Clark Lake, within walking distance of the Missouri River, fine restaurants, and downtown. Listed on the National Register of Historic Places.

Hosts: Gerrald and Millie Cameron
Rooms: 6 (2PB; 4SB) $35-52
Continental Breakfast (Full Breakfast extra charge)
Credit Cards: A, B
Notes: 2, 5, 7, 8, 9, 10

Tennessee

Natchez Trace Bed and Breakfast Reservation Service

PO Box 193, **Hampshire,** 38461
(931) 285-2777; (800) 377-2770
E-mail: natcheztrace@worldnet.att.net
Web site: http://www.bbonline.com/natcheztrace

This reservation service is unusual in that all the homes are close to the Natchez Trace, the delightful National Parkway running from Nashville, Tennessee, to Natchez, Mississippi. Kay Jones can help plan your trip along the Trace, with homestays in interesting and historic homes. Locations of homes include Ashland City, Columbia, FairView, Franklin, Hohenwald, and Nashville, **Tennessee;** Florence and Cherokee, **Alabama;** and Church Hill, Corinth, French Camp, Kosciusko, Lorman, Natchez, New Albany, Tupelo, and Vicksburg, **Mississippi.** Rates $60-125.

ATHENS

Woodlawn B&B

110 Keith Lane, 37303
(423) 745-8211; (800) 745-8213
Web site: http://www.woodlawn.com

Woodlawn, an elegant Greek Revival antebellum home, circa 1858, is listed on the National Historic Register. It was a Union hospital during the Civil War. It is furnished with gorgeous antique pieces and Oriental rugs that add to its warm feel. Located on 5 acres in the heart of downtown Athens, a charming historic town filled with antique and specialty shops. Pool onsite; golf and tennis nearby; white-water rafting on the Ocoee River, 30 minutes away.

Woodlawn Bed and Breakfast

Hosts: Susan and Barry Willis
Rooms: 4 (PB) $69-145
Full Breakfast
Credit Cards: A, B, D
Notes: 2, 5, 8, 9, 10, 12

BRISTOL

New Hope B&B

822 Georgia Avenue, 37620
(423) 989-3343; (888) 989-3343

New Hope has all the charm of a late Victorian home, yet comfort and convenience

---

welcome; 7 Children welcome; 8 Tennis nearby; 9 Swimming nearby; 10 Golf nearby; 11 Skiing nearby; 12 May be booked through travel agent.

TENNESSEE

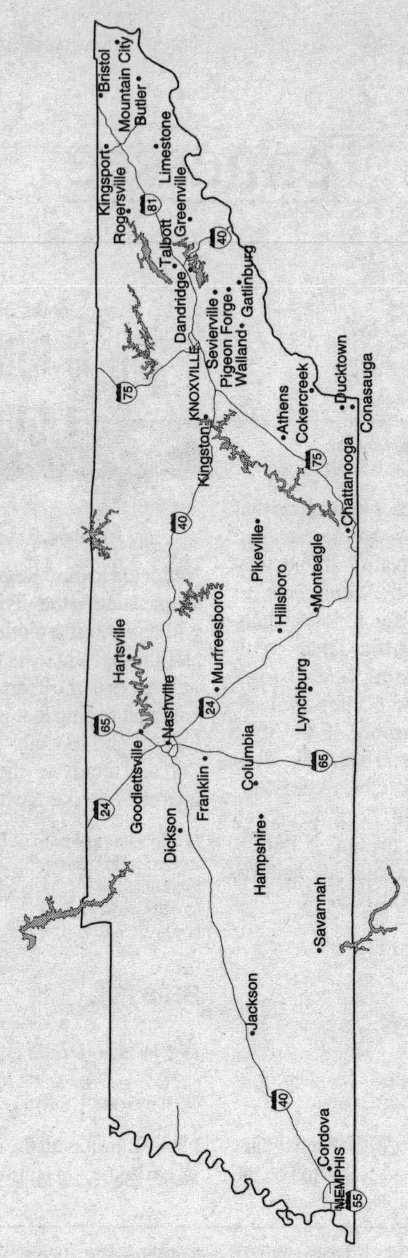

Bristol
Mountain City
Butler
Kingsport
Rogersville
Limestone
Greenville
81
Talbott
40
Dandridge
Gatlinburg
Sevierville
Pigeon Forge
Walland
KNOXVILLE
75
Ducktown
Cokercreek
Athens
Conasauga
Kingston
75
Chattanooga
40
Pikeville
Monteagle
Hillsboro
Murfreesboro
Hartsville
Lynchburg
24
65
Nashville
Goodlettsville
Columbia
65
Franklin
24
Dickson
Hampshire
Savannah
Jackson
40
Cordova
MEMPHIS
55

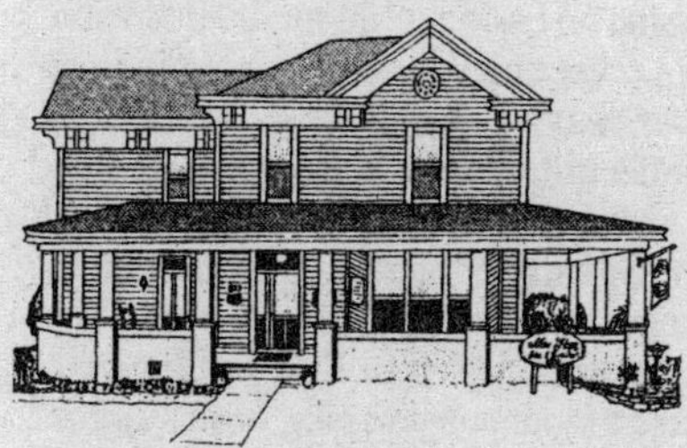

New Hope Bed and Breakfast

were high on the agenda when decorative decisions were being made. Our guests often tell us, "I feel so at home." There are four guest rooms, each with a large, private bath. Our beds are either twin, queen, or king. A full breakfast is served each morning in the dining room or on the wraparound porch, or you may have it brought to your room.

Hosts: Tom and Tonda Fluke
Rooms: 4 (PB) $75-105
Full Breakfast
Credit Cards: A, B, C
Notes: 2, 5, 10, 11, 12

BUTLER

Doe Mountain Inn Bed and Breakfasts

412 K&R Road, 37640
(423) 727-2726

Doe Mountain Inn is the perfect, quiet getaway with warm hospitality and pleasant, comfortable accommodations. Our deluxe suites offer privacy, with more than 875 square feet of living comfort and a spectacular view of the surrounding mountains. Our convenient location puts you within minutes of Watauga Lake, Roan Valley Golf Estates, and many area antique and craft shops in Boone, North Carolina. Hot tub suite available with wood-burning fireplaces. Home-cooked breakfast served daily. Group packages available for family reunions, church retreats, conferences, weddings, receptions, and other social events.

Hosts: Jerry and Teresa Calhoun
Rooms: 2 (PB) $75-95
Full Breakfast
Credit Cards: A, B
Notes: 2, 5, 7, 9, 10, 11

Iron Mountain Inn Bed and Breakfast

138 Moreland Drive, 37640
(423) 768-2446 (voice and FAX)
E-mail: ironmtn@preferred
Web site: http://www.bbonline.com/tn/ironmtn

Secluded mountain hideaway in northeastern Tennessee, "the quiet corner," where three states join hands. Warm hospitality, 40 miles of views from wraparound decks and porches. All baths have whirlpool tubs—a respite from the "real" world. Rest, relax, rock, read, hike, sail, fish. Skiing nearby, horseback riding (bring your own horse, or trail ride on a gentle one from the neighbor's herd), antiquing, bluegrass music, storytelling. No smoking; no pets; no children.

Hostess: Vikki Woods
Rooms: 4 (PB) $100-130
Full Breakfast
Credit Cards: A, B, C
Notes: 2, 11

NOTES: Credit cards accepted: A Master Card; B Visa; C American Express; D Discover; E Diners Club; F Other; 2 Personal checks accepted; 3 Lunch available; 4 Dinner available; 5 Open all year; 6 Pets welcome; 7 Children welcome; 8 Tennis nearby; 9 Swimming nearby; 10 Golf nearby; 11 Skiing nearby; 12 May be booked through travel agent.

CHATTANOOGA

Adams Hilborne Mansion Inn

801 Vine Street, 37403
(423) 265-5000; (888) IINNJOY (446-6569);
FAX (423) 265-5555
Web site: http://www.innjoy.com

Cornerstone to Chattanooga's Fort Wood Historic District; mayor's mansion in 1889. Rare Victorian Romanesque design with original coffered ceilings, hand-carved oak stairway, beveled-glass windows, and ceramic tile embellishments. Old-world charm and hospitality in a tree-shaded setting rich with Civil War history and turn-of-the-century architecture. Small, European-style hotel accommodations in ten tastefully restored, exquisitely decorated guest rooms. Awarded National Trust Home Beautiful, 1997. Private baths, fireplaces, and complimentary breakfast for guests. Fine dining nightly at the restaurant; wine and liquors available. Ballroom, meeting and reception areas, private dining, and catering available to the public by arrangement. Minutes from Chattanooga museums, fine shops and restaurants, the aquarium, UTC arena, and other cultural attractions. Offstreet parking.

Hosts: Wendy and David Adams
Rooms: 10 (PB) $100-275
Continental Breakfast
Credit Cards: A, B, C
Notes: 2, 3, 4, 5, 7 (by arrangement), 8, 9, 10, 12

Alford House

5515 Alford Hill Drive, 37419
(423) 821-7625

A taste of Chattanooga past and present surrounds you in this seventeen-room home on Lookout Mountain. Interesting collections stir your interest, including more than sixty antique glass baskets, soft drink collectibles, trains, carousel horses, and much more. Many items are for sale. You'll enjoy early coffee and breakfast on the upper deck surrounded by towering trees or in our dining room. Relax in the gazebo, take a mountain trail hike, or sit by a cozy fire on wintry nights. Only minutes from all major attractions, including the Tennessee Aquarium, Rock City, Ruby Falls, Civil War battlefield, museums, and dining. Off-season discounts. Reservations preferred.

Hostess: Rhoda Alford
Rooms: 3 + 3-room suite (PB) $65-145
Full or Continental Breakfast
Credit Cards: none
Notes: 2, 8, 9, 10, 11, 12

COKER CREEK

Mountain Garden Inn

PO Box 171, 37314
(423) 261-2689

Enjoy luxurious, romantic suites and cozy bedrooms, all with private baths and air-conditioning. A stately cypress log inn with wraparound porches and rockers galore. A family-style B&B specializing in reunions—special group rates. Very peaceful setting with a panoramic, three-state view overlooking the Cherokee National Forests of North Carolina, Georgia, and Tennessee. Adjacent to the historic "Trail of Tears," waterfall hiking, gold panning, and horseback riding.

Hosts: Stephen and Pam Wentworth
Rooms: 4 (PB) $40-80
Full Breakfast
Credit Cards: none
Notes: 2, 5, 7

NOTES: Credit cards accepted: A Master Card; B Visa; C American Express; D Discover; E Diners Club; F Other; 2 Personal checks accepted; 3 Lunch available; 4 Dinner available; 5 Open all year; 6 Pets

COLUMBIA

Locust Hill B&B

1185 Mooresville Pike, 38401
(931) 388-8531; (800) 577-8264;
FAX (931) 570-8719
E-mail: locust@edge.net

Historic 1840 home and two-story smokehouse, both furnished with family antiques, handmade quilts, and embroidered linens. Pamper yourself with morning coffee in your room and evening refreshments at the fireside. Spacious rooms with private baths and comfortable sitting areas. The gourmet breakfasts feature country ham, feather-light biscuits, and homemade jams. Five fireplaces. Relax in the library, flower gardens, or on the three porches to make this a perfect getaway. Gourmet dining available by reservation.

Hosts: Bill and Beverly Beard
Rooms: 4 (PB) $90-125
Full Breakfast
Credit Cards: A, B, C, D
Notes: 2, 4, 5, 8, 10, 12

CONASAUGA

Chestnut Inn Bed and Breakfast

Box 124, Delta Drive, 37316
(423) 338-7873; (800) 993-7873;
FAX (423) 338-3974
Web site: www.bbonline.com/tn/chestnut/

A Dutch Colonial home built in 1940, paneled with American chestnut in the entrance, dining room, and parlor. Furnished with antiques and collectibles. Three guest rooms each have private baths. Full breakfast served in the dining room or on the screened porch. Set in a quiet rural community at the foot of the Cherokee National Forest. Near white-water rafting, hiking, fishing, mountain biking, horseback riding, and swimming.

Hosts: Larry and Lynne Bivens
Rooms: 3 (PB) $70
Full Breakfast
Credit Cards: A, B
Notes: 2, 5, 7 (11 and up)

DANDRIDGE

Mill Dale Farm Bed and Breakfast

140 Mill Dale Road, 37725
(423) 397-3470; (800) 767-3471
Web site: http://www.bbonline.com/tn/milldale

Nineteenth-century farmhouse located in Tennessee's second-oldest town. Floating staircase leads to three guest rooms, all with private baths. Nearby is fishing, boating, swimming, tennis, golf, the Great Smoky Mountains, Gatlinburg, and Pigeon Forge. Delicious country breakfast.

Hostess: Lucy Franklin
Rooms: 3 (PB) $55-72
Full Breakfast
Credit Cards: none
Notes: 2, 5, 7, 8, 9, 10, 11

DICKSON

East Hills Bed and Breakfast Inn

100 East Hill Terrace (on Highway 70), 37055
(615) 441-9428; FAX (615) 446-2181
Web site: http://www.bbonline.com/tn/easthills

Fully restored traditional home with southern charm, built in the late '40s on four acres with lots of big, tall trees. The home has five bedrooms and a cottage with private baths and cable TVs, a large living room, library/den with fireplaces, and an enclosed back porch. Beautifully decorated and furnished throughout with period antiques and designer reproductions. Located on Highway 70 near Luther Lake and the GreyStone golf course, 6 miles from Montgomery Bell State Park. Convenient to shopping, restaurants, downtown areas, historic Charlotte, and Cumberland Furnace. Rates include afternoon tea and muffins and a full breakfast in the morning. No smoking, no alcohol.

Hosts: John and Anita Luther
Rooms: 5 (PB) $65-95
Full Breakfast
Credit Cards: A, B, C, D
Notes: 2, 5, 10

DUCKTOWN

The Company House Bed and Breakfast Inn

125 Main Street; PO Box 154, 37326
(423) 496-5634; (800) 343-2909
Web site: http://www.bbonline.com/tn/companyhouse

Built in 1850, The Company House is listed on the National Historic Register. Recently restored, it has all the charm of yesteryear with the conveniences of today. Each bedroom is individually decorated with antiques and has a private bath. Guests can enjoy the big-screen television in the parlor or relax on the rocking chair porch. Wake up to a sumptuous breakfast served family style. The area offers white-water rafting, kayaking and canoeing, swimming, fishing, hiking, biking, horseback riding, and golfing. Antique shops and flea markets abound. Located in the southeastern corner of Tennessee.

Hosts: Mike and Margie Tonkin
Rooms: 6 (PB) $69-75
Full Breakfast
Credit Cards: A, B
Notes: 2, 5, 9, 10, 12

The White House Bed and Breakfast

104 Main Street; PO Box 668, 37326
(423) 496-4166; (800) 775-4166

Embracing the elegance of the past and the convenience of today. Relax on our lovely rocking chair porch. The home is air-conditioned. Three guest bedrooms, one with private bath and two sharing. Full country breakfast included.

Hosts: Mardee and Dan Kauffman
Rooms: 3 (1PB; 2SB) $60-70
Full Breakfast
Credit Cards: A, B, D, F (traveler's checks)
Notes: 2, 5, 7 (over 10), 9, 10, 12

FRANKLIN

Namaste Acres Barn Bed and Breakfast

5436 Leipers Creek Road, 37064
(615) 791-0333; FAX (615) 591-0665
E-mail: namaste@aol.com
Web site: http://www.bbonline.com/tn/namaste

Quiet valley setting. Poolside deck and hot tub, hiking, horseback trails. Country inn offers four theme suites, including the Loft, Bunkhouse, Cabin, and Franklin. In-room coffee, phone, and refrigerator; TV/VCR (movies). Private entrance and bath. Featured in *Southern Living Magazine,*

Namaste Acres Barn Bed and Breakfast

Horse Illustrated, and *Western Horseman*. One mile from Natchez Trace Parkway, 11 miles from historic Franklin, and 23 miles from Nashville. Established 1993. Reservation requested; weekday discounts. AAA three-diamond rating. Guided trail rides are available.

Hostess: Bill and Lisa Winters
Rooms: 4 (PB) $75-85
Full and Continental Breakfast
Credit Cards: all major
Notes: 2, 5, 7 (12 and older), 9, 10, 12

GATLINBURG

7th Heaven Log Inn Bed and Breakfast

3944 Castle Road, 37738
(423) 430-5000; (800) 248-2923;
FAX (423) 436-7748
E-mail: heaveninn@icx.net
Web sites: http://www.pwgroup.com/7heaven
http://www.7-heaven.com

The inn is nestled on the seventh green of the Bent Creek Golf Resort. Experience log home living with all the modern conveniences. One suite has a private bath. Four knotty pine rooms also have private baths. Private guest entrances are provided. Exciting murder mystery weekend packages are available. Call today—truly heaven on earth.

Hosts: Dan and Cheryl Roese
Rooms: 5 (PB) $97-127
Full Breakfast
Credit Cards: A, B
Notes: 2, 5, 7, 9, 10, 11, 12

Butcher House in the Mountains

1520 Garrett Lane, 37738
(423) 436-9457

Nestled 2,800 feet above the main entrance to the Smokies, Butcher House in the Mountains offers mountain seclusion as well as convenience. The Swisslike cedar-and-stone chalet enjoys one of the most beautiful views in the state. Antiques are tastefully placed throughout the house, and a guest kitchen is available for coffee and lavish dessert. European gourmet brunch. AAA three-diamond-rated; ABBA-rated, excellent. Hospitality is our gift.

Hosts: Hugh and Gloria Butcher
Rooms: 5 (PB) $89-129
Full European Gourmet Breakfast
Credit Cards: A, B, C
Notes: 2, 5, 8, 9, 10, 11, 12

Butcher House in the Mountains

welcome; 7 Children welcome; 8 Tennis nearby; 9 Swimming nearby; 10 Golf nearby; 11 Skiing nearby; 12 May be booked through travel agent.

The Colonel's Lady Inn

1120 Tanrac Trail, 37738
(423) 436-5432; (800) 515-5432;
FAX (423) 436-7855
E-mail: colonel@colonelsladyinn.com
Web site: http://www.colonelsladyinn.com

Wandering through the picturesque country of the Great Smoky Mountains arts and crafts community, travelers often find "mountain treasures" around each bend. One splendid treasure is found sitting grandly atop a buttress ridge just outside the national park: a gracious, charming bed and breakfast known as The Colonel's Lady Inn, handsomely decorated with antiques, paintings, and family heirlooms.

Hosts: Anita and Bill Cate
Rooms: 8 (PB) $89-159
Full Breakfast
Credit Cards: A, B, C, D
Notes: 8, 9, 10, 11, 12

Cornerstone Inn Bed and Breakfast

3966 Regal Way; PO Box 1600, 37738
(423) 430-5064
Web site: http://www.bbonline.com/tn/cornerstone

A delightful country inn with a 50-foot front porch overlooking a magnificent mountain view. Although very near the arts and crafts community, Dollywood, and the Great Smoky Mountains National Park, the Cornerstone Inn provides privacy and a warm, comfortable atmosphere. Private baths, full breakfast. Open all year. Smoking on porches only.

Hosts: Kay and Don Cooper
Rooms: 3 (PB) $85-95
Full Breakfast
Credit Cards: A, B, C, D
Notes: 2, 5, 7, 10, 12

Eight Gables Inn

Eight Gables Inn

219 N. Mountain Trail, 37738
(423) 430-3344; (800) 279-5716;
FAX (423) 430-3344, *51
E-mail: 8gables@eightgables.com
Web site: http://www.eightgables.com

For the perfect bed and breakfast getaway, Eight Gables is the answer. Reserve your accommodations from among twelve spacious guest rooms that appeal to even the most discriminating taste. At the foot of the Great Smoky Mountains National Park, Eight Gables Inn's location is easily accessible to all area attractions. The inn offers bedrooms with private baths and luxurious living space, and has a covered porch area. It is AAA-approved, four diamonds. Family-owned and -operated.

Hosts: Don and Kim Cason
Rooms: 12 (PB) $109-179
Full Breakfast
Credit Cards: A, B, C, D, E, F
Notes: 2, 3 and 4 (on request), 5, 7, 8, 10, 11, 12

Olde English Tudor Inn

135 W. Hollyridge Road, 37738
(423) 436-7760; (800) 541-3798;
FAX (423) 430-7308
E-mail: tudorinn@smoky-mtns.com
Web site: http://www.smoky-mtns.com/gatlinburg/bb

The Olde English Tudor Inn bed and breakfast is set on a hillside overlooking

NOTES: Credit cards accepted: A Master Card; B Visa; C American Express; D Discover; E Diners Club; F Other; 2 Personal checks accepted; 3 Lunch available; 4 Dinner available; 5 Open all year; 6 Pets

the beautiful mountain resort of Gatlinburg. Ideally located within a few minutes' walk of downtown and a few minutes' drive of the Great Smoky Mountains National Park. The inn has seven spacious guest rooms with their own modern baths and cable TVs (HBO). Each guest is made to feel at home in the large community room furnished with television/VCR and free-standing wood-burning stove. Call toll-free for a brochure.

Hosts: Linda and Steve Pickel
Rooms: 7 (PB) $79-109
Full Breakfast
Credit Cards: A, B, C, D
Notes: 2, 5, 7, 8, 9, 10, 11, 12

GREENEVILLE

Hilltop House Bed and Breakfast Inn

6 Sanford Circle, 37743
(423) 639-8202

Denise serves a full breakfast in the formal dining room; she has a different menu for every day of the month, featuring eggs cooked in a variety of ways, pancakes, crepes stuffed with apples, French toast, and other delectables. Many guests are outdoors types who enjoy hiking, fishing, mountain biking, and white-water rafting at the nearby Appalachian Trail, Nolichucky River, and several lakes. Hiking, trout fishing, horseback riding, river rafting, and scenic/historic tours available.

Hosts: Denise M. Ashworth
Rooms: 3 (PB) $75-80
Full Breakfast
Credit Cards: A, B, C
Notes: 2, 5, 7 (3+), 9 (3 miles), 10, 12

HARTSVILLE

Miss Alice's Bed and Breakfast

8325 Highway 141 S., 37074
(615) 374-3015; (615) 444-4401
Web site: http://www.bbonline.com/tn/missalices

Relax! Enjoy Tennessee's southern hospitality in a restored early-1900s farmhouse. Choose a beautiful bedroom or the cabin. The cabin takes you back to an era without modern conveniences. Walk through the woods, read, play horseshoes, lie in the hammock, or sip lemonade in the well house. Wake up with a cup of gourmet coffee and a farmer's breakfast. Area attractions include Nashville, Vice President Gore's hometown, and many antique shops nearby.

Hostess: Volene B. Barnes
Rooms: 2 + cabin (1PB; 2SB) $65
Full Breakfast
Credit Cards: none
Notes: 2, 9, 10

HILLSBORO

Lord's Landing Bed and Breakfast

375 Lord's Landing Lane, 37342
(931) 467-3830; FAX (931) 467-3032
E-mail: lordslanding@blomand.net
Web site: http://kristallnet.com/lordslanding

Central Tennessee's 50-acre paradise awaits guests from near and far. You may drive in for a relaxing retreat or fly into our 2,400 x 80-foot turf airstrip for a quiet getaway. Located near the base of the Cumberland Plateau, the main house has breathtaking views from every window. A

Lord's Landing Bed and Breakfast

leisurely stroll takes guests to the eight-bedroom, seven-bath country cottage, beautifully decorated with antiques and fine furnishings. Fireplaces and Jacuzzi tubs in most rooms. Outdoor pool.

Hosts: Denny and Pam Neilson
Rooms: 7 (PB) $95-150
Full Breakfast
Credit Cards: A, B, D
Notes: 2, 3, 4, 5, 7, 10, 12

JACKSON

Highland Place Bed and Breakfast

519 N. Highland Avenue, 38301
(901) 427-1472; FAX (901) 422-7994
E-mail: grwjpw@usit.net
Web site: http://www.bbonline.com/tn/highlandplace

Highland Place Bed and Breakfast is a stately home of distinct charm, offering comfortable accommodations and southern hospitality. Highland Place is west Tennessee's 1995 Designers Showplace. Each room, hall, staircase, and hidden nook has been designed and decorated by outstanding designers. Experience the pleasure of sharing the surroundings of one of the state's finest homes. Built circa 1911, the inn was totally renovated and reopened in 1995.

Hosts: Glenn and Janice Wall
Rooms: 4 (PB) $75-135
Full Breakfast
Credit Cards: A, B, C
Notes: 2, 3, 4, 5, 10, 12

KINGSPORT

Warrior's Rest

1000 Colonial Heights Road, 37663
(423) 239-8838

Nestled in the rolling foothills of the east Tennessee mountains, Warrior's Rest is the ideal place to withdraw from the battles of everyday life. Spend time with family, friends, or just by yourself. The 90-year-old farmhouse is within 5 minutes of golfing, swimming, boating, horseback riding, and hiking at Warrior's Path State Park. The scenic Blue Ridge Parkway and historic Jonesborough are nearby.

Hosts: Charlie and Suzanne Buchleiter
Rooms: 3 (PB) $65-85
Full Breakfast
Credit Cards: none
Notes: 2, 5, 7, 8, 9, 10

KINGSTON

Whitestone Country Inn

1200 Paint Rock Road, 37763
(423) 376-0113; (888) 247-2464;
FAX (423) 376-4454
E-mail: moreinfo@whitestones.com
Web site: http://www.whitestones.com

AAA four-diamond country inn. Twelve bedrooms, each with fireplace, whirlpool,

NOTES: Credit cards accepted: A Master Card; B Visa; C American Express; D Discover; E Diners Club; F Other; 2 Personal checks accepted; 3 Lunch available; 4 Dinner available; 5 Open all year; 6 Pets

TV/VCR, telephone. Set on a 275-acre country estate with 7,000 feet of frontage on Watts Bar Lake. Recreation room, exercise equipment, sauna, steam showers. Seven miles of hiking trails, canoes, paddleboats, great fishing. Dinner $18.95. Special rates for pastors. Central to all attractions. Find sanctuary for the soul in the tranquillity of God's creation.

Hosts: Paul and Jean Cowell
Rooms: 12 (PB) $85-160
Full Breakfast
Credit Cards: A, B, C, D
Notes: 2, 3, 4, 5, 7 (over 6 yrs), 8, 9, 10, 11 (90 minutes), 12

LIMESTONE

Snapp Inn

1990 Davy Crockett Park Road, 37681
(423) 257-2482

Gracious circa-1815 Federal-style home furnished with antiques. Come to the country for a relaxing weekend getaway. Enjoy the peaceful mountain view or play a game of pool. Close to Davy Crockett Birthplace State Park. A 15-minute drive from historic Jonesborough or Greenville.

Hosts: Dan and Ruth Dorgan
Rooms: 2 (PB) $65
Full Breakfast
Credit Cards: A, B, D
Notes: 2, 5, 6, 7 (1 only), 8, 9, 10, 12

LYNCHBURG

Cedar Lane B&B

Route 3, Box 155E, 37352
(931) 759-6891 (voice and FAX)

Located on the outskirts of historic Lynchburg (home of Jack Daniel's Distillery). This newly built farmhouse offers comfort and relaxation. You can spend your time antiquing in nearby shops or reading a book in the sunroom. The rooms are beautifully decorated in rose, blue, peach, and green with queen and twin beds. Phones and TVs are available.

Hosts: Elaine and Chuck Quinn
Rooms: 4 (PB) $65-75
Continental Plus Breakfast
Credit Cards: A, B, C
Notes: 2, 4 (by reservation), 5, 7 (over 10), 9, 10

Lynchburg B&B

Lynchburg B&B

Mechanic Street; PO Box 34, 37352
(931) 759-7158

Lynchburg's first B&B, open since 1985, is within walking distance of Jack Daniel's Distillery and shopping area. The quaint atmosphere of this two-story home (circa 1877), provides relaxation and enjoyment in a small town. Each room is decorated with antiques. Big front porch for a quiet afternoon view of the beautiful hills.

Hosts: Mike and Virginia Tipps
Rooms: 2 (PB) $60-65
Continental Breakfast
Credit Cards: A, B
Notes: 2, 5, 7, 9

MEMPHIS AREA

The Bridgewater House Bed and Breakfast

7015 Raleigh LaGrange Road, **Cordova,** 38018
(901) 384-0080
E-mail: kmistilis@worldnet.att.net

The Bridgewater House is a Greek Revival home converted from a schoolhouse that is more than 100 years old. It is a lovely, elegant dwelling filled with remembrances of travels, antiques, family heirlooms, and Oriental rugs. The Bridgewater House has original hardwood floors cut from trees on the property; enormous rooms; high ceilings; leaded-glass windows; and deep, hand-marbleized moldings. There are two spacious bedrooms with private baths. A certified chef and a food and beverage director serve a full gourmet breakfast and pamper guests with refreshments upon arriving. The house is located 1 mile from the largest city park in the United States, which offers sailing, walking and biking trails, horseback riding, fishing, canoeing, and more.

Hosts: Katherine and Steve Mistilis
Rooms: 2 (PB) $90-100
Full Gourmet Breakfast
Credit Cards: A, B, D
Notes: 2, 5

MONTEAGLE

Adams Edgeworth Inn

Monteagle Assembly, 37403
(931) 924-4000; FAX (931) 924-3236
Web site: http://www.innjoy.com

Circa 1896, Adams Edgeworth Inn celebrates a century of fine lodging and still is a leader in elegance and quality. Recently refurbished in country chintz decor, the inn is a comfortable refuge of fine antiques, original paintings, and quaint atmosphere. Stroll through the 96-acre private Victorian village that surrounds the inn, or drive 6 miles to the Gothic campus of Sewanee, University of the South. Cultural activities year-round. Nearby are 150 miles of hiking trails, scenic vistas, and waterfalls, as well as tennis, swimming, golf, and riding. Fine candlelight dining. "One of the best inns I've ever visited anywhere. . . ." (Sara Pitzer, recommended by "Country Inns" in *Country Inns Magazine*).

Hosts: Wendy and Dave Adams
Rooms: 12 (PB) $75-205
Full Breakfast
Credit Cards: A, B, C
Notes: 2, 4, 5, 7, 8, 9, 10, 12

MOUNTAIN CITY

Prospect Hill Bed and Breakfast Inn

801 W. Main Street; Highway 67, 37683
(423) 727-0139

Unusual tranquillity; superb mountain views; and proximity to nature hikes, fishing, boating, festivals, caverns, galleries, and shopping. Between the mountains where Tennessee, North Carolina, and Virginia join hands. Circa-1889 brick mansion built by a local prospector who served in the Union Army. Huge rooms, modern romantic baths, comfortable beds, fireplaces. Decorated in the second owner's period (1910) with Stickley reproductions and antique dining set. A parklike setting on 2½ acres. Comfortable hospitality from

---

NOTES: Credit cards accepted: A Master Card; B Visa; C American Express; D Discover; E Diners Club; F Other; 2 Personal checks accepted; 3 Lunch available; 4 Dinner available; 5 Open all year; 6 Pets

experienced innkeepers who found the best small town in northeast Tennessee.

Hosts: Robert and Judy Hotchkiss
Rooms: 6 (3PB; 3SB) $89-199
Full Breakfast
Credit Cards: A, B
Notes: 2, 3, 5, 7, 8, 9, 10, 11, 12

MURFREESBORO

Clardy's Guest House

435 E. Main Street, 37130
(615) 893-6030
E-mail: rdeaton@bellsouth.net
Web site: http://www.bbonline.com/tn/clardys

This large Victorian home was built in 1898 and is located in Murfreesboro's historic district. You will marvel at the ornate woodwork, beautiful fireplaces, and magnificent stained glass overlooking the staircase. The house is filled with antiques, as are local shops and malls. The hosts will help you with dining, shopping, and touring plans.

Hosts: Barbara and Robert Deaton
Rooms: 3 (2PB; 1SB) $45-53
Continental Plus Breakfast
Credit Cards: none
Notes: 2, 5, 8, 9, 10

Simply Southern, A Bed and Breakfast

211 N. Tennessee Boulevard, 37130
(615) 896-4988
Web site: http://www.bbonline.com/tn/simplysouthern

In the heart of Tennessee. Four-story home built in 1907. Four spacious rooms plus a suite. Professionally decorated, casual elegance, private baths, sitting areas, and large rec room with pool table, player piano, karaoke, etc. Old advertising and soft drink memorabilia. Amenities reflect the innkeepers' desire to provide an experience, not just a place to stay. Across the street from Middle Tennessee State University's beautiful campus. Horse farms, Civil War sites, quaint villages nearby. Near Nashville. No smoking.

Simply Southern, A Bed and Breakfast

Hosts: Carl and Georgia Buckner
Rooms: 4 + suite that sleeps 4 (PB) $80-140
Full Breakfast
Credit Cards: A, B, D
Notes: 2, 5, 8, 9, 10, 12

NASHVILLE

Applebrook Bed and Breakfast and Barn

9127 Highway 100, 37221–4502
(615) 646-5082
Web site: http://members.tripod.com/~APPLEBROOK/index.html

Enjoy rural Nashville in an elegant turn-of-the-century farmhouse circa 1896. All private baths. Full, delicious country breakfast, swimming pool (in season). Nestled on 5 panoramic acres. Minutes

Applebrook Bed and Breakfast and Barn

from historic Second Avenue or historic Franklin; only 2.5 miles from Natchez Trace Parkway. If you enjoy history, antiques, lovely rolling hills, and nature walks, Applebrook B&B is the place for you to stay in Nashville. Open year-round. Please call for reservations.

Hosts: Don and Cynthia VanRyen
Rooms: 4 (PB) $95-115
Full or Continental Breakfast
Credit Cards: A, B, D, F (Trade Bank)
Notes: 2, 5, 7, 9, 10, 12

Bed and Breakfast About Tennessee RSO

PO Box 110227, 37222
(615) 331-5244; FAX (615) 833-7701
E-mail: fodom71282@aol.com

From the Great Smoky Mountains to the Mississippi, here is a diversity of attractions that includes fabulous scenery, Tennessee's Grand Ole Opry and Opryland, universities, Civil War sites, horse farms, and much more. With Bed and Breakfast About Tennessee, you make your visit a special occasion. An intimate alternative to hotels and motels. You will stay in a private home or inn with a host who can share firsthand knowledge of the area. This home-style atmosphere includes the offer of a freshly prepared continental breakfast. Confirmation and directions sent immediately upon reservation.

Hostess: Fredda Odom
Rooms: 80 (PB) $60-150
Continental Breakfast
Credit Cards: A, B, C, D, E
Notes: 5, 12

Crocker Springs B&B

2382 Crocker Springs Road, **Goodlettsville,** 37072
(615) 876-8502; FAX (on demand) (615) 876-4083
E-mail: crockersprings@juno.com
Web site: http://www.bbonline.com/tn/crockersprings

This haven hidden just 14 miles from downtown Nashville offers peace and tranquillity. Guests stay in the 1890s farmhouse with high ceilings and restored wood floors, furnished with many antiques. Relax and enjoy our beautiful country location (4 miles from I–24 and Old Hickory Boulevard, north of the city), southern hospitality, and full breakfasts complete with sweetbreads. Guest rooms with private bath, heat/AC, and ceiling fan await you.

Hosts: Jack and Bev Spangler
Rooms: 3 + master suite that sleeps 4 (PB) $85-135
Full Breakfast
Credit Cards: C, D
Notes: 2, 5, 7, 8, 9, 10, 12

PIGEON FORGE

Day Dreams Country Inn

2720 Colonial Drive, 37863
(423) 428-0370; (800) 377-1469;
FAX (423) 428-2622
E-mail: daydreams@sprynet.com
Web site: http://www.daydreamscountryinn.com

Delight in the true country charm of this antique-filled, secluded, two-story log

Day Dreams Country Inn

home with its six uniquely decorated guest rooms. Enjoy an evening by our cozy fireplace, relax on the front porch to the soothing sound of Mill Creek, or take a stroll around our 3 wooded acres. Treat your tastebuds to our bountiful country breakfast each morning. Within walking distance of the Parkway. Perfect for family reunions and retreats. From the Parkway, take 321 south, go 1 block, turn left onto Florence Drive, go 3 blocks, and turn right onto Colonial Drive.

Hosts: Bob and Joyce Guerrera
Rooms: 6 (PB) $79-119
Full Breakfast
Credit Cards: A, B, D
Notes: 2, 3, 4, 5, 7, 8, 9, 10, 11, 12

PIKEVILLE

Fall Creek Falls Bed and Breakfast Inn

Route 3, Box 298B, 37367
(423) 881-5494; FAX (423) 881-5040
Web site: http://www.bbonline.com/tn/fallcreek

Elegant mountain inn featured in the August '94 *Tennessee* magazine and August '96 *Country* magazine. Seven guest rooms and one suite, all with private baths and air-conditioning. Some rooms have heart-shaped whirlpools and fireplaces. Victorian or country decor. One mile from nationally acclaimed Fall Creek Falls State Resort Park. Beautiful mountains, waterfalls, golfing, boating, fishing, tennis, hiking, horseback riding, and biking trails. AAA-rated. No smoking. Full breakfast. Romantic, scenic, and quiet.

Hosts: Doug and Rita Pruett
Rooms: 8 (PB) $75-130
Full Breakfast
Credit Cards: A, B, C, D
Notes: 2, 8, 9, 10, 12

ROGERSVILLE

The Guest House

272 Blevins Road, 37857
(423) 272-0861 or (423) 272-2984

View miles of mountain beauty from our front porch or meditate in the woods or at the creek. For great day adventures, we're within 2 hours of the Great Smokies; Lost Sea; Abingdon, Virginia; or Biltmore in Asheville, North Carolina. Fifty dollars per night includes continental breakfast, or rent by the week/month and do your own cooking in our full kitchen.

Hosts: Ellen and Harold McCoy
Rooms: 3 (PB) $50
Continental Breakfast
Credit Cards: A, B
Notes: 3 (make your own), 5, 7, 8, 9, 10 (15 miles), 11 (50 miles), 12

Hale Springs Inn, Since 1824

Town Square, 37857
(423) 272-5171

Tennessee's oldest operational inn, built in 1824 and recently restored to its former glory. AC, central heat. Most rooms have working fireplaces. Private, modern baths, antique furniture, poster beds. Dine at fireside in the candlelit dining room. Presidents Jackson, Polk, and Andrew Johnson stayed here. An easy 1-hour drive from historic sites and mountain resorts.

Hosts: Capt. and Mrs. Carl Netherland-Brown
Rooms: 9 (PB) $45-70
Continental Breakfast
Credit Cards: A, B, C
Notes: 3, 4, 5, 7, 8, 9, 10, 12

SAVANNAH

White Elephant B&B Inn

304 Church Street, 38372
(901) 925-6410
Web site: http://www.bbonline.com/tn/elephant

Stately 1901 Queen Anne Victorian home on 1½ shady acres in the historic district. Within walking distance of the Tennessee River, downtown shopping, restaurants, and churches. Nearby golf courses and Civil War attractions; 10 miles from Shiloh National Military Park (the innkeeper offers battlefield tours); 12 miles from Pickwick Dam and Lake. Three individually decorated rooms feature antiques, queen beds. Two parlors, antiques, central heat and air, wraparound porches, croquet. No smoking or pets. See the Elephant!

White Elephant Bed and Breakfast Inn

Hosts: Ken and Sharon Hansgen
Rooms: 3 (PB) $65-95
Full Breakfast
Credit Cards: none
Notes: 2, 5, 8, 10, 12

SEVIERVILLE

Blue Mountain Mist Country Inn

1811 Pullen Road, 37862
(423) 428-2335; (800) 497-2335;
FAX (423) 453-1720
E-mail: blumtnmist@aol.com
Web site: http://www.bbonline.com/tn/bluemtnmist

Experience the silent beauty of mountain scenery while rocking on the big wraparound porch of this Victorian-style farmhouse. Common rooms filled with antiques lead to individually decorated guest rooms. Enjoy many special touches such as old-fashioned claw-foot tubs, high antique headboards, quilts, and Jacuzzi. Nestled in the woods behind the inn are five cottages designed for romantic getaways. The Great Smoky Mountains National Park and Gatlinburg are only 20 minutes away.

Hosts: Norman and Sarah Ball
Rooms: 12 + 5 cottages (PB) $98-140
Full Breakfast
Credit Cards: A, B
Notes: 2, 5, 7, 8, 9, 10, 11, 12

Calico Inn

Calico Inn

757 Ranch Way, 37862
(423) 428-3833; (800) 235-1054

Voted 1998 "Inn of the Year." The Calico Inn is located in the Smoky Mountains near Gatlinburg and Dollywood. It is an authentic log inn with touches of elegance. Decorated with antiques, collectibles, and country charm. Enjoy the spectacular mountain view, surrounded by 25 acres of peace and tranquillity. Minutes from fine dining, live entertainment shows, shopping, hiking, fishing, golfing, horseback riding, and all other attractions the area has to offer, yet completely secluded.

Hosts: Lill and Jim Katzbeck
Rooms: 3 (PB) $85-95
Full Breakfast
Credit Cards: A, B
Notes: 2, 5, 7, 8, 9, 10, 11, 12

Edelweiss Bed and Breakfast

1531 Providence Hills Road, 37876
(423) 429-4771

Just before you get to the Great Smoky Mountain National Park, you will find the Edelweiss. You will enjoy the European hospitality and your morning coffee while overlooking the panoramic view of rolling hills from the wraparound porch. We have four bedrooms with private baths, and serve a hefty country German breakfast.

Hosts: Joachim and Heidi Matheurs
Rooms: 4 (PB) $79-99
Full Breakfast
Credit Cards: A, B, C, D
Notes: 2, 5, 7, 10, 11

Little Greenbrier Lodge

3685 Lyon Springs Road, 37862–8257
(423) 429-2500; (800) 277-8100
E-mail: littlegreenbrier@worldnet.att.net
Web site: http://www.bbonline.com/tn/lgl

Borders national park entrance. Historical lodge on mountainside overlooking beautiful Wears Valley in the Great Smoky Mountains. Antique decor, very secluded and peaceful. Great hiking. The aroma of hot Pecan Pull Apart Bread is mouthwatering. Just 150 yards from hiking trails. Or rock on the porch with a lemonade and great book.

Hosts: Charles and Susan Lebon
Rooms: 10 (8PB; 2SB) $95-110
Full Breakfast
Credit Cards: A, B, D
Notes: 2, 3, 5, 9, 10, 11, 12

Persephone's Farm Retreat

2279 Hodges Ferry Road, 37876
(423) 428-3904; FAX (423) 453-7089
E-mail: vnicholson@smokymtnmall.com
Web site: http://www.smokymtnmall.com

A peaceful, rural estate nestled in a grove of huge shade trees. Convenient to Gatlinburg, Pigeon Forge, and Knoxville, but ideal for rest and relaxation from busy tourist activities. An elegant two-story home offers extremely comfortable bedrooms with private baths and large porches overlooking pastures and a beautiful river valley. Enjoy spacious grounds, yard games, farm animals, miniature horses, and hiking. Children welcome.

Hosts: Bob Gonia and Victoria Nicholson
Rooms: 2 (PB) $95
Full Breakfast
Credit Cards: A, B, C
Notes: 2, 7, 8, 9, 10, 11, 12

Von-Bryan Inn

2402 Hatcher Mountain Road, 37862
(423) 453-9832; (800) 633-1459;
FAX (423) 428-8634
E-mail: von-bryan-inn@juno.com
Web site: http://www.bbonline.com/tn/vonbryan

A mountaintop log inn with an unsurpassed, panoramic view of the Great Smoky Mountains. Greet the sunrise with singing birds and the aroma of breakfast. Swim, hike, rock, rest, read, and relax the day away, then watch the sunset just before the whippoorwills begin to call. Swimming pool, hot tub, whirlpool tubs, steam shower, library, complimentary dessert, refreshments, and breakfast. Our three-bedroom log chalet is great for families.

Hosts: The Vaughns (D.J., JoAnn, David, Patrick)
Rooms: 7 + 3-bedroom log cabin (PB) $90-200
Full Breakfast
Credit Cards: A, B, C, D
Notes: 2, 5, 7, 9 (onsite), 10, 11, 12

Von-Bryan Inn

TALBOTT

Arrow Hill B&B

6622 W. Andrew Johnson Highway, 37877
(423) 585-5777
Web site: http://www.bbonline.com/tn/arrowhill

Arrow Hill, circa 1857 and listed on the National Historic Register, retains the ambience of the antebellum era with its 12-foot ceilings, three-story spiral staircase, original carved woodwork, and widow's walk. Three 1850s-style guest rooms invite a step back in time. Author Helen T. Miller wrote many of her fifty-four novels in the comfortably furnished library, where you may enjoy reading them today. In the morning, a delightful breakfast is served in the elegant tradition of the Old South.

Hosts: Gary and Donna Davis
Rooms: 3 (2PB; 1SB) $55-65
Full Breakfast
Credit Cards: A, B, C, D
Notes: 2, 4, 5, 7, 8, 9, 10, 11, 12

WALLAND

Misty Morning B&B

5515 Old Walland Highway, 37886
(423) 681-6373 (voice and FAX)

A three-story log home on 8 beautiful acres nestled in the foothills of the Smoky Mountains. The B&B offers a sense of family and southern hospitality, with full amenities. A restful getaway convenient to Pigeon Forge, Knoxville, Gatlinburg, Cade's Cove, and Knoxville Airport.

Hosts: Darnell and Herman Davis
Rooms: 2 (PB) $69-89
Full Breakfast
Credit Cards: A, B, D
Notes: 9 (onsite), 10, 11

NOTES: Credit cards accepted: A Master Card; B Visa; C American Express; D Discover; E Diners Club; F Other; 2 Personal checks accepted; 3 Lunch available; 4 Dinner available; 5 Open all year; 6 Pets

Texas

Reservation Service—Bed and Breakfast Texas Style, Inc.

4224 W. Red Bird Lane, **Dallas,** 75237-2016
(972) 298-8586; (800) 899-4538;
FAX (972) 298-7118
E-mail: bdtxstyle1@aol.com
Web site: http://www.bnbtexasstyle.com

Bed and Breakfast Texas Style, Inc., is a reservation service established in 1982. We offer you a wide variety of accommodations in private homes, cottages, and small inns. We carefully inspect and approve lodgings to ensure guests' comfort and convenience. If you prefer more privacy, you may choose a log cabin on a ranch, cottage on a farm, or guest house in the woods. Many of our bed and breakfasts are historical mansions with Victorian decor. Let us know your desire; we will try to find just the right place for your special needs.

AUSTIN

Austin's Governors' Inn

1900 David Street, 78705
(512) 477-0711; (800) 871-8908;
FAX (512) 476-4769
E-mail: governorsinn@earthlink.net
Web site: http://www.citysearch.com/aus/carringtonsbluff

Built in 1897, this neoclassical Victorian inn is furnished with beautiful and tasteful antiques. All of the ten guest rooms have private baths, telephones, and cable televisions. Every morning, a full breakfast will satisfy your appetite for fine food. The inn lies only a few blocks from the University of Texas, the state capitol grounds, and all Austin has to offer. Governors' Inn is perfect for business or pleasure. It was awarded 1997 "Best Bed & Breakfast in Austin" by the *Austin Chronicle*. The Governors' Inn also was one of only three Texas bed and breakfasts to be featured

---

welcome; 7 Children welcome; 8 Tennis nearby; 9 Swimming nearby; 10 Golf nearby; 11 Skiing nearby; 12 May be booked through travel agent.

TEXAS

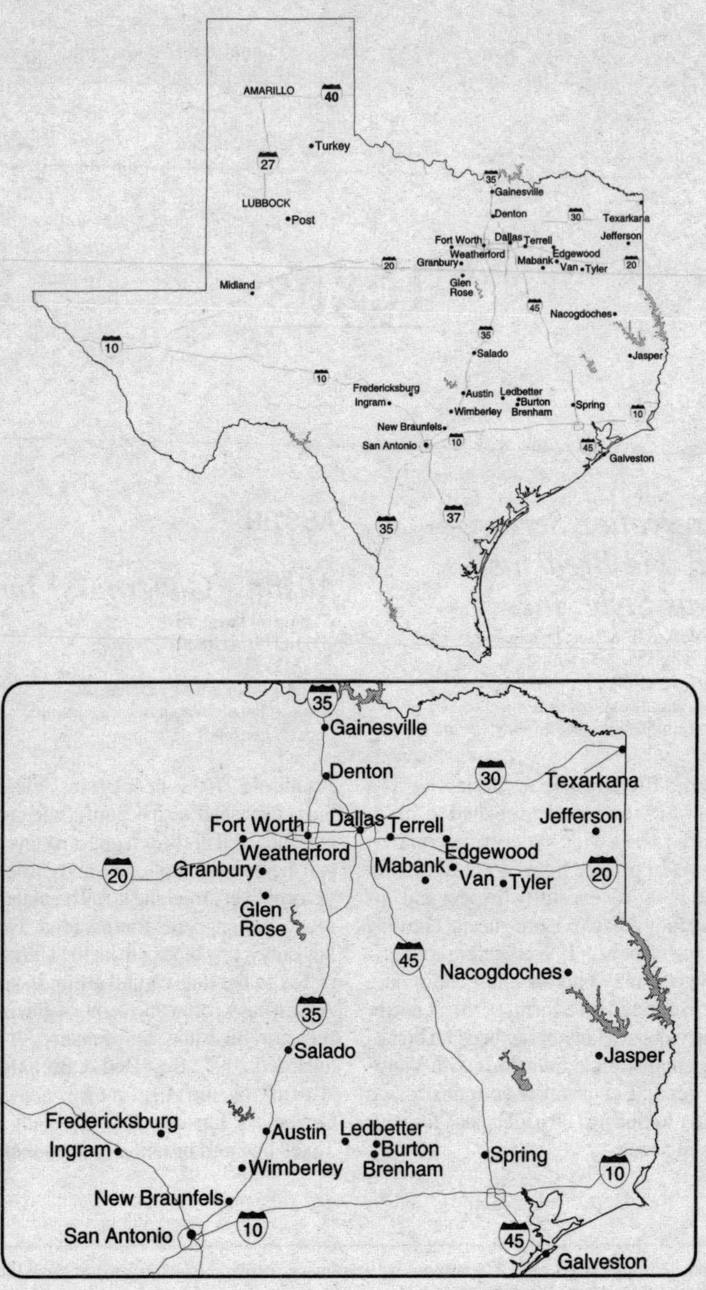

AMARILLO
40
Turkey
27
LUBBOCK
Post
35
Gainesville
Denton
30
Texarkana
Jefferson
Fort Worth
Dallas
Terrell
Weatherford
Edgewood
20
Granbury
Mabank
Van
Tyler
Glen Rose
Midland
45
Nacogdoches
10
Salado
Jasper
Fredericksburg
Ingram
Austin
Ledbetter
Burton
Brenham
Wimberley
Spring
New Braunfels
San Antonio
Galveston
37

on the Travel Channel's "Romantic Inns of America."

Hosts: Lisa and Ed Mugford
Rooms: 10 (PB) $59-119
Full Breakfast
Credit Cards: A, B, C, D, E, F
Notes: 2, 5, 6, 7, 8, 9, 10, 12

Austin's Wildflower Inn

1200 W. 22½ Street, 78705
(512) 477-9639; FAX (512) 474-4188
E-mail: kjackson@io.com
Web site: http://www.io.com/~kjackson

Austin's Wildflower Inn, built in the early 1930s, is a lovely Colonial-style, two-story home with a spacious porch. Every room has been restored carefully to create an atmosphere of warmth and comfort. A gourmet breakfast is served each day. We are tucked away in a very quiet neighborhood in the center of Austin. I invite you to come and relax here and enjoy our beautiful grounds and gardens.

Hostess: Kay Jackson
Rooms: 4 (2PB; 2SB) $74-89
Full Breakfast
Credit Cards: A, B, C
Notes: 2, 5, 8, 9, 10

Lake Travis Bed and Breakfast, Inc.

4446 Eck Lane, 78734
(512) 266-3386; FAX (512) 266-9490
E-mail: jdwyer1511@aol.com
Web site: http://www.laketravisbb.com

Lake Travis Bed and Breakfast, a unique waterfront retreat, is a 20-minute scenic drive from downtown Austin. A cliff, crystal water, hills, and expansive view create the setting for your luxurious getaway. The natural beauty of the surroundings is reflected in the hill country home. Each room has a king bed, private bath, and deck with a panoramic view of the lake. "Intimate resort" best describes the amenities: private boat dock, pool, hot tub, fitness center, massage and spa services, and sailing/boat charters. Inside is a stone fireplace, game room, pool table, and library/theater. Nearby are boat and jet ski rentals, golf, tennis, horseback riding, bicycling, hiking, a steam train, and wineries to tour.

Hosts: Judy and Vic Dwyer
Rooms: 4 (PB) $145-225
Full Breakfast
Credit Cards: A, B, C
Notes: 2, 5, 9, 10, 12

BRENHAM

Capt. Clay Home Bed and Breakfast

9445 FM 390 E., 77833
(409) 836-1916 (voice and FAX)

Come experience a quiet, tranquil stay at the Capt. Clay Home. Witness the breathtaking countryside view for miles. Watch colts frolic in the pasture, or take a stroll along the rippling, spring-fed creek. For your evening comfort, choose between a room with a king four-poster bed or two four-poster double beds. Each antique bed has been fitted with a comfortable, custom mattress. The original Cistern House with twin beds and private bath also is available—small but cozy. We offer a six-person spa enclosed in a gazebo. In the morning, sit down to a country breakfast with farm-fresh eggs from our own henhouse. Reservations required.

Hostess: Thelma Zwiener
Rooms: 4 (3PB; 3SB) $50-75
Full Breakfast
Credit Cards: none
Notes: 2, 5, 7 (sometimes), 10

CANTON AREA

Heavenly Acres B&B

Route 3, Box 470, **Mabank,** 75147
(903) 887-3016; (800) 283-0341;
FAX (903) 887-6108
E-mail: habb@vzinet.com
Web site: http://www.heavenlyacres.com

Heavenly Acres is a working ranch with three spring-fed fishing lakes, 12 miles southwest of Canton. Each private cabin provides a unique decor with kitchen, TV/VCR, and porches with rockers that overlook the water. Guests can enjoy the video library, billiards, outdoor game field, mountain bikes, fishing and paddleboats, a barnyard petting zoo, and walking paths. Special group packages and a large meeting/dining hall are available for groups and reunions. Group cabins and conference center available. No smoking indoors.

Hosts: Vickie J. and Marshall E. Ragle
Rooms: 6 cabins (PB) $95 (ask about group rates)
Full Breakfast
Credit Cards: A, B, C, D
Notes: 2, 3, 4, 5, 8, 9, 10, 12

Texas Star B&B

Route 1, Box 187-1, **Edgewood,** 75117
(903) 896-4277
E-mail: ohohm@aol.com

The east Texas countryside dotted heavily with large oak and cedar trees hosts our guest house. Four bedrooms with private baths/private patios and two additional rooms with a shared bath are in the main house. Each room reflects a different phase of Texas history and/or culture. Enjoy an exhilarating game of volleyball, horseshoes, or croquet, or relax on the porch. Homemade bread and jams are featured in our family-style country breakfast. A few miles from the world-famous Trade Days (flea market) of Canton.

Hosts: David and Marie Stoltzfus
Rooms: 6 (4PB; 2SB) $65-85
Full or Continental Breakfast
Credit Cards: A, B, C, D
Notes: 4, 5, 7, 10, 12

Tumble on Inn

PO Box 1249, **Van,** 75790
(903) 963-7669; (888) 707-3992;
FAX (903) 963-5413
E-mail: tumbloninn@aol.com
Web site: http://members.aol.com/tumbloninn

Casual country comfort, surrounded by pastures and pines. Deck and balcony overlooking hot tub and open fields. Perfect for stargazing or relaxing under the stars. Private, quiet, serene. Full breakfast. Various discounts. Five minutes from Canton First Monday Grounds.

Hosts: Gordon and Jean Jensen
Rooms: 5 (SB) $75
Full Breakfast
Credit Cards: A, B
Notes: 2, 3, 4, 5, 7 (over 12), 10, 12

DALLAS/FORT WORTH AREA

St. Botolph Inn

808 S. Lamar Street, **Weatherford,** 76086
(817) 594-1455 (voice and FAX); (800) 868-6520

A beautifully restored 1897 Queen Anne–style Victorian mansion set on a 5–acre hilltop in a historic residential area. Five guest rooms and a carriage house suite all have baths; some have whirlpool tubs and spas/hot tubs. Afternoon tea is served on the veranda; a full gourmet breakfast is served in your room, the formal dining room, on the veranda, or around the pool. Weatherford was established in 1856 and is part of the Dallas/Fort Worth metroplex.

Hosts: Dan and Shay Buttolph
Rooms: 6 (PB) $80-150
Full Breakfast
Credit Cards: A, B
Notes: 2, 5, 7, 9 (pool), 10, 12

The Redbud Inn Bed and Breakfast

DENTON

The Redbud Inn Bed and Breakfast

815 N. Locust Street, 76201
(940) 565-6414; (888) 565-6414;
FAX (940) 565-6515
E-mail: redbudbb@gte.net
Web site: http://www.bbhost.com/redbudbb

The Redbud Inn has become home away from home for many business travelers. We welcome you to make our three rooms and four suites your second home. Historic Denton is within walking distance, as are the storytelling and jazz festivals each spring.

Hosts: John and Donna Morris
Rooms: 7 (PB) $56-125
Full Breakfast
Credit Cards: A, B, C, D
Notes: 2, 4, 5, 7, 9, 10, 12

FORT WORTH

The Texas White House Bed and Breakfast

1417 Eighth Avenue, 76104
(817) 923-3597; (800) 279-6491;
FAX (817) 923-0410
E-mail: txwhitehou@aol.com

This historically designated, award winning, country-style home has been restored to its original 1910 grandeur of simple, yet elegant decor. It is centrally located within 5 minutes of downtown, the medical center, the Forth Worth Zoo, cultural district, Botanical Gardens, Water Gardens, and TCU. The guest rooms are furnished with luxurious queen beds with your choice of pillows, relaxing sitting areas, and private baths with claw-foot tubs for showers or soaking in bubble baths by candlelight. Guests have complete privacy; however, if desired, they may enjoy the parlor, living room with fireplace, dining room, and wraparound porch. Breakfast, described by one guest as, "fit for visiting royalty," will be a gourmet treat with fresh fruit or baked fruit in compote (seasonal), baked egg casseroles, homemade breads and muffins, juices, coffee, and tea served on antique china with sterling silver and crystal. Phone, TV, early-morning coffee on request, afternoon snacks and beverages, secretarial services, laundry service for extended stays, and offstreet parking.

Hosts: Jamie and Grover McMains
Rooms: 3 (PB) $85-105
Full Breakfast
Credit Cards: A, B, C, D
Notes: 2, 5, 9, 10, 12

FREDERICKSBURG

Hill Country Guesthouse

407 W. Austin Street, 78624
(210) 997-2689 or (210) 997-5612 (reservations);
FAX (830) 997-8282
E-mail: gasthaus@ktc.com

This 1921 bungalow-style family home in the historic district was refurbished by one of the eleven children and her husband, maintaining the charm of yesterday while adding the comforts of today. Original furnishings and family heirlooms convey German traditions. Country gardens, limestone walks, old-fashioned swept yard, and 10-foot picnic table under the old pecan tree create the perfect ambience for relaxation. Neighborhood Sunday morning church bells welcome all visitors.

Hosts: Peter and Corinne Danysh
Rooms: 2 (PB) $75-95
Full Breakfast
Credit Cards: A, B, C, D
Notes: 2, 5, 8, 9, 10, 12

Hill Country Guesthouse

Magnolia House Bed and Breakfast

101 E. Hackberry Street, 78624
(830) 997-0306; (800) 880-4374;
FAX (830) 997-0766
E-mail: magnolia@hctc.net
Web site: http://www.magnolia-house.com

Built circa 1923, restored in 1991. Enjoy southern hospitality in a grand and gracious manner. Outside are lovely magnolias and a bubbling fishpond. Inside, a beautiful living room and formal dining room provide areas for guests to mingle. There are two romantic suites with fireplaces and three rooms—all appointed with your comfort in mind. You'll find a relaxing patio and porches. The beautiful, bountiful breakfast makes this a truly memorable experience.

Hosts: Joyce and Patrick Kennard
Rooms: 5 (5PB) $85-125
Full Breakfast
Credit Cards: A, B, C, D
Notes: 2, 5, 8, 9, 10

Schildknecht-Weidenfeller House Bed and Breakfast

Gästehaus Schmidt Reservation Service: 231 W. Main, 78624
(830) 997-5612; FAX (830) 997-8282
E-mail: gasthaus@ktc.com
Web site: http://www.speakez.net/schildknecht

Relive history in this house in the heart of Fredericksburg's historic district. Decorated with antiques and handmade quilts, this guest house accommodates up to ten people. A German-style breakfast is left for you to enjoy at your leisure around the antique farm table in the kitchen. The 1870s German limestone house has been featured on tours of historic homes and in

Schildknecht-Weidenfeller House B&B

Country Decorating Ideas. Member of Historic Accommodations of Texas.

Hosts: Ellis and Carter Schildknecht
Rooms: entire house (8 rooms + 2 baths) $125 and up, according to party size
Expanded Continental (German-Style) Breakfast
Credit Cards: A, B, D
Notes: 2, 5, 7 (12 and older), 8, 9, 10, 12

Way of the Wolf B&B/Retreats

HC 12, Box 92H, 78624
(830) 997-0711; (888) 929-9653
E-mail: wawolf@ktc.com
Web site: http://www.wayofthewolf.com

This B&B retreat on 61 acres in the hill country offers a pool, space for picnics and hikes, wildlife, and scenic views. The four bedrooms and common living area with fireplace are furnished with antiques. A reconstructed Civil War–era cabin is also available. This destination B&B is peaceful and secluded, but only 15 minutes from shopping, golf, and churches in Kerrville or Fredericksburg. Assistance in preparing personal or group retreats is available.

Hosts: Ron and Karen Poidevin
Rooms: 5 (3PB; 2SB) $75-125
Full Breakfast
Credit Cards: none
Notes: 2, 5, 9 (onsite), 10, 12

The Yellow House

231 W. Main, 78624
(830) 997-5612; FAX (830) 997-8282

The Yellow House is an original Sunday House built at the turn of the century. It is known as the "little yellow house under the big oak tree." Featured in the June 1994 *Country Living Magazine,* this home has three rooms. The front porch leads you to the bedroom/sitting room with a four-poster queen-size bed situated high off the floor with a fluffy comforter. There is also a fully equipped kitchen and bath with shower.

Hosts: Dan and Donna Mittel
Rooms: 1 (PB) $85
Continental Breakfast
Credit Cards: A, B, D

GAINESVILLE (WHITESBORO)

Alexander Bed and Breakfast Acres Inc.

Route 7, Box 788, 76240
(903) 564-7440 (voice and FAX; call before FAXing); (800) 887-8794
E-mail: abba@texoma.net
Web site: http://www.bbhost.com/alexanderbbacres

A three-story Queen Anne home and guest house nestled peacefully on 65 acres of woods and meadows just south of Whitesboro between Lakes Texoma and Ray Roberts. Both houses are available for small retreats. The main house offers a wraparound porch for relaxing, a parlor, and full breakfast in the dining room; five guest bedrooms with private baths plus a third-floor sitting area with television/VCR.

The two-story guest house has three bedrooms sharing one bath, and full kitchen facilities—perfect accommodations for families with children.

Hosts: Pamela and Jimmy Alexander
Rooms: 5 + cottage (5PB; 3SB) $60-125
Full Breakfast (at main house)
Credit Cards: A, B, D
Notes: 2, 4, 5, 7 (at guest house), 9, 10, 11 (water), 12

The Victorian Inn Bed and Breakfast

GALVESTON

The Victorian Inn Bed and Breakfast

511 17th Street, 77550
(409) 762-3235; FAX (409) 762-6351

Elegantly decorated in turn-of-the-century antiques. Relax on the veranda, nap in the hammock, picnic in the rose garden. Suites all have private baths; kings share a central bath. Breakfast buffet, 8–10 AM. Unique and exceptional charm. Two-night minimum on weekends.

Hostess: Marcy Hanson
Rooms: 6 (3PB; 3SB) $100-125
Breakfast Buffet
Credit Cards: A, B, C
Notes: 5, 8, 9, 10

GLEN ROSE

"A Touch of Germany" Popejoy Haus

PO Box 2023, 76043
(800) 897-3521

If you are looking for a quiet place to relax, you've reached the end of your search. Unwind and enjoy 18 secluded acres with one cottage and two cabins. Amenities include king bed, private hot tub, fireplace, kitchenette, and homemade German pastries. Just 3 miles from downtown Glen Rose. *Wir sprechen Deutsch!*

Hosts: Kody and Klare Popejoy
Rooms: 4 (PB) $75-95
Full or Continental Breakfast
Credit Cards: A, B
Notes: none

Bussey's Something Special Bed &B

202 Hereford Street; PO Box 1425, 76043
(254) 897-4843; (800) 700-4843, 13

The cozy Victorian cottage has a king bed, jet tub/shower, and kitchenette. The country arts and crafts cottage has king and full beds, full kitchen, living room, and bath with shower. Nestled in the heart of Glen Rose. Relax in the porch swing; leisurely stroll to the historic town square for shopping and lunch. Historic buildings and museums are close by. Walk to the river or explore the countryside to experience the heart of Texas! Free fossil hunts for guests! Note: Hosts not on the premises.

Hosts: Susan and Morris Bussey
Rooms: 2 (PB) $80-100
Continental Breakfast
Credit Cards: A, B, C
Notes: 2, 5, 7, 8, 9, 10

The Captain's House on the Lake

GRANBURY

The Captain's House on the Lake—Historic Bed and Breakfast

123 W. Doyle, 76048
(817) 579-6664; FAX (817) 579-0213
E-mail: captain@itexas.net
Web site: http://www.hat.org

Just a few blocks from the historic square, this pristine, elegant Queen Anne Victorian property offers guests the "best of the past to enjoy in the present...the place where excellent service is a way of life." Guests are offered desserts and drinks upon arrival and are served hot breakfast trays to their suites in the morning. Each guest also selects a brunch or lunch each day at the historic bakery on the square. The B&B is an approved member of the Historic Accommodations of Texas.

Hosts: Bob and Julia Pannell
Rooms: 5 (3 main house; 2 in offsite cottage) (PB) $88-135
Continental Gourmet Breakfast
Credit Cards: none
Notes: 2, 3 (provided), 5, 7 (at cottage), 8, 9, 10, 11 (water), 12 (commission paid during week)

Dabney House B&B

106 S. Jones, 76048
(817) 579-1260; (800) 566-1260
E-mail: dabney@safeweb.net

Craftsman-style, one-story home built in 1907 by a local banker and furnished with antiques. It features hardwood floors and original woodwork. Long-term business rates available per request; romance dinner by reservation only. We offer custom, special-occasion baskets in the room on arrival, by advance order only. Book the whole house for family occasions, staff retreats, or Bible retreats at discount rates. Hot tub available for all registered guests.

Hosts: John and Gwen Hurley
Rooms: 4 (PB) $60-105
Full Breakfast
Credit Cards: A, B, C
Notes: 2, 5, 8, 9, 10, 12

INGRAM

Lazy Hills Guest Ranch

PO Box G, 78025
(830) 367-5600; (800) 880-0632;
FAX (830) 367-5667
E-mail: lhills@ktc.com
Web site: http://www.lazyhills.com

Guest rooms are furnished with comfortable twin or queen beds and will sleep from four to six people comfortably. Rooms have electric heat, air conditioning, bathrooms with showers, and pleasant porches. Some of the rooms have wood-burning fireplaces. American Plan—rates are per person, per night, and are based on same occupancy. Rates are subject to change without notice (not after confirmation). Rates include lodging, three meals daily, and the use of all ranch facilities (not including horseback riding). Weekly rates include six horseback rides per person. Rates do not include tax and gratuities.

Hosts: Bob and Carol Steinruck
Rooms: 25 (PB) $75-95
Full Breakfast
Credit Cards: A, B, C, D
Notes: 5, 7, 8, 9, 10, 12

JASPER

The Swann Hotel

250 N. Main Street, 75951
(409) 384-2341; (888) 776-SWAN (7926);
FAX (409) 384-3287
E-mail: swan@jas.net

Enjoy the fine southern hospitality offered by this jewel of Jasper. Known throughout Texas for comfortable rooms and tasty meals, this elegantly restored Victorian classic awaits the beautiful pineywoods traveler. Built in 1901 and established in 1915, this elegant bed and breakfast offers seven charming rooms tastefully decorated with beautiful period furnishings.

Hosts: Dave and Katrina Henegar
Rooms: 7 (5PB; 2SB) $55-95
Full Breakfast
Credit Cards: A, B, C
Notes: 2, 5, 7, 8, 9, 10

JEFFERSON

1st Bed and Breakfast in Texas—Pride House

409 Broadway, 75657
(903) 665-2675; (800) 894-3526;
FAX (903) 665-3901
E-mail: jefftx@mind.net
Web site: http://www.jeffersontexas.com

Breathtaking Victorian mansion in a historic steamboat port—Texas' favorite small town, where a weekend is never enough. Luscious interiors, luxurious accommodations, legendary breakfasts. Sink into footed tubs with bubbles and bath pillows, and big beds with triple sheets and fireplaces. Wake up to sunlight streaming through stained glass and our own Jefferson Pecan Coffee. Three hours east of Dallas. A captivating, continuously updated Web site has the latest events, attractions, discounts. Guests enjoy the home tours, antique shops, live theater, and paddlewheel steamboat.

Hosts: Carol Abernathy and Christel Frederick
Rooms: 10 (PB) $42.50-135
Full Breakfast
Credit Cards: A, B, C, D
Notes: 2, 5, 7, 10, 12

McKay House Bed and Breakfast Inn

306 E. Delta Street, 75657
(903) 665-7322; (800) 468-2627;
FAX (903) 665-8551
E-mail: mckaybb@aol.com
Web site: http://www.bbonline.com/tx/mckayhouse

Jefferson is a town where one can relax rather than get tired. The McKay House, an 1851 Greek Revival cottage, features a pillared front porch and many fireplaces. It offers genuine hospitality in a Christian atmosphere. Heart-of-pine floors, 14-foot ceilings, and documented wallpapers complement antique furnishings. Enjoy a full "gentleman's" breakfast each morning. Victorian nightshirts and gowns await pampered guests in each bedchamber.

Hosts: Lisa and Roger Cantrell
Rooms: 7 (PB) $89-165 (corporate rates available)
Full Breakfast
Credit Cards: A, B, C
Notes: 2, 5, 10, 12

LEDBETTER

Ledbetter Bed and Breakfast

PO Box 212, 78946
(409) 249-3066; (800) 240-3066;
FAX (409) 249-3330
E-mail: jjervis@fais.net
Web site: http://www.ledbetter-tx.com

Ledbetter B&B, established in 1988, is a collection of multigeneration, family, 1800–1900s homes within walking distance of the remaining 1870s downtown businesses. A full country breakfast buffet can serve up to seventy guests daily. Walks, hayrides, fishing, horse-and-buggy rides, games, Christmas lights, chuck wagon, romantic dinners, indoor heated swimming pool, VCR, TV. A phone can be made available on advance request. Each unit accommodates approximately four people. Only nonalcoholic beverages are allowed outside private quarters. Only outdoor smoking is allowed.

Hosts: Chris and Jay Jervis
Rooms: 20 (PB) $55-150
Full or Continental Breakfast
Credit Cards: A, B, C
Notes: 2, 3, 4, 5, 7, 8, 9, 10, 11 (water), 12

MIDLAND

Top o' the Mark

112 Loraine South, In the Penthouse, 79701
(915) 682-4560; FAX (915) 570-7250

From our stunning sunrises and famous sunsets obscured by the towering buildings of downtown Midland to heavenly stargazing, Top o' the Mark is a beautiful streamline New York–style penthouse overlooking Midland from three directions. You will be immersed in deep navy blue, mystical red, and ether gray as Midland's big sky floods your moods with sunlight or starlight. For a romantic weekend, business trip, celebration, or sales meeting, Top o' the Mark will help ensure success.

Hosts: Mark Kimball, Mrs. Kennie Clabaugh
Rooms: 4 (SB) $71-105
Continental Breakfast
Credit Cards: A, B
Notes: 2, 5

NACOGDOCHES

Anderson Point B&B

29 E. Lake Estates, 75964
(409) 569-7445
Web site: http://www.virtualcities.com

You won't want to leave this lovely, two-story, French-style home surrounded by 300 feet of lake frontage. Enjoy sweeping views of the water from every room and a double veranda for dining and dozing. You can stroll around the beautiful grounds or go fishing off the pier. Don't miss the glorious sunsets as you gather in the fireplace sitting room for coffee and conversation. A breakfast pantry is available every morning. The home and grounds are unique in that no toxic chemicals or fragrances are used. The most severe allergy sufferers will be safe in this pristine environment.

Hostess: Rachel Anderson
Rooms: 2 (SB) $58-68
Continental Plus Breakfast
Credit Cards: A, B
Notes: 2, 5, 6, 7, 9

PineCreek Lodge

Route 3, Box 1238, 75964
(409) 560-6282; (888) 714-1414;
FAX (409) 560-1675
E-mail: pitts@lcc.net
Web site: http://www.pinecreeklodge.com

On a beautiful, tree-covered hill overlooking a spring-fed creek sits PineCreek Lodge. Built on a 140-acre property with lots of lawns, rose gardens, and a multitude of flowers deep in the east Texas woods, yet only 10 miles from historic Nacogdoches. Our rustic lodge features king-size beds in tastefully decorated rooms with phone, TV/VCR, lots of decks, swimming pool, spa, fishing, biking, and much more. We have become the destination for many city dwellers.

Hosts: The Pitts Family
Rooms: 9 + cottage (PB) $55-95
Full Breakfast
Credit Cards: A, B, C, D
Notes: 2, 3, 4, 5, 7, 9, 10

NEW BRAUNFELS

Aunt Nora's Countryside Inn

120 Naked Indian Trail, 78132–1865
(830) 905-3989; (800) 687-2887
Web site: http://www.texasbedandbreakfast.com/auntnoras.htm

Our private cottage suites are cozy, with country Victorian decor, including handbuilt furnishings, antiques, and old bridal heirlooms—a truly romantic getaway with hill country elegance. The buildings are reminiscent of early Texas, overlooking picturesque hillsides along with a wedding gazebo and arched bridge atop two goldfish ponds with waterfalls. Located just minutes away from New Braunfels, Gruene, the Guadalupe River, and Canyon Lake. Private baths, kitchens, decks, patio hot tub.

Hosts: Alton and Iralee Haley
Rooms: 4 cottages (PB) $85-125
Full Breakfast
Credit Cards: A, B
Notes: 2, 5, 7, 8, 9, 10, 12

Hotel Garza

POST

Hotel Garza Historic Inn and Conference Center

302 E. Main Street, 79356
(806) 495-3962

When you check into Hotel Garza, you'll experience the ambience of a 1915 western inn. More than 80 years later, with modern conveniences, this fine establishment offers overnight accommodations, wonderful home cooking, and Texas hospitality. Post

NOTES: Credit cards accepted: A Master Card; B Visa; C American Express; D Discover; E Diners Club; F Other; 2 Personal checks accepted; 3 Lunch available; 4 Dinner available; 5 Open all year; 6 Pets

is a Texas Main Street City founded by cereal king C.W. Post. Within walking distance of Hotel Garza you'll find theaters, museums, fine gift shops, boutiques, and Old Mill Trade Days. A new guest cottage now is available.

Hosts: Janice and Jim Plummer
Rooms: 12 + cottage (9PB; 4SB) $40-105
Full Breakfast, weekends; Continental, weekdays
Credit Cards: A, B, C
Notes: 2, 4, 5, 7, 8, 9, 10, 12

SALADO

The Inn at Salado

7 N. Main Street, 76571
(254) 947-0027; (800) 724-0027;
FAX (254) 947-3144
E-mail: innstay@stonemedia.com
Web site: www.inn-at-salado.com

Salado's first bed and breakfast is located in the heart of the historic district. Renovated to its original 1872 splendor, the inn displays both a Texas historical marker and a National Register listing. The inn's ambience is enhanced by its antique furniture, porch swings, and live oak trees, all on 2 beautifully landscaped acres. A wedding chapel, meeting rooms, and catering complete the amenities offered by the inn.

Hosts: Rob and Suzanne Petro
Rooms: 9 (PB) $70-110
Full Breakfast
Credit Cards: A, B, C, D
Notes: 2, 5, 9, 10

The Rose Mansion

PO Box 613, 76571
(254) 947-8200; (800) 948-1004
Web site: http://www.touringtexas.com/rose

Nestled among towering oaks, the traditional Greek Revival–style mansion and

The Rose Mansion

complementary cottage and 1850s log cabins offer a return to yesterday, with class. Four acres of beautiful grounds, memorabilia, antiques, shaded seating, swings, and games are complemented by a gourmet breakfast, queen beds, private baths, fireplace, and central heat and air. Elegance in a cozy atmosphere.

Hosts: Neil and Carole Hunter
Rooms: 10 (PB) $90-120
Full Breakfast
Credit Cards: A, B, C, D
Notes: 2, 5, 10

SAN ANTONIO

Adams House B&B

231 Adams Street, 78210
(210) 224-4791; (800) 666-4810;
FAX (210) 223-5125
E-mail: innkeeper@san-antonio-texas.com
Web site: http://www.san-antonio-texas.com

Enjoy gracious southern hospitality at the Adams House B&B, located in the King William historic district of downtown San Antonio. The River Walk, the Alamo Mission, and River Center Shopping are within easy walking distance. The two-story home has been lovingly restored to its original 1902 splendor. Full-width verandas grace both floors, front and back. All rooms are furnished with period antiques, Oriental rugs, and handmade reproductions. AAA, Mobil Travel Guide ratings.

Hosts: Nora Peterson and Richard Green
Rooms: 4 (PB) $89-119
Full Breakfast
Credit Cards: A, B, C, D
Notes: 2, 12

Beckmann Inn and Carriage House

222 E. Guenther Street, 78204
(210) 229-1449; (800) 945-1449;
FAX (210) 229-1061
Web site: http://www.beckmanninn.com

A wonderful Victorian house (1886) located in the King William historic district, across the street from the start of the Riverwalk. Beautifully landscaped, it will take you on a leisurely stroll to the Alamo, downtown shops, and restaurants. You also can take the trolley, which stops at the corner, and within minutes you're there in style. The beautiful wraparound porch welcomes you to the main house and warm, gracious, Victorian hospitality. The large guest rooms feature antique, ornately carved, Victorian queen beds; private baths; and ceiling fans. TVs, phones, refrigerators, desks, and robes. Gourmet breakfast, with breakfast dessert, is served in the dining room with china, crystal, and silver. Warm, gracious hospitality at its best. AAA-, IIA-, and Mobil-rated, excellent.

Hosts: Betty Jo and Don Schwartz
Rooms: 5 (PB) $99-140
Full Breakfast
Credit Cards: A, B, C, D, E
Notes: 2, 5, 7 (over 12), 10, 12

Brackenridge House

230 Madison Street, 78204
(210) 271-3442; (800) 221-1412;
FAX (210) 226-3139
E-mail: benniesueb@aol.com
Web site: http://www.brackenridgehouse.com

Native Texan owners and innkeepers will guide you through your visit from their beautiful Greek Revival home in historic King William. Gourmet breakfast served in formal dining room or veranda. Hot tub, private baths, and country Victorian decor add to your comfort and pleasure. Walk to the Riverwalk and trolley to Market Square. Pets and children are welcome in the carriage house.

Hosts: Bennie and Sue Blansett
Rooms: 6 (PB) $89-125
Full and Continental Breakfast
Credit Cards: A, B, C, D, E
Notes: 2, 5, 6 and 7 (in carriage house), 8, 9, 10, 12

The Ogé House Inn on the Riverwalk

209 Washington Street, 78204
(210) 223-2353; (800) 242-2770;
FAX (210) 226-5812
E-mail: ogeinn@swbell.net
Web site: http://www.ogeinn.com

This elegant, historic antebellum mansion is privately located on 1½ landscaped acres along the famous Riverwalk. The inn is decorated in European antiques. A gourmet breakfast is served on Wedgewood china with silver and crystal. For business or pleasure, come enjoy quiet comfort and luxury. Mobil IIA-rated.

Hosts: Sharrie and Patrick Magatagan
Rooms: 10 (PB) $145-225
Full Breakfast
Credit Cards: A, B, C, D, E
Notes: 2, 5, 8, 10

NOTES: Credit cards accepted: A Master Card; B Visa; C American Express; D Discover; E Diners Club; F Other; 2 Personal checks accepted; 3 Lunch available; 4 Dinner available; 5 Open all year; 6 Pets

Riverwalk Inn

329 Old Guilbeau, 78204
(210) 212-8300; (800) 254-4440;
FAX (210) 229-9422

The Riverwalk Inn is comprised of five two-story homes, circa 1840, which have been restored on the downtown San Antonio Riverwalk. Period antiques create an ambience of "country elegance." Rock on our 80-foot porch. Enjoy Aunt Martha's evening desserts and local storytellers who join us for breakfast. Fireplaces, refrigerators, private baths, phones, balconies, TV, and conference room. A Texas tradition with a Tennessee flavor awaits you. Call for brochure.

Hosts: Johnny Halpenny and Tammy Hill
Rooms: 11 (PB) $110-155
Full Breakfast
Credit Cards: A, B, C, D
Notes: 2, 5, 12

A Victorian Lady Inn

421 Howard Street, 78212
(210) 224-2524; (800) 879-7116;
FAX (210) 224-5123
E-mail: vli@swbell.net
Web site: http://www.viclady.com

This 1898 mansion features grand guest rooms with period antiques. Your pampered retreat includes a private bath, fireplace, veranda, television, and phone. Fabulous breakfasts are served in the majestic dining room. Relax in our hot tub surrounded by tropical palms and banana trees. Walk or trolley to the Riverwalk, Alamo, or Convention Center. AAA rating, three diamonds.

A Victorian Lady Inn

Hosts: Kate and Joe Bowski
Rooms: 8 (PB) $69-139
Full Breakfast
Credit Cards: B
Notes: 5, 8, 9, 10, 12

SPRING

McLachlan Farm Bed and Breakfast

PO Box 538, 77383
(281) 350-2400; (800) 382-3988;
FAX (281) 288-1011

The 1911 McLachlan family homestead was restored and enlarged in 1989 by the great-granddaughter, and her husband, of the original McLachlan family who settled the land in 1862. Set back among 35 acres of towering sycamore and pecan trees, neatly mowed grounds, and winding forest trails. It is a quiet oasis that returns guests to a time when life was simpler. Visitors may swing on the porches, walk in the woods, or visit Old Town Spring (1 mile south) where there are more than 100 shops to enjoy.

Hosts: Jim and Joycelyn Clairmonte
Rooms: 3-4 (3PB or 2SB) $75-85
Full Country Breakfast
Credit Cards: A, B, C, D
Notes: 2, 5, 10, 12

TERRELL

The Bluebonnet Inn

310 W. College Street, 75160
(972) 524-2534; (888) 258-4124;
FAX (972) 524-2534, Ext.124
E-mail: bjobe@flash.net
Web site: http://www.virtualcities.com

Built before the turn of the century, this Victorian home was part of Terrell's grand old days. Relax in our large rooms, all with private baths. Enjoy this house full of antiques with its two parlors, sunroom dining, country kitchen, and service area where you can help yourself to snacks and fountain sodas. A full breakfast is served each morning at 9—or choose a private continental breakfast at your leisure.

Hosts: Bryan and Jan Jobe
Rooms: 4 (PB) $75-105
Full Breakfast
Credit Cards: A, B, C, D
Notes: 2, 4, 5, 8, 9, 10, 11 (water)

TEXARKANA

Mansion on Main Bed and Breakfast Inn

802 Main Street, 75501
(903) 792-1835; FAX (903) 793-0878
E-mail: mansionbnb@aol.com
Web site: http://www.bestinns.net/usa/tx/mansion.html

"Twice as Nice," the motto of Texarkana (Texas and Arkansas), is standard practice at Mansion on Main. The 1895 neoclassical Colonial mansion, surrounded by fourteen tall columns, recently was restored by the owners of McKay House, the popular bed and breakfast in nearby Jefferson. Six bedchambers vary from the

Mansion on Main Bed and Breakfast Inn

Governor's Suite to the Butler's Garret. Guests enjoy southern hospitality, period furnishings, fireplaces, and a gentleman's breakfast. Thirty miles away is the town of Hope, birthplace of President Clinton.

Hosts: Lee and Inez Hayden
Rooms: 6 (PB) $60-109
Full Breakfast
Credit Cards: A, B, C
Notes: 2, 5, 10, 12

TURKEY

Hotel Turkey

3rd and Alexander; PO Box 37, 79261
(806) 423-1151; (800) 657-7110
E-mail: suziej@caprock-spur.com
Web site: http://www.llano.net/turkey/hotel

This 1927 hotel is like a step back in time—period furnishings, vintage clothing, and local memorabilia. Enjoy a "peace" of the past, 15 miles from the beautiful Caprock Canyons State Park. The Bob Wills Museum is located here. We are listed on the state and national historic registers. Smoke-free environment.

Hosts: Gary and Suzie Johnson
Rooms: 15 (7PB; 8SB) $69-89
Full Breakfast
Credit Cards: A, B, C
Notes: 2, 5, 7, 8, 10, 12

Rosevine Inn

TYLER

Rosevine Inn

415 S. Vine, 75702
(903) 592-2221; FAX (903) 593-9500
E-mail: rosevine@iamerica.net

Rosevine Inn is a quaint two-story home complete with a white picket fence, located in the Brick Street District of Tyler. The inn offers many amenities, including a covered hot tub outdoors and a courtyard with both a fountain and a fireplace. In the lodge-style game room, you may enjoy billiards, lots of board-type games, cards, darts, horseshoes, and washers, as well as volleyball and badminton. Outdoor fires are a common nightly occurrence. A full, formal breakfast includes omelets or quiches, coffee cakes, muffins, fresh fruit, coffee, teas—more than you can eat! The hosts can direct you to great restaurants, antique shops, museums, lakes, the zoo, the rose garden, and other sites throughout Tyler and the surrounding area.

Hosts: Bert and Rebecca Powell
Rooms: 5 (PB) $65-95
Full Breakfast
Credit Cards: A, B, C, D, E
Notes: 2, 3 (picnic), 5, 7, 8, 9, 10, 12

WIMBERLEY

Rancho Cama B&B

2595 Flite Acres Road, 78676–5706
(512) 847-2596; (800) 594-4501;
FAX (512) 847-7135
E-mail: ranchocama@aol.com
Web site: http://members.aol.com/ranchocama

Rancho Cama Bed and Breakfast offers country comfort, scenic beauty, and adorable animals—miniature horses and donkeys, Nigerian dwarf goats—on a 50-acre hill country ranch with individual guest house and two-bedroom bunkhouse nestled beneath spreading live oaks. Enjoy privacy, home-cooked breakfasts, a beautiful pool, a hot tub, and swings or rockers on every porch. The quaint village of Wimberley has antiques, crafts, galleries, and outstanding restaurants.

Hosts: Curtis and Nell Cadenhead
Rooms: 3 (1PB; 2SB) $70-85
Full Breakfast
Credit Cards: none
Notes: 2, 5, 8, 9, 10

UTAH

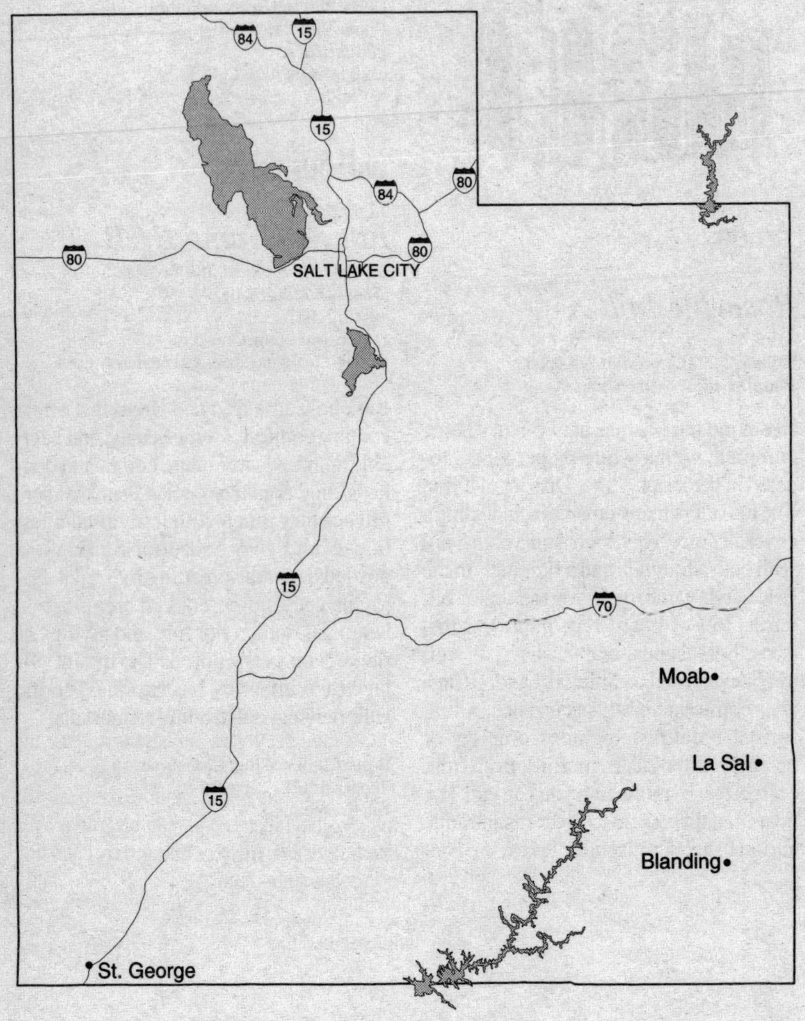

84
15
15
84
80
80
80
SALT LAKE CITY
15
70
Moab
La Sal
15
Blanding
St. George

Utah

Advance Reservations Inn Arizona/Mi Casa Su Casa/Old Pueblo Homestays B&B RSO

PO Box 950, **Tempe, AZ,** 85280–0950
(602) 990-0682; (800) 456-0682 (reservations);
FAX (602) 990-3390
E-mail: micasa@primenet.com
Web site: http://www.micasa.com

Since 1981, we have listed inspected, clean, comfortable homestays, inns, cottages, and ranches in Arizona and the Southwest. We list about 200 modest-to-luxurious, historic-to-contemporary B&Bs. In **Utah,** we list Alton, Cedar City, Moab, Monroe, Monticello, St. George, Salt Lake City, Springdale, Torrey, and Tropic. (See also our entries in Arizona, Nevada, and New Mexico.) We also represent two luxury villas, one in Puerto Vallarto, **Mexico,** and the second in the Costa Brava area of **Spain.** Most rooms have private baths and range from $50 to $275, based on double occupancy. Continental to gourmet breakfasts. A book with individual descriptions and pictures of the different venues is available for $9.50. Ruth Young, coordinator.

BLANDING

Grayson Country Inn

118 E. 300 S., 84511
(435) 678-2388; (800) 365-0868
E-mail: lgutke@bes.sanjuan.k12.ut.us

Located a block east of Main Street at 300 South. We offer country hospitality while adding modern conveniences. A private bath and cable TV are available in eight guest rooms. A three-bedroom cottage has three baths, living room, and kitchen for larger groups or a family. We specialize in a home atmosphere! We do not encourage pets.

Hosts: Dennis and Lurlene Gutke
Rooms: 11 (PB) $49-59
Full Breakfast
Credit Cards: A, B, C
Notes: 5, 7, 12

NOTES: Credit cards accepted: A Master Card; B Visa; C American Express; D Discover; E Diners Club; F Other; 2 Personal checks accepted; 3 Lunch available; 4 Dinner available; 5 Open all year; 6 Pets welcome; 7 Children welcome; 8 Tennis nearby; 9 Swimming nearby; 10 Golf nearby; 11 Skiing nearby; 12 May be booked through travel agent.

Home Away From Home
(Arches National Park)

MOAB

Home Away From Home

122 Hillside Drive, 84532
(435) 259-6276

This bed and breakfast is minutes from Arches National Park, Canyonlands Air Field Airport, and Colorado River rafting, jet-skiing, and kayaking. It is within walking distance of markets and shops, mountain biking, and hiking. Horseback riding, water slides, a pool, and golf are a short distance away. Some may enjoy tent camping at the enclosed minipark backyard of the bed and breakfast. Colorado Connection for deer or elk hunting—bow or rifle. Three hours from Telluride. Ski chairlift, winter and summer. TBN dish viewing available in the large living room for guests upon request.

Host: E. M. Smith
Rooms: 4 (2PB; 2SB) $38.75-78.13
Continental Breakfast
Credit Cards: none
Notes: 2, 5, 7, 8, 9, 10, 11, 12

MOUNTAIN GREEN

Hubbard House Bed and Breakfast Inn

5648 W. Old Highway Road, 84050
(801) 876-2020 (voice and FAX)
E-mail: hubbhouse@aol.com
Web site: http://members.aol.com/hubbhouse/hpg.htm

Built in the 1920s, the Hubbard House Bed and Breakfast Inn has the warmth and charm of days gone by, with hardwood floors and stained-glass windows. It has awesome views of God's majestic mountains. Three ski resorts are in the area, as are fishing, boating, hiking, and golfing. Piano in dining room. Outdoor whirlpool spa. Additional rooms planned. Can accommodate horses. About 1 mile east from Exit 92 off I–84.

Hosts: Donald and Gloria Hubbard
Rooms: 4 (2PB; 2SB) $60-100
Full Breakfast
Credit Cards: A, B, C
Notes: 2, 4, 5, 7, 9, 10, 11

OLD LASAL

Mt. Peale Country Inn/Bed and Breakfast & Information Center

1415 E. Highway 46, 84530
(435) 686-2284 (voice and FAX); (888) 687-3253
E-mail: mtpeale@moab-canyonlands.com
Web site: http://www.moab-canyonlands.com/mtpeale

Our inn is located at the base of the La Sal Mountains and offers every traveler a wonderful place to relax and play. The resort provides day tours through the La

Sal Mountain Express to Monument Valley, Canyonlands, Arches National Park, and Mesa Verde, Telluride or Ouray, Colorado. Our country inn is a log home. We currently have three guest rooms, a glassed dining area, a fireplaced comfort room, and an outdoor deck and hot tub. It is the perfect place for contemplation, adventure, and romance.

Hosts: Teague Eskelsen and Lisa Ballantyne
Rooms: 3 (PB) $65-85
Full Breakfast
Credit Cards: A, B
Notes: 2, 3, 4 (restaurant onsite), 5, 7 (call), 9, 10, 11, 12

ST. GEORGE

Greene Gate Village Historic Bed and Breakfast

76 W. Tabernacle Street, 84770
(435) 628-6999; (800) 350-6999;
FAX (435) 628-6989
E-mail: stay@greenegate.com
Web site: http://www.greenegate.com

Greene Gate Village consists of nine restored pioneer homes operated collectively as an inn. The homes sit side by side on one city block, surrounded by wide lawns, flower gardens, swimming pool, hot tub. Each room is furnished with antiques in mint condition, fireplaces, cable TV, VCR, in-room telephones. Many have large whirlpool tubs, king beds, kitchens. We cater to family reunions and corporate retreats, with large meeting rooms.

Host: John Greene
Rooms: 19 (PB) $55-125
Breakfast Not Included
Credit Cards: A, B, C, D, E
Notes: 2, 3, 4, 5, 6, 7, 8, 9, 10, 11, 12

Seven Wives Inn

217 N. 100 W., 84770
(435) 628-3737; (800) 600-3737;
FAX (435) 673-0165
E-mail: seven@infowest.com

The inn consists of two adjacent pioneer adobe homes with massive hand-grained moldings that frame windows and doors. Bedrooms are furnished with period antiques and handmade quilts. Some rooms have fireplaces; three have whirlpool tubs. Swimming pool on the premises.

Hosts: Jay and Donna Curtis, Bob and Claudia Tribe
Rooms: 13 (PB) $55-125
Full Breakfast
Credit Cards: A, B, C, D, E
Notes: 2, 3, 5, 7, 8, 9, 10, 12

Anton Boxrud Bed and Breakfast

SALT LAKE CITY

Anton Boxrud B&B

57 S. 600 E., 84102
(801) 363-8035; (800) 524-5511;
FAX (801) 596-1316
E-mail: antonboxrud@inquo.net
Web site: http://www.netoriginals.com/antonboxrud

When you are looking for a warm home base from which to explore Salt Lake City and the Wasatch ski resorts, come stay in

welcome; 7 Children welcome; 8 Tennis nearby; 9 Swimming nearby; 10 Golf nearby; 11 Skiing nearby; 12 May be booked through travel agent.

casual elegance. Return to a time of polished woods, leaded-glass windows, and hand-woven lace, all wrapped inside a three-story Victorian home built in 1901. Hearty, homemade breakfast features cinnamon buns and is served on real Bavarian china. Chosen "best place to stay" by numerous B&B guides. AAA three stars.

Hostess: Jane E. Johnson
Rooms: 7 (5PB; 2SB) $74-134
Full Breakfast
Credit Cards: A, B, C, D, E
Notes: 2, 5, 7, 8, 9, 10, 11, 12

Armstrong Mansion

667 E. 100 S., 84102
(801) 531-1333; (800) 708-1333;
FAX (801) 531-0282
E-mail: armstrong@vii.mail.com
Web site: http://www.armstrong.bb.com

Enjoy the warm, elegant atmosphere of the Armstrong Mansion without sacrificing convenience to the downtown Salt Lake area. Located close to everything! The airport is only 12 minutes away. The mansion is within walking distance of downtown businesses, shopping, entertainment, the Salt Lake Convention Center, the historic Temple Square, and many other cultural attractions. But don't limit yourself to the city center attractions; exciting winter and summer recreational activities await in the beautiful mountains that surround Salt Lake City. A 30- to 45-minute drive will take you from the Armstrong Mansion to any of nine world-class ski resorts. You'll also find four championship golf courses within a 15-minute drive of the mansion.

Hosts: Kurt and Andrea Horning
Rooms: 13 (PB) $99-229
Full Breakfast
Credit Cards: A, B, C, D, E
Notes: 2, 5 (closed Dec. 24-26), 11, 12

Vermont

ALBURG

Thomas Mott Homestead Bed and Breakfast

Blue Rock Road on Lake Champlain (Route 2, Box 149-B), 05440–9620
(802) 796-3736 (voice and FAX); (800) 348-0843
Web site: http://www.go-native.com/Inns/0162.html

Formerly an importer and distributor of fine wines, your host also enjoys gourmet cooking. His completely restored farmhouse has a guest living room with television and fireplace overlooking the lake, game room with bumper pool and darts, and quilt decor. Full view of Mount Mansfield and Jay Peak. One hour from Montreal/Burlington; 1½ hours from Lake Placid and Stowe. Lake activities in winter and summer. Amenities include Ben & Jerry's ice cream, lawn games, and horseshoes. Internet access; boat dock. Gift certificates available.

Host: Patrick J. Schallert
Rooms: 5 (PB) $75-95
Full Breakfast
Credit Cards: A, B, C, D
Notes: 2, 5, 7 (over 6), 8, 9, 10, 11, 12

Arlington Inn

ARLINGTON

Arlington Inn

Historic Route 7A, 05250
(802) 375-6532; (800) 443-9442
Web site: http://www.arlingtoninn.com

A stately Greek Revival mansion set on lush, landscaped lawns. Elegantly appointed rooms filled with antiques and amenities. All rooms have private baths and air-conditioning and include breakfast. The Arlington Inn is located between Bennington and Manchester. Antique shops, boutiques, museums, skiing, hiking, biking, canoeing, fly-fishing, golf, and other outdoor activities are nearby. Tennis on our private court. Outstanding cuisine is served by romantic candlelight in our award-winning, fireplaced dining room.

---

welcome; 7 Children welcome; 8 Tennis nearby; 9 Swimming nearby; 10 Golf nearby; 11 Skiing nearby; 12 May be booked through travel agent.

VERMONT

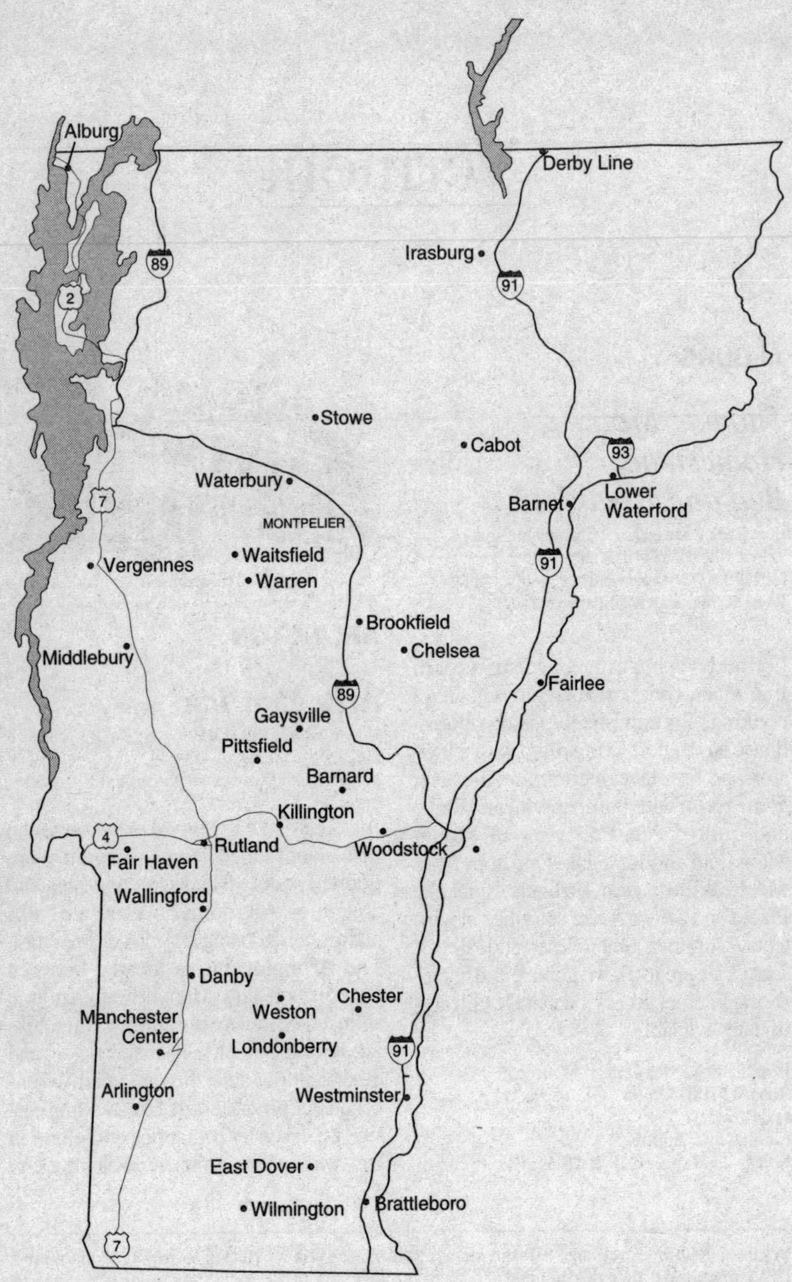
Alburg
Derby Line
89
Irasburg
91
2
Stowe
Cabot
93
Waterbury
Lower
Waterford
Barnet
7
MONTPELIER
Waitsfield
91
Vergennes
Warren
Brookfield
Chelsea
Middlebury
Fairlee
89
Gaysville
Pittsfield
Barnard
Killington
4
Rutland
Woodstock
Fair Haven
Wallingford
Danby
Chester
Weston
Manchester
Center
Londonberry
91
Arlington
Westminster
East Dover
Wilmington
Brattleboro
7

No smoking. Rated AAA three diamonds; Mobil three stars.

Hosts: Deborah and Mark Gagnon
Rooms: 19 (PB) $70-205
Full Breakfast
Credit Cards: A, B, C, D, E
Notes: 2 (deposit only), 4, 5, 7, 8, 9, 10, 11, 12

Country Willows B&B

332 E. Arlington Road, 05250
(800) 796-2585
Web site: http://www.bbonline.com/vt/countrywillows/index.html

An 1850s Victorian with wraparound porch. Quiet village setting; mountain views. Spacious rooms (some with fireplaces), queen beds, air-conditioning, TV. Beautifully decorated with antiques and handmade quilts. Walking distance to Norman Rockwell Gallery and shops.

Hosts: Craig and Kathleen Yanez
Rooms: 4 (PB) $65-145
Full Breakfast
Credit Cards: none
Notes: 2, 5, 7, 8, 9, 10, 11, 12

Hill Farm Inn

RR 2, Box 2015, 05250
(802) 375-2269; (800) 882-2545;
FAX (802) 375-9918
E-mail: hillfarm@vermontel.com
Web site: http://www.hillfarminn.com

Hill Farm Inn is one of Vermont's original farmsteads granted from King George III in 1775. It has been an inn since 1905 and still retains the character of an old farm vacation inn on 50 beautiful acres between the Taconic and Green Mountains, with a mile of frontage on the Battenkill River. We specialize in warm country hospitality. Outside, relax and enjoy the magnificent views from our porches. Inside, savor the aromas of homemade bread fresh from the oven, soup simmering on the stove, and apple crisp baking. Hiking, biking, canoeing, fishing, skiing, and shopping are all nearby. Friendly conversation everywhere.

Hill Farm Inn

Hosts: George and Joanne Hardy
Rooms: 13 (8PB; 5SB) $70-125
Full Hot Country Breakfast
Credit Cards: A, B, C, D
Notes: 2, 4, 5, 6 (limited), 7, 8, 9, 10, 11, 12

BARNET

The Old Homestead

1573 U.S. Route 5 S.; PO Box 150, 05821
(802) 633-4016; (877) 653-4663;
FAX (802) 633-4924

Vermont's Northeast Kingdom is truly God's Kingdom, and He will shine in your

The Old Homestead

NOTES: Credit cards accepted: A Master Card; B Visa; C American Express; D Discover; E Diners Club; F Other; 2 Personal checks accepted; 3 Lunch available; 4 Dinner available; 5 Open all year; 6 Pets welcome; 7 Children welcome; 8 Tennis nearby; 9 Swimming nearby; 10 Golf nearby; 11 Skiing nearby; 12 May be booked through travel agent.

smile as you enjoy antiques, treasures, collectibles, a cozy fire, a warm sunporch, and lovely gardens. Awaken to the sunrise over the White Mountains and Connecticut River and the smell of coffee and fresh-baked breads. Come early and enjoy our afternoon fellowship time.

Hostess: Gail Warnaar
Rooms: 4 (2PB; 2SB) $55-85
Full Breakfast
Credit Cards: A, B, D
Notes: 2, 7, 9, 10, 11, 12

BELLOWS FALLS

Blue Haven Christian Bed and Breakfast

6963 U.S. Route 5, 05158
(802) 463-9008; (800) 228-9008
E-mail: bluhaven@sover.net
Web site: http://www.virtualvermont.com/bandb/bluehaven

Explore Vermont's beauty from our 1830 restored schoolhouse. Experience canopy beds, hand-painted touches, and a big country kitchen where hearth-baked Vermont breakfasts are served. Have teatime treats at the antique glass-laden sideboard or in the ruddy pine common room. Expect a peaceful and pleasant time here. Christian retreat groups welcome at special rates. Open to one and all in God's love. Please come!

Hosts: Helene Champagne and son Victor
Rooms: 4 (PB) $60-110
Full Breakfast weekends, Continental Breakfast weekdays
Credit Cards: A, B, C
Notes: 2, 7, 8, 10, 12

BRATTLEBORO

Crosby House 1868

45 Western Avenue, 05301
(802) 257-4914; (800) 528-1868
E-mail: tomlynn@sover.net
Web site: http://www.sover.net/~tomlynn

Built in 1868, this restored Italianate Victorian beckons with historic architecture and a beguiling opportunity to walk back in time. Bedrooms offer fireplaces, whirlpool, air-conditioning, TV/VCR, personal bathrobes, and other luxury amenities. We also have a two-bedroom apartment suite. There are miles of trails onsite. It is a short walk downtown, where you will find many unique shops and restaurants, and a short drive to several major ski areas, antiquing, and cultural events.

Hosts: Tom and Lynn Kuralt
Rooms: 3 rooms + 1 suite (PB) $90-130
Full Breakfast
Credit Cards: A, B, C, D
Notes: 2, 3 (picnic), 5, 7 (limited), 8, 9, 10, 11, 12

BROOKFIELD

Green Trails Inn

By the Floating Bridge, 05036
(802) 276-3412; (800) 243-3412
E-mail: greentrails@quest-net.com

Relax and be pampered. . . .Enjoy comfortable elegance and true Vermont hospitality on our 17-acre country estate in the heart of historic Brookfield. Outdoor lover's paradise—biking, hiking, fishing, swimming, canoeing, ice-skating, and cross-country skiing (more than 30 kilometers) from our front door. Scrumptious meals, spacious lounging areas, and comfy beds to fall into at night. Twin-, double-, and queen-bedded guest rooms, some with Jacuzzis or fireplaces. Fabulous antique clock collection!

Hosts: Mark and Sue Erwin
Rooms: 13 (9PB; 4SB) $79-149
Full Breakfast
Credit Cards: A, B, D
Notes: 2, 4, 5, 7 (10 and over), 9, 10, 11, 12

CABOT

Creamery Inn Bed and Breakfast

PO Box 187, 05647
(802) 563-2819

This bed and breakfast is not Christian in name only. Its owners have dedicated it to the Lord and put their hearts into providing an atmosphere that witnesses to the Lord's presence. Grace is offered before breakfast. Daily shared morning and evening prayer is available, if desired. The home is used for retreats and teaching seminars. Matthew 11:28: "Come unto Me, all ye that labor and are heavy laden, and I will give you rest."

Hosts: Dan and Judy Lloyd
Rooms: 4 (PB) $55-75
Full Breakfast
Credit Cards: none
Notes: 2, 4, 5, 7, 8, 9, 11, 12

Creamery Inn Bed and Breakfast

CHELSEA

Shire Inn Bed and Breakfast

Main Street, 05038
(802) 685-3031; (800) 441-6908
E-mail: CBB@shireinn.com
Web site: http://www.shireinn.com

Vermont before ski resorts and factory outlets? Come to Chelsea! Dairy farms, forests, trout streams, covered bridges, birds, deer, friendly folks, unbelievable starry nights. Stay in a bright, comfortable room with wood-burning fireplace in this 1832 mansion. Begin and end each day with fabulous meals. Between, enjoy our tours of vintage Vermont, hike the nearby hills, bike or cross-country ski this beautiful valley. Or just relax by the fire, on the porch, or on 23 acres by the stream. Experience a simpler life. . .as you'd expect it to be. Come unwind!

Hosts: Jay and Karen Keller
Rooms: 6 + cottage (PB) $95-145
Full Breakfast
Credit Cards: A, B, D
Notes: 2, 4, 5, 9, 10, 11

CHESTER

Hugging Bear Inn and Shoppe

244 Main Street, 05143
(800) 325-0519; FAX (802) 875-3823
Web site: http://www.huggingbear.com

Teddy bears peek out the windows and are tucked in all the corners of this beautiful Victorian house built in 1850. If you love teddy bears, you'll love the Hugging Bear. There are six guest rooms with private shower baths and a teddy bear in

welcome; 7 Children welcome; 8 Tennis nearby; 9 Swimming nearby; 10 Golf nearby; 11 Skiing nearby; 12 May be booked through travel agent.

every bed. Full breakfast and afternoon snack are served.

Hostess: Georgette Thomas
Rooms: 6 (PB) $85-115
Full Breakfast
Credit Cards: A, B, C, D
Notes: 2, 5, 6 (limited), 7, 8, 9, 10, 11

Silas Griffith Inn

DANBY

Silas Griffith Inn

RR 1, Box 66F, 05739
(802) 293-5567; (800) 545-1509;
FAX (802) 293-5559

Built by Vermont's first millionaire, this Victorian inn was constructed in 1891 in the heart of the Green Mountains, with a spectacular mountain view. It features seventeen delightful, antique-furnished rooms and a fireplace in the living and dining room. Hiking, skiing, and antiquing nearby. Come and enjoy our elegant meals and New England hospitality.

Hosts: Paul and Lois Dansereau
Rooms: 17 (14PB; 3SB) $72-107
Full Breakfast
Credit Cards: A, B
Notes: 2, 4, 5, 7, 9, 10, 11, 12

DERBY LINE

Derby Village Inn

46 Main Street; PO Box 1085, 05830
(802) 873-3604; FAX (802) 873-3047
E-mail: dvibandb@together.net
Web site: http://homepages.together.net/~dvibandb

Come visit us in the Northeast Kingdom where the rivers run north and the views of the mountains provide peace and tranquillity. Derby Line borders Quebec, Ontario, and is at the midpoint between the equator and the North Pole. The Northeast Kingdom is host to many outdoor activities. We invite you to enjoy our warm hospitality and delicious home cooking at our relaxing and friendly inn.

Hostesses: Sheila Steplar and Catherine McCormick
Rooms: 5 (PB) $75-100
Full Breakfast
Credit Cards: A, B, C, D
Notes: 2, 5, 7, 8, 9, 10, 11, 12

EAST DOVER

Cooper Hill Inn

Cooper Hill Road; PO Box 146, 05341
(802) 348-6333; (800) 783-3229
E-mail: cooperhill@juno.com
Web site: http://www.virtualvermont.com/countryinn/cooperhill

Set high on a hill in southern Vermont's Green Mountains, Cooper Hill Inn commands a view to the east proclaimed by the *Boston Globe* as "one of the most spectacular mountain panoramas in all New England." A small portion of the inn was a farmhouse built in 1797. The inn has ten rooms, all with private baths. The atmosphere is always homey and informal. Families welcome.

Hosts: Pat and Marilyn Hunt
Rooms: 10 (PB) $72-120
Full Country Breakfast
Credit Cards: A, B, D
Notes: 2, 4, 5, 7, 8, 9, 10, 11, 12

FAIR HAVEN

Maplewood Inn

Route 22A S., 05743
(802) 265-8039; (800) 253-7729;
FAX (802) 265-8210
E-mail: maplewd@sover.net
Web site: http://www.sover.net/~maplewd

Rediscover romance in this exquisite, National Historic Register Greek Revival. Elegant rooms and suites boast antiques, fireplaces, AC, cable TVs, radios, optional phone, and turndown service. Gathering room with library, parlor with games and complimentary cordials. Hot beverages and snacks. Near lakes, skiing, dining, attractions. AAA three diamonds, Mobil three stars. Recommended by more than thirty guidebooks. A four-season inn!

Hosts: Cindy and Doug Baird
Rooms: 5 (PB) $80-135
Continental Plus Breakfast
Credit Cards: A, B, C, D
Notes: 2, 5, 7 (over 5), 8, 9, 10, 11, 12

FAIRLEE

Silver Maple Lodge and Cottages

RR 1, Box 8, 05045
(802) 333-4326; (800) 666-1946

A historic bed and breakfast country inn is located in a four-season recreational area. Enjoy canoeing, fishing, golf, tennis, and skiing within a few miles of the lodge. Visit nearby flea markets and country auctions. Choose a newly renovated room in our antique farmhouse or a handsome, pine-paneled cottage room. Three cottages with working fireplaces. Many fine restaurants nearby; Dartmouth College 17 miles away. Hot-air balloon packages, inn-to-inn bicycling, canoeing, and walking tours. Brochures available.

Hosts: Sharon and Scott Wright
Rooms: 16 (14PB; 2SB) $56-82
Continental Breakfast
Credit Cards: A, B, C, D
Notes: 2, 5, 6 (in cottages), 7, 8, 9, 10, 11, 12

GAYSVILLE

Laolke Lodge

PO Box 107, 05746–0107
(802) 234-9205
E-mail: laolke@juno.com

Enjoy a relaxing vacation at this authentic log house. Built in 1964 especially to be a lodge. Centrally located for scenic day trips and convenient to major ski areas.

Hostess: Olive Pratt
Rooms: 5 (PB) $25-35
Full Breakfast
Credit Cards: none
Notes: 2, 4, 5, 6, 7, 8, 9, 10, 11, 12

IRASBURG

Brick House B&B

Route 14; PO Box 33, 05845
(802) 754-2108 (voice and FAX)
E-mail: Vermont.Life@connriver.net
Web site: http://www.connriver.net/VermontLife/Home

This 1870s brick Victorian home is in the historic town of Irasburg in the beautiful

---

welcome; 7 Children welcome; 8 Tennis nearby; 9 Swimming nearby; 10 Golf nearby; 11 Skiing nearby; 12 May be booked through travel agent.

Brick House Bed and Breakfast

Northeast Kingdom. One bedroom has twin beds and a private bath. Room with lace-topped canopy bed, queen- and full-size antique brass bedroom share a bath. A full breakfast is served country-style and is meant to spoil our guests. In business since 1988. Guest comment: "Everything was wonderful. Every need and more was taken care of."

Hosts: Jo and Roger Sweatt
Rooms: 3 (1PB; 2SB) $45-50
Full Breakfast
Credit Cards: none
Notes: 2, 5, 6, 7, 9, 10, 11

KILLINGTON

The Peak Chalet

South View Path; PO Box 511, 05751
(802) 422-4278
E-mail: homes@thepeakchalet.com
Web site: http://www.thepeakchalet.com

A four-room bed and breakfast located within the beautiful Green Mountains. The exterior is authentically European Alpine. The interior is furnished with a fine country inn flavor and reflects high quality with attention to detail. Panoramic mountain views with a cozy stone fireplace to unwind by. All rooms have queen beds. Centrally located within Killington Ski Resort, this is a truly relaxing experience. AAA three-diamond- and Mobil-rated.

Hosts: Diane and Greg Becker
Rooms: 4 (PB) $50-110
Continental Breakfast
Credit Cards: A, B, C, E
Notes: 2, 5, 7 (over 12), 8, 9, 10, 11, 12

The Peak Chalet

LONDONBERRY

Blue Gentian Lodge

RR 1, Box 29, 05148
(802) 824-3357; (800) 456-2405;
FAX (802) 824-3531
E-mail: kenalberti@csi.com
Web site: http://ourworld.compuserve.com/homepages/kenalberti

A special place to stay, nestled at the foot of Magic Mountain. All rooms have private baths and cable color TV and include a full breakfast in the dining room. Seasonal activities on the grounds, a heated swimming pool, and walking trails. Recreation Room offers Ping-Pong, bumper pool, board games, and library. There is golf, tennis, fishing, outlet shopping, antiquing, horseback riding, and skiing (downhill and cross-country) nearby.

Hosts: The Alberti Family
Rooms: 13 (PB) $50-80
Full Breakfast
Credit Cards: A, B
Notes: 2, 5, 7, 8, 9, 10, 11

LOWER WATERFORD

Rabbit Hill Inn Bed and Breakfast

Box 55, Route 18, 05848
(802) 748-5168; (800) 76-BUNNY (762-8669);
FAX (802) 748-8342

Nestled between a river and the mountains, in a village untouched by time, sits the historic Rabbit Hill Inn. Escape to this tranquil place and experience the gentle comforts of enchanting guest rooms and suites, a Jacuzzi by candlelight, memorable gourmet dining, and pampering service. Enjoy a variety of activities or simply relax. We await you with truly heartfelt hospitality unlike any you've experienced. Meals included. Award-winning, nationally acclaimed inn, rated four stars by Mobil and four diamonds by AAA.

Hosts: Brian and Leslie Mulcahy
Rooms: 21 (PB) $210-355
Full Breakfast
Credit Cards: A, B, C
Notes: 2, 4, 5, 8, 9, 10, 11, 12

MANCHESTER CENTER

River Meadow Farm

PO Box 822, 05255
(802) 362-1602

The oldest portion of the New England farmhouse was built in the late 18th century. During one part of its history, the home served as the Manchester Poor Farm. It is located at the end of a country lane with beautiful mountain views and is bordered on one side by the Battenhill River. All of the house and 90 acres are open for guests to enjoy. Five bedrooms share 2½ baths.

Hostess: Patricia J. Dupree
Rooms: 5 (SB) $30 per person
Full Breakfast
Credit Cards: none
Notes: 2, 5, 7, 8, 9, 10, 11

The Middlebury Inn

MIDDLEBURY

The Middlebury Inn

14 Courthouse Square, 05753
(802) 388-4961; (800) 842-4666;
FAX (802) 388-4563
E-mail: midinnvt@sover.net
Web site: http://www.middleburyinn.com

This 1827 landmark overlooks the village green in a picturesque New England college town. Discover Middlebury: the splendor of its historic district, Vermont State Craft Center, Middlebury College, boutique shopping, and four-season recreation. Elegantly restored rooms, telephone, color TV, and AC (in season). The inn offers breakfast, lunch, dinner, seasonal porch dining, afternoon tea, and Sunday brunch. Recommended by AAA; member of Historic Hotels of America.

Hosts: The Emanuel Family
Rooms: 75 (PB) $86-275
Continental Breakfast
Credit Cards: A, B, C, D, E
Notes: 2, 3, 4, 5, 6, 7, 8, 9, 10, 11, 12

PITTSFIELD

Swiss Farm Lodge

PO Box 630, 05762
(802) 746-8341
Web site: http://www.mediausa.com/vt/swissfarmlodge

Working Hereford beef farm. Enjoy the casual, family-type atmosphere in our living room with fireplace and TV or in the game room. Home-cooked meals and baking, served family-style. Our own maple syrup, jams, and jellies. Walk-in cooler available for guests' use. Two rooms have queen beds. Cross-country trails onsite. B&B available all year. MAP provided November to April only. Mountain bike trails close by. Owned and operated by the same family for fifty years. Lower rates for children who stay in the same room as parents.

Hosts: Mark and Sandy Begin
Rooms: 17 (14PB; 3SB) $50-70
Full Breakfast
Credit Cards: A, B
Notes: 2, 4, 5, 7, 8, 9, 10, 11, 12

RUTLAND

The Inn at Rutland

70 N. Main Street (Route 7), 05701
(802) 773-0575; (800) 808-0575;
FAX (802) 775-3506
E-mail: inrutlnd@vermontel.com
Web site: http://www.innrutland@qpg.com

Come stay in our elegant 1890s Victorian mansion. All rooms have private bathrooms, TVs, telephones, and great views. Our deluxe rooms are air-conditioned and have VCRs. Two large common rooms, front wraparound porch. Nonsmoking. Close to all Vermont attractions. Minutes

The Inn at Rutland

from Killington ski resort. Why stay in a motel when you can sleep in a mansion?

Hosts: Bob and Tanya Liberman
Rooms: 12 (PB) $59-179
Full Breakfast in season, Continental off season
Credit Cards: A, B, C, D, E
Notes: 5, 7, 8, 9, 10, 11, 12

STOWE

Brass Lantern Inn

717 Maple Street, 05672
(802) 253-2229; (800) 729-2980;
FAX (802) 253-7425
E-mail: brasslntrn@aol.com
Web site: http://www.stoweinfo.com/saa/brasslantern

An award-winning traditional bed and breakfast in the heart of Stowe overlooking Mount Mansfield, Vermont's most prominent mountain. Period antiques, handmade quilts, local artisan wares, AC. Most rooms have views; some have fireplaces; some have whirlpools. An intimate inn for romantics. Special packages include honeymoon/anniversary, romance, skiing, golf, historic, and more. No smoking.

Host: Andy Aldrich
Rooms: 9 (PB) $80-225
Full Breakfast
Credit Cards: A, B, C
Notes: 2, 5, 8, 9, 10, 11, 12

NOTES: Credit cards accepted: A Master Card; B Visa; C American Express; D Discover; E Diners Club; F Other; 2 Personal checks accepted; 3 Lunch available; 4 Dinner available; 5 Open all year; 6 Pets

The Siebeness Inn

3681 Mountain Road, 05672
(802) 253-8942; (800) 426-9001;
FAX (802) 253-9232
E-mail: siebenes@together.net
Web site: http://stoweinfo.com/saa/siebeness

A warm welcome awaits you at our charming country inn nestled in the foothills of Mount Mansfield. Romantic rooms have country antiques, private baths, and air-conditioning; some have fireplaces. New mountain-view suites have Jacuzzis, fireplaces, feather beds—and views! Hearty New England breakfast. Relax in our outdoor hot tub in winter or our pool with mountain views in summer. Fireplace in lounge. Bike, walk, or cross-country ski from the inn on a recreational path. Honeymoon, golf, and ski packages.

Hosts: Sue and Nils Andersen
Rooms: 12 (PB) $70-200
Full Breakfast
Credit Cards: A, B, C, D
Notes: 2, 5, 7, 8, 9, 10, 11, 12

VERGENNES

Strong House Inn

82 W. Main Street, 05491
(802) 877-3337; FAX (802) 877-2599

Experience elegant lodging in a grand 1834 Federal home listed on the National Register of Historic Places. The inn, fully air-conditioned, is situated on 6 acres with walking trails and gardens and offers snowshoeing and sledding in the winter. Located in the heart of the Champlain Valley, the area offers cycling, golf, skiing, and the Shelburne Museum. All rooms have private baths. Room rates include afternoon snacks and beverages and a full country breakfast.

Hostess: Mary Bargiel
Rooms: 12 (PB) $75-200
Full Breakfast
Credit Cards: A, B, C
Notes: 5, 9, 10, 11, 12

WAITSFIELD

The Mad River Inn

PO Box 75, 05673
(802) 496-7900; (800) 832-8278;
FAX (802) 496-5390
E-mail: madinn@madriver.com

Romantic 1860s country Victorian inn along Mad River. Elegant but comfortable. Picturesque mountain views, flower-filled porches, gardens, and gazebo. Feather beds, private baths, Jacuzzi, and family room with cable TV and billiards. Gourmet breakfast and afternoon tea. Recreation path and swimming along the river. Horseback riding, golf, tennis, Sugarbush and Mad River Glen Ski Resorts, Ben & Jerry's, and Cold Hollow cider mill are nearby. Weddings and groups welcome.

Host: Luc Maranda
Rooms: 10 (PB) $69-125
Full Gourmet Breakfast
Credit Cards: A, B, C
Notes: 2, 5, 7, 8, 9, 10, 11, 12

---

welcome; 7 Children welcome; 8 Tennis nearby; 9 Swimming nearby; 10 Golf nearby; 11 Skiing nearby; 12 May be booked through travel agent.

Mountain View Inn

RR 1, Box 69, 05673
(802) 496-2426

The Mountain View Inn is an old farmhouse, circa 1826, that was made into a lodge in 1948 to accommodate skiers at nearby Mad River Glen. Today it is a charming country inn with seven rooms. Meals are served family-style around the antique harvest table where good fellowship prevails. Sip mulled cider and swap tales of the day's activities around the crackling fire in the living room when the weather turns chilly.

Hosts: Fred and Susan Spencer
Rooms: 7 (PB) $90-130
Full Breakfast
Credit Cards: none
Notes: 2, 5, 7, 8, 9, 10, 11, 12

I.B. Munson House B&B Inn

WALLINGFORD

I.B. Munson House Bed and Breakfast Inn

7 S. Main Street, 05773
(802) 446-2860; (888) 519-3771
E-mail: ibmunson@vermontel.com
Web site: http://www.ibmunsoninn.com

The I.B. Munson House is an 1856 Italianate Victorian totally and lovingly restored. It features high ceilings, beautiful chandeliers, and five wood-burning fireplaces. Guest rooms and common rooms are finely decorated and furnished with comfortable period antiques and fine art. The grounds and gardens are expertly maintained. Offstreet parking is provided. The inn is located in a quaint, historic village. Boyhood home of Paul Harris, founder of Rotary International.

Hosts: Karen and Phil Pimental
Rooms: 7 (PB) $85-145
Full Gourmet Breakfast
Credit Cards: A, B, C, D, F
Notes: 2, 5, 7 (12 and older), 8, 9, 10, 11, 12

WARREN

Beaver Pond Farm Inn

Golf Course Road, 05674
(802) 583-2861; FAX (802) 583 2860
E-mail: beaverpond@madriver.com
Web site: http://www.beaverpondfarminn.com

Beaver Pond Farm Inn, a small, gracious country inn near the Sugarbush ski area, is located 100 yards from the first tee of the Sugarbush Golf Course, transformed into 25 kilometers of cross-country ski trails in the winter. *Bed and Breakfast in New England* calls it "the best of the best." Rooms have down comforters and beautiful views. Hearty breakfasts are served, and snacks are enjoyed by the fireplace. Continental dinners are offered three times a week during the winter. Hiking, biking, soaring, and fishing are nearby. Bob will take guests out for fly-fishing instruction. Ski and golf packages are available.

Hosts: Betty and Bob Hansen
Rooms: 5 (PB) $82-118
Full Breakfast
Credit Cards: A, B
Notes: 2, 4 (occasionally), 8, 9, 10, 11, 12

WATERBURY (STOWE)

Grünberg Haus Bed and Breakfast and Cabins

RR 2, Box 1595-CB; Route 100 S., 05676
(802) 244-7726; (800) 800-7760;
FAX (802) 244-1283
E-mail: grunhaus@aol.com
Web site: http://www.bestinns.net/usa/vt/grun.html

Grünberg Haus is a handbuilt Austrian inn offering romantic guest rooms (each with balcony, antiques, comforters, and quilts), secluded cabins (each with fireplace and mountain-view deck), and a carriage house suite (with sky window, kitchen, sitting area, and two balconies). The central location is close to Stowe, Burlington, Sugarbush, and Montpelier. All accommodations include a full, musical breakfast. Enjoy our Jacuzzi, sauna, BYOB pub, fireplaces, tennis court, and groomed cross-country ski trails. Help Mark feed the chickens.

Hosts: Chris Sellers and Mark Frohman
Rooms: 14 (9PB; 5SB) $59-145
Full Breakfast
Credit Cards: A, B, D
Notes: 2, 5, 7, 8, 9, 10, 11, 12

Inn at Blush Hill

RR 1, Box 1266, 05676
(802) 244-7529; (800) 736-7522;
FAX (802) 244-7314
E-mail: inn@blushhill.com
Web site: http://www.blushhill.com

Inn at Blush Hill Bed and Breakfast, circa 1790, sits on 5 acres, high on a hilltop, with unsurpassed views of the mountains. Choose from five individually decorated guest rooms with private baths, featuring colonial antiques, canopy beds, down comforters, and a fireplace or Jacuzzi tub. The large common rooms are spacious and warm, filled with books, antiques, and fireplaces. A full breakfast with many Vermont specialty food products is served by the garden in summer and fireside in winter. The inn is located "back to back" with Ben & Jerry's ice cream factory, and the skiing at Stowe and Sugarbush is only minutes away. AAA- and Mobil-rated.

Hostess: Pam Gosselin
Rooms: 5 (PB) $59-130
Full Breakfast
Credit Cards: A, B, C, D
Notes: 2, 5, 7 (over 6), 8, 9, 10, 11, 12

WESTON

The Colonial House

287 Route 100, 05161
(802) 824-6286; (800) 639-5033;
FAX (802) 824-3934
E-mail: cohoinn@sover.net
Web site: http://www.sover.net/~cohoinn

The Colonial House is a unique country inn and motel offering a full breakfast with its rooms. Dinner is available on Friday and Saturday nights year-round and midweek during the summer, fall, and winter holiday periods. Rooms are light and airy. The guest living room has an attached solarium where coffee, tea, and fresh-baked goods are offered each afternoon. Convenient to all southern Vermont attractions.

Hosts: John and Betty Nunnikhoven
Rooms: 15 (9PB; 6SB) $50-88
Full Breakfast
Credit Cards: A, B, D
Notes: 2, 4, 5, 7, 8, 9, 10, 11

welcome; 7 Children welcome; 8 Tennis nearby; 9 Swimming nearby; 10 Golf nearby; 11 Skiing nearby; 12 May be booked through travel agent.

The Wilder Homestead Inn

25 Lawrence Hill Road, 05161–5600
(802) 824-8172; FAX (802) 824-5054
E-mail: whomesteadinn@juno.com
Web site: http://www.wilderhomestead.com

An 1827 brick home on the National Historic Register with Rumford fireplaces and 1830 original Moses Eaton stenciling. The inn has been carefully restored and has quiet surroundings and antique furnishings. Walk to the village for shopping, museums, theater, and dining. Nearby are skiing, golfing, hiking, the Weston Priory (Benedictine monks sing all services). Weston is a village that takes you back in time. No smoking. Common rooms where TV, phone, wet bar (tea, coffee, and sodas), and library are for your use.

Hosts: Peggy and Roy Varner
Rooms: 7 (5PB; 2SB) $69-125
Full Breakfast
Credit Cards: A, B
Notes: 2, 5, 7 (over 6), 8, 9, 10, 11, 12 (no fee)

WILMINGTON

Shearer Hill Farm Bed and Breakfast

PO Box 1453, 05363
(802) 464-3253; (800) 437-3104
E-mail: puseyshf@sover.net

Wake to the aroma of freshly brewed coffee, homemade muffins, and bread at this small working farm on a quiet, pristine country road. Large rooms, delicious Vermont breakfast. In summer, enjoy the Marlboro Music Festival, golf, swimming, fishing, horseback riding, hiking. In winter, enjoy groomed cross-country ski trails on the property and snowmobiling. Near Mt. Snow ski area. Distances: 210 miles to NYC, 120 to Boston, 70 to Albany.

Hosts: Bill and Patti Pusey
Rooms: 6 (PB) $90
Full Breakfast
Credit Cards: A, B, C, D
Notes: 2, 5, 7, 8, 9, 10, 11, 12

The White House of Wilmington Bed and Breakfast

178 Route 9 E., 05363
(802) 464-2135; (800) 541-2135;
FAX (802) 464-5222
E-mail: whitehse@sover.net
Web site: http://www.whitehouseinn.com

The White House of Wilmington—voted "one of the most romantic Inns. . ." (*New York Times*). The 1915 Victorian mansion, converted to an elegant country inn in 1978, sits on the crest of a high, rolling hill amid bubbling fountains and formal gardens. Sixteen elegant guest rooms are available in the main inn, nine with fireplaces and four with two-person whirlpool tubs. Seven rooms are at the adjacent guest house, all with private baths. Award-winning cuisine served by romantic candlelight in front of roaring fireplaces in three dining rooms. Full-service patio lounge. Indoor and outdoor pools, whirlpool and sauna. Cross-country ski touring center onsite. Tubing on the premises.

Host: Robert Grinold
Rooms: 23 (PB) $98-195
Full Breakfast
Credit Cards: A, B, C, D, E
Notes: 2, 3, 4, 5, 7, 8, 9, 10, 11, 12

NOTES: Credit cards accepted: A Master Card; B Visa; C American Express; D Discover; E Diners Club; F Other; 2 Personal checks accepted; 3 Lunch available; 4 Dinner available; 5 Open all year; 6 Pets

Applebutter Inn

WOODSTOCK

Applebutter Inn

Happy Valley Road, **Taftsville,** 05073
Mail: PO Box 24, Woodstock, 05091
(802) 457-4158 (voice and FAX); (800) 486-1734
E-mail: aplbtrn@aol.com

The Applebutter Inn is nestled in the quiet and peaceful hamlet of Taftsville, 3 miles from the centers of Woodstock and Quechee. Get away from the hustle and bustle of the villages and enjoy the breathtaking views of the Green Mountains and the landscaped grounds. Take walks on the country roads by the inn, the Taftsville covered bridge over the Ottauquechee River, and the rushing waterfalls. On our 12 acres you can picnic, read, and relax in season, or in winter go sledding and practice cross-country skiing.

Hosts: Beverlee and Andy Cook
Rooms: 6 (PB) $70-135
Full Breakfast
Credit Cards: A, B
Notes: 2, 3 (on request), 5, 6 (special arrangements), 7 (with parental supervision), 8, 9, 10, 12

Barr House

55 South Street, 05091
(802) 457-3334
Web site: http://www.pbpul.com

We are a 19th-century saltbox situated on 1¾ acres in the village near the green. Our B&B overlooks golf and cross-country ski courses but is away from busy thoroughfares. Small and unique. Two charming rooms are hosted by a sixth-generation Vermont native. Full Vermont breakfast. Public room. Gift certificates. Children over 12. Nonsmoking. No pets.

Hosts: Katharine and Jim Paul
Rooms: 2 (SB) $60-75 (double)
Full Breakfast
Credit Cards: none
Notes: 2, 5, 8, 10, 11

Deer Brook Inn

HCR 68, Box 443, 05091
(802) 672-3713
Web site: http://www.bbhost.com/deerbrookinn

Handmade quilts, original pine floors, and an immaculately maintained country decor are just a few of the charming features of this 1820 farmhouse. Five spacious guest rooms, one of which is a two-room suite, with private baths and queen or king beds. Enjoy a crackling fire in winter or a view of the Ottauquechee River from the porch in summer. A bountiful breakfast provides the perfect start for your day. Cable TV, AC. AAA three diamonds.

Hosts: Brian and Rosemary McGinty
Rooms: 5 (PB) $75-125
Full Breakfast
Credit Cards: A, B, C
Notes: 2, 5, 7, 8, 9, 10, 11, 12

The Jackson House Inn

37 Old Route 4 W., 05091
(802) 457-2095; (800) 448-1890;
FAX (802) 457-9290
E-mail: innkeeper@jacksonhouse.com
Web site: http://www.jacksonhouse.com

Fine dining and luxurious accommodations in an 1890 Victorian mansion. On the

The Jackson House Inn

National Register of Historic Places, located in charming Woodstock. Fifteen guest rooms, including six suites with fireplaces. Memorable gourmet breakfast and evening wine/champagne bar included. Spa with steam room. Enjoy elegant new American cuisine prepared by Chef Brendan Nolan, formerly of Aujourd' hui at The Four Seasons Hotel/Boston. Exquisite dining room features open-hearth fireplace, cathedral ceilings, and spectacular garden views.

Hosts: Juan and Gloria Florin
Rooms: 15 (PB) $170-260
Full Breakfast
Credit Cards: A, B, C
Notes: 2, 4, 5, 8, 9, 10, 11, 12

The Maple Leaf Inn

PO Box 273, **Barnard,** 05031
(802) 234-5342; (800) 51-MAPLE (516-2753)
E-mail: mapleafinn@aol.com
Web site: http://www.mapleleafinn.com

The Maple Leaf is an elegant Victorian-style inn resplendent with gables, dormers, wraparound porch, gazebo, gingerbread trim, and soaring chimneys, nestled within 16 acres of maple and birch trees. All of our guest rooms have a king-size bed, sitting area, TV/VCR/telephone, and private bath—most with whirlpool tubs. Wood-burning fireplaces grace most of our guest rooms, as well. Stenciling, stitchery, and handmade quilts blend with antique and reproduction furnishings to give each guest room a warm and welcoming individuality. The aroma of our gourmet breakfast will entice you to our dining room, where your candlelit table awaits. The Maple Leaf Inn has been honored with the AAA four-diamond award.

Hosts: Gary and Janet Robison
Rooms: 7 (PB) $110-175
Full Breakfast
Credit Cards: A, B, C, D, E, F
Notes: 2, 5, 8, 9, 10, 11, 12

The Woodstocker Bed and Breakfast

61 River Street (Route 4), 05091
(802) 457-3896; FAX (802) 457-3897

This delightful bed and breakfast sits snugly at the foot of Mt. Tom in one of the country's most picturesque villages. It offers a casual, unpretentious atmosphere where everyone feels welcome. The rooms are exceptionally large and tastefully appointed. The full breakfast buffet and afternoon refreshments are always delicious. In-room kitchens are available—particularly nice for families traveling with small children. The private, five-person whirlpool is a big hit during the winter months.

Hosts: Nancy and Tom Blackford
Rooms: 9 (PB) $85-155
Full Breakfast
Credit Cards: A, B
Notes: 2, 5, 7, 8, 9, 10, 11, 12

NOTES: Credit cards accepted: A Master Card; B Visa; C American Express; D Discover; E Diners Club; F Other; 2 Personal checks accepted; 3 Lunch available; 4 Dinner available; 5 Open all year; 6 Pets

Virginia

ALSO SEE LISTINGS UNDER THE DISTRICT OF COLUMBIA.

APPOMATTOX

The Babcock House Bed and Breakfast

106 Oakleigh Avenue; Route 6, Box 1421, 24522
(804) 352-7532; (800) 689-6208;
FAX (800) 752-7329
E-mail: richguild@earthlink.net
Web site: http://www.information.com/va/babcock

We are located in historic Appomattox, less than 5 miles from the famous surrender site that ended the Civil War. The Babcock House is a restored turn-of-the-century inn with five rooms and one suite. All rooms have private baths, ceiling fans, and AC. A full breakfast is included with all room rates.

Hosts: Debbie Powell, Luella Coleman, Lynah Guild
Rooms: 5 + 1 suite (PB) $85-110
Full Breakfast
Credit Cards: A, B, C, D
Notes: 2, 5, 7, 8, 10, 12

ARLINGTON

Alexandria B&B Network

PO Box 25319, 22202–9319
(703) 549-3415; (888) 549-3415;
FAX (703) 549-3415
E-mail: aabbn@juno.com

Centered in Old Town Alexandria, this network offers stays in a breathtaking range of homes—1750s Old Town town houses to 1990 luxury high-rise apartments. We have private homes, B&Bs, inns, country inns, and boutique hotels throughout DC, Virginia, and Maryland.

Hostess: Leslie Garrison
Rooms: more than 100 (most PB; 10SB) $60-325
Full or Continental Breakfast
Credit Cards: A, B, C
Notes: 2, 5, 6, 7, 8, 9, 10, 12

BASYE

Sky Chalet

Route 263, 280 Sky Chalet Lane; PO Box 300, 22810
(540) 856-2147; FAX (540) 856-2436
E-mail: skychalet@skychalet.com
Web site: http://www.skychalet.com

Rustic, comfortable, romantic mountaintop hideaway in the Shenandoah Valley. The

---

welcome; 7 Children welcome; 8 Tennis nearby; 9 Swimming nearby; 10 Golf nearby; 11 Skiing nearby; 12 May be booked through travel agent.

VIRGINIA

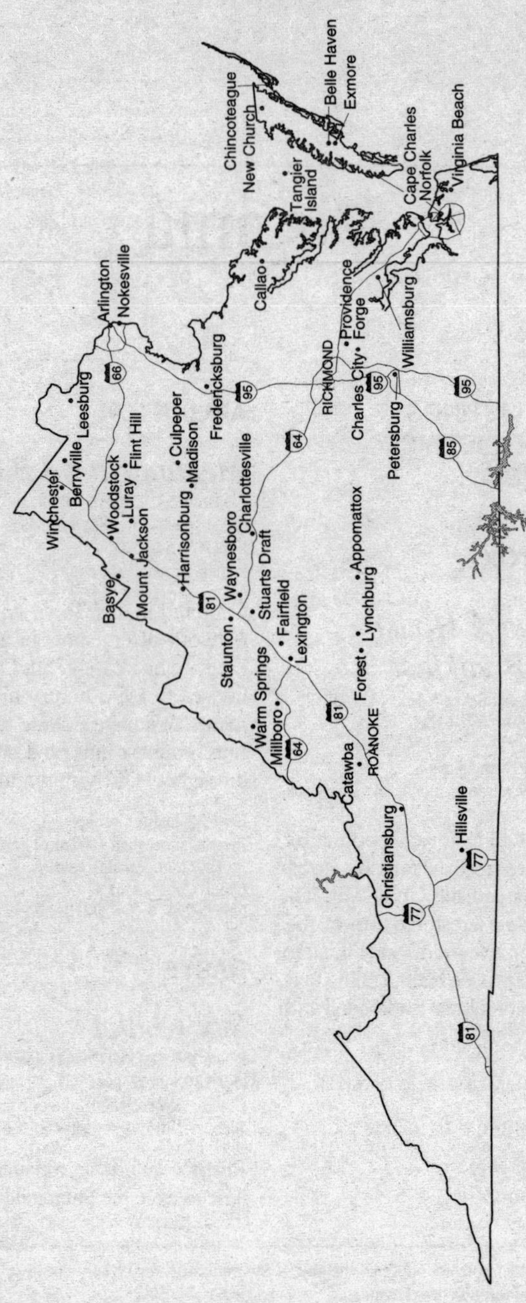

Chincoteague
New Church
Belle Haven
Exmore
Tangier Island
Cape Charles
Norfolk
Virginia Beach
Arlington
Nokesville
Callao
Providence Forge
Williamsburg
Fredericksburg
RICHMOND
Charles City
Petersburg
Leesburg
Berryville
Winchester
Woodstock
Flint Hill
Luray
Culpeper
Madison
Mount Jackson
Harrisonburg
Charlottesville
Waynesboro
Stuarts Draft
Appomattox
Basye
Staunton
Fairfield
Lexington
Lynchburg
Forest
Warm Springs
Millboro
ROANOKE
Catawba
Christiansburg
Hillsville
66
95
64
85
81
77

Sky Chalet

property features spectacular views. Delivered continental breakfast. The Ridge Lodge has rooms with private baths. The Treetop Lodge features rooms, private baths, living rooms, fireplaces, decks. Welcome honeymooners, couples, groups, retreats, children, pets. Unique Main Old World Lodge features European architecture, fireplaces, ambience, verandas, and unchallenged views for wedding receptions, reunions, seminars, special events. Hiking, attractions, activities.

Hosts: Ken and Mona Seay
Rooms: 9 (PB) $34-79
Continental Breakfast
Credit Cards: A, B, D, E, F (Carte Blanche)
Notes: 2, 5, 6, 7, 8, 9, 10, 11, 12

BELLE HAVEN

Bay View Waterfront Bed and Breakfast

35350 Copes Drive, 23306
(757) 442-6963; (800) 442-6966
E-mail: browning@shore.intercon.net
Web site: http://www.bbhost.com/bvwaterfront

Bay View is on a hill overlooking Occohannock Creek with an expansive view to the Chesapeake Bay and a dock to deep water. Guests can enjoy a superb view, reading, fishing, crabbing, biking, swimming in the pool or the creek, a small beach, croquet, basketball, volleyball, a full country breakfast, 140 acres of woods, farmland, and creek shore to hike and explore—and a large, gracious home.

Hosts: Wayne and Mary Will Browning
Rooms: 4 (2PB; 2SB) $95
Full Breakfast
Credit Cards: none
Notes: 2, 5, 7, 8, 9 (onsite), 10, 12

BERRYVILLE

Blue Ridge Bed and Breakfast Reservation Service

Rocks and Rills Farm, Route 2, Box 3895, 22611
(540) 955-1246; (800) 296-1246;
FAX (540) 955-4240
E-mail: blurdgbb@shentel.net
Web site: http://www.BlueRidgeBB.com

Beautiful, antique-filled Colonial Williamsburg reproduction nestled in the foothills of the Blue Ridge Mountains, near the Shenandoah River on 11 acres of fragrant Christmas trees. Perfect getaway; ideal for weekend bikers and hikers. Only 90 minutes from Washington, DC. Also a reservation service for numerous host homes.

Hosts: Rita Z. Duncan, Rolando A. Amador
Rooms: numerous (most PB) $50-150
Full Breakfast
Credit Cards: A, B, C
Notes: 2, 3 and 4 (some, with reservations), 5, 6, 7, 8, 9, 10, 11, 12

NOTES: Credit cards accepted: A Master Card; B Visa; C American Express; D Discover; E Diners Club; F Other; 2 Personal checks accepted; 3 Lunch available; 4 Dinner available; 5 Open all year; 6 Pets welcome; 7 Children welcome; 8 Tennis nearby; 9 Swimming nearby; 10 Golf nearby; 11 Skiing nearby; 12 May be booked through travel agent.

CALLAO

"His Place"

PO Box 126, 22435
(804) 529-7014; FAX (804) 529-7187

Come to Virginia's Northern Neck to relax where the only sounds are the singing of birds and the humming of lawn mowers. You may stay in the 1974 main house and share Gene's love of music—perhaps play her baby grand—or choose the private cottage. Furnishings are a mixture of antiques, Early American, and traditional pieces. "His Place" sits on a cove of the Yeocomico River, which runs into the Potomac and leads out into the Chesapeake. Explore the homes of Lee and Washington (30 miles). Play golf at the course 2 miles away, or use the owner's paddleboat. If you are cruising the bay or Potomac, you may dock on the property if your boat's draft is no more than 3 feet—there's a tide. (Nearby marinas take larger craft; pickup can be arranged.) Callao is 55 miles from Williamsburg, 65 from Richmond, and 115 from Washington.

Hostess: "Gene" Pehovic
Rooms: 1 + guest house (PB) $50-70
Full Breakfast
Credit Cards: none
Notes: 2, 3, 4, 5, 10

CAPE CHARLES

Chesapeake Charm B&B

202 Madison Avenue, 23310
(757) 331-2676; (800) 546-9215
E-mail: chesapeakecharminfo@prodigy.net
Web site: http://www.inngetaways.com/va/chesape.html

Discover one of the last unspoiled treasures of Virginia: Cape Charles on the Eastern Shore. A perfect setting for a special birthday, anniversary, or just an escape from the pressures of today, the B&B offers all the modern conveniences of today in yesterday's setting. Period antiques and individually controlled heating and AC. Stroll 2 blocks to enjoy sunning on the Chesapeake Bay beach or the Eastern Shore's spectacular sunsets. Bicycles are available. Enjoy the historic architecture of Cape Charles. Golf, tennis, chartered fishing available. Hike at the National Wildlife Refuge or Kiptopeke State Park.

Hostess: Phyllis S. Tyndall
Rooms: 3 (PB) $65-85
Full Breakfast
Credit Cards: A, B
Notes: 2, 7, 8, 9, 10, 12

Sea Gate Bed and Breakfast

Sea Gate B&B

9 Tazewell Avenue, 23310
(757) 331-2206; FAX (757) 331-2207
E-mail: seagate@pilot.infi.net
Web site: http://www.bbhost.com/seagate

Located in the quiet, sleepy town of Cape Charles, just steps from the Chesapeake Bay on Virginia's undiscovered Eastern Shore. My home is your home! Begin the day with a full breakfast followed by leisure or hiking, birding, bathing, or exploring our historic area. Tea prepares you for

NOTES: Credit cards accepted: A Master Card; B Visa; C American Express; D Discover; E Diners Club; F Other; 2 Personal checks accepted; 3 Lunch available; 4 Dinner available; 5 Open all year; 6 Pets

the most glorious sunsets on the East Coast. Sea Gate is perfect for resting, relaxing, and recharging away from the crush of modern America.

Host: Chris Bannon
Rooms: 4 (2PB; 2SB) $75-85
Full Breakfast
Credit Cards: none
Notes: 2, 5, 8, 9, 10, 12

Wilson-Lee House

403 Tazewell Avenue, 23310–3217
(757) 331-1954; FAX (757) 331-8133
E-mail: WLHBnB@aol.com
Web site: http://www.wilsonleehouse.com

Wilson-Lee House invites you to come visit Cape Charles on the Eastern Shore of Virginia—"the land that time forgot." Only 45 minutes from the hustle and bustle of Norfolk/Virginia Beach, you will be transported 50 years back in time. The pace is deliciously slow, and sunsets on the Chesapeake are breathtaking. Rock on our porch, ride our bicycle-built-for-two, and let us arrange a romantic sunset sail, followed by a relaxing cookout on our deck.

Hosts: David Phillips and Leon Parham
Rooms: 6 (PB) $85-120
Full Breakfast
Credit Cards: A, B, C
Notes: 2, 8, 9, 10, 12

CATAWBA

Crosstrails B&B

5880 Blacksburg Road, 24070
(540) 384-8078
E-mail: xtrails@roanoke.infi.net
Web site: http://www.crosstrails.com

A mountain valley getaway in scenic Catawba Valley, where the Appalachian

Crosstrails Bed and Breakfast

Trail and TransAmerica Bicycle Trail cross between Roanoke and Blacksburg. Excellent out-the-door hiking and biking and wonderful views, as our 15 acres join national park property. Cross-country skiing, snow tubing, and fly-fishing in season. Discount golf nearby. Hearty breakfast. Porches, patio, decks, hot tub, and library provide relaxing, romantic atmosphere. Remote carriage house bedroom. Virginia Tech, Roanoke College, Hollins University, and Homeplace Restaurant nearby.

Hosts: Bill and Katherine Cochran
Rooms: 3 (PB) $70-75
Full Breakfast
Credit Cards: none
Notes: 2, 5, 7 (over 10 years), 10

CHARLES CITY

North Bend Plantation

12200 Weyanoke Road, 23030
(804) 829-5176
Web site: http://www.inngetaways.com/va/north.html

North Bend is a National Register property, circa 1819, a 500-acre James River plantation that remains under cultivation by the owner, the great-great-grandson of agriculturist Edmund Ruffin. Rich Civil War history, original antiques, full breakfast served in dining room with original china, rare book library, billiard room. Thirty minutes from Colonial Williamsburg. Croquet, horseshoes, bicycles, volleyball, pool onsite. Williamsburg Pottery, tennis, golf, horse racing, Busch Gardens nearby.

Hosts: George and Ridgely Copland
Rooms: 4 + 1 suite (4PB; 1SB) $115-135
Full Country Breakfast
Credit Cards: A, B
Notes: 2, 5, 7 (over 6), 8, 9 (on site), 10, 12

Orange Hill B&B

18401 Glebe Lane, 23030
(804) 829-5936; (888) 889-7781

Located in the middle of 50 acres of working farmland, this newly renovated farmhouse offers the charm and quiet of the country with the luxuries of the '90s. In the heart of historic James River Plantation and only 20 minutes from Colonial Williamsburg, shopping, and golf courses. Breakfast is served in the dining room; refreshments are served in the afternoon.

Hosts: Skip and Dorothy Bergoine
Rooms: 3 (2PB; 1SB) $80-110
Full Breakfast
Credit Cards: A, B
Notes: 2, 5, 7 (12 and over), 10, 12

CHARLOTTESVILLE

The Inn at Monticello

Route 20 S., 1188 Scottsville Road, 22902
(804) 979-3593; FAX (804) 296-1344
E-mail: innatmonticello@mindspring.com
Web site: http://www.innatmonticello.com

A charming country manor house built in 1850. The inn sits cradled in the valley at the foot of Thomas Jefferson's Monticello mountain. It looks out on landscaped grounds toward the mountains. Inside, we offer beautifully decorated rooms full of antique and period pieces. Some rooms have fireplaces, canopy beds, or a private porch. A gourmet breakfast is served.

Hosts: Norm and Becky Lindway
Rooms: 5 (PB) $125-145
Full Gourmet Breakfast
Credit Cards: A, B
Notes: 2, 5, 8, 9, 10, 11, 12

CHINCOTEAGUE

The Garden and the Sea

4188 Nelson Road, **New Church,** 23415
(757) 824-0672; (800) 824-0672
E-mail: baker@shore.intercom.net

Casual elegance and warm hospitality await you at this European-style country inn with its romantic, candlelit, fine-dining restaurant. Near Chincoteague wildlife refuge and Assateague Island's beautiful beach. Large, luxurious guest rooms, beautifully designed; spacious private baths, some with whirlpools; Victorian detail and stained glass; Oriental rugs; antiques; bay windows; and patios and gardens. We are open mid-March through November 29.

Hosts: Tom and Sara Baker
Rooms: 6 (PB) $75-165
Continental Plus Breakfast
Credit Cards: A, B, C, D
Notes: 2, 3, 4, 6, 7 (limited), 8, 9, 10, 12

The Inn at Poplar Corner

4248 Main Street, 23336
(757) 336-6115; (800) 336-6787;
FAX (757) 336-5776
Web site: http://www.chincoteague.com/b-b/popinn.html

The Inn at Poplar Corner is romantically decorated in Victorian style. Guest rooms are furnished with walnut beds, marble-top dressers, and wash stands; they have air-conditioning, ceiling fans, and large private baths with whirlpool tubs. Enjoy your full breakfast and afternoon tea on a wrap-around veranda. The Chincoteague National Wildlife Refuge and beach are only a few minutes away. Take advantage of our free use of bicycles to tour the refuge. This is a great way to appreciate the broad variety of wildlife.

Hosts: Tom and Jacque Derrickson, David and JoAnne Snead
Rooms: 4 (PB) $109-149
Full Breakfast
Credit Cards: A, B
Notes: 2, 7 (10 and older), 8, 9, 10

The Watson House Bed and Breakfast

The Watson House Bed and Breakfast

4240 Main Street, 23336
(757) 336-1564; (800) 336-6787;
FAX (757) 336-5776
Web site: http://www.chincoteague.com/b-b/watson.html

Featured on The Learning Channel's "Romantic Escapes," The Watson House is a recently restored Victorian country home built in the late 1800s by David Robert Watson. Nestled in the heart of Chincoteague, it is within walking distance of favorite shops and restaurants. We have six guest rooms furnished with antiques, private baths, AC, and ceiling fans. Full breakfast and afternoon tea with refreshments are served in the dining room or on the veranda. Complimentary use of bicycles, beach chairs, and beach towels to enjoy our beautiful beach. Also, we have cottages with Jacuzzis, pool access, and limited water view.

Hosts: Tom and Jacque Derrickson, David and JoAnne Snead
Rooms: 6 (PB) $69-115
Full Breakfast
Credit Cards: A, B
Notes: 7 (10 and older), 8, 9, 10

CHRISTIANSBURG

"Evergreen"— The Bell-Capozzi House

201 E. Main Street, 24073
(540) 382-7372; (800) 905-7372;
FAX (540) 382-4376
Web site: http://www.bnt.com/evergreen

A circa-1890 Victorian mansion located in the historic area just off I–81 (Exit 114). Private baths, TV/VCRs in rooms, central air, heated pool, poster beds, parlors, library, fireplaces, gallery of local artists, traditional southern breakfasts. Members of PAII and BBAV. Saturday tea. VIB Bears. Forty-eight-hour cancellation. Nonsmoking inn.

Hosts: Rocco and Barbara Bell Capozzi
Rooms: 5 + cottage (PB) $90-125
Full Breakfast
Credit Cards: A, B, C, D
Notes: 5, 10

CULPEPER

Fountain Hall B&B

609 S. East Street, 22701
(540) 825-8200; (800) 29-VISIT (298-4748);
FAX (540) 825-7716
E-mail: fhbnb@aol.com

This grand 1859 Colonial Revival home features tastefully restored and decorated rooms, some with private porch, whirlpool, or sitting room. Common rooms for reading, relaxing, TV, and conversation. Complimentary beverages. Gardens, stately trees, and mature boxwoods. Walk to the quaint historic district; visit antique and gift shops, restaurants, bookstores, and the museum. One mile from Highway 29 between Charlottesville, Washington, Richmond, and the Blue Ridge Mountains. Golf and dinner packages. AAA three diamonds, Mobil three stars.

Hosts: Steve and Kathi Walker
Rooms: 6 (PB) $95-150
Continental Breakfast
Credit Cards: A, B, C, D, E
Notes: 2, 5, 7, 8, 10, 12

EXMORE

The Gladstone House

12108 Lincoln Avenue, 23350–0296
(757) 442-4614; (800) BNB-GUEST (262-48378);
FAX (757) 442-4678
E-mail: egan@gladstonehouse.com
Web site: http://www.gladstonehouse.com

Gracious southern hospitality awaits your arrival (Romans 12:13). Spacious room with en suite baths, TV, central AC, VCR, complimentary video library. Morning brings coffee to your door and then a delicious four-course breakfast. Centrally located between Chincoteague and Cape Charles. Antiquing, cycling routes available. Good restaurants nearby. AAA-rated, three diamonds.

Hosts: Pat and Al Egan
Rooms: 3 (PB) $65-85
Full Breakfast
Credit Cards: A, B, C, D
Notes: 2, 5, 12

FAIRFIELD

Angels Rest Farm

471 Sunnybrook Road, 24435
(540) 377-6449

Angels Rest Farm is located in the beautiful Shenandoah valley just 8 miles north of Lexington. Lexington is home of VMI and Washington and Lee University, as well as a number of historic landmarks and museums. Our home, located on a country road, is nestled in a quiet valley surrounded by pastures with grazing cattle and horses nearby. The pond provides good fishing and a reflected view of the woods from either porch. A pool is available in summer, a hot tub year-round.

Hosts: John and Carol Nothwang
Rooms: 2 (PB) $60-70
Continental Breakfast
Credit Cards: none
Notes: 2, 5, 9, 11

FOREST

The Summer Kitchen at West Manor

3594 Elkton Farm Road, 24551
(804) 525-6208

Come enjoy a romantic English country cottage located on a beautiful working dairy farm. This private, restored summer kitchen, circa 1840, sleeps four with fireplace, loft, sunroom, and Jacuzzi. Enjoy a full country breakfast while overlooking 600 acres of rolling cropland, pastures, cattle, and mountains. Afternoon tea and strolls through the gardens complete each day. Come escape to our country haven. Area points of interest include Thomas Jefferson's Poplar Forest, antique shops, and the Blue Ridge Mountains.

Hosts: Sharon and Greg Lester
Rooms: 1 cottage, sleeps 4 (SB) $135-170
Full Breakfast
Credit Cards: none
Notes: 2, 5, 7, 9, 10

FREDERICKSBURG

Fredericksburg Colonial Inn

1707 Princess Anne Street, 22401
(540) 371-5666

A restored country inn in the historic district has thirty-two antique-appointed rooms, private baths, phones, TV, refrigerator, and Civil War motif. Complimentary continental breakfast included. Suites and family rooms available. Wonderful restaurants within walking distance. Beautiful churches nearby! More than 200 antique dealers, twenty major tourist attractions, and battlefields. A great getaway! One hour from Washington, Richmond, Charlottesville. Open year-round. (Prices subject to change.)

Host: B.J. Fletcher
Rooms: 32 (PB) $55-85
Continental Breakfast
Credit Cards: A, B, C
Notes: 2, 5, 7, 10

La Vista Plantation

La Vista Plantation

4420 Guinea Station Road, 22408–8850
(540) 898-8444; (800) 529-2823;
FAX (540) 898-9414
E-mail: lavistabb@aol.com
Web site: http://www.bbonline.com/va/lavista

An 1838 Classical Revival country home nestled amid ancient tulip poplars, cedars, and hollies, surrounded by pastures, woods, and fields. The house retains its original charm, with intricate acorn-and-oak leaf moldings, high ceilings, wide pine floors, and a two-story front portico. Choose a two-bedroom apartment (sleeps six) or huge formal room with mahogany, rice-carved, king poster bed. Both have AC, fireplaces, TV/radios, refrigerators. Brown-egg breakfast and stocked pond.

Hosts: Michele and Edward Schiesser
Rooms: 1 + 2-bedroom apartment (PB) $95
Full Breakfast
Credit Cards: A, B
Notes: 2, 5, 7, 8, 10, 12

HARRISONBURG

Kingsway B&B

3955 Singers Glen Road, 22802–0711
(540) 867-9696

Your hosts make your comfort their priority. The home is in a quiet rural area with a view of the mountains in the beautiful Shenandoah Valley. Hosts' carpentry and homemaking skills, house plants and outdoor flowers, a large lawn, and the inground pool help make your stay restful. Just 4½ miles from downtown. Nearby is Skyline Drive, caverns, historic sites, antique shops, and flea markets.

Hosts: Chester and Verna Leaman
Rooms: 3 (1PB; 2SB) $50-55
Full Breakfast
Credit Cards: none
Notes: 2, 5, 7, 9, 10, 12

HILLSVILLE

Bray's Manor

PO Box 385, 24343
(540) 728-7901; (800) 753-2729
E-mail: bramanor@swva.net
Web site: http://www.swva.net/braymanor/

Bray's Manor is situated above the surrounding countryside in a pastured setting. The house has a deck in the rear overlooking flowerbeds and the forest, and a front porch with beautiful long views of the valley below.

Hosts: Dick and Helen Bray
Rooms: 3 (PB) $75
Full Breakfast
Credit Cards: A, B, D
Notes: 2, 5, 7, 8, 9, 10, 12

LEESBURG

The Norris House Inn

108 Loudoun Street SW, 20175–2909
(703) 777-1806; (800) 644-1806;
FAX (703) 771-8051
E-mail: inn@norrishouse.com
Web site: http://norrishouse.com

Elegant accommodations in the heart of Leesburg's historic district. Six guest rooms furnished with antiques, and three wood-burning fireplaces. Full country breakfast. Convenient location with fine restaurants within easy walking distance. An hour's drive from Washington, DC, in Virginia's hunt country, rich in colonial and Civil War history, antiquing, and quaint villages. Perfect for romantic getaways, small meetings, and weddings. Open daily by reservation. Stone House Tea Room located on the inn's right.

Hosts: Pam and Don McMurray
Rooms: 6 (SB) $95-145
Full Breakfast
Credit Cards: A, B, C, D, E, F
Notes: 2, 5, 8, 9, 10, 12

LEXINGTON

B&B at Llewellyn Lodge

603 S. Main Street, 24450
(540) 463-3235; (800) 882-1145
E-mail: lll@rockbridge.net
Web site: http://www.llodge.com

This charming brick Colonial is located in a quiet neighborhood, just a few minutes' walk from the historic district, museums, Washington & Lee University, Virginia Military Institute, shops, and restaurants. John and Ellen Roberts will make sure your visit is a memorable one, giving you lots of advice on historic sites, hiking, theater, scenic driving, fishing, and other activities. Ellen's fantastic full breakfasts bring many repeat visitors. John is a Lexington native, born in the Stonewall Jackson Hospital (once a hospital, now a museum).

Hosts: John and Ellen Roberts
Rooms: 6 (PB) $55-98
Full Breakfast
Credit Cards: A, B, C, D
Notes: 2, 5, 8, 9, 10, 11, 12

Stoneridge Bed and Breakfast

Stoneridge Bed and Breakfast

Stoneridge Lane; PO Box 38, 24450
(540) 463-4090; (800) 491-2930;
FAX (540) 463-6078
Web site: http://www.webfeat-inc.com/stoneridge

Romantic 1829 antebellum home on 36 secluded acres of fields, streams, and woodlands. Five guest rooms with private baths, queen beds, and ceiling fans, most featuring private balconies or porches, double Jacuzzis, and fireplaces. Large front porch with wonderful mountain views and spectacular sunsets. Virginia wines are available, and a full gourmet country breakfast is served in the candlelit dining room or on the patio. Central AC. Five minutes south of historic Lexington.

Hosts: Norm and Barbara Rollenhagen
Rooms: 5 (PB) $115-160
Full Breakfast
Credit Cards: A, B, C, D
Notes: 2, 5, 7 (over 12 years), 12

LURAY

The Woodruff House

330 Mechanic Street, 22835
(540) 743-1494; FAX (540) 743-1722
Web site: http://www.bbonline.com/va/woodruff

"Prepare to be pampered!" Our chef-owned 1882 fairytale Victorian offers an inclusive stay with candlelit, fireside parlors, romantic fireside Jacuzzi rooms, and our "rooftop skylight fireside Jacuzzi suite!" A "candlelit dessert tea" welcomes you. Romantic candlelit gourmet dinner is included. Two outdoor hot tubs. AAA three diamonds; Mobil three stars.

Hosts: Lucas and Deborah Woodruff
Rooms: 6 (PB) $98-225
Full Breakfast
Credit Cards: A, B, D
Notes: 2, 4, 5, 8, 9, 10, 11, 12

The Woodruff House

LYNCHBURG

Federal Crest Inn Bed and Breakfast

1101 Federal Street, 24504
(804) 845-6155; (800) 818-6155;
FAX (804) 845-1445
Web site: http://www.inmind.com/federalcrest

A warm and relaxing atmosphere awaits every guest at this elegant 1909 Georgian Revival mansion in the Federal Hill Historic District. Magnificent woodwork and architectural details. Amenities include queen canopy beds, whirlpool tub, bedroom fireplaces, AC, luxury linens and robes, refreshments, full country breakfast, gift shop, much more! Convenient to all area colleges, Appomattox, golf, vineyards, antiquing, and museums.

Hosts: Ann and Phil Ripley
Rooms: 5 (4PB; 1SB) $85-125
Full Breakfast
Credit Cards: A, B, C, D
Notes: 2, 3 and 4 (with notice), 5, 8, 9, 10, 11, 12

Lynchburg Mansion Inn

Lynchburg Mansion Inn

405 Madison Street, 24504
(804) 528-5400; (800) 352-1199;
FAX (804) 847-2545

Luxurious accommodations in the historic district. A 9,000-square-foot Spanish Georgian mansion, king beds, fireplaces, outdoor spa, verandas, gardens, and gazebo. Mobil three stars. Civil War sites, near mountains and Blue Ridge Parkway.

Hosts: Bob and Mauranna Sherman
Rooms: 5 (PB) $109-144
Full Breakfast
Credit Cards: A, B, C, E
Notes: 2, 5, 7, 10, 12

Once Upon a Time

1102 Harrison Street, 24504
(804) 845-3561
E-mail: hughest@inmind.com
Web site: http://www.inmind.com/b_and_b

Our family waits to welcome you to Once Upon a Time, where the food is great, the beds are just right, and the atmosphere is friendly. This 1874 French Second Empire Victorian-style home in Lynchburg's Federal Hill Historic District provides guest rooms decorated after fairytale themes; they contain some antiques, clawfoot tubs, and plush Oriental rugs. So whether you're young at heart or just young, come be a part of our extended family when you travel to Lynchburg.

Hosts: Loriann and Tom Hughes
Rooms: 2 (PB) $65-90
Full Breakfast
Credit Cards: A, B, C
Notes: 2, 5, 7, 8, 9, 12

MADISON

Shenandoah Springs Country Inn

PO Box 770, 22727
(540) 923-4300; (540) 923-4109;
FAX (540) 923-4109
E-mail: farmern@summit.net
Web site: http://www.inngetaways.com/va/shenando.html

You will lodge in the pre-Civil War home of American Walker Yowell. The bedrooms are cozily decorated. Enjoy the open fireplace and candlelit breakfast beside a crackling fire, served by a gracious and competent host. Added to all this are the scenic views of the rolling hills, the Shenandoah National Park, and miles of pastoral farmland.

Hosts: Anne and Doug Farmer
Rooms: 5 (3PB; 2SB) $75-100
Full Breakfast
Credit Cards: none
Notes: 2, 3 and 4 (weekends), 5, 7 (over 6), 9, 10

MT. JACKSON

Widow Kip's Country Inn

355 Orchard Drive, 22842–9753
(540) 477-2400; (800) 478-8714
E-mail: widow@shentel.net
Web site: http://www.widowkips.com

A stately 1830 Colonial on 7 rural acres in the Shenandoah Valley overlooking the Blue Ridge Mountains. Romantic getaway. Five rooms with fireplaces/antiques, and two cottages. Locally crafted quilts adorn the four-poster, canopy, and sleigh beds. Civil War battlefields and museums, caverns, canoeing, hiking, horseback riding, golf, fishing and skiing, and pool. A comment by a recent guest: "You have set a standard of professional excellence; we will be back."

Hosts: Betty and Bob Luse
Rooms: 5 + 2 courtyard cottages (PB) $65-85
Full Breakfast
Credit Cards: A, B
Notes: 2, 5, 6 and 7 (in cottages), 8, 9, 10, 11, 12

MILLBORO

Ft. Lewis Lodge

HCR 3, Box 21A, 24460
(540) 925-2314; FAX (540) 925-2352
E-mail: ftlewis@va.tas.net
Web site: http://www.svta.org/ftlewis

A full-service country inn at the heart of a 3,200-acre mountain estate. Outdoor activities abound, with miles of river trout and bass fishing, swimming, extensive hiking trails, mountain biking, magnificent views, and abundant wildlife. The main lodge features wildlife art and locally handcrafted furniture. Three "in the round" silo bedrooms and two hand-hewn log cabins with stone fireplaces are perfect for a romantic getaway. Evenings are highlighted by contemporary American-style cuisine served in the historic Lewis Gristmill.

Hosts: John and Caryl Cowden
Rooms: 13 (PB) $140-195 for 2 MAP, dinner and breakfast
Full Breakfast
Credit Cards: A, B
Notes: 2, 3, 4, 7, 9, 10, 12

NATURAL BRIDGE

Burgers Country Inn

305 Rices Hill Road, 24578
(540) 291-2464

This historic country inn has been in the Burger family since our grandmother operated it as Patricia Inn in 1921. On 10 wooded acres near Natural Bridge, the farmhouse is furnished with antiques and collectibles. Its four bedrooms, parlor, living room, dining room, and porch all welcome guests. Play croquet in the summer, relax in front of the fire in the winter. Call or write for reservations or a brochure.

Host: John W. Burger
Rooms: 4 (2PB; 2SB) $60
Continental Plus Breakfast
Credit Cards: none
Notes: 2, 5, 6, 7, 8, 9, 10

NOKESVILLE

Shiloh Bed and Breakfast

13520 Carriage Ford Road, 20181
(703) 594-2664
E-mail: shilohbb@aol.com

Elegant white Georgian-style home sits high on a hill amidst 153 acres, overlooking a

5-acre bass lake. Beautifully decorated with country French decor that allows for the graciousness of the Old South to live on forever. Located near Manassas Civil War battlefield. One hour from Washington, DC, in one direction and the Blue Ridge Mountains in the other. Privacy and seclusion are emphasized; both rooms have private entrances, bathrooms, and kitchens, and are very spacious. Patio hot tub available. Romantic getaway.

Hosts: Alan and Carolee Fischer
Rooms: 2 (PB) $105-150
Full Breakfast
Credit Cards: A, B
Notes: 2, 5, 7, 8, 9, 10

NORFOLK

Old Dominion Inn

4111 Hampton Boulevard, 23504
(757) 440-5100; (800) 653-9030;
FAX (757) 423-5238

Our sixty-room inn opened in 1989 and takes its name from the Commonwealth of Virginia, "The Old Dominion." Located in the heart of Norfolk's west side, just 1 block south of the Old Dominion University campus and only a short drive up or down Hampton Boulevard from many of the area's busiest facilities. Each Old Dominion Inn room has a remote-controlled, color TV with cable service, ceiling fan, and individually controlled heat and air-conditioning. The James W. Sherrill family invite you to share in the warm hospitality of the inn. As a family-owned business, it is our desire that you feel right at home when you stay with us. We treat our guests like part of "our family." Be our guest for a complimentary, light breakfast each morning of your stay.

Hosts: The Sherrill Family
Rooms: 60 (PB) $70-138
Continental Breakfast
Credit Cards: A, B, C, D, E
Notes: 2, 5, 7, 8, 9, 10, 12

The Owl and the Pussycat

PETERSBURG

The Owl and the Pussycat

405 High Street, 23803
(804) 733-0505; (888) 733-0505;
FAX (804) 862-0698
E-mail: owlcat@ctg.net
Web site: http://wwwctg.net/owlcat

Enjoy a stay at a beautiful Queen Anne Victorian mansion near Old Towne. We have lovely, large bedrooms and offer a generous buffet breakfast. Only 5 minutes from highways 85 and 95, but quiet and surrounded by a garden. We are near numerous Civil War sites and some splendid plantations. A "purrfect" place to stay on your travels!

Hosts: Juliette and John Swenson
Rooms: 6 (4PB; 2SB) $70-110
Full Breakfast weekends, Continental weekdays
Credit Cards: A, B, C, D, F
Notes: 2, 5, 6, 7, 8, 10, 12

PROVIDENCE FORGE

Jasmine Plantation Bed and Breakfast Inn

4500 N. Courthouse Road, 23140
(804) 966-9836; (800) NEW KENT (639-5368);
FAX (804) 966-5679
Web site: http://www.bbonline.com/va/jasmine

Jasmine Plantation is a restored 1750s farmhouse convenient to Williamsburg, Richmond, and the James River plantations. Genuine hospitality, historical setting, and rooms decorated in period antiques await the visitor. The home was settled prior to 1683. Guests are invited to walk the 47 acres and use their imaginations as to what events have occurred here during the inn's 300-year history. Just 2.4 miles from I–64, Jasmine Plantation offers both convenience and seclusion to travelers. Fine dining can be enjoyed nearby.

Hosts: Joyce and Howard Vogt
Rooms: 6 (4PB; 2SB) $80-120
Full Breakfast
Credit Cards: A, B, C
Notes: 2, 5, 7 (over 12), 10, 12

RICHMOND

Be My Guest Bed and Breakfast

2926 Kensington Avenue, 23221
(804) 358-9901

Elegant 1918 home in the historic district of Richmond. Near the Virginia Museum of Fine Arts and the Virginia Historical Society. Four blocks from charming Carytown with wonderful shops and restaurants. Convenient to I–95 and I–64, as well as the downtown area.

Hosts: Bertie and Bill Selvey
Rooms: 3 (1PB; 2SB) $60-110
Full Breakfast
Credit Cards: none
Notes: 2, 5, 7, 10, 12

The William Catlin House

2304 E. Broad Street, 23223
(804) 780-3746

Richmond's first and oldest bed and breakfast features antiques, canopy poster beds, and working fireplaces. A delicious full breakfast is served in the elegant dining room. Built in 1845, this richly appointed home is in the Church Hill historic district and was featured in *Colonial Homes* and *Southern Living* magazines. Across from St. John's Church, where Patrick Henry gave his famous "liberty or death" speech. Just 2 minutes from I–95 and Route 64.

Hosts: Robert and Josephine Martin
Rooms: 5 (3PB; 2SB) $95
Full Breakfast
Credit Cards: A, B, D
Notes: 2, 5, 12

STAUNTON

Ashton Country House

1205 Middlebrook Avenue, 24401
(540) 885-7819; (800) 296-7819;
FAX (540) 885-6029
Web site: http://www.bbhost.com/ashtonbnb

Ashton Country House is a delightful blend of town and country. This 1860 Greek

Revival home is located on 24 acres, yet is only a mile from the center of Staunton. There are five air-conditioned, comfortable, attractive bedrooms, each with a private bath. Guests start each day with a hearty country breakfast. Afternoon tea is served in the grand living room or on any porch. Ashton Country House is the perfect place to soothe the spirit, share a weekend with friends, celebrate a special anniversary, or escape to the serenity of the countryside.

Hosts: Dorie DiStefano
Rooms: 5 (PB) $75-125
Full Breakfast
Credit Cards: A, B
Notes: 2, 7, 8, 9, 10, 11, 12

Frederick House

Frederick House

28 N. New Street, 24401
(540) 885-4220; (800) 334-5575;
FAX (540) 885-5180
E-mail: ejharman@frederickhouse.com
Web site: http://www.frederickhouse.com

Frederick House is a small historic hotel in the European tradition. Six restored homes are situated across from Mary Baldwin College in Staunton, the oldest city in the Shenandoah Valley. You can walk to restaurants, antique shops, galleries, and museums.

Hosts: Joe and Eve Harman
Rooms: 17 (PB) $75-170
Full Breakfast
Credit Cards: A, B, C, D, E
Notes: 2, 5, 7, 8, 9, 10, 11, 12

Montclair Bed and Breakfast

Montclair B&B

320 N. New Street, 24401
(540) 885-5761
E-mail: msbang@juno.com
Web site: http://www.bbonline.com

Conveniently located in historic downtown Staunton, Montclair offers deluxe, personal service and overnight accommodations with a choice of twin, double, and queen rooms. Central AC, private phones, and modern baths add to the luxury of this beautifully restored Italianate town home. Built in 1880, Montclair received an award for historic restoration in 1994. Guests are welcomed with afternoon tea in the English tradition and are encouraged to relax in the parlor, library, or sitting room.

Hosts: Sheri and Mark Bang
Rooms: 4 (3PB; 1SB) $75-85
Full Breakfast
Credit Cards: A, B
Notes: 2, 5, 7 (12+), 8, 9, 10, 11

Thornrose House at Gypsy Hill

531 Thornrose Avenue, 24401
(540) 885-7026; (800) 861-4338;
FAX (540) 885-6458
Web site: http://www.bbhsv.org/thornrose

Outside, this turn-of-the century Georgian residence has a wraparound veranda, Greek colonnades, and lovely gardens. Inside, a fireplace and grand piano create a formal but comfortable atmosphere. Five attractive bedrooms with private baths await on the second floor. Your hosts offer afternoon tea, refreshments, and conversation. Adjacent to a 300-acre park that is great for walking, with tennis, golf, and ponds. Nearby attractions include the Blue Ridge National Park, natural chimneys, Skyline Drive, Woodrow Wilson's birthplace, and the Museum of American Frontier Culture.

Hosts: Otis and Suzanne Huston
Rooms: 5 (PB) $69-95
Full Breakfast
Credit Cards: A, B, C
Notes: 2, 5, 7 (over 6), 8, 9, 10

STUARTS DRAFT

Restful Haven

3007 Lyndhurst Road, **Lyndhurst**, 22952
(Mail: Route 2, Box 416K, Stuarts Draft, 24477)
(540) 943-7812

Located on the entire upper floor of a tidy Cape Cod house, via a separate spiral staircase entrance. The neatly furnished bedroom, small den, breakfast nook, and ¾ bath retain the sweet, country charm of our lovely Shenandoah Valley area. The self-serve, dry cereal/soup items in the "welcome basket" can be cooked/chilled in the small refrigerator and microwave provided. Accommodations are equipped with AC, extension phone (with separate "ring"/number), color TV (for VCR use only), and private "prayer closet."

Hostess: Mrs. Lolly Johnson Hoover
Rooms: 1 (PB) $10/person/day suggested
Continental Breakfast (self-serve dry cereal/soup)
Credit Cards: none
Notes: 2, 3 (dried soup), 5, 9, 11

TANGIER

Shirley's Bay View Inn

PO Box 183, 23440
(757) 891-2396

Enjoy a pleasant and restful visit to one of the last quiet and remote fishing villages on the Chesapeake Bay. You will stay at one of the oldest homes on Tangier Island, filled with the beauty and charm of days gone by. The beautiful beaches, sunsets, and customs of Tangier Island will make your stay a memorable one, and your hostess will make you feel you are part of the family.

Hostess: Shirley Pruitt
Rooms: 7 (4PB; 3SB) $40-70
Full Breakfast
Credit Cards: none
Notes: 2, 5, 7, 9

VIRGINIA BEACH

Barclay Cottage B&B

400 16th Street, 23451
(757) 422-1956

Barclay Cottage offers casual sophistication in a warm, historic, innlike atmosphere. Designed in turn-of-the-century style, the

Barclay Cottage Bed and Breakfast

cottage is 2 blocks from the beach, in the heart of the Virginia Beach recreational area. The inn is completely restored with antique furniture to bring together the feeling of yesterday with the comfort of today. Formerly the home of Lillian S. Barclay, the inn has been a guest home for many years. We have kept the historic ambience of the inn while modernizing it significantly to meet today's needs. We look forward to welcoming you to Barclay Cottage, where the theme is "We go where our dream leads us."

Hosts: Peter and Claire
Rooms: 5 (3PB; 2SB) $78-108
Full Breakfast
Credit Cards: A, B, C
Notes: 8, 9, 10, 12

WARM SPRINGS

Three Hills Inn

PO Box 9, Route 220, 24484
(540) 839-5381; (888) 23-HILLS (234-4557);
FAX (540) 839-5199

A premier country inn in the heart of Bath County. Enjoy a casually elegant retreat in a beautifully restored historic manor. You'll have spectacular mountain views, acres of woods and trails—serenity at its best! Elegant suites are available, some with kitchens and fireplaces. The inn is located 4 miles from the historic Homestead Resort. Your hosts have missionary backgrounds and speak fluent Spanish. From a romantic getaway to an executive retreat (a meeting/conference facility is available), Three Hills Inn is a perfect choice for the discriminating traveler. Afternoon tea, weekends.

Hosts: Doug and Charlene Fike
Rooms: 14 (PB) $69-189
Full Gourmet Breakfast
Credit Cards: A, B, D
Notes: 2, 5, 6, 7, 8, 9, 10, 11, 12

WASHINGTON

Caledonia Farm—1812

47 Dearing Road, **Flint Hill,** 22627
(540) 675-3693 (voice and FAX);
(800) BNB-1812 (262-1812)
Web site: http://www.bnb-n-va.com/cale1812.htm

Enjoy ultimate hospitality, comfort, scenery, and recreation adjacent to Virginia's Shenandoah National Park. This romantic getaway to history and nature includes outstanding full breakfasts, fireplaces, air-conditioning, hayrides, bicycles, lawn games, VCR, and piano. Fine dining, caves, Skyline Drive, battlefields, stables, antiquing, hiking, and climbing are all nearby. Washington, DC, is 68 miles away; Washington, Virginia, just 4 miles. A Virginia historic landmark, the farm is listed on the National Register of Historic Places. Unwind in our new spa.

Host: Phil Irwin
Rooms: 4 (2PB; 2SB) $80-140
Full Breakfast
Credit Cards: A, B, D
Notes: 2, 5, 7 (over 12), 8, 9, 10, 11, 12

WAYNESBORO

The Iris Inn Bed & Breakfast

191 Chinquapin Drive, 22980
(540) 943-1991
E-mail: irisinn@cfw.com
Web site: http://www.irisinn.com

The charm and grace of southern living in a totally modern facility, nestled in a wooded tract on the western slope of the Blue Ridge, overlooking the historic Shenandoah Valley—that's what awaits you at The Iris Inn. It's ideal for a weekend retreat, a refreshing change for the business traveler, and a tranquil spot for the tourist to spend a night or a week. Guest rooms are spacious, comfortably furnished, and delightfully decorated in nature and wildlife motifs. Each room has individual temperature control.

Hosts: Wayne and Iris Karl
Rooms: 9 (PB) $80-140
Full Breakfast
Credit Cards: A, B, C
Notes: 2, 5, 7 (over 12), 8, 9, 10, 11

WILLIAMSBURG

Applewood Colonial Bed and Breakfast

605 Richmond Road, 23185
(757) 229-0205; (800) 899-2753;
FAX (757) 229-9401
E-mail: applewood@tni.net
Web site: http://www.applewoodbnb.com

An "Applewood" a day, for a memorable stay. This Flemish bond brick home was built in 1929 by the construction manager for the Colonial Williamsburg restoration

Applewood Colonial Bed and Breakfast

and features many finely crafted colonial details of the 18th century. Antiques and 20th-century comfort throughout the house are accented by the owner's unique apple collection. Guests enjoy a full breakfast served by candlelight in the elegant dining room. Refreshments, including sparkling cider, Virginia peanuts, and homebaked cookies, are continually available. Cable TV in the parlor, with a VCR featuring informative Colonial Williamsburg videotapes. Guest phone, FAX capabilities, and full concierge service.

Hosts: Van Pepper, Marty and Roger Jones
Rooms: 4 (PB) $70-150
Full Breakfast
Credit Cards: A, B
Notes: 2, 5, 7 (restricted), 8, 9, 10

Colonial Gardens Bed and Breakfast

1109 Jamestown Road, 23185
(757) 220-8087; (800) 886-9715
E-mail: colgdns@widomaker.com
Web site: http://www.ontheline.com/cgbb

This beautiful home is conveniently located just 4 minutes from Colonial Williamsburg and 5 minutes from Jamestown. Situated on a heavily wooded lot in the heart of the city, Colonial Gardens Bed and Breakfast

Colonial Gardens Bed and Breakfast

offers the weary traveler a quiet haven of rest and relaxation. The home features English and early-1800s American antiques. Bedrooms are beautifully decorated. Suites available. A full plantation breakfast is served. Experience true southern hospitality and Williamsburg elegance at its best.

Hosts: Scottie and Wilmot Phillips
Rooms: 4 (PB) $105-130
Full Breakfast
Credit Cards: A, B, C
Notes: 2, 5, 7, 8, 9, 10, 12

Fox and Grape B&B

701 Monumental Avenue, 23185
(757) 229-6914; (800) 292-3699

Here you'll find genteel accommodations 5 blocks north of Virginia's restored colonial capital. This lovely two-story Colonial with its spacious wraparound porch is a perfect place to enjoy your morning coffee, plan your day's activities in Williamsburg, or relax with your favorite book. Furnishings include antiques, counted cross-stitch, duck decoys, and folk-art Noah's arks made by your host. Pat enjoys doing counted cross-stitch; Bob carves walking sticks and makes nursery rhyme collectibles.

Hosts: Pat and Robert Orendorff
Rooms: 4 (PB) $85-105
Full Breakfast
Credit Cards: A, B, D
Notes: 2, 5, 7, 8, 9, 10, 12

Hite's Bed and Breakfast

704 Monumental Avenue, 23185
(757) 229-4814

Charming Cape Cod within a 7-minute walk of Colonial Williamsburg. Large rooms are cleverly furnished with antiques and collectibles. Each room has phone, TV, radio, coffeemaker, robes, and beautiful bathrooms with old claw-foot tubs. A suite is available, with a nice romantic setting and a large sitting room. In the parlor for our guests' enjoyment is an antique pump organ and hand-crank Victrola. You can relax in the garden and enjoy the swing, birds, flowers, and goldfish pond.

Hosts: James and Faye Hite
Rooms: 2 (PB) $85-100
Full Breakfast
Credit Cards: none
Notes: 2, 5, 7, 10, 12

Hughes Guest Home

106 Newport Avenue, 23185–4212
(757) 229-3493

The Hughes Guest Home, lodging only, has been in operation since 1947, located directly opposite Williamsburg Lodge. It is a lovely 2-minute stroll from Colonial Williamsburg's restored district, golfing, and numerous dining facilities, including the Colonial Taverns. The College of William and Mary, Merchant's Square, and Civil

War museums are also within easy walking distance. We welcome you to stay in our home during your visit to Williamsburg. The home is decorated lavishly with family antiques. Do come and enjoy our southern hospitality.

Hostess: Genevieve O. Hughes
Rooms: 3 (1PB; 2SB) $50
No Breakfast
Credit Cards: none
Notes: 2, 5, 7, 10

Liberty Rose B&B

1022 Jamestown Road, 23185
(757) 253-1260; (800) 545-1825
Web site: http://www.libertyrose.com

Williamsburg's only four-diamond award B&B. This perfectly romantic bed and breakfast is truly in a class of its own. A hilltop setting of gardens, courtyards, and century-old trees. Great breakfast served at intimate "tables for two" in the windowed parlor porch. All of the finely detailed rooms have queen beds, luxurious linens, beautiful baths, TV/VCRs, movies, private phones, and chocolates!

Hosts: Brad and Sandra Hirz
Rooms: 4 (PB) $135-195
Full Breakfast
Credit Cards: A, B, C
Notes: 2, 5, 8, 10

Newport House Bed & Breakfast

710 S. Henry Street, 23185
(757) 229-1775; FAX (757) 229-6408

A reproduction of a 1756 home, Newport House has museum-standard period furnishings, including canopy beds. Only a 5-minute walk to the historic area. Breakfast with colonial recipes; colonial dancing in the ballroom Tuesday evenings (beginners welcome). The host is a historian/author (including a book on Christ) and former museum director. The hostess is a gardener, beekeeper, 18th-century seamstress, and former nurse. A pet rabbit entertains at breakfast. No smoking.

Hosts: John and Cathy Millar
Rooms: 2 (PB) $130-160
Full Breakfast
Credit Cards: none
Notes: 2, 5, 7, 8, 9, 10, 12

A Primrose Cottage

706 Richmond Road, 23185
(757) 229-6421; (800) 522-1901;
FAX (757) 259-0717
Web site: http://www.primrose-cottage.com

A nature lover's delight. In the spring, the front walkway is lined with primroses. Thousands of tulips bloom in April and May, and even in cooler months something adds color to this award-winning garden. There are four rooms, all spacious, bright, and lovingly decorated with antiques. Each has its own television and bath. Two of the bathrooms have Jacuzzis. You are invited to play the harpsichord built by the innkeeper. Wonderful hot breakfasts are served every morning.

Host: Inge Curtis
Rooms: 4 (PB) $85-115
Full Breakfast
Credit Cards: A, B
Notes: 2, 5, 8, 9, 10, 12

Williamsburg Manor

600 Richmond Road, 23185
(757) 220-8011 (voice and FAX); (800) 422-8011

A 1927 Georgian home built during the reconstruction of Colonial Williamsburg.

It recently was restored to the manor's original elegance and furnished with exquisite pieces, including antiques and collectibles. Well-appointed guest rooms, each with private bath, TV, and central AC. A lavish fireside breakfast is prepared by the executive chef. The home is available for weddings, private parties, dinners, and meetings. Ideal location, within walking distance of the historic area. Onsite parking. Off-season rates.

Hostess: Laura Reeves
Rooms: 5 (PB) $75-115 (seasonal)
Full Breakfast
Credit Cards: A, B
Notes: 2, 4, 5, 7, 8, 10, 12

Williamsburg Sampler Bed and Breakfast

Williamsburg Sampler Bed and Breakfast

922 Jamestown Road, 23185
(757) 253-0398; (800) 722-1169;
FAX (757) 253-2669
E-mail: WbgSampler@aol.com

This 18th-century, plantation-style Colonial was proclaimed "Inn of the Year" by Virginia's governor. This is a AAA three-diamond and Mobil three-star home within walking distance of the historic area. Richly furnished bedrooms and suites with king- or queen-size beds, private baths, fireplaces, and rooftop garden. A collection of antiques, pewter, and samplers is displayed throughout the house. A "skip lunch" breakfast is served. The Williamsburg Sampler is internationally recognized as a favorite spot for a romantic honeymoon or anniversary.

Hosts: Helen and Ike Sisane
Rooms: 2 + 2 suites (PB) $100-150
Full Breakfast
Credit Cards: A, B
Notes: 2, 5, 8, 9, 10, 12

WINCHESTER

Brownstone Cottage Bed and Breakfast

161 McCarty Lane, 22602
(540) 662-1962
Email: brnstone@winchesterva.com
Web site: http://www.nvim.com/brownstonebnb

Enjoy the quiet and peaceful country setting of Brownstone Cottage, a private home in the Shenandoah Valley outside historic Winchester. Hospitality and individual attention highlight your stay. Step across the threshold of this bed and breakfast and feel right at home as you relax in your room or the sitting room, or on the outside deck. Wake to the aroma of fresh-brewed coffee and the beginning of a full country breakfast, featuring Chuck's homemade pancakes or bread.

Hosts: Chuck and Sheila Brown
Rooms: 2 (PB) $95
Full Breakfast
Credit Cards: A, B
Notes: 2, 5, 8, 10

NOTES: Credit cards accepted: A Master Card; B Visa; C American Express; D Discover; E Diners Club; F Other; 2 Personal checks accepted; 3 Lunch available; 4 Dinner available; 5 Open all year; 6 Pets

WOODSTOCK

Azalea House B&B

551 S. Main Street, 22664
(540) 459-3500
Web site: http://www.azaleahouse.com

A large Victorian house built in 1892, featuring family antiques and stenciled ceilings. It initially was used as a parsonage, serving a church 3 blocks away for about 70 years. Located in the historic Shenandoah Valley, it is close to Skyline Drive and the mountains. Many Civil War sites are within a short driving distance. Nearby activities include antiquing, hiking, and horseback riding.

Hosts: Margaret and Price McDonald
Rooms: 4 (PB) $55-75
Full Breakfast
Credit Cards: A, B, C
Notes: 2, 7 (over 6), 9, 10, 11

Azalea House Bed and Breakfast

The Inn at Narrow Passage

PO Box 608, 22664
(540) 459-8000; (800) 459-8002;
FAX (540) 459-8001
Web site: http://www.innatnarrowpassage.com

This cozy, historic inn has been welcoming travelers along the Great Wagon Road (now U.S. 11) through the Shenandoah Valley since the 1740s. In the main building, guests can enjoy the large common room with its gleaming pine floors, wing chairs, and massive limestone fireplace. A hearty, fireside breakfast is served in the paneled dining room each morning. Fine restaurants can be found nearby for other meals. The oldest guest accommodations in the inn feature wood floors, stenciling, and the atmosphere of colonial times. Rooms from later additions are decorated in the same style, but open onto porches, with marvelous views of the Shenandoah River and the Massanutten Mountains to the east. The inn is fully air-conditioned, and most rooms have private baths and working fireplaces.

Hosts: Ellen and Ed Markel
Rooms: 12 (PB) $90-145
Full Breakfast
Credit Cards: A, B, D
Notes: 2, 5, 7 (well-behaved), 8, 9, 10, 11, 12

---

welcome; 7 Children welcome; 8 Tennis nearby; 9 Swimming nearby; 10 Golf nearby; 11 Skiing nearby; 12 May be booked through travel agent.

WASHINGTON

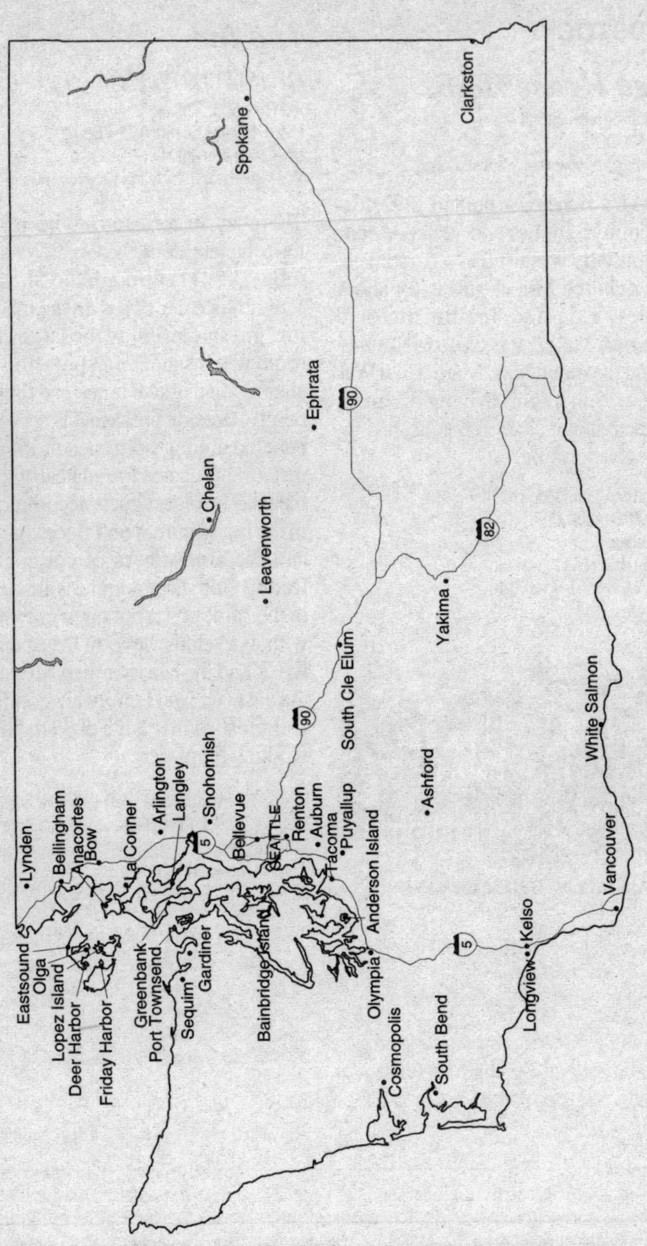

Clarkston
Spokane
Ephrata
90
Chelan
Leavenworth
82
Yakima
South Cle Elum
90
White Salmon
Ashford
Snohomish
Arlington
Langley
Bellingham
Anacortes
Bow
La Conner
Lynden
Bellevue
SEATTLE
Renton
Auburn
Puyallup
Tacoma
5
Anderson Island
Vancouver
Kelso
5
Longview
Olympia
Bainbridge Island
Gardiner
Sequim
Port Townsend
Greenbank
Eastsound
Olga
Lopez Island
Deer Harbor
Friday Harbor
Cosmopolis
South Bend

Washington

Bed and Breakfast Service (BABS)

445 W. Lake Samish Drive, **Bellingham,** 98226
(360) 733-8642

BABS is an RSO (reservation service organization). Our hosts nationwide have modest prices and feature lodging in the European tradition.

Hosts: Delores and George Herrmann
Rooms: many (PB&SB)
Full and Continental Breakfasts
Credit Cards: none
Notes: 2, 5, 12

ABERDEEN/COSMOPOLIS

Cooney Mansion Bed and Breakfast

1705 Fifth Street, Box 54, **Cosmopolis,** 98537
(360) 533-0602; (800) 9-SPRUCE (977-7823)
E-mail: cooney@techline.com
Web site: http://www.techline.com/~cooney

Cooney Mansion Bed and Breakfast

The Cooney Mansion is located 2 minutes from Aberdeen. This 1908 National Historic Register home, situated in wooded seclusion, was built by Neil Cooney, owner of one of the largest sawmills of the time. It captures the adventure of the Northwest. Share the lumber baron's history and many of his original Craftsman-style antiques. Enjoy eighteen holes of golf (in the backyard) or a leisurely walk around Mill Creek Park. Relax in the sauna and Jacuzzi, curl up with one of the many books from the library, or watch TV in the ballroom or living room. Award-winning breakfast. Highly rated.

Hosts: Judi and Jim Lohr
Rooms: 8 (5PB; 3SB) $75-165
Full "Lumber Baron's" Breakfast
Credit Cards: all
Notes: 5, 8, 10

NOTES: Credit cards accepted: A Master Card; B Visa; C American Express; D Discover; E Diners Club; F Other; 2 Personal checks accepted; 3 Lunch available; 4 Dinner available; 5 Open all year; 6 Pets welcome; 7 Children welcome; 8 Tennis nearby; 9 Swimming nearby; 10 Golf nearby; 11 Skiing nearby; 12 May be booked through travel agent.

ANACORTES

Hasty Pudding House

1312 8th Street, 98221
(360) 293-5773 (voice and FAX); (800) 368-5588
E-mail: hasty@mail1.halcyon.com
Web site: http://www.hastypudding.net/hasty

Celebrate romance in a delightful 1913 heritage home with Victorian decor, fresh flowers, and cozy window seats. Snuggle in king and queen top-quality beds; private baths. Breakfast is fabulous! A great getaway anytime.

Hosts: Mike and Melinda Hasty
Rooms: 4 (PB) $75-109
Full Breakfast
Credit Cards: A, B, C, D
Notes: 2, 5, 8, 9, 10, 12

Sunset Beach B&B

100 Sunset Beach, 98221
(360) 293-5428; (800) 359-3448
Web site: http://www.whidbey.com/sunsetbeach

On exciting Rosario Straits. Relax and enjoy the view of seven major islands from our decks, stroll the beach, or walk in the beautiful Washington Park, adjacent to our private gardens. Also enjoy boating, hiking, and fishing. Three bedrooms with private baths; one with a Jacuzzi; a hot tub is available in a separate building. Private entry and TV. Five minutes to San Juan ferries, fine restaurants, and marina. A convenience store is nearby. Sunsets are outstanding! No smoking.

Hosts: Joann and Hal Harker
Rooms: 3 (PB) $79-95 (seasonal)
Full Breakfast
Credit Cards: A, B
Notes: 2, 5, 7 (over 6), 9, 10, 11, 12

ANDERSON ISLAND

The Inn at Burg's Landing

8808 Villa Beach Road, 98303
(253) 884-9185; (800) 431-5622
E-mail: innatburgslandingmailexcite.com

Catch the ferry from Steilacoom to stay at this contemporary log homestead built in 1987. It offers spectacular views of Mt. Rainier, Puget Sound, and the Cascade Mountains and is located south of Tacoma off I–5. Choose from three guest rooms, including the master bedroom with queen-size "log" bed, skylight above, and private whirlpool bath. The inn has a private beach. Collect seashells and agates, swim on two freshwater lakes nearby, and/or enjoy a game of tennis or golf. Tour the island by bicycle or on foot and watch for sailboats and deer. Hot tub. Full breakfast. Families welcome. No smoking.

Hosts: Ken and Annie Burg
Rooms: 4 (2PB; 2SB) $70-110
Full Breakfast
Credit Cards: A, B
Notes: 2, 5, 7, 8, 9, 10, 11, 12

ARLINGTON

Mt. Higgins House

29805 SR 530 NE, 98223
(360) 435-8703; (888) 296-3777;
FAX (360) 435-9757
E-mail: mthigginshouse@juno.com

A peaceful, secluded retreat on a 70-acre farm in the Stillaguamish River Valley, 17 miles east of Arlington and 11 miles west of Darrington. All rooms have mountain views; a large deck overlooks a stocked trout pond. The common areas include the living room with a river rock fireplace, piano, satellite TV, and CD player; a large dining area; and a cozy library. Enjoy birding, fishing, and hiking. River access. Adult, smoke-free. A generous buffet breakfast is included.

Hostess: Renee Ottersen
Rooms: 2 (PB) $85-110
Full Breakfast
Credit Cards: A, B

ASHFORD

Mountain Meadows Inn

28912 State Route 706 E.; PO Box 291, 98304
(360) 569-2788
E-mail: mtmeadow@mashell.com
Web site: http://www.bbchannel.com

Experience the authentic Northwest! Built in 1910 as the home of a mill superintendent, Mountain Meadows Inn is on 11 quiet acres of tall cedars amongst the grandeur of the northwestern landscape. Guests enjoy privacy and hospitality on their romantic getaway weekends. Historic John Muir and Native American displays. Close to Mt. Rainier National Park but away from the crowds.

Hosts: Harry and Michelle Latimer
Rooms: 6 (PB) $75-115
Full Breakfast
Credit Cards: A, B
Notes: 2, 5, 7 (4 and up), 9, 10, 11, 12

AUBURN

Rose Arbor Inn B&B and Massage

514 A Street NE, 98002
(253) 931-8564
Web site: http://www.moriah.com/inns

Relaxing, homey atmosphere with old-fashioned decor that helps you step back in time to a slower, gentler place. We have four lovely guest rooms and a hot tub. Bathrobes are provided. Swedish massage is available by appointment. Ample vegetarian breakfasts are served, including homemade breads and granola. Irish chocolate chip cookies are in the rooms; fresh fruit, pop, and juice are available.

Hostess: Rae Boggs
Rooms: 4 (1PB; 3SB) $60-90
Full Breakfast
Credit Cards: A, B
Notes: 2, 5, 8, 9, 10, 11

BAINBRIDGE ISLAND

The Woodsman B&B

7700 Springridge Road NE, 98110
(206) 842-7386

The Woodsman B&B is nestled on 5 acres amidst beautiful gardens and tall trees. The tastefully decorated guest room has a private entrance and offers a hot tub. Breakfast is a memorable event, served in the formal dining room or sunroom. Close to good restaurants, parks, lovely Bloedel gardens, and a ferry ride from Seattle.

Hosts: Bill and Joyce Ostling
Rooms: 1 (PB) $75-80
Full Breakfast
Credit Cards: none

BELLEVUE

Petersen Bed and Breakfast

10228 SE 8th, 98004
(425) 454-9334

We offer guest lodging 5 minutes from Bellevue Square with wonderful shopping, half a block from the bus line to Seattle.

Rooms have down comforters, and we have a hot tub on the deck. Children are welcome. No smoking.

Hostess: Eunice A. Petersen
Rooms: 2 (SB) $60-75
Full Breakfast
Credit Cards: none
Notes: 2, 5, 7

CHELAN

Highland Guest House

121 E. Highland Avenue; PO Box 2089, 98816
(509) 682-2892; (800) 681-2892
Web site: http://www.lakechelan.com/highland.htm

Homesteaded in 1896, this Queen Anne–style Victorian was finished in 1902. The home is in the process of being listed on the National Register of Historic Places. The mansion is situated on the north hill overlooking Lake Chelan and is a short walk from downtown or the lake. The view is breathtaking from the huge wraparound veranda or the private porch off the Rose and Wicker Rooms. All rooms are theme-decorated and hand-stenciled. During the summer, enjoy your gourmet breakfast and fresh-ground coffee on the veranda.

Hosts: Brad and Marilee Stolzenburg
Rooms: 3 (PB) $55-114
Gourmet Breakfast
Credit Cards: A, B
Notes: 2, 3, 5, 7, 8, 9, 10, 11, 12

CLARKSTON

The Cliff House B&B

1227 Westlake Drive, 99403
(509) 758-1267

"Breathtaking" is one of the best ways to describe The Cliff House view of the Snake River, 500 feet below. Jet-boat trips and white-water rafting can be arranged. Chief Timothy State Park, named for the Nez Percé Indian leader, lies along the river. Varied wildlife may be viewed. North America's deepest gorge, Hell's Canyon, is nearby. Relax in king-size beds.

Hosts: Yvonne and Everett Dickerson
Rooms: 2 (PB) $70-75
Full Breakfast
Credit Cards: none
Notes: 2, 7 (by arrangement), 9, 10

CLE ELUM, SOUTH

The Moore House Bed and Breakfast Inn

526 Marie Avenue; PO Box 629, 98943
(509) 674-5939; (800) 2-2-TWAIN (228-9246; OR/WA only)

Former 1909 Milwaukee Railroad Crew Hotel, now offering twelve bright and airy rooms ranging from economical to exquisite and including two genuine cabooses and a bridal suite with jetted tub. On the National Register, the inn has a museumlike atmosphere with an extensive collection of railroad memorabilia and artifacts. Nestled in the Cascade Mountain foothills, the house is close to cross-country

NOTES: Credit cards accepted: A Master Card; B Visa; C American Express; D Discover; E Diners Club; F Other; 2 Personal checks accepted; 3 Lunch available; 4 Dinner available; 5 Open all year; 6 Pets

skiing, hiking, biking, rafting, horseback riding, fishing, and fine dining.

Hosts: Eric and Cindy Sherwood
Rooms: 12 (6PB; 6SB) $50-125
Full Breakfast
Credit Cards: A, B, C, D
Notes: 2, 5, 7, 10, 11, 12

EPHRATA

Ivy Chapel Inn

164 D Street SW, 98823
(509) 754-0629
Web site: http://www.quikpage.com/i/ivychapel

The Ivy Chapel Inn is located in the former Presbyterian Church at the corner of Second SW and D streets. The original brick building was constructed in the 1940s. The inn is the result of a long-time dream. Love and hard work have maintained the stately grace and charm of the recently refurbished building, while still offering the conveniences of a modern facility. Breakfast is served in the sunny morning room on the second floor. An open-air deck with a large hot tub is provided.

Hosts: Kirk and Cheryl McClelland
Rooms: 6 (PB) $75-100
Full Breakfast
Credit Cards: A, B, C, D
Notes: 2, 5, 7, 9, 10

FRIDAY HARBOR

Halvorsen House

1165 Halvorsen Road, 98250
(360) 378-2707 (voice and FAX); (888) 238-4187
E-mail: johnpatten@interisland.net
Web site: http://www.friday-harbor.net/halvorsen

Halvorsen House Bed and Breakfast offers beautiful, pastoral views of the nearby valley. The serenity of an island forest welcomes you to this traditional country home, located just 2 miles from Friday Harbor, San Juan Island. Our guest rooms feature queen beds, private baths, floral wallpaper, and lace curtains. Children are welcome in these rooms, which have phones and TV/VCRs.

Hosts: John and Cindy Patten
Rooms: 4 (PB) $70-160
Full Breakfast
Credit Cards: A, B, C, D, F
Notes: 2, 5, 7

States Inn

States Inn

2039 W. Valley Road, 98250
(360) 378-6240; FAX (360) 378-6241

Situated in a scenic valley 7 miles from town, the inn is situated on a 60-acre horse ranch on the west side of the island. We offer diverse rooms with private baths, and one three-room suite. Each is individually decorated with the flavor of a state's name. Three-diamond AAA rating. This is a high-quality inn, located in the middle of the Northwest's most scenic vacation area.

Hosts: Alan and Julia Paschal
Rooms: 10 (8PB; 2SB) $85-125
Full Breakfast
Credit Cards: A, B
Notes: 2, 5, 12

GARDINER

Diamond Point Inn

241 Sunshine Road, 98334
(360) 797-7720; (888) 797-0393
E-mail: dpinn@olypen.com
Web site: http://www.dynamicgraphics.com/diamondpoint

We are a refuge away from the stress of work and city living. In the center of 10 acres, we offer tranquillity in a country setting. Comfortable furnishings and cozy woodstoves beckon you to rest and rejuvenate. The main house offers two rooms with queen beds and private baths and two rooms with shared bath—one with queen bed and one with twin beds. There are two cottage units with queen beds, private baths, coffeemakers, refrigerators.

Hosts: Barbara and Doug Billings
Rooms: 6 (4PB; 2SB) $75-125
Full Breakfast
Credit Cards: A, B
Notes: 2, 5, 10, 12

GREENBANK

Guest House Cottages

3366 S. Highway 525, 98253
(360) 678-3115 (voice and FAX)
E-mail: guesthse@whidbey.net
Web site: http://www.whidbey.net/logcottages

Discover privacy, peace, and pampering in each of our six individually designed cottages in Greenbank, Whidbey Island. (Four of the cottages are log houses.) Each cottage has a private setting on 25 acres of island greenery. Every cottage features personal Jacuzzis, fireplaces, kitchens, and TV/VCRs. More than 500 complimentary movies, an outdoor swimming pool, and a hot tub make for a relaxing retreat for two.

Guest House Cottages

Hosts: Don and MaryJane Creger
Rooms: 6 cottages (PB) $160-285
Full Breakfast
Credit Cards: A, B, C, D
Notes: 2, 5, 8, 9, 10, 12

KELSO

Longfellow House B&B Cottage

203 Williams-Finney Road, 98626
(360) 423-4545
E-mail: lngfelhs@pacifier.com
Web site: http://www.pacifier.com/~lngfelhs

Longfellow House is the ideal private destination for your special occasion or business trip. A secluded cottage for two in a rural setting, 1 mile east of I–5. The main

Longfellow House Bed and Breakfast Cottage

NOTES: Credit cards accepted: A Master Card; B Visa; C American Express; D Discover; E Diners Club; F Other; 2 Personal checks accepted; 3 Lunch available; 4 Dinner available; 5 Open all year; 6 Pets

floor is yours alone. Enjoy our 1913 player piano and collection of works by and about Henry Wadsworth Longfellow. Sleep as long as you like. Wake to the smell of gourmet coffee and the breakfast you've selected being prepared. Fine teas are our specialty. Offstreet parking, phone, modem jack, and business services. Visit Mount St. Helens, Pacific beaches, and Columbia River Gorge.

Hosts: Dick and Sally Longfellow
Rooms: 1 (PB) $89
Full Breakfast
Credit Cards: none
Notes: 2, 5, 8, 9, 10, 11

LA CONNER

Benson Farmstead Bed and Breakfast

1009 Avon-Allen Road, **Bow,** 98232
(360) 757-0578; (800) 685-7239, 1930
Web site: http://www.bbhost.com/bensonbnb

Located just minutes from the Skagit Valley, tulip fields, the historic town of LaConner, and ferries to the San Juan Islands, the Benson Farmstead is a beautiful, restored farmhouse. The Bensons are a friendly couple who serve homemade desserts in the evening and a wonderful breakfast. They have filled their home with charming antiques, old quilts, and curios from their Scandinavian heritage. The extensive yard features an English garden and the fields beyond are home to trumpeter swans.

Hosts: Jerry and Sharon Benson
Rooms: 4 (PB) $75-85 (spring and summer rates)
Full Breakfast
Credit Cards: A, B
Notes: 2, 5 (weekends only, September–March), 7, 8, 9, 10, 11

Katy's Inn

503 S. Third; PO Box 869, 98257
(360) 466-3366; (800) 914-7767
Web site: http://home.ncia.com/katysinn

This is a charming Victorian nestled on the hillside, 2 blocks above the town and its quaint shops, galleries, and antique stores. Four of our rooms are upstairs, with little French doors opening onto a wraparound porch with town and water views. The main-floor suite looks out on gardens, pond, and waterfall. Evening cookies/beverages; brunch-style breakfast served in dining room or tray at door; hot tub!

Hosts: Bruce and Kathie Hubbard
Rooms: 5 (3PB; 2SB) $72-120
Full Breakfast
Credit Cards: A, B, D
Notes: 2, 5, 8, 10, 11, 12 (10-percent commission)

Rainbow Inn B&B

1075 Chilberg Road; PO Box 15, 98257
(360) 466-4578; (888) 266-8879;
FAX (360) 466-3844
E-mail: tom@rainbowinnbandb.com
Web site: http://www.rainbowinnbandb.com

For a romantic, peaceful repose in a 1908 Craftsman home where Jesus' love flows, relax in a hammock or hot tub with a view of rich Skagit Valley farmlands and Mount Baker. Fine dining, antiques, quaint shops, kayaking, hot-air balloons, and bird- and whale-watching are available from La Conner. Miles of flat roads for biking and mountains for hiking and skiing. Grandma's cookies await you after your fun-filled day.

Hosts: The Squires Family (Tom, Patsy, Bruce, and Laureen)
Rooms: 8 (5PB; 3SB) $80-115 (seasonal)
Full Breakfast
Credit Cards: A, B, D
Notes: 2, 5, 7, 8, 9, 10, 11, 12

LANGLEY

Log Castle B&B

4693 Saratoga Road, 98260
(360) 221-5483; FAX (360) 221-6249
E-mail: innkeeper@whidbey.com
Web site: http://www.whidbey.com/logcastle

The Log Castle Bed and Breakfast is a charming country lodge located directly on the beach of the Saratoga Passage. Delight in our magnificent views of the sound, Mount Baker, and the Cascade Mountains. Enjoy beach walks, wooded trails. Relax by the large stone fireplace. Breakfasts at the "Castle" are legendary.

Hosts: Rep. Jack and Norma Metcalf, Karen and Phil Holdsworth
Rooms: 4 (PB) $95-120
Full Breakfast
Credit Cards: A, B, D
Notes: 2, 5, 7 (10 and over), 8, 9, 10, 12

LEAVENWORTH

All Seasons River Inn

8751 Icicle Road; PO Box 788, 98826
(509) 548-1425; (800) 254-0555
E-mail: allriver@rightathome.com
Web site: http://www.allseasonsriverinn.com

A feeling of calm and solitude consumes you as you enter this home wrapped in evergreens on the banks of the Wenatchee River. The beauty and warmth of the decor and welcome hospitality are additional reasons why so many have chosen All Seasons River Inn. This feeling continues as you enter the guest rooms, each unique in its antique decor and amenities, all with private bath, river view, and queen bed; most have a Jacuzzi. Suites and fireplaces are available. You will sleep lulled by the river. Awaken to a bountiful gourmet breakfast. Explore the many hiking, biking, and cross-country ski trails of this magnificent Alpine setting with its abundant wildlife. Just 1½ miles from Leavenworth Village. Complimentary bikes. Adults only. Totally nonsmoking.

Hosts: Kathy and Jeff Falconer
Rooms: 6 (PB) $85-145
Full Breakfast
Credit Cards: A, B
Notes: 2, 5, 10, 11

Bosch Gärten B&B

9846 Dye Road, 98826
(509) 548-6900; (800) 535-0069;
FAX (509) 548-6076
Web site: http://www.boschgarten.com

Quiet elegance within walking distance of Leavenworth, a Bavarian theme village. Spectacular view of the Cascade Mountains. The facility features warm Christian hospitality, beautiful gardens, king beds, TV, AC, and soundproofing, along with a library, hot tub, fireplace, and multicourse fresh breakfasts. A great area for golf, tennis, rock climbing, hiking, river rafting, downhill and cross-country skiing, sleighing, snowmobiling, etc.

Hosts: Cal and Myke Bosch
Rooms: 3 (PB) $98
Full Breakfast
Credit Cards: A, B, D
Notes: 2, 5, 8, 10, 11, 12

Run of the River

PO Box 285, 98826
(509) 548-7171; (800) 288-6491;
FAX (509) 548-7547
E-mail: rofther@rightathome.com
Web page: http://www.runoftheriver.com

Imagine the quintessential northwestern log bed and breakfast inn. Spacious rooms feature private baths, hand-hewn log beds, and fluffy down comforters. Celebrate in a suite with your own heart-warming woodstove, Jacuzzi surrounded by river rock, and bird's-eye loft to laze about with a favorite book. From your room's log porch swing, view the Icicle River, surrounding bird refuge, and Cascade peaks, appropriately named the "Enchantments." To explore the Icicle Valley, get off the beaten path with hiking, biking, and driving guides written just for you by the innkeepers—avid bikers and hikers. Take a spin on complimentary mountain bikes. In winter months, try the new Redfeather snowshoes. A hearty breakfast sets the day in motion.

Hosts: Monty and Karen Turner
Rooms: 6 (PB) $100-155
Full Breakfast
Credit Cards: A, B, D
Notes: 2, 5, 8, 9, 10, 11, 12

LONGVIEW

Misty Mountain Llamas Bed and Breakfast

1033 Stella Road, 98632
(360) 577-4772
E-mail: bljoy@kalama.com

The hosts welcome you to their little piece of heaven: a 5-acre llama ranch. The beautiful new custom home offers two bedrooms, one with queen and one with twin beds, that share a bath. Large sitting room with woodstove, TV/VCR, games, and large covered patio, with a view of the Columbia River through the wonderful trees. You may take a quiet walk through the woods or visit the llamas. Enjoy a continental plus breakfast in our great room while watching the llamas graze. Gourmet dinner available with advance notice. No smoking or pets.

Hosts: Doug and Barbara Joy
Rooms: 2 (SB) $85-90
Continental Plus Breakfast
Credit Cards: none
Notes: 2, 4, 5, 7 (over 12), 9 (Columbia River), 10, 12

LOPEZ

Aleck Bay Inn

Route 1, Box 1920, 98261
(360) 468-3535; FAX (360) 468-3533
E-mail: abi@pacificrim.net

Aleck Bay Inn provides the luxurious, quiet, and personal care needed for guests celebrating special events, having a romantic getaway, or just wishing a relaxing time by the fireplace. Coffee always hot, pastry ever present. Repeatedly visited by national and state dignitaries. The inn hosts small weddings, business meetings, retreats, and church outings. Guests can walk our beaches, hike through original forests, relax in a hot tub, enjoy the game room, and watch the wildlife. Near island churches, golf courses, and tennis courts. Kayak instruction and bike rentals available. Special breakfasts are served in our lovely dining room or in the solarium; they begin with fresh fruit and are followed by a large portion of gourmet selections. Breakfast piano concerts on weekends. Chinese and Spanish spoken.

Hosts: David and May Mendez
Rooms: 4 (PB) $79-159
Full Breakfast
Credit Cards: A, B, C, D, E
Notes: 2, 3, 4, 5, 7, 8, 9, 10, 12

LYNDEN

Century House Bed and Breakfast

401 S. British Columbia Avenue, 98264
(360) 354-2439; (800) 820-3617;
FAX (360) 354-6910

Located on 35 acres at the edge of town, Century House Bed and Breakfast is a 109-year-old Victorian home. You'll find this completely restored bed and breakfast is a quiet retreat with spacious gardens and lawns for your enjoyment. The quaint Dutch village of Lynden, an easy walk away, boasts the best museums in the area and gift shops galore. . .but sorry, the town is closed on Sundays. You can take day trips to the Cascade Mountains and Mount Baker, the sea, Seattle, Vancouver, or Victoria, British Columbia.

Hosts: Jan and Ken Stremler
Rooms: 4 (2PB; 2SB) $65-95
Full Breakfast
Credit Cards: A, B
Notes: 2, 5, 7, 8, 9, 10, 11

OLYMPIA

Swantown Bed and Breakfast Inn

1431 11th Avenue SE, 98501
(360) 753-9123
E-mail: swantown@olywa.net
Web site: http://www.olywa.net/swantown

Located in an elegant 1893 Victorian mansion in the heart of Olympia, the Swantown Inn can be your headquarters to exploring the Puget Sound region or your refuge for a quiet retreat. Queen beds with cozy down comforters, private baths, beautiful views of the sunset over the capitol dome, an inviting gazebo, and gourmet breakfasts are but some of the ingredients for a memorable visit.

Swantown Bed and Breakfast Inn

Hosts: Lillian and Ed Peeples
Rooms: 3 (PB) $75-115 (seasonal)
Full Breakfast
Credit Cards: A, B
Notes: 2, 5, 7 (over 10), 12

ORCAS ISLAND —DEER HARBOR

Palmer's Chart House

PO Box 51, 98243
(360) 376-4231

The first bed and breakfast on Orcas Island (since 1975) with a magnificent water view. The 33-foot private yacht *Amante* is available for a minimal fee, with

NOTES: Credit cards accepted: A Master Card; B Visa; C American Express; D Discover; E Diners Club; F Other; 2 Personal checks accepted; 3 Lunch available; 4 Dinner available; 5 Open all year; 6 Pets

skipper Don. Low-key, personal attention makes this B&B unique and attractive. Well-traveled hosts speak Spanish.

Hosts: Don and Majean Palmer
Rooms: 2 (PB) $60-70
Full Breakfast
Credit Cards: none
Notes: 2, 5, 7 (over 12), 8, 10, 11, 12

ORCAS ISLAND—EASTSOUND

Turtleback Farm Inn & The Orchard House

Route 1, Box 650, 98245
(360) 376-4914; (800) 376-4914;
FAX (360) 376-5329
Web site: http://www.turtlebackinn.com

Turtleback Farm Inn is noted for detail-perfect restoration, elegantly comfortable and spotless rooms, glorious setting, and award-winning breakfasts. You will be made welcome and pampered by the warm hospitality of Bill and Susan Fletcher and their staff. Orcas Island is a haven for anyone who enjoys spectacular scenery, varied outdoor activities, unique shopping, and superb food. As spring turns to summer, the warm days encourage your enjoyment of nature at its best. Flowers are in full bloom; birds flutter; whales, seals, and porpoises coast lazily through the simmering waters of the sound. After a day of hiking, fishing, bicycling, kayaking, sailing, windsurfing, or just reading by our pond, return to Turtleback for a relaxing soak in your private bath or a sherry on the deck overlooking the valley below. After a tasty dinner at one of the island's fine restaurants and perhaps a performance at the Orcas Center, guests can snuggle under a custom-made woolen comforter and doze off with visions of the delicious breakfast awaiting you in the morning.

Hosts: William C. and Susan C. Fletcher
Rooms: 11 (PB) $80-210
Full Breakfast
Credit Cards: A, B, D
Notes: 2, 5, 7 (8 and over, by arrangement), 8, 9, 10, 12

ORCAS ISLAND—OLGA

Buck Bay Farm B&B

Star Route Box 45, 98279
(360) 376-2908
Web site: http://www.rockisland.com/~paperjom/Buck/BuckBay.html

Buck Bay Farm is located on beautiful Orcas in the San Juan Islands of Washington State. Orcas is an idyllic vacation destination with lots of outdoor fun: hiking, bicycling, boating or kayaking, whale-watching, golf, fishing, and much more. The B&B is a farmhouse recently rebuilt by the owner. A warm welcome and hearty, home-style breakfast await you.

Hosts: Rick and Janet Bronkey
Rooms: 5 (3PB; 2SB) $85-115
Full Breakfast
Credit Cards: A, B, C, D
Notes: 2, 5, 7 (by arrangement), 8, 9, 10

PORT TOWNSEND

Ann Starrett Mansion

744 Clay Street, 98368
(360) 385-3205; (800) 321-0644;
FAX (360) 385-2976
Web site: http://www.olympus.net/starrett

A destination with a sense of history is a vacation with "Romance." The 1889 mansion was built as a wedding gift. Authentic antiques and ambience will take you back to a gentler time. The inn won a National Trust for Historic Preservation "Great American Home Award." The lovely views and scrumptious breakfast will make you want to stay forever.

Hostess: Edel Sokol
Rooms: 11 (PB) $85-225
Full Breakfast
Credit Cards: A, B, C, D
Notes: 2, 5, 7, 8, 9, 10, 11, 12

PUYALLUP

Tayberry Victorian Cottage

7406 80th Street E., 98371
(253) 848-4594
E-mail: tayberrybb@aol.com
Web site: http://www.bbonline.com

Nestled in a peaceful country setting with Norman Rockwell views of the valley, this lovely Victorian offers beautiful rooms with queen beds, TV/VCR, private baths, feather beds, robes, and a delightful hot tub. Lose yourself in down-appointed beds and awaken to scrumptious breakfasts. Five miles to Tacoma, 20 miles to Seattle.

Hosts: Terry and Vicki Chissus
Rooms: 3 (PB) $75-95
Full Breakfast
Credit Cards: A, B, C, D
Notes: 2, 5, 7, 10, 11, 12

RENTON

Holly Hedge House

908 Grant Avenue S., 98055
(425) 226-2555 (voice and FAX); (888) 226-2555
E-mail: holihedg@nwlink.com
Web site: http://www.nwlink.com/~holihedg

Nestled high atop a scenic hill lies your oasis of tranquillity and seclusion. Only 8 minutes from a major airport and 15 minutes from downtown Seattle and major attractions. The Holly Hedge House is a painstakingly restored, award-winning 1901 English country cottage for two. Private outdoor pool, hot tub under gazebo, hammock, beautifully manicured grounds, whirlpool tub, full kitchen, queen-size "heaven" bed, gas log fireplace, vast CD/video/reading library, and glassed-in veranda that overlooks the Green River Valley and Olympic Mountains.

Hosts: Lynn and Marian Thrasher
Rooms: 1 cottage (PB) $100-135
Full and Continental Breakfast
Credit Cards: A, B
Notes: 2, 5, 8, 9, 10, 11, 12

SEATTLE

85 Street Guest House and Apartments

731 85th Street, 98103
(206) 439-7677; (800) 684-2932;
FAX (206) 431-0932
E-mail: pacificb@nwlink.com
Web site: http://www.seattlebedandbreakfast.com/85st.html

For large families, reunions, group travel, or extended stays, nothing compares to the convenience and privacy of this 1920s Tudor-style home or any of the suites that are in the rear. Children welcome. Full kitchens are stocked with breakfast food in every unit. Totally nonsmoking. No pets. You'll find TVs, VCRs, phones, cribs, and a cooperative innkeeper.

Host: "T.H." Monroe
Rooms: 6 (PB) $55-125
Full Breakfast (self-serve; food provided)
Credit Cards: none
Notes: 2, 5, 7, 8, 9, 10

NOTES: Credit cards accepted: A Master Card; B Visa; C American Express; D Discover; E Diners Club; F Other; 2 Personal checks accepted; 3 Lunch available; 4 Dinner available; 5 Open all year; 6 Pets

Hill House Bed and Breakfast

1113 E. John Street, 98102
(206) 720-7161; (800) 720-7161;
FAX (206) 323-0772
E-mail: hillhouse@foxinternet.net
Web site: http://www.foxinternet.net/business/hillhouse

A 1903 Victorian just minutes from downtown Seattle. It features superb gourmet breakfasts served on china and crystal and seven rooms, tastefully appointed with antiques. All rooms have queen beds with down comforters, crisp linens, and plenty of pillows. Walk to numerous shops and restaurants just blocks away. Located ¾ mile from downtown attractions, the Convention Center, Pike Place Market. Close to transportation. Offstreet parking. AAA three diamonds; Seattle B&B Association, "Best Places to Kiss in the Northwest."

Hosts: Herman and Alea Foster
Rooms: 7 (5PB; 2SB) $75-135
Gourmet Breakfast
Credit Cards: A, B, C, D, E
Notes: 2, 4, 5, 10

SEQUIM

Greywolf Inn

395 Keeler Road, 98382
(360) 683-5889; (800) 914-WOLF (9053);
FAX (360) 683-1487
E-mail: grywolf@olypen.com
Web site: http://www.northolympic.com/greywolf

Nestled in a crescent of towering evergreens, this northwestern country estate overlooks the Dungeness Valley. An ideal starting point for year-round, light adventure on the Olympic peninsula—hiking, fishing, biking, boating, bird-watching, sight-seeing, and golf. Enjoy Greywolf's sunny decks, Japanese-style hot tub, and meandering 5-acre woodswalk, or curl up by the fire with a good book. Then retire to one of the cozy, comfortable theme rooms for the night.

Hosts: Peggy and Bill Melang
Rooms: 5 (PB) $68-120
Full Breakfast
Credit Cards: A, B, C, D
Notes: 2, 5, 7 (over 12), 8, 9, 10, 11, 12

Redmond House Bed and Breakfast

SNOHOMISH

Redmond House Bed and Breakfast

317 Glen Avenue, 98290
(360) 568-2042

Enter a world of comfort, luxury, and simple elegance that makes time stand still. Located in the Victorian-era town of Snohomish, Redmond House is within walking distance of the "Antique Capital of the Northwest" with 400 antique dealers, gift shops, and restaurants. The house is graced by beautiful gardens and a wraparound porch. Period antiques. Luxurious bedrooms filled with quilts, linens, and queen feather beds are available with claw-foot soaking tubs. Hiking, boating, golf, skiing, hot-air ballooning, parachuting, wineries, and sports are nearby.

Hosts: Mary and Ken Riley
Rooms: 4 (2PB; 2SB) $85-100
Full Breakfast
Credit Cards: A, B
Notes: 2, 5, 7, 8, 9, 10, 11

SOUTH BEND

Maring's Courthouse Hill Bed and Breakfast

602 W. 2nd Street; PO Box 34, 98586
(360) 875-6519; (800) 875-6519
E-mail: maringbb@willapabay.org
Web site: http://www.willapabay.org/~maringbb

An 1892 church, now a historic home with tasteful decor. River views in picturesque South Bend. Comfort and warm hospitality. Spacious guest rooms. Queen/twin beds, cable television, private baths, full breakfast. Quiet location with wildlife. Situated 5 blocks off 101, a short walk from downtown.

Hosts: Ed and Frances Maring
Rooms: 3 (2PB; 1SB) $55-65
Full Breakfast
Credit Cards: A, B, C
Notes: 2, 5, 7 (well-behaved), 8, 10

SPOKANE

Marianna Stoltz House Bed and Breakfast

427 E. Indiana Avenue, 99207
(509) 483-6773; (800) 978-6587;
FAX (509) 483-6773
Web site: http://www.go-native.com/inns/0082.shtml

Established in 1987, The Marianna Stoltz House has earned a reputation for pampering its guests. This 1908 Historic Landmark is beautifully decorated. Private baths with a tub for two, air-conditioning, and cable TV are just a few of the amenities that await you. Minutes from I–90, downtown, Spokane Arena, Opera House, Convention Center, Centennial Trail, and Gonzaga University.

Hosts: Jim and Phyllis Maguire
Rooms: 4 (2PB; 2SB) $75-95
Full Breakfast
Credit Cards: A, B, C, D
Notes: 2, 5, 8, 9, 10, 11, 12

Oslo's Bed and Breakfast

1821 E. 39th Avenue, 99203
(509) 838-3175; (888) 838-3175
Web site: http://www.innkeepersonly.com

Oslo's Bed and Breakfast is an attractive South Hill home on a quiet street. It offers comfortable bedrooms with private baths. In the living room, you may relax and read or visit in a Norwegian atmosphere. The home has central AC. A large terrace overlooking the garden may be enjoyed with a full breakfast served at 9 AM—Scandinavian cuisine, if desired. An earlier breakfast may be arranged, if planned in advance. A small park is located a half block away; it has tennis courts, exercise stops, and paths for walking. The network of skywalks in downtown Spokane is worth investigating, as are the Cheney Cowles Museum and the Bing Crosby Library at Gonzaga University.

Host: Aslaug Stevenson
Rooms: 2 (PB) $55-70
Full Breakfast
Credit Cards: none
Notes: 2, 5, 6, 8, 10, 11, 12

TACOMA/SEATTLE

Commencement Bay Bed and Breakfast

3312 N. Union Avenue, 98407
(253) 752-8175; FAX (253) 759-4025
E-mail: greatviews@aol.com
Web site: http://www.bestinns.net/usa/wa/cb.html

An elegant Colonial home in scenic North Tacoma with dramatic bay and mountain views. Located in a historic area near quaint shops, numerous fine restaurants, and waterfront parks. Featured in "Northwest Best Places," the inn serves fantastic breakfasts and offers large rooms, private baths, a relaxing fireside area, a secluded garden hot tub, and full services for business guests. Gourmet coffees are served each day.

Hosts: Sharon and Bill Kaufmann
Rooms: 3 (PB) $85-125
Full Breakfast
Credit Cards: A, B, C, D
Notes: 2, 5, 8, 9, 10, 11, 12

VANCOUVER

Vintage Inn Bed and Breakfast

310 W. 11th Street, 98660–3146
(360) 693-6635; (888) 693-6635
E-mail: info@vintage-inn.com
Web site: http://www.vintage-inn.com

Hospitality plus! One of Vancouver's original mansions built in 1903 in the heart of downtown, with elegant antiques throughout. On the National Historic Register. Large rooms with comfortable queen beds. Bountiful breakfasts. Fine restaurants, antique shops, theater, and art galleries—all within walking distance. Fort Vancouver National Historic site, 7 blocks away. Easy freeway access. Fifteen minutes from downtown Portland, Oregon, and airport. No smoking, pets, alcohol.

Hosts: Mike and Doris Hale
Rooms: 4 (SB) $80-85
Full Breakfast
Credit Cards: A, B
Notes: none

WHITE SALMON

Llama Ranch Bed and Breakfast

1980 Highway 141, 98672
(509) 395-2786; (800) 800-LAMA (5262)
E-mail: lama1@linkport.com

Llama Ranch Bed and Breakfast is nestled in a peaceful valley with spectacular views of two mountains. Unforgettable beauty! Enjoy free llama walks with hands-on experience. See nature in all its splendor as you horseback ride, white-water raft, windsurf, fish, hunt, cross-country ski, snowmobile, bike, pick huckleberries, or explore caves in the area. Hike through the lush mountain forests and wildflower-filled meadows, along bubbling streams and cascading waterfalls. Separate bed and breakfast area is complete with kitchen, dining room, living room, and queen beds. Suitable for small group retreats. Children and pets okay.

Hosts: Jerry Stone and Dee Kern
Rooms: 7 (2PB; 5SB) $79-99
Full Breakfast
Credit Cards: A, B, D
Notes: 2, 5, 6, 7, 10, 11, 12

welcome; 7 Children welcome; 8 Tennis nearby; 9 Swimming nearby; 10 Golf nearby; 11 Skiing nearby; 12 May be booked through travel agent.

YAKIMA

The Orchard Inn

1207 Pecks Canyon Road, 98908
(509) 966-1283; (888) 858-8284;
FAX (509) 972-0726

Cherry orchard setting. . . . Put yourself in a place where you can slow down, tune out the clamor, and listen to the quiet. Private baths, jetted tubs, down comforters, and custom-made mattresses make you feel as if the innkeepers had you personally in mind when they built this bed and breakfast in 1996. Leaving The Orchard Inn will be hard the next morning, after you have enjoyed a mug of locally roasted coffee and a satisfying breakfast and made new friends!

Hosts: Ben and Shari Dover
Rooms: 3 (PB) $65-80
Full Breakfast
Credit Cards: A, B, C, D
Notes: 2, 5, 7, 8, 9, 10, 11, 12

West Virginia

BERKELEY SPRINGS

Cacapon B&B

Route 1, Box 301-A, 25411
(304) 258-1442; (888) 629-3309;
FAX (304) 258-3310
E-mail: curtis@nfis.com
Web site: http://www.mariasgarden.com

While Cacapon B&B is a converted mom and pop motel, the room amenities and location make it ideal. Located at the entrance of the 6,000-acre Cacapon State Park, with eighteen-hole golf, swimming, horseback riding, hiking, fishing, and more. Our rooms offer queen beds, quilted spreads, cable TV. Private baths, full country breakfast, tanning beds, beauty salon, wicker furniture, and craft and gift shop.

Host: Curtis Perry
Rooms: 8 (PB) $39-59
Full Breakfast
Credit Cards: A, B, D
Notes: 6 (in some rooms), 7

Maria's Garden and Inn

201 Independence Street, 25411
(304) 258-2021; (888) 629-2253;
FAX (304) 258-5915
E-mail: curtis@nfis.com
Web site: http://www.mariasgarden.com

Nestled in the heart of town in two homes built in the '20s, Maria's Garden is the creation of Peg Perry. A devout Catholic, Peg shares her faith, poetry, and Christian insights with guests and bus groups. Maria's is close to the Roman baths, local spas, antiques, golfing, horseback riding, fishing on two rivers, two state parks, and great local restaurants. Romantic couples and families welcome.

Hostess: Peg Perry
Rooms: 12 (6PB; 6SB) $50-120
Full Breakfast
Credit Cards: A, B, D
Notes: 2, 3, 4, 5, 7, 8, 9, 10, 11, 12

BLUEFIELD

Country Chalet Bed and Breakfast

Route 1, Box 176 B, 24701
(304) 487-2120 (voice and FAX);
(800) CALL WVA (225-5982; for reservations)
E-mail: maxnshar@juno.com
Web site: http://bbonline.com/wv/countrychalet

Conveniently located on Route 20 between Bluefield and Princeton, the Country Chalet is surrounded by nature. The cedar shake A-frame provides a cozy, casual atmosphere sure to help busy travelers and business folks relax. Read by the large stone fireplace in the A-room with

---

welcome; 7 Children welcome; 8 Tennis nearby; 9 Swimming nearby; 10 Golf nearby; 11 Skiing nearby; 12 May be booked through travel agent.

WEST VIRGINIA

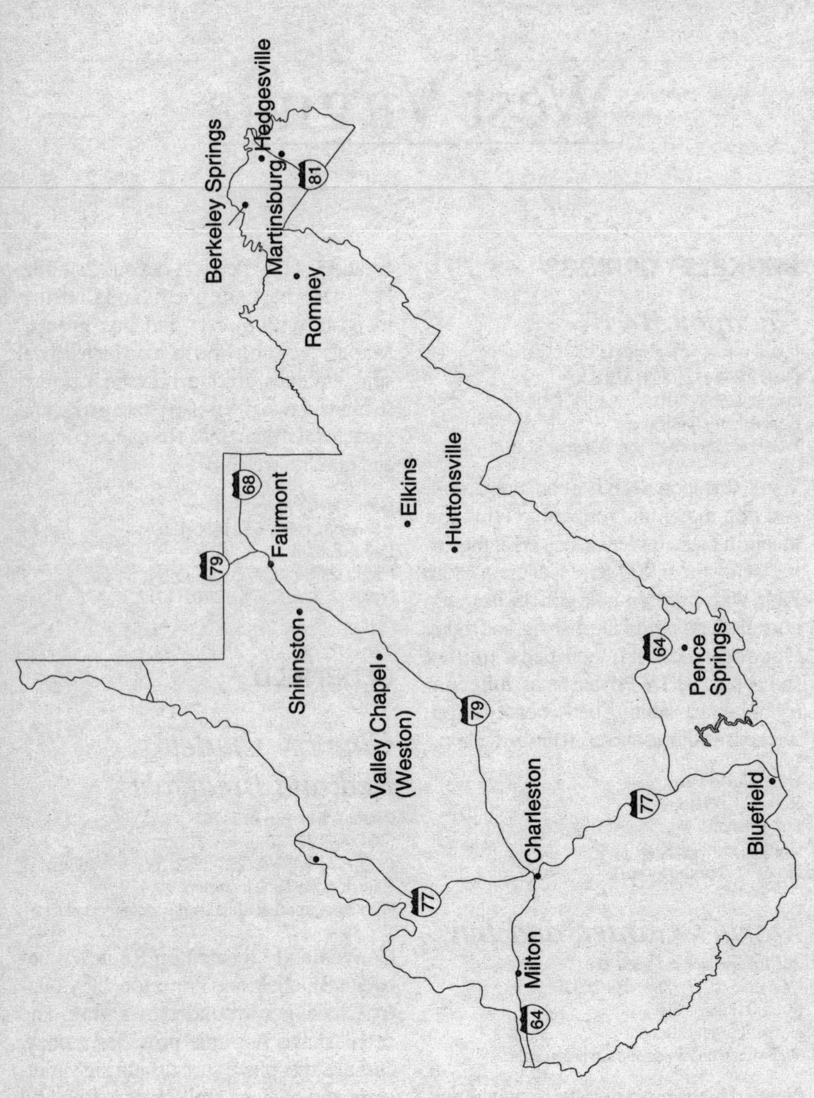

24-foot ceiling and windowed wall, sun on the deck, stroll around the country landscaped yard, visit the fishpond, or snooze on the shaded porch. Sharon's famous sourdough bread is the specialty of the house, and the glorious spring-to-fall flower garden is a specialty from God. Two bedrooms on the second floor are simply yet tastefully furnished in a country motif. The queen Country Garden Room may be rented with private bath, or a party of four in two bedrooms will share the carpeted, windowed bath. A treadmill, microwave, mini-frige, phone, piano, and table games are provided. We provide a smoke- and alcohol-free environment.

Hosts: Max and Sharon Hudson
Rooms: 2 (1PB; 2SB) $40-70
Full or Continental Breakfast
Credit Cards: none
Notes: 2, 5, 7 (by permission), 8, 9, 10, 11

CHARLESTON

Brass Pineapple B&B

1611 Virginia Street E., 25311
(304) 344-0748 (voice and FAX);
(800) CALL WVA (225-5982)
Web site: http://wvweb.com/www/brass.pineapple_bandb

This cozy but elegant 1910 brick home is in Charleston's historic district within half a block of the capitol complex. The house has been carefully restored to its original grandeur, with antiques throughout. Guest rooms have private baths, phones with voice mail, and cable TV/VCR. Free VCR movies. AC, robes, hair dryers. Candlelight breakfast is accented with crystal and silver; tea is available, 5–7 PM. Friendly professional staff and great food. Traveler's checks okay. We welcome the opportunity to care for your gentle spirit.

Brass Pineapple Bed and Breakfast

Hostess: Sue Pepper
Rooms: 6 (PB) $79-109
Full Breakfast
Credit Cards: A, B, C, E, F (travelers checks)
Notes: 2, 5 (except major holidays), 7, 8, 9, 10, 12

Historic Charleston B&B

110 Elizabeth Street, 25311
(304) 345-8156; (800) CALL WVA (225-5982);
FAX (304) 342-1572

This is a nonsmoking home. Affordable elegance. Breakfast includes Jean's famous egg soufflé and is enjoyed with fresh fruit,

Historic Charleston Bed and Breakfast

NOTES: Credit cards accepted: A Master Card; B Visa; C American Express; D Discover; E Diners Club; F Other; 2 Personal checks accepted; 3 Lunch available; 4 Dinner available; 5 Open all year; 6 Pets welcome; 7 Children welcome; 8 Tennis nearby; 9 Swimming nearby; 10 Golf nearby; 11 Skiing nearby; 12 May be booked through travel agent.

juice, more. Close to art glass/hand-blown glass factories, antique shops, and museums. Refreshments on arrival, if desired. No pets. Your home away from home is furnished with antiques and collectibles.

Hosts: Bob and Jean Lambert
Rooms: 4 (3PB; 1SB) $65-80, $15 for child's room
Full Breakfast
Credit Cards: A, B, C
Notes: 2, 5, 7 (over 10), 8, 9, 10, 11 (1 hour away)

The Warfield House

ELKINS

Tunnel Mountain B&B

Route 1, Box 59-1, 26241
(304) 636-1684; (888) 211-9123
Web site: http://www.wvonline.com/shareourbeds/tunnelmtn

Charming three-story fieldstone home nestled on 5 private, wooded acres surrounded by scenic peaks, lush forests, and sparkling rivers. Finished in pine and rare wormy chestnut woodwork. Tastefully decorated with antiques, collectibles, and crafts. Near Monongahela National Forest, Blackwater Falls, Seneca Rocks, Spruce Knob, Snowshoe, Cass Railroad, Dolly Sods, country/downhill skiing, historic sites, festivals, and shops.

Hosts: Anne and Paul Beardslee
Rooms: 3 (PB) $70-75
Full Breakfast
Credit Cards: none
Notes: 2, 5, 8, 9, 10, 11

The Warfield House

318 Buffalo Street, 26241
(304) 636-4555; (800) 636-4555;
FAX (304) 636-1457
Web site: http://www.bbonline.com/wv/warfield

Casual atmosphere in elegant turn-of-the-century home nestled among towering oaks, hemlocks, and pines on a quiet corner. Serene setting across from forested City Park in scenic mountain town. Within walking distance of restaurants, shops, and theaters. A sumptuous breakfast of fresh fruit, home-baked breads/pastries, and hot entrée will ready you for the day's activities or a nap on the broad front porch. Nearby historic attractions, antiquing, hiking, biking, fishing, and festivals.

Hosts: Connie and Paul Garnett
Rooms: 5 (PB) $75-95
Full Breakfast
Credit Cards: none
Notes: 2, 5, 8, 9, 10, 11

FAIRMONT

Acacia House Bed and Breakfast

158 Locust Avenue, 26554
(304) 367-1000 (voice and FAX); (888) 269-9541
E-mail: acacia@wv.com
Web site: http://www.wvonline.com/acacia

Shop on the premises with antiques and collectibles. Five minutes from Fairmont State College and Fairmont Hospital; 30 minutes from WVU stadium and hospital.

Location: I–79, Exit 137, Route 310 to Fairmont Avenue, right on Fourth Street, right to Locust Avenue, ¼ mile on right.

Hosts: George and Kathy Sprowls
Rooms: 4 (2PB; 2SB) $60-65
Full Breakfast
Credit Cards: A, B, C, D, E

The Farmhouse on Tomahawk Run

HEDGESVILLE

The Farmhouse on Tomahawk Run

1 Tomahawk Run Place, 25427
(304) 754-7350 (voice and FAX)
E-mail: tomahawk@intrepid.net
Web site: http://www.travelwv.com/bed5.htm

Ten miles west of I–81, near Martinsburg. In addition to B&B guests, we host small group retreats for up to sixteen persons. We are trained by the Association of Couples in Marriage Enrichment to lead marriage retreats, which we hold twice a year. Our farmhouse, built during the Civil War, stands beside the springhouse (on the National Register of Historic Places) and the foundation of the old log cabin. Nestled in a secluded valley by a meandering stream, it is surrounded by woods, hills, and meadows with walking paths. A stone fireplace in the large gathering room has a roaring log fire on cold evenings. Wraparound porch, rocking chairs, and Jacuzzi available. A bountiful three-course breakfast is served by candlelight.

Hosts: Judy and Hugh Erskine
Rooms: 5 (PB) $75-115
Full Breakfast
Credit Cards: A, B, C, D, E
Notes: 2, 5, 7, 10, 12

HUTTONSVILLE

Hutton House B&B

Routes 250 and 219; PO Box 88, 26273
(304) 335-6701
Web site: http://www.wvonline.com/shareourbeds/hutton

Meticulously restored and decorated, this Queen Anne Victorian on the National Register of Historic Places is convenient to Elkins, Cass Railroad, and Snowshoe Ski Resort. It has a wraparound porch and deck for relaxing and enjoying the view, TV, game room, lawn for games, and friendly kitchen. Breakfast and afternoon refreshments are served at your leisure; other meals are available with prior reservation or good luck! Come see us!

Hosts: Loretta Murray and Dean Ahren
Rooms: 6 (PB) $75-80
Full Breakfast
Credit Cards: A, B
Notes: 2, 7, 10, 11, 12

MARTINSBURG

Boydville, The Inn at Martinsburg

601 S. Queen Street, 25401
(304) 263-1448

A stone manor house set well back from Queen Street. To reach the front door, you

welcome; 7 Children welcome; 8 Tennis nearby; 9 Swimming nearby; 10 Golf nearby; 11 Skiing nearby; 12 May be booked through travel agent.

turn up a drive through 10 acres with overarching maples on both sides of the road. This is an experience in itself; it feels as if you are being led away from a busy world into an earlier, peaceful time. Handsomely appointed and furnished with English and American antiques, the inn dates to 1812. Enjoy leisurely walks on the grounds, in the brick-walled courtyard, and in the surrounding gardens. Boydville is ideal for a business retreat or romantic getaway. On the National Register of Historic Places.

Hosts: LaRue Frye and Pete Bailey
Rooms: 6 (4PB; 2SB) $90-110, 2-night stay
Full Breakfast
Credit Cards: A, B
Notes: 2, 5 (except August), 7 (over 12), 10, 11, 12

MILTON

The Cedar House

92 Trenol Heights, 25541
(304) 743-5516; (888) 743-5516
E-mail: vickersc@marshall.edu
Web site: http://www.bbonline.com/wv/cedarhouse

Enjoy the convenience of a contemporary home with old-fashioned hospitality. A spacious hilltop, AC, trilevel-style cedar house with a panoramic view of surrounding hills awaits visitors on 5½ acres that provide quiet and privacy within a mile of I–64, Exit 28. Relax in front of the family room fireplace, or play pool, games, or piano in the game room. Use the treadmill or roller traction table. Blenko Glass Company, antiques, crafts, flea market nearby. Hand-dipped chocolates a specialty.

Hostess: Carole Vickers
Rooms: 3 (PB) $65-75
Full Breakfast
Credit Cards: A, B, C, D
Notes: 2, 5, 10

The Pence Springs Hotel

PENCE SPRINGS

The Pence Springs Hotel

PO Box 90, 24962
(304) 445-2606; (800) 826-1829;
FAX (304) 445-2204
E-mail: omc01508@mail.wvnet.edu

Known as The Grand Hotel, this National Register Inn is one of the historic mineral spas of the Virginias. A premier retreat from 1897 until the Great Depression, Pence Springs was the most popular and expensive hotel in West Virginia. At the 1904 World's Fair in St. Louis, Pence Mineral Water won an award as the finest in the world. An elegant brick structure, The Pence Springs Hotel has served several purposes over the years, including a finishing school established by Eleanor Roosevelt and the West Virginia State Prison for Women. The hotel is closed January–March.

Hosts: O. Ashby Berkley and Rosa Lee Berkley Miller
Rooms: 24 (15PB; 9SB) $70-100
Full Breakfast
Credit Cards: A, B, C, D, E
Notes: 2, 3, 4, 6 (basement only, with deposit), 7, 9, 10, 11, 12

NOTES: Credit cards accepted: A Master Card; B Visa; C American Express; D Discover; E Diners Club; F Other; 2 Personal checks accepted; 3 Lunch available; 4 Dinner available; 5 Open all year; 6 Pets

ROMNEY

Hampshire House 1884

165 N. Grafton Street, 26757
(304) 822-7171; FAX (304) 822-7582

Hampshire House is a completely renovated brick 1884 Federal-style home. Period furnishings, private baths, AC, health spa, massage available. Full breakfast of your choice. Private sitting area, room for group visiting and game playing.

Hosts: Jane and Scott Simmons
Rooms: 5 (PB) $65-85
Full Breakfast
Credit Cards: A, B, C, D, E
Notes: 2, 5, 7, 8, 9, 10, 11 (1½ hours), 12

Gillum House Bed and Breakfast

SHINNSTON

Gillum House Bed and Breakfast

35 Walnut Street, 26431–1154
(304) 592-0177; (888) 592-0177;
FAX (304) 592-1882
E-mail: gillum@westvirginia.net
Web site: http://www.callwva.com/gillum

Near I–79, Shinnston is a hub to see all of north-central West Virginia. The Gillum House is 4 blocks from the West Fork River Trail; 16+ miles of trail for bicyclists, hikers, and equestrians; bicycle rentals and stable facilities can be arranged. Experience "front porch," small-town America and tantalize your tastebuds with wonderful homemade, heart-healthy foods. Special diets accommodated. Member, Mountainside Association of Bed and Breakfasts. A smoke-free, pet-free facility.

Hostess: Kathleen Panek
Rooms: 3 (SB) $55-60
Continental Breakfast
Credit Cards: A, B
Notes: 2, 5, 7, 10

VALLEY CHAPEL (WESTON)

Ingeberg Acres Bed and Breakfast

PO Box 199, 26446
(304) 269-2834 (voice and FAX);
(800) CALL WVA (225-5982)
E-mail: u1a00779@wvnvm.wvnet.edu
Web site: http://www.tiac.net/users/mann

A unique experience can be yours at this scenic, 450-acre horse and cattle farm. Ingeberg Acres is located in the heart of West Virginia, 7 miles from Weston, overlooking its own private valley. Hiking, swimming, hunting, and fishing—or just relaxing—can be the order of the day. Observe or participate in farm activities. Craft outlets and antique stores nearby. Come enjoy the gardens, the pool, and the friendly atmosphere. German spoken.

Hosts: John and Inge Mann
Rooms: 3 (SB) $59; cabin $80
Full Breakfast
Credit Cards: none
Notes: 2, 5, 7, 9, 10

WISCONSIN

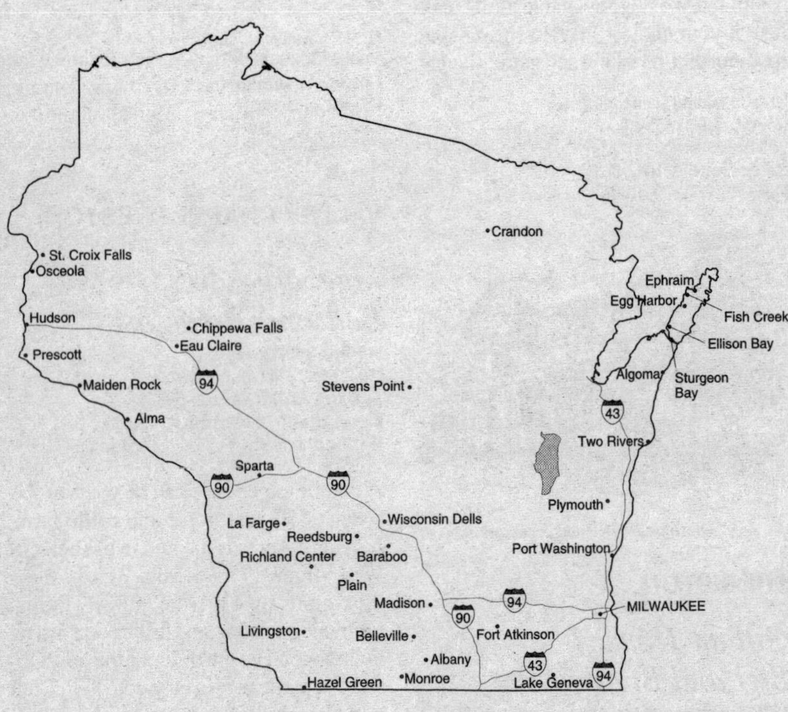

Crandon
St. Croix Falls
Osceola
Hudson
Chippewa Falls
Eau Claire
Prescott
Maiden Rock
Alma
94
Stevens Point
Ephraim
Egg Harbor
Fish Creek
Ellison Bay
Algoma
Sturgeon Bay
43
Two Rivers
Sparta
90
90
Plymouth
La Farge
Wisconsin Dells
Reedsburg
Richland Center
Baraboo
Port Washington
Plain
Madison
94
MILWAUKEE
90
Livingston
Belleville
Fort Atkinson
Albany
43
94
Hazel Green
Monroe
Lake Geneva

Wisconsin

ALBANY

Albany Guest House

405 S. Mill Street, 53502
(608) 862-3636
E-mail: bobbrae@brodnet.com
Web site: http://www.cruising-america.com/albany

A 2-acre, parklike setting, with flower gardens galore and a brick walk, is where you'll find the restored 1908 three-story block home. With blooming plants everywhere, you'll find king- and queen-size beds, and a wood-burning fireplace in the master bedroom. Be amazed with the complete, antique, four-piece, solid bird's-eye maple bedroom set, a family heirloom. After a full, wholesome breakfast, recover on the porch swing or rocker, or stroll the grounds before exploring, biking, tubing, or canoeing the river. A great reunion or retreat site.

Albany Guest House

Hosts: Bob and Sally Braem
Rooms: 6 (5PB; 1SB) $60-80
Full Breakfast
Credit Cards: A, B
Notes: 2, 5, 7 (disciplined), 8, 10, 11

Oak Hill Manor Bed and Breakfast

401 E. Main Street; PO Box 190, 53502
(608) 862-1400; FAX (608) 862-1403
E-mail: innkeeper@oakhillmanor.com
Web site: http://www.oakhillmanor.com

Step back into time in our 1908 manor home. Enjoy rich oak woodwork, gasoliers, and period furnishings. Spacious, sunny corner rooms have queen-size beds and cozy reading areas. Choose a room with a fireplace, porch, or canopy bed. Relax in our English country garden with gazebo, or lounge in a wicker rocker on our spacious porch. Sumptuous breakfast served by fireside and candlelight. Wake-up coffee. Canoe/fish on the Sugar River

---

NOTES: Credit cards accepted: A Master Card; B Visa; C American Express; D Discover; E Diners Club; F Other; 2 Personal checks accepted; 3 Lunch available; 4 Dinner available; 5 Open all year; 6 Pets welcome; 7 Children welcome; 8 Tennis nearby; 9 Swimming nearby; 10 Golf nearby; 11 Skiing nearby; 12 May be booked through travel agent.

or ride/hike the bike trail. Complimentary guest bikes. No smoking. Great for reunions and business retreats! Gift certificates available.

Hosts: Donna and Glen Rothe
Rooms: 4 (PB) $70-80
Full Breakfast
Credit Cards: A, B
Notes: 2, 5, 7 (12 and older), 8, 9, 10, 11 (cross-country)

Amberwood Bed and Breakfast Inn

ALGOMA

Amberwood B&B Inn

N. 7136 Highway 42, 54201
(920) 487-3471
Web site: http://www.amberwoodinn.com

Lake Michigan beachfront. Private wooded acreage on the shores of Lake Michigan, less than 5 miles from Door County. We have large luxury suites, each with private bath, fireplace, and double French doors with private decks opening to the beach. Whirlpool tub, wet bars, refrigerators. Finnish sauna. Sleep to the sound of the waves; awaken to a sunrise over the water. Inquire about accommodations for children. No smoking.

Hosts: Karen and Mark Rittle
Rooms: 7 (PB) $75-105
Full Breakfast
Credit Cards: A, B
Notes: 2, 5, 8, 9, 10

ALMA

Laue House Inn

Box 176, 54610
(608) 685-4923

Comfortable, cozy, and affordable. Within walking distance of all the stores and shops of the city. Watch the train and barges go by from the front porch, or hike in the hills behind the house. The Laue House is a fine example of Italianate architecture, designed by Charles Maybury. The house was placed on the National Register of Historic Places in 1979 by the hosts, who saved and restored this charming old structure. Player piano in the lounge with which to sing along. Refrigerator for refreshments and coffee bar for chatting with friends by the fireplace.

Hosts: Jan and Jerry Schreiber
Rooms: 6 (SB) $25-35
Continental Breakfast
Credit Cards: none
Notes: 2, 6, 7, 8, 9, 10, 11

BARABOO

Pinehaven Bed and Breakfast

E. 13083 Highway 33, 53913
(608) 356-3489

Located in a scenic valley with a small, private lake and Baraboo Bluffs in the background. The guest rooms are distinctly different, with wicker furniture and antiques, queen and twin beds. Take a walk in this peaceful country setting. Area activities include Devil's Lake State Park, Circus World Museum, Wisconsin Dells, and ski resorts. Ask about our private guest cottage. No pets, no smoking. Gift certificates available. Closed in March.

Hosts: Lyle and Marge Getschman
Rooms: 4 (PB) $70-135
Full Breakfast
Credit Cards: A, B
Notes: 2, 5, 7 (over 5), 9, 10, 11

Abendruh Bed and Breakfast Swisstyle

BELLEVILLE

Abendruh B&B Swisstyle

7019 Gehin Drive, 53508–9752
(608) 424-3808

Experience B&B Swisstyle. This highly acclaimed Wisconsin B&B offers true Swiss charm and hospitality. The serenity of this retreat is one of many treasures that keep guests coming back. Spacious guest rooms are adorned with beautiful family heirlooms. The sitting room has a high cathedral ceiling and a cozy fireplace. An Abendruh breakfast is a perfect way to start a new day or end a peaceful stay.

Hostess: Mathilde S. Jaggi
Rooms: 2 (PB) $65-70
Full or Continental Breakfast
Credit Cards: none
Notes: 2, 5, 8, 9, 10, 11, 12

CHIPPEWA FALLS

McGilvray's Victorian Bed and Breakfast

312 W. Columbia Street, 54729
(715) 720-1600; (888) 324-1893

Experience the Midwest in this friendly, historic city. Once a booming lumber town, Chippewa Falls has many beautiful homes built at the turn of the century. Warm hospitality and a scrumptious breakfast are top priority in this beautifully restored B&B. Relax by the fireplace on a chilly evening or enjoy one of the four porches on a summer day. There is much to do in the area: antiquing, biking, fishing, boating, skiing, and golf courses.

Hostess: Melanie J. Berg
Rooms: 3 (PB) $60-75
Full Breakfast
Credit Cards: none
Notes: 2, 5, 7 (over 12), 8, 9, 10, 11

Pleasant View Bed and Breakfast

16649 96th Avenue, 54729
(715) 382-4401
E-mail: info@pleasantviewbb.com
Web site: http://www.pleasantviewbb.com

Pleasant View Bed and Breakfast is a newly remodeled lake home nestled in the woods overlooking 6,300-acre Lake Wissota. There are four beautifully decorated theme rooms: Wind and Waves, Northwoods, Cozy Corner, and Secret Garden. While each room has a whirlpool, private bath, and queen-size bed, their decor is distinctively different. Pleasant View features a gathering room with a fireplace, as well as a sitting area in the atrium.

Hosts: Jeanine and Michael Adams
Rooms: 4 (PB) $79-129
Full Breakfast
Credit Cards: A, B, D
Notes: 2, 5, 8, 9, 10

Courthouse Square Bed and Breakfast

CRANDON

Courthouse Square B&B

210 E. Polk Street, 54520
(715) 478-2549
E-mail: chousebb@newnorth.net
Web site: http://www.innsite.com/wbba

Guests frequently comment about the peace and tranquillity of the setting. Enjoy birds and squirrels at the many benches placed throughout the flower and herb gardens, or stroll down the hill to the lake through the forget-me-nots and view the wildlife. *The Rhinelander Daily News* wrote: "Traditional hospitality is emphasized at Courthouse Square B&B, and it's evident from the moment you enter this delightful home where tranquillity and peace abound. You will no doubt smell something delicious baking in Bess's kitchen as gourmet cooking is one of her specialties." Forty minutes from Northland Baptist Bible College. Churches within walking distance.

Hosts: Les and Bess Aho
Rooms: 3 (1PB; 2SB) $52-70
Full Gourmet Candlelit Breakfast
Credit Cards: C
Notes: 2, 5, 7 (ask about 12+), 8, 9, 10, 11

DOOR COUNTY
(SEE—EGG HARBOR, EPHRAIM, GILLS ROCK, AND STURGEON BAY)

EAU CLAIRE

The Atrium B&B

5572 Prill Road, 54701
(715) 833-9045; (888) 773-0094
E-mail: atrium@eau-claire.com
Web site: http://www.eau-claire.com/atrium

The heart of this contemporary home lies in its 20 x 20-foot garden room with trickling fountain, palm trees, and bougainvillea vines stretching up to the windowed ceiling. Enjoy the exquisite antique stained-glass windows that grace the home. Explore the lovely gardens and wooded creekside trails. Nearby you'll find bicycling, cross-country skiing, canoeing, antiquing, and an Amish community. The

The Atrium Bed and Breakfast

NOTES: Credit cards accepted: A Master Card; B Visa; C American Express; D Discover; E Diners Club; F Other; 2 Personal checks accepted; 3 Lunch available; 4 Dinner available; 5 Open all year; 6 Pets

Atrium B&B offers the best of both worlds: relaxed seclusion only minutes from numerous restaurants, shopping, and the downtown area.

Hosts: Celia and Dick Stoltz
Rooms: 4 (PB) $70-129
Full Breakfast
Credit Cards: A, B
Notes: 2, 5, 7 (12+), 8, 9, 10, 11 (cross-country)

Otter Creek Inn

2536 Highway 12, 54701
(715) 832-2945; FAX (715) 832-4607
E-mail: hansen@werewolf.net
Web site: http://www.werewolf.net/~hansen

Pamper yourself! Each antique-filled guest room has a double whirlpool, private bath, phone, AC, and cable TV. Our breakfast menu allows a choice of entrées and breakfast in bed! This spacious inn (more than 6,000 square feet) is a three-story English Tudor with country Victorian decor. Nestled on a wooded acre adjacent to, but high above, the Otter Creek, the inn is less than a mile from numerous restaurants and shops. Inground pool. Otter Creek Inn is AAA-rated.

Hosts: Shelley and Randy Hansen
Rooms: 6 (PB) $79-159
Full Breakfast
Credit Cards: A, B, C, D, E, F
Notes: 2, 5, 8, 9, 10, 11

EGG HARBOR (DOOR COUNTY)

The Wildflower B&B

7821 Church Street; PO Box 34, 54209
(920) 868-9030

"Charming and intimate" describe Egg Harbor's only bed and breakfast, situated just a short stroll down the wildflower path from all village activities. This new home has blended together contemporary amenities with antique decor. All the Wildflower's rooms enjoy cool bay breezes from the private balconies and include fireplaces, television, and air-conditioning. Common area with wet bar, microwave, and refrigerator. Refreshments available at all times. Warm hospitality and relaxation abound—where friends meet!

Hostess: Judy LaMacchia
Rooms: 3 (PB) $90-135
Full Breakfast
Credit Cards: A, B, D
Notes: 2, 5, 9, 10, 11

EPHRAIM

Hillside Hotel of Ephraim

9980 Water Street (Highway 42), 54211–0017
(920) 854-2417; (800) 423-7023;
FAX (920) 854-4240
E-mail: kjmcneil@juno.com

An authentic, restored country Victorian inn featuring full, specialty breakfasts and afternoon tea, feather beds, original antiques, gorgeous harbor view, 100-foot veranda overlooking the harbor, individually decorated guest rooms, claw-foot tubs with showers, and brass fixtures. We have 15 years' experience and enjoyment here, and are so blessed. Let us share our home with you!

Hosts: Dave and Karen McNeil
Rooms: 11 (SB) + 2 cottages (PB) $74-94
Full Breakfast
Credit Cards: A, B, D
Notes: 2, 5, 7, 8, 9, 10, 11

Thorp House Inn and Cottages

FISH CREEK

Thorp House Inn and Cottages

4135 Bluff Lane; PO Box 490, 54212
(920) 868-2444
Web site: http://www.thorphouseinn.com

Find history and romance in the heart of a charming waterfront village. Choose from authentic antique-filled rooms or a private cottage, most with whirlpool, fireplace, and bay view. Featured in *McCall's* as one of "America's Most Charming Inns." Inspiration for LaVyrle Spencer's best-seller *Bittersweet*. Listed on the National Register of Historic Places. Brochure.

Hosts: Christine and Sverre Falck-Pedersen
Rooms: 5 + 6 cottages (PB) $85-165
Continental Breakfast
Credit Cards: none
Notes: 2, 5, 7 (in cottages), 8, 9, 10, 11

FORT ATKINSON

Lamp Post Inn

408 S. Main Street, 53538
(920) 563-6561

We welcome you to the charm of our 122-year-old Victorian home filled with beautiful antiques. Five gramophones for your listening pleasure. For the modern, one of our baths features a large Jacuzzi. We are located 7 blocks from the famous Fireside Playhouse. You come a stranger, but leave here a friend. No smoking.

Hosts: Debbie and Mike Rusch
Rooms: 3 (2PB; 1SB) $65-95
Full Breakfast
Credit Cards: none
Notes: 2, 5, 7, 8, 9, 10, 11

Harbor House Inn

GILLS ROCK (DOOR COUNTY)

Harbor House Inn

12666 Highway 42, 54210
(920) 854-5196; FAX (920) 854-9717

A 1904 Victorian bed and breakfast with a new Scandinavian country wing overlooking the quaint fishing harbor, bluffs, and sunsets. The inn has been restored to its original charm and tastefully done in period furniture. All rooms have private baths, air-conditioning, and TVs (most have microwaves and refrigerators). Two cottages are also available, one with a fireplace. Enjoy the inn's sauna, whirlpool, beach, gazebo, and gardens. Close to the ferry, shops, and dining. Home of Door County's newest lighthouse. The inn provides a

NOTES: Credit cards accepted: A Master Card; B Visa; C American Express; D Discover; E Diners Club; F Other; 2 Personal checks accepted; 3 Lunch available; 4 Dinner available; 5 Open all year; 6 Pets

beautiful two-room suite with fireplace and Jacuzzi inside.

Hosts: David and Else Weborg
Rooms: 15 (PB) $54-149
Continental Plus Breakfast
Credit Cards: A, B, C
Notes: 2, 6, 7, 9, 10

HAZEL GREEN

Wisconsin House Stage Coach Inn

2105 E. Main Street, 53811
(608) 854-2233

Built as a stage coach inn in 1846, the inn now offers six rooms and two suites for your comfort. Join us for an evening's rest. Dine and be refreshed in the parlor, where Gen. Grant spent many evenings with his friend Jefferson Crawford. Most conveniently located for all the attractions of the tri-state area. Galena, Illinois, is 10 minutes away; Dubuque, Iowa, 15 miles away; and Platteville, 20 miles away.

Hosts: Pat and Ken Disch
Rooms: 8 (6PB; 2SB) $55-115
Full Breakfast
Credit Cards: A, B, C, D
Notes: 2, 5, 7, 8, 9, 10, 11

HUDSON

The Grapevine Inn Bed and Breakfast

702 Vine Street, 54016
(715) 386-1989; FAX (715) 386-5047
E-mail: grpvine@pressenter.com

Casual elegance, European cottage style, invites you to relax and unwind in this historic home built by H.J. Andersen (Andersen windows). Enjoy quiet conversation in the front parlor or library. Sleep well in our beautiful guest rooms with queen beds and private baths. Morning brings a wake-up tray and full breakfast. Summer pool, front porch breakfasts. Located in Hudson on the St. Croix River—close to the Twin Cities, Mall of America, and Stillwater.

Hosts: Avery and Barbara Dahl
Rooms: 4 (PB) $89-149
Full Breakfast
Credit Cards: A, B, D
Notes: 2, 5, 8, 9, 10, 11

Jefferson Day House

Jefferson Day House

1109 Third Street, 54016
(715) 386-7111
Web site: http://www.jeffersondayhouse.com

The quiet, tree-lined street of a romantic river town is home to this luxurious, historic bed and breakfast. The home offers beautifully designed guest accommodations, each with private bath, queen bed, double whirlpool, and gas fireplace. Wood-burning fireplaces grace the home's formal dining room. Well-planted grounds create a sense of enclosure in the large, private courtyard. Just a short walk away are Hudson's charming downtown streets with one-of-a-kind shops and restaurants.

This beautiful house was restored from top to bottom in 1996.

Hosts: Tom and Sue Tyler
Rooms: 5 (PB) $99-179
Full Breakfast
Credit Cards: A, B, D
Notes: 2, 5, 6 and 7 (inquire), 9, 10, 11, 12

Phipps Inn Bed and Breakfast

Phipps Inn Bed and Breakfast

1005 3rd Street, 54016
(715) 386-0800; FAX (715) 386-0509

Listed on the National Register of Historic Places, this Queen Anne Victorian offers comfort, romance, and elegance. All rooms are nonsmoking and include whirlpools, private baths, and full breakfasts. All but one have a fireplace. Located 30 minutes from the Mall of America and St. Paul/Minneapolis.

Hosts: Cyndi and John Berglund
Rooms: 6 (PB) $99-189
Full Breakfast
Credit Cards: A, B, C, D
Notes: 2, 5, 8, 9, 10, 11, 12

LA FARGE

Trillium

Route 2, Box 121, 54639
(608) 625-4492

The guest cottage is on our farm and can accommodate several adults and one infant at a time (double beds, single beds, and a portable crib). Much wildlife is to be observed, including owls, hawks, wild turkeys, deer, pheasant, rabbits, songbirds, and more. The cottage is completely furnished and includes kitchen utensils, bed linens, bath towels, etc. A generous farm cottage breakfast is provided for each guest each morning. Other meals may be provided by guests, as they choose. Three nearby towns offer a good selection of restaurants for dining out.

Host: Trillium R. Bazctt
Rooms: 2 cottages (PB) $75-85
Full Breakfast
Credit Cards: none
Notes: 2, 5, 7, 8, 9, 10, 11

LAKE GENEVA

Eleven Gables Inn on the Lake

493 Wrigley Drive, 53147
(414) 248-8393
E-mail: egi@lkgeneva.com
Web site: http://www.lkgeneva.com

Nestled in evergreen amid giant oaks in the Edgewater Historical District, this quaint lakeside Carpenter's Gothic inn offers privacy and a prime location. Romantic bedrooms, bridal chamber, and unique country cottages all have fireplaces, down comforters, baths, TVs, wet bars, or cocktail refrigerators. Some have lattice courtyards, balconies, and private entrances. A private pier provides exclusive water activities. Bike rentals available. This charming "Newport of the Midwest" community provides fine dining, boutiques, and entertainment year-round.

Host: A. Milliette
Rooms: 10 (PB)
Full Breakfast
Credit Cards: A, B, C, D, E
Notes: 5, 6, 7, 8, 9, 10, 12

T.C. Smith Historic Inn

T.C. Smith Historic Inn

865 Main Street, 53147
(414) 248-1097; (800) 423-0233;
FAX (414) 248-1672
Web site: http://wwte.com/tcinn.htm

National historic landmark. The downtown lake-view, circa-1845 mansion offers spacious whirlpool and fireplace suites with fine antiques, museum paintings, and Oriental carpets. Magnificent honeymoon suites. Visualize your visit: You will experience 19th-century light fixtures that once were gas lights illuminating the parquet foyer floor, hand-tooled black walnut balustrades and staircase, and hand-painted walls with miniature oil paintings and original trompe l'oeil by Chicago artist John Bullock. You will feel the depth of history in a mansion built 150 years ago.

Hosts: The Marks Family
Rooms: 8 (PB) $115-350
Full Breakfast
Credit Cards: A, B, C, D, E
Notes: 2, 5, 7, 8, 9, 10, 11, 12

LIVINGSTON

Oak Hill Farm

9850 Highway 80, 53554
(608) 943-6006

A comfortable country home with a warm, hospitable atmosphere that is enhanced with fireplaces, porches, and facilities for picnics, bird-watching, and hiking. In the area you will find state parks, museums, and lakes.

Hosts: Elizabeth and Victor Johnson
Suites: 4 (1PB; 3SB) $45-50
Continental Breakfast
Credit Cards: none
Notes: 2, 6, 7, 8, 9, 10, 11, 12

MADISON

Annie's Bed and Breakfast

2117 Sheridan Drive, 53704
(608) 244-2224 (voice and FAX)
Web site: http://www.bbinternet.com/annies

When you want the world to go away, come to Annie's, the quiet inn on Warner

welcome; 7 Children welcome; 8 Tennis nearby; 9 Swimming nearby; 10 Golf nearby; 11 Skiing nearby; 12 May be booked through travel agent.

Park with the beautiful view. Luxury accommodations—a full floor of space all to yourself, including a master bedroom; a smaller bedroom; connecting full bath; whirlpool room; pine-paneled library with fireplace; and dining room opening to lovely gardens, gazebo, and shaded terrace. Miles of nature trails to lake, marshes, and woods to enjoy wildlife and sports. Only 6 minutes from downtown Madison and the UW campus. Central AC.

Hosts: Anne and Larry Stuart
Suites: 5-room suite (2PB) $128-259
Full Breakfast
Credit Cards: A, B, C
Notes: 2, 5, 7 (over 12), 8, 9, 10, 11

Mansion Hill Inn Bed and Breakfast

424 N. Pinckney Street, 53703
(608) 255-3999; (800) 798-9070;
FAX (608) 255-2217
Web site: http://www.mansionhillinn.com

The Mansion Hill Inn offers eleven luxurious rooms, each with a sumptuous bath. Whirlpool tubs with stereo headphones, hand-carved marble fireplaces, minibars, and elegant Victorian furnishings help make this restored mansion into a four-diamond inn. A private wine cellar, VCRs, and access to private dining and athletic clubs are available on request. Guests are treated to turndown service and evening refreshments in our parlor. The Mansion Hill Inn is ideal for honeymoons. It is listed on the National Register of Historic Places.

Hostess: Janna Wojtal
Rooms: 11 (PB) $120-300
Continental, Silver-Service Breakfast
Credit Cards: A, B, C
Notes: 2, 5, 9, 12

MAIDEN ROCK

Harrisburg Inn Bed and Breakfast

W. 3334 Highway 35; PO Box 15, 54750
(715) 448-4500; FAX (715) 448-3908

Our slogan, "a view with a room," does not begin to describe the sweeping vista enjoyed from every room. Miles of Mississippi Valley spread out with boating, fishing, bird-watching, and biking readily available. The Harrisburg Inn nestles on a bluff with the ambience of yesteryear in simple country decor and the beauty of nature pleasing the eye. Hearty food and happy hosts welcome you to Wisconsin's west coast. Explore twelve vintage villages of the Lake Pepin area and "inn-joy."

Hosts: Bern Paddock and Carol Crisp (Paddock)
Rooms: 4 (PB) $68-98
Full Breakfast
Credit Cards: A, B, D
Notes: 2, 7 (weekdays), 9, 10, 11

MONROE

Victorian Garden Bed and Breakfast

1720 16th Street, 53566–2643
(608) 328-1720; FAX (608) 328-1722
E-mail: vicgard@uteko.tds.net
Web site: http://apu.com/vicgard

This 1890 Victorian home has a wraparound porch and a large flower garden. The light and airy interior welcomes you into a pet- and smoke-free home. The sitting room with a baby grand piano, a formal parlor, and an informal parlor with a television are for your enjoyment. A

Victorian Garden Bed and Breakfast

three-course breakfast is served in the formal dining room. The new kitchen is always a favorite spot to enjoy the view of the yard from the bay window.

Hosts: Jane and Pete Kessenich
Rooms: 3 (PB) $75-85
Full Breakfast
Credit Cards: A, B, D
Notes: 2, 5, 8, 9, 11 (cross-country), 12

OSCEOLA

Pleasant Lake Bed and Breakfast

2238 60th Avenue, 54020–4509
(715) 294-2545; (800) 294-2545
E-mail: pllakebb@centuryinter.net

Enjoy a romantic getaway on beautiful Pleasant Lake. While here, you may take a leisurely walk in the woods, watch the birds and other wildlife, enjoy the lake in the paddleboat or canoe, sit around the bonfire, and watch the moon and stars reflecting on the lake. Then relax in one of the whirlpools and enjoy a fireplace. Savor a full country breakfast.

Pleasant Lake Bed and Breakfast

Hosts: Richard and Charlene Berg
Rooms: 7 (PB) $60-125
Full Breakfast
Credit Cards: A, B
Notes: 2, 5, 9, 10, 11

PLAIN

Bettinger House Bed and Breakfast

855 Wachter Avenue, Highway 23, 53577
(608) 546-2951 (voice and FAX)
Web site: Spring Green Chamber of Commerce

The Bettinger House is the hostess's grandparents' 1904 Victorian farmhouse; Grandma was a midwife who delivered 300 babies in this house. Choose from five spacious bedrooms that blend the old with the new, each named after noteworthy persons of Plain. The home is centrally air-conditioned. Start your day with one of the old-fashioned, full-course breakfasts for which we are famous. The Bettinger House is located near "House on the Rock," Frank Lloyd Wright's original Taliesen, American Players Theater, White Mound Park, and many more attractions.

Hosts: Jim and Marie Neider
Rooms: 5 (2½PB; 2½SB) $55-70
Full Breakfast
Credit Cards: A, B
Notes: 2, 5, 7 (inquire first), 8, 9, 10, 11, 12

PLYMOUTH

52 Stafford, An Irish Guest House

52 Stafford Street; PO Box 217, 53073
(920) 893-0552; (800) 421-4667;
FAX (920) 893-1800
Web site: http://www.classicinns.com

52 Stafford is in Plymouth, in the heart of the Kettle Moraine area. The 1892 building was originally a hotel and now is listed on the National Register of Historic Places. Our flagship inn offers exquisite cuisine in the restaurant and a congenial atmosphere in the authentic Irish pub.

Rooms: 19 (PB) $79.50-129.50
Full Breakfast weekends, Continental weekdays
Credit Cards: A, B, C, D, E
Notes: 2, 4, 5, 6, 7, 8, 9, 10, 11

PORT WASHINGTON

The Inn at Old Twelve Hundred

806 W. Grand Avenue, 53074
(414) 268-1200; FAX (414) 284-6885
Web site: http://www.southeastwis.com

The Inn at Old Twelve Hundred is a beautifully restored and decorated Queen Anne. All rooms are spacious and have queen or king beds; some offer whirlpools, fireplaces, private sitting rooms, and/or porches. Guest house rooms offer all amenities, including a wet bar, plus privacy. TV/VCRs. AC. No smoking.

Hosts: Stephanie and Ellie Bresette
Rooms: 6 (PB) $95-175
Continental Breakfast (no breakfast in guest house)
Credit Cards: A, B, C
Notes: 2, 5

PRESCOTT

The Arbor Inn

434 N. Court Street, 54021
(715) 262-4522; (888) 262-1090;
FAX (715) 262-5644
E-mail: arborinn@pressenter.com
Web site: http://www.pressenter.com/~arborinn

A quiet, peaceful haven with a St. Croix River View. Enjoy our 1902 home with fieldstone and grapevine breakfast porches. Four guest rooms with whirlpools—or relax in the hot tub under the stars! A four-course breakfast is served at the time and place you choose. Just 45 minutes from Mall of America. Walk to river cruises or waterfront restaurants. Near golf, antique shopping, and ski hills.

Hosts: Marv and Linda Kangas
Rooms: 4 (PB) $120-149
Full Breakfast
Credit Cards: A, B, C
Notes: 2, 5, 7 (inquire), 9, 10, 11

REEDSBURG

Parkview Bed and Breakfast

211 N. Park Street, 53959
(608) 524-4333; FAX (608) 524-1172
E-mail: parkview@jvlnet.com
Web site: http://www.jvlnet.com/~parkview

Our 1895 Queen Anne Victorian home overlooks City Park in the historic district. Many of the original features of the home remain, such as hardware, hardwood floors, intricate woodwork, leaded and etched windows, plus a suitor's window. Wake-up coffee is followed by a full, homemade breakfast. Central air and ceiling fans add to guests' comfort. Located 1 block from downtown. Close to Wisconsin Dells, Baraboo, and Spring Green. Three blocks from 400 Bike Trail.

Hosts: Tom and Donna Hofmann
Rooms: 4 (2PB; 2SB) $65-80
Full Breakfast
Credit Cards: A, B, C
Notes: 2, 5, 7 (inquire), 8, 10, 11, 12

Lamb's Inn Bed and Breakfast

RICHLAND CENTER

Lamb's Inn Bed and Breakfast

23761 Misslich Road, 53581
(608) 585-4301
E-mail: lambsinn@mwt.net
Web site: http://www.bbonline.com/wi/wbba

Relax on our 180-acre farm located in a scenic valley surrounded by spectacular hills. Beautifully renovated farmhouse furnished with country antiques. . .porch for watching deer and other wildlife. . .cozy library for rainy days. Our new cottage has a spiral stair to the loft and a deck on which to relax. Large, homemade breakfasts are served at the bed and breakfast with homemade breads, egg dishes, and often old-fashioned bread pudding. Twenty-five miles from Spring Green with American Players Theater, House on the Rock, and Taliesen. Close to biking trails and Amish.

Hosts: Dick and Donna Messerschmidt
Rooms: 7 (PB) $80-120
Full Breakfast in B&B; Continental in cottage
Credit Cards: A, B
Notes: 2, 5, 7 (in cottage), 8, 9, 10, 12

ST. CROIX FALLS

Wissahickon Farms Country Inn

2263 Maple Drive, 54024
(715) 483-3986

"Rustic country lodging with a touch of class." Located on a 30-acre hobby farm secluded by God's creative handiwork, our country inn portrays an old country store from a bygone era. Relax on the porch, enjoy the two-person whirlpool, or hike the many surrounding trails, including an ice age trail. The "Gandy Dancer" bicycle/snowmobile trail runs right through the farm. Furnishings include queen-size camelback bed, hide-a-bed sofa for two ($15 per extra person), and glider rocker. The small efficiency kitchen contains a refrigerator, microwave, etc. Guests have a TV with VCR. The inn is air-conditioned. No smoking, no pets. Bicycles are provided to ride the trail and snowshoe in winter. Come see what the St. Croix River Valley has to offer!

Hosts: Steve and Sherilyn Litzkow
Rooms: 1 (PB) $125
Continental Breakfast
Credit Cards: A, B
Notes: 2, 5, 9, 10, 11

SPARTA

The Franklin Victorian Bed and Breakfast

220 E. Franklin Street, 54656
(608) 269-3894; (800) 845-8767
Web site: http://www.spartan.org/fvbb

This turn-of-the-century home welcomes you to bygone elegance with small-town quiet and comfort. The four spacious bedrooms provide a perfect setting for ultimate relaxation. A full, home-cooked breakfast is served before starting your day of hiking, biking, skiing, canoeing, antiquing, or exploring this beautiful area.

Hosts: Lloyd and Jane Larson
Rooms: 4 (2PB; 2SB) $75-95
Full Breakfast
Credit Cards: A, B
Notes: 2, 5, 8, 9, 10, 11

Strawberry Lace Inn Bed and Breakfast

603 N. Water Street, 54656
(608) 269-7878
E-mail: strawberry@centuryinter.net
Web site: http://www.spartan.org/sbl

Return to an era of romance and elegance. The home is an excellent example of an Italianate Victorian (circa 1875). Rest in your own private retreat with private bath, king or queen bed with mountains of pillows, and distinctive antique decor. Partake in your hosts' four-course breakfast, presented on crystal and linen. Relax by visiting, reading, or playing games on the four-season porch. Known as "the biking capital of America," the area offers bike trails, golf, water sports, antiquing, restaurants, winter sports, and many more attractions year-round.

Strawberry Lace Inn Bed and Breakfast

Hosts: Jack and Elsie Ballinger
Rooms: 5 (PB) $79-125
Full Breakfast
Credit Cards: A, B
Notes: 2, 5, 9, 10, 11, 12

STEVENS POINT

Dreams of Yesteryear Bed and Breakfast

1100 Brawley Street, 54481
(715) 341-4525; FAX (715) 344-3047
E-mail: dreams@coredcs.com
Web site: http://www.coredcs.com/~dreams

Featured in *Victorian Homes Magazine* and listed on the National Register of Historic Places. Your hosts are from Stevens Point and enjoy talking about the restoration of their turn-of-the-century home, which has been in the same family for three generations. All rooms are furnished in antiques. Guests enjoy the use of parlors, porches, and gardens. Two blocks from the historic downtown, antique and specialty shops, picturesque Green Circle Trails, the university, and more. Truly "a Victorian dream come true."

Hosts: Bonnie and Bill Maher
Rooms: 6 (4PB; 2SB) $55-135
Full Breakfast
Credit Cards: A, B, C, D
Notes: 2, 5, 7 (over 12), 8, 9, 10, 11, 12

STURGEON BAY

Hearthside B&B

2136 Taube Road, 54235
(920) 746-2136

Our 1800s farmhouse has a blend of contemporary and antique furnishings. The old barn still stands nearby. Within easy driving distance are fantastic state parks, beaches for swimming in summer, and areas for skiing in winter. Lighthouses, U.S. Coast Guard Station, lake cruises, airport, ship building, and weekend festivals. The rooms are charming—three with queen beds. Our family room has twin beds with an adjoining room that has a double bed. TVs, VCRs, living room, and sunroom.

Hosts: Don and Lu Klussendorf
Rooms: 4 (PB) $45-65
Full Breakfast
Credit Cards: none
Notes: 2, 5, 7, 8, 9, 10, 11

The Scofield House Bed and Breakfast

908 Michigan Street, 54235–1849
(920) 743-7727 (voice and FAX); (888) 463-0204
E-mail: scofhse@mail.wiscnet.net
Web site: http://www.scofieldhouse.com

The Scofield House Bed and Breakfast

"Door County's most elegant bed and breakfast." This 1902 multicolored, three-story Victorian was restored in 1987 by the present hosts. Guests keep coming back for Bill's wonderful gourmet breakfasts and Fran's homemade "sweet treats" served fresh daily. The Scofield House has six guest rooms, of which four are suites; all have private baths, color television/VCRs, and a "free" video library. Double whirlpools, fireplaces, and central AC. Smoke-free environment.

Hosts: Bill and Fran Cecil
Rooms: 6 (PB) $93-196 (seasonal)
Full Breakfast
Credit Cards: none
Notes: 2, 5, 8, 9, 10, 11, 12

TWO RIVERS

Red Forest Bed and Breakfast

1421 25th Street, 54241
(920) 793-1794; (888) 250-2272;
FAX (920) 793-3056
Web sites: http://www.insite.com/wbba
http://www.innsandouts.com

We invite you to step back in time to 1907 and enjoy our gracious, three-story shingle-style home. Highlighted with stained-glass windows, heirloom antiques, and cozy

welcome; 7 Children welcome; 8 Tennis nearby; 9 Swimming nearby; 10 Golf nearby; 11 Skiing nearby; 12 May be booked through travel agent.

fireplace. Four beautifully appointed guest rooms await your arrival. Stroll along our sugar sand beaches or through downtown antique shops. The Red Forest is located on Wisconsin's east coast, minutes from Manitowoc, Wisconsin's port city, and the Lake Michigan car ferry. Also located midway between Chicago and the Door County Peninsula.

Hosts: Kay and Alan Rodewald
Rooms: 4 (2PB; 2SB) $65-85
Full Breakfast
Credit Cards: A, B, C, D
Notes: 2, 5, 7 (older), 8, 9 (beach), 10, 11, 12

WISCONSIN DELLS

The Buckley House Bed and Breakfast

PO Box 598, 53965
(608) 586-5752; (888) 689-4875;
FAX (608) 586-4744

An early 1900s country Victorian home with an inviting wraparound porch, nestled on 6 acres with a pond and a breathtaking view of the rolling countryside. A Currier and Ives setting. Enjoy antiques, queen-size brass beds, in-room whirlpools, quilts, fresh air, flower gardens, bright skies, and moonlight. Hiking, bicycling, skiing, snowmobiling, bird-watching, hot-air balloon rides, antiquing, and auctions. All this and just minutes from golf courses, fishing lakes, and Wisconsin Dells.

Hosts: Michael and Kathie Lake
Rooms: 3 (PB) $60-150
Full Breakfast
Credit Cards: A, B
Notes: 2, 5, 9, 10, 11

Historic Bennett House

825 Oak Street, 53965
(608) 254-2500
Web site: http://www.dells.com/bennett

The 1863 home of pioneer photographer H.H. Bennett is warm and inviting in its casual elegance and welcoming atmosphere. Traveling with another couple? We have the ideal situation for you. Two lovely bedrooms, one with queen canopy bed and English armoire and the other with queen brass bed with wicker accents. Share a carpeted bedroom-size bath with Italian sinks and Bennett's claw-foot tub. You may, of course, reserve just one room. The library has become part of a two-room suite with private bath. View a favorite movie from our 100-plus collection. Savor a delicious gourmet breakfast, and visit Dells attractions; state parks; Bennett, Rockwell, Circus, and Railroad museums; riverboat tours; skiing; Crane Foundation.

Hosts: Gail and Rich Obermeyer
Rooms: 3 (1PB; 2SB) $70-95
Full Breakfast
Credit Cards: none
Notes: 2, 5, 8, 9, 10, 11

Terrace Hill B&B

922 River Road, 53965
(608) 253-9363
E-mail: terrace.hill@mail.maqs.net
Web site: http://www.maqs.net/~lnovak

Our 100-year-old, yellow Victorian home is located atop a small bluff near the sandstone cliffs of the Upper Dells on scenic River Road, just 1 block from downtown Dells. Enjoy old-world charm, browse our electronic library, experience serendipity. Pamper yourself with a little respite from the busy world in which we live. Private parking, private baths, in-room whirlpool, AC. Children welcome.

Hosts: The Novak family
Rooms: 5 (PB) $65-110
Full Breakfast
Credit Cards: A, B, C, D
Notes: 2, 5, 7, 8, 9, 10, 11, 12

The White Rose B&B Inn

910 River Road, 53965
(608) 254-4724; (800) 482-4724
E-mail: whiterose@jvlnet.com

A romantic retreat or family fun getaway. Your comfort and relaxation are our pleasure. The White Rose B&B Inn invites you to visit our gardens, relax in the parlor, or experience rich indulgence at the Secret Garden Cafe, located at the lower level of the Victorian B&B, offering the famous international cuisine of the Cheese Factory Restaurant. Doubles, queens, or suites available, all with private baths. Heated outdoor pool.

Hosts: Marty and Shionagh Stuehler
Rooms: 5 (PB) $65-115
Full Breakfast
Credit Cards: A, B, C
Notes: 2, 3, 4, 5, 7, 9, 10, 11, 12

WYOMING

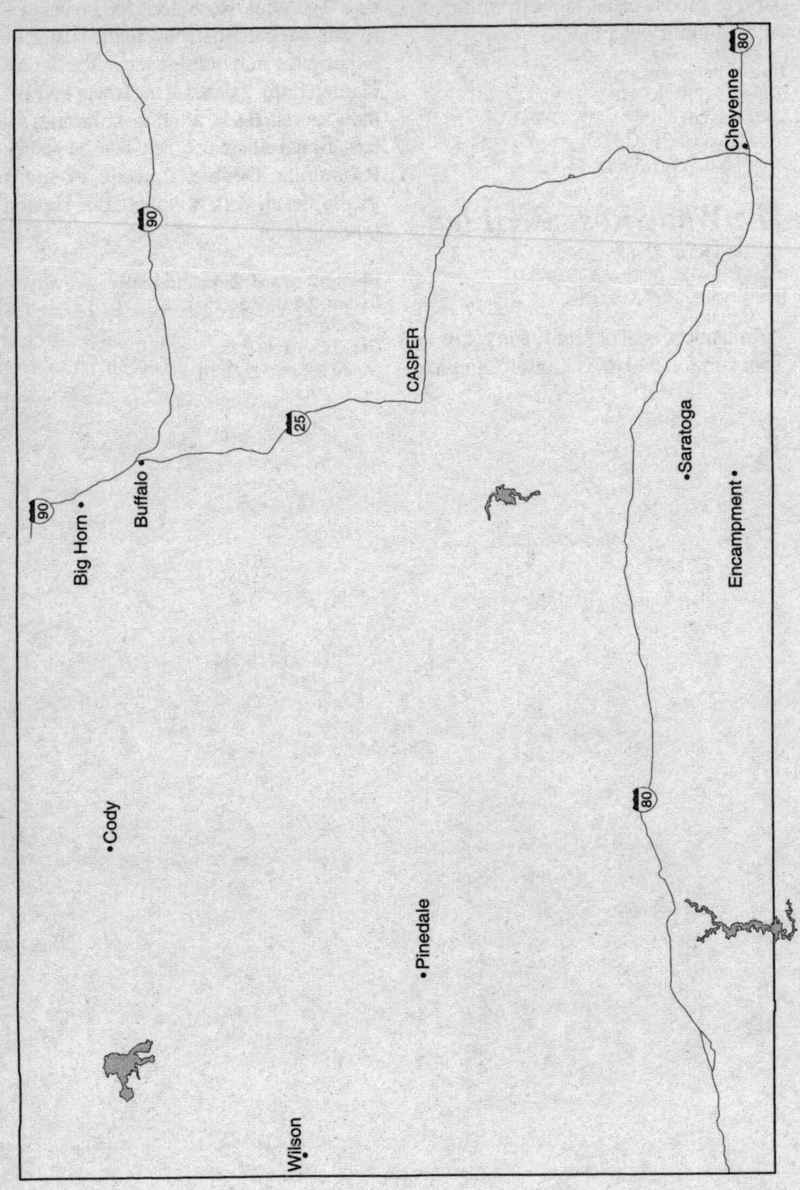

90
Big Horn
Buffalo
25
90
CASPER
Cheyenne
80
Saratoga
Encampment
80
Cody
Pinedale
Wilson

Wyoming

BIG HORN

Spahn's Bighorn Mountain Bed and Breakfast

PO Box 579, 82833
(307) 674-8150
E-mail: spahnbb@wave.sheridan.wy.us
Web site: http://wave.sheridan.wy.us/~spahnbb

Towering log home and secluded guest cabins on the mountainside in whispering pines. Borders 1 million acres of public forest with deer and moose. A gracious mountain breakfast is served on the deck with binoculars so you can enjoy the 100-mile view. The owner is a former Yellowstone park ranger. Located 10 minutes from I–90, near Sheridan.

Hosts: Ron and Bobbie Spahn
Rooms: 3 + 2 cabins (PB) $75-125
Full Breakfast
Credit Cards: none
Notes: 4, 5, 7

BUFFALO

Historic Mansion House Inn

313 N. Main Street, 82834
(307) 684-2218; (888) 455-9202

Seven western Victorian guest rooms on historic Main Street. Eleven comfortable motel rooms in annex. Continental breakfast, spa, color cable TV, AC. Located on historic Main Street and Highway 16—scenic route to Yellowstone National Park. Open year-round.

Hosts: Phil and Diane Mehlhaff
Rooms: 18 (PB) $40-65
Continental Breakfast
Credit Cards: A, B, D
Notes: 5, 7, 8, 9, 10, 11, 12

NOTES: Credit cards accepted: A Master Card; B Visa; C American Express; D Discover; E Diners Club; F Other; 2 Personal checks accepted; 3 Lunch available; 4 Dinner available; 5 Open all year; 6 Pets welcome; 7 Children welcome; 8 Tennis nearby; 9 Swimming nearby; 10 Golf nearby; 11 Skiing nearby; 12 May be booked through travel agent.

A. Drummond's Ranch

CHEYENNE/LARAMIE

A. Drummond's Ranch

399 Happy Jack Road, 82007
(307) 634-6042 (voice and FAX)
E-mail: adrummond@juno.com
Web site: http://www.cruising-america.com/drummond.html

A quiet, gracious retreat situated on 120 acres near Medicine Bow National Forest and Curt Gowdy State Park. Between Cheyenne and Laramie at an elevation of 7,500 feet. We provide privacy with personalized service. Hiking, mountain biking, cross-country skiing, llama packing, or simply relaxing. Outdoor hot tubs and glorious night skies. Boarding for horses and pets in transit. Dietary restrictions accommodated, when possible. No smoking, please. Reservations required.

Hostess: Taydie Drummond
Rooms: 4 (2PB; 2SB) $65-155
Full Breakfast
Credit Cards: A, B, D, F (Novus)
Notes: 2, 3, 4, 5, 6, 7, 10, 11, 12

The Storyteller Pueblo

5201 Ogden Road, 82009
(307) 634-7036; FAX (307) 635-9117

Native American art from more than thirty tribes: pottery, beadwork, baskets, and rugs. Contemporary home of country and primitive antiques. Down-home hospitality on a quiet street. Convenient to shopping and major restaurants. Breakfast with all the amenities. Fireplaces and family rooms for your enjoyment. Reservations recommended. Special rates during the last ten days of July.

Hosts: Howard and Peggy Hutchings
Rooms: 3 (1PB; 2SB) $40-55
Full Breakfast
Credit Cards: none
Notes: 2, 5, 7 (by arrangement), 8, 9, 10, 11, 12

The Lockhart Bed and Breakfast Inn

CODY

The Lockhart B&B Inn

109 W. Yellowstone Avenue (U.S. 14, 16, 20), 82414
(307) 587-6074 (voice and FAX); (800) 377-7255
E-mail: CBaldwin@wyoming.com

Truly your "home away from home" for people who enjoy personal service as well as western hospitality. Enjoy fresh mountain air, blue skies, and beautiful mountain views as you relax on the spacious veranda outside the inn. The historic home of authoress Caroline Lockhart has been beautifully restored with the grace and country charm befitting its tranquil setting in the majestic Rocky Mountains.Only minutes from the Buffalo Bill Historical Center, Old Trail Town, and Cody Nite Rodeo. Twenty-five miles from Shoshone

NOTES: Credit cards accepted: A Master Card; B Visa; C American Express; D Discover; E Diners Club; F Other; 2 Personal checks accepted; 3 Lunch available; 4 Dinner available; 5 Open all year; 6 Pets

National Forest, 50 miles from the entrance to Yellowstone National Park.

Hostess: Cindy Baldwin
Rooms: 14 (PB) $65-95
Full Breakfast
Credit Cards: A, B, C, D, E
Notes: 2, 3, 5, 7, 8, 9, 10, 11, 12

ENCAMPMENT

Rustic Mountain Lodge

Star Route, Box 49, 82325
(307) 327-5539

A peaceful mountain view from a working ranch with wholesome country atmosphere and lots of western hospitality. Enjoy daily fishing on a private pond, big-game trophy hunts, cookouts, retreats, pack trips, photo safaris, youth programs, cattle drives, trail rides, hiking, rock hunting, many ranch activities, mountain biking and four-wheeling trails, and survival workshops. Individuals, families, groups welcome! Terrific atmosphere for workshops. Lodge and cabin rentals available. Reservations only. Private fishing cabins available May–September. Write for brochure!

Hosts: Mayvon Platt
Rooms: 4 (1PB; 3SB) $65
Full Breakfast
Credit Cards: none
Notes: 2, 3, 4, 5, 6, 7, 8, 9, 10, 11

Rustic Mountain Lodge

JACKSON HOLE

Nowlin Creek Inn

660 E. Broadway; PO Box 2766, 83002
(307) 733-0882; FAX (307) 733-0106
E-mail: nowlin@sisna.com
Web site: http://www.JacksonHoleNet.com/b&bsl

Nowlin Creek Inn is located in Jackson Hole, gateway to Yellowstone and Grand Teton National Parks. Located across from the National Elk Refuge, Nowlin Creek is convenient for walking or driving to the many area attractions and activities: hiking, biking, fishing, boating, rafting, sight-seeing. The inn offers many features typical of high-quality bed and breakfasts. We work hard to find those special services like evening beverages, those fine details like thick terry robes, and that extra measure of graciousness that will make your stay memorable so you want to return. Gas log fireplace in the king suite; other fireplaces are being added. Two-room luxury cabin has gas log fireplace, full kitchen, bath, and laundry room. Enjoy western hospitality at its finest!

Hosts: Susan and Mark Nowlin
Rooms: 5 (PB) $95-210
Full Breakfast
Credit Cards: A, B, C, D
Notes: 2, 5, 7, 8, 9, 10, 11, 12

PINEDALE

Pole Creek Ranch Bed and Breakfast

PO Box 278, 82941
(307) 367-4433
Web site: http://www.bbonline.com/wy/polecreek

Relive the charm of the Old West in our rustic log home with a superb view of the spectacular Wind River Mountains. Enjoy horse, wagon, and sleigh rides; hiking; backpacking; fishing. Then relax on the front porch or in the hot tub. It's *sooo* peaceful. We cater especially to families and can help you prepare for a personal pack trip in the Bridger Wilderness.

Hosts: Dexter and Carole Smith
Rooms: 3 (1PB; 2SB) $55
Full Breakfast
Credit Cards: none
Notes: 2, 3, 4, 5, 6, 7, 8, 9, 10, 11

SARATOGA

Far Out West Bed and Breakfast

304 N. 2nd Street; PO Box 1230, 82331
(307) 326-5869; FAX (307) 326-9864
E-mail: fowbnb@union-tel.com
Web site: http://www.cruising-america.com/farout.html

This historic home has six guest rooms that are decorated comfortably with a country flair. All have private baths. Three rooms have king-size beds. We are located 2 blocks from downtown and 1½ blocks from the N. Platte River, where we have the best fly-fishing in the country. We offer a hot tub, exercise equipment, and large-screen TV in the great room that has a large, round fireplace. Open year-round. No smoking.

Hosts: Bill and B.J. Farr
Rooms: 6 (PB) $95
Full Breakfast
Credit Cards: A, B
Notes: 2, 5, 7, 9, 10, 11

WILSON

Teton View Bed and Breakfast

2136 Coyote Loop; PO Box 652, 83014
(307) 733-7954

Rooms have mountain views. The lounge/eating area, where homemade pastries, fresh fruit, and coffee are served, connects to a private upper deck with fantastic mountain and ski resort views. Private guest entrance. Convenient to Yellowstone and Grand Teton National Parks. Located approximately 4 miles from the ski area. Closed April and October–November.

Hosts: John and Joanna Engelhart
Rooms: 3 (1PB; 2SB) $70-90
Full Breakfast
Credit Cards: none
Notes: 2, 4, 7, 8, 9, 10, 11, 12

Alberta

AIRDRIE

Big Springs Bed and Breakfast

RR 1, T4B 2A3
(403) 948-5264; FAX (403) 948-5851
E-mail: bigsprings@bigsprings-bb.com
Web site: http://www.bigsprings-bb.com

Overlooking a picturesque valley on 35 very private pastoral acres. Beautifully landscaped and treed. Five-thousand-square-foot hillside bungalow. Choose from four beautifully decorated rooms: the Bridal Suite, featuring a hydro-massage tub; the Manor Room; the Victorian Room; or the Arbour Room. Relax in our secluded English Garden sitting room, where furniture groupings are situated so that the garden atmosphere continues to the surrounding green of the outdoors. Elegant gourmet breakfast by certified and experienced hosts. Fireplace, hot tub, evening beverages, and "goodies." You'll find extra personal touches; we pamper our guests. Indoor sauna. Nature trail that winds along rock formations in the valley. Fifteen minutes from Calgary city limits; 25 minutes from airport. Great access to Banff, Lake Louise, Kananaskis Country, Calgary Stampede, and Calgary Zoo. Canada Select three-star rating.

Hosts: Earle and Carol Whittaker
Rooms: 4 (PB) $95-125 (Canadian)
Full Breakfast
Credit Cards: A, B
Notes: 5, 7, 9, 10, 11, 12

DeWitt's B&B

RR 1, T4B 2A3
(403) 948-5356; FAX (403) 912-0788
E-mail: dewitbnb@cadvision.com
Web site: http://www.cadvision.com/dewitbnb

Enjoy warm hospitality and tantalizing breakfast served in the flower-filled patio or in our dining room, viewing the Rocky Mountains through the trees. Nearby are the world-famous Calgary Stampede, the Western Heritage Center, Calaway Park, Spruce Meadows Equestrian Center, and the many attractions of Kananaskis Country and Banff National Park. Ten-and-three-quarters kilometers west of Airdrie/ Highway 2 on the southern junction of highways 567 and 772; 20 minutes from Calgary and the international airport.

Hosts: Irene DeWitt and Wendy Kelly
Rooms: 3 (1PB; 2SB) $75-85 (Canadian)
Full or Continental Breakfast
Credit Cards: B
Notes: 5, 7, 9, 10, 11

---

welcome; 7 Children welcome; 8 Tennis nearby; 9 Swimming nearby; 10 Golf nearby; 11 Skiing nearby; 12 May be booked through travel agent.

ALBERTA

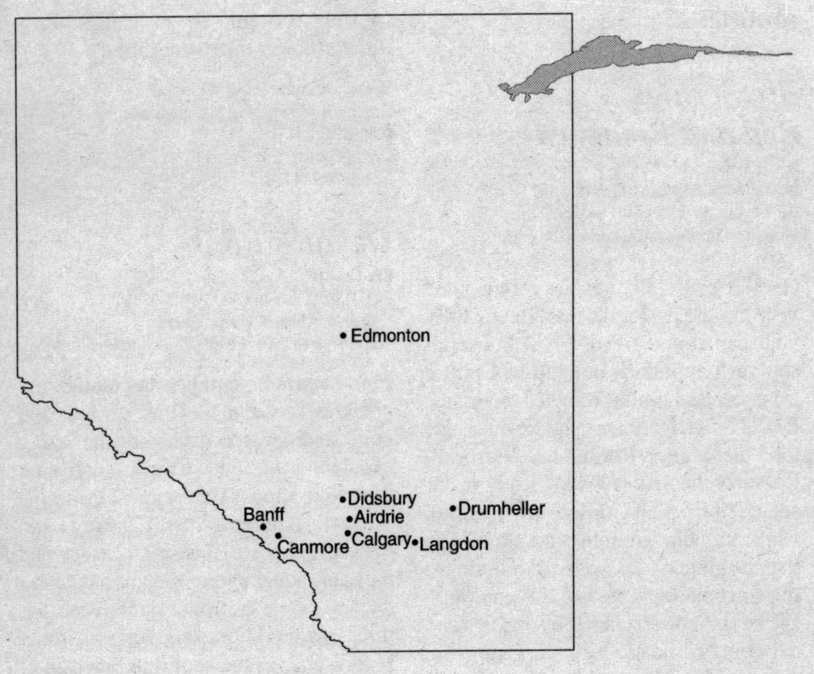

Edmonton
Didsbury
Banff
Airdrie
Drumheller
Canmore
Calgary
Langdon

BANFF

Spray Valley

Box 184, T0L 0C0
(403) 762-2846
E-mail: spraybb@telusplanet.net

"A home away from home" close to the famous Banff Springs Hotel Conference Center and Golf Course. Restaurant is three houses away, downtown center 5 minutes. Hostess is knowledgeable of the area and will help with your itineraries. Sitting room with fireplace, cable TV, and library. Hostess is a Toastmaster, enjoys good conversation, speaks English and German. Cash and traveler's checks accepted. Come and enjoy.

Hostess: Marvelyne Yarmoloy
Rooms: 3 (PB) $95-135 (prices subject to change)
Continental Breakfast
Credit Cards: none
Notes: 5, 8, 9, 10, 11, 12

CALGARY

Paradise Acres Bed and Breakfast

243105 Paradise Road, Box 20, Site 2, RR 6, T2M 4L5
(403) 248-4748; (403) 235-3916
E-mail: paradise@cwave.com
Web site: http://www.cwave.com/paradise

Come enjoy our friendly and luxurious setting with country quietness and city access. Paradise Acres features choice of breakfasts, queen-size beds, private baths, plus guest sitting rooms with TV/VCR. Located close to the Trans Canada Highway and Calgary airport with a city and mountain view. Airport pickup available.

Hosts: Brian and Char Bates
Rooms: 4 (PB) $67.50-82.50
Full Breakfast
Credit Cards: A, B, C
Notes: 2, 5, 8, 9, 10, 11, 12

Rosedale House Bed and Breakfast

Rosedale House B&B

1633-7A Street NW, T2M 3K2
(403) 284-0010 (voice and FAX)
E-mail: rosedale@cadvision.com
Web site: http://www.cadvision.com/rosedale/index.htm

This large, executive home offers the charm of a turn-of-the-century home with all the modern conveniences. The guest rooms have en suite bathrooms, excellent queen beds, writing tables, and phone jacks. The lounge offers a TV, VCR, fireplace, pool table, and beverage station with microwave. Breakfast is served in a formal dining room with linen and china. Excellent central location.

Hosts: Dennis and Beth Palmquist
Rooms: 3 (PB) $80-110 (Canadian)
Full Breakfast
Credit Cards: A, B, C
Notes: 2, 5, 7, 8, 9, 10, 11, 12

NOTES: Credit cards accepted: A Master Card; B Visa; C American Express; D Discover; E Diners Club; F Other; 2 Personal checks accepted; 3 Lunch available; 4 Dinner available; 5 Open all year; 6 Pets welcome; 7 Children welcome; 8 Tennis nearby; 9 Swimming nearby; 10 Golf nearby; 11 Skiing nearby; 12 May be booked through travel agent.

CANMORE

Cougar Creek Inn Bed and Breakfast

240 Grizzly Crescent, T1W 1B5
(403) 678-4751; FAX (403) 678-9529

Quiet, rustic, cedar chalet with mountain views in every direction. Grounds border on Cougar Creek and are surrounded by rugged mountain scenery that invites all types of outdoor activity. Hostess has strong love for the mountains and can assist with plans for local hiking, skiing, canoeing, mountain biking, backpacking, etc., as well as scenic drives. The inn has a private entrance with sitting area, fireplace, games, TV, sauna, and reading materials for guests. Two large guest rooms, one with three double beds, the other with two double beds. Breakfasts are hearty and wholesome, with many home-baked items. Open May–September.

Hostess: Mrs. Patricia Doucette
Rooms: 2 (SB) $60-65 (Canadian)
Full Breakfast
Credit Cards: none
Notes: 2, 3, 7, 8, 9, 10, 11

DIDSBURY

Grimmon House Bed and Breakfast

1610 Fifteen Avenue; PO Box 1268, T0M 0W0
(403) 335-8353; FAX (403) 335-3640

"Love in any language, color, or creed fluently spoken here." Relax and enjoy the benefits of a rural experience just 45 minutes from Calgary. Three rooms charmingly furnished with brass beds, antiques, and quilts. Hearty breakfast overlooking the garden, private entrance, and offstreet parking. Wake-up coffee brought to your door. Lemonade and evening outdoor fire, weather permitting.

Grimmon House Bed and Breakfast

Hosts: John and Myrna Grimmon
Rooms: 3 (SB) $55-65
Full Breakfast
Credit Cards: none
Notes: 2, 5, 7 (by arrangement), 8, 9, 10, 11, 12

DRUMHELLER

The Victorian House B&B

541 Riverside Drive W., T0J 0Y3
(403) 823-3535
Web site: http://www.bbcanada.com/269.html

Nonsmoking, pet-free accommodations within walking distance of downtown. We have queen, double, and single beds, and private and shared bathrooms. Breakfast served from 6 to 10, with a full menu to choose from. Enjoy a view of the river and Badlands from our veranda and balcony. A quiet location. Guest lounge has TV/VCR with many classical videos.

Hosts: Jack and Florence Barnes
Rooms: 4 (1PB; 3SB) $50-65
Full Breakfast
Credit Cards: A, B
Notes: 5, 7, 8, 9, 10, 11, 12

NOTES: Credit cards accepted: A Master Card; B Visa; C American Express; D Discover; E Diners Club; F Other; 2 Personal checks accepted; 3 Lunch available; 4 Dinner available; 5 Open all year; 6 Pets

EDMONTON

Alberta's B&B and Reservation Agency

11216 48th Avenue, T6H 0C7
(780) 434-6098 (voice and FAX)
Web site: http://www.bbcanada.com/1301.html

Tastefully decorated, smoke-free home with friendly atmosphere in quiet park setting. Close to university, West Edmonton Mall, International Airport, City Centre. There is office equipment for business travelers. Enjoy all-you-can-eat gourmet breakfast in dining area overlooking flower garden. Hostess has many years' experience in the travel industry and can help with your entire travel itinerary in Canada and the U.S. Traveler's checks accepted.

Hosts: Gordon and Betty Mitchell
Rooms: 2 (PB) $60-85
Full Breakfast
Credit Cards: A, B
Notes: 5, 8, 9, 10, 11, 12

LANGDON

Merrywood Bed and Breakfast and Crafts

23 Newton Street, T0J 1X0
(403) 936-5796

Enjoy relaxed accommodations in a quiet hamlet east of Calgary. Merrywood is in a rural setting central to the Canadian Rockies, Banff, Lake Louise, Jasper, Waterton Park, Glacier National Park, the Calgary Stampede, West Edmonton Mall, dinosaur areas, dinner theaters, birding and rock-hounding locations, fishing holes, and gardens. Fenced yard for small dog. Reservations required.

Host: G.M. Chappell
Rooms: 2 (SB) $45-55
Full Breakfast
Credit Cards: some
Notes: 5, 6

---

welcome; 7 Children welcome; 8 Tennis nearby; 9 Swimming nearby; 10 Golf nearby; 11 Skiing nearby; 12 May be booked through travel agent.

BRITISH COLUMBIA

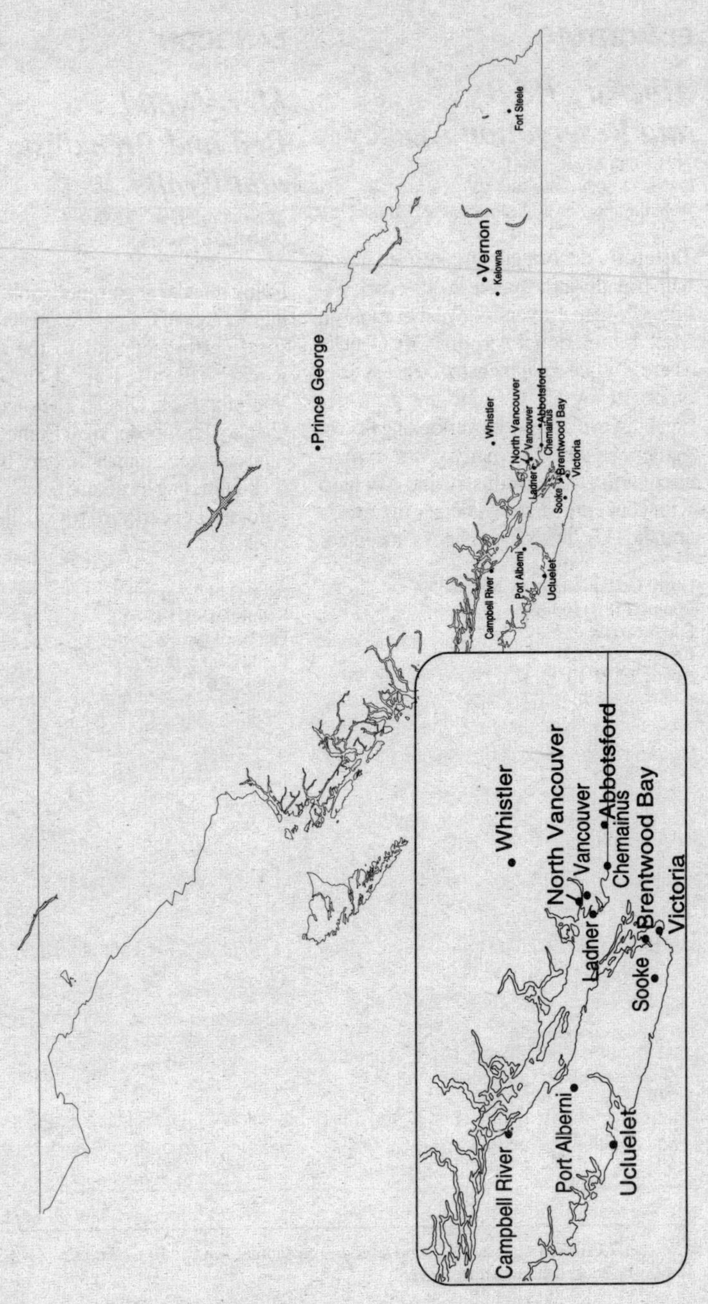

British Columbia

ABBOTSFORD

Everett House B&B

1990 Everett Road, V2S 7S3
(604) 859-2944; FAX (604) 859-9180
E-mail: everettbb@bc.sympatico.ca
Web site: http://www.vancouver-bc.com/everettbb

We invite you to join us in our Victorian-style home. Easily accessible to the freeway and overlooking the Fraser Valley, our home is the perfect retreat removed from the hustle of the city. It is also that "someplace special" for you while you conduct your business in the Fraser Valley. A stay at our home will provide you with a refreshing break from ordinary life.

Hosts: Cindy and David Sahlstrom
Rooms: 2 (PB) $85-125
Full Breakfast
Credit Cards: A, B
Notes: 5, 7, 8, 9 (public pools), 10, 11, 12

BRENTWOOD BAY

Seascape Oceanfront

740 Sea Drive, V8M 1B1
(250) 652-9628 (voice and FAX); (888) 791-1192
E-mail: seascape@bctravel.com

A contemporary waterfront home in a country setting only 3 minutes from Butchart Gardens. Guests enjoy private baths, queen-size beds, antique furnishings, outstanding views from every room, private decks, guest lounges, hearty breakfasts (muffins, scones, marvelous breads, preserves—all homemade). We offer government-approved, luxurious accommodations. Relax on our deck, swim, boat, and fish. Watch seals, otters, bird life, and sunsets. Deep-water moorage close to fine dining. Twenty minutes to Victoria. No smoking, no pets.

Hosts: Ray and Judith Sam
Rooms: 3 (2PB; 2SB)
Full Breakfast
Credit Cards: A, B
Notes: 5, 9

CAMPBELL RIVER

Arbour's Guest House Bed and Breakfast

375 S. Murphy Street, V9W 1Y8
(250) 287-9873; FAX (250) 287-2353
E-mail: crfish@oberon.ark.com

Arbour's Guest House is a large residential treed property with mountain and

---

NOTES: Credit cards accepted: A Master Card; B Visa; C American Express; D Discover; E Diners Club; F Other; 2 Personal checks accepted; 3 Lunch available; 4 Dinner available; 5 Open all year; 6 Pets welcome; 7 Children welcome; 8 Tennis nearby; 9 Swimming nearby; 10 Golf nearby; 11 Skiing nearby; 12 May be booked through travel agent.

ocean views, suites and theme rooms, queen beds, private and shared baths, sitting rooms, and televisions. Located near golf, downtown, boat rentals, salmon guided service. Adult-oriented. Smoking outside only.

Hosts: Ted and Sharon Arbour
Rooms: 4 (1PB; 3SB) $70-95
Continental Breakfast
Credit Cards: A, B
Notes: 5, 8, 9, 10, 11, 12

Campbell River Lodge and Fishing Resort

1760 Island Highway, V9W 2E7
(250) 287-7446; (800) 663-7212;
FAX (250) 287-4063
E-mail: crlodge@oberon.ark.com
Web site: http://www.vquest.com/crlodge

The Campbell River Lodge and Fishing Resort is a small lodge nestled on the banks of the "famous" Campbell River. The lodge itself was built from logs in 1948, in the style of the Hudson Bay trading posts. Magnificent wood carvings adorn many of the beams, walls, and railings inside the lodge. Our surrounding grounds host an extraordinary collection of chainsaw carvings. We boast great food and great fun, all provided in clean, comfortable riverside accommodations. One of our experienced guides will take you saltwater salmon sport fishing or on one of our many adventure tours.

Hosts: Ted and Sharon Arbour
Rooms: 28 (PB) $55-94
Continental Breakfast
Credit Cards: A, B
Notes: 3, 4, 5, 6, 7, 8, 9, 10, 11, 12

CHEMAINUS

Sea-Breeze Tourist Home

2912 Esplanade; PO Box 1362, V0R 1K0
(250) 246-4593 (voice and FAX)
Web site: http://www.virtualcities.com

Turn-of-the-century home, beautifully appointed. Steps from the beach and boat ramp. Almost waterfront. Beautiful views from every room. One complete suite including kitchen. Enjoy watching sails and seals from an old-fashioned veranda. The Sea-Breeze is surrounded by clean, fresh breezes and sparkling water. *Wir sprechen Deutsch*! Picturesque town of Chemainus on Vancouver Island.

Hosts: John and Christa Stegemann
Rooms: 4 (PB) $60-65 (Canadian)
Full Breakfast
Credit Cards: none
Notes: 5, 6 (1 small pet), 7, 8, 9, 10, 12

FORT STEELE

Emery's Mountain View Bed and Breakfast

183 Wardner–Fort Steele Road; PO Box 60, V0B 1N0
(250) 426-2756 (voice and FAX)
Web site: http://www.islandnet.com/~pixsell/bebbd/5/5000027.htm

Three hours from Banff, Alberta; 4 hours from Spokane, Washington; 5 minutes from Fort Steele heritage town. Located on 37 scenic acres above a creek and a marsh where animals and birds live and feed. Our home and cabin have porches, patios, and a gazebo where guests can relax and enjoy views of the Rocky Mountains. Hiking trails, hot springs, historic sites, golf courses, and churches are

---

NOTES: Credit cards accepted: A Master Card; B Visa; C American Express; D Discover; E Diners Club; F Other; 2 Personal checks accepted; 3 Lunch available; 4 Dinner available; 5 Open all year; 6 Pets

nearby. No pets—two dogs in residence. Smoking outside.

Hosts: John and Joanna Emery
Rooms: 3 (1PB; 2SB) $60-95
Full Breakfast
Credit Cards: B
Notes: 5, 7, 9, 10, 11, 12

KELOWNA

A View to Remember B&B

1090 Trevor Drive, V1Z 2J8
(250) 769-4028 (voice and FAX)
E-mail: bnbview@cnx.net

Welcome to our enchanting home offering antique decor and a spectacular view, close to Highway 97. Quiet area, minutes from downtown. Air-conditioned, deluxe accommodations include elegant and spacious guest rooms, en suite bathrooms, private entrance, guest parlor, gourmet breakfast (served outdoors in summer), large covered patio, attractive gardens. Government-inspected. No smoking. Adult-oriented. Well-traveled Australian hosts enjoy sharing with guests.

Hostess: Celia Jarman
Rooms: 3 (PB) $70-85 (Canadian)
Full Breakfast
Credit Cards: A, B
Notes: 5, 8, 9, 10, 11

LADNER

Primrose Hill Guest House B&B

4919 48th Avenue, V4K 1V4
(604) 940-8867; FAX (604) 940-0234
Web site: http://www.primrose-hill.com

A 1913 Craftsman-style home that reflects the Edwardian era. Furnished with antiques. Curl up on a wrought-iron and brass bed or canopy bed after a soak in a claw-foot tub. Come spend a restful night or two. Join us in the dining room for a delightful homemade breakfast. We are 10 minutes from the Tsawwassen ferry terminal, with sailing to Victoria, Nanaimo, and the Gulf Islands; 25 minutes from the U.S. border and Vancouver International Airport; 35 minutes from downtown Vancouver.

Hosts: Christine and James
Rooms: 6 (PB) $85-125
Full Breakfast
Credit Cards: A, B, C
Notes: 5, 7, 8, 9, 10, 12

Grand Manor Guest House

NORTH VANCOUVER

Grand Manor Guest House

1617 Grand Boulevard, V7L 3Y2
(604) 988-6082; FAX (604) 988-4596
E-mail: donna@helix.com
Web site: http://users.imag.net/~srydonna/default.html

Grand Manor was built in 1912 for the Gill family. James Gill was the reeve of the district of North Vancouver. This four-story stone Edwardian home is located in the heart of North Vancouver, 5 blocks from Londale. Rooms have water, mountain, and city views. A guest cottage at the back (sleeps six) is fully self-contained.

Hostess: Donna Patrick
Rooms: 6 (2PB; 4SB) $70-130
Full or Continental Breakfast
Credit Cards: B
Notes: 5, 7, 8, 9, 11, 12

PORT ALBERNI

Lakewoods B&B

Site 339, C5, RR3, V9Y 7L7
(250) 723-2310 (voice and FAX)
Web site: www.bbcanada.com/82.html

We welcome adult travelers to our peaceful waterfront home in a garden setting on the shore of beautiful Sproat Lake. Excellent base for day trips on the *MV Lady Rose* down the Alberni Inlet. Go to Pacific Rim Park and the villages of Tofino and Ucluelet. Walking trails, forestry and mill tours. Enjoy a swim before turning in or before we serve your homemade breakfast. Dutch is spoken. Open year-round to accommodate you.

Hosts: Dick and Jane Visee
Rooms: 3 (1PB; 2SB) $60-80
Full Breakfast
Credit Cards: none
Notes: 2, 5, 8, 9, 10, 11, 12

PRINCE GEORGE

Beaverly B&B

12725 Miles Road, V2N 5C1
(250) 560-5255; FAX (250) 560-5211
Web site: http://www.bbcanada.com/339.htm

Beaverly B&B is located 18 kilometers west of Prince George on 10 acres of beautiful British Columbia wilderness. You will feel very welcome and comfortable in our new home. Many trees surround us, and it is a birder's paradise. We serve a luxurious, full breakfast, and you will enjoy our Dutch touch.

Hosts: Anneke and Adrian VanPeenen
Rooms: 2 (PB) $45-55
Full Breakfast
Credit Cards: none
Notes: 5, 9, 10, 11, 12

SOOKE

Ocean Wilderness Inn and Spa Retreat

109 West Coast Road, V0S 1N0
(250) 646-2116; (800) 323-2116;
FAX (250) 646-2317
E-mail: ocean@sookenet.com
Web site: http://www.sookenet.com/ocean

Nine guest rooms on 5 forested acres of oceanfront with breathtaking views. Large, beautifully decorated rooms with private baths and canopied beds. A silver service of coffee, etc., is delivered to your door as a gentle wake-up. Country breakfast from local produce is a wonderful treat. The ocean water hot tub is popular with weary travelers. Book for a private soak. There are several in-room soaker tubs for two, overlooking the ocean. Arrange a stress-relieving massage, mud facial, or seaweed/herb wrap. Perfect for small seminars, family reunions, weddings.

Hosts: Marion Rolston
Rooms: 9 (PB) $75-165 (May–October)
Full Breakfast
Credit Cards: A, B, C
Notes: 2, 5, 6, 7, 9, 10, 12

NOTES: Credit cards accepted: A Master Card; B Visa; C American Express; D Discover; E Diners Club; F Other; 2 Personal checks accepted; 3 Lunch available; 4 Dinner available; 5 Open all year; 6 Pets

UCLUELET

Burley's Lodge Bed and Breakfast

1073 Helen Road; Box 550, V0R 3A0
(250) 726-4444 (voice and FAX)

A waterfront home on a "drive to" island at the harbor mouth in friendly Ucluelet. A view from every window, large living room, decks, fireplace, books, recreation room with pool table. Enjoy the open ocean, sandy beaches, lighthouse lookout, nature walks, charter fishing, diving, fisherman's wharves, cruises for whale-watching and sight-seeing—or later, the exhilarating winter storms. No pets. Adult-oriented. No smoking. *Français aussi.*

Hosts: Ron and Micheline Burley
Rooms: 6 (SB) $45-65
Continental Breakfast
Credit Cards: A, B
Notes: 8, 9, 10

VANCOUVER

Beautiful Bed and Breakfast

428 W. 40th Avenue, V5Y 2R4
(604) 327-1102; FAX (604) 327-2299
E-mail: sandbbb@portal.ca
Web site: http://www.fleethouse.com/fhcanada/bed/beautiful/bea-hom.htm

Gorgeous Colonial-style home with antiques, fresh flowers, views. Breakfast is served in the formal dining room with silver, linens, antiques. Unbeatable location at 40th Avenue and Cambie Street. Buses directly to and from the ferry, airport, downtown, the University of British Columbia, and Victoria are all just ¾ block away. We are on a quiet street in a great central location, minutes from downtown and within walking distance of tennis, golf, swimming pools, hospitals, three cinemas, fine restaurants, and a major shopping center. Queen Elizabeth Park and Van Dusen Gardens are only a few blocks down the street.

Hosts: Corinne and Ian Sanderson
Rooms: 5 (1PB; 4SB) $90-150 (US)
Full or Continental Breakfast
Credit Cards: none
Notes: 2, 5, 8, 9, 10, 11, 12

Beautiful Bed and Breakfast

Diana's Luxurious Accommodations Bed and Breakfast

1019 E. 38th Avenue, V5W 1J4
(604) 321-2855; FAX (604) 321-3411
E-mail: stayhere@dianasluxury.com
Web site: http://www.dianasluxury.com

Diana's Bed and Breakfast has been serving tourists from all over the world since 1985. Her freshly brewed coffee, breads, and seasonal fruits start your day off right. Diana's exceptional service has earned her a golden reputation among travelers and earned her many awards. She has lived in

Vancouver since 1972, and would be happy to direct you to must-see attractions and the most popular restaurants.

Hostess: Diana Piwko
Rooms: 11 (6PB; 5SB) $95-140
Full Breakfast
Credit Cards: A, B, C
Notes: 5, 7, 8, 9, 10, 11, 12

Laburnum Cottage Bed and Breakfast

1388 Terrace Avenue, **North Vancouver,** V7R 1B4
(604) 988-4877 (voice and FAX)

This charming home with a Victorian air and antiques is set in ½ acre of beautifully kept English gardens surrounded by virgin forest. Yet it is only 15 minutes from downtown Vancouver or Horseshoe Bay, 90 minutes from Whistler ski resorts, and 5 minutes from Grouse Mountain and other tourist attractions.

Host: Delphine Masterton
Rooms: 4 +2 cottages (PB) $95-195 (US)
Full Breakfast
Credit Cards: A, B
Notes: 2, 5, 7, 8, 9, 10, 11, 12

Tall Cedars B&B

720 Robinson Street, **Coquitlam,** V3J 4G1
(604) 936-6016 (voice and FAX)
E-mail: tallcedars_bnb@bc.sympatico.ca
Web site: http://www.bbcanada.com/2490.html

Tall Cedars B&B is inspected and approved by British Columbia Ministry of Tourism. This B&B is tastefully decorated with ceiling fans and eiderdowns and has bright, clean rooms with comfy beds. Enjoy complimentary refreshments on the lovely lighted garden/covered balcony while you relax and unwind at the end of the day. And in the morning, let breakfast be your choice. Try our lemon-glazed poppyseed candied ginger biscuits, great grandmother's rhubarb rolls (ask for the recipe), and homemade jams, or have the traditional eggs, ham, and toast. This is a B&B you can afford! You'll feel like you're at home. Your gracious hosts have been in the B&B business for 12 years.

Hosts: Dwyla and Ed Beglaw
Rooms: 3 (1PB; 2SB) $55-85 (Canadian)
Full Breakfast
Credit Cards: F
Notes: 3, 4, 5, 7 (call first), 8, 9, 10, 11, 12

Wrays Lakeview Bed and Breakfast

VERNON

Wrays Lakeview Bed and Breakfast

7368 L&A Road, V1B 3S6
(250) 545-9821; FAX (250) 545-9924

Come and relax in the peace and seclusion of our cozy, air-conditioned home in a beautiful country setting. We offer accommodations for up to eight adults. Our guest rooms have private bathrooms. A guest sitting room has a piano and TV,

NOTES: Credit cards accepted: A Master Card; B Visa; C American Express; D Discover; E Diners Club; F Other; 2 Personal checks accepted; 3 Lunch available; 4 Dinner available; 5 Open all year; 6 Pets

along with a private entrance and parking. Enjoy the view from the deck or balcony. A full breakfast is served in our formal dining room. Warm hospitality is guaranteed. Adults only. No smoking or pets. Easy access to skiing, golfing, boating, beaches, hiking, dining, and shopping.

Hosts: Irma and Gord Wray
Rooms: 3 (PB) $69
Full Breakfast
Credit Cards: A, B
Notes: 5, 8, 9, 10, 11

VICTORIA

AA-Accommodations West Reservation Service

660 Jones Terrace, V8Z 2L7
(250) 479-1986; FAX (250) 479-9999
E-mail: dwensley@vanisle.net
Web site: http://www.bctravel.com/gardencity

No reservation fee. More than sixty choice locations inspected and approved. Ocean views, farm tranquillity, cozy cottage, city convenience, and historic heritage. Assistance with itineraries that include **Victoria, Vancouver Island,** and some adjacent islands. For competent, caring service, call Doreen 9 AM–9 PM Monday–Saturday or 2 PM–9 PM Sunday (P.T.L.).

Manager: Doreen Wensley
Credit Cards: A, B, C
Notes: 2, 5, 7, 8, 9, 10, 12

Battery Street Guesthouse

670 Battery Street, V8V 1E5
(250) 385-4632

Comfortable, 100-year-old home only 1 minute away from ocean and Beacon Hill Park. It is a 20-minute walk to the heart of town. Quiet and peaceful. Dutch and English spoken. Home away from home!

Hostess: Pamela Verdvyn
Rooms: 6 (2PB; 4SB) $65-95
Full Breakfast
Credit Cards: none
Notes: 2, 5, 8

Beaconsfield Inn

Beaconsfield Inn

998 Humboldt Street, V8P 5E9
(250) 384-4044; FAX (250) 384-4052
E-mail: beaconsfield@islandnet.com
Web site: http://www.islandnet.com/beaconsfield

"International Bed and Breakfast of the Year" award winner by *Andrew Harper's Hideaway Report*, this luxury small inn 3 blocks from the harbor and downtown offers fine art, antiques, flowers, Jacuzzis for two, fireplaces, and English gardens in a heritage manor of sophisticated charm. Afternoon tea at fireside in the library; full breakfast in the sunroom or dining room. No smoking. Complimentary parking. Complete fitness facilities nearby.

Hosts: Con and Judy Sallid
Rooms: 9 (PB) $145-350 (Canadian) (seasonal discounts available)
Full Breakfast
Credit Cards: A, B
Notes: 5, 8, 9, 10

welcome; 7 Children welcome; 8 Tennis nearby; 9 Swimming nearby; 10 Golf nearby; 11 Skiing nearby; 12 May be booked through travel agent.

The Edwardian Inn Bed and Breakfast

The Edwardian Inn Bed and Breakfast

135 Medana Street, V8V 2H6
(250) 380-2411; (888) 388-0334;
FAX (250) 380-4743
E-mail: edwardianinn@pacificcoast.net
Web site: http://www.victoriabc.com/accom/edwardan.htm

The Edwardian Inn is an elegant 1907 Edwardian character home located just steps from the Inner Harbour, Parliament buildings, museum, U.S. ferries, and Beacon Hill Park, as well as miles of oceanfront walkways. You can snuggle under duvets in our bright, charming rooms. Private and shared baths are available. The Edwardian Inn features fresh flowers, delicious breakfasts, and a warm and friendly welcome to travelers.

Hosts: Eric and Edith Klippenstein
Rooms: 6 (2PB; 4SB) $55-80 (US)
Full Breakfast
Credit Cards: A, B
Notes: 2, 5, 7 (10+), 8, 9, 10, 12

Gregory's Guest House

5373 Patricia Bay Highway (Route 17), V8Y 2N9
(250) 658-8404; (888) 658-8404;
FAX (250) 658-4604
E-mail: gregorys@direct.ca

Circa-1919 English country restored farmstead with 2 acres overlooks Elk Lake. Enjoy our water gardens, farm animals, exotic birds. Convenient location only 10 kilometers (6 miles) from Victoria and minutes from Butchard Gardens, ferries, and airport. Included is our bountiful country breakfast, cozy parlor with fireplace, fine character rooms with antique furnishings, down quilts, and private baths. Lake activities include swimming, hiking, canoeing, and windsurfing. Children welcome.

Hosts: Elizabeth and Paul Gregory
Rooms: 4 (2PB; 2SB) $65-85
Full Breakfast
Credit Cards: A, B
Notes: 2, 5, 7, 8, 9, 10, 12

Heathergate House

122 Simcoe Street, V8V 1K4
(250) 383-0068; (888) 683-0068;
FAX (250) 383-4320

Situated in the heart of Victoria close to the Inner Harbour and all downtown attractions, this acclaimed bed and breakfast with its well-appointed guest rooms and private baths is fashioned in the comforts and antiques of a small English inn. Guest rooms include bathrobes, down comforters, and Casablanca fans. Early-morning silver tray coffee service in rooms, with a full breakfast served in the dining room. Complimentary tea service in the guest lounge. A private two-bedroom cottage is available at the same location, with

Heathergate House

a continental breakfast brought there each morning. Off-season discounts available.

Hosts: Ann and Ned Easton
Rooms: 3 + cottage (PB) $65-100 (US)
Full Breakfast
Credit Cards: A, B
Notes: 2, 5, 8, 9, 10, 12

Hibernia B&B

747 Helvetia Circle, V8Y 1M1
(250) 658-5519; FAX (250) 658-0588

Off Highway 17 on a cul-de-sac. Pastoral setting. Full Irish breakfast served on terrace. Comfortable home with antiques, artwork, Oriental rugs, memorabilia. Fifteen minutes from Butchart Gardens, Victoria Ferries, Airport. Two rooms: one queen, one double. Duvets, handmade quilts. Fresh flowers. Guest lounge with grand piano, books, TV/VCR, games. Extensive grounds with flower gardens, trees, vines.

Hostess: Mrs. Aideen Lydon
Rooms: 2 (PB) $70-75 (Canadian)
Full Breakfast
Credit Cards: A, B
Notes: 5, 8, 9, 10, 12

Oak Bay Guest House

1052 Newport Avenue, V8S 5E3
(250) 598-3812; (800) 575-3812;
FAX (250) 598-0369
E-mail: oakbay@beds-breakfasts.com
Web site: http://beds-breakfasts.com/oakbay

Located in Victoria's genteel suburb of Oak Bay, our classic English Tudor-style B&B offers affordable elegance in an old-world setting. Our rooms all are individually decorated and designed to meet the needs and budgets of all our guests. Like a boutique hotel, our house offers separate dining tables and scrumptious breakfasts. Off-season discounts.

Hosts: Jackie and Karl Morris
Rooms: 11 (PB) $85-160 (Canadian)
Full Breakfast
Credit Cards: A, B, C
Notes: 5, 8, 9, 10, 12

Oak Bay Guest House

A Sea Rose Bed and Breakfast

1250 Dallas Road, V8V 1C4
(250) 381-7932; (888) 335-7673;
FAX (250) 480-1298
E-mail: searose@compuserve.com
Web site: www.bctravel.com/searose.html

A 1921 house remodeled in 1987 and redecorated in 1994. Located on Victoria's

---

welcome; 7 Children welcome; 8 Tennis nearby; 9 Swimming nearby; 10 Golf nearby; 11 Skiing nearby; 12 May be booked through travel agent.

scenic marine drive, offering panoramic views of Juan de Fuca Strait and the snow-capped Olympic Mountains. Each suite is self-contained, including bathroom and fully furnished kitchen. Beds are comfortable twin-, queen-, and king-size, with down duvets. Delicious breakfasts are served in the dining room. The Sea Rose is located within walking distance of restaurants, downtown, beaches, a seaside path, and a park.

Hostess: Pauline Boytim
Rooms: 4 (PB) $75-170 (Canadian; seasonal)
Full Breakfast
Credit Cards: A, B, C
Notes: 2, 5, 7, 8, 9, 10, 12

Top o'Triangle Mountain Bed and Breakfast

3442 Karger Terrace, V9C 3K5
(250) 478-7853; (800) 870-2255;
FAX (250) 478-2245

As I gaze out the window of our solid cedar home atop Triangle Mountain at the splendor of the Olympic Mountains, Juan de Fuca Strait, and the City of Victoria, all agleam in the afternoon sun, I stand in awe at God's handiwork. I thank Him for all the wonderful friends we have made during our 12 years of welcoming guests into our home. Good food, warm hospitality, and clean, comfortable accommodations await you.

Hosts: Henry and Pat Hansen
Rooms: 3 (PB) $70-90 (Canadian)
Full, Home-Cooked Breakfast
Credit Cards: A, B
Notes: 5, 7, 8, 9, 10, 12

Golden Dreams Bed and Breakfast

WHISTLER

Golden Dreams B&B

6412 Easy Street, V0N 1B6
(604) 932-2667; (800) 668-7055;
FAX (604) 932-7055
E-mail: goldendreams@whistlerweb.net
Web site: http://www.cantravel.ab.ca/goldendr.html

Enjoy our world-class, year-round resort just 2 hours from Vancouver. Be surrounded by nature's beauty and pampered with a wholesome breakfast, homemade jams, and fresh breads. Unique theme rooms feature cozy duvets and sherry decanters. Relax in the outdoor hot tub with mountain views! Family room with wood fireplace. Full guest kitchen. Located just 1 mile from village express gondolas. Valley trail system and bus route at our doorstep. Bike rentals onsite. Many seasonal activities. Now in two locations! Whistler Town Plaza is within walking distance of express ski lifts, fabulous restaurants, and new shops. These new condos feature gas fireplace, entertainment center, full kitchen, spa access, and underground parking.

Hosts: Ann and Terry Spence
Rooms: 3 + 2 condos (PB&SB) $75-125
Full Breakfast
Credit Cards: A, B
Notes: 2, 5, 7, 8, 9, 10, 11

NOTES: Credit cards accepted: A Master Card; B Visa; C American Express; D Discover; E Diners Club; F Other; 2 Personal checks accepted; 3 Lunch available; 4 Dinner available; 5 Open all year; 6 Pets

Manitoba

ROSSBURN

Maple Grove Bed and Breakfast

PO Box 471, R0J 1V0
(204) 859-2221; (204) 859-3064;
FAX (204) 859-2145

Trees, birds, wildlife, grain fields, and conservation area surround our Victorian country home, built in 1910. Enjoy the quiet, relaxing surroundings, sunsets, and wild berries in season. Full breakfast served. Evening meals available with advance notice, at extra charge. Complimentary tea and coffee. Smoking allowed on the veranda. Only 11 kilometers from Rossburn, 11 kilometers from Arrow Lake and 25 kilometers from Rossman Lake for fishing, golfing, boat launching, and ice fishing. Cross-country skiing and snowmobiling in the area. Riding Mountain National Park is only 45 minutes away. The B&B is open year-round.

Hosts: Bert and Kathy Swann
Rooms: 3-4 (PB) $30 single, $40 double
Full Breakfast
Credit Cards: none
Notes: 2, 3, 4, 5, 7, 10, 12

WINNIPEG

Elsa's Hideaway Bed and Breakfast

303 Marshall Bay, R3T 0R8
(204) 284-3176

Enjoy the seclusion of our pleasant backyard. Quiet surroundings. Indoor and outdoor hot tubs and pool in season. Easy access from Perimeter. Off Pembina Highway, near the university, parks, shopping mall, and restaurants. Easy access to anywhere in the city. Interests include travel, reading, Scrabble®, quilting.

Hosts: Werner and Elsa Neufeld
Rooms: 4 (2PB; 2SB) $40-50
Full Breakfast
Credit Cards: none
Notes: 2, 7, 9, 10

Oakdale Bed and Breakfast

15 Oakdale Drive, R3R 0Z3
(204) 896-1354

A charming mix of contemporary home and antique furnishings awaits you in a quiet

---

welcome; 7 Children welcome; 8 Tennis nearby; 9 Swimming nearby; 10 Golf nearby; 11 Skiing nearby; 12 May be booked through travel agent.

MANITOBA

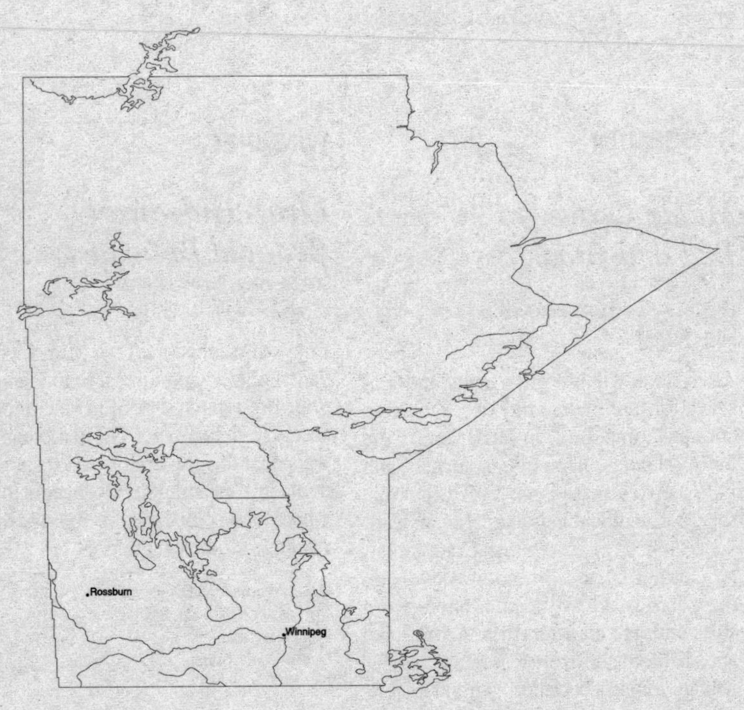

residential neighborhood. Large, private backyard with deck. Direct bus route to city center; easy access to airport, Perimeter, and Trans Canada highway. Located close to Assiniboine Park and Zoo, golf courses, and most major shopping centers. Enjoy your breakfast in the great room with the sun shining through the skylight. Your hostess is a music teacher; you are welcome to play and enjoy the piano. German is spoken here.

Hostess: Wilma Poetker
Rooms: 2 (SB) $40 single, $50 double
Full Breakfast
Credit Cards: none
Notes: 5, 8, 10, 12

NOTES: Credit cards accepted: A Master Card; B Visa; C American Express; D Discover; E Diners Club; F Other; 2 Personal checks accepted; 3 Lunch available; 4 Dinner available; 5 Open all year; 6 Pets welcome; 7 Children welcome; 8 Tennis nearby; 9 Swimming nearby; 10 Golf nearby; 11 Skiing nearby; 12 May be booked through travel agent.

NEW BRUNSWICK

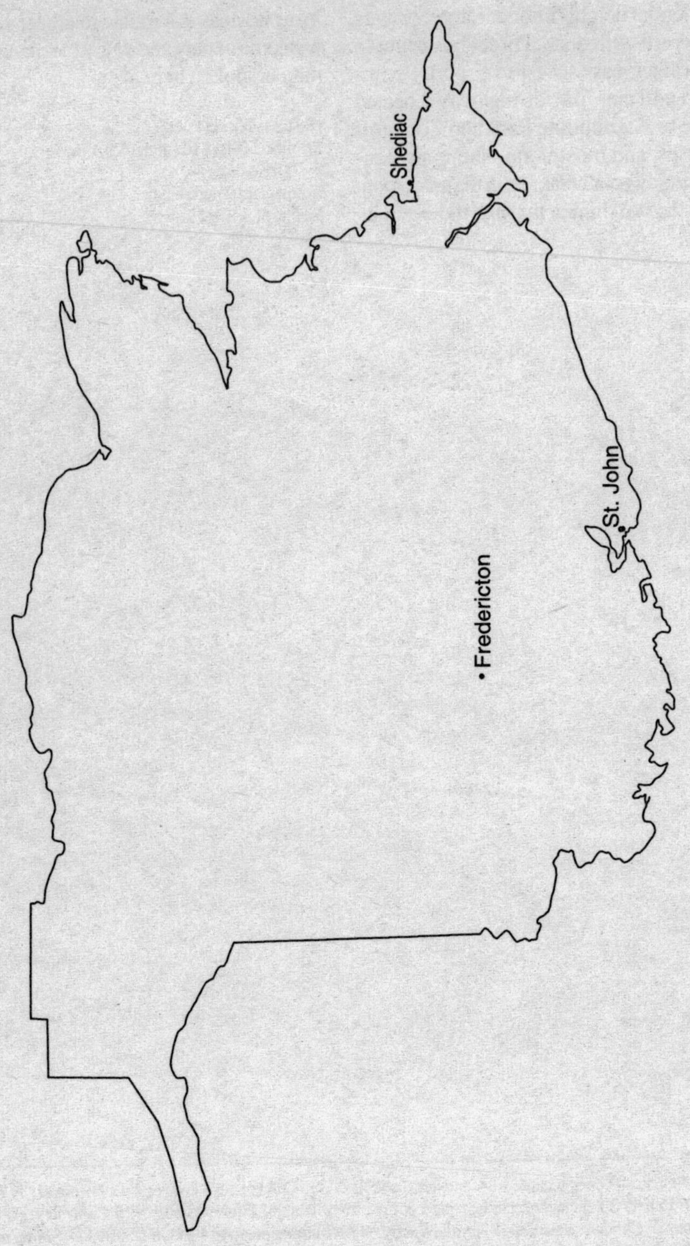

New Brunswick

FREDERICTON

Appelot Bed and Breakfast

1272 Route 105 Highway, E3A 7K2
(506) 444-8083
Web site: http://www.bbcanada.com/187.htm

An attractive farmhouse overlooking the St. John River. Three bedrooms with a view in the restful country atmosphere. Full homemade breakfast served on the spacious sunporch. Orchards and woodlands with walking trails—"a bird-watcher's delight." Board games, TV, VCR, books, and piano inside; picnic table, BBQ, and lawn swing outside. Area attractions include several golf courses, Mactaquac Park, Kings Landing Historical Village, museums in Fredericton, the Beaverbrook Art Gallery, and the Provincial archives.

Hostess: Elsie Myshrall
Rooms: 3 (1PB; 2SB) $60
Full Breakfast
Credit Cards: none
Notes: 2, 9, 10

Carriage House Inn Bed and Breakfast

Carriage House Inn Bed and Breakfast

230 University Avenue; PO Box 1088, E3B 5C2
(506) 452-9924; (800) 267-6068;
FAX (506) 458-0799
E-mail: chinn@nbnet.nb.ca
Web site: http://www.cygnus.nb.ca/carriagehouseinn.html

A Victorian mansion built by Mayor Beckwith in 1875. An elegant ballroom, sun-filled solarium, and antiques will take you back in time to a bygone era. The inn is surrounded by stately elms and is located near the heart of town beside the

---

NOTES: Credit cards accepted: A Master Card; B Visa; C American Express; D Discover; E Diners Club; F Other; 2 Personal checks accepted; 3 Lunch available; 4 Dinner available; 5 Open all year; 6 Pets welcome; 7 Children welcome; 8 Tennis nearby; 9 Swimming nearby; 10 Golf nearby; 11 Skiing nearby; 12 May be booked through travel agent.

beautiful St. John River and the Trans Canada Trail/Sentier NB Trail.

Hosts: Nathan and Joan Gorham
Rooms: 11 (PB) $60-85
Full Breakfast
Credit Cards: A, B, C, E
Notes: 2, 5, 7, 8, 9, 10, 11, 12

ST. JOHN

Mahogony Manor

220 Germain Street, E2L 2G4
(506) 636-8000; FAX (506) 636-8001
E-mail: leavittr@nbnet.nb.ca
Web site: http://www.sjnow.com/mm

The graceful elegance of a bygone era greets you in this restored home dating to the turn of the century. Each guest room is decorated with antique or heirloom furniture and has a private bathroom and a queen- or king-size bed. Located on a quiet residential street in the midst of historic St. John, we are within walking distance of tourist attractions, restaurants, shops, and entertainment. Make yourself at home—your comfort is our pleasure!

Hosts: Ross Leavitt/Wayne Harrison
Rooms: 5 (PB) $60-65
Full Breakfast
Credit Cards: A, B
Notes: 5, 7, 10

SHEDIAC

Seaside Haven Manor and Suites

75 Calder Street (off Main Street); Box 1921, E0A 3G0
(506) 532-9025

Seaside Haven Manor is a rambling Victorian, circa 1890, featuring rooms with beautiful antique furniture. Come relax with a book in our glassed-in porch furnished with 1810 Louis XV mahogony furniture, or relax on the piazza. The adjacent Seaside Haven Suites are a newer addition, modernly furnished with kitchenettes; they have been a delightful convenience for our treasured guests. Experience the warmth, comfort, and genuine hospitality of a New Brunswick welcome.

Hostess: Lynne Leger
Rooms: 7 (PB) $80-150
Continental Breakfast
Credit Cards: A, B
Notes: 7, 8, 9

NOTES: Credit cards accepted: A Master Card; B Visa; C American Express; D Discover; E Diners Club; F Other; 2 Personal checks accepted; 3 Lunch available; 4 Dinner available; 5 Open all year; 6 Pets

Nova Scotia

CHESTER

Smithaven Bed and Breakfast

Highway 103, Exit 8; PO Box 15, B0J 1J0
(902) 275-2380; FAX (902) 275-4460

Smithaven Bed and Breakfast invites you to discover our new, large, well-appointed guest rooms. Each has a private, three-piece washroom. A full breakfast is provided in the formal dining room from 7:30 to 9 AM. There are many places for guests to sit and walk by the ocean, 10 minutes from Smithaven, and there are a number of nearby gift shops in which to browse. Restaurants are available for casual or fine dining—or you may take in one of many church suppers that are well-known to the area. Smithaven is open year-round. The season extends May 1–October 30; off-season accommodations by arrangement.

Rooms: 4 (PB) $70
Full Breakfast
Credit Cards: B
Notes: 7, 8, 9, 10 (40 miles), 11, 12

MASSTOWN/DEBERT

Shady Maple B&B

11207 Highway 2, B0M 1G0
(902) 662-3565 (voice and FAX)
E-mail: emeisses@ns.sympatico.ca

Welcome to our fully operating farm. Exit 12 off Highway 104; travel 1½ miles into Masstown. Or take Exit 14A off Highway 102; 6 miles to Masstown. Walk through fields and wooded trails, view the milking, pet the animals, have a swim in our heated outdoor pool, and enjoy the outdoor, year-round spa. In the evening, sit by the fireplace in our country home. Close to the Tidal Bore, Truro, and Ski Wentworth, and only 45 minutes from Halifax Airport. We offer homemade jams, jellies, and maple syrup. Farm-fresh eggs and an in-house gift shop. Cribs and cots available. Honeymoon package available. Evening snack. Open May 1–October 31.

Hosts: James and Ellen Eisses
Rooms: 3 (1PB; 2SB) $40-75
Full Breakfast
Credit Cards: B
Notes: 5, 6, 7, 9, 10, 11, 12

---

welcome; 7 Children welcome; 8 Tennis nearby; 9 Swimming nearby; 10 Golf nearby; 11 Skiing nearby; 12 May be booked through travel agent.

QUEENSLAND

Surfside Inn

RR 2, Hubbards, 9609 St. Margarets Bay Road,
B0J 1T0
(902) 857-2417; (800) 373-2417
E-mail: dbrown20_glid@sympatico.ca
Web site: http://www.bbcanada.com/524.html

The inn overlooks Queensland Beach and is 30 minutes from Halifax, Peggy's Cove, and Lunenburg. This sea captain's home, circa 1880, has been restored, keeping the Victorian elegance with all the modern amenities. Rooms feature color televisions, whirlpools, and special luxuries for guests' enjoyment. Guests will feel like royalty sleeping in one of our massive antique mahogany beds, which come complete with Beautyrest® mattress and cozy duvet. There is also an in-ground pool for guests. Off-season rates available.

Hosts: Michelle and Bill Batcules
Rooms: 4 (PB) $69-110 (Canadian)
Continental Plus Breakfast
Credit Cards: A, B, C, D
Notes: 5, 8, 9, 10, 11, 12

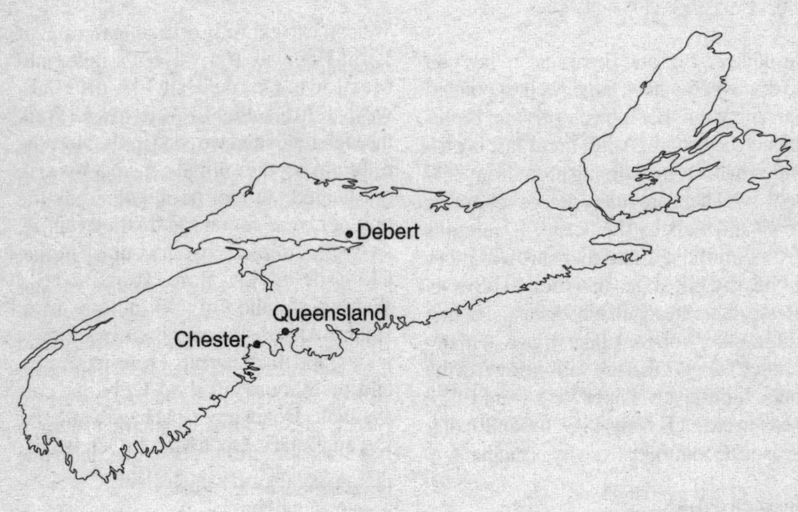

Ontario

BARRIE

Cozy Corner Bed and Breakfast

2 Morton Crescent, L4N 7T3
(705) 739-0157; (705) 323-3471

A popular location with Georgian Bay—30,000 islands, Wasaga Beach—on our doorstep. Close to the Muskoka Lakes, vacationland to many from the U.S. and Canada. Site of summer homes of Hollywood celebrities (Kurt Russell, Goldie Hawn, Rodney Dangerfield, and others). Only 36 miles from Toronto. Our elegant home offers luxurious and safe accommodations. Deluxe bedding, hair dryers, private TV, parking. Suite has private bath with Jacuzzi. Delicious breakfasts and a *joie de vivre* are standard. Brochure available on request.

Hosts: Charita and Harry Kirby
Rooms: 3 (1PB; 2SB) $65-110
Full Breakfast
Credit Cards: B
Notes: 2, 4, 5, 8, 9, 10, 11, 12

CARLETON PLACE

The Carleton Heritage Victorian Inn

7 Bridge Street, K7C 2V2
(613) 253-6058; FAX (613) 253-6027
E-mail: carltnhertg@sprint.ca

Originally constructed in the mid-1800s, this stunning Victorian heritage inn has been fully restored to its original splendor. Discover what makes The Carleton so exceptional: luxuriously appointed facilities with antique furnishings, modern amenities, and fine dining prepared by our award-winning chef, in a relaxing atmosphere. It's all here, including our grand imperial suite, king-size bed, bathroom with double Jacuzzi and separate shower, fifteen guest rooms, aesthetics salon, a genuine Asian artifacts boutique, and a fine dining facility and banquet hall.

Host: Gerard Weller
Rooms: 15 + Grand Imperial Suite (PB) $90-100
Credit Cards: A, B, C
Notes: 3, 4, 5, 7, 10, 11

ONTARIO

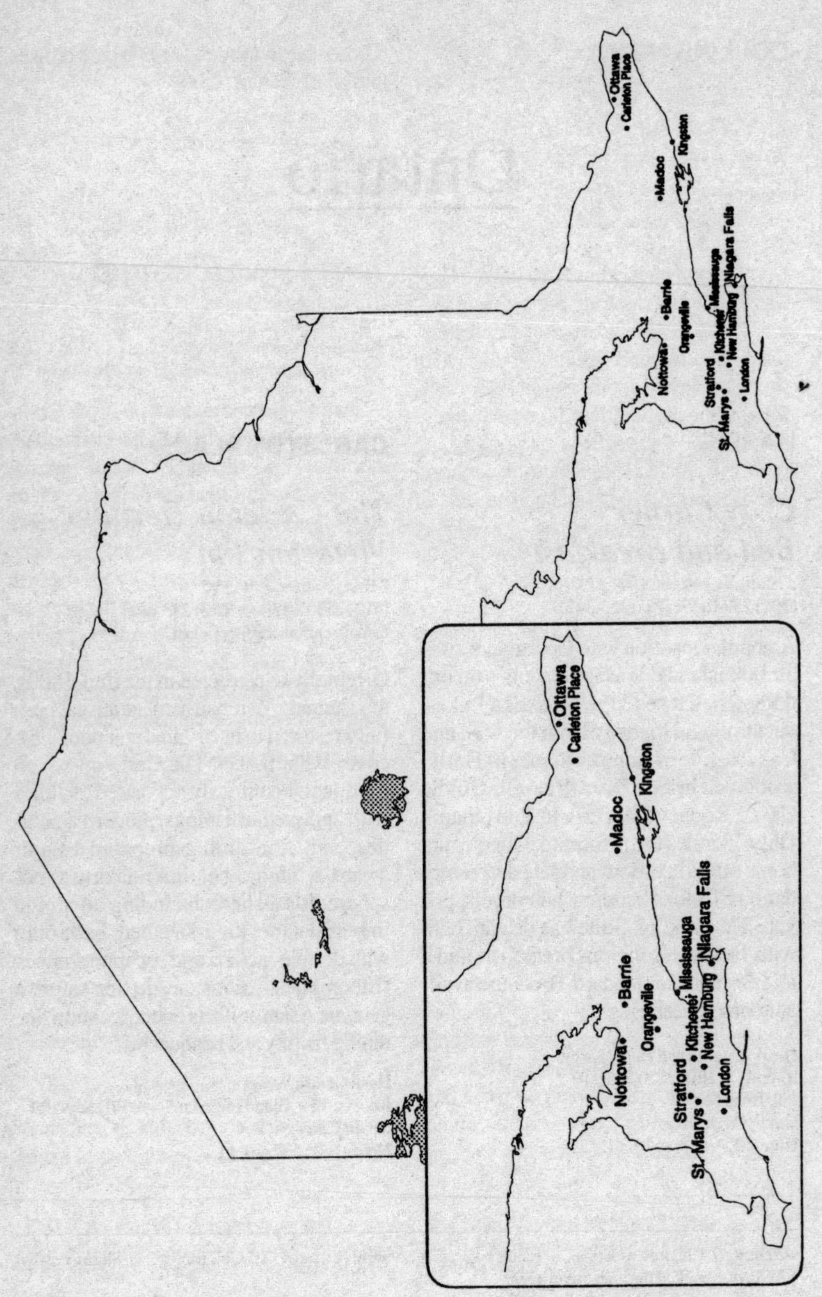
Ottawa
Carleton Place
Kingston
Madoc
Barrie
Orangeville
Mississauga
Niagara Falls
Kitchener
New Hamburg
Nottowa
Stratford
St. Marys
London

COLLINGWOOD

Pretty River Valley Country Inn

RR 1, **Nottawa,** L0M 1P0
(705) 445-7598 (voice and FAX)

Cozy, quiet country inn in the scenic Blue Mountains overlooking Pretty River Valley Wilderness Park. Choose from distinctive pine-furnished studios and suites with fireplaces and in-room whirlpools for two. Spa and air-conditioning. Close to Collingwood, beaches, golfing, fishing, hiking (Bruce Trail), bicycle paths, antique shops, and restaurants. Complimentary tea served on arrival. Studios and suites are available. No smoking.

Hosts: Steve and Diane Szelestowski
Rooms: 6 studios, 2 suites (PB) $79-120 (Canadian)
Full Breakfast
Credit Cards: A, B, C, E
Notes: 5, 7 (well-behaved), 8, 9, 10, 11, 12

KINGSTON

Painted Lady Inn

181 William Street, K7L 2E1
(613) 545-0422
Web site: http://www.travel.nx.com (under "Bed and Breakfasts")

Built in 1972, this grand Victorian offers seven elegant guest rooms, all with private baths. Luxury rooms feature Jacuzzis, fireplaces, and sofas. Gourmet breakfasts served in the dining room—waffles, French toast, eggs Benedict. Central air. Parking. Close to downtown, 1,000 Island cruises, and Fort Henry.

Hostess: Carol Franks
Rooms: 7 (PB) $75-125 (US)
Full Breakfast
Credit Cards: A, B, C
Notes: 5, 8, 9, 10, 12

Roses and Blessings

112 High Acres Crescent, N2N 2Z9
(519) 742-1280; FAX (519) 742-8428
E-mail: nmwarren@golden.net
Web site: http://www.bbcanada.com/2077.html

A warm welcome awaits you in our Christian home featuring friendly hospitality, cozy comfort, and renowned home baking. Breakfast is served in the dining room, on the patio, or in the intimacy of our sunroom with orchids and tropical plants. Relax by the fire, in the hot tub, or in your room in an easy chair, or work out on the exercise equipment. We can help with excursions and information about the Mennonite community. Close to the farmers markets, St. Jacobs, the universities, and Stratford.

Hosts: Marg and Norm Warren
Rooms: 2 (PB) $45 single, $60 double (Canadian)
Full Breakfast
Credit Cards: A
Notes: 2, 5, 7, 8, 9, 10, 11, 12

LONDON

Idlewyld Inn

36 Grand Avenue, N6C 1K8
(519) 433-2891 (voice and FAX); (800) 267-0525
E-mail: idlewyld@lonet.ca
Web site: http://www.someplacedifferent.com

Surround yourself in the luxury and charm of this 1878 Victorian mansion in a quiet residential neighborhood. Close to theater, restaurants, and shopping. Each of our guest rooms boasts its own unique decor, a subtle blending of antique furnishings and modern amenities. Several suites offer either Jacuzzi tubs or decorative fireplaces. Each morning, a light breakfast is yours to enjoy in our cheerful breakfast room or on our garden patio.

Hostess: Dawn Lashbrook
Rooms: 27 (PB) $85-169 (Canadian)
Continental Breakfast
Credit Cards: A, B, C, E
Notes: 5, 7, 8, 9, 10, 12

MADOC

Camelot Country Inn

RR 5, K0K 2K0
(613) 473-0441 (voice and FAX)

Relax in the quiet, country setting of our 1853 brick-and-stone home. It is surrounded by plantings of red-and-white pine on 25 acres of land in the heart of Hastings County. Original woodwork and oak floors have been lovingly preserved. There are three guest rooms, two with doubles, one with twins. Breakfast may be chosen from the country breakfast or one of two gourmet breakfasts.

Camelot Country Inn

Hostess: Marian Foster
Rooms: 3 (SB) $35-45
Full Breakfast
Credit Cards: none
Notes: 2, 4, 5, 7, 8, 9, 10

MISSISSAUGA

Country Cottage B&B

1531 Glenburnie Road, L5G 3C9
(905) 274-5720

Sheltered by evergreens on ½ acre. Country casual; quiet, safe, and comfortable. Veranda with fireplace in pine kitchen and dining room. Healthy lifestyle meals. Close to airport, public transportation, and churches. Very quiet, private, peaceful.

Hostess: Irene Donovan
Rooms: 2 suites + 1 double room (1PB; 2SB) $49 (Canadian)
Full Breakfast
Credit Cards: none
Notes: 5

NEW HAMBURG

The Waterlot Restaurant and Inn

17 Huron Street, N0B 2G0
(519) 662-2020; FAX (519) 662-2114
E-mail: waterlot@sympatico.ca

The Waterlot is the recipient of the Travel Holiday Fine Dining Award out of New York and The Gourmet Club of America Silver Spoon Award (fewer than 300 awarded in North America). A lot of very dedicated and hard-working staff appreciated the recognition and support. The Waterlot offers private-label Canadian wines, private imports, and now at The Wine Bar: very fine wines by the taster or by the glass.

Hosts: Gord and Leslie Elkeer
Credit Cards: A, B, C, E
Notes: 2, 3, 4, 8, 9, 10

NIAGARA FALLS

Bed of Roses B&B

4877 River Road, L2E 3G5
(905) 356-0529 (voice and FAX)
Web site: http://www.v-ip.com/roses

Christian hosts welcome you. We have two efficiency units with bedroom, living room with pull-out sofa bed, furnished kitchenette, dining area, bath, and private entrance. A full breakfast is served "room service-style." We are located on the famous River Road near Niagara Falls, bridges to the U.S., bike and hiking trails, golf course, and all major attractions. Free pick-up from bus and train station. Family units suitable for up to five people. Come and enjoy your stay in Niagara Falls.

Hostess: Norma Lambertson
Rooms: 2 (PB) $85-140
Full Breakfast
Credit Cards: A, B
Notes: 5, 7, 10

Gretna Green B&B

5077 River Road, L2E 3G7
(905) 357-2081
Web site: http://www.bbcanada.com/262.html

A warm welcome awaits you in this Scots-Canadian home overlooking the Niagara River Gorge. All rooms have AC and TVs. Included in the rate is a full breakfast with homemade scones and muffins. We pick up at the train or bus station. Many people have called this a "home away from home."

Hosts: Stan and Marg Gardiner
Rooms: 4 (PB) $45-75
Full Breakfast
Credit Cards: none
Notes: 5, 7, 8, 10

ORANGEVILLE

Country Host B&B Network

Headwaters Hideaway, RR 5, L9W 2Z2
(519) 942-0686 (voice and FAX)
Web site: http://www.travelinx.com

Heritage and restored country and Victorian homes in Hockley Valley, Caledon Hills, Belefountain, Primrose, and Meaford. Next to provincial parks, on the Niagara escarpment and Bruce Trail. Fly-fishing, McMichael Collection, art studios, antiques, festivals, country markets galore. One hour north of Toronto, Paramount Canada's Wonderland, and the Skydome and C.N. Tower.

Hostess: Lesley Burns
Rooms: 2-3 each location (40%PB; 60%SB) $55-85
Full Breakfast
Credit Cards: none
Notes: 2, 3, 4, 5, 6 (small), 7, 9, 10, 11

OTTAWA

Australis Guest House

35 Marlborough Avenue, K1N 8E6
(613) 235-8461 (voice and FAX)
E-mail: waters@intranet.ca
Web site: http://www.bbcanada.com/1463.html

We are the oldest established and still-operating bed and breakfast in the Ottawa area. Located on a quiet, tree-lined street 1 block from the Redeau River with ducks and swans, and Strathcona Park; a 20-minute walk from the Parliament buildings. This period house boasts leaded-glass windows, fireplaces, oak floors, and unique stained-glass windows overlooking the hall. Hearty breakfasts with home-baked breads and pastries. Past winner of the Ottawa Hospitality Award and Gold Award recipient for Star of City for Tourism. Recommended by *Newsweek* and *Travel Scoop* and featured in *Ottawa Sun* for breakfast recipes. Carol is co-author of *The Cookbook: A Breakfast Companion of Whispered Recipes.*

Hosts: Carol, Brian, and Olivia Waters
Rooms: 3 (1PB; 2SB) $62-78 (Canadian)
Full Breakfast
Credit Cards: none
Notes: 5, 7, 8

ST. MARYS

Eagleview Manor B&B

178 Widder Street E.; Box 3183, N4X 1A8
(519) 284-1811

"St. Marys is a town time forgot." Beautiful Victorian home overlooking a quaint, peaceful town. Minutes from London and Stratford. Sweeping staircase, stained-glass windows, Jacuzzi, quilts, antiques, fireplaces, in-ground pool, large guest rooms. Nanny's Tea Room available for afternoon or Victorian teas. Reservations necessary. Year-round. Theme weekends and retreats. Amtrak stops here. Future home of Canadian Baseball Hall of Fame.

Eagleview Manor Bed and Breakfast

Hosts: Bob and Pat Young
Rooms: 4 (SB) $50-70 (Canadian)
Full Menu Breakfast
Credit Cards: none
Notes: 2, 5, 7, 8, 9, 10, 11, 12

STRATFORD

Burnside Guest House

139 William Street, N5A 4X9
(519) 271-7076; FAX (519) 271-0265

Burnside is a turn-of-the-century Queen Anne Revival home on the north shore of Lake Victoria, the site of the first Stratford logging mill. The home features many family heirlooms and antiques and is centrally air-conditioned. Our rooms have been redecorated in light, cheery colors. Relax in the gardens overlooking the Avon River on hand-crafted furniture amid the rose, herb, herbaceous, and annual flower gardens. A home-cooked, nutritional breakfast is provided. Within walking distance of Shakespearean theaters. Close to Protestant and Roman Catholic churches of Stratford. Stratford is the home of a world-renowned Shakespearean festival from early May to mid-November.

Host: Lester J. Wilker
Rooms: 4 (SB) $50-75
Full Breakfast
Credit Cards: none
Notes: 2, 5, 7, 8, 9, 10, 11

Prince Edward Island

ALBANY

The Captain's Lodge

Seven Mile Bay, RR 2, C0B 1A0
(902) 855-3106; (800) 261-3518
Web site: http://www.bbcanada.com/559.html

A quiet, secluded B&B surrounded by flower gardens and fields of clover, grain, and potato blossoms. A short walk from a red sand beach; 7 kilometers from our new Confederation Bridge that links Prince Edward Island to the mainland. Queen beds; one room with twins. Ceiling fans, fresh flowers, duvets, slippers, gourmet breakfasts, and evening desserts spoil our guests. Off-season rates and senior discounts. No smoking. Resident cat, dog, and bunny. Deposit required. Cancellation policy. Open May 15-October 15.

Hosts: Jim and Sue Rogers
Rooms: 3 (PB) $70-80
Full Breakfast
Credit Cards: A, B
Notes: 2, 9, 10

MONTAGUE

VanDykes' Lake View Bed and Breakfast

RR3, C0A 1R0
(902) 838-4408

Only 20 miles from Charlottetown. The beginning of Confederation, our home is unique, as our living/dining area was built in 1885 and is an Orkney Island–style structure. We have two rooms with queen beds; the other two have twin and double beds. Close to golf, beaches, museum, horseback riding, live theater, and shops. Breakfast is continental with the room. Large deck overlooking small lake.

Hosts: Lorraine and John VanDyke
Rooms: 4 (1PB; 3SB) $25-50
Continental Breakfast
Credit Cards: none
Notes: 3, 8, 9, 10, 11 (cross-country)

MURRAY RIVER

Bayberry Cliff Inn

RR 4, Little Sands, C0A 1W0
(902) 962-3395 (voice and FAX); (800) 668-3395
E-mail: dgregori@bud.peinet.pe.ca
Web site: http://www.bbcanada.com/528.html

Eight kilometers east of Wood Islands Ferry. All rooms have private baths and private porches. Rooms have antiques, quilts, and rustic decor. Double, single, and queen beds. Two remodeled post-and-beam barns in a scenic farming area "on the edge" of Northumberland Strait cliffs. Swimming, restaurants, seal-watching, Rossignal Winery, craft stores nearby. Evening meals are served. Not suitable for children under 5. Early registration suggested; deposit required. Open May 15–September 30.

Hosts: Nancy and Don Perkins
Rooms: 4 (PB) $90-130
Full Breakfast
Credit Cards: A, B
Notes: 4, 7 (6+), 9, 10, 12

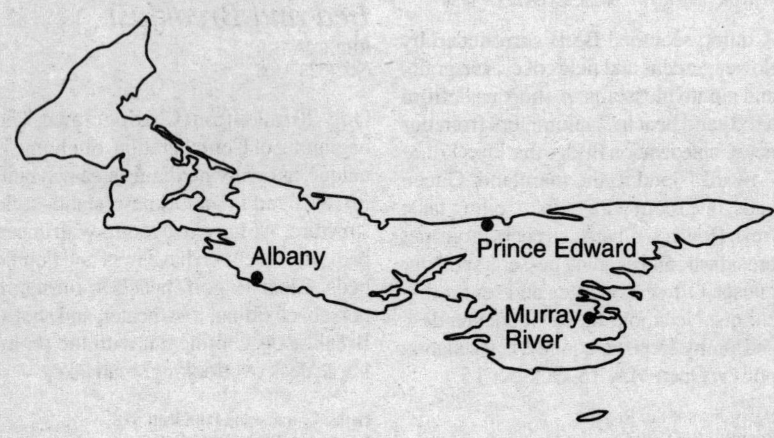

NOTES: Credit cards accepted: A Master Card; B Visa; C American Express; D Discover; E Diners Club; F Other; 2 Personal checks accepted; 3 Lunch available; 4 Dinner available; 5 Open all year; 6 Pets

Quebec

DESCHAMBAULT

Auberge Chemin du Roy

106 St-Laurent, G0A 1S0
(418) 286-6958

First step in the Quebec City region, Deschambault invites guests to discover its historic past by staying at this Victorian Inn. The antiques evoke a feeling of serenity and romance near the fireplace. Guests also can relax with the murmuring waterfall in front of the house and the St. Lawrence River breezes.

Hosts: Francine and Gilles
Rooms: 8 (6PB; 2SB) $64-94
Full Breakfast
Credit Cards: A, B
Notes: 4, 5, 9, 10

MONTREAL

Auberge de la Fontaine

1301 Rachel Street E., H2J 2K1
(514) 597-0166; (800) 597-0597;
FAX (514) 597-0496
E-mail: info@aubergedelafontaine.com
Web site: http://www.aubergedelafontaine.com

The Auberge de la Fontaine is a nice stone house, newly renovated, where the rooms in a warm and modern decor are of unique

Auberge de la Fontaine

style in Montreal. Located in front of a magnificent park. Comfortable, friendly atmosphere and attentive, personal service are greatly appreciated by our corporate and leisure travelers. Each room is tastefully decorated. The suites with whirlpool baths, as well as the luxurious rooms, have brick walls and exclusive fabrics. It will settle you in an elegant and quiet environment. Duvet and decorative pillows will ensure cozy comfort. Breakfast is a given at the Auberg. A delicious variety of breakfast foods are set out each morning,

---

welcome; 7 Children welcome; 8 Tennis nearby; 9 Swimming nearby; 10 Golf nearby; 11 Skiing nearby; 12 May be booked through travel agent.

QUEBEC

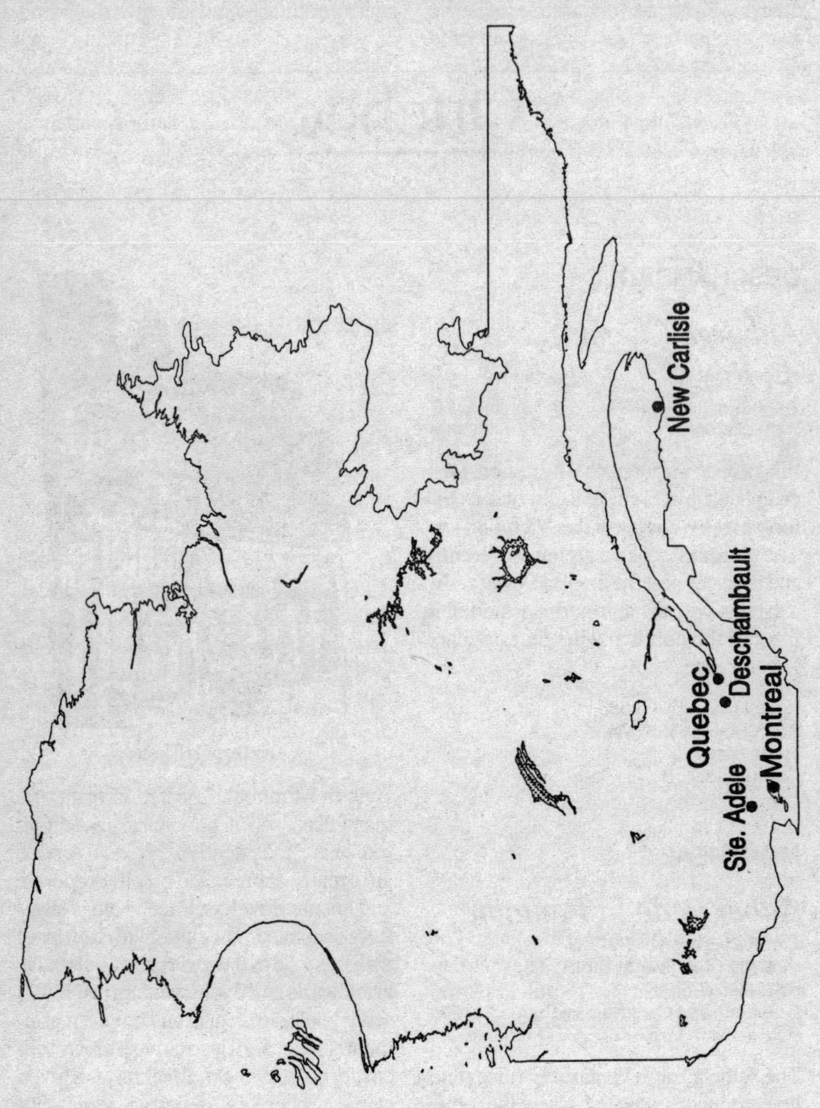

and you have access to the kitchen for snacks. There are no parking fees. We want our guests to feel comfortable and to be entirely satisfied with their stay. Discover the exclusive shops, restaurants, and art galleries of the Plateau Mont-Royal, which is typical of French Montreal.

Hostesses: Celine Boudreau and Jean Lamothe
Rooms: 21 (PB) $109-190 (Canadian)
Continental Buffet Breakfast
Credit Cards: A, B, C, E
Notes: 5, 7, 8, 9, 10, 12

Bay View Manor/Manoir Bay View

NEW CARLISLE

Bay View Manor/ Manoir Bay View

395 Route 132, Bonaventure E. (Mail: PO Box 21, New Carlisle), G0C 1Z0
(418) 752-2725; (418) 752-6718

Comfortable, two-story, wood frame home on the beautiful Gaspé Peninsula across the highway from the beach and beside an eighteen-hole golf course. The building was once a country store and rural post office. Stroll our quiet, natural beach; see nesting seabirds along the rocky cliffs; watch fishermen tend their nets and lobster traps; enjoy beautiful sunrises and sunsets; view the lighthouse beacon on the nearby point; and fall asleep to the sound of waves on the shore. Museums, archaeological caves, fossil site, bird sanctuary, Bristish Heritage Village. Hike, fish, canoe, horseback ride, or bird-watch.

Hostess: Helen Sawyer
Rooms: 5 + cottage (1PB; 4SB) $35
Full Breakfast
Credit Cards: none
Notes: 5, 7, 8, 9, 10, 11

NEW CARLISLE WEST

Bay View Farm

337 Main Highway, Route 132; Box 21, G0C 1Z0
(418) 752-2725; (418) 752-6718

On the coastline of Quebec's picturesque Gaspé Peninsula, guests are welcomed into our comfortable home located on Route 132, Main Highway. Enjoy fresh sea air from our wraparound veranda; walk or swim at the beach. Visit natural and historic sites. Country breakfast; fresh farm, garden, and orchard produce; home baking; and genuine Gaspésian hospitality. Light dinners by reservation. Craft, quilting, and folk music workshops. August Folk Festival. A small cottage also is

Bay View Farm

NOTES: Credit cards accepted: A Master Card; B Visa; C American Express; D Discover; E Diners Club; F Other; 2 Personal checks accepted; 3 Lunch available; 4 Dinner available; 5 Open all year; 6 Pets welcome; 7 Children welcome; 8 Tennis nearby; 9 Swimming nearby; 10 Golf nearby; 11 Skiing nearby; 12 May be booked through travel agent.

available for $350 per week. English and French spoken.

Hostess: Helen Sawyer
Rooms: 5 (1PB; 4SB) $35
Full Breakfast
Credit Cards: none
Notes: 3, 4, 5, 7, 8, 9, 10, 11

QUEBEC

Manoir Des Remparts

3½ Rue des Remparts, G1R 3R4
(301) 692-2056; FAX (301) 692-1125

Located minutes from the train/bus terminal and the famed Chateau Frontenac, with some rooms overlooking the majestic St. Lawrence River, the Manoir des Remparts boasts one of the most coveted locations available in the old city of Quebec. Newly renovated, it can offer its guests a vast choice of rooms, ranging from a budget room with shared washrooms to an all-inclusive room with private terrace.

Hostess: Sitheary Ngor
Rooms: 36 (22PB; 14SB) $35-75
Continental Breakfast
Credit Cards: A, B, C, E
Notes: 5, 7, 11, 12

SAINTE-ADELE

Auberge Beaux Reves (Sweet Dreams Inn)

2310 Boulevard Sainte-Adele, J0R 1L0
(450) 229-9226; (800) 279-7679;
FAX (450) 229-2999
E-mail: welcome@beauxreves.com
Web site: www.beauxreves.com

Located on an enchanted river with natural river whirlpools, Beaux Reves (Sweet Dreams) offers you a unique, relaxing experience. Old stone sauna, exterior spa, relaxation pavilion. Massages, wooded path, delicious breakfast, and personalized rooms await your visit. Golf, skiing, hiking, snowmobiling, cycling, swimming, shopping, and great dining are available within a few minutes' drive.

Host: Hannes Lamothe
Rooms: 6 (PB) $75-100 (Canadian)
Full Breakfast
Credit Cards: B
Notes: 5, 7, 8, 9, 10, 11, 12

Puerto Rico

CABO ROJO

Parador Perichi's

HC 01; Box 16310, 00623
(787) 851-3131; (800) 435-7197;
FAX (787) 851-0560

Parador Perichi's Hotel, Restaurant, and Cocktail Lounge is in Joyuda, site of Puerto Rico's famous resorts of the west. Seventeen years of hospitality and service. Rooms have air-conditioning, wall-to-wall carpet, private balconies, color TVs, and telephones. Award-winning restaurant. After sunset, meet friends in the well-stocked, cozy lounge. The banquet room accommodates 300 persons.

Hosts: Julio C. Perichi
Rooms: 49 (PB) $65-80
Full and Continental Breakfast
Credit Cards: A, B, C, D, E
Notes: 3, 4, 5, 7, 8, 9, 10, 12

LAJAS

Parador Villa Paraguera

PO Box 273, 00667
(787) 899-7777; FAX (787) 899-6040

Within our facilities are sixty-nine double bedrooms with color TV, telephone, AC, and private bath; half of them have a very nice ocean view with balconies. We have a large swimming pool, restaurant, bar, gift shop, children's playground, convention center, meeting room facilities, and a big patio surrounded by the Caribbean Sea. Boat services nearby to the world-famous Phosphorescent Bay. Diving, snorkeling, and kayaking nearby!

Host: Nelson Mercado
Rooms: 69 (PB) $90
Full Breakfast
Credit Cards: A, B, C, D, E
Notes: 3, 4, 5, 7, 9, 12

SAN JUAN

El Canario Inn

1317 Ashford Avenue - Condado, 00907
(787) 722-3861; (800) 533-2649;
FAX (787) 722-0391
E-mail: canariopr@aol.com
Web site: http://www.canariohotels.com

A historic and unique B&B inn. All guest rooms are air-conditioned with private baths, cable TVs, and telephones, and come with a complimentary continental breakfast. Our tropical patios and sundeck provide a friendly and informal atmosphere. Centrally located near the beach, casinos, restaurants, boutiques, and public transportation.

Hosts: Jude and Keith Olson
Rooms: 25 (PB) $75-99
Continental Breakfast
Credit Cards: A, B, C, D, E
Notes: 5, 7, 9, 12

Hotel La Playa

Calle Amapola #6, Isla Verde, 00979
(787) 791-1115; FAX (787) 791-4650

Welcome to the Enchanted Island. Since we are a small, family-oriented hotel, we welcome the opportunity to provide a relaxing atmosphere. Our open-air restaurant and cocktail lounge with deck enjoy a cool breeze. Each room has cable TV and AC. Public phones are available in our courtyard. We are located on the beach, and all beaches here are in the public domain.

Hosts: Barbara and David Yourch, Manuel Godinez
Rooms: 15 (PB) $65-105
Continental Breakfast
Credit Cards: A, B, C
Notes: 3, 4, 5, 7, 9, 10, 12

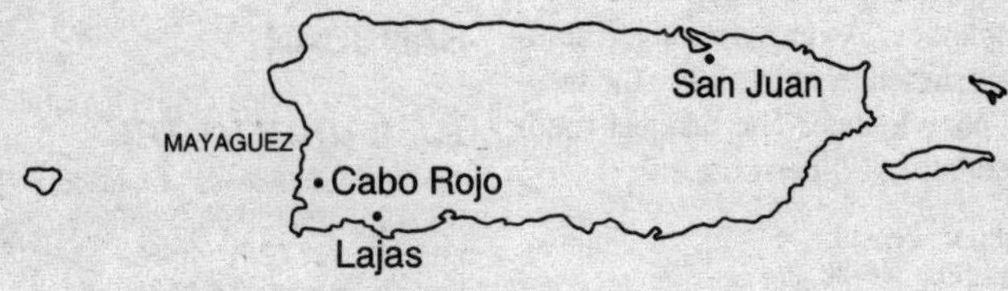

U.S. Virgin Islands

FREDERIKSTED, ST. CRIOX

Sprat Hall Plantation

Route 63 N. at 58, 00841
(340) 772-0305; (800) 843-3584;
FAX (340) 772-2880

Beautiful country inn featuring the oldest privately owned building in the Caribbean. Antique and modern rooms, efficiency suites in duplex cottages, one- and two-bedroom houses. Private beach, calm, clean water, beach restaurant for lunch—gourmet food. Riding stables, hiking trails, tropical fruit overhead.

Hosts: Joyce and Jim Hurd
Rooms: 8 plus 8 efficiency suites
Continental Breakfast
Credit Cards: none
Notes: 2, 3, 4, 5, 7, 8, 9, 12

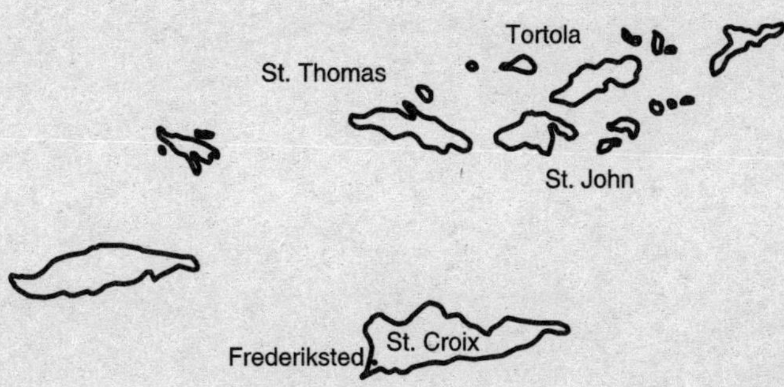

6 Pets welcome; 7 Children welcome; 8 Tennis nearby; 9 Swimming nearby; 10 Golf nearby; 11 Skiing nearby; 12 May be booked through travel agent.

The Christian Bed & Breakfast Directory

P.O. Box 719
Uhrichsville, OH 44683

INN EVALUATION FORM

Please copy and complete this form for each stay and mail to the address above. Since 1990 we have maintained files that include thousands of evaluations from travelers. We value your comments. These help us to keep abreast of the hundreds of new inns that open each year and to follow the changes in established inns.

Name of inn: ____________________

City and State: ____________________

Date of stay: ____________________

Length of stay: ____________________

Please use the following rating scales for the next items.
A: Outstanding B: Good C: Average D: Fair F: Poor

Attitude of innkeepers: ________	Attitude of helpers: ________
Food Service: ________	Handling of Reservations: ________
Cleanliness: ________	Privacy: ________
Beds: ________	Bathrooms: ________
Parking: ________	Worth of price: ________

Comments on the above: ____________________

What did you especially like? ____________________

Suggestions for improvements: ____________________

1999-2000

RECOMMENDATION FORM

As *The Christian Bed & Breakfast Directory* gains approval from the traveling public, more and more bed and breakfast establishments are asking to be included on our mailing list. If you know of another bed and breakfast which may not be on our list, give them a great outreach and advertising opportunity by providing us with the following information:

1) B&B Name ____________________

Host's Name ____________________

Address ____________________

City ____________ State ____________ Zip Code ______

Telephone ____________ FAX ____________

2) B&B Name ____________________

Host's Name ____________________

Address ____________________

City ____________ State ____________ Zip Code ______

Telephone ____________ FAX ____________

3) B&B Name ____________________

Host's Name ____________________

Address ____________________

City ____________ State ____________ Zip Code ______

Telephone ____________ FAX ____________

Please return this form to: The Christian Bed & Breakfast Directory
PO Box 719, Uhrichsville, OH 44683
(740) 922-6045; FAX (740) 922-5948